NO LONGER PROPERTY OF
ANYTHINK LIBRARIES/
RANGEVIEW LIBRARY DISTRICT

GUN TRADER'S GUIDE TO RIFLES

A Comprehensive, Fully Illustrated Reference for Modern Rifles with Current Market Values

Edited by Stephen D. Carpenteri

Skyhorse Publishing, Inc.
New York

Copyright © 2013 by Skyhorse Publishing, Inc.

All Rights Reserved. No part of this book may be reproduced in any manner without the express written consent of the publisher, except in the case of brief excerpts in critical reviews or articles. All inquiries should be addressed to Skyhorse Publishing, 307 West 36th Street, 11th Floor, New York, NY 10018.

Skyhorse Publishing books may be purchased in bulk at special discounts for sales promotion, corporate gifts, fund-raising, or educational purposes. Special editions can also be created to specifications. For details, contact the Special Sales Department, Skyhorse Publishing, 307 West 36th Street, 11th Floor, New York, NY 10018 or info@skyhorsepublishing.com.

Skyhorse® and Skyhorse Publishing® are registered trademarks of Skyhorse Publishing, Inc.®, a Delaware corporation.

Visit our website at www.skyhorsepublishing.com.

10 9 8 7 6 5 4 3 2 1

Library of Congress Cataloging-in-Publication Data

Gun trader's guide to rifles : a comprehensive, fully illustrated reference for modern rifles with current market values / edited by Stephen D. Carpenteri.
    pages cm.
Includes index.
 ISBN 978-1-62636-026-6 (pbk. : alk. paper) 1. Rifles--Catalogs. 2. Rifles--Prices. 3. Rifles--Collectors and collecting. I. Carpenteri, Stephen D.
TS536.4.G89 2013
683.4'22--dc23
                     2013027945 ISBN: 978-1-62636-026-6

Introduction

Welcome to Skyhorse Publishing's *Gun Trader's Guide to Rifles*. This book is designed to provide the professional and amateur rifle enthusiast with all the information he will need to buy, sell, or trade the most popular rifles of the smokeless powder era.

Fans of the *Gun Trader's Guide,* another Skyhorse Publishing publication that has been a standard reference for gun collectors for over fifty years, will find the same level of detail and accuracy in this and other related books in the Skyhorse collectibles series. We work hard to provide accurate descriptions of listed firearms and their variations, plus up-to-date values for each listing.

Over two million gun buffs have found the *Gun Trader's Guide* a useful reference and a valuable aid in the identification and comparison of sporting, military, and law enforcement rifles, including some rare and unusual collectibles and commemoratives. This first edition of *Gun Trader's Guide to Rifles* continues that theme, offering thousands of listings accompanied by hundreds of illustrations of the most popular collectible rifles manufactured since the late 1800s, with detailed descriptions of the most common modern smokeless-powder rifles. Not every rifle ever made can be listed in any catalog of this size, but we have made every effort to include the makes and models that are most commonly encountered by American traders and collectors. Please note that the *Gun Trader's Guide to Rifles* does not include recent or antique blackpowder arms or the newest modern firearms that currently have little or no collectible value.

Collectors should also understand that there is often a wide variation in value in various models. This is caused by a number of factors including quality of original manufacture, the condition of the firearm, and the popularity of the item among collectors, dealers, and auctioneers. It makes sense that any "New in the Box" rifle will have the highest value because it is in pristine condition, has never been fired, and shows no signs of wear or use; it is as perfect as the day it left the factory. Such rifles command premium prices and, to the right collector, may bring offers that are substantially higher than the values stated here.

Rifles in "Excellent" condition show few signs of wear or damage, function perfectly, and have had no upgrading, alterations, or repairs. A rifle that is in excellent condition should generate considerable interest from collectors or traders seeking to add the piece to their own collections or who know other collectors who have shown interest in that particular rifle.

Rifles in "Good" condition are often sought by beginning collectors who want to establish a grouping of rifles representative of the manufacturer's catalog but who do not want to pay top dollar for them. This is a good way to start a collection of specific model firearms, gradually trading up in condition and price until the grouping is complete.

The format of the *Gun Trader's Guide to Rifles* is simple and straightforward, listing rifles manufactured or imported since the late 1800s in the United States and abroad. Most entries include complete specifications, including model number and name, caliber, barrel length, overall length, weight, distinguishing features, variations, the dates of manufacture (when they can be accurately determined), and date of discontinuation. Photos accompany the text to help the reader with identifications and comparisons. Also, first/last entries are listed at the top of the page for additional ease in finding a particular manufacturer.

The *Gun Trader's Guide to Rifles* will be revised periodically to ensure that its wealth of information is both current and detailed. The principal features that contribute to the unique nature of this rifle reference guide include its extensive pictorial format and accompanying comprehensive specifications. It provides a convenient avenue for identifying popular collectible rifles while simultaneously determining their current value.

Values shown are based on national averages obtained by conferring with knowledgeable gun dealers, traders, collectors, and auctioneers around the country, not by applying an arbitrary mathematical formula that could produce unrealistic figures. The values listed accurately reflect the nationwide average at the time of publication and are updated from time to time. Users should keep in mind that the stated values are averages based on a wide spectrum of variables. No price given in any such catalog should be considered the "one and only" value for a particular firearm. That figure is ultimately determined by final agreement between the buyer and seller.

Rifle values are also affected by regional preferences. For example, the Marlin Model 336 lever-action in .30-30 caliber is extremely popular on the East Coast and will command higher prices than it would in other parts of the country, where long-range bolt-action rifles, or the

so-called "bean field rifles," are more desirable among shooters, hunters, and others who seek these models. In some cases collectors will purchase regionally-popular models elsewhere at relative bargain prices and then offer them for sale later in regions where they are considered more valuable.

Successful collecting of any valuable commodity—from rifles to rugs—requires patience, research, and experience. Never be in a hurry to buy, sell, or trade any rifle no matter how attractive the offer. Study the sale and consult with known experts before closing a sale. Be sure you know what you have and what it is worth before buying, selling, or trading it away.

Rare or one-of-a-kind items are not listed here because very little trading takes place. Most of these transactions are private sales between individuals or their agents with few opportunities for public bidding. In such cases it is nearly impossible to set or obtain current market values. Rifles that are worth $20,000 to $1 million or more are offered for sale only at exclusive gun shows or private auctions. The occasional gem squeaks through the system (usually during estate sales when the owners are unaware of the value of a particular item), but those opportunities are extremely rare.

However, many of these ultra-valuable rifles may be found in the most recent edition of the *Gun Trader's Guide*, along with more

detailed descriptions of their history, variations, and value.

Listings Organization

Manufacturers' listings in the *Gun Trader's Guide to Rifles* are organized chronologically by date of production whenever possible, as many gun-making companies used the date that a particular model was introduced as its model number. For example, the Winchester Model 94 was introduced in 1894. However, during the first quarter of the twentieth century, gun makers began assigning names and numbers that did not relate to the year the rifle was introduced. As these recent models and their variations multiplied through the years, it became increasingly difficult to track them by date, especially for the less-experienced collector.

As a result, Winchester rifles are grouped alphanumerically in two different groups: early Winchesters manufactured before 1920 under the four-digit model-date designations, and guns manufactured after 1920 with their revised model format designations. The case is the same with rifles manufactured by other long-term companies. If any difficulty is encountered in locating a particular model, the different models and their variations are cross-referenced in the index.

To make specific models easier to find, rifles have also been grouped according to action type, including: single-shot rifles, bolt-action, slide actions, semi-automatic, and so forth. Our surveys indicate that this is the easiest way for readers to locate a specific firearm. The index may be helpful when searching for a particular model.

In researching data for this edition, some manufacturers' records were unavailable and/or some information was unobtainable. For example, many early firearms production records were destroyed in a fire that ravaged the Winchester plant. Other manufacturers' records have been lost or were simply not maintained accurately. These circumstances result in some minor deviations in the presentation format of certain model listings. For example, production dates or discontinuation dates may not be listed when manufacturing records are unclear or unavailable. Approximate dates of manufacture may be listed to reflect the availability of guns from a manufacturer or distributor, although these figures may represent disposition dates indicating when that particular model was shipped to a distributor or importer. Frequently, and especially with foreign manufacturers, production records are inaccurate or unavailable. Therefore, availability information is often based on importation records that reflect domestic distribution only.

A Caution to the Reader

Because state and federal laws vary and may change annually, it is in the collector's best interest to inquire about the legality of ownership, concealment, or display of specific firearms and accessories in his state, county, or municipality. Firearms restrictions are not universal and ignorance of the law is not a legal defense. Protect yourself by knowing which rifles you may own, purchase, and transport under the laws of your state as well as in the state where you intend to display them.

The publisher wishes to express special thanks to the many collectors, dealers, manufacturers, shooting editors, and other industry professionals who provided product information and willingly shared their knowledge in compiling the *Gun Trader's Guide to Rifles*. Also, our appreciation is extended to the firearm firms and distributors' public relations, production personnel, and research staff who provide us with specifications and updates throughout the year. We are especially grateful for their assistance and cooperation in compiling information and for providing us with photographs and illustrations of their collectible firearms.

Researching Your Rifle

To realize the greatest profit from or simply to establish the current value of a used rifle, the trader must learn everything he can about the piece. Some standard rifle models are easy to identify (Winchester's Model 70, the Marlin 336, or the Savage Model 99), but even among those listings one may encounter variations in caliber, barrel length, composition, metal finish, or stock configurations. Any or all of these may affect the value of a particular rifle. Guessing or assuming that a given rifle is what it appears to be based on a cursory examination could prove costly at auction or in a private sale. To make the most of your trading dollar, it makes sense to positively identify each rifle.

Few firearms enthusiasts are completely familiar with the make, model, and version of every rifle ever made, but the most experienced gun traders know where to look for verification. It is folly to attempt to sell (or buy) a rifle when you do not know its true value. The offered price may be too high or too low, and many times the difference between variations (particularly years of manufacture) can mean a value range spanning hundreds, perhaps thousands, of dollars. Bottom line: Never buy or sell a collectible rifle until you can positively identify it, establish its condition, and ascertain its current value. Proceeding with a sale or trade without this knowledge invariably means that you will come out on the short end of the trade.

Interestingly, many trades are based on a "I paid this much and I want this much" approach, which is the most common procedure for backyard trading. In these transactions a 50 or 100 percent profit is acceptable, but somewhere along the line one of the players will take the time to research the item and discover one of two things: the rifle is either over-valued or under-valued. It's usually at the point where the asking price of a given rifle seems overly ambitious, and this is where the buyer's experience kicks in. He'll take the time to do some research, evaluate the condition of the rifle, and come to the appropriate conclusion. Normally, once a rifle has peaked at a certain price it will stall in the last buyer's hands, often for years, until it appreciates enough for the owner to risk sending it through the trading mill once more.

How to Research a Collectible Rifle

Every rifle has a value. The trick is determining just how much it is worth on the current market. Assigning a random value to the piece may fool a few buyers, but an experienced trader knows that verification and documentation are the keys to a satisfying sale. Not every rifle is worth top dollar, but many are worth that and more. An accurate, final determination can only be

achieved through research.

This also applies to rifles you wish to insure against fire, theft, or loss. Most insurance companies will require a certified appraisal of any rifle valued at over $500. These requirements vary, but this is a good way to go if you want to realize top dollar for your investment. Of course, over time the insurance premiums may amount to total more than the total value of the rifle, but this is not usually a consideration when insuring family heirlooms or high-end collectibles. When owning the rifle is all that matters, the cost of ownership is a minor factor.

To assess the true, current value of any rifle, begin by making a list of what is known about the item: model number, magazine capacity, caliber, barrel length, action type, stock configuration, metal and wood finishes, accessories (iron sights, sling studs, or swivels; engraving or checkering) proof marks, and any other identifying details.

With this information in hand, begin by studying the manufacturer's catalog. Many of these documents are available online by simply typing in the manufacturer's name or, in some cases, the model number of the rifle. Information about most late-year rifle models may be found this way, but in many cases older-model rifles and their catalog listings are not available via the Internet.

The next step is to write to the manufacturer's archivist or historian, whose

contact information may also be found online. In most cases a nominal fee is charged to research a specific rifle, usually using its serial number and any other marks or details that can be provided. This process merely establishes when the rifle was made and, in some cases, when it was shipped from the factory. Some archivists will also provide a manufacturer's suggested retail price for the rifle, although that figure is rarely used when determining a collectible's value. However, this information will be useful in determining the exact model and date of manufacture of the rifle—a great help in establishing its market value.

Another option is to take the rifle to a certified auctioneer, gun dealer, or trader for identification and appraisal. There may also be a fee involved when taking this route, depending on the time it takes to make a positive identification. Not every rifle is a mystery, but some models will require additional time for confirmation.

The National Rifle Association's archivist (available online) may be another source of identification, especially in the case of old, rare, or obscure models. There are also many online blogs that are dedicated to specific manufacturers or models, but the information gleaned from these sites is not always accurate nor can it be considered the final word in identifying a particular rifle.

Gather all the information you can until you are certain of your rifle's make, model, and year of manufacture. If it has other unique features (special finishes, engraving, checkering, etc.) keep these in mind as you continue your research into the current collectible value of the piece.

The next step is to gather as many current collectible references as possible including Skyhorse's *Gun Trader's Guide* and similar catalogs dedicated to modern firearms values. Most of these publications offer detailed descriptions of the various firearms models, their manufacturers, and dates of production, which will also help in identifying a particular rifle. Also, they offer listings of current market values for rifles in new, excellent, and good condition. All of these catalogs use a variety of sources to determine the general market value of rifles based on auction records, sales reports, trader's guides, and similar resources. However, keep in mind that any published value for any rifle is merely a guide, not a final determination. In most cases, especially when trading with dealers, guns shops, pawn shops, and other commercial entities, the price you will be offered may be much less than the catalog listing. The dealer must factor in his cost of doing business, shelf time for the rifle as he waits for a chance to sell it, his time, and what he thinks the real chances are for a resale. Expect to receive 20 percent (or more) below

the book value of your rifle. Certainly exceptions exist in the case of rare, desirable, or unusual items, but it's not often that any rifle, even one that's new in the box, will bring top dollar in a commercial sale. If you are in a hurry and must sell the rifle, a buyer will sense your impatience and likely offer you 50 percent of its listed value. When it comes to collectibles, patience is the key! If you want the full value of your rifle, learn to wait for the right buyer and don't accept a penny less than what you know your rifle is worth.

To avoid disappointment, it's best to sell or trade with other interested individuals. Ideally, you'll want to find a person who needs that particular rifle to complete a collection or to begin one, in which case he may be willing to pay a premium for it. Again, never trade or sell a used rifle until you know exactly what it is and also its current value. You may not be able to sell it for top dollar, either, but you will at least walk away with something closer to its true market value.

Documentation

Any rifle is worth a great deal more when it is accompanied by certified documentation. It starts with the gun in its original box, ideally with a sample factory target, and all of the original paperwork (including the original serial numbers) and accessories. Some rifles are shipped with

extra magazines, iron sights or scope mounts, sling swivels, cleaning gear, or other options. When all of these are included the value of the piece will be nearer its book value.

As is the case in any field of collectibles there is always an element of fraud. For this reason, and especially when dealing with an unusual, rare, or preferred item, have it inspected and verified (in writing) by a certified expert. There are many copies, reproductions, and repaired versions of firearms in circulation, as well as guns that were made from crates full of leftover, interchangeable parts. When none of the serial numbers or proof marks seem to match, that's a red flag that should not be ignored.

As is the case with all collectibles including furniture, jewelry, artwork, or rifles, verification of authenticity is the most important first step in determining the true, current market value of a given item. Leave no stone unturned in your search and maintain a file of documentation for each rifle in your collection. When it comes time to sell or trade, you will reap the benefits of your meticulous research. In some instances the effort may mean the difference in hundreds if not thousands of dollars in market value.

Rifle Collecting Strategies

It's the rare trader in used rifles who starts his career with a barn full of prized firearms, a lively network of buyers and sellers, and enough cash on hand to buy any rifle (or collection) that catches his eye. This is where most avid, life-long traders hope to end up—and good luck in your quest. However, the more honest scenario is that a novice collector owns a few rifles sold or given to him by friends or relatives and wants to know not only what they are, but also how much they are worth. Open the door to the world of collectible rifles and you will feel like Alice in Wonderland, falling head over heels into a remarkable, interesting, and sometimes surprising universe where the smallest details (proof marks, model variations, dates of manufacture, and values) will lead you on a merry chase through a rabbit hole. Don't shy away from rifle collecting simply because it is new to you or even initially confusing. Instead, embrace the art and science of gun collecting for fun, education, and, at the end of the day, profit.

The most common entry into rifle collecting involves just one rifle, passed on from generation to generation, and accompanied by a rich familial history. Or, a trusted friend or neighbor, in the midst of cleaning out his attic or garage, no longer needs the old guns

that have been standing in a corner for years and wants to be rid of them. Being in the right place at the right time is often all it takes to send a new collector on his way. In any case, whether the rifle enthusiast owns one gun or one hundred, one good experience and he's hooked for life. Buying, selling, trading, and appraising rifles soon turns from a simple passion to a lucrative hobby—or even a profitable business.

One of the most successful rifle collectors I've met was actually a cattle auctioneer by trade. Many of the farmers he worked with had old guns hanging around the barn and a need to buy or sell milk or beef cows to keep the family going. Dickering over guns for bovines was an enjoyable side job for this trader, who ended up opening a used gun shop with an inventory of new and used guns that, at one point, was valued at over $2 million!

The transition took many years, of course, but over time this man learned as much about firearms as he did about cows, and that, in essence, is what rifle collecting is all about. You buy, sell, trade, and bid on the firearms that are of most interest to you and learn by your mistakes (and victories) as you go along.

The absolute beginner rifle trader is best advised

to start out small—and cheap. For example, it is possible to collect a "blue collar" manufacturer's entire inventory of rifles for much, much less than the cost of just one rifle from a high-end maker. Every rifle ever made by such companies as Marlin, Savage, H&R, or Mossberg can be acquired for a small percentage of the value of a single pre-World War II Purdey or Boss. Many more of the low-end rifles were made and can often be purchased for $100 or less, depending on their condition. Of course, a complete collection of a specific company's rifles will be worth more per gun than individual pieces in an incomplete collection, so there is incentive there.

Also, beginning collectors who are willing to settle for rifles in "Good" or "Average" condition can complete a collection of representative rifles from a specific manufacturer at much less than half the cost of a collection of rifles that are in "New in the Box" or "Excellent" condition. Not every trader insists on every rifle being in mint condition, opening a wide variety of options for the new or low-end collector.

The list of options is varied. Some collectors will focus on a single manufacturer, or they will focus on just lever-actions or bolt-actions. The categories can be as vertical as the collector wishes to make it: rifles of only one caliber, rifles with just walnut stocks, rifles with engraving, iron sights, or certain custom features . . . the list is endless. The odds are that no matter how you slice it there is a collector out there with the same interest and focus. Find each other, agree on a price, and away you go.

Completing a collection of rifles can be a daunting endeavor depending on how specific the collector wishes to get. Standard models are usually more abundant and generally lower in value than deluxe or custom-shop models. Some short run, commemorative, or special-event models are extremely rare and may be valued many times higher than the standard model. A collector whose goal is acquiring all of a company's standard models will pay less for and have an easier time completing his collection.

Venturing into the unusual, unique, short-lived, or extremely rare collectibles is going to cost more time, money, and energy. Trading in high-end collectible rifles requires a great deal of effort and capital because some of the more desirable items may sell for $100,000 or more, and rarely, if ever, come up for auction or sale. Trading in one-of-a-kind rifles most often occurs in the later years of a collector's career, at a point when money is no object and the trader is willing to give up an entire collection (or several of them) to acquire a

single important, significant, or unique piece.

Trading in collectible rifles can be as simple as, "I'll give you $50 for it," to "I'll have my banker wire a certified check." Most collectible rifle transactions are closer to the former than the latter, but the variables are infinite. For example, some "trades" include cash, other rifles, or even shotguns or handguns. I once traded a mint condition Winchester Model 94 in .32 Special for some cash, two lesser rifles, an oak hutch, a cord of white cedar, and a pig! I made good use of all those items but, forty years later, I wish I had kept the .32 Special! Such is the world of collectible gun trading.

It's best to have a long-term strategy in mind when trading, buying, or selling collectible rifles. This makes it much easier to evaluate and appraise guns that are merely being used as stepping stones to other transactions. En route to owning a full collection of Marlin rifles, for example, it may be necessary to orchestrate a trade involving several other desirable firearms. This, in turn, creates an opportunity to start a new collection of rifles, a common dilemma when trading in a wide variety of guns. As the Marlin collection is nearing completion it becomes apparent that another manufacturer's line-up of rifles is ripe for the taking; perhaps several hard-to-find models were part of an earlier trade. The process continues as quickly as new trades are made, leaving

the collector with a dozen incomplete collections. Without a clear strategy the random rifle collector can end up with a mish-mash of guns, all with some degree of collectible value, but few complete collections, which can often bring higher prices.

In most cases novice collectors will be least satisfied with sales or trades conducted in pawn shops, guns shops, or most gun shows. These traders know the value of each gun they sell and must make a profit, and so they will rarely dicker over price. If you must have the rifle and are willing to pay any price for it, these outlets may well be the best bet, but most collectors are also "horse traders" in the traditional sense, always looking to get a good deal on an item they must have. Private sales, auctions, and estate sales are the best places to find bargains when it comes to collectible firearms. A shrewd collector can often acquire the same item at half the price (or much less) when dealing with someone who is not a collector, has no idea what the gun is worth, or just wants to get rid of it for the sake of the estate. My father, one of the most accomplished traders I know, was able to buy a pre-64 Model 70 Supergrade in .220 Swift (worth over $5,000) by telling the seller that he really did not want or need the gun but that he'd "Take it off your hands" for $100. Lucky break? For sure, but there's no doubt that an experienced dealer would never have let such a rare rifle go for that much less than its book value.

Stories of this type are common in the collectible field, whether the item being sought is a tea cup, piece of jewelry, or a rifle. The easiest route to productive collecting is to spend time at auctions, estate sales, and gun and pawn shops. Know what you are looking for (or looking at) and, keeping your long-term strategy in mind, be able to negotiate a price that works for you.

Occasionally the collector will encounter a situation where an entire collection of guns is for sale but no individual rifles are offered. It's all or nothing, and sometimes the selling price is equal to or slightly higher than the current value of the collection. In this case it may be a good idea to evaluate each rifle in the collection, keeping close tabs on condition, age, and value, and then decide if the collection is truly worth the asking price. Except in extreme cases it is in fact cheaper to buy all of the guns in a collection instead of battling over one specific model. Time is always on the collector's side, and most modern firearms will appreciate about 10 percent annually. Factor this into your decision and decide if you have the time (and money) to invest in a complete collection that may, in ten years' time, be worth substantially more than its current value. This is where access to references, experience, and knowledge of the local trading community can come in very handy.

Do your research, study current catalogs, and ask questions of auctioneers, dealers, and brokers. The more you know, the more profitable your collecting will be.

The Art of Rifle Trading

Most folks are drawn into the world of collectible rifle trading the day they inherit, find, or are given an old rifle that Grandpa used "during the war" or "up to camp" fifty years ago or more. Even the most naive of collectors will think (or be told) that if a rifle is old, in good condition, and is no longer manufactured that it must be extremely valuable. This is where the charade begins, and after a great deal of effort and research, there are only two ways the game can end: in disappointment or joy. The truth is that the former is more likely than the latter for any number of reasons, the most likely culprit being that Grandpa's well-used deer rifle has only one thing going for it: age. Many standard model rifles were manufactured by the millions. For example, the revered Winchester Model 94 in its many variations passed the three million mark in the mid-1960s and many more were produced in later years.

The search for true value begins with research, and it is during this process that the eager rifle owner will discover why his item is worth a lot . . . or not.

There is much to know about gun values, condition, and scarcity. Sad to say but not every rifle ever made is that "One in a Million" that will bring top dollar on the auction block or collector's table. The curious and persistent collector will take the time to research the manufacturing and collectible background of a particular rifle model and goes into the trading world confident that he knows what he has in his hands, its history, and what it is worth in the nebulous world of firearms values. This will allow the seller or trader to realize the maximum "real" value of his rifle and not go away thinking that he's been had. Rare, valuable rifles have been, and continue to be, sold for pennies on the dollar. Anyone who's ever bought, sold, or traded a used firearm has at least one "Got it for a steal" story. It has happened before and will happen again—but don't let it happen to you!

To avoid being taken at the trader's table, you must do your homework. Upon discovery or receipt of a rifle you think is valuable, take it home and study it. Gather as many current firearms reference books as you can find and try to determine your rifle's make, model, and date of manufacture based on the serial number and other markings. Look for information on how many such rifles were produced, where, and when. The fun begins when you discover that your rifle is a special, unusual, or custom model; perhaps it was made at a different factory or for a different retailer. Its identifying marks (proof marks) may indicate that it was part of an earlier (or later) production run, or that those marks do not match from receiver to frame or barrel, indicating that the rifle has been reconditioned, rebuilt, or assembled from random, leftover parts.

Already we can see that identifying your specific rifle can lead you on a wild goose chase through reams of paperwork, piles of reference books, and, if necessary, to a manufacturer's representative or archivist who can tell you when, where, and how many of your particular item were made. Also, visit local and regional auction houses, collectors, and dealers and get a representative assessment of your rifle. Ask for appraisals as well (expect some dealers to levy a fee for an "official" appraisal), and don't be shocked if none of the figures are comparable.

It takes time to glean this information and the process is often discouraging or confusing. One word of advice: Never sell a rifle you have not positively identified.

The ringers are often the ones that are worth 100 times more than the standard production rifle. Know exactly what you have in hand before you offer it for sale, and don't let anyone tell you it's not what you think it is unless they have irrefutable written documentation. Word-of-mouth pronouncements or "I sold one just like it last week," is not good enough. If you are in desperate need for cash and just want to sell the rifle, go ahead and take your chances; but if you want full value for each rifle you sell, be patient and persistent in determining exactly what it is you have to sell and how much it is worth in the local collectible market.

When you have accurately and satisfactorily established the make, model, and year of manufacture of your rifle it is time to determine its dollar value. This can be even more daunting than the identification process. Everyone wants to realize the most from their collectible investment, but the only ones who ever achieve that goal are those who insure their property based on a certified appraiser's written estimate. Even then, there is wiggle room (for the insurance company) because a rifle that's appraised at "$5,000 to $10,000" instantly presents a range of value that varies by 100 percent! In these cases it's best to insure the item for the maximum value and pay the associated premium to protect it; but even then it is only going to be worth

top dollar if it is stolen, permanently lost, or irreparably damaged. From this perspective, your $10,000 rifle is essentially worthless while it is in your possession because it will only pay off when it no longer belongs to you!

In-hand values of actively traded rifles vary tremendously. Never assume that because a rifle is listed in a collector's catalog that it will always be worth top dollar during every transaction. None of the top values listed in any collectible catalog are cast in stone, required by law, or guaranteed in any other way. They are merely reflections of what other collectors, auctioneers, or traders have been willing to pay for that particular rifle.

Consult as many collectibles references as you can find to establish your rifle's true value. Estimates may vary from book to book for any number of reasons, but in most cases the book values given are likely to be within 10 percent or so, depending on the source. If you notice an unusually wide range of values for your particular rifle, perform additional studies to determine why. If necessary, contact the reference book's editor or publisher for clarification. It is always worth the effort in determining what a collectible firearm may be worth. Never conclude a sale unless you are absolutely certain of your rifle's identification, condition, and value.

No collectible item's value is absolute, however. Prices and enthusiasm for a given model change with the passing years, and some collectibles actually lose value exponentially as they lose favor with dealers and collectors. Fortunately, most firearms appreciate in value as time goes on, if only at the rate of a few dollars per year. Also, interest in some models may continue unabated for decades as shown by collectors' endless love affair with Savage Model 99s, Winchester Model 94s and Model 70s (pre-64, of course), early Remingtons, and the original Henry rifles. Certain custom, centennial, and commemorative models also increase in value at higher, nearly immeasurable, or unpredictable rates. For example, custom double-barrel rifles produced by James Purdey & Sons prior to World War II are worth upwards of $50,000, with the Nitro Express calibers demanding $85,000 and more. Some of these exceptionally valuable rifles are in the "Are you kidding me?" range and will quite honestly never be seen on the open collectible market except through some extreme and outrageous mistake. If you happen to bump into such a rifle in a rural roadside yard sale, forget everything we've discussed here and just buy it!

In the real world of collectible rifles there is plenty of room for doubt, dickering, horse trading, and speculation. This is why learning all you can about your rifle is imperative if you want to get the highest value for it in a sale or trade.

In addition to age, condition is an important, often deciding, factor in trading and collecting. Any rifle that is "New in the Box" will bring higher prices than a rifle that is obviously, albeit occasionally, used. A rifle that has lost much of its original wood or metal finish, has been repaired, tampered with, or rebuilt, has major cracks in the stock, forearm, or frame, shows rust and pitting, has lost or broken parts, and so forth will give the buyer plenty of room to argue for a reduction in its value. Generally, a rifle with all of its original parts but showing signs of normal wear and use will be worth more than the same model that has been refurbished, rebuilt, or repaired. Learn to develop a keen eye for after-market repairs and trust your instincts: If it looks too good to be true it probably is unless the piece comes with written affirmation from the manufacturer, archivist, or a certified appraiser.

The trading game is a simple one that has been played by experts of varying degree for ages. Ideally, the transaction ends with each party walking away thinking they came out ahead. If you've ever played checkers or chess you already understand the process: move and countermove until one party or the other runs out of options. The seller can always withdraw if he thinks his rifle is worth substantially more than the standing offer, or he can continue to parry in hopes of getting full price for the item. At this point it's a matter of how much the buyer wants the rifle. A buyer that is anxious to complete a collection or knows someone who simply must have the piece will pay much more than the collector who always adheres to the "buy low, sell high" mantra. In a well choreographed dance both parties shake hands and walk away satisfied, but in the back of their minds they always wonder: "What if?" Only years of experience and the sting of a few trades gone wrong can reduce the number of disappointing transactions. The most sensible approach is to have a price in mind for your collectible rifle based on your research and not wavering from it. If one buyer won't pay your price for it, conclude the transaction and wait for another opportunity to sell. Rifles have sat on dealers' shelves for years before the appropriate trade was made. In general, the player who is the greatest hurry to close on a sale is the one who will likely lose the most.

Remember, patience and persistence is the key to a successful, satisfying collectible transaction.

Trading Tips from a Used Gun Pro

There are plenty of picnic table gun experts out there and some of them do know a little about the used gun trade. But when it comes time to sell, trade, or barter a particular rifle or collection, it's best to consult with a certified, knowledgeable trader. The difference in a specific rifle's value could be in the hundreds if not thousands of dollars. Many a priceless gem sneaks through because one of the parties involved hadn't done his research.

"Don't be in a hurry to sell a rifle you've inherited or discovered in your grandfather's attic," advised Dave Michniewicz (pronounced "mick-nivits"), chief used gun coordinator at Kittery Trading Post, in Kittery, Maine. "Look at as many reference books as you can, attend auctions and gun shows, and look at www.gunbroker.com to establish a positive identification of the rifle and its current value."

Michniewicz, who trades an average of 1,200 guns each month, has over 20 years of experience in the used gun trade. He recently purchased a Winchester Model 1873 lever-action rifle for $7,500 and also brokered a deal on a pair of Rigby bolt-action rifles that were worth more than $16,000 each. The most valuable firearm brought into the Kittery Trading Post during his tenure was an original Parker double-barrel shotgun worth over $25,000.

"Know what you have before you sell or trade it," Michniewicz said. "Many rifles acquired in estate sales or 'sidewalk auctions' may be worth far more than the owner realizes. Never rush into a sale or trade until you know exactly what you have, it's condition, and its current value."

When considering a purchase or sale, Michniewicz advises traders to begin by establishing the condition of the rifle. "Know and understand the NRA Standards of Condition and apply them to the rifle in question. If there are doubts, concerns, or uncertainties, consult with a certified used gun dealer, trader, auctioneer, or other expert before you sell," he said.

"A rifle in original condition, no matter how bad it may look, could be worth substantially more than the same model rifle that has been altered, refinished, or repaired," Michniewicz noted. "Look for defects in wood and metal parts as well as barrel condition because all of these can affect the value of the firearm."

Overall, Michniewicz said that the highest value for any used firearm will

Dave Michniewicz, chief used gun coordinator at Maine's Kittery Trading Post, urges novice traders to research each rifle they plan to buy or sell before placing it on the market.

Michniewicz advises consulting with other knowledgeable experts on a rifle's condition and current value before offering for sale.

likely be realized in a private sale. Because dealers, brokers, and other professionals must factor in their costs, overhead, profit margin, and other considerations, the price they offer for a rifle may be somewhat lower than its "book" value or the amount an eager private collector may offer.

Be Patient

According to Michniewicz, the biggest mistake beginners in the collectible trade make is rushing a sale. A hurried transaction could result in a huge loss.

"This usually happens when a rifle is found in an attic or barn and is quickly sold to make a fast buck," Michniewicz said. "Quite often the seller does not know the true market value of the firearm or simply wants to get rid of the piece because he has no interest in it. Take the time to research each piece you intend to sell

and don't accept any offers until you can positively identify the rifle, know something of its history, and can determine what it is worth on today's market.

"Whenever there is a question about a particular model, continue researching until you know exactly what you have and what its current value is depending on where and to whom you decide to sell it," Michniewicz said, adding, "It's important to remember that any published value is merely a guide. The final determination of value of any given firearm could be much higher or lower depending on its condition, location of sale, and other factors."

Location and Condition

Michniewicz noted that in many cases firearms can be more valuable in certain parts of the country due to local popularity or history.

"For example," he said, "a Marlin .30-30 maybe be more valuable in the Northeast than it would be in the Southwest or California, where bolt-action rifles are more popular."

In addition, Michnievicz suggested that collectors try to purchase firearms that are in the best possible condition. "While all guns have value, rifles that are in the best condition will bring the highest premiums," he said. "Minor imperfections will not affect the ultimate value of a collectible rifle, but be on the lookout for shoddy repairs, replacement parts, or refinished metal or wood."

Watch the Market

Michniewicz also cautioned traders about investing during periods of volatility in the market. "A recent surge in AR sales had prices spiking ten to fifteen percent for a short period of time," Michniewicz noted. "Usually after such a jump prices will quickly go back down. A buyer who paid top dollar during the spike in sales may have to wait a considerable length of time before values increase to that level again."

The Reality of Gun Trading

Michniewicz, who purchases more than a thousand firearms each month, offered some advice for clients interested in selling or trading used rifles. Most traders come to Michniewicz's shop having little or no knowledge of the age, condition, or value of the gun they are

The Kittery Trading Post's used gun buyers process more than 1,000 rifles, shotguns, and handguns each month. Many end up on the shops used gun racks for sale, trade, or barter.

offering for sale. Once they are shown the appropriate references, understand its condition issues, and know the current value of the piece, the majority are at least pleased, if not happily surprised, at the offer that is made.

"Some clients come in expecting to sell the gun for a higher price, and there are times when they decide not to accept my offer," Michniewicz admitted. "However, I feel confident that my appraisals are accurate and in keeping with current market values. Some clients simply expect to get more for their gun and I respect that. If a person is patient and persistent he

may be able to get the price he wants through a private sale or auction."

Michniewicz noted that while he often offers clients "close to" the "book" value of a particular firearm, it's important to remember that there is a cost of doing business that must be factored into the sale.

"If a client wants top dollar for the piece, I'd suggest that he try selling it privately, online, or through collectors of that particular make and model who may be willing to offer more for the piece," Michniewicz said.

Michniewicz had one final piece of advice for prospective rifle traders: "Always make sure that

each firearm you bring in for an appraisal is unloaded. You'd be surprised at how often a customer will come in with a gun that has a live round in the chamber or magazine."

To contact Dave Michniewicz or to find out more about the Kittery Trading Post's used firearms program or listings, email him at davemich@ktp. com. For a complete listing of used guns available at the Kittery Trading Post, log onto www.ktpguns.com or call (800) USA-GUNS (878-4867).

GUN TRADER'S GUIDE TO RIFLES

Action Arms Timber Wolfe

Alpha Arms Custom

Alpha Arms Alaskan

Alpha Arms Jaguar

A.A. ARMS — Monroe, North Carolina

AR-9 SEMIAUTOMATIC CARBINE . . . **NiB $797 Ex $635 Gd $435**
Semiautomatic recoil-operated rifle w/side-folding metal stock design. Fires from a closed bolt. Caliber: 9mm Parabellum. 20-round magazine. 16.25-inch bbl., 33 inches overall. Weight: 6.5 lbs. Fixed blade, protected postfront sight adjustable for elevation, winged square notched rear. Matte phosphate/blue or nickel finish. Checkered polymer grip/frame. Made 1991 to 1994 (banned)

ACTION ARMS — Philadelphia, Pennsylvania

MODEL B SPORTER
SEMI-AUTOMATIC CARBINE . . . . . **NiB $644 Ex $566 Gd $377**
Caliber: 9mm Parabellum, 10-round magazine. 16-inch bbl. Weight: 8.75 lbs. Post front sight; adj. rear. Imported 1994.

TIMBERWOLF REPEATING RIFLE
Calibers: .357 Mag./.38 Special and .44 Mag. slide-action. Tubular magazine holds 10 and 8 rounds, respectively. 18.5-inch bbl. 36.5 inches overall. Weight: 5.5 lbs. Fixed blade front sight; adj. rear. Receiver w/integral scope mounts. Checkered walnut stock. Imported from 1989 to 1993.

Blued model . . . . NiB $335 Ex $271 Gd $190
Chrome model, add $75
.44 Mag., add $125

ALPHA ARMS, INC. — Dallas, Texas

CUSTOM BOLT-ACTION RIFLE . . . . . . **NiB $1690 Ex $1335 Gd $867**
Calibers: .17 Rem. thru .338 Win. Mag. Right or left-hand action in three action lengths w/three-lug locking system and 60-degree bolt rotation. 20- to 24-inch round or octagonal bbl. Weight: 6 to 7 lbs. No sights. Presentation-grade California Claro walnut stock w/hand-rubbed oil finish, custom inletted sling swivels and ebony forend tip. Made from 1984 to 1987.

ALASKAN BOLT-ACTION RIFLE . . . . . . **NiB $1689 Ex $1334 Gd $869**
Similar to Custom model but w/stainless-steel bbl. and receiver w/all other parts coated w/Nitex. Weight: 6.75 to 7.25 lbs. Open sights w/bbl-band sling swivel. Classic-style Alpha wood stock w/Niedner-style steel grip cap and solid recoil pad. Made from 1985 to 1987.

GRAND SLAM
BOLT-ACTION RIFLE . . . . **NiB $1309 Ex $1065 Gd $795**
Same as Custom model but has Alphawood (fiberglass and wood) classic-style stock featuring Niedner-style grip cap. Wt: 6.5 lbs. Left-hand models same value. Made 1985 to 1987.

AMT (Arcadia Machine & Tool)

CUSTOM BOLT-ACTION RIFLE

Same as Custom Rifle except designed on Mauser-style action w/claw extractor drilled and tapped for scope. Originally designated Alpha Model 1. Calibers: .243, 7mm-08, .308 original chambering (1984 to 1985) up to .338 Win. Mag. in standard model; .338 thru .458 Win. Mag. in Big Five model (1987). Teflon-coated trigger guard/floorplate assembly. Made from 1984 to 1987.

Jaguar Grade I . . . . NiB $1025 Ex $855 Gd $624
Jaguar Grade II . . . . NiB $1255 Ex $684 Gd $700
Jaguar Grade III . . . . NiB $1306 Ex $1046 Gd $756
Jaguar Grade IV . . . . NiB $1410 Ex $1056 Gd $755
Big Five model . . . . NiB $1700 Ex $1198 Gd $977

AMERICAN ARMS — N. Kansas City, Missouri

1860 HENRY . . . . NiB $908 Ex $698 Gd $530

Replica of 1860 Henry rifle. Calibers: .44-40 or .45 LC. 24.25-inch half-octagonal bbl. 43.75 inches overall. Weight: 9.25 lbs. Brass frame and appointments. Straight-grip walnut buttstock.

1866 WINCHESTER

Replica of 1866 Winchester. Calibers: .44-40 or .45 LC. 19-inch round tapered bbl. (carbine) or 24.25-inch tapered octagonal bbl. (rifle). 38 to 43.25 inches overall. Weight: 7.75 or 8.15 lbs. Brass frame, elevator and buttplate. Walnut buttstock and forend.

Carbine . . . . NiB $736 Ex $625 Gd $409
Rifle . . . . NiB $736 Ex $625 Gd $409

1873 WINCHESTER

Replica of 1873 Winchester rifle. Calibers: .44-40 or .45 LC. 24.25-inch tapered octagonal bbl. w/tubular magazine. Color casehardened steel frame w/brass elevator and ejection port cover. Walnut buttstock w/steel buttplate.

Standard model . . . . NiB $867 Ex $710 Gd $419
Deluxe model . . . . NiB $1130 Ex $924 Gd $640

AMERICAN SPIRIT ARMS CORP. — Scottsdale, Arizona

ASA BULL BARREL FLATTOP RIFLE . . . . NiB $1033 Ex $709 Gd $533

Semi-automatic. Caliber: ..223 Rem. Patterned after AR-15. Forged steel lower receiver, aluminum flattop upper receiver, 24-inch stainless bull barrel, free-floating aluminum hand guard, includes Harris bipod.

ASA BULL BARREL A2 RIFLE . . . . NiB $979 Ex $733 Gd $535

Similar to Flattop Rifle except has A2 upper receiver with carrying handle and sights. Introduced 1999.

OPEN MATCH RIFLE . . . . NiB $1456 Ex $1097 Gd $745

Caliber: .223 Rem. Bbl.: 16-inch fluted and ported stainless steel match with round shroud. Flattop without sights, forged upper and lower receiver, match trigger. Introduced 2001.

LIMITED MATCH RIFLE . . . . NiB $1397 Ex $900 Gd $579

Caliber: .223 Rem. Bbl.: 16-inch fluted stainless steel match with round shroud. National Match front and rear sights; match trigger.

DCM SERVICE RIFLE . . . . NiB $1398 Ex $915 Gd $618

Caliber: .223 Rem. Bbl.: 20-inch stainless steel match type with free-floating shroud. National Match front and rear sights; match trigger; pistol grip.

ASA M4 RIFLE . . . . NiB $935 Ex $679 Gd $477

Caliber: .223 Rem. Non-collapsible stock, M4 hand guard, 16-inch bbl. w/muzzle brake; aluminum flattop upper receiver.

ASA A2 RIFLE . . . . NiB $908 Ex $633 Gd $509

Caliber: .223 Rem. A2 receiver; 20-inch National Match barrel. Introduced in 1999.

ASA CARBINE . . . . NiB $1066 Ex $700 Gd $589

Caliber: .223 Rem. or Short. Side-charging, flattop receiver; M4 hand guard; 16-inch National Match bbl. w/slotted muzzle brake.

POST-BAN CARBINE . . . . NiB $900 Ex $690 Gd $477

Caliber: .223 Rem. Wilson 16-inch National Match bbl.; non-collapsible stock. Introduced 1999.

BULL BARREL A2 INVADER . . . . NiB $1022 Ex $710 Gd $544

Caliber: .223 Rem. Similar to ASA 24-inch bull bbl. rifle except has 16-inch stainless steel bbl.. Introduced 1999.

A2 CAR CARBINE . . . . NiB $1031 Ex $703 Gd $544

Caliber: 9mm Parabellum. Forged receiver, non-collapsible stock. Bbl.: 16-inch Wilson w/o muzzle brake, bird cage flash hider (pre-ban) or muzzle brake (post-ban).

FLATTOP CAR RIFLE . . . . NiB $1031 Ex $703 Gd $544

Caliber: 9mm Parabellum. Similar to A2 CAR Rifle except flattop design w/o sights. Introduced 2002.

ASA TACTICAL RIFLE . . . . NiB $1788 Ex $1096 Gd $780

Caliber: .308 Win. Bbl.: 16-inch stainless steel regular or match; side-charging handle; pistol grip.
Match model (w/fluted bbl. match trigger, chrome finish) add . . . $525

ASA 24-INCH MATCH RIFLE . . . . . . NiB $1780 Ex $1106 Gd $789

Caliber: .308 Win. Bbl.: 24-inch stainless steel match with or w/o fluting/porting. Side-charging handle; pistol grip. Introduced 2002.

AMT (ARCADIA MACHINE & TOOL) — Irwindale, California

BOLT-ACTION REPEATING RIFLE

Winchester-type push-feed or Mauser-type controlled-feed short-, medium- or long-action. Calibers: .223 Remington, .22-250 Remington, .243 A, .243 Winchester, 6mm PPC, .25-06 Remington, 6.5x08, .270 Winchester, 7x57 Mauser, 7mm-08 Remington, 7mm Remington Mag., 7.62x39mm, .308 Winchester, .30-06, .300 Winchester Mag., .338 Winchester Mag., .375 H&H, .416 Remington, .416 Rigby, .458 Winchester Mag. 22- to 28-inch number 3 contour bbl. Weight: 7.75 to 8.5 lbs. Sights: None furnished; drilled and tapped for scope mounts. Classic composite or Kevlar stock. Made from 1996 to 1997.

Standard model . . . . NiB $890 Ex $720 Gd $531
Deluxe model . . . . NiB $1076 Ex $830 Gd $529

BOLT-ACTION SINGLE-SHOT RIFLE

Winchester-type cone breech push-feed or Mauser-type controlled-feed action. Calibers: .22 Hornet, .22 PPC, .222 Remington, .223 Remington, .22-250 Remington, .243 A, .243 Winchester, 6mm PPC, 6.5x08, .270 Win., 7mm-08 Remington, .308 Winchester 22- to 28-inch #3 contour bbl. Weight: 7.75 to 8.5 lbs. Sights: None furnished; drilled and tapped for scope mounts. Classic composite or Kevlar stock. Made from 1996.

Standard model . . . . NiB $856 Ex $733 Gd $520
Deluxe model . . . . NiB $1066 Ex $744 Gd $500

AMT (Arcadia Machine & Tool)

Anschutz Model 54.18MS-REP

CHALLENGER AUTOLOADING TARGET RIFLE SERIES I, II & III
Similar to Small Game Hunter except w/McMillan target fiberglass stock. Caliber: .22 LR. 10-round magazine. 16.5-, 18-, 20-, or 22-inch bull bbl. Drilled and tapped for scope mount; no sights. Stainless steel finish. Made from 1994 to 1998.
Challenger I Standard . . . . NiB $814 Ex $577 Gd $409
Challenger II w/muzzle brake. . . . . NiB $908 Ex $755 Gd $554
Challenger III w/bbl extension . . . . NiB $966 Ex $588 Gd $452
W/jeweled trigger, add $225

LIGHTNING 25/22
AUTOLOADING RIFLE . . . . NiB $313 Ex $237 Gd $170
Caliber: .22 LR. 25-round magazine. 18-inch tapered or bull bbl. Weight: 6 lbs. 37 inches overall. Sights: Adj. rear; ramp front. Folding stainless-steel stock w/matte finish. Made 1986 to 1993.

SMALL GAME HUNTER SERIES
Similar to AMT 25/22 except w/conventional matte black fiberglass/nylon stock. 10-round rotary magazine. 22-inch bbl. 40.5 inches overall. Weight: 6 lbs. Grooved for scope; no sights. Made from 1986 to 1994 (Series I), and 1993 (Series II).
Hunter I . . . . NiB $330 Ex $218 Gd $155
Hunter II (w/22-inch
heavy target bbl.) . . . . NiB $267 Ex $223 Gd $159

MAGNUM HUNTER AUTO RIFLE . . . . NiB $490 Ex $455 Gd $240
Similar to Lightning Small Game Hunter II model except chambered in .22 WRF w/22-inch match-grade bbl. Made from 1995 to 1998.

ANSCHUTZ RIFLES — Ulm, Germany.
Currently imported by Merkel USA.

Anschutz models 1407 ISU, 1408-ED, 1411, 1413, 1418, 1432, 1433, 1518, and 1533 were marketed in the United States by Savage Arms. Further, Anschutz models 1403, 1416, 1422D, 1441, 1516, and 1522D were sold as Savage/Anschutz with Savage model designations (see also listings under Savage Arms).

MODEL 54.18MS . . . . NiB $733 Ex $569 Gd $469
Bolt-action, single-shot, Caliber: .22 LR. 22-inch bbl. European hardwood stock w/cheekpiece. Stipple-checkered forend and Wundhammer swell pistol-grip. Receiver grooved, drilled and tapped for scope blocks. Weight: 8.4 lbs. Imported from 1982 to 1997.

MODEL 54.18MS-REP REPEATING RIFLE
Same as model 54.18MS except w/repeating action and 5-round magazine. 22- to 30-inch bbl. 41-49 inches overall. Avg. weight: 7 lbs., 12 oz. Hardwood or synthetic gray thumbhole stock. Imported from 1989 to 1997.
Standard MS-REP model . . . . NiB $733 Ex $569 Gd $469
Left-hand model . . . . NiB $745 Ex $579 Gd $479

MODEL 64S BOLT-ACTION SINGLE-SHOT RIFLE
Bolt-action, single-shot. Caliber: .22 LR. 26-inch bbl. Checkered European hardwood stock w/Wundhammer swell pistol-grip and adj. buttplate. Single-stage trigger. Aperture sights. Weight: 8.25 lbs. Imported from 1963 to 1981.
Standard . . . . NiB $1408 Ex $730 Gd $515
Left-hand model . . . . NiB $1408 Ex $730 Gd $515

MODEL 64MS BOLT-ACTION SINGLE-SHOT RIFLE
Bolt-action, single-shot. Caliber: .22 LR. 21.25-inch bbl. European hardwood silhouette-style stock w/cheekpiece. Forend base and Wundhammer swell pistol-grip, stipple-checkered. Adj. two-stage trigger. Receiver grooved, drilled and tapped for scope blocks. Weight: 8 lbs. Imported from 1982 to 1996.
Standard or Featherweight
(disc. 1988) . . . . NiB $1133 Ex $780 Gd $620
Left-hand model . . . . NiB $1133 Ex $780 Gd $620

MODEL 64MSR BOLT-ACTION REPEATER
Similar to Anschutz Model 64MS except repeater w/5-round magazine. Imported from 1996.
Standard model. . . . . NiB $1045 Ex $789 Gd $603
Left-hand model . . . . NiB $1045 Ex $789 Gd $603

MODEL 520/61 SEMIAUTOMATIC . . . . . . NiB $331 Ex $270 Gd $165
Caliber: .22 LR. 10-round magazine. 24-inch bbl. Sights: Folding leaf rear, hooded ramp front. Receiver grooved for scope mounting. Rotary-style safety. Monte Carlo stock and beavertail forend, checkered. Weight: 6.5 lbs. Imported from 1982 to 1983.

MODEL 525 AUTOLOADER
Caliber: .22 LR. 10-round magazine. 20- or 24-inch bbl. 39 to 43 inches overall. Weight: 6.1 to 6.5 lbs. Adj. folding rear sight; hooded ramp front. Checkered European hardwood Monte Carlo style buttstock and beavertail forend. Sling swivel studs. Imported from 1984 to 1995.
Carbine model
(disc. 1986) . . . . NiB $452 Ex $324 Gd $225
Rifle model (24-inch bbl.) . . . . NiB $540 Ex $443 Gd $319

MODEL 1403B . . . . NiB $935 Ex $745 Gd $440
A lighter-weight model designed for Biathlon competition. Caliber: .22 LR. 21.5-inch bbl. Adj. two-stage trigger. Adj. grooved wood buttplate, stipple-checkered deep thumb-rest flute and straight pistol-grip. Weight: 9 lbs. w/sights. Imported from 1990 to 1992.

MODEL 1403D MATCH SINGLE-SHOT TARGET RIFLE
Caliber: .22 LR. 25-inch bbl. 43 inches overall. Weight: 8.6 lbs. No sights, receiver grooved for Anschutz target sights. Walnut-finished hardwood target stock w/adj. buttplate. Importation disc. 1992.
Standard model. . . . . NiB $700 Ex $567 Gd $417
W/match sights. . . . . NiB $988 Ex $779 Gd $555

Anschutz Rifles

Anschutz Model 1416D

Anschutz Model 1418

Anschutz Model 1422D

MODEL 1407 ISU MATCH 54 RIFLE
Bolt-action, single-shot, caliber: .22 LR. 26.88-inch bbl. Scope bases. Receiver grooved for Anschutz sights. Single-stage adj. trigger. Select walnut target stock w/deep forearm for position shooting, adj. buttplate, hand stop and swivel. Weight: 10 lbs. Imported from 1970 to 1981.
Standard model . . . . NiB $633 Ex $535 Gd $291
Left-hand model . . . . NiB $633 Ex $535 Gd $291
W/international sights, add. $75

MODEL 1408 . . . . NiB $466 Ex $408 Gd $366
Bolt-action, single-shot, caliber: .22 LR. 23.5-inch bbl. w/sliding weights. No metallic sights. Receiver drilled and tapped for scope-sight bases. Single-stage adj. trigger. Oversize bolt knob. Select walnut stock w/thumbhole, adj. comb and buttplate. Weight: 9.5 lbs. Introduced 1976. Disc.
Model 1408ED, add $175

MODEL 1411 MATCH 54 RIFLE
Bolt-action, single-shot. Caliber: .22 LR. 27.5-inch extra heavy bbl. w/mounted scope bases. Receiver grooved for Anschutz sights. Single-stage adj. trigger. Select walnut target stock w/cheekpiece (adj. in 1973 and later production, full pistol-grip, beavertail forearm, adj. buttplate, hand stop and swivel. Model 1411-L has left-hand stock. Weight: 11 lbs. Disc.
W/non-adj. cheekpiece . . . . NiB $678 Ex $423 Gd $267
W/adj. cheekpiece . . . . NiB $703 Ex $532 Gd $402
W/Anschutz
International sight set, add $300

MODEL 1413 SUPER MATCH 54 RIFLE
Freestyle international target rifle w/specifications similar to those of Model 1411, except w/special stock w/thumbhole, adj. pistol grip, adj. cheekpiece in 1973 and later production, adj. hook buttplate, adj. palmrest. Model 1413-L has left-hand stock. Weight: 15.5 lbs. Disc.
W/non-adj. cheekpiece . . . . NiB $822 Ex $733 Gd $400
W/adj. cheekpiece . . . . NiB $704 Ex $566 Gd $399
W/Anschutz
International sight set, add $300

MODEL 1416D . . . . NiB $590 Ex $577 Gd $368
Bolt-action sporter. Caliber: .22 LR. 22.5-inch bbl. Sights: Folding leaf rear; hooded ramp front. Receiver grooved for scope mounting. Select European stock w/cheekpiece, skip-checkered pistol grip and forearm. Weight: 6 lbs. Imported from 1982 to 2007.

MODEL 1416D CLASSIC/CUSTOM SPORTERS
Same as Model 1416D except w/American classic-style stock (Classic) or modified European-style stock w/Monte Carlo roll-over cheekpiece and Schnabel forend (Custom). Weight: 5.5 lbs. (Classic); 6 lbs. (Custom). Imported from 1986 to 2007.
Model 1416D Classic . . . . NiB $966 Ex $549 Gd $377
Model 1416D Classic,
"True" left-hand . . . . NiB $1009 Ex $577 Gd $419
Model 1416D Custom   NiB $946 Ex $530 Gd $377
Model 1416D fiberglass (1991–92) NiB $966 Ex $623 Gd $445

MODEL 1418 BOLT-ACTION
SPORTER. . . . . NiB $412 Ex $322 Gd $200
Caliber: .22 LR. 5- or 10-round magazine. 19.75-inch bbl. Sights: Folding leaf rear; hooded ramp front. Receiver grooved for scope mounting. Select walnut stock, Mannlicher type w/cheekpiece, pistol-grip and forearm skip checkered. Weight: 5.5 lbs. Introduced 1976. Disc.

MODEL 1418D BOLT-ACTION
SPORTER. . . . . NiB $1008 Ex $886 Gd $533
Caliber: .22 LR. 5- or 10-round magazine. 19.75-inch bbl. European walnut Monte Carlo stock, Mannlicher type w/cheekpiece, pistol-grip and forend skip-line checkered, buffalo horn Schnabel tip. Weight: 5.5 lbs. Imported from 1982 to 1995, and 1998 to 2003.

MODEL 1422D CLASSIC/CUSTOM RIFLE
Bolt-action sporter. Caliber: .22 LR. Five-round removable straight-feed clip magazine. 24-inch bbl. Sights: Folding leaf rear; hooded ramp front. Select European walnut stock, classic type (Classic); Monte Carlo w/hand-carved rollover cheekpiece (Custom). Weight: 7.25 lbs. (Classic) 6.5 lbs. (Custom). Imported from 1982 to 1989.
Model 1422D Classic . . . . NiB $833 Ex $670 Gd $432
Model 1422D Custom. . . . . NiB $896 Ex $833 Gd $479

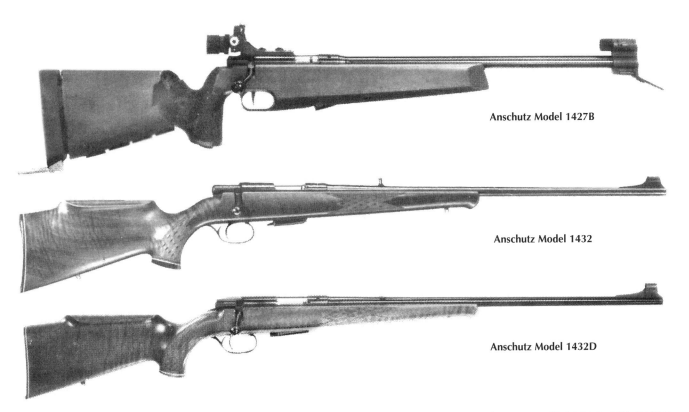

Anschutz Model 1427B

Anschutz Model 1432

Anschutz Model 1432D

MODEL 1827B BIATHLON RIFLE   NiB $1943 Ex $1377 Gd $937
Bolt-action clip repeater. Caliber: .22 LR. 21.5-inch bbl. Two-stage trigger w/wing-type safety. Hardwood stock w/deep fluting, pistol grip and deep forestock with adj. hand stop rail. Target sights w/ adjustable weights. Imported from 1982 to date as Model 1827B.

MODEL 1430D MATCH . . . . NiB $966 Ex $644 Gd $429
Improved version of Model 64S. Bolt-action, single-shot. Caliber: .22 LR. 26-inch medium-heavy bbl. Walnut Monte Carlo stock w/ cheekpiece, adj. buttplate, deep midstock tapered to forend. Pistol-grip and contoured thumb groove w/stipple checkering. Single-stage adj. trigger. Target sights. Weight: 8.38 lbs. Imported from 1982 to 1990.

MODEL 1432 BOLT-ACTION SPORTER
Caliber: .22 Hornet. 5-round box magazine. 24-inch bbl. Sights: Folding leaf rear, hooded ramp front. Receiver grooved for scope mounting. Select walnut stock w/Monte Carlo comb and cheekpiece, pistol-grip and forearm skip-checkered. Weight: 6.75 lbs. Imported from 1974 to 1987. (Reintroduced as 1700/1730 series.)
Early model
(1974–85) . . . . NiB $1344 Ex $988 Gd $721
Late model
(1985–87) . . . . NiB $1145 Ex $933 Gd $631

MODEL 1432D CLASSIC/CUSTOM RIFLE
Bolt-action sporter similar to Model 1422D except chambered for Caliber: .22 Hornet. 4-round magazine. 23.5-inch bbl. Weight: 7.75 lbs. (Classic); 6.5 lbs. (Custom). Classic stock on Classic model; fancy-grade Monte Carlo w/hand-carved rollover cheekpiece (Custom). Imported from 1982 to 1987. (Reintroduced as 1700/1730 series.)
Model 1432D Classic . . . . NiB $1344 Ex $982 Gd $733
Model 1432D Custom. . . . . NiB $1175 Ex $923 Gd $634

MODEL 1433 BOLT-ACTION SPORTER . . . . . NiB $1131 Ex $916 Gd $644
Caliber: .22 Hornet. 5-round box magazine. 19.75-inch bbl. Sights: Folding leaf rear, hooded ramp front. Receiver grooved for scope mounting. Single-stage or double-set trigger. Select walnut Mannlicher stock; cheekpiece, pistol-grip and forearm skip-checkered. Weight: 6.5 lbs. Imported from 1976 to 1986.

MODEL 1448D. . . . . NiB $421 Ex $324 Gd $236
Similar to Model 1449 except chambered for Caliber: .22 LR. w/22.5-inch smooth bore bbl. and no sights. Walnut-finished hardwood stock. Imported from 1999 to 2001.

MODEL 1449D YOUTH SPORTER. . .NiB $300 Ex $233 Gd $177
Bolt-action sporter version of Model 2000. Caliber: .22 LR. 5-round box magazine. 16.25-inch bbl. Weight: 3.5 lbs. Hooded ramp front sight, addition. Walnut-finished hardwood stock. Imported from 1990 to 1991.

MODEL 1450B TARGET RIFLE . . . . NiB $703 Ex $533 Gd $397
Biathlon rifle developed on 2000 Series action. 19.5-inch bbl. Weight: 5.5 lbs. Adj. buttplate. Target sights. Imported from 1993 to 1994.

MODEL 1451 E/R SPORTER/TARGET
Bolt-action, single-shot (1451E) or repeater (1451R). Caliber: .22 LR. 22- or 22.75-inch bbl. w/o sights. Select hardwood stock w/stippled pistolgrip and vented forearm. beavertail forend, adj. cheekpiece, and deep thumb flute. Weight: 6.5 lbs. Imported from 1996 to 2001.
Model 1451E (disc. 1997) . . . . NiB $487 Ex $366 Gd $254
Model 1451R . . . . NiB $479 Ex $455 Gd $310

MODEL 1451D CLASSIC/CUSTOM RIFLE
Same as Model 1451R except w/walnut-finished hardwood stock (Classic) or modified European-style walnut stock w/Monte Carlo rollover cheekpiece and Schnabel forend (Custom). Weight: 5 lbs. Imported from 1998 to 2001.
Model 1451D Classic (Super) . . . . . NiB $367 Ex $288 Gd $199
Model 1451D Custom. . . . . NiB $488 Ex $455 Gd $321

Anschutz Rifles

Anschutz Model 1700

Anschutz Model 1803D

Anschutz Model 1907

MODEL 1451 ST- R RIFLE . . . . **NiB $499 Ex $454 Gd $342**
Same as Model 1451R except w/two-stage trigger and walnut-finished hardwood uncheckered stock. Imported from 1996 to 2001.

MODEL 1516D CLASSIC/CUSTOM RIFLE
Same as Model 1416D except chambered for Caliber: .22 Magnum RF, with American classic-style stock (Classic) or modified European-style stock w/Monte Carlo rollover cheekpiece and Schnabel forend (Custom). Weight: 5.5 lbs. (Classic), 6 lbs. (Custom). Imported from 1986 to 2003.
Model 1516D Classic . . . . **NiB $704 Ex $566 Gd $379**
Model 1516D Custom . . . . **NiB $639 Ex $600 Gd $423**

MODELS 1518/1518D SPORTING RIFLES
Same as Model 1418 except chambered for .22 Magnum RF, 4-round box magazine. Model 1518 intro. 1976. Disc. Model 1518D has full Mannlicher-type stock. Imported from 1982 to 2001.
Model 1518 . . . . **NiB $766 Ex $644 Gd $423**
Model 1518D . . . . **NiB $974 Ex $788 Gd $544**
W/set trigger, add **$150**

MODEL 1522D CLASSIC/CUSTOM RIFLE
Same as Model 1422D except chambered for .22 Magnum RF, 4-round magazine. Weight: 6.5 lbs. (Custom). Fancy-grade Classic or Monte Carlo stock w/hand-carved rollover cheekpiece. Imported from 1982 to 1989. (Reintroduced as 1700D/1730D series.)
Model 1522D Classic . . . . **NiB $1197 Ex $869 Gd $633**
Model 1522D Custom . . . . **NiB $1197 Ex $869 Gd $633**

MODEL 1532D CLASSIC/CUSTOM RIFLE
Same as Model 1432D except chambered for .222 Rem. Three-round mag. Weight: 6.5 lbs. (Custom). Classic stock on Classic Model; fancy-grade Monte Carlo stock w/handcarved rollover cheekpiece (Custom). Imported from 1982 to 1989. (Reintroduced as 1700D/174 D0 series.)
Model 1532D Classic . . . . **NiB $1019 Ex $795 Gd $448**
Model 1532D Custom . . . . **NiB $1297 Ex $996 Gd $698**

MODEL 1533 . . . . **NiB $1090 Ex $844 Gd $589**
Same as Model 1433 except chambered for .222 Rem. Three-shot box magazine. Imported from 1976 to 1994.

MODEL 1700 SERIES BOLT-ACTION REPEATER
Match 54 Sporter. Calibers: .22 LR., .22 Magnum, .22 Hornet, .222 Rem. Five-shot removable magazine 24-inch bbl. 43 inches overall. Weight: 7.5 lbs. Folding leaf rear sight, hooded ramp front. Select European walnut stock w/cheekpiece and Schnabel forend tip. Imported from 1989 to 2001.
Standard Model 1700
Bavarian — rimfire cal. . . . .**NiB $1018 Ex $933 Gd $580**
Standard Model 1700
Bavarian — centerfire cal. . . . .**NiB $1342 Ex $1056 Gd $697**
**Model 1700D Classic (classic
stock, 6.75 lbs.) rimfire cal.** . . . .**NiB $1179 Ex $994 Gd $698**
Model 1700D Classic — centerfire cal. . . . .**NiB $1279 Ex $1044 Gd $748**
Model 1700D Custom — rimfire cal. . . . .**NiB $1094 Ex $893 Gd $633**
Model 1700D Custom — centerfire cal. . . . . .**NiB $1332 Ex $1088 Gd $775**
**Model 1700D Graphite Cust. (McMillan graphite
reinforced stock, 22-inch bbl., intro. 1991)** . .**NiB $1156 Ex $985 Gd $635**
Select walnut and gold trigger, add. **$200**
**Model 1700 FWT (featherweight, 6.5 lbs.) –
rimfire cal.** . . . .**NiB $1122 Ex $909 Gd $635**
Model 1700 FWT — centerfire cal. . . . .**NiB $1289 Ex $1136 Gd $703**

Anschutz Model 2013

MODEL 1733D MANNLICHER........ NiB $1366 Ex $1168 Gd $860
Same as Model 1700D except w/19-inch bbl. and Mannlicher-style stock. 39 inches overall. Weight: 6.25 lbs. Imported from 1993 to 1995 (Reintroduced in 1998, disc; 2001).

MODEL 1740 MONTE CARLO SPORTER
Caliber: .22 Hornet or .222 Rem. Three and 5-round magazines respectively. 24-inch bbl. 43.25 inches overall. Weight: 6.5 lbs. Hooded ramp front, folding leaf rear. Drilled and tapped for scope mounts. Select European walnut stock w/roll-over cheekpiece, checkered grip and forend. Imported from 1998 to 2006.
Model 1740 Classic
(Meistergrade)............... NiB $1504 Ex $1237 Gd $866
Model 1740 Custom.......... NiB $1366 Ex $1089 Gd $733

MODEL 1743 MONTE CARLO
SPORTER.................. NiB $1366 Ex $1132 Gd $769
Similar to Model 1740 except w/Mannlicher full stock. Imported from 1997 to 2001.

MODEL 1803D MATCH SINGLE-SHOT TARGET RIFLE
Caliber: .22 LR. 25.5-inch bbl. 43.75 inches overall. Weight: 8.5 lbs. No sights; receiver grooved, drilled and tapped for scope mounts. Blonde or walnut-finished hardwood stock w/adj. cheekpiece, stippled grip and forend. Left-hand version. Imported from 1987 to 1993.
Right-hand model
(Reintroduced as 1903D) .... NiB $1006 Ex $844 Gd $544
Left-hand model .... NiB $1108 Ex $866 Gd $633

MODEL 1807 ISU
STANDARD MATCH......... NiB $1359 Ex $1094 Gd $708
Bolt-action single-shot. Caliber: 22 LR. 26-inch bbl. Improved Super Match 54 action. Two-stage match trigger. Removable cheekpiece, adj. buttplate, thumbpiece and forestock w/stipple-checkered. Weight: 10 lbs. Imported from 1982 to 1988. (Reintroduced as 1907 ISU.)

MODEL 1808ED SUPER RUNNING TARGET
Bolt-action single-shot. Caliber: .22 LR. 23.5-inch bbl. w/sliding weights. Improved Super Match 54 action. Heavy beavertail forend w/adj.cheekpiece and buttplate. Adj. single-stage trigger. Weight: 9.5 lbs. Imported from 1982 to 1998.
Right-hand model........... NiB $1677 Ex $1328 Gd $869
Left-hand model .... NiB $1688 Ex $1377 Gd $973

MODEL 1808MS-R
METALLIC SILHOUETTE...... NiB $2021 Ex $1565 Gd $932
Bolt-action repeater. Caliber: .22 LR. 19.2-inch bbl. w/o sights. Thumbhole Monte Carlo stock w/grooved forearm enhanced w/ "Anschutz" logo. Weight: 8.2 lbs. Imported from 1998 to date.

MODEL 1810 SUPER MATCH II...... NiB $1979 Ex $1440 Gd $937
A less detailed version of the Super Match 1813 model. Tapered forend w/deep receiver area. Select European hardwood stock. Weight: 13.5 lbs. Imported from 1982 to 1988 (reintroduced as 1910 series).

MODEL 1811 PRONE MATCH....... NiB $1843 Ex $1623 Gd $877
Bolt-action single-shot. Caliber: .22 LR. 27.5-inch bbl. Improved Super Match 54 action. Select European hardwood stock w/beavertail forend, adj. cheekpiece, and deep thumb flute. Thumb groove and pistol grip w/stipple checkering. Adj. buttplate. Weight: 11.5 lbs. Imported from 1982 to 1988. (Reintroduced as 1911 Prone Match.)

MODEL 1813 SUPER MATCH
Bolt-action single-shot. Caliber: .22 LR. 27.5-inch bbl. Improved Super Match 54 action w/light firing pin, one-point adj. trigger. European walnut thumbhole stock, adj. palm rest, forend and pistol grip stipple checkered. Adj. cheekpiece and hook buttplate. Weight: 15.5 lbs. Imported from 1979 to 1988. (Reintroduced as 1913 Super Match.)
Right-hand model .... NiB $2310 Ex $1989 Gd $879
Left-hand model.............. NiB $2366 Ex $1909 Gd $1343
W/laminated stock, add $150
W/stainless steel bbl., add $175

MODEL 1827B BIATHLON RIFLE
Bolt-action clip repeater. Caliber: .22 LR. 21.5-inch bbl. 42.5 inches overall. Weight: 8.5 to 9 lbs. Slide safety. Adj. target sight set w/snow caps. European walnut stock w/cheekpiece, stippled pistol grip and forearm w/adj. weights. Fortner straight pull bolt option offered in 1986. Imported from 1982 to date.
W/Super Match 54 action........... NiB $2476 Ex $2240 Gd $1116
Left-hand model .... NiB $2240 Ex $1899 Gd $1433
Model 1827BT w/Fortner
option, right-hand................. NiB $2655 Ex $2365 Gd $1144
Model 1827BT, left-hand .... NiB $2734 Ex $2266 Gd $1733
Model 1827BT w/laminated stock, add $175
W/stainless steel bbl., add $200

MODEL 1907 ISU INTERNATIONAL MATCH RIFLE
Updated version of Model 1807 w/same general specifications as Model 1913 except w/26-inch bbl. 44.5 inches overall. Weight: 11 lbs. Designed for ISU 3-position competition. Fitted w/vented beechwood or walnut, blonde or color-laminated stock. Imported from 1989 to date.
Right-hand model .... NiB $2000 Ex $1477 Gd $954
Left-hand model .... NiB $1886 Ex $1588 Gd $1099
W/laminated stock, add $180
W/walnut stock, add $150
W/stainless steel bbl., add $175

MODEL 1910 INTERNATIONAL SUPER MATCH RIFLE
Updated version of Model 1810 w/same general specifications Model 1913 except w/less-detailed hardwood stock w/tapered forend. Weight: 13.5 lbs. Imported from 1989 to 1998.
Right-hand model .... NiB $2733 Ex $2166 Gd $1188
Left-hand model .... NiB $2700 Ex $2166 Gd $1175

MODEL 1911 PRONE MATCH RIFLE
Updated version of Model 1811 w/same general specifications Model 1913 except w/specialized prone match hardwood stock w/ beavertail forend. Weight: 11.5 lbs. Imported from 1989 to date.
Right-hand model .... NiB $1955 Ex $1700 Gd $1035

GRADING: **NiB** = New in Box   **Ex** = Excellent or NRA 95%   **Gd** = Good or NRA 68%   **9**

Armalite, Inc.

Anschutz Achiever

MODEL 1912
LADIES' SPORT RIFLE........ NiB $1837 Ex $1932 Gd $865
Similar to the Model 1907 designed for ISU 3-position competition w/same general U.I.T. specifications except w/shorter dimensions to accomodate smaller competitors. Weight: 11.4 lbs. Imported from 1999 to date.

MODEL 1913 STANDARD RIFLE ...... NiB $1611 Ex $1235 Gd $900
Similar to 1913 Super Match w/economized appointments. Imported from 1997 to date.

MODEL 1913 SUPER MATCH RIFLE
Bolt-action single-shot Super Match (updated version of Model 1813). Caliber: .22 LR. 27.5-inch bbl. Weight: 14.2 lbs. Adj. two-stage trigger. Vented International thumbhole stock w/adj. cheekpiece, hand and palm rest, fitted w/10-way butthook. Imported from 1989 to date.
Right-hand model . . . . NiB $2377 Ex $2110 Gd $955
Left-hand model . . . . NiB $2475 Ex $1780 Gd $1455
W/stainless steel bbl., add $200

MODEL 2007 ISU STANDARD RIFLE
Bolt-action single-shot. Caliber: .22 LR. 19.75-inch bbl. 43.5 to 44.5 inches overall. Weight: 10.8 lbs. Two-stage trigger. Standard ISU stock w/adj. cheekpiece. Imported from 1992 to date.
Right-hand model . . . . NiB $1997 Ex $1529 Gd $900
Left-hand model . . . . NiB $2040 Ex $1719 Gd $1244
W/stainless steel bbl., add $175

MODEL 2013
LADIES' SPORT RIFLE........ NiB $2197 Ex $2021 Gd $933
Similar to the Model 2007 designed for ISU 3-position competition w/same general U.I.T. specifications except w/shorter dimensions to accomodate smaller competitors. Weight: 11.4 lbs. Imported from 1999 to date.

MODEL 2013
BENCHREST RIFLE (BR-50).... NiB $1889 Ex $1624 Gd $877
Bolt-action single-shot. Caliber: .22 LR. 19.6-inch bbl. 43 inches overall. Weight: 10.3 lbs. Adjustable trigger for single or two-stage function. Benchrest-configuration stock. Imported from 1999 to date.

MODEL 2013 SILHOUETTE RIFLE ....NiB $2187 Ex $1655 Gd $944
Bolt-action single-shot. Caliber: .22 LR. 20-inch bbl. 45.5 inches overall. Weight: 11.5 lbs. Two-stage trigger. Thumbhole black synthetic or laminated stock w/adj. cheekpiece, hand and palm rest. Imported from 1994 to date.

MODEL 2013 SUPER MATCH RIFLE
Bolt-action single-shot. Caliber: .22 LR. 19.75- or 27.1-inch bbl. 43 to 50.1 inches overall. Weight: 15.5 lbs. Two-stage trigger. International thumbhole, black synthetic or laminated stock w/ adj. cheekpiece, hand and palm rest; fitted w/10-way butthook. Imported from 1992 to date.
Right-hand model . . . . NiB $2566 Ex $2317 Gd $1149
Left-hand model . . . . NiB $2588 Ex $1290 Gd $1477
W/laminated stock, add $200

ACHIEVER BOLT-ACTION RIFLE........ NiB $422 Ex $337 Gd $219
Caliber: .22 LR. 5-round magazine. Mark 2000-type repeating action. 19.5-inch bbl. 36.5 inches overall. Weight: 5 lbs. Adj. open rear sight; hooded ramp front. Plain European hardwood target-style stock w/vented forend and adj. buttplate. Imported from 1987 to 1995.

ACHIEVER ST-SUPER TARGET..... NiB $559 Ex $431 Gd $269
Same as Achiever except single-shot w/22-inch bbl. and adj. stock. 38.75 inches overall. Weight: 6.5 lbs. Target sights. Imported from 1994 to 1995.

BR-50 BENCH REST RIFLE .... NiB $2123 Ex $1690 Gd $1026
Single-shot. Caliber: .22 LR. 19.75-inch bbl. (23 inches w/muzzle weight). 37.75-42.5 inches overall. Weight: 11 lbs. Grooved receiver, no sights. Walnut-finished hardwood or synthetic benchrest stock w/adj. cheekpiece. Imported from 1994 to 1997. (Reintroduced as Model 2013 BR-50.)

KADETT BOLT-ACTION
REPEATING RIFLE............. NiB $366 Ex $241 Gd $198
Caliber: .22 LR. 5-round detachable box magazine. 22-inch bbl. 40 inches overall. Weight: 5.5 lbs. Adj. folding leaf rear sight; hooded ramp front. Checkered European hardwood stock w/ walnut-finish. Imported 1987.

MARK 2000 MATCH........... NiB $448 Ex $355 Gd $221
Takedown, bolt-action single-shot. Caliber: .22 LR. 26-inch heavy bbl. Walnut stock w/deep-fluted thumb-groove, Wundhammer swell pistol grip, beavertail forend. Adj. buttplate, single-stage adj. trigger. Weight: 8 lbs. Imported from 1982 to 1988.

ARMALITE, INC. — Geneseo, Illinois (formerly Costa Mesa, California)
Armalite was in Costa Mesa, California, from 1959—73. Following the acquisition by Eagle Arms in 1995, production resumed under the Armalite, Inc. Logo in Geneseo, Illinois.

AR-7 EXPLORER SURVIVAL RIFLE .... NiB $169 Ex $145 Gd $90
Takedown. Semiautomatic. Caliber: .22 LR. Eight-round box magazine. 16-inch cast aluminum bbl. w/steel liner. Sights: Peep rear; blade front. Brown plastic stock, recessed to stow barrel, action, and magazine. Weight: 2.75 lbs. Will float stowed or assembled. Made from 1959–1973 by Armalite; from 1974–90 by Charter Arms; from 1990–97 by Survival Arms, Cocoa, FL.; from 1997 to date by Henry Repeating Arms Co., Brooklyn, NY.

AR-7 EXPLORER CUSTOM RIFLE ... NiB $225 Ex $190 Gd $109
Same as AR-7 Survival Rifle except w/deluxe walnut stock w/cheekpiece and pistol grip. Weight: 3.5 lbs. Made from 1964 to 1970.

Armalite, Inc.

Armalite AR-7 Explorer Rifle
NRA NATIONAL FIREARMS MUSEUM

Armalite AR-10

Armalite AR-10 (T) Target Carbine

Armalite M-15A2 National Match

Armalite M-15A2 HBAR

Armscor (Arms Corp.)

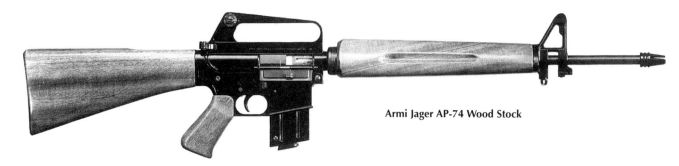

Armi Jager AP-74 Wood Stock

AR-180 SEMIAUTOMATIC RIFLE
Commercial version of full automatic AR-18 Combat Rifle. Gas-operated semiautomatic. Caliber: .223 Rem. (5.56mm). 5-, 20-, 30-round magazines. 18.25-inch bbl. w/flash hider/muzzle brake. Sights: Flip-up "L" type rear, adj. for windage; post front, adj. for elevation. Accessory: 3x scope and mount (add $60 to value). Folding buttstock of black nylon, rubber buttplate and pistol grip, heat dissipating fiberglass forend (hand guard), swivels, sling. 38 inches overall, 28.75 inches folded. Weight: 6.5 lbs.

Armalite AR-180 (mfg. by
Armalite-Costa Mesa) . . . . NiB $2189 Ex $1543 Gd $1033
Armalite AR-180 (mfg. by Howa) . . . . . . NiB $2209 Ex $1535 Gd $990
Armalite AR-180 (mfg. by Sterling) . . . . . NiB $1809 Ex $1404 Gd $933
W/3x scope and mount, add. $250

AR-10 SEMIAUTOMATIC SERIES
Gas-operated semiautomatic action. Calibers: .243 Win. or .308 Win. (7.62 x 51mm). 10-round magazine. 16- or 20-inch bbl. 35.5 or 39.5 inches overall. Weight: 9 to 9.75 lbs. Post front sight, adj. aperature rear. Black or green composition stock. Made from 1995 to date.

AR-10 A2 (Std. carbine) . . . . . . NiB $2590 Ex $1688 Gd $1027
AR-10 A2 (Std. rifle) . . . . NiB $2632 Ex $1144 Gd $1009
AR-10 A4 (S.P. carbine). . . . . . . NiB $2632 Ex $1144 Gd $1009
W/stainless steel bbl., add $150

AR-10 (T) TARGET
Similar to Armalite Model AR-10A except in National Match configuration w/three-slot short Picatinny rail system and case deflector. 16- or 24-inch bbl. Weight: 8.25 to 10.4 lbs. Composite stock and handguard. No sights. Optional National Match carry handle and detachable front sight. Made from 1995 to 2004.

AR-10 T (Rifle) . . . . NiB $2579 Ex $1789 Gd $1033
AR-10 T (Carbine). . . . . NiB $2579 Ex $1789 Gd $1033

MODEL AR-50 SS BOLT-ACTION
RIFLE. . . . . NiB $2598 Ex $2045 Gd $1366
Caliber: .50 BMG. 31-inch bbl. w/muzzle brake. 59 inches overall. Weight: 41 lbs. Modified octagonal-form receiver, drilled and slotted for scope rail. Single-stage trigger. Triple front-locking bolt lug w/ spring-loaded plunger for automatic ejection. Magnesium phosphate steel, hard-anodized aluminum finish. Made from 1999 to date.

M15 SERIES
Gas-operated semiautomatic w/A2-style forward-assist mechanism and push-type pivot pin for easy takedown. Caliber: .223. 7-round magazine. 16-, 20- or 24-inch bbl. Weight: 7-9.2 lbs. Composite or retractable stock. Fully adj. sights. Black anodized finish. Made from 1995 to date.

M-15A2 (Carbine) . . . . NiB $927 Ex $800 Gd $647
M-15A2 (Service Rifle) . . . . NiB $989 Ex $845 Gd $655
M-15A2 (National Match). . . . . NiB $1350 Ex $1123 Gd $770
M-15A2
(Golden Eagle heavy bbl.). . . . . NiB $1332 Ex $1086 Gd $730

M-15A2 M4C
(retractable stock, disc. 1997) . . . . NiB $1299 Ex $1021 Gd $698
M-15A4 (Action Master, disc. 1997). . . . . NiB $1139 Ex $934 Gd $670
M-15A4 (Predator) . . . . NiB $977 Ex $855 Gd $654
M-15A4 (S.P. Rifle) . . . . NiB $956 Ex $799 Gd $535
M-15A4T (Eagle Eye Carbine). . . . . NiB $1326 Ex $1090 Gd $775
M-15A4T (Eagle Eye Rifle) . . . . NiB $1377 Ex $1030 Gd $755

ARMI JAGER — Turin, Italy

AP-74 COMMANDO . . . . NiB $322 Ex $248 Gd $166
Similar to standard AP-74 but styled to resemble original version of Uzi 9mm submachine gun w/wood buttstock. Lacks carrying handle and flash suppressor. Has different type front sight mount and guards, wood stock, pistol grip and forearm. Introduced 1976. Disc.

AP-74 SEMIAUTOMATIC RIFLE
Styled after U.S. M16 military rifle. Caliber: .22 LR, .32 Auto (pistol cartridge). Detachable clip magazine; capacity: 14 rounds caliber .22 LR, 9 rounds .32 ACP. 20-inch bbl. w/flash suppressor. Weight: 6.5 lbs. M16 type sights. Stock, pistol-grip and forearm of black plastic, swivels and sling. Introduced 1974. Disc.
.22 LR. . . . . NiB $359 Ex $290 Gd $200
.32 Auto . . . . NiB $379 Ex $322 Gd $209

AP-74 WOOD STOCK MODEL
Same as standard AP-74 except w/wood stock, pistol-grip and forearm weight: 7 lbs. Disc.
.22 LR . . . . NiB $448 Ex $377 Gd $250
.32 Auto . . . . NiB $448 Ex $377 Gd $250

ARMSCOR (Arms Corp.) — Manila, Philippines (imported by Armscor Precision Int'l.)

MODEL 20 AUTO RIFLE
Caliber: .22 LR. 15-round magazine. 21-inch bbl. 39.75 inches overall. Weight: 6.5 lbs. Sights: Hooded front; adj. rear. Checkered or plain walnut finished mahogany stock. Blued finish. Imported from 1990 to 1991. (Reinstated by Ruko in the M series.)
Model 20 (checkered stock) . . . . NiB $165 Ex $130 Gd $97
Model 20C (carbine-style stock). . . . NiB $143 Ex $122 Gd $98
Model 20P (plain stock) . . . . NiB $125 Ex $100 Gd $78

MODEL 1600 AUTO RIFLE
Caliber: .22 LR. 15-round magazine. 19.5-inch bbl. 38 inches overall. Weight: 6 lbs. Sights: Post front; aperture rear. Plain mahogany stock. Matte black finish. Imported from 1987 to 1991. (Reinstated by Ruko in the M series.)
Standard model. . . . . NiB $180 Ex $155 Gd $100
Retractable stock model . . . . NiB $190 Ex $165 Gd $110

Armscor (Arms Corp.)

A-Square — Hannibal

MODEL AK22 AUTO RIFLE
Caliber: .22 LR. 15- or 30-round magazine. 18.5-inch bbl. 36 inches overall. Weight: 7 lbs. Sights: Post front; adj. rear. Plain mahogany stock. Matte black finish. Imported from 1987 to 1991.
Standard model . . . . NiB $179 Ex $150 Gd $110
Folding stock model . . . . NiB $269 Ex $220 Gd $166

MODEL M14 SERIES BOLT-ACTION RIFLE
Caliber: .22 LR. 10-round magazine. 23-inch bbl. Weight: 6.25 lbs. Open sights. Walnut or mahogany stock. Imported from 1991 to 1997.
M14P Standard model . . . . NiB $129 Ex $98 Gd $70
M14D Deluxe model
(checkered stock, disc. 1995) . . . . . NiB $149 Ex $110 Gd $90

MODEL M20 SERIES SEMIAUTOMATIC RIFLE
Caliber: .22 LR. 10- or 15-round magazine. 18.25- or 20.75-inch bbl. Weight:5.5 to 6.5 lbs. 38 to 40.5 inches overall. Hooded front sight w/windage adj. rear. Walnut finished mahogany stock. Imported from 1990 to 1997.
M20C (carbine model) . . . . NiB $144 Ex $109 Gd $80
M20P (standard model) . . . . NiB $128 Ex $100 Gd $78
M20S Sporter Deluxe (w/checkered
mahogany stock) . . . . NiB $167 Ex $150 Gd $97
M20SWC Super Classic (w/checkered
walnut stock) . . . . NiB $281 Ex $225 Gd $108

MODEL M1400 BOLT-ACTION RIFLE
Similar to Model 14P except w/checkered stock w/Schnabel forend. Weight: 6 lbs. Imported from 1990 to 1997.
M1400LW (Lightweight, disc. 1992) . . . . . NiB $239 Ex $199 Gd $137
M1400S (Sporter) . . . . NiB $177 Ex $150 Gd $100
M1400SC (Super Classic) . . . . NiB $300 Ex $255 Gd $179

MODEL M1500 BOLT-ACTION RIFLE
Caliber: .22 Mag. 5-round magazine. 21.5-inch bbl. Weight: 6.5 lbs. Open sights. Checkered mahogany stock. Imported from 1991 to 1997.
M1500 (standard) . . . . NiB $198 Ex $137 Gd $105
M1500LW (Euro-style walnut
stock, disc. 1992) . . . . NiB $219 Ex $188 Gd $135
M1500SC (Monte Carlo stock) . . . . NiB $224 Ex $190 Gd $140

MODEL M1600 AUTO RIFLE
Rimfire replica of Armalite Model AR 180 (M16) except chambered for Caliber .22 LR. 15-round magazine. 18-inch bbl. Weight: 5.25 lbs. Composite or retractable buttstock w/composite handguard and pistol grip. Carrying handle w/adj. aperture rear sight and protected post front. Black anodized finish. Imported from 1991 to 1997.
M1600 (standard w/fixed stock) . . . . . NiB $190 Ex $149 Gd $110
M1600R (retractable stock) . . . . NiB $200 Ex $161 Gd $120

MODEL M1800 BOLT-ACTION RIFLE
Caliber: .22 Hornet. 5-round magazine. 22-inch bbl. Weight: 6.6 lbs. Checkered hardwood or walnut stock. Sights: Post front; adj. rear. Imported from 1996 to 1997.
M1800 (standard) . . . . NiB $310 Ex $233 Gd $175
M1800SC (checkered walnut stock) . . . . . NiB $400 Ex $327 Gd $255

MODEL M2000 BOLT-ACTION RIFLE
Similar to Model 20P except w/checkered mahogany stock and adj.

sights. Imported from 1991 to 1997.
M2000S (standard) . . . . NiB $177 Ex $139 Gd $100
M2000SC (checkered walnut stock) . . . . . NiB $279 Ex $220 Gd $165

ARNOLD ARMS — Arlington, Washington

AFRICAN SAFARI
Calibers: .243 to .458 Win. Magnum. 22- to 26-inch bbl. Weight: 7-9 lbs. Scope mount standard or w/optional M70 Express sights. Chrome-moly in four finishes. "A" and "AA" Fancy Grade English walnut stock with number 5 standard wraparound checkering pattern. Ebony forend tip. Made from 1994 to 2001.
W/"A" Grade English
walnut stock, blue finish . . . . NiB $4732 Ex $3841 Gd $2690
Std. polish . . . . NiB $4969 Ex $4000 Gd $2821
Hi-Luster . . . . NiB $5189 Ex $4290 Gd $2950
Stainless steel matte . . . . NiB $4733 Ex $3847 Gd $2993
W/"AA" Grade English
walnut stock, C-M matte blue finish . . . NiB $4700 Ex $3810 Gd $2688
Std. polish . . . . NiB $4988 Ex $4037 Gd $2835
Hi-Luster . . . . NiB $5188 Ex $4200 Gd $2969
Stainless steel matte finish . . . . NiB $4700 Ex $3875 Gd $2710

ALASKAN TROPHY
Calibers: .300 Magnum to .458 Win. Magnum. 24- to 26-inch bbl. Weight: 7-9 lbs. Scope mount w/Express sights standard. Stainless steel or chrome-moly Apollo action w/fibergrain or black synthetic stock. Barrel band on 357 H&H and larger magnums. Made from 1996 to 2000.
Matte finish . . . . NiB $3300 Ex $2680 Gd $1900
Std. polish . . . . NiB $3559 Ex $2900 Gd $2044
Stainless steel . . . . NiB $3356 Ex $2744 Gd $1935

A-SQUARE COMPANY INC. — Glenrock, Wyoming

CAESAR BOLT-ACTION RIFLE
Custom rifle built on Remington's 700 receiver. Calibers: Same as Hannibal, Groups I, II and III. 20- to 26-inch bbl. Weight: 8.5 to 11 lbs. Express 3-leaf rear sight, ramp front. Synthetic or classic Claro oil-finished walnut stock w/flush detachable swivels and Coil-Chek recoil system. Three-way adj. target trigger; 3-position safety. Right- or left-hand. Made from 1986 to date.
Synthetic stock model . . . . NiB $3412 Ex $2790 Gd $1947
Walnut stock model . . . . NiB $3044 Ex $2379 Gd $1756

GENGHIS KHAN BOLT-ACTION RIFLE
Custom varmint rifle developed on Winchester's M70 receiver; fitted w/heavy tapered bbl. and Coil-Chek stock. Calibers: .22-25 Rem., .243 Win., .25-06 Rem., 6mm Rem. Weight: 8-8.5 lbs. Made from 1995 to date.
Synthetic stock model . . . . NiB $3566 Ex $2312 Gd $2044
Walnut stock model . . . . NiB $3477 Ex $2854 Gd $2023

Austrian Military Rifles

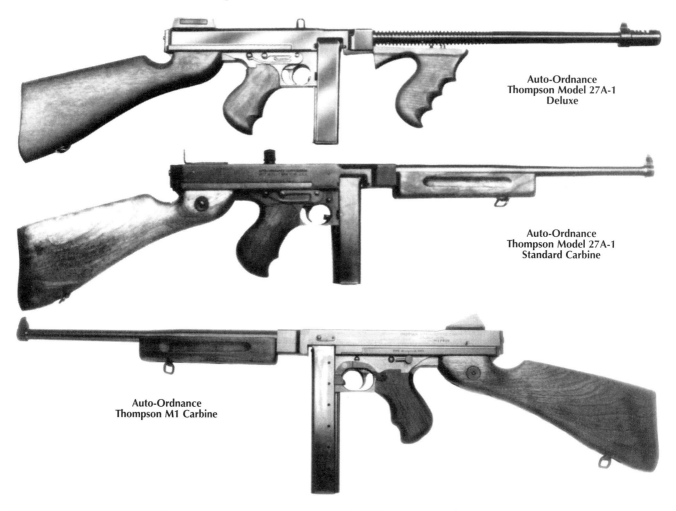

**Auto-Ordnance
Thompson Model 27A-1
Deluxe**

**Auto-Ordnance
Thompson Model 27A-1
Standard Carbine**

**Auto-Ordnance
Thompson M1 Carbine**

HAMILCAR BOLT-ACTION RIFLE
Similar to Hannibal Model except lighter. Calibers: .25-06, .257 Wby., 6.5x55 Swedish, .270 Wby., 7x57, 7mm Rem., 7mm STW, 7mm Wby., .280 Rem., .30-06, .300 Win., .300 Wby., .338-06, 9.3x62. Weight: 8-8.5 lbs. Made from 1994 to date.
Synthetic stock model . . . . NiB $3554 Ex $2909 Gd $2011
Walnut stock model . . . . NiB $3508 Ex $2866 Gd $2009

HANNIBAL BOLT-ACTION RIFLE
Custom rifle built on reinforced P-17 Enfield receiver. Calibers: Group I: 30-06; Group II: 7mm Rem. Mag., .300 Win. Mag., .416 Taylor, .425 Express, .458 Win. Mag.; Group III: .300 H&H, .300 Wby. Mag., 8mm Rem. Mag., .340 Wby. Mag., .375 H&H, .375 Wby. Mag., .404 Jeffery, .416 Hoffman, .416 Rem Mag., .450 Ackley, .458 Lott; Group IV: .338 A-Square Mag., .375 A-Square Mag., .378 Wby. Mag., .416 Rigby, .416 Wby. Mag., .460 Short Square Mag., .500 A-Square Mag. 20- to 26-inch bbl. Weight: 9 to 11.75 lbs. Express 3-leaf rear sight, ramp front. Classic Claro oil-finished walnut stock or synthetic stock w/flush detachable swivels and Coil-Chek recoil system. Adj. trigger w/2-position safety. Made from 1986 to date.
Synthetic stock model . . . . NiB $3614 Ex $2870 Gd $1921
Walnut stock model . . . . NiB $3700 Ex $2795 Gd $2021

**AUSTRIAN MILITARY RIFLES — Steyr, Austria.
Manufactured at Steyr Armory**

MODEL 90
STEYR-MANNLICHER RIFLE . . . . . . NiB $334 Ex $189 Gd $139
Straight-pull bolt action. Caliber: 8mm. 5-round magazine. Open sights. 10-inch bayonet. Cartridge clip forms part of the magazine mechanism. Some of these rifles were provided with a laced canvas hand guard, others were made wood.

MODEL 90
STEYR-MANNLICHER CARBINE . . . . NiB $339 Ex $228 Gd $139
Same general specifications as Model 90 rifle except w/19.5-inch bbl., weight 7 lbs. No bayonet stud or supplemental forend grip.

MODEL 95
STEYR-MANNLICHER CARBINE . . . . NiB $329 Ex $250 Gd $141
Same general specifications as Model 95 rifle except w/19.5-inch bbl., weight 7 lbs. Post front sight; adj. rear carbine sight.

MODEL 95 STEYR-MANNLICHER
SERVICE RIFLE . . . . NiB $299 Ex $190 Gd $137
Straight-pull bolt action. Caliber: 8x50R Mannlicher (many of these rifles were altered during World War II to use the 7.9mm German service ammunition). 5-round Mannlicher-type box magazine. 30-inch bbl. Weight: 8.5 lbs. Sights: Blade front; rear adj. for elevation. Military-type full stock. Many of these rifles were altered during WWII to accept 7.9mm German service ammunition.

Auto-Ordnance Corporation

Ballard No. 5 Pacific Rifle
NRA NATIONAL FIREARMS MUSEUM

AUTO-ORDNANCE CORPORATION — Worcester, Massachusetts

THOMPSON
MODEL 22-27A-3 . . . . **NiB $790 Ex $654 Gd $498**
Same-bore version of Deluxe Model 27A-1. Same general specifications except 22 LR w/lightweight alloy receiver, weight 6.5 lbs. Magazines include 5-, 20-, 30- and 50-round box types, 80-round drum. Made from 1977 to 1994.

THOMPSON MODEL 27A-1 DELUXE
Same as Standard Model 27A-1 except w/finned bbl. w/compensator, adj. rear sight, pistol-grip forestock. Caliber: .22 LR, l0mm (1991 to 1993) or 45 ACP. Weight: 11.5 lbs. Made from 1976 to 1999.
.22 LR (limited production). . . . . **NiB $1390 Ex $1123 Gd $770**
10mm or .45 ACP . . . . **NiB $790 Ex $679 Gd $530**
50-round drum magazine, add $275
100-round
drum magazine, add $75
Violin carrying case, add $125

THOMPSON MODEL 27A-1 STANDARD SEMIAUTO
CARBINE . . . . **NiB $689 Ex $635 Gd $440**
Similar to Thompson submachine gun ("Tommy Gun") except has no provision for automatic firing. Caliber: .45 Auto. 20-round detachable box magazine (5-,15- and 30-round box magazines, 39-round drum also available). 16-inch plain bbl. Weight: 14 lbs. Sights: Aperture rear; blade front. Walnut buttstock, pistol grip and grooved forearm, sling swivels. Made from 1976 to 1986.

THOMPSON 27A-1C
LIGHTWEIGHT CARBINE . . . . . . **NiB $845 Ex $677 Gd $480**
Similar to Model 27A-1 except w/lightweight alloy receiver. Weight: 9.25 lbs. Made 1984 to date.

THOMPSON M1
SEMI-AUTOMATIC CARBINE . . . . **NiB $791 Ex $660 Gd $479**
Similar to Model 27A-1 except in M-1 configuration w/side cocking lever and horizontal forearm. Weight: 11.5 lbs. Made from 1986 to date.

BALLARD RIFLE LLC — Cody, Wyoming

BALLARD 1-1/2
HUNTER'S RIFLE . . . . **NiB $3200 Ex $2440 Gd $1833**
Calibers: Seven calibers from .22 LR to .50-70. Single trigger, S-style lever action; uncheckered stock. Weight: 10.5 lbs.

BALLARD 1-3/4
FAR WEST RIFLE . . . . **NiB $2902 Ex $2045 Gd $1456**
Calibers: Eight calibers from .32-40 WCF to .50-90 SS. Patterned after original Ballard Far West model. 30 or 32-inch bbl., standard or heavyweight octagon; double set triggers; ring-style lever. Weight: 9.75 to 10.5 lbs.

BALLARD NO. 5
PACIFIC . . . . **NiB $3208 Ex $2460 Gd $1996**
Calibers: Nine calibers between .32-40 WCF and .50-90 SS. Similar to No. 1-3/4 Far West model but with under-barrel wiping rod.

BALLARD NO. 4-1/2
MID-RANGE RIFLE . . . . **NiB $2900 Ex $2080 Gd $1765**
Calibers: .Five calibers between .32-40 WCF and .45-110. Designed for black powder silhouette shooting. 30 or 32-inch bbl., half-octagonal heavyweight; single or double set triggers; pistol grip stock; full loop lever; hard rubber Ballard buttplate; Vernier tang sight. Weight: 10.75 to 11.5 lbs.

BALLARD NO. 7
LONG-RANGE RIFLE . . . . **NiB $3369 Ex $2390 Gd $1479**
Caliber: Five calibers between .40-65 Win. and .45-110. Similar to No. 4-1/2 Mid-Range Rifle; designed for long-range shooting. 32 or 34-inch half-octagon standard or heavyweight bbl.

MODEL 1885 HIGH WALL RIFLE
Calibers: Various. Exact replica of Winchester Model 1885 (parts are interchangeable). 30 or 32-inch bbl., octagon; case-colored receiver, uncheckered straight-grip stock and forearm. Weight: Approx. 9 lbs. Introduced 2001.
Standard model . . . . **NiB $3190 Ex $2444 Gd $1954**
Deluxe model, add $1700
Sporting model, add $250
Shuetzen model, add $400

BANSNER'S ULTIMATE RIFLES, LLC — Established in 1981 in Adamstown, Pennsylvania, as Basner's Gunsmithing Specialties. Company name changed in 2000

ULTIMATE
ONE RIFLE . . . . **NiB $5540 Ex $3766 Gd $3060**
Calibers: Various. Bolt-action, modeled on Winchester M70 and Remington 700 actions. Various metal finishes; muzzle brake; custom trigger; custom stock; Pachmayer decelerator pad; custom scope mounts and bases.

Belgian Military Rifles

HIGH TECH SERIES RIFLE
Calibers: Various. Steel or stainless steel action with factory bbl. Bansner's synthetic stock and Pachmayer decelerator pad.
Standard model . . . . .NiB $1022 Ex $790 Gd $635
Stainless steel model, add $300

SAFARI
HUNTER RIFLE . . . . .NiB $6200 Ex $4356 Gd $2398
Calibers: Various dangerous game calibers. Based on Model 70 Classic action; muzzle brake; Lilja Precision stainless steel barrel; synthetic stock; matte black Teflon metal finish. Introduced 2003.

WORLD SLAM LIMITED EDITION
RIFLE. . . . . .NiB $5345 Ex $3850 Gd $2300
Calibers: Various. Customized Model 700 action; fluted bold body. jeweled trigger. three-position safety; synthetic stock. Only 25 to 50 of limited edition models were made beginning in 2003.

BARRETT FIREARMS MFG., INC. — Murfreesboro, Tennessee

MODEL 82 A-1
SEMI-AUTOMATIC RIFLE. . . . NiB $9144 Ex $7644 Gd $4588
Caliber: .50 BMG. 10-round detachable box magazine. 29-inch recoiling bbl. w/muzzle brake. 57 inches overall. Weight: 28.5 lbs. Open iron sights and 10x scope. Composit stock w/Sorbothance recoil pad and self-leveling bipod. Blued finish. Made in various configurations from 1985 to date.

MODEL 90
BOLT-ACTION RIFLE . . . . NiB $3530 Ex $3099 Gd $2020
Caliber: .50 BMG. Five round magazine. 29-inch match bbl. 45 inches overall. Weight: 22 lbs. Composite stock w/retractable bipod. Made from 1990 to 1995.

MODEL 95 BOLT-ACTION. . . NiB $6635 Ex $4890 Gd $3530
Similar to Model 90 bullpup design chambered for .50 BMG except w/improved muzzle brake and extendable bipod. Made from 1995 to date.

BEEMAN PRECISION ARMS INC. — Santa Rosa, California

Since 1993, all European firearms imported by Beeman have been distributed by Beeman Outdoor Sports, Div., Roberts Precision Arms, Inc., Santa Rosa, CA.

WEIHRAUCH HW MODELS 60J AND 60J-ST
BOLT-ACTION RIFLES
Calibers: .22 LR (60J-ST), .222 Rem. (60J). 22.8-inch bbl. 41.7 inches overall. Weight: 6.5 lbs. Sights: Hooded blade front; open adj. rear. Blued finish. Checkered walnut stock w/cheekpiece. Made from 1988 to 1994.
Model 60J . . . . NiB $835 Ex $746 Gd $615
Model 60J-ST. . . . . NiB $655 Ex $539 Gd $398

WEIHRAUCH HW MODEL 60M
SMALL BORE RIFLE. . . . . NiB $690 Ex $579 Gd $389
Caliber: .22 LR. Single-shot. 26.8-inch bbl. 45.7 inches overall. Weight: 10.8 lbs. Adj. trigger w/push-button safety. Sights:

Hooded blade front on ramp, precision aperture rear. Target-style stock w/stippled forearm and pistol grip. Blued finish. Made from 1988 to 1994.

WEIHRAUCH HW
MODEL 660 MATCH RIFLE . . . . NiB $1023 Ex $855 Gd $445
Caliber: .22 LR. 26-inch bbl. 45.3 inches overall. Weight: 10.7 lbs. Adj. match trigger. Sights: globe front, precision aperture rear. Match-style walnut stock w/adj. cheekpiece and buttplate. Made from 1988 to 1994.

FEINWERKBAU MODEL 2600 SERIES TARGET RIFLE
Caliber: .22 LR. Single-shot. 26.3-inch bbl. 43.7 inches overall. Weight: 10.6 lbs. Match trigger w/fingertip weight adjustment dial. Sights: Globe front; micrometer match aperture rear. Laminated hardwood stock w/adj. cheekpiece. Made from 1988 to 1994.
Standard Model 2600
(left-hand) . . . . .NiB $1733 Ex $1360 Gd $944
Standard Model 2600
(right-hand) . . . . NiB $1560 Ex $1239 Gd $816
Free Rifle Model 2602
(left-hand) . . . . NiB $2196 Ex $1755 Gd $1024
Free Rifle Model 2602
(right-hand) . . . . NiB $2196 Ex $1755 Gd $1024

BELGIAN MILITARY RIFLES — Manufactured by Fabrique Nationale D'Armes de Guerre, Herstal, Belgium; Fabrique D'Armes de L'Etat, Lunich, Belgium

Hopkins & Allen Arms Co. of Norwich, CT as well as contractors in Birmingham, England, also produced these guns during World War I.

MODEL 1889 MAUSER
MILITARY RIFLE . . . . NiB $279 Ex $230 Gd $156
Caliber: 7.65mm Belgian Service (7.65mm Mauser). 5-round projecting box magazine. 30.75-inch bbl. w/jacket. Weight: 8.5 lbs. Adj. rear sight, blade front. Straight-grip military stock. This, and the carbine version, was the principal weapon of the Belgian Army at the start of WWII. Made from 1889 to c.1935.

MODEL 1916
MAUSER CARBINE . . . . NiB $300 Ex $240 Gd $190
Same as Model 1889 Rifle except w/20.75-inch bbl. Weighs 8 lbs. and has minor differences in the rear sight graduations, lower band closer to the muzzle and swivel plate on side of buttstock.

MODEL 1935 MAUSER
MILITARY RIFLE . . . . NiB $370 Ex $292 Gd $169
Same general specifications as F.N. Model 1924; minor differences. Caliber: 7.65mm Belgian Service. Mfd. by Fabrique Nationale D'Armes de Guerre.

MODEL 1936 MAUSER
MILITARY RIFLE . . . . NiB $378 Ex $290 Gd $166
An adaptation of Model 1889 w/German M/98-type bolt, Belgian M/89 protruding box magazine. Caliber: 7.65mm Belgian Service. Mfd. by Fabrique Nationale D'Armes de Guerre.

Benton & Brown Firearms, Inc.

**Beretta 501
Bolt-Action Sporter**

Beretta AR-70

BENTON & BROWN FIREARMS, INC. — Fort Worh, Texas

MODEL 93 BOLT-ACTION RIFLE
Similar to Blaser Model R84 (the B&B rifle is built on the Blaser action, see separate listing) with an interchangeable bbl. system. Calibers: .243 Win., 6mm Rem., .25-06, .257 Wby., .264 Win., .270 Win., .280 Rem., 7mm Rem Mag., .30-06, .308, .300 Wby., .300 Win. Mag., .338 Win., .375 H&H. 22- or 24-inch bbl. 41 or 43 inches overall. Bbl.-mounted scope rings and one-piece base; no sights. Two-piece walnut or fiberglass stock. Made from 1993 to 1996.
Walnut stock model. . . . . . . NiB $1896 Ex $1744 Gd $1012
Fiberglass stock model, add $225
Extra bbl. assembly, add $525
Extra bolt assembly, add $450

BERETTA U.S.A. CORP. — Accokeek, Maryland. Manufactured by Fabbrica D'Armi Pietro Be.etta, S.P.A., Gardone Val Trompia (Brescia), Italy

500 BOLT-ACTION SPORTER
Centerfire bolt-action rifle w/Sako A I short action. Calibers: .222 Rem., .223 Rem. Five round magazine. 23.63-inch bbl. Weight: 6.5 lbs. Available w/ or w/o iron sights. Tapered dovetailed receiver. European walnut stock. Disc. 1998.
Standard . . . . NiB $700 Ex $590 Gd $475
DL model . . . . NiB $1590 Ex $1288 Gd $900
500 EELL Engraved . . . . NiB $1650 Ex $1465 Gd $990
W/iron sights, add 10%

501 BOLT-ACTION SPORTER
Same as Model 500 except w/Sako A II medium action. Calibers: .243 Win., .308 Win. Weight: 7.5 lbs. Disc. 1986.
Standard . . . . NiB $625 Ex $466 Gd $420
Standard w/iron sights . . . . NiB $700 Ex $644 Gd $430
DL model . . . . NiB $1386 Ex $1097 Gd $944
501 EELL (engraved) . . . . NiB $1607 Ex $1329 Gd $979
W/iron sights, add 10%

502 BOLT-ACTION SPORTER
Same as Model 500 except w/Sako A III long action. Calibers: .270 Win., 7mm Rem. Mag., .30/06, 375 H&H. Weight: 8.5 lbs. Disc. 1986.
Standard model. . . . . NiB $675 Ex $534 Gd $460
DL model . . . . NiB $1565 Ex $1299 Gd $980
502 EELL (engraved) . . . . NiB $1607 Ex $1344 Gd $1088
W/iron sights, add 10%

AR-70 SEMIAUTOMATIC
RIFLE. . . . . NiB $2020 Ex $1788 Gd $1077
Caliber: .223 Rem. (5.56mm). 30-round magazine. 17.75-inch bbl. Weight: 8.25 lbs. Sights: Rear peep adj. for windage and elevation; blade front. High-impact synthetic buttstock. Imported from 1984 to 1989.

EXPRESS S686/S689 SILVER SABLE O/U RIFLE
Calibers: .30-06 Spfld., 9.3x74R, and .444 Marlin. 24-inch bbl. Weight: 7.7 lbs. Drilled and tapped for scope mount. European-style cheek rest and ventilated rubber recoil pad. Imported from 1995.
Model S686/S689 Silver Sable II. . . . . . NiB $4720 Ex $3800 Gd $2244
Model S689 Gold Sable . . . . NiB $6344 Ex $5329 Gd $3144
Model S686/S689 EELL
W/extra bbl. set, add $350
W/detachable claw mounts, add $645

Blaser U.S.A., Inc.

Blaser Model R84

MATO

Calibers: .270 Win., .280 Rem., 7mm Rem. Mag., .300 Win. Mag., .338 Win. Mag., .375 H&H. 23.6-inch bbl. Weight: 8 lbs. Adjustable trigger. Drop-out box magazine. Drilled and tapped for scope w/ or w/o adj. sights. Walnut or synthetic stock. Manufactured based on Mauser 98 action. Made from 1997 to 2002.

Standard model. . . . . NiB $1015 Ex $733 Gd $533
Deluxe model . . . . NiB $2015 Ex $1723 Gd $966
.375 H&H w/iron sights, add $350

SMALL BORE SPORTING CARBINE/TARGET RIFLE

Semiautomatic w/bolt handle in raised or conventional single-shot bolt-action w/handle in lowered position. Caliber: .22 LR. Four, 5-, 8-, 10- or 20-round magazines. 20.5-inch standard or heavy bbl. Sights: 3-leaf folding rear, partridge front. Target or sporting stock w/checkered pistol grip and forend and sling swivels. Weight: 5.5 to 6 lbs.

Sporter model (Super Sport X) . . . . . NiB $420 Ex $343 Gd $235
Target model (Olympia X). . . . . NiB $294 Ex $472 Gd $317

BERNARDELLI, VINCENZO — Brescia, Italy

Currently headquartered in Brescia, Italy, Bernardelli arms were manufactured from 1721 to 1997 in Gardone, Italy. Imported and distributed by Armsport, Inc., Miami, Florida. Also handled by Magnum Research, Inc., Quality Arms, Inc., Armes De Chasse, Stoeger, and Action Arms.

EXPRESS VB

Double barrel. Calibers: Various. Side-by-side sidelock action. Ejectors, double triggers. Imported from 1990 to1997.

Standard model. . . . . NiB $5768 Ex $4755 Gd $3690
Deluxe model (w/double triggers), add $1125

EXPRESS 2000

Calibers: .30-06, 7x65R, 8x57JRS, 9.3x74R. Over/under boxlock design. Single or double triggers, extractors. Checkered walnut stock and forearm. Imported from 1994 to 1997.

Standard model. . . . . NiB $2700 Ex $2025 Gd $1580
Single trigger, add $200

MINERVA EXPRESS . . . . NiB $5200 Ex $3890 Gd $4098
Caliber: Various. Exposed hammers. Extractors, double triggers. Moderate engraving. Imported from 1995 to 1997.

CARBINA .22 . . . . NiB $5150 Ex $3896 Gd $3987
Semi-auto. Caliber: .22 rimfire. Blow-back action. Imported from 1990 to 1997.

MODEL 120 . . . . NiB $2120 Ex $1587 Gd $1100
Combination gun; over-under boxlock; 12 gauge over .22 Hornet, .222 Rem., 5.6x50R Mag., .243 Win., 6.5x57R, .270 Win., 7x57R, .308 Win., .30-06, 6.5x55, 7x65R, 8x57JRS, 9.3x74R. Iron sights. Checkered walnut stock and forearm. Double triggers, automatic ejectors or extractors. Ventilated recoil pad. Engraved action. Made in Italy. Discontinued.

MODEL 190 . . . . NiB $1489 Ex $1129 Gd $1069
Combination gun; over-under boxlock. Calibers: 12, 16 or 20 ga. Over .222 Rem., .243 Win., .30-06, .308 Win., 5.6x50R Mag., .5.6x57R, 6.5x55, 6.5x57R, 7x57R, 7x65R, 8x57JRS, 9.3x74R. Iron sights. Checkered walnut stock. Double triggers; extractors. Made in Italy. Introduced in 1969, discontinued 1989.

MODEL 2000

Combination gun; over-under boxlock action. Calibers: 12, 16 or 20 ga. Over .222 Rem., .22 Hornet, 5.6x50R Mag., .243 Win., 6.5x55, 6.5x57R, .270 Win., 7x57R, .308 Win., .30-06, 8x57JRS, 9.3x74R. Bbl: 23 inches. Sights: Blade front, open rear. Hand checkered, oil-finished select European walnut stock, double-set triggers, auto ejectors. Silvered, engraved action. Made in Italy. Introduced in 1990, discontinued 1991.

Standard model. . . . . NiB $2713 Ex $1866 Gd $1390
Extra bbl. assembly, add $595

BLASER U.S.A., INC. — Fort Worth, Texas. Manufactured by Blaser Jagdwaffen GmbH, Germany (imported by Sigarms, Exeter, New Hampshire; Autumn Sales, Inc., Fort Worth, Texas)

MODEL R84 BOLT-ACTION RIFLE

Calibers: .22-250, .243, 6mm Rem., .25-06, .270, .280 Rem., .30-06- .257 Wby. Mag., .264 Win. Mag., 7mm Rem Mag., .300 Win. Mag., .300 Wby. Mag., .338 Win. Mag., .375 H&H. Interchangeable bbls. w/standard or Magnum bolt assemblies. Bbl. length: 23 inches (standard); 24 inches (Magnum). 41 to 42 inches overall. Weight: 7 to 7.25 lbs. No sights. Bbl.-mounted scope system. Two-piece Turkish walnut stock w/solid black recoil pad. Imported from 1989 to 1994.

Model R84 Standard . . . . NiB $2245 Ex $1725 Gd $1190
Model R84 Deluxe
(engraved game scene) . . . . NiB $2400 Ex $2021 Gd $1200
Model R84 Super Deluxe
(Gold and silver inlays) . . . . NiB $2449 Ex $1990 Gd $1590
Left-hand model, add $150
Extra bbl. assembly, add $600

MODEL R93 SAFARI SERIES BOLT-ACTION REPEATER

Similar to Model R84 except restyled action w/straight-pull bolt, unique safety and searless trigger mechanism. Additional chamberings: 6.5x55, 7x57, .308, .416 Rem. Optional open sights. Imported from 1994 to 1998.

Model R93 Safari . . . . NiB $3598 Ex $2277 Gd $1844
Model R93 Safari Deluxe . . . . NiB $3943 Ex $4134 Gd $3297
Model R84 Safari Super Deluxe . . . . . . NiB $4854 Ex $4326 Gd $3458
Extra bbl. assembly, add $600

MODEL R93 CLASSIC SERIES BOLT-ACTION REPEATER

Similar to Model R93 Safari except w/expanded model variations. Imported from 1998 to 2002.

Model R93 Attache
(Premium wood, fluted bbl.) . . . . NiB $3566 Ex $3887 Gd $3110
Model R93 Classic
(.22-250 to .375 H&H) . . . . NiB $3525 Ex $2889 Gd $2009
Model R93 Classic Safari (.416 Rem.) . . . . .NiB $3535 Ex $3279 Gd $2250
Model R93 LX (.22-250 to .416 Rem.) . . . . .NiB $1799 Ex $1445 Gd $996
Model R93 Synthetic (.22-250
to .375 H&H) . . . . NiB $1908 Ex $1235 Gd $855
Extra bbl. assembly, add $600

Brno Model II

Brno Model 21H
Bolt-Action Sporting Rifle

Brno Model 22F

Brno Hornet
Bolt-Action Sporting Rifle

BRITISH MILITARY RIFLES — Manufactured at Royal Small Arms Factory, Enfield Lock, Middlesex, England, private contractors

RIFLE NO. 1 MARK III . . . . **NiB $335 Ex $209 Gd $144**
Short magazine Lee-Enfield (S.M.L.E.). Bolt action. Caliber: .303 British. 10-round box magazine. 25.25-inch bbl. Weight: 8.75 lbs. Sights: Adj. rear; blade front w/guards. Two-piece, full-length military stock. Note: The earlier Mark III (approved 1907) is virtually the same as Mark III adopted in 1918, except for sights and different magazine cut-off (eliminated on the newer version).

RIFLE NO. 3 MARK I (PATTERN 14). . . . . . **NiB $344 Ex $255 Gd $160**
Modified Mauser-type bolt action. Except for caliber .303 British and long-range sight, this rifle is the same as U.S. Model 1917 Enfield. See listing for general specifications.

RIFLE NO. 4 MARK I . . . . **NiB $275 Ex $230 Gd $155**
Post-World War I modification of the S.M.L.E. intended to simplify mass production. General specifications same as Rifle No. 1 Mark III except w/aperture rear sight and minor differences in construction. Weight 9.25 lbs.

LIGHT RIFLE NO. 4 MARK I. . . . . . **NiB $225 Ex $170 Gd $133**
Modification of the S.M.L.E. Caliber: .303 British. 10-round box magazine. 23-inch bbl. Weight: 6.75 lbs. Sights: Micrometer click rear peep; blade front. One-piece military-type stock w/recoil pad. Made during WWII.

RIFLE NO. 5 MARK I . . . . **NiB $365 Ex $244 Gd $175**
Jungle Carbine. Modification of the S.M.L.E. similar to Light Rifle No. 4 Mark I except w/20.5-inch bbl. w/flash hider, carbine-type stock. Made during WWII. Originally designed for use in the Pacific Theater.

BRNO SPORTING RIFLES — Brno, Czech Republic. Manufactured by Ceska Zbrojovka; Imported by Euro-Imports, El Cajon, CA (previously by Bohemia Arms & Magnum Research)

See also CZ rifles.

MODEL I BOLT-ACTION
SPORTING RIFLE . . . . **NiB $680 Ex $615 Gd $437**
Caliber: .22 LR. Five round detachable magazine. 22.75-inch bbl. Weight: 6 lbs. Sights: three-leaf open rear; hooded ramp front. Sporting stock w/checkered pistol grip, swivels. Made from 1946 to 1973.

MODEL II BOLT-ACTION
SPORTING RIFLE . . . . **NiB $635 Ex $543 Gd $444**
Same as Model I except w/deluxe grade stock. Made from 1949 to 1957.

MODEL III BOLT-ACTION
TARGET RIFLE. . . . . **NiB $700 Ex $567 Gd $490**
Same as Model I except w/heavy bbl. and target stock. Made from 1948 to 1956.

MODEL IV BOLT-ACTION
TARGET RIFLE. . . . . **NiB $755 Ex $587 Gd $488**
Same as Model III except w/improved target trigger mechanism. Made from 1956 to 1962.

MODEL V BOLT-ACTION
SPORTING RIFLE . . . . **NiB $789 Ex $633 Gd $456**

Brown Precision Company

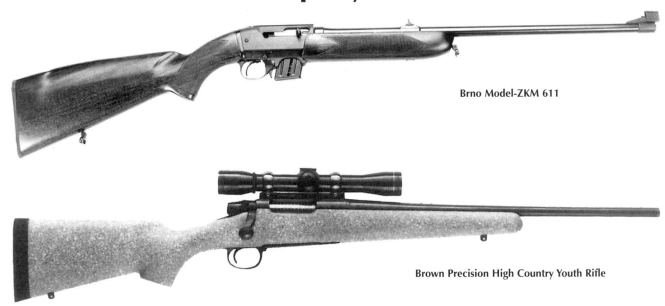

Brno Model-ZKM 611

Brown Precision High Country Youth Rifle

Same as Model I except w/improved trigger mechanism. Made from 1956 to 1973.

MODEL 21H BOLT-ACTION
SPORTING RIFLE . . . . NiB $1590 Ex $1325 Gd $1009
Mauser-type action. Calibers: 6.5x57mm, 7x57mm 8x57mm. Five round box magazine. 20.5-inch bbl. Double set trigger. Weight: 6.75 lbs. Sights: Two-leaf open rear-hooded ramp front. Half-length sporting stock w/cheekpiece, checkered pistol-grip and forearm; swivels. Made from 1946 to 1955.

MODEL 22F . . . . NiB $1408 Ex $1010 Gd $679
Same as Model 21H except w/full-length Mannlicher-type stock. Weight: 6 lbs., 14 oz. Disc.

MODEL 98 STANDARD
Calibers: .243 Win., .270 Win., .30-06, .308 Win., .300 Win. Mag., 7x57mm, 7x64mm, or 9.3x62mm. 23.8-inch bbl. Overall 34.5 inches. Weight: 7.25 lbs. Checkered walnut stock w/Bavarian cheekpiece. Imported from 1998. Disc.
Standard calibers . . . . NiB $560 Ex $435 Gd $300
Calibers .300 Win. Mag., 9.3x62mm . . . . . NiB $580 Ex $469 Gd $386
W/single set trigger, add. $150

MODEL 98 MANNLICHER
Similar to Model 98 Standard except full length stock and set triggers. Imported from 1998. Disc.
Standard calibers . . . . NiB $724 Ex $545 Gd $390
Calibers .300 Win. Mag., 9.3x62mm . . . . . NiB $755 Ex $600 Gd $445

ZKB-110 SINGLE-SHOT
Calibers: .22 Hornet, .222 Rem., 5.6x52R, 5.6x50 Mag., 6.5x57R, 7x57R, and 8x57JRS. 23.8-inch bbl. Weight: 6.1 lbs. Walnut checkered buttstock and forearm w/Bavarian cheekpiece. Imported from 1998 to 2003.
Standard model. NiB $279 Ex $218 Gd $177
Lux model. . . . . NiB $448 Ex $330 Gd $266
Calibers 7x57R and 8x57 JRS, add $50
W/interchangeable 12 ga.
shotgun bbl., add $150

HORNET BOLT-ACTION
SPORTING RIFLE . . . . NiB $1275 Ex $1043 Gd $689
Miniature Mauser action. Caliber: .22 Hornet. Five-round detachable

box magazine. 23-inch bbl. Double set trigger. Weight: 6.25 lbs. Sights: Three-leaf open rear hooded ramp front. Sporting stock w/ checkered pistol grip and forearm, swivels. Made 1949-74. Note: This rifle was also marketed in U.S. as "Z-B Mauser Varmint Rifle" and reintroduced as the Model KZB 680.

MODEL ZKB 680
BOLT-ACTION RIFLE . . . . NiB $477 Ex $345 Gd $296
Calibers: .22 Hornet, .222 Rem. Five-round detachable box magazine. 23.5-inch bbl. Weight: 5.75 lbs. Double-set triggers. Adj. open rear sight, hooded ramp front. Walnut stock. Imported from 1985 to 1992.

MODEL ZKM 611 SEMIAUTOMATIC RIFLE
Caliber: .22 WMR. Six-round magazine. 20-inch bbl. 37 inches overall. Weight: 6.2 lbs. Hooded front sight; mid-mounted rear sight. Checkered walnut or beechwood stock. Single thumb-screw takedown. Grooved receiver for scope mounting. Imported from 2006 to date.
Standard beechwood model . . . . . . NiB $503 Ex $412 Gd $389
Deluxe walnut model . . . . NiB $600 Ex $477 Gd $328

BROWN PRECISION COMPANY — Los Molinos, California

MODEL 7 SUPER LIGHT SPORTER . . . . NiB $1128 Ex $1086 Gd $775
Lightweight sporter built on a Remington Model 7 barreled action w/18-inch factory bbl. Weight: 5.25 lbs. Kevlar stock. Made from 1984 to 1992.

HIGH COUNTRY BOLT-ACTION SPORTER
Custom sporting rifles built on Blaser, Remington 700, Ruger 77 and Winchester 70 actions. Calibers: .243 Win., .25-06, .270 Win., 7mm Rem. Mag., .308 Win., .30-06. Five-round magazine (4-round in 7mm Mag.). 22- or 24-inch bbl. Weight: 6.5 lbs. Fiberglass stock w/recoil pad, sling swivels. No sights. Made from 1975 to 1992.
Standard High Country . . . . NiB $1624 Ex $1033 Gd $855
Custom High Country . . . . NiB $4490 Ex $3124 Gd $1876
Left-hand action, add $250
Stainless bbl., add. $250
70, 77, or Blaser actions, add $150
70 SG action, add $400

Brown Precision Company

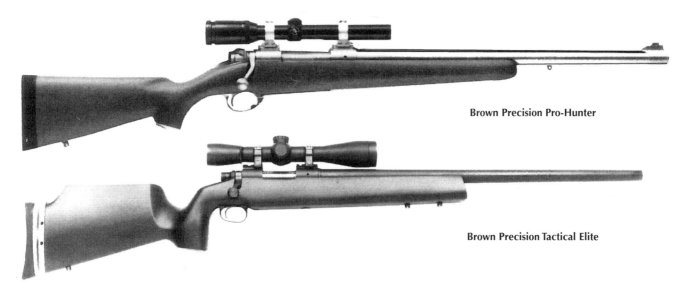

Brown Precision Pro-Hunter

Brown Precision Tactical Elite

HIGH COUNTRY YOUTH RIFLE . . . . . . **NiB $1336 Ex $1023 Gd $688**
Similar to standard Model 7 Super Light except w/Kevlar or graphite stock, scaled-down to youth dimensions. Calibers: .223, .243, 6mm, 7mm-08, .308. Made from 1993 to 2000.

PRO-HUNTER BOLT-ACTION RIFLE
Custom sporting rifle built on Remington 700 or Winchester 70 SG action fitted w/match-grade Shilen bbl. chambered in customer's choice of caliber. Matte blued, nickel or Teflon finish. Express-style rear sight hooded ramp front. Synthetic stock. Made from 1989 to date.
Standard Pro-Hunter . . . . **NiB $4597 Ex $3150 Gd $2366**
Pro-Hunter Elite (1993 to date) . . . . . . **NiB $6066 Ex $3886 Gd $2125**

PRO-VARMINTER BOLT-ACTION RIFLE
Custom varminter built on a Remington 700 or 40X action fitted w/ Shilen stainless steel benchrest bbl. Varmint or benchrest-style stock. Made from 1993 to date.
Standard Pro-Varminter . . . . **NiB $3735 Ex $2966 Gd $969**
Pro-Hunter w/Rem 40X action, add **$650**

SELECTIVE TARGET MODEL . . . . . **NiB $1044 Ex $835 Gd $590**
Tactical law-enforcement rifle built on a Remington 700V action. Caliber: .308 Win. 20-, 22- or 24-inch bbl. Synthetic stock. Made from 1989 to 1992.

TACTICAL ELITE RIFLE . . . . **NiB $4566 Ex $3290 Gd $1977**
Similar to Selective Target Model except fitted w/select match-grade Shilen benchrest heavy stainless bbl. Calibers: .223, .308, .300 Win. Mag. Black or camo Kevlar/graphite composite fiberglass stock w/ adj. buttplate. Non-reflective black Teflon metal finish. Made from 1997 to date.

BROWNING RIFLES — Morgan, Utah.
Manufactured for Browning by Fabrique Nationale d'Armes de Guerre (now Fabrique Nationale Herstal), Herstal, Belgium; Miroku Firearms Mfg. Co., Tokyo, Japan; A.T.I., Salt Lake City, Utah; Oy Sako Ab, Riihimaki, Finland

.22 AUTOMATIC RIFLE, GRADE I
Similar to discontinued Remington Model 241A. Autoloading. Take-down. Calibers: .22 LR. .22 Short (not interchangeably). Tubular magazine in buttstock holds 11 LR. 16 Short. Bbl. lengths: 19.25 inches (.22 LR), 22.25 inches (.22 Short). Weight: 4.75 lbs. (.22 LR); 5 lbs. (.22 Short). Receiver scroll engraved. Open rear sight, bead front. Checkered pistol-grip buttstock, semibeavertail forearm. Made from 1956 to 1972 by FN; from 1972 to date by Miroku.
FN manufacture . . . . **NiB $890 Ex $500 Gd $265**
Miroku manufacture . . . . **NiB $644 Ex $398 Gd $327**

.22 AUTOMATIC RIFLE, GRADE II
Same as Grade I except satin chrome-plated receiver engraved w/ small game animal scenes, gold-plated trigger select walnut stock and forearm. .22 LR only. Made from 1972 to 1984.
FN manufacture . . . . **NiB $1200 Ex $900 Gd $365**
Miroku manufacture . . . . **NiB $554 Ex $435 Gd $300**

.22 AUTOMATIC RIFLE, GRADE III
Same as Grade I except satin chrome-plated receiver elaborately hand-carved and engraved w/dog and game-bird scenes, scrolls and leaf clusters: gold-plated trigger, extra-fancy walnut stock and forearm, skip-checkered. .22 LR only. Made from 1972 to 1984.
FN manufacture . . . . **NiB $1500 Ex $1125 Gd $880**
Miroku manufacture . . . . **NiB $822 Ex $590 Gd $480**

.22 AUTOMATIC, GRADE VI . . . . **NiB $1190 Ex $798 Gd $600**
Same general specifications as standard .22 Automatic except for engraving, high-grade stock w/checkering and glossy finish. Made by Miroku from 1986 to date.

MODEL 52 BOLT-ACTION RIFLE . . . . **NiB $800 Ex $655 Gd $443**
Limited edition of Winchester Model 52C Sporter. Caliber: .22 LR. Five-round magazine. 24-inch bbl. Weight: 7 lbs. Micro-Motion trigger. No sights. Checkered select walnut stock w/rosewood forend and metal grip cap. Blued finish. 5,000 made from 1991 to 1992.

MODEL 53 LEVER-ACTION RIFLE . . . . **NiB $833 Ex $724 Gd $480**
Limited edition of Winchester Model 53. Caliber: .32-20. Seven-round tubular half-magazine. 22-inch bbl. Weight: 6.5 lbs. Adj. rear sight, bead front. Select walnut checkered pistol-grip stock w/high-gloss finish. Classic-style forearm. Blued finish. 5,000 made in 1990.

Browning Rifles

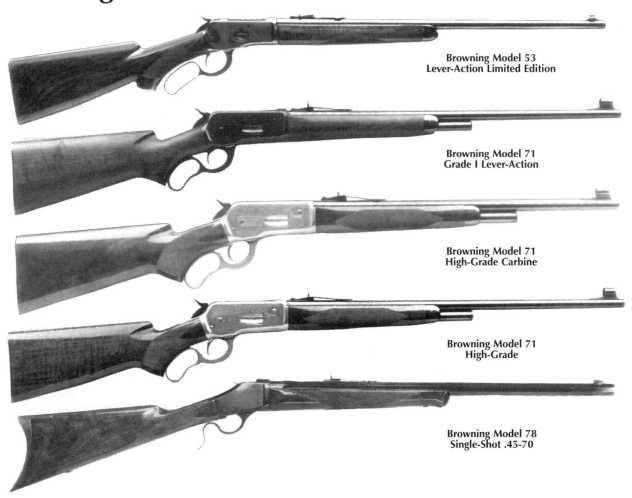

Browning Model 53
Lever-Action Limited Edition

Browning Model 71
Grade I Lever-Action

Browning Model 71
High-Grade Carbine

Browning Model 71
High-Grade

Browning Model 78
Single-Shot .45-70

MODEL 65 GRADE I
LEVER-ACTION RIFLE . . . . NiB $620 Ex $445 Gd $366
Caliber: .218 Bee. 7-round tubular half-magazine. 24-inch bbl.
Weight: 6.75 lbs. Sights: Adj. buckhorn-style rear, hooded bead front.
Select walnut pistol-grip stock w/high-gloss finish. Semibeavertail
forearm. Limited edition of 3,500 made in 1989.

MODEL 65 HIGH GRADE RIFLE . . . . NiB $909 Ex $733 Gd $528
Same general specifications as Model 65 Grade I except w/engrav-
ing and gold-plated animals on grayed receiver. Cut checkering on
pistol grip and forearm. Limited edition of 1,500 made in 1989.

MODEL 71 GRADE I CARBINE . . . . NiB $800 Ex $640 Gd $455
Same general specifications as Model 71 Grade I Rifle except
carbine w/20-inch round bbl. and weighs 8 lbs. Limited edition of
4,000 made in 1986 to 1987.

MODEL 71 GRADE I
LEVER-ACTION RIFLE. . . . . NiB $916 Ex $710 Gd $497
Caliber: .348 Win. 4-round magazine. 24-inch round bbl. Weight:
8 lbs., 2 oz. Open buckhorn sights. Select walnut straight grip stock
w/satin finish. Classic-style forearm, flat metal buttplate. Limited
edition of 3,000 made in 1986 to 1987.

MODEL 71 HIGH-GRADE CARBINE . . . . .NiB $1312 Ex $1123 Gd $765
Same general specifications as Model 71 High Grade Rifle, except
carbine w/20-inch round bbl. Limited edition of 3,000 made 1986
to 1988.

MODEL 71 HIGH-GRADE RIFLE . . . . . . NiB $1440 Ex $1110 Gd $823
Caliber: .348 Win. Four round magazine. 24-inch round bbl. Weight:
8 lbs., 2 oz. Engraved receiver. Open buckhorn sights. Select walnut
checkered pistol-grip stock w/high-gloss finish. Classic-style forearm,
flat metal buttplate. Limited edition of 3,000 made in 1987.

M-78 BICENTENNIAL SET . . . . NiB $3866 Ex $3121 Gd $2140
Special Model 78 .45-70 w/same specifications as standard type,
except sides of receiver engraved w/bison and eagle, scroll engraving on top of receiver, lever, both ends of bbl. and buttplate; high-
grade walnut stock and forearm. Accompanied by an engraved
hunting knife and stainless steel commemorative medallion, all in
an alder wood presentation case. Each item in set has matching
serial number beginning with "1776" and ending with numbers 1
to 1,000. Edition limited to 1,000 sets. Made in 1976.

MODEL 78 SINGLE-SHOT RIFLE
Falling-block lever-action similar to Winchester 1885 High Wall single-shot
rifle. Calibers: .22-250, 6mm Rem., .243 Win., .25-06, 7mm Rem. Mag.,
.30-06, .45-70 Govt. 26-inch octagon or heavy round bbl.; 24-inch octagon
bull bbl. on .45-70 model. Weight: 7.75 lbs. w/octagon bbl.; w/round bbl.,
8.5 lbs.; .45-70, 8.75 lbs. Furnished w/o sights except .45-70 model w/open
rear sight, blade front. Checkered fancy walnut stock and forearm. .45-70
model w/straight-grip stock and curved buttplate; others have Monte Carlo
comb and cheekpiece, pistol-grip w/cap, recoil pad. Made from 1973 to
1983 by Miroku. Reintroduced in 1985 as Model 1885.
All calibers except .45-70 . . . . . NiB $1489 Ex $1274 Gd $1010
.45-70 . . . . NiB $970 Ex $766 Gd $523

Browning Model 1885
High-Wall Single-Shot

Browning Model 1885
High-Wall Traditional Hunter

Browning Model 1885
Low-Wall Single-Shot

Browning Model 1885
BPCR Single-Shot

MODEL 1885 SINGLE-SHOT RIFLE
Calibers: .22 Hornet, .223, .243, (Low Wall); .357 Mag., .44 Mag., .45 LC (L/W Traditional Hunter); .22-250, .223 Rem., .270 Win., 7mm Rem. Mag., .30-06, .454 Casull Mag., .45.70 (High Wall); .30.30 Win., .38-55 WCF, .45 Govt. (High Wall Traditional Hunter); .40-65, .45 Govt. and .45.90 (BPCR). 24-, 28-, 30 or 34-inch round, octagonal or octagonal and round bbl. 39.5, 43.5, 44.25 or 46.125 inches overall. Weight: 6.25, 8.75, 9, 11, or 11.75 lbs. respectively. Blued or color casehardened receiver. Gold-colored adj. trigger. Drilled and tapped for scope mounts w/no sights or vernier tang rear sight w/globe front and open sights on .45-70 Gov't. Walnut straight-grip stock and Schnabel forearm w/cut checkering and high-gloss or oil finish. Made from 1985 to 2001.

Low Wall model w/o sights (intro. 1995) . . NiB $1500 Ex $976 Gd $540
Traditional Hunter model (intro. 1998) . . NiB $1440 Ex $990 Gd $575
High Wall model w/o sights (intro. 1985) . . NiB $1390 Ex $1020 Gd $770
Traditional Hunter model (intro. 1997) . . NiB $1390 Ex $1020 Gd $770
BPCR model w/no ejector (intro. 1996) . . . . NiB $1733 Ex $1432 Gd $1041
BPCR Creedmoor Model .45-90
(intro. 1998) . . . . NiB $1733 Ex $1432 Gd $1041

MODEL 1886 MONTANA
CENTENNIAL RIFLE . . . . NiB $2120 Ex $1650 Gd $1097
Same general specifications as Model 1886 High Grade lever-action except w/specially engraved receiver designating Montana Centennial; also different stock design. Limited issue made in 1986, by Miroku.

MODEL 1886 GRADE I
LEVER-ACTION RIFLE . . . . NiB $1035 Ex $712 Gd $490

Caliber: .45-70 Govt., 8-round magazine. 26-inch octagonal bbl. 45 inches overall. Weight: 9 lbs., 5 oz. Deep blued finish on receiver. Open buckhorn sights. Straight-grip walnut stock. Classic-style forearm. Metal buttplate. Satin finish. Limited issue of 7,000 made in 1986, by Miroku.

MODEL 1886 HIGH-
GRADE LEVER-ACTION RIFLE . . NiB $1707 Ex $1359 Gd $933
Same general specifications as the Model 1886 Grade I except receiver is grayed, steel embellished w/scroll; elk and American bison engraving. High-gloss stock. Limited issue of 3,000 made in 1986, by Miroku.

MODEL 1895 GRADE I LA RIFLE . . . . . . NiB $1679 Ex $1011 Gd $765
Caliber: .30-06, .30-40 Krag. Four round magazine. 24-inch round bbl. 42 inches overall. Weight: 8 lbs. French walnut stock and Schnabel forend. Sights: Rear buckhorn; gold bead on elevated ramp front. Limited issue of 8,000 made in 1986, by Miroku; 2,000 in .30-40 Krag and 6,000 in .30-06

MODEL 1895 HIGH-
GRADE LA RIFLE . . . . NiB $1503 Ex $1379 Gd $996
Same general specifications as Model 1895 Grade I except engraved receiver and Grade III French walnut stock and forend w/fine checkering. Made in 1985 in limited issue of 1,000 in each caliber by Miroku.

MODEL A-BOLT .22 RIFLE
Calibers: .22 LR. .22 Magnum. Five- and 15-round magazines. 22-inch round bbl. 40.25 inches overall. Weight: 5 lbs., 9 oz. Gold-colored adj. trigger. Laminated walnut stock w/checkering. Rosewood forend grip cap; pistol grip. With or w/o sights. Ramp

Browning Rifles

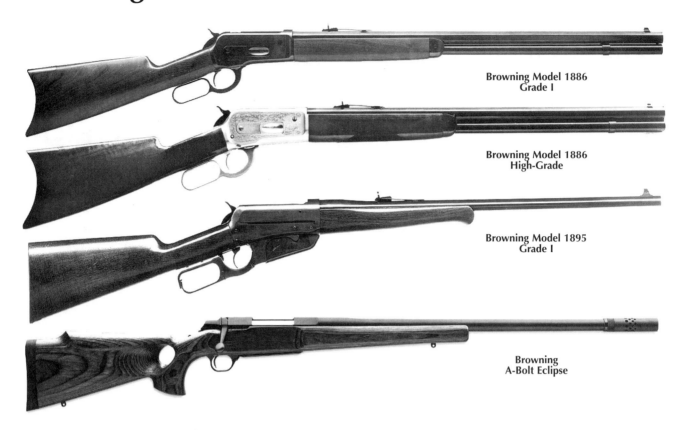

Browning Model 1886
Grade I

Browning Model 1886
High-Grade

Browning Model 1895
Grade I

Browning
A-Bolt Eclipse

front and adj. folding leaf rear on open sight model. 22 LR made from 1985 to 1996; 22 Magnum made from 1990 to 1996.

Grade I .22 LR	NiB $534	Ex $340	Gd $255
Grade I .22 Magnum	NiB $500	Ex $423	Gd $267
Deluxe Grade Gold Medallion	NiB $616	Ex $479	Gd $354

MODEL A-BOLT ECLIPSE BOLT RIFLE
Same general specifications as Hunter Grade except fitted w/gray and black laminated thumbhole stock. Available in both short and long action w/two bbl. configurations w/BOSS. Made from 1996 to 2006 by Miroku

Eclipse w/standard bbl.	NiB $955	Ex $821	Gd $677
Eclipse Varmint w/heavy bbl.	NiB $1123	Ex $978	Gd $720
Eclipse M-1000 Target (.300 Win. Mag.)	NiB $1304	Ex $1038	Gd $796

MODEL A-BOLT EURO-BOLT RIFLE
Same general specifications as Hunter Grade except w/checkered satin-finished walnut stock. W/continental-style cheekpiece, palm-swell grip and Schnabel forend. Mannlicher-style spoon bolt handle and contoured bolt shroud. 22- or 26-inch bbl. w/satin blued finish. Weight: 6.8 to 7.4 lbs. Calibers: .22-250 Rem., .243 Win., .270 Win., .30.06, .308 Win., 7mm Rem. Mag. Made from 1993 to 1994, 1994 to 1996 (Euro-Bolt II) by Miroku.

Euro-Bolt	NiB $679	Ex $536	Gd $369
Euro-Bolt II	NiB $755	Ex $640	Gd $470
BOSS option, add			$100

MODEL A-BOLT HUNTER GRADE RIFLE
Calibers: .22 Hornet, .223 Rem., .22-250 Rem., .243 Win., .257 Roberts, 7mm-08 Rem., .308 Win., (short action) .25-06 Rem., .270 Win., .280 Rem., .284 Win., .30-06, 7mm Rem. Mag., .300 Win. Mag., .338 Win. Mag. Four-round magazine (standard), 3-round (magnum). 22-inch bbl. (standard), 24-inch (magnum). Weight: 7.5 lbs. (standard), 8.5 lbs. (magnum). With or w/o sights. Classic-style walnut stock. Produced in

two action lengths w/nine locking lugs, fluted bolt w/60 degree rotation. Mfd. from 1985 to 1993; and from 1994 to 2007 (Hunter II) by Miroku.

Hunter	NiB $489	Ex $333	Gd $269
Hunter II	NiB $590	Ex $389	Gd $310
Hunter Micro	NiB $596	Ex $395	Gd $317
BOSS option, add			$100
Open sights, add			$75

MODEL A-BOLT MEDALLION GRADE RIFLE
Same as Hunter Grade except w/high-gloss deluxe stock rosewood grip cap and forend; high-luster blued finish. Also in .375 H&H w/open sights. Left-hand models available in long action only. Made from 1988 to 1993 and from 1994 to 2009 (Medallion II, Bighorn Sheep edition) by Miroku.

.270 Win. (600 made in 1986)	NiB $1398	Ex $1096	Gd $790
Gold Medallion Deluxe Grade	NiB $679	Ex $500	Gd $346
Gold Medallion II Deluxe Grade	NiB $670	Ex $525	Gd $377
Medallion, Standard Grade	NiB $633	Ex $488	Gd $354
Medallion II, Standard Grade	NiB $655	Ex $500	Gd $397
Medallion, .375 H&H	NiB $999	Ex $770	Gd $488
Medallion II, .375 H&H	NiB $1012	Ex $790	Gd $497
Micro Medallion	NiB $690	Ex $557	Gd $367
Micro Medallion II	NiB $700	Ex $569	Gd $415
Pronghorn Antelope Ltd. Ed. 243 Win. (500 made in 1987,)	NiB $1266	Ex $1139	Gd $923
W/BOSS option, add			$100
W/open sights, add			$75

MODEL A-BOLT STALKER RIFLE
Same general specifications as Model A-Bolt Hunter Rifle except w/ checkered graphite-fiberglass composite stock and matte blued or stainless metal. Non-glare matte finish of all exposed metal surfaces. 3 models: Camo Stalker orig. w/multi-colored laminated wood stock, matte blued metal; Composite Stalker w/graphite-fiberglass stock, matte blued metal; w/composite stock, stainless metal. Made

Browning Rifles

Browning A-Bolt .22

Browning A-Bolt
Euro-Bolt

Browning A-Bolt
Hunter

Browning A-Bolt
Hunter with BOSS

Browning A-Bolt
Medallion Custom Trophy

Browning A-Bolt
Medallion White Gold

Browning A-Bolt
Medallion

Browning A-Bolt
Medallion (Left-Handed)

Browning Rifles

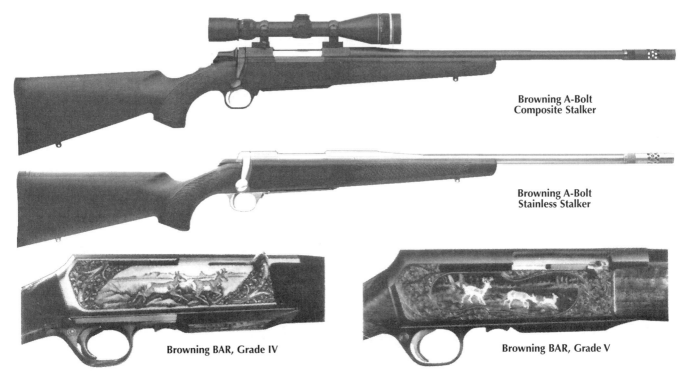

Browning A-Bolt Composite Stalker

Browning A-Bolt Stainless Stalker

Browning BAR, Grade IV

Browning BAR, Grade V

from 1987 to 1993 and from 1994 to date (Stalker II) by Miroku.

Camo Stalker (w/laminated stock)	NiB $960	Ex $709	Gd $350
Composite Stalker.	NiB $990	Ex $656	Gd $433
Composite Stalker II	NiB $990	Ex $656	Gd $433
Stainless Stalker	NiB $1045	Ex $745	Gd $500
Stainless Stalker II.	NiB $876	Ex $655	Gd $571
Stainless Stalker, .375 H&H	NiB $900	Ex $808	Gd $667
W/BOSS option, add.			$100
Left-hand model, add			$100

MODEL A-BOLT
VARMINT II RIFLE . . . . NiB $797 Ex $723 Gd $577
Same general specifications as Stalker model except w/22-inch heavy bbl. w/BOSS system and varmint-style black laminated wood stock. Calibers: .22-250, .223 or .308. No sights. Bright blue or satin finish. Made from 2002 to 2008 by Miroku

MODEL B-92 LEVER-ACTION RIFLE . . . . . NiB $534 Ex $467 Gd $288
Calibers: .357 Mag. and .44 Rem. Mag. 11-round magazine. 20-inch round bbl. 37.5 inches overall. Weight: 5.5 to 6.4 lbs. Seasoned French walnut stock w/high gloss finish. Cloverleaf rear sight; steel post front. Made from1979 to 1989 by Miroku.

BAR AUTOMATIC RIFLE,
GRADE I, STANDARD CALIBERS . . . . NiB $797 Ex $ 623 Gd $455
Gas-operated semiautomatic. Calibers: .243 Win., .270 Win., .280 Rem., .308 Win., .30-06. Four-round box magazine. 22-inch bbl. Weight: 7.5 lbs. Folding leaf rear sight, hooded ramp front. French walnut stock and forearm checkered, QD swivels. Made from 1967 to 1992 by FN.

BAR, GRADE I, MAGNUM CALIBERS . . . . . . .NiB $809 Ex $733 Gd $590
Same as BAR in standard calibers, except w/24-inch bbl. 7mm Rem. Mag. or .300 Win. Mag. .338 Win. Mag. w/3-round box magazine and recoil pad. Weight: 8.5 lbs. Made from 1969 to 1992 by FN.

BAR, GRADE II
Same as Grade I except receiver engraved w/big-game heads (deer and antelope on standard-caliber rifles, ram and grizzly on Magnum-caliber) and scrollwork, higher grade wood. Made from 1967 to 1974 by FN.

Standard calibers	NiB $1229	Ex $966	Gd $657
Magnum calibers	NiB $1338	Ex $875	Gd $617

BAR, GRADE III
Same as Grade I except receiver of grayed steel engraved w/big-game heads (deer and antelope on standard-caliber rifles, moose and elk on Magnum-caliber) framed in fine-line scrollwork, gold-plated trigger, stock and forearm of highly figured French walnut, hand-checkered and carved. Made from 1971 to 1974 by FN.

Standard calibers	NiB $1665	Ex $1105	Gd $644
Magnum calibers	NiB $1756	Ex $1376	Gd $893

BAR, GRADE IV
Same as Grade I except receiver of grayed steel engraved w/full detailed rendition of running deer and antelope on standard-caliber rifles, moose and elk on Magnum-caliber gold-plated trigger, stock and forearm of highly figured French walnut, hand checkered and carved. Made from 1971 to 1986 by FN.

Standard calibers	NiB $2490	Ex $1546	Gd $1110
Magnum calibers	NiB $2669	Ex $1721	Gd $1300

BAR, GRADE V
Same as Grade I except receiver w/complete big-game scenes executed by a master engraver and inlaid w/18K gold (deer and antelope on standard-caliber rifles, moose and elk on Magnum caliber), gold-plated trigger, stock and forearm of finest French walnut, intricately hand-checkered and carved. Made from 1971 to 1974 by FN.

Standard calibers	NiB $6457	Ex $4700	Gd $2897
Magnum calibers	NiB $6844	Ex $5110	Gd $3194

BAR MARK II SAFARI AUTOMATIC RIFLE
Same general specifications as standard BAR semiautomatic rifle, except w/redesigned gas and buffer systems, new bolt release lever, and engraved receiver. Made from 1993 to date.

Standard calibers	NiB $1019	Ex $700	Gd $505
Magnum calibers	NiB $1040	Ex $808	Gd $617
Lightweight (alloy receiver w/20-inch bbl.)	NiB $765	Ex $588	Gd $377

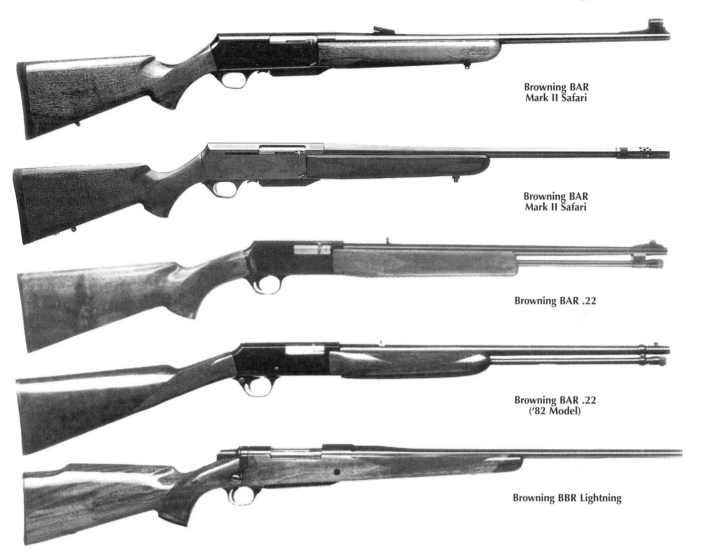

Browning BAR Mark II Safari

Browning BAR Mark II Safari

Browning BAR .22

Browning BAR .22 ('82 Model)

Browning BBR Lightning

BAR MK II Grade III (intro. 1996) .... **NiB $3520 Ex $2377 Gd $1290**
BAR MK II Grade IV (intro. 1996) .... **NiB $3609 Ex $2303 Gd $1829**
W/BOSS option, add **$75**
W/open sights, add **$25**

BAR .22 AUTOMATIC RIFLE
Semiautomatic. Caliber: .22 LR. Tubular magazine holds 15 rounds. 20.25-inch bbl. Weight: 6.25 lbs. Sights: Folding-leaf rear, gold bead front on ramp. Receiver grooved for scope mounting. French walnut pistol-grip stock and forearm checkered. Made from 1977 to 1985.
Grade I .... **NiB $635 Ex $365 Gd $322**
Grade II .... **NiB $1011 Ex $555 Gd $375**

BBR LIGHTNING BOLT-ACTION RIFLE ... NiB $606 Ex $490 Gd $400
Bolt-action rifle w/short bolt throw of 60 degrees. Calibers: .25-06 Rem., .270 Win., .30-06, 7mm Rem. Mag., .300 Win. Mag. 24-inch bbl. Weight: 8 lbs. Made from 1979 to 1984.

BL-.22 LEVER-ACTION REPEATING RIFLE
Short-throw lever-action. Caliber: .22 LR, Long, Short. Tubular magazine holds 15 LR, 17 Long 22 Short rounds. 20-inch bbl. Weight: 5 lbs. Sights: Folding leaf rear; bead front. Receiver grooved for scope mounting. Walnut straight-grip stock and forearm, bbl. band. Made from 1970 to date by Miroku.
Grade I .... **NiB $445 Ex $379 Gd $290**
Grade II (w/scroll engraving) ..... **NiB $498 Ex $390 Gd $300**

BLR LEVER-ACTION REPEATING RIFLE
Calibers: (short action only) .243 Win., .308 Win., .358 Win. Four round detachable box magazine. 20-inch bbl. Weight: 7 lbs. Sights: Windage and elevation adj. open rear; hooded ramp front. Walnut straight-grip stock and forearm, checkered, bbl. band, recoil pad. Made in 1966 by BAC/USA; from 1969 to 1973 by FN; from 1974 to 1980 by Miroku. USA manufacture of this model was limited to prototypes and pre-production guns only and may be identified by the "MADE IN USA" roll stamp on the bbl.
FN model .... **NiB $1000 Ex $699 Gd $554**
Miroku model .... **NiB $690 Ex $500 Gd $398**
USA model .... **NiB $1245 Ex $1097 Gd $686**

BLR LIGHTNING MODEL
Lightweight version of the Browning BLR '81 w/forged alloy receiver and redesigned trigger group. Calibers: Short-action models: .22-250 Rem., .223 Rem., .243 Win., 7mm-08 Rem., .308 Win.; Long-action models: .270 Win., 7mm Rem. Mag., .30-06, .300 Win. Mag; 3- or 4-round detachable box magazine. 20-, 22- or 24-inch bbl.

Browning Rifles

Browning BL-22 II

Browning BL-.22, Grade I

Browning BPR Pump Rifle

Weight: 6.5 to 7.75 lbs. Pistol-grip style walnut stock and forearm, cut checkering and recoil pad. Made from 1995 to 2002 by Miroku.
Short-action model . . . . NiB $690 Ex $586 Gd $390
Long-action model . . . . NiB $700 Ex $596 Gd $400

BLR MODEL '81
Redesigned version of the Browning BLR. Calibers: .222-50 Rem., .243 Win., .308 Win., .358 Win; Long-action: .270 Win., 7mm Rem. Mag., .30-06. Four round detachable box magazine. 20-inch bbl. Weight: 7 lbs. Walnut straight-grip stock and forearm, cut checkering, recoil pad. Made from 1981 to 1995 by Miroku. Long-action models introduced 1991.
Short-action model . . . . NiB $696 Ex $592 Gd $396
Long-action model . . . . NiB $803 Ex $505 Gd $390

BPR-22 PUMP RIFLE
Hammerless slide-action repeater. Specifications same as for BAR-.22, except also available in .22 WMR; magazine capacity, 11 rounds. Made from 1977 to 1982 by Miroku.
BPR model, standard calibers . . . . . NiB $736 Ex $533 Gd $390
BPR model, magnum calibers, add. $75

BPR PUMP RIFLE
Slide-action repeater based on proven BAR designs w/forged alloy receiver and slide that cams down to clear bbl. and receiver. Calibers: .243 Win., .308 Win., .270 Win., .30-06, 7mm Rem. Mag. .300 Win. Mag.; 3- or 4-round detachable box magazine. 22- or 24-inch bbl. w/ramped front sight and open adj. rear. Weight: 7.2 to 7.4 lbs. Made from 1997 to 2001 by Miroku.
Standard . . . . NiB $775 Ex $620 Gd $447
Magnum calibers, add. $100

HIGH-POWER BOLT-ACTION
RIFLE, MEDALLION GRADE. . . . . NiB $3877 Ex $3488 Gd $1967
Same as Safari Grade except receiver and bbl. scroll engraved; ram's head engraved on floorplate; select walnut stock w/rosewood forend tip and grip cap. Made from 1961 to 1974.

HIGH-POWER BOLT-ACTION
RIFLE, OLYMPIAN GRADE. . . . . NiB $3831 Ex $3435 Gd $1925

Same as Safari Grade except receiver and bbl. engraved; receiver, trigger guard and floorplate satin chrome-plated and engraved w/game scenes appropriate to caliber; finest figured walnut stock w/rosewood forearm tip and grip cap, latter w/18K-gold medallion. Made from 1961 to 1974.

HIGH-POWER BOLT-ACTION RIFLE,
SAFARI GRADE, MEDIUM ACTION . . . . . NiB $1433 Ex $988 Gd $733
Same as Standard except medium action. Calibers: .22-250, .243 Win., .264 Win. Mag., .284 Win. Mag., .308 Win. Mag. Bbl.: 22-inch lightweight bbl.; .22-250 and .243 also available w/24-inch heavy bbl. Weight: 6 lbs., 12 oz. (lightweight bbl.), 7 lbs., 13 oz. (heavy bbl.). Made 1963 to 1974 by Sako

HIGH-POWER BOLT-ACTION RIFLE,
SAFARI GRADE, SHORT ACTION . . . . . . NiB $1722 Ex $933 Gd $747
Same as Standard except short action. Calibers: .222 Rem., .222 Rem. Mag. 22-inch lightweight or 24-inch heavy bbl. No sights. Weight: 6 lbs., 2 oz. w/lightweight bbl.; 7.5 lbs. w/heavy bbl. Made from 1963 to 1974 by Sako.

HIGH-POWER BOLT-ACTION RIFLE,
SAFARI GRADE, STANDARD ACTION . . NiB $1523 Ex $1133 Gd $944
Mauser-type action. Calibers: .270 Win., .30-06, 7mm Rem. Mag., .300 H&H Mag., .300 Win. Mag., .308 Norma Mag., .338 Win. Mag., .375 H&H Mag., .458 Win. Mag. Capacity: 6 rounds in .270, .30-06, four in magnum calibers. Bbl.: 22 inches in .270 and .30-06; 24 inches in magnum calibers. Wgt.: 7 lbs., 2 oz. in .270 and .30-06; 8.25 lbs. in magnum calibers. Folding leaf rear sight, hooded ramp front. Checkered Monte Carlo stock w/pistol grip; recoil pad on magnum calibers. QD swivels. Made from 1959 to 1974 by FN.

T-BOLT T-1 .22 REPEATING RIFLE
Straight-pull bolt action. Caliber: .22 LR. Five round clip magazine. 24-inch bbl. Peep rear sight w/ramped blade front. Plain walnut stock w/pistol grip and laquered finish. Weight: 6 lbs. Made from 1965 to 1974 by FN.
Right-hand model . . . . NiB $644 Ex $469 Gd $300
Left-hand model . . . . NiB $675 Ex $512 Gd $409

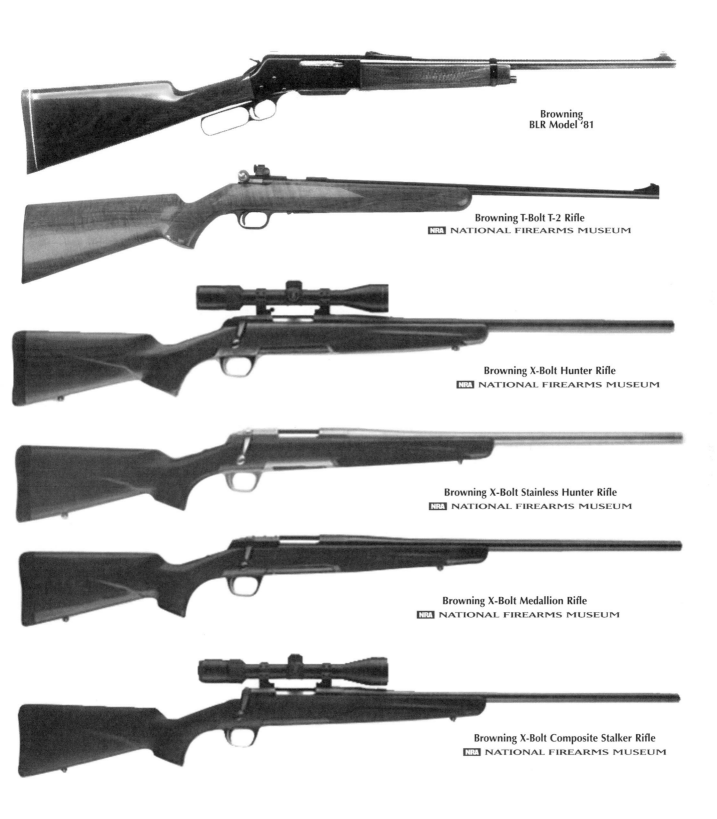

Browning
BLR Model '81

Browning T-Bolt T-2 Rifle
NRA NATIONAL FIREARMS MUSEUM

Browning X-Bolt Hunter Rifle
NRA NATIONAL FIREARMS MUSEUM

Browning X-Bolt Stainless Hunter Rifle
NRA NATIONAL FIREARMS MUSEUM

Browning X-Bolt Medallion Rifle
NRA NATIONAL FIREARMS MUSEUM

Browning X-Bolt Composite Stalker Rifle
NRA NATIONAL FIREARMS MUSEUM

Bsa Guns Ltd.

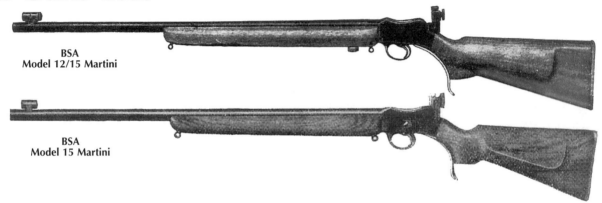

BSA Model 12/15 Martini

BSA Model 15 Martini

T-BOLT T-2
Same as T-1 Model except w/checkered fancy figured walnut stock. Made from 1966-74 by FN. (Reintroduced briefly during the late 1980s with oil-finished stock.)
Original model . . . . NiB $900 Ex $579 Gd $289
Reintroduced model . . . . .NiB $589 Ex $433 Gd $266

X-BOLT HUNTER . . . . .NiB $899 Ex $625 Gd $400
Calibers: Various, short and long action, three- or four-round detachable rotary mag. Bbl.: 22 to 26 inches, no sights; X-lock scope mounting system (four screws per base); adj. trigger. Satin finished walnut stock, low luster blue finish; soft recoil pad. Wgt.: 6.5 to 7 lbs. Introduced. 2008, disc. 2013.

X-BOLT STAINLESS HUNTER . . . . .NiB $1120 Ex $600 Gd $450
Similar to X-Bolt Hunter except w/matte finished stainless steel receiver and bbl. Wgt.: 8 lbs. Introduced. 2009. Disc. 2013.

X-BOLT MEDALLION . . . . .NiB $1025 Ex $675 Gd $450
Same as X-Bolt Hunter except w/gloss-finished walnut stock, rosewood pistol grip and forend caps. Introduced 2008. Disc. 2013.

X-BOLT COMPOSITE STALKER . . . .NiB $900 Ex $600 Gd $405
Similar to X-Bolt Hunter. Bbl.: 22 or 26 inches. Matte blue receiver and bbl. Matte black checkered composite stock w/palm swell, DuraTouch Armor coating. Wgt.: 6 lbs, 5 oz. to 6 lbs., 13 oz. Introduced 2008. Disc. 2013.

FN. BROWNING FAL SEMIAUTOMATIC RIFLE
Same as FN FAL Semiautomatic Rifle. See FN listing for specifications. Sold by Browning for a brief period c. 1960.
F.N. FAL standard model (G-series) . . . . . . .NiB $4977 Ex $3677 Gd $2928
F.N. FAL lightweight model (G-series) . . . . .NiB $5310 Ex $4400 Gd $3090
F.N. FAL heavy bbl.. model (G-series) . . . . .NiB $7175 Ex $6230 Gd $4956
BAC FAL model .NiB $5320 Ex $4902 Gd $4915

BSA GUNS LTD. — Birmingham, England (previously imported by Samco Global Arms, BSA Guns Ltd and Precision Sports)

NO. 12 MARTINI SINGLE-SHOT
TARGET RIFLE. . . . . NiB $766 Ex $567 Gd $433
Caliber .22 LR. 29-inch bbl. Weight: 8.75 lbs. Parker-Hale Model 7 rear sight and Model 2 front sight. Straight-grip stock, checkered forearm. Note: This model was also available w/open sights or w/ BSA No. 20 and 30 sights. Made before WWII.

MODEL 12/15 MARTINI HEAVY . . . . NiB $765 Ex $544 Gd $379
Same as Standard Model 12/15 except w/extra heavy bbl.,

MODEL 12/15 MARTINI
SINGLE-SHOT TARGET RIFLE . . . . . NiB $644 Ex $479 Gd $355
Caliber: .22 LR. 29-inch bbl. Weight: 9 lbs. Parker-Hale No. PH-7A rear sight and No. FS-22 front sight. Target stock w/high comb and cheekpiece, beavertail forearm. This is a post-WWII model; however, a similar rifle, the BSA-Parker Model 12/15, was produced c. 1938.

NO. 13 MARTINI SINGLE-SHOT
TARGET RIFLE. . . . . NiB $756 Ex $579 Gd $443
Caliber: .22 LR. Lighter version of the No.12 w/same general specifications except w/25-inch bbl., weighs 6.5 lbs Made before WWII.

NO. 13 SPORTING RIFLE
Same as No. 13 Target except fitted w/Parker-Hale "Sportarget" rear sight and bead front. Also available in .22 Hornet. Made before WWII.
.22 Long Rifle . . . . NiB $756 Ex $579 Gd $443
.22 Hornet . . . . NiB $976 Ex $800 Gd $579

MODEL 15 MARTINI
SINGLE-SHOT TARGET RIFLE. . . . . .NiB $765 Ex $577 Gd $335
Caliber: .22 LR. 29-inch bbl. Weight: 9.5 lbs. BSA No. 30 rear sight and No. 20 front sight. Target stock w/cheekpiece and pistol-grip; long, semi-beavertail forearm. Made before WWII.

CENTURION MODEL MATCH RIFLE . . .NiB $522 Ex $423 Gd $320
Same general specifications as Model 15 except w/Centurion match bbl. Made before WWII.

CF-2 BOLT-ACTION HUNTING RIFLE . . .NiB $543 Ex $399 Gd $265
Mauser-type action. Calibers: 7mm Rem. Mag., .300 Win. Mag. Three-round magazine. 23.6-inch bbl. Weight: 8 lbs. Sights: Adj. rear; hooded ramp front. Checkered walnut stock w/Monte Carlo comb, rollover cheekpiece, rosewood forend tip, recoil pad, sling swivels. Made from 1975 to 1987.

CF-2 STUTZEN RIFLE . . . . NiB $577 Ex $437 Gd $333
Calibers: .222 Rem., .22-250, .243 Win., .270 Win., .308 Win. .30-06. Four round capacity (5 in 222 Rem.). 20.6-inch bbl. 41.5 inches (approx.) overall length. Weight: 7.5 to 8 lbs. Williams front and rear sights. Hand-finished European walnut stock. Monte Carlo cheekpiece and Windhammer palm swell. Double-set triggers. Importation disc. 1987.

CFT TARGET RIFLE . . . . NiB $917 Ex $735 Gd $533
Single-shot bolt-action. Calibers: 7.62mm (.308 Win.) Bbl.: 26.5 inches. Lgt.: 47.5 inches. Weight.: 11 lbs. Importation disc. 1987.

MAJESTIC DELUXE FEATHERWEIGHT BOLT-ACTION HUNTING RIFLE
Mauser-type action. Calibers: .243 Win., .270 Win., .308 Win., .30-06, .458 Win. Mag. Four round magazine. 22-inch bbl. w/BESA recoil reducer. Weight: 6.25 lbs.; 8.75 lbs. in 458. Folding leaf rear sight, hooded ramp front. Checkered European-style walnut stock w/cheekpiece, pistol-grip, Schnabel forend, swivels, recoil pad. Made from 1959 to 1965.
.458 Win. Mag. caliber . . . . NiB $644 Ex $508 Gd $377
Other calibers. . . . . NiB $506 Ex $433 Gd $298

BSA CFT Target

BSA
Martini-International ISU Match

BSA
Martini-International Mark V Match

BSA
Martini-International MK III Match

BSA
Monarch Deluxe Varmint

BSA MAJESTIC DELUXE
STANDARD WEIGHT . . . . **NiB $503 Ex $332 Gd $255**
Same as Featherweight model except w/heavier bbl. and no recoil
reducer. Calibers: .22 Hornet, .222 Rem., .243 Win., 7x57mm, .308
Win., .30-06. Weight: 7.25 to 7.75 lbs. Disc.

MARTINI-INTERNATIONAL
ISU MATCH RIFLE . . . . **NiB $944 Ex $708 Gd $577**
Similar to MK III, but modified to meet International Shooting Union
"standard rifle" specifications. 28-inch standard weight bbl. Weight:
10.75 lbs. Redesigned stock and forearm attached to bbl. w/"V" section alloy strut. Introduced 1968. Disc.

MARTINI-INTERNATIONAL
MARK V MATCH RIFLE . . . . **NiB $1066 Ex $897 Gd $623**
Same as ISU model except w/heavier bbl. Weight: 12.25 lbs. Introduced 1976. Disc.

MARTINI-INTERNATIONAL MATCH
RIFLE SINGLE-SHOT HEAVY PATTERN . . . **NiB $866 Ex $630 Gd $443**
Caliber: .22 LR. Bbl. Heavy, 29—inches. Weight: 14 lbs. Parker-Hale
"International" front and rear sights. Target stock w/full cheekpiece and pis-
tol grip, broad beavertail forearm; and stop and swivels. Right- or left-hand
models made from 1950 to 1953.

MARTINI-INTERNATIONAL
MATCH RIFLE — LIGHT PATTERN. . . . . **NiB $1033 Ex $720 Gd $630**
Same general specifications as Heavy Pattern except w/26-inch
lighter weight bbl. Weight: 11 lbs. Disc.

MARTINI-INTERNATIONAL
MK II MATCH RIFLE . . . . **NiB $1044 Ex $812 Gd $613**
Same general specifications as original model. Heavy and
Light Pattern. Improved trigger mechanism and ejection system.
Redesigned stock and forearm. Made from 1953 to 1959.

Canadian Military Rifles

MARTINI-INTERNATIONAL
MK III MATCH RIFLE . . . . **NiB $1233 Ex $1088 Gd $780**
Same general specifications as MK II Heavy Pattern. Longer action frame w/I-section alloy strut to which forearm is attached; bbl. is fully floating. Redesigned stock and forearm. Made from 1959 to 1967.

MONARCH DELUXE BOLT-ACTION
HUNTING RIFLE . . . . **NiB $714 Ex $349 Gd $260**
Same as Majestic Deluxe Standard Weight model except w/redesigned stock of U.S. style w/contrasting hardwood forend tip and grip cap. Calibers: .222 Rem., .243 Win., .270 Win., 7mm Rem. Mag., .308 Win., .30-06. 22-inch bbl. Weight: 7 to 7.25 lbs. Made from 1965 to 1974.

MONARCH DELUXE
VARMINT RIFLE . . . . **NiB $710 Ex $420 Gd $290**
Same as Monarch Deluxe except w/24-inch heavy bbl. Calibers: .222 Rem., .243 Win. Weight: 9 lbs.

BUSHMASTER FIREARMS
(Quality Parts Company) — Windham, Maine

M17S BULLPUP . . . . **NiB $735 Ex $600 Gd $466**
Caliber: .223. 21.5-inch bbl. Weight: 8.2 lbs. Polymer stocks. Handle w/fixed open sights w/Weaver-type rail for any optics. Semi-auto, self-compensating short stroke gas piston. Forward trigger/grip w/rear chamber. Bullpup style. Alloy receiver. Synthetic lower receiver is hinged to upper w/hinged takedown system. Accepts M-16 type magazines. Made from 1992 to 2005.

MODEL XM15 E2S SERIES
Caliber: .223 Rem. Bbl.: 16, 20, 24 or 26 inches. Weight: 7 to 8.6 lbs. Polymer stocks. Adj. sights w/dual flip-up aperture. Optional flattop rail accepts scope mounts. Direct gas-operated w/rotating bolt. Forged alloy receiver. All steel coated w/manganese phosphate. Accepts M-16-type mags. Made from 1989 to date.
XM15 E2S Carbine . . . . **NiB $1210 Ex $979 Gd $750**
XM15 E2S Target Rifle . . . . **NiB $1244 Ex $1018 Gd $700**

CABELA'S, INC. — Sidney, Nebraska

Cabela's is a sporting goods dealer and catalog company headquartered in Sidney, Nebraska. Cabela's imports black powder cartridge Sharps replicas, revolvers, and other reproductions and replicas manufactured in Italy by A. Uberti, Pedersoli, Pietta, and others.

1858 HENRY REPLICA . . . . **NiB $700 Ex $599 Gd $524**
Lever-action. Modeled after the original Henry rifle. Caliber: .44-40. Thirteen-round magazine; Bbl: 24 inches. Overall length: 43 inches. Weight: 9 pounds. European walnut stock. Sights: Bead front, open adjustable rear. Brass receiver and buttplate. Introduced 1994.

1866 WINCHESTER REPLICA . . . . . **NiB $599 Ex $425 Gd $344**
Lever-action. Modeled after the Model 1886 rifle. Caliber: .44-40; 13-round mag. Bbl.: 24 inches, octagonal. Lgt.: 43 inches. Weight: 9 lbs. European walnut stock, brass receiver, buttplate and forend cap. Bead front, open adj. rear sights.

1873 WINCHESTER REPLICA
Lever-action modeled after the original Model 1873 rifle. Caliber: .44-40, .45 Colt. Thirteen-round magazine. Bbl: 30 inches. Overall length: 43 inches. Weight: 8 pounds. European walnut stock. Sights: Bead front, open adjustable rear or globe front and tang rear. Color case-hardened steel receiver. Introduced 1994.
Standard model. . . . . **NiB $525 Ex $455 Gd $390**
W/tang rear sight, globe front, add $175

1873 SPORTING MODEL REPLICA
Same as 1873 Winchester except with 24-inch bbl.
Standard model. . . . . **NiB $655 Ex $577 Gd $500**
W/half-round, half-octagonal bbl., half magazine, add $125

CATTLEMAN CARBINE. . . . . **NiB $355 Ex $290 Gd $225**
Revolver with shoulder stock. Caliber: .44-40; six-round cylinder. Bbl: 18 inches. Overall length: 34 inches. Weight: 4 pounds. European walnut stock. Sights: Blade front, notch rear. Color case-hardened frame, remainder blued. Introduced 1994.

SHARPS SPORTING RIFLE . . . . **NiB $879 Ex $779 Gd $576**
Single-shot. Caliber: .45-70. Bbl: tapered octagon, 32 inches. Length: 47 inches. Weight: 9 pounds. Checkered walnut stock. Sights: Blade front, open adjustable rear. Color case-hardened receiver and hammer; remainder blued. Introduced 1995.

CALICO LIGHT WEAPONS SYSTEMS —
Bakersville, California

LIBERTY 50/100 Semi-automatic RIFLE
Retarded blowback action. Caliber: 9mm. 50- or 100-round helical-feed magazine. 16.1-inch bbl. 34.5 inches overall. Weight: 7 lbs. Adjustable post front sight and aperture rear. Ambidextrous rotating safety. Glass-filled polymer or thumbhole-style wood stock. Made from 1995 to 2001; reintro. 2007.
Model Liberty 50 . . . . **NiB $800 Ex $668 Gd $410**
Model Liberty 100 . . . . **NiB $900 Ex $869 Gd $490**

MODEL M-100 Semi-Automatic SERIES
Similar to the Liberty 100 Model except chambered for .22 LR. Weight: 5 lbs. 34.5 inches overall. Folding or glass-filled polymer stock and forearm. Made from 1986 to 1994; reintro. 2007.
Model M-100 w/folding stock (disc. 1994). . . **NiB $600 Ex $355 Gd $300**
Model M-100 FS w/fixed stock disc. 1996 . . . . **NiB $400 Ex $379 Gd $320**

MODEL M-105 SEMI-AUTOMATIC
SPORTER. . . . . **NiB $688 Ex $492 Gd $330**
Similar to the Liberty 100 Model except fitted w/walnut buttstock and forearm. Made from 1989 to 1994.

MODEL M-900 SEMIAUTOMATIC CARBINE
Caliber: 9mm Parabellum. 50- or 100-round magazine. 16.1-inch bbl. 28.5 inches overall. Weight: 3.7 lbs. Post front sight adj. for windage and elevation, fixed notch rear. Collapsible steel buttstock and glass-filled polymer grip. Matte black finish. Made from 1989 to 1990, 1992 to 1993, and 2007.
Model M-100 w/folding stock (disc. 1994) . . . . **NiB $808 Ex $497 Gd $338**
Model M-100 FS w/fixed stock (intro. 1996). . . .**NiB $677 Ex $533 Gd $390**

MODEL M-951 TACTICAL CARBINE
Similar to Model 900 except w/long compensator and adj. forward grip. Made from 1990 to 1994.
Model 951 . . . . **NiB $725 Ex $533 Gd $445**
Model 951-S . . . . **NiB $725 Ex $533 Gd $445**

CANADIAN MILITARY RIFLES — Quebec,
Canada. Manufactured by Ross Rifle Co.

MODEL 1907 MARK II
ROSS MILITARY RIFLE . . . . **NiB $409 Ex $299 Gd $277**
Straight-pull bolt-action. Caliber: .303 British; five-round box mag. Bbl.: 28 inches. Weight: 8.5 lbs. Adj. rear, blade front sights. Military-style full stock. The Ross was originally issued as a Canadian service rifle in 1907. There were several variations of this model. It was the official service weapon at the start of WWII but has been obsolete for many years. For more Ross products, see the Ross Rifle Company listings.

Century International Arms, Inc.

CENTURY INTERNATIONAL ARMS, INC. — Delray Beach, Florida

CENTURION M38/M96 BOLT-ACTION SPORTER
Sporterized Swedish M38/96 Mauser action. Caliber: 6.5x55mm. Five-round magazine. 24-inch bbl. 44 inches overall. Adj. rear sight. Blade front. Black synthetic or checkered European hardwood Monte Carlo stock. Holden Ironsighter see-through scope mount. Imported from 1987 to date.

W/hardwood stock . . . . NiB $277 Ex $190 Gd $133
W/synthetic stock . . . . NiB $280 Ex $198 Gd $143

CENTURION M98 BOLT-ACTION SPORTER
Sporterized VZ24 or 98 Mauser action. Calibers: .270 Win., 7.62x39mm, .308 Win., .30-06. Five round magazine. 22-inch bbl. 44 inches overall. Weight: 7.5 lbs. W/Millet or Weaver scope base(s), rings and no iron sights. Classic or Monte Carlo laminated hardwood, black synthetic or checkered European hardwood stock. Imported from 1992 to date.

M98 Action w/black
synthetic stock (w/o rings) . . . . NiB $300 Ex $220 Gd $167
M98 Action w/hardwood Stock(w/o rings) . . . . NiB $290 Ex $190 Gd $125
VZ24 action w/laminated
hardwood stock (Elite) . . . . NiB $355 Ex $289 Gd $188
VZ24 action w/black synthetic stock . . . NiB $335 Ex $269 Gd $175
W/Millet base and rings, add $45

CENTURION P-14 SPORTER
Sporterized P-14 action. Caliber: 7mm Rem. Mag., .300 Win. Mag. Five-round magazine. 24-inch bbl. 43.4 inches overall. Weight: 8.25 lbs. Weaver-type scope base. Walnut stained hardwood or fiberglass stock. Imported from 1987 to date.

W/hardwood stock . . . . NiB $267 Ex $211 Gd $157
W/fiberglass stock. . . . . NiB $299 Ex $223 Gd $165

ENFIELD SPORTER 4 BOLT-ACTION RIFLE
Sporterized Lee-Enfield action. Caliber: .303 British. 10-round magazine. 25.25-inch bbl. 44.5 inches overall. Blade front sight, adj. aperture rear. Sporterized beechwood military stock or checkered walnut Monte Carlo stock. Blued finish. Imported from 1987 to date.

W/sporterized military stock . . . . NiB $169 Ex $128 Gd $90
W/checkered walnut stock . . . . NiB $223 Ex $190 Gd $135

L1A1 FAL SPORTER . . . . NiB $944 Ex $749 Gd $588
Sporterized L1A1 FAL semiautomatic. Caliber: .308 Win. 20.75-inch bbl. 41 inches overall. Weight: 9.75 lbs. Protected front post sight, adj. aperture rear. Matte blued finish. Black or camo Bell & Carlson thumbhole sporter stock w/rubber buttpad. Imported from 1988 to 1998

M-14 SPORTER . . . . NiB $460 Ex $335 Gd $255
Sporterized M-14 gas operated semiautomatic action. Caliber: .308 Win. 10-round magazine. 22-inch bbl. 41 inches overall. Weight: 8.25 lbs. Blade front sight, adj. aperture rear sight. Parkerized finish. Walnut stock w/rubber recoil pad. Forged receiver. Imported from 1991 to date.

TIGER DRAGUNOV . . . . NiB $1023 Ex $790 Gd $545
Russian SVD semiautomatic sniper rifle. Caliber: 7.62x54R; five-round mag. Bbl.: 21 inches. Lgt.: 43 inches. Weight: 8.5 lbs. Blade front, adj. rear. Blued finish. Laminated European hardwood thumbhole stock. 4x range-finding scope w/lighted reticle and sun shade. QD scope mount. Imported from 1994 to 1995.

GAMESTALKER . . . . NiB $1399 Ex $1088 Gd $946
Cal.: .243 WSSM, .25 WSSM, .300 WSSM. Bbl.: 22 inches, stainless steel, flattop upper, free-floating aluminum hand guard. ACE skeleton stock with ERGO Sure Grip. 100% camo. Weight: 7 lbs.

Century International Arms GP WASR-10

Century International Arms Tantal Sporter

Century International Arms VZ 2008 Sporter

Century International Arms GP 1975

Century International Arms Degtyarev DP28

Century International Arms Sterling SA

G-3 SPORTER . . . . NiB $866 Ex $633 Gd $425
Semi-auto. Cal.: .308 Win. Made from G3 parts, American-made receiver with integrated scope rail. Bbl.: 19 inches. 20-round mag. Pistol grip stock, matte black finish. Weight: 9.3 pounds. Imported 1999 to 2006.

Cimarron Arms

CETME SPORTER . . . . **NiB $754 Ex $577 Gd $387**
Cal.: .308 Win. Bbl.: 19.5 inches. 20-round mag. Blue or Mossy Oak Break-Up camo finish, wood or synthetic stock w/pistol grip. Vented forearm. Weight: 9.7 lbs.

S.A.R. 1 . . . . **NiB $835 Ex $600 Gd $377**
AK-47-type by Romarm. Cal.: 7.62x39mm. Bbl.: 16 inches. Wood stock and forearm. Includes one 10 and one 30-round double-stack magazine. Disc. 2003
S.A.R. 2 (5.45x39mm) . . . . **NiB $835 Ex $600 Gd $377**
S.A.R. 3 (.223 Rem.) . . . . **NiB $835 Ex $600 Gd $377**

MODEL B-82 . . . . **NiB $835 Ex $600 Gd $377**
Limited production Italian police model; serial no. with "D" suffix. Cal.: .30 Luger, .32 ACP, 9 mm Ultra.

GP WASR-10 . . . . **NiB $555 Ex $366 Gd $244**
AK-47 type by Romarm. Cal.: 7.62x39mm. Bbl.: 16.25 inches. Wood stock and forearm, includes one 5- and one 10-round mag. Weight: 7.5 lbs.
High-Cap series . . . . **NiB $529 Ex $345 Gd $221**

L1A1/R1A1 SPORTER . . . . **NiB $1044 Ex $835 Gd $229**
Modeled after British L1A1. Cal.: .308 Win. Bbl.: 22.5 inches. Carrying handle, synthetic furn. 20-round mag. Folding rear sight. Weight: 9.5 lbs.

GOLANI SPORTER . . . . **NiB $835 Ex $644 Gd $456**
Made in Israel. Cal.: .223 Rem. Bbl.: 21 inches. Folding stock, opt. bayonet lug., 35-round mag. Weight: 8 lbs.

TANTAL SPORTER . . . . **NiB $735 Ex $555 Gd $455**
Cal.: 5.45x39mm. Bbl.: 18 inches, flash hider. Folding wire stock. Parkerized finish. Includes extra mag. Weight: 8 lbs.

VZ 2008 SPORTER . . . . **NiB $856 Ex $645 Gd $465**
Copy of the Czech V258. Cal.: 7.62x39mm. Bbl.: 16.25 inches; steel receiver w/matte finish; wood or plastic stock. Weight: 7 lbs.

M-76 SNIPER . . . . **NiB $1956 Ex $1538 Gd $967**
Semi-auto version of Yugoslav M76. Cal.: 8mm Mauser. Bbl.: 21.5 inches. U.S.-made receiver. Includes scope, mount and 10-round mag. Weight: 11.3 lbs.

GP 1975 . . . . **NiB $644 Ex $440 Gd $300**
Cal.: 7.62x39mm. Bbl.: 16.25 inches. Black synthetic furniture, U.S.-made receiver and bbl. Weight: 7.4 lbs.

DEGTYAREV DP28 . . . . **NiB $4125 Ex $3155 Gd $2390**
Semi-auto, top-mounted magazine. Cal.: 7.62x54R. Gas operated. Full stock. 47- to 50-round mag. Weight: 10 lbs.
DPM 28 (pistol grip) . . . . . **NiB $3970 Ex $3289 Gd $2410**
DPX Tank Model . . . . **NiB $3970 Ex $3289 Gd $2410**

STERLING SA . . . . **NiB $745 Ex $560 Gd $380**
Semi-auto version of Sterling sub-machine gun. Cal.: 9mm Para., 34-round mag. Bbl.: 16 inches. U.S.-made receiver and bbl., crinkle finish; folding stock.

PAR 1 . . . . **NiB $439 Ex $300 Gd $218**
AK-47 receiver, made by PAR. Cal.: 7.62x39mm; 10-round mag. Bbl.: 20.9 inches. Weight: 7.6 lbs. Imported 2002 to 2009.
PAR 3 (.223 Rem.) . . . . **NiB $439 Ex $300 Gd $218**

CHARTER ARMS CORPORATION — Shelton, Connecticut

AR-7 EXPLORER SURVIVAL RIFLE . . . . **NiB $139 Ex $120 Gd $99**

Same as Armalite AR-7 except w/black wood-grain plastic stock. See listing of that rifle for specs. Made from 1973 to 1990.

CHIPMUNK RIFLES — Prospect, Oregon. Manufactured by Rogue Rifle Company (formerly Oregon Arms Company and Chipmunk Manufacturing, Inc.)

BOLT-ACTION SINGLE-SHOT RIFLE
Calibers: .22 LR. or .22 WMR. 16.13-inch standard or 18.13-inch bull bbl. Weight: 2.5 lbs. (standard) or 4 lbs. (Bull bbl.) Peep sight rear; ramp front. Plain or checkered American walnut, laminated or black hardwood stock. Made from 1982 to 2007.
Standard model
w/plain walnut stock . . . . **NiB $235 Ex $156 Gd $103**
Standard model
w/black hardwood stock . . . . **NiB $195 Ex $155 Gd $99**
Standard model
w/camouflage stock . . . . **NiB $225 Ex $170 Gd $130**
Standard model
w/laminated stock . . . . **NiB $200 Ex $160 Gd $125**
Deluxe grade
w/checkered walnut stock . . . . **NiB $289 Ex $225 Gd $144**
.22 WMR, add **$40**

CHURCHILL RIFLES — High Wycombe, England

HIGHLANDER BOLT-ACTION RIFLE . . . .**NiB $435 Ex $367 Gd $298**
Calibers: .243 Win., .25-06 Rem., .270 Win., .308 Win., .30-06, 7mm Rem. Mag., .300 Win. Mag. Four round magazine (standard); 3-round (magnum). Bbl. length: 22-inch (standard); 24-inch (magnum). 42.5 to 44.5 inches overall. Weight: 7.5 lbs. Adj. rear sight, blade front. Checkered European walnut pistol-grip stock. Imported from 1986 to 1991.

"ONE OF ONE THOUSAND"
RIFLE . . . . **NiB $4220 Ex $2535 Gd $1966**
Made for Interarms to commemorate the firm's 20th anniversary. Mauser-type action. Calibers: .270 Win., 7mm Rem. Mag., .308 Win., .30-06, .300 Win. Mag., .375 H&H Mag., .458 Win. Mag,; five-round mag. (three rounds in magnum calibers). Bbl.: 24 inches. Weight: 8 lbs. Classic-style French walnut stock w/cheekpiece, black forend tip, checkered pistol grip and forearm; swivel-mounted recoil pad w/cartridge trap, pistol-grap cap w/trap for extra front sight; barrel-mounted sling swivel. Limited issue of 2,000 rifles made in 1973.

REGENT BOLT-ACTION RIFLE . . . . **NiB $577 Ex $423 Gd $290**
Caliber: .243 Win., .25-06 rem., .270 Win., .308 Win., .30-06, 7mm Rem., Mag., .300 Win. Mag.; four-round mag. Bbl.: 22 inches, round. Length. 42.5 inches. Weight: 7.5 lbs. Ramp gold bead front, adj. rear sights. Hand-checkered Monte-Carlo-style stock of select European walnut; recoil pad. Made from 1986 to 1988.

CIMARRON ARMS — Fredericksburg, Texas

1860 HENRY LEVER-ACTION REPLICA
Replica of 1860 Henry w/original Henry loading system. Calibers: .44-40, .44 Special, .45 Colt. 13-round magazine. 22-inch bbl. (carbine) or 24.25-inch bbl. (rifle). 43 inches overall (rifle). Weight: 9.5 lbs. (rifle). Bead front sight, open adj. rear. Brass receiver and buttplate. Smooth European walnut buttstock. Imported from 1991.
Carbine model . . . . **NiB $1460 Ex $1096 Gd $735**
Rifle model . . . . **NiB $1390 Ex $1076 Gd $675**

Churchill "One of One Thousand"

Churchill Regent

Civil War model
(U.S. issue, martially marked). . . **NiB $1466 Ex $1100 Gd $709**
W/standard engraving add $2550
W/standard engraving, deluxe wood, add. $3150
W/Lincoln hand engraving (disc. 2009), add $4500
W/Lincoln hand engraving,
deluxe wood (disc. 2009), add $5000

1866 YELLOWBOY LEVER-ACTION
Replica of 1866 Winchester. Calibers: .22 LR, 22WMR, .38 Special, .44-40, .45 Colt. 16-inch round bbl. (Trapper), 19-inch round bbl. (Carbine) or 24.25-inch ocatagonal bbl. (rifle). 43 inches overall (rifle). Weight: 9 lbs. (rifle). Bead front sight, open adj. rear. Brass receiver, buttplate and forend cap. Smooth European walnut stock. Imported from 1991 to date.
Carbine . . . . .NiB $1075 Ex $787 Gd $581
Rifle . . . . .NiB $1050 Ex $612 Gd $406
Indian model (disc.) . . . . NiB $895 Ex $585 Gd $379
Trapper Model (.44-40 WCF only, disc.) . . . . . .NiB $995 Ex $756 Gd $502
W/A-engraving, add. $2025
W/B-engraving, add. $2500
W/C-engraving, add. $3000

1873 LEVER-ACTION
Replica of 1873 Winchester. Calibers: .22 LR. .22WMR, .357 Magnum, .44-40 or .45 Colt. 16-inch round bbl. (Trapper), 19-inch round bbl. (SRC), 20-inch octagonal bbl. (short rifle), 24.25-inch octagonal bbl. (sporting rifle) and 30-inch octagonal bbl. (express rifle). 43 inches overall (sporting rifle). Weight: 8 lbs. Fixed blade front sight, adj. semi-buckhorn rear or tang peep sight. Walnut stock and forend. Color case-hardened receiver. Imported from 1989 to date.
Express Rifle . . . . NiB $1235 Ex $960 Gd $677
Short Rifle (disc.) . . . . NiB $1235 Ex $960 Gd $677
Sporting Rifle . . . . NiB $1235 Ex $960 Gd $677
SRC Carbine . . . . NiB $1235 Ex $960 Gd $677
Trapper (disc.) . . . . .NiB $1255 Ex $980 Gd $697
One of 1,000 engraved model . . . . . . NiB $2409 Ex $2033 Gd $1354

1874 FALLING BLOCK SPORTING RIFLE
Replica of 1874 Sharps Sporting Rifle. Calibers: .45-65, .45-70, .45-90 or .45-120. 32- or 34-inch round or octagonal bbl. Weight: 9.5 to 10 lbs. Blade or globe front sight w/adj. open rear or sporting tang peep sight. Single or double set triggers. Checkered walnut stock and forend w/nose cap. Color case-hardened receiver. Imported from 1997 to date.
Billy Dixon Model . . . . NiB $1714 Ex $1289 Gd $1100
Quigley Model . . . . NiB $1356 Ex $1178 Gd $909
Sharps Sporting No. 1 Rifle . . . . NiB $1577 Ex $1133 Gd $908

1883 BURGESS RIFLE . . . . NiB $1489 Ex $1077 Gd $744
Caliber: .45 Long Colt. Bbl.: 20 or 25 ½ inches. Reproduction.

Importation began in 2010.
LIGHTNING MAGAZINE RIFLE . NiB $1488 Ex $1088 Gd $755
Reproduction of Colt Lightning Rifle. Cal.: .357 Mag., .44-40 WCF or .45 Long Colt. Bbl.: round; 20 or 24 inches; octagon: 20, 24, or 26 inches. Blue or case-colored frame.
W/octagon bbl., add $150
Color case-hardened frame, add $300

MODEL 1871 ROLLING BLOCK
BABY CARBINE . . . . NiB $379 Ex $290 Gd $195
Remington repro. Caliber: .22 LR, .22 Hornet, .22 Mag. Or .357 Mag. Bbl: 22 inches. Walnut stock and forearm. Brass trigger guard and buttplate. Disc. 1990.
Deluxe model . . . . NiB $785 Ex $580 Gd $335

LONG RANGE CREEDMOOR. . . . . . . NiB $1279 Ex $890 Gd $655
Cal.: .45-70 Gov't. Barrel: 30-inch octagon. Deluxe checkered walnut stock.

ADOBE WALLS FALLING
BLOCK RIFLE . . . . .NiB $1754 Ex $1310 Gd $966
Cal.: .45-70 Gov't. Bbl.: 30 inches, octagon. Case hardened receiver, hand checkered walnut stock, German silver nose cap. Optional Creedmoor sights.

SHARPS NO. 1 RIFLE . . . . NiB $1076 Ex $755 Gd $544
Sharps reproduction. Cal.: .40-65 Win. or .45-70 Gov't. Bbl.: 32 inches, octagon; pistol grip stock. Imported 2000 to 2002.
No. 1 Silhouette . . . . NiB $1588 Ex $1011 Gd $744

MODEL 1874 SPORTING RIFLE . . . NiB $1377 Ex $986 Gd $644
Armi-Sport Billy Dixon model. Cal.: .38-55 WCF, .45-70 Gov't., .45-90 Win., .45-110, .50-90. Bbl.: 32 inches. Checkered deluxe walnut stock. Double set triggers.
Pedersoli model . . . . NiB $1809 Ex $1335 Gd $1088
Quigley II model. . . . . NiB $1469 Ex $1104 Gd $854
Pedersoli Quigley . . . . NiB $2188 Ex $1598 Gd $1077
Big 50 model. . . . . NiB $2769 Ex $1988 Gd $1369
Sharps Pride model . . . . NiB $2240 Ex $1654 Gd $1290
Pride II model. . . . . NiB $1544 Ex $1068 Gd $900
Professional Hunter . . . . NiB $1344 Ex $1068 Gd $900
Texas Ranger . . . . NiB $1271 Ex $933 Gd $730

SHARPS ROCKY MOUNTAIN II
MODEL 74 . . . . NiB $1498 Ex $1033 Gd $677
Repro. Cal.: .45-70 Gov't. Bbl.: 30 inches, octagon. Silver receiver, checkered walnut stock. Optional 6x Malcolm rifle scope.
W/scope, add $650

Clifton Arms

MODEL 1860 SPENCER RIFLE . . **NiB $1645 Ex $1154 Gd $933**
By Armi Sport. Cal.: 56-50. Bbl.: 30 inches. Plain walnut stock and forearm. Case hardened receiver, trigger guard and hammer. Three barrel bands.

**MODEL 1865 SPENCER
REPEATING RIFLE** . . . . **NiB $1490 Ex $1167 Gd $770**
By Armi Sport. Cal.: .44-40 WCF, .45 Schofield, .45 Long Colt, .56-50. Bbl.: 20 or 30 inches (in 56-50 only, disc. 2009). Blue finish, color case hardened frame. Straight grip walnut stock.
W/30-inch bbl., add **$225**

CIVIL WAR HENRY RIFLE . . . . . . **NiB $1644 Ex $1269 Gd $976**
By Uberti. Cal.: .44-40 WCF or .45 Long Colt. Bbl.: 24 inches. Includes military inspector's marks and cartouche; military-type sling swivels.

1866 YELLOWBOY CARBINE . . . **NiB $1192 Ex $1054 Gd $593**
By Uberti. Cal.: .32-20 WCF, .38 SP, .38-55 WCF, .44 SP, .44-40 WCF, .45 Long Colt. Similar to Model 1866 Sporting Rifle except w/19-inch round bbl., two barrel bands, saddle ring, smooth walnut stock, and forearm.
Trapper model. . . . . **NiB $1167 Ex $866 Gd $546**
Indian Carbine model . . . . **NiB $1056 Ex $679 Gd $496**
Red Cloud model . . . . **NiB $1056 Ex $679 Gd $496**

1873 SADDLE RING CARBINE . . **NiB $1355 Ex $1089 Gd $733**
Cal.: .22 LR, .22 Mag., .32-20 WCF, .357 Mag./.38 SP, .38-40 WCF, .44 SP, .44-40 WCF, .45 Long Colt. Bbl.: 19 inches, round. Blued receiver, saddle ring.
Trapper Carbine . . . . **NiB $1490 Ex $1100 Gd $977**

**1876 CENTENNIAL
SPORTING RIFLE** . . . . **NiB $1525 Ex $1250 Gd $995**
Cal.: .40-60 WCF, .45-60 WCF, .45-70 WCF, .50-95 WCF; bbl.: 22 or 28 inches, octagon. Blue finish, case hardened frame. Full-length magazine, iron sights, walnut stock, and forearm.

1876 CARBINE . . . . **NiB $1788 Ex $1388 Gd $1100**
By Uberti. Cal.: .45-60 WCF, .45-75. Bbl.: 22 inches, round. Full length fore end and barrel band. Canadian NWMP model has blued frame and saddle ring.

1885 HI-WALL RIFLE . . . . **NiB $1169 Ex $977 Gd $749**
Cal.: .30-40 Krag, .348 Win., .38-55 Win., .405 Win., .40-65 WCF, .45-70 Gov't., .45-90 WCF, .45-120 WCF. Bbl.: 28 or 30 inches, octagon. Case hardened finish frame. Iron sights standard or optional aperture rear and globe front offered.
Pedersoli mode . . . . **NiB $2378 Ex $1956 Gd $1100**

1885 LOW-WALL RIFLE . . . . **NiB $1077 Ex $800 Gd $654**
Cal.: .22 LR, .22 Hornet, .22 Mag., .30-30 Win., .32-20 WCF, .357 Mag., .38-40 WCF, .44 Mag., .38-55, .44-40 WCF, .45-70 Gov't., .45 Long Colt. Bbl.: 30 inches. Hand checkered walnut stock, single- or double-set trigger.
Deluxe model, add **$200**
Standard custom engraving, add **$1750**
Double set triggers, add **$400**

1892 RIFLE . . . . **NiB $1288 Ex $800 Gd $643**
Cal.: .357 Mag., .44 Mag., .44-40 WCF, .45 Long Colt. Bbl.: 20 or 24 inches. Solid or take-down frame, smooth walnut stock and forearm, case colored receiver.
W/take-down frame, add **$200**
.44-40 WCF, .44 Mag., add **$50**

1892 CARBINE . . . . **NiB $1235 Ex $866 Gd $644**
Cal.: .357 Mag., .44 Mag., .44-40 WCF, .45 Long Colt. Bbl.: 16 (Trapper model) or 20 inches. Solid frame, choice of big loop lever (El Dorado) or standard with 20-inch bbl. Saddle ring with 20-inch bbl. only.

CLERKE RECREATION PRODUCTS — Santa Monica, California

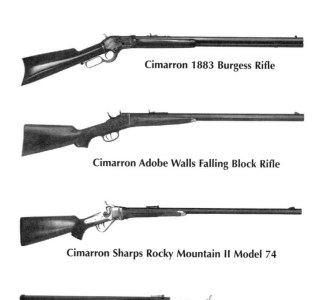

Cimarron 1883 Burgess Rifle

Cimarron Adobe Walls Falling Block Rifle

Cimarron Sharps Rocky Mountain II Model 74

Cimarron Civil War Henry Rifle

Cimarron 1876 Centennial Sporting Rifle

Cimarron 1892 Carbine

DELUXE HI-WALL. . . . . **NiB $337 Ex $290 Gd $219**
Same as standard model, except w/adj. trigger, half-octagon bbl., select wood, stock w/cheekpiece and recoil pad. Made 1972 to 1974.

HI-WALL SINGLE-SHOT RIFLE . . . . **NiB $310 Ex $234 Gd $177**
Falling-block lever-action similar to Winchester 1885 High Wall S.S. Color casehardened investment-cast receiver. Calibers: .222 Rem., .22-250, .243 Rem., 6mm Rem., .25-06, .270 Win., 7mm Rem. Mag., .30-06, .45-70 Govt. 26-inch medium-weight bbl. Weight: 8 lbs. Furnished w/o sights. Checkered walnut pistol-grip stock and Schnabel forearm. Made from 1972 to 1974.

CLIFTON ARMS — Medina, Texas

SCOUT BOLT-ACTION RIFLE
Custom rifle built on the Dakota M76, Ruger M77 or Winchester M70 action. Shilen match-grade bbl. Clifton composite custom-fitted stock. Made from 1992 to 1997.
AfricanScout . . . . **NiB $3175 Ex $2690 Gd $2310**
Pseudo Scout . . . . **NiB $3160 Ex $2211 Gd $1589**
Standard Scout . . . . **NiB $3122 Ex $2520 Gd $1433**
Super Scout. . . . . **NiB $3145 Ex $2175 Gd $1590**

Colt AR-15 A2

Colt AR-15 A2 Delta Match H-BAR

Colt AR-15 A2 Government Model

Colt AR-15 Sporter Competition H-BAR

COLT'S MFG. CO., INC. — West Hartford, Connecticut

NOTE: *Add $200 to pre-ban models made prior to October 13, 1994*

AR-15 A2 DELTA
MATCH H-BAR RIFLE . . . . **NiB $1794 Ex $1677 Gd $1492**
Similar to AR-15A2 Government Model except w/standard stock and heavy refined bbl. Furnished w/3-9x rubber armored scope and removeable cheekpiece. Made from 1986 to 1991.

Colt's Mfg. Co., Inc.

Colt Stagecoach

Colteer 1-.22

Colteer .22 Autoloader

Coltsman Deluxe

Coltsman 1957 Standard

AR-15 A2 GOVERNMENT
MODEL CARBINE . . . . **NiB $1945 Ex $1044 Gd $813**
Caliber: .223 Rem., Five-round magazine. 16-inch bbl. w/flash suppressor. 35 inches overall. Weight: 5.8 lbs. Telescoping aluminum buttstock; sling swivels. Made from 1985 to 1991.

AR-15 A2 SPORTER II . . . . **NiB $1937 Ex $1344 Gd $1136**
Same general specifications as standard AR-15 Sporter except heavier bbl., improved pistol-grip. Weight 7.5 lbs.; optional 3x or 4x scope. Made from 1985 to 1989.

AR-15 COMPACT 9MM CARBINE . . . . **NiB $2023 Ex $1590 Gd $1176**
Semiautomatic. Caliber: 9mm NATO, 20-round detachable mag. Bbl.: 16 inches, round. Ribbed round handguard. Made from 1985 to 1986.

AR-15 SEMIAUTOMATIC SPORTER
Commercial version of U.S. M-16 rifle. Gas-operated. Takedown. Caliber: .223 Rem. (5.56mm); 20-round mag w/spacer to reduce capacity to five rounds. Bbl.: 20 inches, flash suppressor. Adj. rear peep sight in carrying handle, front adj. for windage. 3x scope and mount optional. Black molded composite buttstock, rubber buttplate. Bbl. surrounded by black fiberglass handguard w/heat reflecting inner shield. Swivels, black web sling strap. Weight: 6.3 lbs. Made from 1964 to 1994.
Standard Sporter . . . . **NiB $1951 Ex $1447 Gd $1133**
W/adj. stock, redesigned
forearm (disc. 1988), add $225
W/3x scope and mount, add $125

AR-15 SPORTER COMPETITION
H-BAR RIFLE . . . . **NiB $1997 Ex $1126 Gd $766**
Similar to AR-15 Sporter Target model except w/integral Weaver-type mounting system on a flat-top receiver. 20-inch bbl. w/counter-bored muzzle and 1:9 rifling twist. Made from 1991 to date.

AR-15 SPORTER
COMPETITION H-BAR (RS) . . . . **NiB $2009 Ex $1143 Gd $931**
Similar to AR-15 Sporter Competition H-BAR Model except "Range Selected" for accuracy w/3x9 rubber-clad scope w/mount. Carrying handle w/iron sights. Made from 1992 to 1994.

AR-15 SPORTER MATCH TARGET LIGHTWEIGHT
Calibers: .223 Rem., 7.62x39mm, 9mm. Five-round magazine. 16-inch bbl. (non-threaded after 1994). 34.5-35.5 inches overall. Weight: 7.1 lbs. Redesigned stock and shorter handguard. Made from 1991 to 2002.
Standard LW Sporter (except 9mm) . . . . . . **NiB $966 Ex $755 Gd $612**
Standard LW Sporter, 9mm . . . . **NiB $1077 Ex $776 Gd $556**
.22 LR conversion (disc. 1994), add $200

AR-15 SPORTER TARGET RIFLE
Caliber: .223 Rem. Five-round magazine. 20-inch bbl. w/flash suppressor (non-threaded after 1994). 39 inches overall. Weight: 7.5 lbs. Black composition stock, grip and handguard. Sights: post front; adj. aperture rear. Matte black finish. Made from 1993 to date.
Sporter Target Rifle . . . . **NiB $1244 Ex $1076 Gd $722**
.22 LR conversion (disc. 1994), add $225

Colt Lightning Magazine Rifle
NRA NATIONAL FIREARMS MUSEUM

Coltsman 1961 Custom

Coltsman 1961 Standard

Colt-Sauer Grand African

LIGHTNING MAGAZINE RIFLE - MEDIUM FRAME

Slide-action. Calibers: .32-20, .38-40, .44-40 w/12-round tubular magazine (Carbine and Baby Carbine) or 15-round tubular magazine (Rifle). Bbl.: 20 inches (Carbine and Baby Carbine) or 26-inch round or octagonal (Rifle). Additional bbl. lengths optional. Weight: 5.5 lbs. (Baby Carbine), 6.25 lbs. (Carbine) or 7 to 9 lbs. (Rifle). Open rear, bead or blade front sights. Walnut stock w/checkered forearm. Blue finish w/color case-hardened hammer. Made from 1884 to 1902. (89,777 produced).

Rifle	NiB $6096	Ex $3822	Gd $2274
Carbine	NiB $7778	Ex $4966	Gd $2988
Baby Carbine	NiB $9380	Ex $5246	Gd $4012

Military model
w/bayonet lug & sling swivels. . NiB $5250   Ex $3844   Gd $2691

LIGHTNING MAGAZINE RIFLE - SMALL FRAME

Similar to Medium Frame model except w/smaller frame and chambered for .22 caliber only. Standard 24-inch round or octagonal bbl. w/half magazine. Additional bbl. lengths optional. Weight: 6 lbs. Sights: Open rear; bead or blade front. Walnut stock and checkered forearm. Made from 1884 to 1902 (89,912 produced).

Standard rifle model. . . . . NiB $5599   Ex $4125   Gd $2889
W/deluxe or optional features, add 25%

STAGECOACH .22 AUTOLOADER . . . . NiB $355   Ex $298   Gd $200
Same as Colteer .22 Autoloader except w/engraved receiver, saddle ring, 16.5-inch bbl. Weight: 4 lbs., 10 oz. Made from 1965 to 1975.

COLTEER 1-.22 SINGLE-SHOT
BOLT-ACTION RIFLE . . . . NiB $303   Ex $197   Gd $159
Caliber: .22 LR. Long, Short. 20- or 22-inch bbl. Sights: Open rear; ramp front. Pistol-grip stock w/Monte Carlo comb. Weight: 5 lbs. Made from 1957 to 1967.

COLTEER .22 AUTOLOADER . . . . . NiB $390   Ex $288   Gd $227
Caliber: .22 LR. 15-round tubular magazine. 19.38-inch bbl. Sights: Open rear; hooded ramp front. Straight-grip stock, Western carbine-style forearm w/bbl. band. Weight: 4.75 lbs. Made 1964 to 1975.

CUSTOM BOLT-ACTION
SPORTING RIFLE . . . . NiB $600   Ex $498   Gd $335
FN Mauser action, side safety, engraved floorplate. Calibers: .30-06, .300 H&H Mag. Five round box magazine. 24-inch bbl., rampfront sight. Fancy walnut stock. Monte Carlo comb, cheekpiece, pistol-grip, checkered, QD swivels. Weight: 7.25 lbs. Made 1957 to 1961.

DELUXE RIFLE . . . . NiB $977   Ex $798   Gd $569
FN Mauser action. Same as Custom model except plain floorplate, plain wood and checkering. Made from 1957 to 1961. Value shown is for rifle w/out sights.

1957 SERIES RIFLES
Built on Sako medium action. Calibers: .243, .309. Weight: 6.75 lbs. Other specs similar to other models with FN actions. Made from 1957 to 1961.

Standard	NiB $755	Ex $486	Gd $417
Custom	NiB $935	Ex $697	Gd $488
Deluxe	NiB $935	Ex $697	Gd $488

Commando Carbines

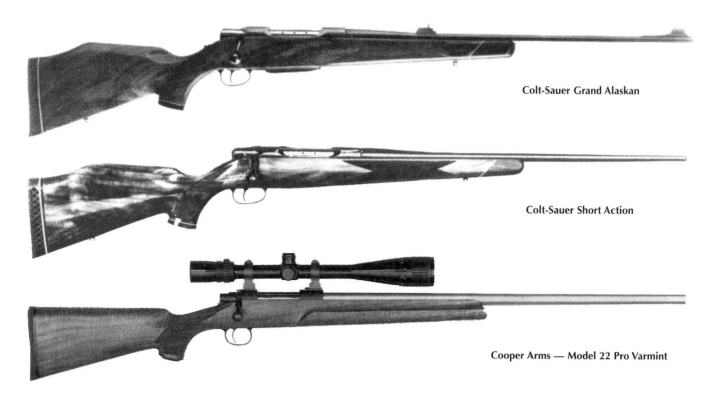

Colt-Sauer Grand Alaskan

Colt-Sauer Short Action

Cooper Arms — Model 22 Pro Varmint

1961 MODEL
CUSTOM RIFLE. . . . . **NiB $733 Ex $568 Gd $422**
Sako action. Calibers: .222, .222 Mag., .223, .243, .264, .270, .308, .30-06, .300 H&H. 23-, 24-inch bbl. Sights: Folding leaf rear; hooded ramp front. Fancy French walnut stock w/Monte Carlo comb, rosewood forend tip and grip cap skip checkering, recoil pad, sling swivels. Weight: 6.5 to 7.5 lbs. Made from 1963 to 1965.

1961 MODEL,
STANDARD RIFLE. . . . . **NiB $744 Ex $578 Gd $432**
Same as Custom model except plainer, American walnut stock. Made from 1963 to 1965.

STANDARD RIFLE. . . . . **NiB $689 Ex $533 Gd $390**
FN Mauser action. Same as Deluxe Rifle except in .243 Win., .30-06, .308 Win., .300 Win. Mag. Stock w/o cheekpiece. Bbl.: 22 inches, no sights. Made from 1957 to 1961.

GRAND AFRICAN . . . . **NiB $2056 Ex $1566 Gd $1049**
Same specifications as standard model except .458 Win. Mag., weight: 9.5 lbs. Sights: Adj. leaf rear; hooded ramp front. Magnum-style stock of Bubinga. Made from 1973 to 1985.

GRAND ALASKAN . . . . **NiB $2006 Ex $1389 Gd $1008**
Same specs as standard model except in .375 H&H Mag. Weight: 8.5 lbs. Adj. leaf rear, hooded ramp front sights. Magnum-style walnut stock.

MAGNUM. . . . . **NiB $1506 Ex $1123 Gd $778**
Same specifications as standard model except calibers 7mm Rem. Mag., .300 Win. Mag., .300 Weatherby. Weight: 8.5 lbs. Made from 1973 to 1985.

SHORT ACTION . . . . **NiB $1390 Ex $1113 Gd $766**
Same specs as standard model except in short-action calibers: .22-250 rem., .243 Win., .308 Win., etc. Weight: 8.25 lbs. No sights.

Drilled and tapped for scope mounts. Made from 1973 to 1988.

SPORTING RIFLE,
STANDARD MODEL. . . . . **NiB $1377 Ex $1105 Gd $766**
Sauer 80 non-rotating bolt action. Calibers: .25-06, .270 Win., .30-06. Three-round detachable box magazine. 24-inch bbl. Weight: 7.75 lbs., 8.5 lbs. (.25-06). Furnished w/o sights. American walnut stock w/Monte Carlo cheekpiece, checkered pistol grip and forearm, rosewood forend tip and pistol-grip cap, recoil pad. Made from 1973 to 1988.

COMMANDO CARBINES — Knoxville, Tennessee (formerly Volunteer Enterprises, Inc.)

MARK III SEMIAUTOMATIC CARBINE
Blow-back action, fires from closed bolt. Caliber: .45 ACP. 15- or 30-round magazine. 16.5-inch bbl. w/cooling sleeve and muzzle brake. Weight: 8 lbs. Sights: peep rear; blade front. "Tommy Gun" style stock and forearm or grip. Made from 1969 to 1976.
W/horizontal forearm. . . . . **NiB $510 Ex $399 Gd $277**

MARK 9
Same specifications as Mark III and Mark 45 except caliber 9mm Luger. Made from 1976 to 1981.
W/horizontal forearm. . . . . **NiB $545 Ex $439 Gd $333**
W/vertical foregrip . . . . **NiB $644 Ex $565 Gd $389**

MARK 45
Same specifications as III w/redesigned trigger housing and magazines. Made from 1976 to 1988.
W/horizontal forearm. . . . . **NiB $545 Ex $439 Gd $333**
W/vertical foregrip . . . . **NiB $596 Ex $484 Gd $341**

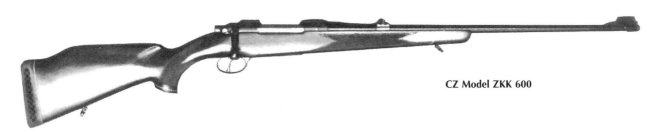

CZ Model ZKK 600

CONTINENTAL RIFLES — Manufactured in Belgium for Continental Arms Corp., New York, New York

DOUBLE RIFLE
Side-by-side. Calibers: .270 Win., .303 Sav., .30-40 Krag., .348 Win., .30-06, .375 H&H. .400 Jeffery, .465, .470, .475 No. 2, .500, .600. Anson-Deeley reinforced boxlock action. Double triggers. Non-automatic safelty. Bbls.: 24 or 26 inches. Express rear, bead front sights. Checkered cheekpiece stock and forend. Weight: from 7 lbs. Imported from 1956 to 1975.

.270 to .348 Win. . . . . NiB $5077 Ex $3966 Gd $3095
.375 H&H & larger calibers, add 60%

COOPER FIREARMS of MONTANA, INC. (Previously COOPER ARMS)—Stevensville, Montana

MODEL 21
Similar to Model 36C except in calibers .17 Rem., .17 Mach IV, .221 Fireball, .222, .223, 6x45, 6x47. 24-inch stainless or chrome-moly bbl. 43.5 inches overall. Weight: 8.75 lbs. Made from 1994 to date.

21 Benchrest. . . . . NiB $1513 Ex $1207 Gd $943
21 Classic . . . . NiB $2223 Ex $1766 Gd $1007
21 Custom Classic . . . . NiB $2178 Ex $1859 Gd $1022
21 Western Classic . . . . NiB $3030 Ex $1956 Gd $1033
21 Varminter. . . . . NiB $1408 Ex $966 Gd $800
21 Varmint Extreme . . . . NiB $1944 Ex $1244 Gd $966

MODEL 22
Bolt-action, single-shot. Calibers: .22 BR. .22-250 Rem., .220 Swift, .243 Win., 6mm PPC, 6.5x55mm, 25-06 Rem., 7.62x39mm 26-inch bbl, 45.63 inches overall. Weight: 8 lbs., 12 oz. Single-stage trigger. AAA Claro walnut stock. Made from 1999 to date.

22 Benchrest. . . . . NiB $1533 Ex $1377 Gd $1079
22 Classic . . . . NiB $2176 Ex $1312 Gd $755
22 Custom Classic. . . . . NiB $1370 Ex $1244 Gd $879
22 Western Classic . . . . NiB $2244 Ex $1359 Gd $954
22 Varminter. . . . . NiB $1468 Ex $934 Gd $644
22 Pro-Varminter Extreme . . . . . NiB $2011 Ex $1143 Gd $836
22 Black Jack . . . . NiB $1895 Ex $1154 Gd $846

MODEL 36 RF/BR 50 . . . . NiB $1608 Ex $1266 Gd $880
Bolt-action, single-shot. Caliber: .22 LR. Bbl.: Stainless, 22 inches, no sights.. Lgt.: 40.5 inches. Weight: 6.8 lbs. Adj. match-grade trigger. McMillan benchrest stock. Made from 1993 to 1999.

MODEL 36 CF BOLT-ACTION RIFLE
Calibers: .17 CCM, .22 CCM, .22 Hornet. Four-round mag. 23.75 inch bbl. 42.5 inch overall. Weight: 7 lbs. Walnut or synthetic stock. Made from 1992 to 1994.

Marksman . . . . NiB $1635 Ex $880 Gd $654
Sportsman . . . . NiB $730 Ex $544 Gd $343
Classic Grade . . . . NiB $1863 Ex $1154 Gd $866

Custom Grade . . . . NiB $1744 Ex $937 Gd $665
Custom Classic Grade. . . . . NiB $1689 Ex $1256 Gd $876

MODEL 36 RF BOLT-ACTION RIFLE
Similar to Model 36CF except in caliber .22 LR. Five round magazine. Weight: 6.5 to 7 lbs. Made from 1992 to 1994.

BR-50 (22-inch stainless bbl.) . . . NiB $1755 Ex $1139 Gd $768
Custom Grade. . . . . NiB $1756 Ex $906 Gd $675
Custom Classic Grade. . . . . NiB $1670 Ex $951 Gd $688
Featherweight . . . . NiB $1617 Ex $988 Gd $709

MODEL 36 TRP-1 SERIES
Similar to Model 36RF except in target configuration w/ ISU or silhouette-style stock. Made from 1992 to 1993.

TRP-1 (ISU single-shot). . . . . NiB $944 Ex $778 Gd $533
TRP-1S (Silhouette). . . . . NiB $944 Ex $778 Gd $533

MODEL 38 SINGLE SHOT
Similar to Model 36CF except in calibers .17 or .22 CCM w/3-round magazine. Weight: 8 lbs. Walnut or synthetic stock. Made from 1992 to 1993.

Standard Sporter. . . . . NiB $1544 Ex $1023 Gd $688
Classic Grade . . . . NiB $2239 Ex $1836 Gd $979
Custom Grade. . . . . NiB $3035 Ex $1997 Gd $977
Custom Classic Grade. . . . . NiB $1570 Ex $1267 Gd $855

MODEL 40 CLASSIC BOLT-ACTION RIFLE
Calibers: .17 CCM, .17 Ackley Hornet, .22 Hornet, .22K Hornet, .22 CCM, 4- or 5-round magazine. 23.75-inch bbl. Checkered oil-finished AAA Claro walnut stock. Made from 1995 to 1996.

Classic. NiB $1644 Ex $1233 Gd $886
Custom Classic . . . . NiB $1844 Ex $1450 Gd $1139
Classic Varminter . . . . NiB $1844 Ex $1450 Gd $1139

CUMBERLAND MOUNTAIN ARMS — Winchester, Tennessee

PLATEAU RIFLE
Falling block action w/underlever. Calibers: .40-65 and .45-70. Bbl.: Round, 32 inches. Lgt.: 48 inches. Weight: 10.5 lbs. Lacquer finish American walnut stock w/crescent buttplate. Bead front, adj. buckhorn rear. Blued finish. Made form 1993 to 1999.

Standard model. . . . . NiB $1133 Ex $829 Gd $631
Deluxe model, add $375

CZ RIFLES — Strankonice, Czechoslovakia (currently Czechpoint, Inc.)

See also listings under Brno Sporting Rifles and Springfield, Inc.

ZKK 600 BOLT-ACTION RIFLE
Calibers: .270 Win., 7x57, 7x64, .30-06. Five round magazine. 23.5- inch bbl. Weight: 7.5 lbs. Adj. folding-leaf rear sight, hooded ramp front. Pistol-grip walnut stock. Imported from 1990 to 1995.

Standard model. . . . . NiB $613 Ex $479 Gd $350
Deluxe model . . . . NiB $688 Ex $554 Gd $400

CZ Rifles

CA Model ZKM 452 LUX Model

CZ 511

CZ Model ZKM 527

CZ 550 LUX Model

ZKK 601 BOLT-ACTION RIFLE
Similar to Model ZKK 600 except w/short-action calibers: .223 rem, .243 Win., .308 Win. Lgt.: 43 inches. Weight: 6 lbs., 13 oz. Checkered Monte Carlo pistol-grip stock. Impored from 1990 to 1995.

Standard model.	NiB $570	Ex $495	Gd $443
Deluxe model	NiB $635	Ex $567	Gd $423

ZKK 602 BOLT-ACTION RIFLE
Similar to Model ZKK 600 except in long-action magnum calibers: .300 Win. Mag., 8x68S, .375 H&H, .458 Win. Mag. Bbl.: 25 inches. Lgt.: 45.5 inches. Weight: 9.25 lbs. Imported from 1990 to 1997.

Standard model.	NiB $727	Ex $644	Gd $468
Deluxe model	NiB $896	Ex $744	Gd $505

ZKM 452 BOLT-ACTION REPEATING RIFLE
Calibers: .22 LR. or .22 WMR. Five, 6- or 10-round magazine. 25-inch bbl. 43.5 inches overall. Weight: 6 lbs. Adj. rear sight, hooded bead front. Oil-finished beechwood or checkered walnut stock w/Schnabel forend. Imported 1995 and 2007.

Standard model (22 LR)	NiB $455	Ex $335	Gd $200
Deluxe model (22 LR)	NiB $455	Ex $335	Gd $200
Varmint model (22 LR)	NiB $458	Ex $370	Gd $215
.22 WMR, add.			$50

ZKM 527 BOLT-ACTION RIFLE
Calibers: .22 Hornet, .222 Rem., .223 Rem., 7.62x39mm. Five round magazine. 23.5-inch bbl. 42.5 inches overall. Weight: 6.75 lbs. Adj. rear sight, hooded ramp front. Grooved receiver. Adj. double-set triggers. Oil-finished beechwood or checkered walnut stock . Imported 1995.

Standard model.	NiB $644	Ex $465	Gd $340
Classic model	NiB $655	Ex $470	Gd $335
Carbine model (shorter configuration)	NiB $600	Ex $466	Gd $345
Deluxe model	NiB $657	Ex $566	Gd $373

ZKM 537 SPORTER BOLT-ACTION RIFLE
Calibers: .243 Win., .270 Win., 7x57mm, .308 Win., .30-06. Four or 5-round magazine. 19- or 23.5-inch bbl. 40.25 or 44.75 inches overall. Weight: 7 to 7.5 lbs. Adj. folding leaf rear sight, hooded ramp front. Shrouded bolt. Standard or Mannlicher-style checkered walnut stock. Imported 1995.

Standard model.	NiB $529	Ex $460	Gd $345
Mountain Carbine model	NiB $555	Ex $439	Gd $326

511 SEMI-AUTO RIFLE
511 SEMI-AUTO RIFLE . . . . NiB $355 Ex $252 Gd $155
Caliber: .22 LR. 8-round magazine. 22- inch bbl., 38.6 inches overall. Weight: 5.39 lbs. Receiver top fitted for telescopic sight mounts. Walnut wood-lacquered checkering stock. Imported 1996, 1998 to 2001, 2005 to 2006.

Mannlicher model	add $125

550 BOLT-ACTION SERIES
Calibers: .243 Win., 6.5x55mm, .270 Win., 7mm Mag., 7x57, 7x64, .30-06, .300 Win Mag., .375 H&H, .416 Rem., .416 Rigby, .458 Win. Mag., 9.3x62. Four or 5-round detachable magazine. 20.5- or 23.6-inch bbl. Weight: 7.25 to 8 lbs. No sights or Express sights on magnum models. Receiver drilled and tapped for scope mount. Standard or Mannlicher-style checkered walnut stock w/ buttpad. Imported 1995 to 2000.

Standard	NiB $510	Ex $423	Gd $326
Magnum	NiB $855	Ex $633	Gd $465
41 Lux	NiB $530	Ex $456	Gd $355
Mannlicher	NiB $817	Ex $579	Gd $366
Calibers .416 Rem., .416 Rigby, .458 Win. Mag., add.			$100

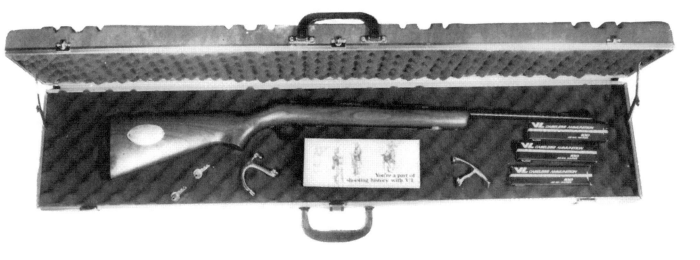

Daisy V/L Collector's Kit

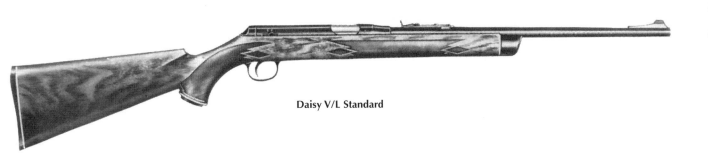

Daisy V/L Standard

CZECHOSLOVAKIAN MILITARY RIFLES — Brno, Czechoslovakia. Manufactured by Ceska Zbrojovka

MODEL 1924 (VZ24)
MAUSER MILITARY RIFLE. . . . . **NiB $331 Ex $243 Gd $176**
Basically same as German Kar., 98k and F.N. (Belgian Model 1924.) Caliber: 7.9mm Mauser. Five round box magazine. 23.25-inch bbl. Weight: 8.5 lbs. Sights: Adj. rear; blade front w/guards. of Belgian-type military stock, full handguard. Made from 1924 thru WWII. Many of these rifles were made for export. As produced during the German occupation, this model was known as Gewehr 24t.

MODEL 1933 (VZ33) MAUSER
MILITARY CARBINE . . . . **NiB $380 Ex $300 Gd $227**
Modification of German M/98 action w/smaller receiver ring. Caliber: 7.9mm Mauser. 19.25-inch bbl. Weight: 7.5 lbs. Sights: Adj. rear; blade front w/guards. Military-type full stock. Mfd. 1933 thru WWII. A similar model, produced during the German occupation, was designated Gew. 33/40.

DAEWOO PRECISION INDUSTRIES — Manufactured in Korea (previously imported by Kimber of America; Daewoo Precision Industries; Nationwide Sports, and KBI, Inc.)

DR200 SA SEMI-AUTOMATIC SPORTER
Caliber: .223 Rem. (5.56mm). 6- or 10-round magazine. 18.4-inch bbl. 39.25 inches overall. Weight: 9 lbs. Protected post front sight, fully-adj. aperture rear. Forged aluminum receiver w/rotating locking bolt assembly. Synthetic sporterized thumbhole stock. Imported from 1994 to 1996.
Sporter model . . . . **NiB $679 Ex $545 Gd $459**
Varmint model . . . . **NiB $644 Ex $579 Gd $356**

DR300 SA SEMI-AUTOMATIC
SPORTER. . . . . **NiB $670 Ex $602 Gd $421**
Similar to Model Daewoo DR200 except chambered for 7.62x39mm. Imported from 1994 to 1996.

DAISY RIFLES — Rogers, Arkansas
Daisy V/L rifles carry the first and only commercial caseless cartridge system. These rifles are expected to appreciate considerably in future years. The cartridge, no longer made, is also a collector's item. Production was discontinued following BATF ruling the V/L model to be a firearm.

COLLECTOR'S KIT . . . . **NiB $590 Ex $427 Gd $304**
Presentation-grade rifle w/gold plate inscribed w/owner's name and gun serial number mounted on the stock. Also includes a special gun case, pair of brass gun cradles for wall-hanging, 300 rounds of 22 V/L ammunition and a certificate signed by Daisy president Cass S. Hough. Approx. 1,000 manufactured from 1968 to 1969.

Dakota Arms, Inc.

Dakota Model 10 Single-Shot Rifle

Dakota Arms Model 76
African Grade

Dakota Arms Model 76
Classic Grade

Dakota Arms Model 97
Hunter

PRESENTATION GRADE........ NiB $344 Ex $296 Gd $245
Same specifications as standard model except w/walnut stock. Approx. 4,000 manufactured from 1968 to 1969.

STANDARD RIFLE............. NiB $267 Ex $224 Gd $175
Single-shot under-lever action. Caliber: .22 V/L (caseless cartridge, propellant ignited by jet of hot air). 18-inch bbl. Weight: 5 lbs. Sights: Adj. open rear, ramp w/blade front. Wood-grained Lustran stock (foam-filled). About 19,000 manufactured from 1968 to 1969.

DAKOTA ARMS, INC. — Sturgis, South Dakota

MODEL 10 SINGLE-SHOT RIFLE
Calibers: Most commercial calibers. Bbl.: 23 inches. Lgt.: 39.5 inches. Weight: 5.5 lbs. Top tang safety. No sights. Checkered pistol-grip and semi-beavertail forearm. QD swivels, rubber recoil pad. Made from 1992 to date.
Standard calibers .... NiB $4279 Ex $3066 Gd $1977
Deluxe model, add $1375

MODEL 22 BOLT-ACTION
SPORTER RIFLE............. NiB $2735 Ex $1217 Gd $823
Calibers: .22 LR. .22 Hornet. Five round magazine. 22-inch bbl. Weight: 6.5 lbs. Adj. trigger. Checkered classic-style Claro or English walnut stock w/black recoil pad. Made from 2003 to 2004.

MODEL 76 AFRICAN
BOLT-ACTION RIFLE .... NiB $7698 Ex $4056 Gd $2597
Same specs as Model 76 Safari. Caliber: .404 Jeffery. .416 Rigby, .416 Dakota, .450 Dakota. Bbl.: 24 inches. Weight: 8 lbs. Checkered select walnut stock w/two crossbolts. "R" prefix on ser. no. Introduced 1989.

MODEL 76 ALPINE
BOLT-ACTION RIFLE .... NiB $4634 Ex $2759 Gd $2009

Same specs as Model 76 Classic except short-action w/blind mag. Calibers: .22-250 Rem., .243 Win., 6mm Rem., .250-3000, 7mm-08, .308 Win. Bbl.: 21 inches. Weight: 7.5 lbs. Made from 1989 to 1992.

MODEL 76 CLASSIC
BOLT-ACTION RIFLE .... NiB $4629 Ex $3467 Gd $2240
Calibers: .257 Roberts, .270 Win., .280 Rem., .30-06, 7mm Rem. Mag., .300 Win. Mag., .338 Win. Mag., .375 H&H Mag., .458 Win. Mag. 21- or 23-inch bbl. Weight: 7.5 lbs. Receiver drilled and tapped for sights. Adj. trigger. Classic-style checkered walnut stock w/steel grip cap and solid recoil pad. Right- and left-hand models. Made from 1987 to date.

MODEL 76 LONGBOW TACTICAL
BOLT-ACTION RIFLE .... NiB $4466 Ex $3459 Gd $2390
Calibers: .300 Dakota Mag., .330 Dakota Mag., .338 Lapua Mag., blind mag. Bbl: Ported, 28 inches. Lgt.: 50 to 51 inches. Weight: 13.7 lbs. Black or olive green fiberglass stock w/adj. cheekpiece and buttplate. Drilled and tapped for one-piece rail mount, no sights. Made from 1997 to 2009.

MODEL 76 SAFARI
BOLT-ACTION RIFLE .... NiB $6433 Ex $3416 Gd $2307
Calibers: .300 Win. Mag., .338 Win. Mag., .375 H&H Mag. .458 Win. Mag. 23-inch bbl. w/bbl. band swivel. Weight: 8.5 lbs. Ramp front sight, standing leaf rear. Checkered fancy walnut stock w/ ebony forend tip and solid recoil pad. Made from 1987 to date.

MODEL 76 TRAVELER SERIES RIFLES
Threadless take-down action w/interchangeable bbl. capability based on the Dakota 76 design. Calibers: .257 through .458 Win (Standard-Classic & Safari) and .416 Dakota, .404 Jeffery, .416 Rigby, .338 Lapua and .450 Dakota Mag. (E/F Family-African Grade.) 23- to 24- inch bbl. Weight: 7.5 to 9.5 lbs. Right or left-hand action. X grade (Classic) or XXX grade (Safari or African) oil finish English Bastogne or Claro walnut stock. Made from 1999 to date.

Dakota Arms, Inc.

Charles Daly Mauser 98 Rifle
NATIONAL FIREARMS MUSEUM

Classic Grade . . . . NiB $5644 Ex $3428 Gd $2380
Safari Grade . . . . NiB $6577 Ex $3502 Gd $2866
African Grade . . . . NiB $7233 Ex $4544 Gd $3209
Interchangeable bbl. assemblies
Classic Grade, add $1275
Safari Grade, add $1520
African Grade, add $1650

MODEL 76 VARMINT
BOLT-ACTION RIFLE . . . . NiB $2510 Ex $1988 Gd $1165
Similar to Model 76 Classic except single-shot w/heavy bbl.
Calibers: .17 Rem. to 6mm PPC. Weight: 13.7 lbs. Checkered
walnut or synthetic stock. No sights; drilled and tapped for scope
mounts. Made from 1994 to date.

MODEL 97 HUNTER BOLT-ACTION SERIES
Calibers: .22-250 Rem. to .330 Dakota Mag.(Lightweight), .25-06 to
.375 Dakota Mag. (Long Range). 22-, 24- or 26-inch bbl. 43 to 46
inches overall. Weight: 6.16 lbs. to 7.7 lbs. Black composite fiberglass
stock w/recoil pad. Adj. match trigger. Made from 1997 to 2004.
Lightweight . . . . NiB $2744 Ex $1655 Gd $944
Long Range . . . . NiB $2744 Ex $1655 Gd $944

MODEL 97 VARMINT HUNTER
BOLT-ACTION RIFLE . . . . NiB $3734 Ex $2566 Gd $1896
Similar to Model 97 Hunter except single-shot w/heavy bbl. Calibers:
.22-250 Rem. to .308 Win. Checkered walnut stock. No sights.
Drilled and tapped for scope mounts. Made from 1998 to 2004.

CHARLES DALY RIFLE — Harrisburg, Pennsylvania. Imported by K.B.I., Inc., Harrisburg, PA (previously by Outdoor Sports Headquarters, Inc.)

EMPIRE GRADE BOLT-ACTION RIFLE (RF)
Similar to Superior Grade except w/checkered California walnut
stock w/rosewood grip cap and forearm cap. High polished blued
finish and damascened bolt. Made from 1998.
Empire Grade (.22 LR) . . . . NiB $366 Ex $324 Gd $223
Empire Grade (.22WMR) . . . . NiB $406 Ex $322 Gd $235
Empire Grade (.22 Hornet) . . . . NiB $556 Ex $444 Gd $320

FIELD GRADE BOLT-ACTION RIFLE (RF)
Single-shot. Caliber: .22 LR; six- or 10-round mag. Bbl.: 16.25, 17.5
or 22.63 inches. Lgt.: 32 to 41 inches. Plain walnut-finished hard-
wood or checkered polymer stock. Blue or stainless finish. Imported
from 1998. Disc.
Standard model w/22.63-inch bbl . . . . NiB $157 Ex $128 Gd $95
Youth model w/17.5-inch bbl . . . . NiB $170 Ex $139 Gd $99
True Youth model
w/16.25-inch bbl. . . . . NiB $188 Ex $155 Gd $131
Polymer w/stainless action . . . . NiB $158 Ex $130 Gd $100

FIELD GRADE HUNTER BOLT-ACTION RIFLE
Calibers: .22 Hornet, .223 Rem., .243 Win., .270 Win., 7mm Rem. Mag.,
.308 Win., .30-06, .300 Win. Mag., .300 Rem. Ultra Mag, .338 Win.

Mag.; three-, four- or 5-round mag. Bbl.: 22 or 24 inches. Weight: 7.2 to
7.4 lbs. Checkered walnut or black polymer stock. Drilled and tapped
for scope mounts. Blue or stainless finish. Imported from 1998. Disc.
W/walnut stock. . . . . NiB $566 Ex $457 Gd $339
W/polymer stock . . . . NiB $589 Ex $478 Gd $339

HORNET RIFLE . . . . NiB $1299 Ex $1088 Gd $759
Same as Herold Rifle. Imported c. 1930. Disc.

MAUSER 98
Calibers: .243 Win., .270 Win., 7mm Rem. Mag., .308 Win., .30-
06, .300 Win. Mag., .375 H&H Mag., .458 Win. Mag.; three- or
four-round mag. Bbl.: 23 inches. Lgt.: 44.5 inches. Weight: 7.5 lbs.
Side safety. Checkered European walnut (Superior mdel) or fiber-
glass/graphite (Field Model) stock w/recoil pad. Ramped front, adj.
rear sights. Drilled and tapped for scope.
Field Grade (standard calibers, disc.). . . . . NiB $466 Ex $423 Gd $155
Field Grade (375 H&H
and 458 Win. Mag.) . . . . NiB $669 Ex $566 Gd $354
Superior Grade (standard calibers, disc.) . . NiB $669 Ex $566 Gd $454
Superior Grade (magnum calibers, disc.) . . NiB $903 Ex $766 Gd $635

MINI-MAUSER 98
Similar to Mauser 98 except w/19.25-inch bbl. chambered for
.22 Hornet, .22-250 Rem., .223 Rem., or 7.62x39mm. Five round
magazine. Imported from 1998. Disc.
Field Grade . . . . NiB $409 Ex $358 Gd $233
Superior Grade . . . . NiB $533 Ex $447 Gd $259

SUPERIOR GRADE BOLT-ACTION RIFLE
Calibers: .22 LR. .22 WMR, .22 Hornet. 20.25- to 22.63-inch bbl.
40.5 to 41.25 inches overall. Five, 6-, or 10-round magazine.
Ramped front sight, adj. rear w/grooved receiver. Checkered walnut
stock. Made from 1998. Disc.
.22 LR . . . . NiB $179 Ex $150 Gd $100
.22 WMR. NiB $244 Ex $190 Gd $145
.22 Hornet . . . . NiB $399 Ex $345 Gd $239

SEMIAUTOMATIC RIFLE
Caliber: .22 LR. 20.75-inch bbl. 40.5 inches overall. 10-round
magazine. Ramped front sight, adj. rear w/grooved receiver.
Plain walnut-finished hardwood stock (Field), checkered walnut
(Superior), checkered polymer stock or checkered California walnut
stock w/rosewood grip cap and forearm cap (Empire). Blue or stain-
less finish. Imported from 1998. Disc.
Field Grade . . . . NiB $145 Ex $125 Gd $85
Field Grade (polymer
w/stainless action) . . . . NiB $161 Ex $136 Gd $92
Superior Grade . . . . NiB $215 Ex $188 Gd $132
Empire Grade . . . . NiB $355 Ex $290 Gd $200

BOLT ACTION RIFLE . . . . NiB $922 Ex $659 Gd $560
Calibers: .22 Hornet. Bbl.: 24 inches. Five round box magazine,
hinged floorplate. Sights: Ramp front, leaf rear. Walnut stock, checkered grip and forearm. Early version introduced in by Franz Jaeger
Co. Discontinued 1939. Imported by Charles Daly but same model
also was imported by A. F. Stoeger as Herold Rifle.

EMF Company, Inc.

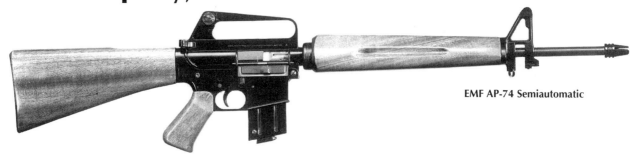

EMF AP-74 Semiautomatic

SUPERIOR
COMBINATION GUN . . . . NiB $1354 Ex $1149 Gd $1013
Calibers: 12 gauge over .22 Hornet, .223 Rem., .22-250 Rem., .243 Win., .270 Win., 30-06. Bbl.: 23.5 inches, chrome-moly steel, gold bead front sight.. Choked Imp. Cyl. Weight: 7.5 lbs. Checkered walnut stock, pistol grip, semi-beavertail forend. Silvered, engraved receiver. Double triggers, extractors. Introduced 1997 and imported by K.B.I.

EMPIRE COMBINATION GUN . . . NiB $1743 Ex $1540 Gd $1179
Similar to Superior Combination Gun but with fancy grade wood, European style comb and cheekpiece, slimmer forend. Introduced 1997 and imported by K.B.I.

FIELD GRADE AUTO RIFLE . . . . NiB $167 Ex $109 Gd $94
Calibers: .22 LR. Semiautomatic, 10-round magazine, shell deflector. Bbl.: 20 3/4 inches. Weight: 6.5 pounds. Overall length: 40.5 inches. Stock: Hardwood, walnut-finished, Monte Carlo style. Sights: Hooded front, adjustable open rear. Grooved for scope mounting. Blued finish. Introduced 1998. Imported by K. B. I.

EMPIRE GRADE AUTO RIFLE . . . . . NiB $210 Ex $166 Gd $135
Similar to Field Grade Auto Rifle but with hand checkered select California walnut stock. Contrasting forend and grip caps. Damascened bolt, high-polish blued finish. Introduced 1998. Disc.

TRUE YOUTH
BOLT-ACTION RIFLE . . . . NiB $156 Ex $100 Gd $75
Bolt-action single-shot. Caliber: .22 LR. Bbl.: 16.25 inches. Weight: 3 lbs. Lgt.: 32 inches. Walnut-finished hardwood stock. Blade front, adj. rear sights. Blued finish. Introduced 1998. Imported by K.B.I.

EAGLE ARMS INC. — Geneseo, Illinois (previously Coal Valley, Illinois)

In 1995, Eagle Arms Inc., became a division of ArmaLite and reintroduced that logo. For current ArmaLite production see models under that listing.
MODEL EA-15 CARBINE
Caliber: .223 Rem. (5.56mm). 30-round magazine. 16-inch bbl. and collapsible buttstock. Weight: 5.75 lbs. (E1); 6.25 lbs. (E2 w/ heavy bbl. & National Match sights). Made from 1990 to 1995; reintroduced from 2002 to 2005.
E1 Carbine . . . . NiB $966 Ex $739 Gd $510
E2 Carbine . . . . NiB $966 Ex $739 Gd $510

MODEL EA-15 GOLDEN
EAGLE MATCH RIFLE . . . . NiB $1244 Ex $977 Gd $657
Same specs as EA-15 Standard except w/E2-style national Match sights. Bbl.: 20 inches, Douglas Heavy Match. National Match trigger and bolt-carrier group. Weight: 12.75 lbs. Made from 1991 to 1995 and reintroduced in 2002.

MODEL EA-15
SEMI-AUTOMATIC RIFLE . . . . NiB $1221 Ex $722 Gd $504
Same as EA-15 Carbine except w/20-inch bbl. Lgt.: 39 inches. Weight: 7 lbs. Made from 1990 to 1993; reintroduced from 2002 to 2005.

EMF COMPANY, INC. — Santa Ana, California

MODEL AP-74
SEMI-AUTOMATIC CARBINE . . . . . NiB $397 Ex $300 Gd $221
Calibers: .22 LR or .32 ACP, 15-round magazine. 20-inch bbl. w/ flash reducer. 38 inches overall. Weight: 6.75 lbs. Protected pin front sight; protected rear peep sight. Plastic buttstock; ventilated snap-out forend. Importation disc. 1989.

MODEL AP74-W
SPORTER CARBINE . . . . NiB $419 Ex $321 Gd $213
Sporterized version of AP-74 w/wood buttstock and forend. Importation disc. 1989.

MODEL AP74 PARATROOPER . . . . NiB $433 Ex $260 Gd $242
Same specifications as Model AP74-W except w/folding tubular buttstock. Made in .22 LR. only. Importation disc. 1987.

MODEL 1860 HENRY RIFLE
Lever-action. Copy of original B. Tyler Henry patent produced by the New Haven Arms Company when Oliver Winchester was president. Calibers: .44-40 and .45 ACP. Bbl.: 24.25 inches, upper half octagonal, one-piece steel magazine tube. Lgt.: 43.75 inches. Weight: 9.25 lbs. Varnished American walnut stock. Polished brass frame and buttplate. Imported from 1987 to 2008.
Deluxe model . . . . NiB $968 Ex $688 Gd $347
Engraved model . . . . NiB $1123 Ex $832 Gd $560

MODEL 1866
YELLOW BOY RIFLE . . . . NiB $754 Ex $558 Gd $359
Lever-action. Calibers: .44-40, .45 LC and .38 Special. Bbl.: 24 inches. Lgt.: 43 inches. Bead front sight. Blued finish, brass frame, walnut stock. Made from 2005 to 2008.

MODEL 1866 YELLOW BOY CARBINE
Same as 1866 Yellow Boy Rifle except carbine length.
Standard carbine . . . . NiB $933 Ex $465 Gd $330
Engraved carbine . . . . NiB $933 Ex $465 Gd $330

MODEL 1873 SPORTING RIFLE
Calibers: .22 LR. .22 WMR, .357 Mag., .44-40 and .45 LC. 24.25-inch octagonal bbl. 43.25 inches overall. Weight: 8.16 lbs. Color casehardened frame w/blued steel magazine tube. Walnut stock and forend.
Standard Rifle . . . . NiB $922 Ex $700 Gd $459
Engraved Rifle . . . . NiB $1007 Ex $657 Gd $477
Boy's Rifle
(Youth Model, .22 LR) . . . . NiB $674 Ex $558 Gd $369

MODEL 1873 SPORTING RIFLE CARBINE
Same as 1873 Sporting Rifle except has 19-inch bbl. Lgt.: 38.25 inches. Weight: 7.38 lbs. Color case-hardened or blued frame. Made from 1988 to 1989.
Standard carbine . . . . NiB $904 Ex $689 Gd $466

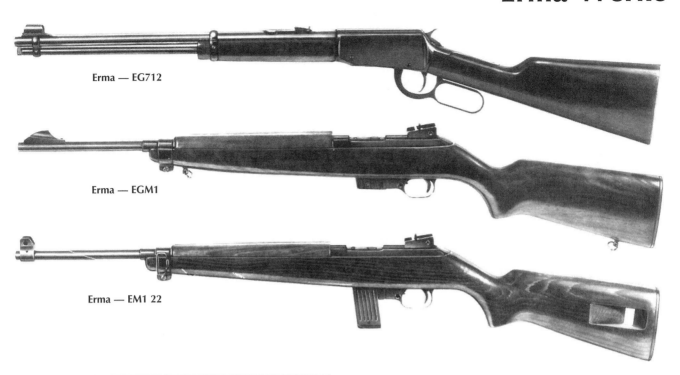

Erma — EG712

Erma — EGM1

Erma — EM1 22

ERMA-WERKE — Dachau, Germany (previously imported by Precision Sales International; Nygord Precision Products; Mandall's Shooting Supplies)

MODEL EG72
PUMP-ACTION REPEATER . . . . NiB $158 Ex $110 Gd $98
Visible hammer. Caliber: .22 LR. 15-round magazine. 18.5-inch bbl. Weight: 5.25 lbs. Sights: open rear; hooded ramp front. Receiver grooved for scope mounting. Straight-grip stock, grooved slide handle. Imported from 1970 to 1976.

MODEL EG73 . . . . NiB $288 Ex $223 Gd $172
Same as Model EG712 except chambered for .22 WMR w/12-round tubular magazine, 19.3-inch bbl. Imported from 1973 to 1997.

MODEL EG712 LEVER-ACTION
REPEATING CARBINE. . . . . NiB $297 Ex $229 Gd $167
Copy of Winchester Model 94. Caliber: .22 LR, Long, Short. 15-round tubular mag. (17 long, 21 Short). Bbl.: 18.5 inches. Weight: 5.5 lbs. Open rear, hooded ramp front sights. Grooved for scope mount. Western carbine-style stock and forearm w/bbl. band. Imported from 1976 to 1997. Note: A similar carbine of Erma manufacture is marketed in the U.S. as Ithaca Model 72 Saddle Gun.

MODEL EGM1 . . . . NiB $290 Ex $247 Gd $180
Same as Model EM1 except w/unslotted buttstock, ramp front sight, 5-round magazine standard. Imported from 1970 to 1995.

MODEL EM1 .22
SEMIAUTOMATIC CARBINE. . . . . . NiB $387 Ex $320 Gd $222
Copy of U.S. M1 Carbine. Caliber: .22 LR; 10 – or 15-round mag. Bbl.: 18 inches. Weight: 5.5 lbs. Carbine-type sights, grooved for scope mount. Military stock/handguard, Imported 1966 to 1997.

EUROPEAN AMERICAN ARMORY — Sharpes, Florida

MODEL HW 660 BOLT-ACTION
SINGLE-SHOT RIFLE . . . . NiB $900 Ex $745 Gd $490
Caliber: .22 LR. 26.8-inch bbl., 45.7 inches overall. Weight: 10.8 lbs. Match-type aperture rear sight; Hooded ramp front. Stippled walnut stock. Imported from 1992 to 1996.

MODEL HW BOLT-ACTION
SINGLE-SHOT TARGET RIFLE. . . . . NiB $895 Ex $740 Gd $485
Same specs as Model HW 660 except w/target stock. Imported from 1995 to 1996.

MODEL SABITTI SP1822
Caliber: .22 LR. 10-round detachable magazine. 18.5 inch bbl. 37.5 inches overall. Weight: 5.25 to 7.15 lbs. No sights. Hammer-forged heavy non-tapered bbl. Scope-mounted rail. Flush-mounted magazine release. Alloy receiver w/non-glare finish. Manual bolt lock. Wide claw extractor. Blowback action. Cross-trigger safety. Imported from 1994 to 1996.
Traditional Sporter model . . . . NiB $259 Ex $206 Gd $149
Thumbhole Sporter
model (synthetic stock). . . . . NiB $379 Ex $312 Gd $221

FABRIQUE NATIONALE HERSTAL — Herstal & Liege, Belgium (formerly Fabrique Nationale d'Armes de Guerre)

MODELS 1924, 1934/30, AND
1930 MAUSER MILITARY RIFLES . . . . NiB $445 Ex $337 Gd $241
Similar to German Kar.98k w/straight bolt handle. Calibers: 7mm, 7.65mm and 7.9mm Mauser; five-round box mag. Bbl.: 23.5 inches. Weight: 8.5 lbs. Adj. rear, blade front sights. Military stock on M/98 pattern w/slight modification. Model differences are minor. Also produced in a short carbine model w/17.25-inch bbl. These rifles were manufactured under contract for Abyssinia, Argentina, Belgium, Bolivia, Brazil, Chile, China, Colombia, Ecuador, Iran , Luxembourg, Mexico, Peru, Turkey, Uruguay and Yugoslavia. Such arms usually bear the coat of arms of the contract country w/the country's coat of arms and date of mfg. Also sold commercially and exported worldwide.

Fabrique Nationale Herstal

F.N. Model 1949

F.N. Model 1950 Mauser

F.N. Deluxe Mauser

F.N. Supreme Mauser

F.N. FAL Semiautomatic

MODEL 1949 SEMI-AUTOMATIC
MILITARY RIFLE . . . . **NiB $799 Ex $647 Gd $328**
Gas-operated. Calibers: 7mm, 7.65mm, 7.92mm, .30-06. 10-round box magazine, clip fed or loaded singly. 23.2-inch bbl. Weight: 9.5 lbs. Sights: Tangent rear-shielded post front. Pistol-grip stock, handguard. Adopted by Belgium in 1949; also by Belgian Congo, Brazil, Colombia, Luxembourg, Netherlands, East Indies, and Venezuela. Approx. 160,000 were made.

MODEL 1950 MAUSER
MILITARY RIFLE . . . . **NiB $533 Ex $360 Gd $287**
Same as previous FN. models of Kar. 98k type except chambered for .30-06.

DELUXE MAUSER BOLT-ACTION
SPORTING RIFLE . . . . **NiB $799 Ex $689 Gd $443**
American calibers: .220 Swift, .243 Win., .244 Rem., .250-3000, .257 Roberts, .270 Win., 7mm, .300 Sav., .308 Win., .30-06. European calibers: 7x57, 8x577JS, 8x60S, 9.3x62, 9.5x57, 10.75x68mm. Five-round box mag. Bbl.: 24 inches. Weight: 7.5 to 8.25 lbs. American model standard w/hooded ramp front and Tri-range rear sights. Continental model w/two-leaf rear sight. Checkered stock w/cheekpiece, pistil-grip, swivels, Made from 1947 to 1963.

DELUXE MAUSER —
PRESENTATION GRADE . . . . **NiB $1334 Ex $1096 Gd $752**
Same as regular model except w/select grade stock; engraving on receiver, trigger guard, floorplate and breech. Disc. 1963.

FAL/FNC/LAR SEMI-AUTOMATIC
Same as standard FAL military rifle except w/o provision for automatic firing. Gas-operated. Calibers: 7.62mm NATO (.308 Win.) or 5.56mm (.223 Rem.). 10- or 20-round box magazine. 25.5-inch bbl. (including flash hider). Weight: 9 lbs. Sights: Post front; aperture rear. Fixed wood or folding buttstock, pistol-grip, forearm/handguard w/carrying handle and sling swivels. Disc. 1988.
LAR model (Light
Automatic Rifle) . . . . **NiB $2594 Ex $2216 Gd $1402**
HB model (heavy bbl.) . . . . **NiB $2955 Ex $2343 Gd $1644**
PARA (Paratrooper) . . . . **NiB $3566 Ex $2886 Gd $1854**
Carbine
model (.223 cal.) . . . . **NiB $2715 Ex $1954 Gd $1294**
Carbine model w/flash
suppresser (.223 cal.) . . . . **NiB $2790 Ex $2033 Gd $1387**

SUPREME MAUSER BOLT-ACTION
SPORTING RIFLE . . . . **NiB $808 Ex $856 Gd $443**
Calibers: .243 Win., .270 Win., 7mm, .308 Win., .30-06; four-round mag. in .243 and .308, five-round capacity in other calibers. Bbl.: 22 inches in .308, .24 inches in other calibers. Hooded ramp front, Tri-Range peep rear sights. Checkered Monte Carlo stock w/pistol grip; swivels. Weight: 7.75 lbs. Made from 1957 to 1975.

SUPREME MAGNUM MAUSER . . . . **NiB $856 Ex $689 Gd $474**
Calibers: .264 Mag., 7mm Mag., .300 Win. Mag. Specifications same as for standard caliber model except 3-round magazine capacity.

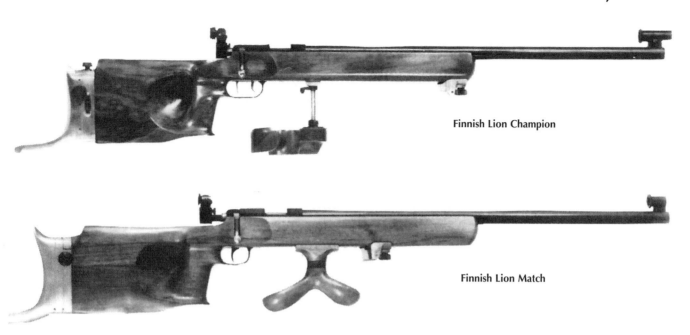

Finnish Lion Champion

Finnish Lion Match

FEATHER INDUSTRIES, INC. — Boulder, Colorado

MODEL AT-9 SEMI-AUTOMATIC RIFLE
Caliber: 9mm Parabellum. 10-, 25-, 32-, or 100-round magazine. 17-inch bbl. 35 inches overall (extended). Hooded post front sight, adj. aperture rear. Weight: 5 lbs. Telescoping wire stock w/composition pistol-grip and barrel-shroud handguard. Matte black finish. Made from 1988 to 1995.

Model AT-9 . . . . NiB $898 Ex $714 Gd $479
W/32-round magazine, add $100
W/100-round magazine, add $300

MODEL AT-22 . . . . NiB $355 Ex $232 Gd $171
Caliber: .22 LR; 20-round mag. Bbl.: 17 inches. Lgt.: 35 inches. Hooded post front, adj. aperture rear sights. Weight: 3.25 lbs. Telescoping wire stock w/composition pistol grip and barrel shroud handguard.

MODEL F2 SA CARBINE. . . . . NiB $331 Ex $258 Gd $149
Similar to AT-22, except w/fixed polymer stock and pistol grip. Made from 1992 to 1995.

MODEL F9 SA CARBINE. . . . . NiB $758 Ex $599 Gd $400
Similar to AT-9, except w/fixed polymer stock and pistol grip. Made from 1992 to 1995.

FINNISH LION RIFLES — Jyväkylylä, Finland. Manufactured by Valmet Oy, Tourula Works

CHAMPION FREE RIFLE . . . . NiB $688 Ex $545 Gd $390
Bolt-action single-shot target rifle. Double set trigger. Caliber: .22 LR. Bbl.: Heavy, 28.75 inches. Weight: 16 lbs. Extension rear peep, aperture front sights. Walnut free-rifle stock w/full pistol grip, thumbhole, beavertail forend, hook buttplate, palm rest, hand stop. Swivels. Made from 1965 to 1972.

STANDARD ISU
TARGET RIFLE. . . . . NiB $421 Ex $334 Gd $213
Bolt-action single-shot. Caliber: .22 LR. Bbl.: 27.5 inches. Weight: 10.5 lbs. Extension rear peep, aperture front sights. Walnut target stock w/full pistol grip, checkered beavertail forearm, adj. buttplate.. Sling swivels. Made from 1966 to 1977.

MATCH RIFLE. . . . . NiB $569 Ex $510 Gd $343
Bolt-action single-shot. Caliber: .22 LR. Bbl.: Heavy, 28.75 inches. Weight: 14.5 lbs. Extension rear peep, aperture front sights. Walnut free-rifle stock w/full pistol grip, thumbhole, beavertail forearm, hook buttplate, palm rest, hand stop. Swivels. Made from 1937 to 1972.

STANDARD TARGET RIFLE
Bolt-action single-shot. Caliber: .22 LR. Bbl.: 17.5 inches. Lgt.: 44.5 inches. Weight: 10.5 lbs. No sights. International-style micrometer rear and globe front sights available. Select walnut stock in target configuration. Made from 1966 to 1997.
Standard
model . . . . NiB $808 Ex $679 Gd $448
Thumbhole
stock model . . . . NiB $893 Ex $733 Gd $533
Deluxe model . . . . NiB $439 Ex $350 Gd $259

LUIGI FRANCHI, S.P.A. — Brescia, Italy

CENTENNIAL AUTOMATIC RIFLE
Semi-automatic. Take-down. Caliber: .22 LR; 11-round magazine in buttstock. Bbl.: 21 inches. Weight: 5.13 lbs. Open rear, gold bead ramp front sights. Checkered walnut stock and forend. Deluxe model w/fully engraved receiver, premium grade wood. Made in 1968. Commemorative for Franchi's 100th anniversary (1868 to 1968). Centennial seal engraved on receiver.
Standard model. . . . . NiB $433 Ex $321 Gd $224
Engraved model . . . . NiB $478 Ex $379 Gd $270

Germany Military Rifles

Franchi Deluxe Centennial

Galil .223 AR Semiautomatic Rifle

FRANCOTTE RIFLES — Leige, Belgium. Imported by Armes de Chasse, Hertford, NC (previously by Abercrombie & Fitch)

BOLT-ACTION RIFLE
Custom rifle built on Mauser-style bolt-action. Available in three action lengths. Calibers: .17 Bee to .505 Gibbs. Bbl.: 21 to 24.5 inches. Weight: 8 to 12 lbs. Stock dimensions, wood type and style to customer's specs. Engraving, appointments and finish to customer's preference. Deduct 20% for rifles with no engraving.
Short action . . . . NiB $9770 Ex $7725 Gd $4690
Standard action. . . . . NiB $7859 Ex $6233 Gd $3834

FRENCH MILITARY RIFLE — Saint Etienne, France

MODEL 1936
MAS MILITARY RIFLE . . . . NiB $209 Ex $170 Gd $103
Bolt-action. Caliber: 7.5mm MAS. Five-round box magazine. 22.5-inch bbl. Weight: 8.25 lbs. Sights: Adj. rear; blade front. Two-piece military-type stock. Bayonet carried in forend tube. Made from 1936 to 1940 by Manufacture Francaise d'Armes et de Cycles de St. Etienne (MAS).

GALIL RIFLES — Manufactured by Israel Military Industries, Israel. Imported by UZI America Inc., North Haven, CT (previously by Action Arms, Springfield Armory and Magnum Research, Inc.)

AR SEMI-AUTOMATIC RIFLE
Calibers: .308 Win. (7.62 NATO), .223 Rem. (5.56mm). 25-round (.308) or 35-round (.223) magazine. 16-inch (.223) or 18.5-inch (.308) bbl. w/flash suppressor. Weight: 9.5 lbs. Folding aperture rear sight, post front. Folding metal stock w/carrying handle. Imported from 1982 to 1994. Select fire models available to law enforcement only.
Model .223 AR . . . . NiB $3233 Ex $1998 Gd $1200
Model .308 AR . . . . NiB $3233 Ex $1998 Gd $1200
Model .223 ARM. . . . . NiB $3225 Ex $2290 Gd $1669
Model .308 ARM. . . . . .NiB $3225 Ex $2290 Gd $1669SPORTER

SEMIAUTOMATIC RIFLE. . . . . NiB $1723 Ex $1009 Gd $700
Same general specifications as AR Model except w/hardwood thumbhole stock and 5-round magazine. Weight: 8.5 lbs. Imported from 1991 to 1994.

GARCIA CORPORATION — Teaneck, New Jersey

BRONCO 22 SINGLE-SHOT RIFLE. . . . . . . NiB $151 Ex $112 Gd $88
Swing-out action. Takedown. Caliber: .22 LR. Long, Short. 16.5-inch bbl. Weight: 3 lbs. Sights: Open rear-blade front. One-piece stock and receiver, crackle finish. Introduced 1967. Disc.

GERMAN MILITARY RIFLES — Manufactured by Ludwig Loewe & Co., Berlin, other contractors, and by German arsenals and various plants under German government control

MODEL 24T (GEW. 24T) MAUSER RIFLE . . . .NiB $598 Ex $443 Gd $300
Same specs as Czech Model 24 (VZ24) Mauser rifle w/minor modifications. Laminated wood stock. Weight: 9.25 lbs. Made in Czechoslovakia during German Occupation; adopted in 1940.

MODEL 29/40 (GEW. 29/40)
MAUSER RIFLE . . . . NiB $433 Ex $329 Gd $244
Same specs as Kar. 98K w/minor differences. Made in Poland during German Occupation; adopted in 1940.

German Military Rifles

MODEL 33/40 (GEW. 33/40)
MAUSER RIFLE . . . . **NiB $1030 Ex $799 Gd $515**
Same specs as Czech Model 33 (VZ33) Mauser Carbine w/minor modifications, laminated wood stock similar to wartime Model 98K carbines. Made in Czechoslovakia during German Occuption; adopted in 1940.

MODELS 41 AND 41-W (GEW. 41, GEW. 41-W)
SEMIAUTOMATIC MILITARY RIFLES
Gas-operated, muzzle cone system. Caliber: 7.9mm Mauser. Ten-round box magazine. 22.5-inch bbl. Weight: 10.25 lbs. Sights: Adj. leaf rear; blade front. Military-type stock w/semi-pistol grip, plastic handguard. Model 41 lacks bolt release found on Model 41-W; otherwise, the models are the same. These early models were mfd. in Walther's Zella-Mehlis plant. Made from c.1941 to 1943.
Model 41 . . . . NiB $4460 Ex $3588 Gd $2510
Model 41-W . . . . NiB $3488 Ex $2789 Gd $1809

MODEL 43 (GEW. 43, KAR. 43)
SEMIAUTO MILITARY RIFLES. . . . . NiB $1399 Ex $1125 Gd $848
Gas-operated, bbl. vented as in Russian Tokarev. Caliber: 7;.9mm Mauser; 10-round detachable box mag. Bbl.: 22 or 24 inches. Weight: 9 lbs. Adj. rear, hooded front sights. Military-style stock w/ semi pistol grip, wooden handguard. Note. These rifles are alike except for minor details. Characteristic late-WWII mfg. shortcuts include cast receiver and bolt cover, stamped steel parts, etc. Gew.43 may have 22- or 24-inch bbl. The former length was standardized in late 1944 when rifle designation was changed to Kar. 43. Made from 1943 to 1945.

MODEL 1888 (GEW. 88) MAUSER-
MANNLICHER SERVICE RIFLE . . . . NiB $433 Ex $265 Gd $221
Bolt-action w/straight bolt handle. Caliber: 7.9mm Mauser (8x57mm). Five round Mannlicher box magazine. 29-inch bbl. w/ jacket. Weight: 8.5 lbs. Fixed front sight, adj. rear. Military-type full stock. Mfd. by Ludwig Loewe & Co., Haenel, Schilling and other contractors.

MODEL 1888 (KAR. 88) MAUSER-
MANNLICHER CARBINE . . . . NiB $334 Ex $249 Gd $245
Same specs as Gew. 88 except w/18-inch bbl. w/o jacket; flat, turned-down bolt handle. Weight: 6.75 lbs. Mfg. by Ludwig Loewe & Co., Haenel, Schilling and other contractors.

MODEL 1898 (GEW. 98)
MAUSER MILITARY RIFLE. . . . . . . NiB $566 Ex $434 Gd $270
Bolt-action with straight bolt handle. Caliber: 7.9mm Mauser (8x57mm); five-round box mag. Bbl.: Stepped, 29 inches. Weight: 9 lbs. Blade front, adj. rear sights. Military-style full stock w/rounded bottom pistol grip. Adopted in 1898.

MODEL 1898A (KAR. 98A)
MAUSER CARBINE . . . . NiB $521 Ex $433 Gd $329
Same specs as Model 1898 (Gew. 98) Rifle except has turned-down bolt handle, smaller receiver ring, lightweight 23-5-inch straight-taper bbl., front sight guards. Sling attaches to left side of stock. Weight: 8 lbs. Note. Some of these carbines are marked "Kar. 98," but the true Kar. 98 is the earlier, original M/98 carbine w/17-inch bbl. and is rarely encountered.

MODEL 1898B (KAR. 98B)
MAUSER CARBINE . . . . NiB $515 Ex $423 Gd $320
Post-WWI model.Same specs as Model 1898 (Gew. 98) Rifle except has turned-down bolt handle and slit attached to left side of stock.

MODEL 1898K (KAR. 98K)
MAUSER CARBINE . . . . NiB $550 Ex $465 Gd $350

Same general specifications as Model 1898 (Gew. 98) Rifle except has turned-down bolt handle, 23.5-inch bbl., may have hooded front sight, sling attached to left side of stock, weighs about 8.5 lbs. Adopted in 1935, this was the standard German service rifle of WWII. Late-war models had stamped sheet steel trigger guards and many of the Model 98K carbines made during WWII had laminated wood stocks that weigh .5 to .75 pound more than the previous Model 98K. Value shown is for the earlier type.

MODEL VK 98
PEOPLE'S RIFLE ("VOLKSGEWEHR") NiB $290 Ex $233 Gd $166
Kar. 98K-type action. Caliber: 7.9mm. Single-shot or repeater (latter w/rough "hole-in-the-stock" five-round "magazine" or fitted w/10-round clip from German Model 43 semi-auto rifle.) Bbl.: 20.9 inches. Weight: 7 lbs. Fixed V-notch rear sight dove-tailed into front receiver ring, front blade welded to bbl. Crude, unfinished, half-length stock w/o buttplate. Note. Of value only as a military arms collectible. This hastily-made rifle should be regarded as unsafe to shoot.

GÉVARM RIFLE — Saint Etienne, France. Manufactured by Gevelot

E-1 AUTOLOADING RIFLE. . . . . . . NiB $234 Ex $190 Gd $150
Caliber: .22 LR. Eight-round clip magazine. 19.5-inch bbl. Sights: Open rear; post front. Pistol-grip stock and forearm of French walnut.

GOLDEN EAGLE RIFLES — Houston, Texas. Manufactured by Nikko Firearms Ltd., Tochigi, Japan

MODEL 7000 GRADE I AFRICAN . . . . NiB $743 Ex $578 Gd $468
Same as Grade I Big Game except: Caliber: .375 H&H Mag. and .458 Win. Mag. Two-round magazine in .458, weight: 8.75 lbs. in .375 and 10.5 lbs. in .458, furnished w/sights. Imported from 1976 to 1981.Model 7000 Big Game Series
Bolt-action. Calibers: .22-250 Rem., .243 Win. .25-06 Rem., .270 Win., .270 Weatherby Mag., 7mm Rem. Mag., .30-06, .300 Weatherby Mag., .300 Win. Mag., .338 Win. Mag. Capacity: four rounds in .22-250, three rounds in others. Bbl.: 24 or 26 inches (in .338 only). No sights. Fancy American walnut stock, skip checkered contrasting wood forend tip and grip cap w/gold eagle head; recoil pad. Imported from 1976 to 1981.
Model 7000 Grade I . . . . NiB $722 Ex $630 Gd $455
Model 7000 Grade II . . . . NiB $755 Ex $680 Gd $479

GREIFELT & CO. — Suhl, Germany

SPORT MODEL 22 HORNET
BOLT-ACTION RIFLE . . . . NiB $2388 Ex $1907 Gd $1398
Caliber: .22 Hornet. Five round box magazine. 22-inch Krupp steel bbl. Weight: 6 lbs. Sights: Two-leaf rear; ramp front. Walnut stock, checkered pistol-grip and forearm. Made before WWII.

CARL GUSTAF RIFLES — Eskilstuna, Sweden. Manufactured by Carl Gustaf Stads Gevärsfaktori

MODEL 2000 BOLT-ACTION RIFLE
Calibers: .243 Win., 6.5x55, 7x64, .270 Win., .308 Win., .30-06, 7mm Rem. Mag., .300 Win. Mag.; three-round mag. Bbl.: 24 inches. Lgt.: 44 inches. Weight: 7.5 lbs. Drilled and tapped for scope mount. Hooded ramp front, open rear sights. Adj. trigger. Checkered

Carl Gustaf Rifles

Carl Gustaf Model 2000

Carl Gustaf Deluxe

Carl Gustaf Grand Prix

Carl Gustaf Sporter

European Monte Carlo walnut stock, Wundhammer palmswell grip. Imported from 1991 to 1995.

W/o sights.	NiB $1433	Ex $1235	Gd $879
W/sights	NiB $1790	Ex $1390	Gd $1009
LUXE	NiB $1744	Ex $1680	Gd $1025

DELUXE . . . . **NiB $700 Ex $579 Gd $522**
Same specifications as Monte Carlo Standard. Calibers: 6.5x55, 308 Win., .30-06, 9.3x62. Four round magazine in 9.3x62. Jeweled bolt. Engraved floorplate and trigger guard. Deluxe French walnut stock w/rosewood forend tip. Imported from 1970 to 1977.

GRAND PRIX SINGLE-SHOT
TARGET RIFLE . . . . **NiB $577 Ex $459 Gd $202**
Bolt-action. Caliber: .22 LR. Bbl.: 26.75 inches, heavy, no sights, w/ adj. trim weight. Weight: 9.75 lbs. Adj. single-stage trigger. Target-type Monte Carlo French walnut stock, cork buttplate. Imported from 1970 to 1977.

MONTE CARLO STANDARD
BOLT-ACTION SPORTING RIFLE . . . . **NiB $507 Ex $422 Gd $366**

Carl Gustaf 1900 action. Calibers: 6.5x55, 7x64, .270 Win., 7mm Rem. Mag., .308 Win., .30-06, 9.3x62. Five round magazine, except 4-round in 9.3x62 and 3-round in 7mm Rem. Mag. 23.5-inch bbl. Weight: 7 lbs. Sights: Folding leaf rear; hooded ramp front. French walnut Monte Carlo stock w/cheekpiece, checkered forearm and pistol grip, sling swivels. Also available in left-hand model. Imported from 1970 to 1977.

SPECIAL . . . . **NiB $575 Ex $401 Gd $376**
Also designated "Grade II" in U.S. and "Model 9000" in Canada. Same specifications as Monte Carlo Standard. Calibers: .22-250, .243 Win., .25-06, .270 Win., 7mm Rem. Mag., .308 Win., .30-06, .300 Win. Mag. Three round magazine in magnum calibers. Select wood stock w/rosewood forend tip. Left-hand model avail. Imported from 1970 to 1977.

SPORTER . . . . **NiB $512 Ex $355 Gd $291**
Also designated "Varmint-target" in U.S. Bolt-action with Bakelite knob. Calibers: .222 Rem., .22-250 Rem., .243 Win., 6.5x55; five-round mag., six rounds in .222 Rem. Bbl.: Heavy, 26.75 inches,w/o sights. Weight: 9.5 lbs. Adj. trigger. Target-type French walnut Monte

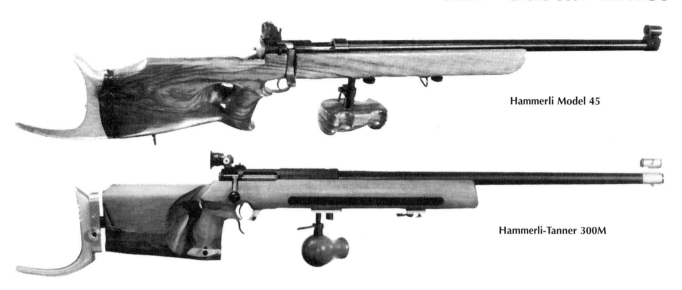

Hammerli Model 45

Hammerli-Tanner 300M

Carlo stock. Imported from 1970 to 1977.

STANDARD . . . . **NiB $512 Ex $355 Gd $291**
Same specifications as Monte Carlo Standard. Calibers: 6.5x55, 7x64, .270 Win., .308 Win., .30-06, 9.3x62. Classic-style stock. Imported from 1970 to 1977.

TROFÉ . . . . **NiB $588 Ex $479 Gd $382**
Also designated "Grade III" in U.S. and "Model 8000" in Canada. Same specifications as Monte Carlo Standard. Calibers: .22-250, .25-06, 6.5x55, .270 Win., 7mm Rem. Mag., .308 Win., .30-06, .300 Win. Mag. Three round magazine in magnum calibers. Furnished w/o sights. Fancy wood stock w/rosewood forend tip, high-gloss lacquer finish. Imported from 1970 to 1977.

C.G. HAENEL — Suhl, Germany

'88 MAUSER SPORTER . . . . **NiB $813 Ex $503 Gd $377**
Same general specifications as Haenel Mauser-Mannlicher except w/ Mauser 5-round box magazine.

MAUSER-MANNLICHER
BOLT-ACTION SPORTING RIFLE . . . . **NiB $821 Ex $566 Gd $400**
Mauser M/88-type action. Calibers: 7x57, 8x57, 9x57; five-round Mannlicher clip-loading box mag. Bbl.: 22 or 24 inches, half or full octagon w/raised, matted rib. Leaf-type open rear, ramp front sights. Double set triggers. Weight: 7.5 lbs. Sporting stock w/cheekpiece, checkered pistol grip, raised side panels, Schnabel forend tip, swivels.

HÄMMERLI AG JAGD-UND-SPORTWAFFENFABRIK — Lenzburg, Switzerland. Imported by Sigarms, Exetre, NH (previously by Hammerli USA; Mandall Shooting Supplies, Inc. & Beeman Precision Arms)

MODEL 45 SMALLBORE BOLT-ACTION
SINGLE-SHOT MATCH RIFLE . . . . **NiB $765 Ex $654 Gd $453**
Caliber: .22 LR, .22 Extra Long. Bbl.: 27.5 inches. Micrometer peep rear, globe front sights. Weight: 15.5 lbs. Free-rifle thumbhole stock w/cheekpiece, full pistol grip, beavertail forearm, palm rest, Swiss-type buttplate, swivels. Made from 1945 to 1957.

MODEL 54 SMALLBORE
MATCH RIFLE . . . . **NiB $709 Ex $544 Gd $423**
Bolt-action single-shot. Caliber: .22 LR. Bbl.: 27.5 inches, heavy. Weight: 15 lbs. Micrometer peep rear, globe front sights. Free-rifle thumbhole stock w/cheekpiece, adj. hook buttplate, palm rest, swivels. Made from 1954 to 1957.

MODEL 503 FREE RIFLE . . . . **NiB $707 Ex $546 Gd $413**
Bolt-action single-shot. Caliber: .22 LR.. Bbl.: 27.5 inches, heavy. Weight: 15 lbs. Micrometer peep rear, globe front sights. Free-rifle thumbhole stock w/cheekpiece, adj. hook buttplate, palm rest, swivels. Made from 1957 to 1962.

MODEL 506 SMALLBORE
MATCH RIFLE . . . . **NiB $769 Ex $644 Gd $439**
Bolt-action single-shot. Caliber: .22 LR. 26.75-inch heavy bbl. Weight: 16.5 lbs. Sights: Micrometer peep rear; globe front. Free-rifle stock w/cheekpiece, thumbhole adj. hook buttplate, palmrest, swivel. Made from 1963 to 1966.

MODEL OLYMPIC 300 METER BOLT-ACTION
SINGLE-SHOT FREE RIFLE . . . . **NiB $905 Ex $755 Gd $556**
Calibers: 7.5mm standard, .30-06, .300 H&H Mag. for U.S.A.; other calibers special order. Bbl.: 29.5 inches, heavy. Double-pull or double set triggers. Micrometer peep rear, globe front sights. Free-rifle thumbhole stock w/cheekpiece, full pistol grip, beavertail forend, palm rest. Swiss-type buttplate, swivels. Made from 1945 to 1959.

TANNER 300 METER FREE RIFLE . . . . **NiB $937 Ex $740 Gd $534**
Bolt-action single-shot. Caliber: 7.5mm standard, available in most centerfire calibers. 29.5-inch heavy bbl. Weight: 16.75 lbs. Sights: Micrometer peep rear; globe front. Free-rifle stock w/cheekpiece, thumbhole, adj. hook buttplate, palmrest, swivel. Introduced 1962. Disc.

HARRINGTON & RICHARDSON, INC. — Gardner, Massachusetts (now H&R 1871, INC., Gardner, Massachusetts)

Harrington & Richardson, Inc.

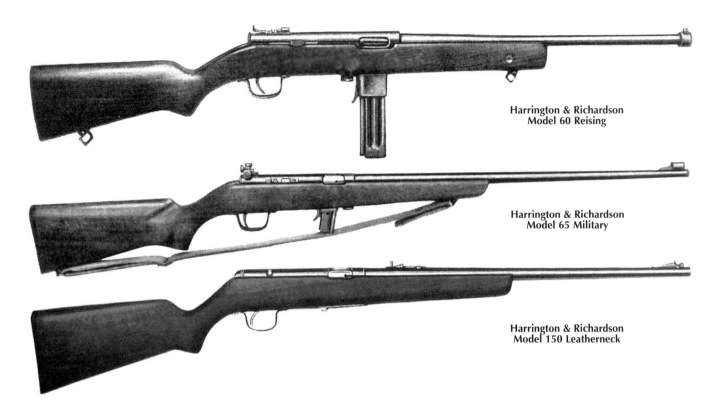

Harrington & Richardson
Model 60 Reising

Harrington & Richardson
Model 65 Military

Harrington & Richardson
Model 150 Leatherneck

**MODEL 60 REISING SEMI-
AUTOMATIC RIFLE** . . . . **NiB $1266 Ex $890 Gd $598**
Caliber: .45 Automatic. 12- and 20-round detachable box magazines.
18.25-inch bbl. Weight: 7.5 lbs. Sights: Open rear; blade front. Plain
pistol-grip stock. Made from 1944 to 1946.

**MODEL 65 MILITARY
AUTOLOADING RIFLE** . . . . **NiB $496 Ex $322 Gd $208**
Also called "General." Caliber: .22 LR; 10-round detachable box
mag. Bbl.: 23 inches, heavy. Redfield 70 rear peep, blade front w/
protecting "ears" sights. Plain pistol-grip stock, Garand dimensions.
Made from 1944 to 1946. This model was used as a training rifle by
the U.S. Marine Corps.

**MODEL 150
LEATHERNECK AUTOLOADER** . . . .**NiB $335 Ex $234 Gd $110**
Caliber: .22 LR; five-round detachable box mag. Bbl.: 22 inches.
Wt.: 7.25 lbs. Open rear, ramp blade front. Plain pistol-grip stock.
Made from 1949 to 1953.

MODEL 151 . . . . **NiB $335 Ex $234 Gd $110**
Same as Model 150 except w/Redfield 70 rear peep sight.

**MODEL 155
SINGLE-SHOT RIFLE** . . . . **NiB $279 Ex $178 Gd $125**
Based on Model 158 action. Calibers: .44 rem., Mag., .45-70 Gov't.
Bbl.: 24 or 28 inches. Weight: 7 or 7.5 lbs. Folding leaf rear, blade
front sights. Straight-grip stock, forearm w/bbl. band. Brass cleaning
rod. Made from 1972 to 1982.

**MODEL 157
SINGLE-SHOT RIFLE** . . . . **NiB $330 Ex $154 Gd $121**

Based on Model 158 action. Calibers: .22 WMR, .22 Hornet, .30-30.
Bbl.: 22 inches. Weight: 6.25 lbs. Folding leaf rear, blade front sights.
Pistol-grip stock, full-length forearm, swivels. Made from 1976 to 1986.

MODEL 158 TOPPER JET SINGLE-SHOT COMBINATION RIFLE
Shotgun-type action w/visible hammer, side lever, auto ejector. Caliber:
.22 Rem. Jet. 22-inch bbl. (interchanges with .30-30, .410 ga., 20 ga.
bbls.). Weight: 5 lbs. Sights: Lyman folding adj. open rear; ramp front.
Plain pistol-grip stock and forearm, recoil pad. Made from 1963 to 1967.
Rifle only. . . . . **NiB $250 Ex $171 Gd $126**
W/interchangeable bbl.
(.30-30 shotgun), add **$75**

MODEL 158C . . . . **NiB $250 Ex $171 Gd $126**
Same as Model 158 Topper Jet except in .22 Hornet, .30-30, .357 Mag.,
.357 Mag., .44 Mag. Straight-grip stock. Made from 1963 to 1986.

**MODEL 163 MUSTANG
SINGLE-SHOT RIFLE** . . . . **NiB $250 Ex $168 Gd $124**
Same as Model 158 Topper except w/gold-plated hammer and trigger,
straight-grip stock and contoured forearm. Made from 1964 to 1967.

**MODEL 165
LEATHERNECK AUTOLOADER** . . . .**NiB $250 Ex $170 Gd $125**
Caliber: .22 LR. 10-round detachable box magazine. 23-inch bbl.
Weight: 7.5 lbs. Sights: Redfield 70 rear peep; blade front, on ramp.
Plain pistol-grip stock, swivels, web sling. Made from 1945 to 1961.

MODEL 171 . . . . **NiB $633 Ex $466 Gd $257**
Model 1873 Springfield Cavalry Carbine replica. Caliber: .45-70.
22-inch bbl. Weight: 7 lbs. Sights: Leaf rear; blade front. Plain walnut stock. Made from 1972 to 1981.

Harrington & Richardson, Inc.

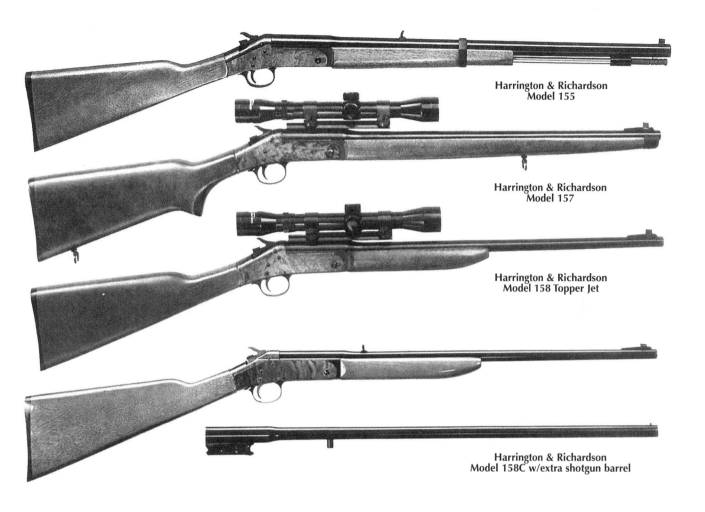

Harrington & Richardson
Model 155

Harrington & Richardson
Model 157

Harrington & Richardson
Model 158 Topper Jet

Harrington & Richardson
Model 158C w/extra shotgun barrel

MODEL 171 DELUXE . . . . NiB $776 Ex $523 Gd $309
Same as Model 171 except w/engraved action and different sights. Made from 1972 to 1986.

MODEL 172 . . . . NiB $759 Ex $588 Gd $454
Same as Model 171 Deluxe except silver-plated, w/fancy checkered walnut stock, grip adapter; tang-mounted aperture sight. Made from 1972 to 1986.

MODEL 173 . . . . NiB $1788 Ex $1009 Gd $983
Model 1873 Springfield Officer's Model replica, same as 100th Anniversary Commemorative except w/o plaque on stock. Made from 1972 to 1986.

MODEL 174 . . . . NiB $1266 Ex $1009 Gd $633
Little Bighorn Commemorative Carbine. Same as Model 171 Deluxe except w/tang-mounted aperture sight, grip adapter. Made from 1972 to 1984.

MODEL 178 . . . . NiB $735 Ex $422 Gd $328
Model 1873 Springfield Infantry Rifle replica. Caliber: .45-70. 32-inch bbl. Weight: 8 lbs. 10 oz. Sights: Leaf rear; blade front. Full-length stock w/bbl. bands, swivels, ramrod. Made from 1973 to 1986.

MODEL 250 SPORTSTER BOLT-ACTION

REPEATING RIFLE. . . . . NiB $220 Ex $111 Gd $80
Caliber: .22 LR. Five-round detachable box magazine. 23-inch bbl. Weight: 6.5 lbs. Sights: Open rear; blade front, on ramp. Plain pistol-grip stock. Made from 1948 to 1961.

MODEL 251 . . . . NiB $255 Ex $128 Gd $90
Same as Model 250 except w/Lyman No. 55H rear sight.

**MODEL 265 "REG'LAR" BOLT-
ACTION REPEATING RIFLE** . . . . NiB $337 Ex $140 Gd $98
Caliber: .22 LR. 10-round detachable box magazine. 22-inch bbl. Weight: 6.5 lbs. Sights: Lyman No. 55 rear peep; blade front, on ramp. Plain pistol-grip stock. Made from 1946 to 1949.

**MODEL 300 ULTRA
BOLT-ACTION RIFLE** . . . . NiB $566 Ex $521 Gd $302
Mauser-type action. Calibers: .22-250 Rem., .243 Win., .270 Win., .30-06, .308 Win., 7mm Rem. Mag., .300 Win. Mag.; three-round mag. in 7mm and .300 Win Mag.; five rounds in other calibers. Bbl.: 22 or 24 inches. Weight: 7.25 lbs. Open rear, ramp front sights. Checkered stock w/rollover cheekpiece and full pistol grip. Contrasting wood forearm tip and grip cap, rubber buttplate, sling swivels. Made from 1965 to 1982.

Harrington & Richardson, Inc.

Harrington & Richardson
Model 171

Harrington & Richardson
Model 171 Deluxe

Harrington & Richardson
Model 172

Harrington & Richardson
Model 173

Harrington & Richardson
Model 174 Little Big Horn Commemorative

Harrington & Richardson
Model 178

Harrington & Richardson, Inc.

Harrington & Richardson
Model 300

Harrington & Richardson
Model 301 Carbine

Harrington & Richardson
Model 317P

Harrington & Richardson
Model 330

Harrington & Richardson
Model 360 Ultra

Harrington & Richardson
Model 370 Ultra Medalist

MODEL 301 CARBINE . . . . NiB $523 Ex $412 Gd $287
Same as Model 300 except w/18-inch bbl., Mannlicher-style stock, weighs 7.25 lbs.; not available in caliber .22-250. Made from 1967 to 1982.

MODEL 308 AUTOMATIC RIFLE . . NiB $531 Ex $390 Gd $277
Original designation of the Model 360 Ultra. Made from 1965 to 1967.

**MODEL 317 ULTRA WILDCAT
BOLT-ACTION RIFLE . . . . NiB $644 Ex $490 Gd $377**
Sako short action. Calibers: .17 Rem. 17/.223 (handload), .222 Rem.,

.223 Rem. Six round magazine. 20-inch bbl. No sights, receiver dovetailed for scope mounts. Checkered stock w/cheekpiece and full pistol grip, contrasting wood forearm tip and pistol-grip cap, rubber buttplate. Weight: 5.25 lbs. Made from 1968 to 1976.

**MODEL 317P
PRESENTATION GRADE. . . . . NiB $710 Ex $546 Gd $488**
Same as Model 317 except w/select grade fancy walnut stock w/ basket-weave carving on forearm and pistol-grip. Made from 1968 to 1976.

Harrington & Richardson, Inc.

Harrington & Richardson
Model 700 Deluxe

Harrington & Richardson
Model 750 Pioneer

Harrington & Richardson
Model 755

MODEL 330 HUNTER'S RIFLE . . . . **NiB $435 Ex $326 Gd $244**
Similar to Model 300 but w/plain stock. Calibers: .243 Win., .270 Win., .30-06, .308 Win., 7mm rem. Mag., .300 Win. Mag. Weight: 7.13 lbs. Made from 1967 to 1972.

MODEL 333 . . . . **NiB $435 Ex $326 Gd $244**
Plainer version of Model 300 w/uncheckered walnut-finished hardwood stock. Calibers: 7mm Rem. Mag. and .30-06. 22-inch bbl. Weight: 7.25 lbs. No sights. Made in 1974.

MODEL 340 . . . . **NiB $450 Ex $341 Gd $259**
Mauser-type action. Calibers: .243 Win., .308 Win., .270 Win., .30-06, 7x57. 22-inch bbl. Weight: 7.25 lbs. Hand-checkered American walnut stock. Made from 1982 to 1984.

MODEL 360
ULTRA AUTOMATIC RIFLE. . . . . . **NiB $534 Ex $377 Gd $300**
Gas-operated semiautomatic. Calibers: .243 Win., .308 Win. Three round detachable box magazine. 22-inch bbl. Sights: Open rear; ramp front. Checkered stock w/rollover cheekpiece, full pistol grip, contrasting wood forearm tip and pistol-grip cap, rubber buttplate, sling swivels. Weight: 7.25 lbs. Made from 1967 to 1978.

MODEL 361 . . . . **NiB $556 Ex $439 Gd $333**
Same as Model 360 except w/full rollover cheekpiece for right- or left-hand shooters. Made from 1970 to 1973.

MODEL 365 ACE BOLT-ACTION
SINGLE-SHOT RIFLE. . . . . **NiB $178 Ex $140 Gd $96**
Caliber: .22 LR. 22-inch bbl. Weight: 6.5 lbs. Sights: Lyman No. 55 rear peep, blade front, on ramp. Plain pistol-grip stock. Made from 1946 to 1947.

MODEL 370 ULTRA MEDALIST . . . **NiB $555 Ex $423 Gd $320**
Varmint and target rifle based on Model 300. Calibers: .22-250, .243 Win., 6mm Rem. Three round magazine. 24-inch varmint weight bbl. No sights. Target-style stock w/semibeavertail forearm. Weight: 9.5 lbs. Made from 1968 to 1973.

MODEL 422 SLIDE-ACTION
REPEATER. . . . .**NiB $375 Ex $234 Gd $141**
Caliber: .22 LR. Long, Short. Tubular magazine holds 21 Short, 17 Long, 15 LR. 24-inch bbl. Weight: 6 lbs. Sights: Open rear; ramp front. Plain pistol-grip stock grooved slide handle. Made from 1956 to 1958.

MODEL 450 . . . . **NiB $403 Ex $221 Gd $130**
Same as Model 451 except w/o sights.

MODEL 451 MEDALIST
BOLT-ACTION TARGET RIFLE. . . . . **NiB $433 Ex $222 Gd $130**
Caliber: .22 LR; five-round detachable box mag. Bbl.: 26 inches. Weight: 10.5 lbs. Lyman No. 524F extension rear, No. 77 front sights; scope bases. Target-style stock w/full pistol grip and forearm, swivels and sling. Made from 1948 to 1961.

Harrington & Richardson
Model 760

Harrington & Richardson
Model 866

Harrington & Richardson
Model 1873 — 100th Anniversary

Harrington & Richardson
Model 5200 Sporter

Harrington & Richardson
Ultra Varmint

MODEL 465 TARGETEER SPECIAL
BOLT-ACTION REPEATER . . . . **NiB $423 Ex $233 Gd $144**
Caliber: .22 LR. 10-round detachable box magazine. 25-inch bbl. Weight: 9 lbs. Sights: Lyman No. 57 rear peep; blade front, on ramp. Plain pistol-grip stock, swivels, web sling strap. Made from 1946 to 1947.

MODEL 700
AUTOLOADER . . . . **NiB $456 Ex $321 Gd $188**
Caliber: .22 WMR; five-round mag. Bbl.: 22 inches. Weight: 6.5 lbs. Folding leaf rear, blade ramp front sights. Monte Carlo-style American walnut stock. Made from 1977 to 1986.

MODEL 700 DELUXE . . . . **NiB $503 Ex $381 Gd $285**
Same as Model 700 Standard except w/select custom polished blued finish. No sights. Fitted w/H&R Model 432 4x scope. Select hand-checkered walnut stock. Made from 1980 to 1986.

MODEL 750 PIONEER BOLT-ACTION
SINGLE-SHOT RIFLE . . . . **NiB $145 Ex $104 Gd $80**
Caliber: .22 LR. Long, Short. 22- or 24-inch bbl. Weight: 5 lbs.

Sights: Open rear; bead front. Plain pistol-grip stock. Made from 1954 to 1981; redesigned 1982. Disc.

MODEL 751 SINGLE-SHOT RIFLE . . . . **NiB $170 Ex $95 Gd $77**
Same as Model 750 except w/Mannlicher-style stock. Made in 1971.

MODEL 755 SAHARA
SINGLE-SHOT RIFLE . . . . **NiB $166 Ex $90 Gd $67**
Blow-back action, auto ejection. Caliber: .22 LR, Long, Short. Bbl.: 18 inches. Weight: 4 lbs. Open rear, military-type front sights. Mannlicher-style stock. Made from 1963 to 1971.

MODEL 760 SINGLE-SHOT . . . . **NiB $188 Ex $100 Gd $80**
Same as Model 755 except w/conventional sporter stock. Made from 1965 to 1970.

MODEL 765 PIONEER BOLT-ACTION
SINGLE-SHOT RIFLE . . . . **NiB $188 Ex $97 Gd $66**
Caliber: .22 LR, Long, Short. Bbl.: 24 inches. Weight: 5 lbs. Open rear, hooded bead front sights. Plain pistol-grip stock Made from 1948 to 1954.

Heckler & Koch, GmbH

MODEL 800 LYNX
AUTOLOADING RIFLE . . . . **NiB $407 Ex $224 Gd $119**
Caliber: .22 LR; five- or 10-round clip mag. Bbl.: 22 inches. Open sights. Weight: 6 lbs. Plain pistol-grip stock. Made from 1958 to 1960.

MODEL 852 FIELDSMAN
BOLT-ACTION REPEATER . . . . **NiB $198 Ex $101 Gd $89**
Caliber: .22 LR, Long, Short; tubular mg., holds 21 Short, 17 Long, 15 LR. Bbl.: 24 inches. Weight: 5.5 lbs. Open rear, bead front sights. Plain pistol-grip stock. Made from 1952 to 1953.

MODEL 865 PLAINSMAN
BOLT-ACTION REPEATER . . . . **NiB $165 Ex $115 Gd $80**
Caliber .22 LR. Long, Short. Five round detachable box magazine. 22- or 24-inch bbl. Weight: 5.25 lbs. Sights: Open rear, bead front. Plain pistol-grip stock. Made from 1949 to 1986.

MODEL 866
BOLT-ACTION REPEATER . . . . **NiB $197 Ex $115 Gd $80**
Same as Model 865, except w/Mannlicher-style stock. Made in 1971.

MODEL 1873 100TH ANNIVERSARY
(1871–1971) COMMEMORATIVE
OFFICER'S SPRINGFIELD REPLICA . . . **NiB $866 Ex $659 Gd $475**
Model 1873 'trap door' single-shot. Engraved breech block, receiver, hammer, lock, band and buttplate. Caliber: .45-70. Bbl.: 26 inches. Peep rear, blade front sights. Checkered walnut stock w/anniversary plaque. Ramrod. Weight: 8 lbs. 10,000 made in 1971.

MODEL 5200 SPORTER . . . . **NiB $677 Ex $376 Gd $277**
Turn-bolt repeater. Caliber: .22 LR Bbl.: 24 inches. Adj. trigger. Peep receiver, hooded ramp front sights. Classic-style American walnut stock. Weight: 6.5 lbs. Disc. 1983.

MODEL 5200 MATCH RIFLE . . . . . **NiB $590 Ex $490 Gd $368**
Same action as 5200 Sporter. Caliber: .22 LR. Bbl.: 22-inch target weight. American walnut target stock. Weight: 11 lbs. Made from 1982 to 1986.

CUSTER MEMORIAL ISSUE
Limited Edition Model 1873 Springfield Carbine replica, richly engraved and inlaid w/gold, fancy walnut stock, in mahogany display case. Made in 1973.
Officers' model
(limited to 25 pieces) . . . . **NiB $4125 Ex $2990 Gd $2423**
Enlisted Men's model
(limited to 243 pieces) . . . . **NiB $2033 Ex $1021 Gd $690**

TARGETEER JR. BOLT-ACTION RIFLE . . . . **NiB $225 Ex $177 Gd $145**
Caliber: .22 LR; five-round detachable box mag. Bbl.: 20 inches. Weight: 7 lbs. Redfield 70 rear peep, Lyman No. 17A front sights. Junior-sized target stock w/pistol grip, swivels and sling. Made from 1948 to 1951.

ULTRA SINGLE-SHOT RIFLE
Side-lever single-shot. Calibers: .22-250 Rem., .223 Rem., .25-06 Rem., .308 Win. 22- to 26-inch bbl. Weight: 7 to 8 lbs. Curly maple or laminated stock. Barrel-mounted scope mount, no sights. Made from 1993 to date.
Ultra Hunter
(.25-06, .308) . . . . **NiB $257 Ex $166 Gd $167**
Ultra Varmint . . . . **NiB $288 Ex $230 Gd $188**

HARRIS GUNWORKS — Phoenix, Arizona (formerly McMillan Gun Works)

Sporting line of firearms discontinued; now specializes in sniper and tactical arms.

SIGNATURE ALASKAN
BOLT-ACTION RIFLE . . . . **NiB $3510 Ex $3108 Gd $2110**
Same general specs as Classic Sporter except w/math-grade bbl. Rings and mounts w/single leaf rear, barrel-band front sights. Checkered Monte Carlo stock w/palm swell and solid recoil pad. Nickel finish. Calibers: Long action (.270 Win., .280 Rem., .30-06), Magnum (7mm Rem. Mag., .300 Win. Mag., .300 Wby. Mag., .340 Wby. Mag., .358 Win., .375 H&H Mag). Made in 1990. Disc.

SIGNATURE CLASSIC SPORTER
Prototype for Harris's Signature Series rifles. Bolt-action available in SA (standard/short) from .22-250 Rem. to .350 Rem. Mag; LA (long) in .25-06 Rem. and .30-06; MA (magnum) in 7mm STW to .426 Rigby; four-round mag. (three in magnum calibers). Pre-64 Win. Mdoel 70-style action for dangerous game calibers. Bbl.: 22, 24 or 26 inches. Weight: 7 lbs. (short action). No sights; rings and bases provided. Harris fiberglass stock, Fibergrain or wood stock optional. Stainless, matte black or lack chrome sulfide finish. Right- or left-hand models. Made from 1987. Disc.
Classic Sporter, standard . . . . . . **NiB $2565 Ex $2344 Gd $1424**
Classic Sporter, stainless . . . . . . **NiB $2565 Ex $2344 Gd $1424**

SIGNATURE
MOUNTAIN RIFLE . . . . **NiB $3037 Ex $2977 Gd $1609**
Same specs as Classic Sporter except w/titanium action and graphite-reinforced fiberglass stock. Weight: 5.5 lbs. Calibers: .270 Win., .280 Rem., .30-06, 7mm Mag., .300 Win. Mag., Other calibers on special order. Made from 1995. Disc.

SIGNATURE
SUPER VARMINTER . . . . **NiB $2512 Ex $2233 Gd $1429**
Same specs as Classic Sporter except w/heavy, countoured bbl., adj. trigger. Fiberglass stock and field bipod. Calibers: .223 Rem., .22-250 Rem., .220 Swift, .244 Win., 6mm Rem., .25-06 Rem., 7mm-08 Rem., .308 Win., .350 Rem. Mag. Made from 1995. Disc.

TALON SAFARI RIFLE
Same specs as Classic Sporter except w/Harris Safari-grade action, match-grade bbl., Safari fiberglass stock. Matte black finish. Calibers: Magnum (.300 H&H Mag., .300 Win. Mag, .300 Wby. Mag., .338 Win. Mag., .240 Wby. Mag, .375 H&H Mag., .404 Jeffrey, .416 Rem. Mag., .458 Win. Mag.; Super Magnum (.300 Phoenix, .338 Lapua, .378 Wby. Mag., .416 Rigby, .416 Wby. Mag., .460 Wby. Mag. Other calibers available on special order. Imported in 1989. Disc.
Safari Magnum . . . . **NiB $3779 Ex $3166 Gd $2179**

HECKLER & KOCH, GMBH — Oberndorf am Neckar, Germany. Imported by Heckler & Koch, Inc., Sterling, Virginia

MODEL 911 SEMIAUTO RIFLE . . . . **NiB $1970 Ex $1723 Gd $1019**
Caliber: .308 (7.62mm). Five-round magazine. 19.7-inch bull bbl. 42.4 inches overall. Sights: Hooded post front; adj. aperture rear. Weight: 11 lbs. Kevlar-reinforced fiberglass thumbhole-stock. Imported from 1989 to 1993.

Heckler & Koch
Model HK91 A-2

Heckler & Koch
Model HK91 A-3

Heckler & Koch
Model HK93 A-2

Heckler & Koch
Model HK940 Carbine

MODEL HK91 A-2
SEMIAUTO . . . . **NiB $2634 Ex $2133 Gd $1388**
Delayed roller-locked blow-back action. Caliber: 7.62mmx51 NATO (.308 Win.); five- or 20-round box mag. Bbl.: 19 inches. Weight: 9.37 lbs. "V" and aperture rear, post front sights. Plastic buttstock and forearm. Disc. 1991.

MODEL HK91 A-3 . . . . **NiB $2721 Ex $2490 Gd $1665**
Same as Model HK91 A-2 except w/retractable metal buttstock, weighs 10.56 lbs. Disc. 1991.

MODEL HK93 SEMIAUTOMATIC
Delayed roller-locked blow-back action. Caliber: 5.56mm x 45 (.223 Rem.). 5- or 20-round magazine. 16.13-inch bbl. Weight: W/o magazine, 7.6 lbs. Sights: "V" and aperture rear; post front. Plastic buttstock and forend. Disc. 1991.
HK93 A-2 . . . . **NiB $2835 Ex $2177 Gd $1198**
HK93 A-3 w/retractable stock . . . . **NiB $3590 Ex $2816 Gd $2021**

MODEL HK94 SEMIAUTOMATIC CARBINE
Caliber: 9mm Para. 15-round magazine. 16-inch bbl. Weight: 6.75 lbs.

Heckler & Koch, GmbH

Heckler & Koch
Model SL-8

Heckler & Koch
Model USC Carbine

Aperture rear sight, front post. Plastic buttstock and forend or retractable metal stock. Imported from 1983 to 1991.

HK94-A2 w/standard stock.........NiB $4054 Ex $3209 Gd $2775
HK94-A3 w/retractable stock, add.........................20%

MODEL HK300 SEMIAUTOMATIC...... NiB $1423 Ex $955 Gd $600
Caliber: .22 WMR. Five- or 15-round box magazine. 19.7-inch bbl. w/polygonal rifling. Weight: 5.75 lbs. Sights: V-notch rear; ramp front. High-luster polishing and bluing. European walnut stock w/cheekpiece, checkered forearm and pistol-grip. Disc. 1989.

MODEL HK630
SEMIAUTOMATIC................. NiB $1733 Ex $1277 Gd $1009
Caliber: .223 Rem. Four- or 10-round magazine. 24-inch bbl. Overall length: 42 inches. Weight: 7 lbs. Sights: Open rear; ramp front. European walnut stock w/Monte Carlo cheekpiece. Imported from 1983 to 1990.

MODEL HK770
SEMIAUTOMATIC.................... NiB $2244 Ex $1703 Gd $1099
Caliber: .308 Win. Three- or 10-round magazine. Overall length: 44.5 inches. Weight: 7.92 lbs. Sights: Open rear; ramp front. European walnut stock w/Monte Carlo cheekpiece. Imported from 1983 to 1986.

MODEL HK940
SEMIAUTOMATIC.................... NiB $2055 Ex $1833 Gd $1079
Caliber: .30-06 Springfield. Three- or 10-round magazine. Overall length: 47 inches. Weight: 8.8 lbs. Sights: Open rear; ramp front. European walnut stock w/Monte Carlo cheekpiece. Imported from 1983 to 1986.

MODEL SL8-1
RIFLE..................... NiB $2006 Ex $1409 Gd $987
Caliber: .223 Rem.; 10-round mag. Bbl.: 20.8 inches. Weight: 8.6 lbs. Gas-operated, short-stroke piston w/rotary locking bolt. Adj. rear sight. Ambidextrous safety selector. Polymer receiver w/adj. buttstock. Intro. In 1999.

MODEL SR-9
SEMIAUTO RIFLE .... NiB $2130 Ex $1850 Gd $1044
Caliber: .308 Win. (7.62mm); five-round mag. Bbl.: 19.7 inches. Lgt.: 42.4 inches. Weight: 11 lbs. Hooded post front, adj. aperture rear sights. Kevlar-reinforced fiberglass thumbhole stock w/wood-grain finish. Imported from 1989 to 1993.

MODEL SR-9
TARGET RIFLE.................... NiB $2844 Ex $2166 Gd $1477
Same specifications as standard SR-9 except w/PSG-1 trigger group and adj. buttstock. Imported from 1992 to 1994.

MODEL USC
CARBINE RIFLE.................... NiB $1655 Ex $1133 Gd $790
Caliber: 45 ACP. 10-round magazine. 16- inch bbl., 35.43 inches overall. Weight: 6 lbs. Blow-back operating system. Polymer receiver w/integral grips. Rear adjustable sight w/ambidextrous safety selector lever. Introduced 1999.

Heym Model 55B Double Rifle
NRA NATIONAL FIREARMS MUSEUM

**Heym
Model SR-20 Standard**

**Heym
Model SR-20L Mannlicher**

HEROLD RIFLE — Suhl, Germany.
Made by Franz Jaeger & Company

BOLT-ACTION REPEATING
SPORTING RIFLE . . . . **NiB $1044 Ex $800 Gd $634**
Miniature Mauser-type action. Caliber: .22 Hornet.; five-round box mag. on hinged floorplate. Double-set triggers. Bbl.: 24 inches. Leaf rear, ramp front sights. Weight: 7.75 lbs. Fancy checkered stock. Made before WWII. These rifles were imported by Charles Daly and A.F. Stoeger, Inc., of New York City, and sold under their names.

HEYM RIFLES AMERICA, INC. —
Manufactured by Heym, GmbH & Co
JAGWAFFEN KD., Gleichamberg, Germany
(previously imported by Heym America, Inc.;
Heckler & Koch; JagerSport, Ltd.)

MODEL 55B DOUBLE RIFLE
Kerston boxlock action w/double cross-bolt and cocking indicators. Calibers: .308 Win., .30-06, .375 H&H Mag., .458 Win. Mag., .470 N.E. Lgt.: 42 inches. Weight: 8.25 inches. Fixed V-type rear, silver bead ramp front sights. Engraved receiver w/optional sidelocks, interchangeable bbls., claw mounts. Checkered European walnut stock. Imported from Germany.
Model 55 (boxlock) . . . . **NiB $6677 Ex $6488 Gd $5745**
Model 55 (sidelock . . . . **NiB $9544 Ex $7890 Gd $6791**
W/extra rifle bbls., add **$6000**
W/extra shotgun bbls., add **$3000**

EXPRESS BOLT-ACTION RIFLE
Same specs as Model SR-20 Safari except w/modified magnum Mauser action. Calibers: .338 Lapua Mag., .375 H&H Mag., .378 Wby. Mag., .416 Rigby, .450 Ackley, .460 Wby. Mag., .500 A-Square, .500 Nitro Express, .600 Nitro Express. Other calibers on special order.. Checkered AAA-grade European walnut stock w/cheekpiece, rosewood forend tip and grip cap. Solid rubber recoil pad. Imported from Germany from 1989 to 1995.
Standard Express Magnum . . . . **NiB $5644 Ex $4490 Gd $3230**
.600 Nitro Express . . . . **NiB $5895 Ex $5133 Gd $3190**
Left-hand models, add **$750**

SR-20 BOLT-ACTION RIFLE
Calibers: .243 Win., .308 Win., .30-06. 7mm Rem. Mag., .300 Win. Mag., .375 H&H Mag.; five-round (standard) or three-round mag. Bbl.: 20. Inches (SR-20L), 24 inches (SR-20N) or 26 inches (SR-20G). Weight: 7.75 lbs. Adj. rear, blade front sights. Checkered French walnut Monte Carlo stock (N&G series) or full Mannlicher (L series). Imported from Germany. Disc. 1992.
SR-20L . . . . **NiB $2316 Ex $1832 Gd $1209**
SR-20N . . . . **NiB $2279 Ex $1856 Gd $1200**
SR-20G . . . . **NiB $2865 Ex $2379 Gd $1600**

SR-20 CLASSIC BOLT-ACTION RIFLES
Same as SR-20 except in .22-250 Rem. and .338 Win. Mag.; metric calibers on request. Bbl.: 24 inches (standard) or 25 inches (magnum). Checkered French walnut stock. Left-hand models were made. Imported from Germany since 1985; Sporter version from 1989 to 1993.
Classic (Standard) . . . . **NiB $1860 Ex $1875 Gd $1423**
Classic (Magnum) . . . . **NiB $2355 Ex $2216 Gd $1466**
**Classic Sporter (std.
w/22-inch bbl.)** . . . . **NiB $2556 Ex $2203 Gd $1499**
**Classic Sporter (magnum cal.
w/24-inch bbl.)** . . . . **NiB $1899 Ex $2288 Gd $1633**
Left-hand models, add **$350**

SR-20 ALPINE, SAFARI AND TROPHY SERIES
Same specs as Model SR-20 Classic Sporter except Alpine Series has 20-inch bbl., Mannlicher stock, standard calibers only; Safari Series w/24-inch bbl., three-leaf Express sights; magnum action in .375 H&H Mag., .404 Jeffrey, .425 Express, .458 Win. Mag.; Trophy

High Standard Sporting Firearms

High Standard
Hi-Power Deluxe

High Standard
Sport-King Autoloading Carbine

High Standard
Sport-King Deluxe Auto

High Standard
Sport-King Field Auto

High Standard
Sport-King Special Auto

Series w/Krupp Special tapered octagon bbl. w/quarter rib and open sights in standard and magnum calibers. Imported from Germany from 1989 to 1993.

Alpine Series . . . . NiB $1969 Ex $1812 Gd $1492
Safari Series . . . . NiB $2308 Ex $2177 Gd $1545
Trophy Series (standard calibers) . . . . . NiB $2589 Ex $2115 Gd $1904
Trophy Series
(magnum calibers) . . . . NiB $2733 Ex $2118 Gd $1944

HI-POINT FIREARMS — Dayton, Ohio

MODEL 995 CARBINE
Semi-automatic recoil-operated carbine. Calibers: 9mm Parabellum or .40 S&W; 10-round mag. Bbl.: 16.5 inches. Lft: 31.5 inches. Protected post front, aperture rear sights w/integral scope mount. Matte blue, chrome or Parkerized finish. Checkered polymer grip./ rame. Made from 1996 to date.

Model 995, 9mm
(blue or Parkerized) . . . . NiB $233 Ex $179 Gd $130
Model 995, .41 S&W
(blue or Parkerized) . . . . .NiB $248 Ex $211 Gd $146
W/laser sights, add $50
W/chrome finish, add $25

HIGH STANDARD SPORTING FIREARMS — East Hartford, Connecticut (formerly High Standard Mfg. Co., Hamden, Connecticut)

A long-standing producer of sporting arms, High Standard discontinued its operations in 1984.

SPORT-KING PUMP RIFLE . . . . NiB $207 Ex $144 Gd $98
Hammerless slide-action. Caliber: .22 LR. .22 Long, .22 Short. Tubular mag. holds 17 LR, 19 Long, or 24 Short. 24-inch bbl. Weight: 5.5 lbs. Sights: Partridge rear; bead front. Monte Carlo stock w/pistol grip, serrated semibeavertail forearm. Made from 1963 to 1976.

HI-POWER DELUXE RIFLE . . . NiB $455 Ex $315 Gd $221
Mauser-type bolt-action, sliding safety. Calibers: .270 Win., .30-06; four-round mag. Bbl.: 22 inches. Weight: 7 lbs. Folding open rear, ramp front sights. Walnut Monte Carlo stock w/checkered pistol grip and forearm; QD swivels. Made from 1962 to 1965.

HI-POWER FIELD BOLT-ACTION RIFLE. . . . . .NiB $255 Ex $179 Gd $126
Same as Hi-Power Deluxe except w/plain field style stock. Made from 1962 to 1966.

Howa
Model 1500 Hunter

Howa
Model 1500 Lightning

SPORT-KING AUTO-
LOADING CARBINE . . . . .NiB $379 Ex $318 Gd $200
Same as Sport-King Field Autoloader except w/18.25-inch bbl.,
Western-style straight-grip stock w/bbl. band, sling and swivels.
Made from 1964 to 1973.

SPORT-KING DELUXE AUTOLOADER . . . . . .NiB $280 Ex $213 Gd $100
Same as Sport-King Special Autoloader except w/checkered stock.
Made from 1966 to 1975.

SPORT-KING FIELD AUTOLOADER . . . . .NiB $229 Ex $130 Gd $90
Calibers: .22 LR, Long, Short; tubular mag. holds 15 LR, 17
Long, 21 Short. Bbl.: 22.25 inches. Weight: 5.5 lbs. Open rear,
beaded post front sights. Plain pistol-grip stock. Made from 1960
to 1966.

SPORT-KING SPECIAL AUTOLOADER . . . . . .NiB $210 Ex $166 Gd $106
Same as Sport-King Field except stock w/Monte Carlo comb and
semi-beavertail forearm. Made from 1960 to 1966.

HOWA RIFLES — Tokyo, Japan. Imported by Legacy Sports Int., Reno, Nevada

MODEL 1500 HUNTER
Similar to Trophy Model except w/standard walnut stock. Imported
from 1988 to 1989.
Standard calibers . . . . NiB $508 Ex $455 Gd $337
Magnum calibers . . . . NiB $520 Ex $466 Gd $350
Stainless steel, add $100

MODEL 1500 LIGHTNING BOLT-ACTION RIFLE
Similar to Hunter model except fitted w/black Bell & Carlson
Carbelite stock w/checkered grip and forend. Weight: 7.5 lbs.
Imported in 1988.
Standard calibers . . . . NiB $479 Ex $336 Gd $267
Magnum calibers . . . . NiB $477 Ex $410 Gd $312

MODEL 1500 PCS BOLT-ACTION RIFLE
Similar to Hunter model except in Police Country-Sniper configuration, chambered for .308 Win. only. Walnut or synthetic
stock w/checkered grip and forend. No sights, drilled and tapped
for scope mounts. Weight: 8.5 to 9.3 lbs. Imported from 1999
to 2000.
PCS Model
w/walnut stock . . . . NiB $433 Ex $334 Gd $249
PCS Model
w/synthetic stock . . . . NiB $479 Ex $388 Gd $307
Stainless steel, add $100

MODEL 1500 REALTREE
CAMO RIFLE . . . . NiB $546 Ex $489 Gd $330
Similar to Trophy model except fitted w/Camo Bell & Carlson
Carbelite stock w/checkered grip and forend. Weight: 8 lbs. Stock,
action and barrel finished in Realtree camo. Imported from 1993
to 1994.

MODEL 1500 TROPHY/VARMINT BOLT-ACTION RIFLE
Calibers: .22-250 Rem., .223 Rem., .243 Win., .270 Win., .308
Win., .30-06, 7mm Rem. Mag., .300 Win. Mag., .338 Win. Mag.
Bbl.: 22 inches (standard), 24 inches (magnum). Lgt.: 42.5 inches.
Weight: 7.5 lbs. Adj. rear, hooded ramp front sights. Checkered wal-
nut Monte Carlo stock. Varmint Model in .22-250 Rem., .223 Rem.
and .308 Win. w/24-inch heavy bbl., Weight: 9.5 lbs. Imported from
1988 to 1992 and 2001 to 2008.
Trophy Standard . . . . NiB $575 Ex $499 Gd $366
Trophy Magnum . . . . NiB $590 Ex $508 Gd $379
Varmint (Parkerized finish) . . . . NiB $602 Ex $488 Gd $377
Stainless steel, add $100

MODEL 1500 WOODGRAIN LIGHTNING RIFLE
Calibers: .243 Win., .270 Win., 7mm Rem. Mag., .30-06; five-
round mag. Bbl.: 22 inches, no sights; drilled and tapped for scope
mounts. Lgt.: 42 inches. Weight: 7.5 lbs. Checkered wood-grain
synthetic polymer stock. Imported from 1993 to 1994.

Husqvarna Vapenfabrik A.B.

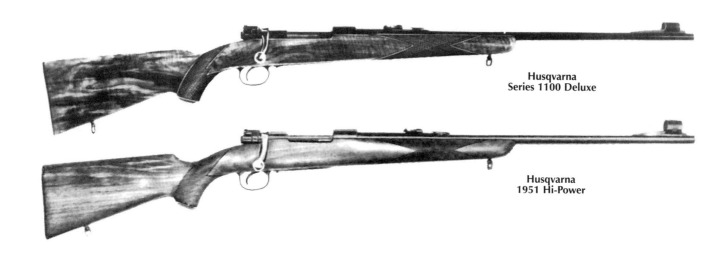

Husqvarna
Series 1100 Deluxe

Husqvarna
1951 Hi-Power

Standard calibers	NiB $488 Ex $419 Gd $374	
Magnum calibers	NiB $500 Ex $443 Gd $399	

H-S PRECISION — Rapid City, South Dakota

PRO-SERIES
Custom rifle built on Remington M700 bolt-action. Calibers: .22 LR to .416 Rigby. Bbl.: 24 or 26 inches w/fluted option. Kevlar/carbon fiber stock built to customer's specs. Aluminum bedding block system w/take-down, other custom options. Mde from 1990 to date.

Sporter model.	NiB $2180 Ex $1830 Gd $1100
Pro-Hunter model (PHR)	NiB $2866 Ex $2033 Gd $1108
Long-Range Model	NiB $4597 Ex $3766 Gd $2080
Long-Range	
takedown model.	NiB $2355 Ex $1944 Gd $1390
Marksman model	NiB $2966 Ex $1830 Gd $1106
Marksman takedown model	NiB $2977 Ex $2133 Gd $1490
Varmint takedown model (VTD).	NiB $4365 Ex $2835 Gd $2000
Left-hand models, add	$225

HUNGARIAN MILITARY RIFLES — Budapest, Hungary. Manufactured at government arsenal

MODEL 1935M MANNLICHER
MILITARY RIFLE . . . . NiB $366 Ex $287 Gd $186
Straight handle bolt-action. Caliber: 8x52mm Hungarian; five-round projecting box mag. Bbl.: 24 inches. Weight: 9 lbs. Adj. leaf rear, hooded front sights. Two-piece military–style stock. Made from 1935 to 1940.

MODEL 1943M (GERMAN GEW 98/40) MANNLICHER
MILITARY RIFLE . . . . NiB $388 Ex $322 Gd $200
Modification of Model 1935M during German Occupation. Caliber: 7.9mm Mauser. Turned-down bolt handle and Mauser M/98-type box mag., other minor differences. Made from 1940 to end of WWII

in Europe.

HUSQVARNA VAPENFABRIK A.B. — Husqvarna, Sweden

MODEL 456 LIGHTWEIGHT
FULL-STOCK SPORTER. . . . . NiB $713 Ex $466 Gd $339
Same as Series 4000/4100 except w/sporting style full stock w/slope-away cheekrest. Weight: 6.5 lbs. Made from 1959 to 1970.

SERIES 1000 SUPER GRADE. . . . . . NiB $566 Ex $479 Gd $339
Same as 1951 Hi-Power except w/European Monte Carlo sporter stock. Made from 1952 to 1956.

SERIES 1100 DELUXE MODEL HI-POWER
BOLT-ACTION SPORTING RIFLE . . . . NiB $557 Ex $468 Gd $339
Same as 1951 Hi-Power, except w/jeweled bolt, European walnut stock. Made from 1952 to 1956.

1950 HI-POWER SPORTING RIFLE . . . . . . NiB $554 Ex $415 Gd $300
Mauser-type bolt-action. Calibers: .220 Swift, .270 Win., .30-06; five-round box mag., Bbl.: 23.75 inches. Weight: 7.75 lbs. Open rear, hooded ramp front sights. Sporting stock of Arctic beech, checkered pistol grip and forearm, swivels. Husqvarna sporters were first intro. In U.S. about 1948. Earlier models were also available in calibers 6.5x55, 8x57. Made from 1946 to 1951.
1951 HI-POWER RIFLE. . . . . NiB $554 Ex $415 Gd $300
Same as 1950 Hi-Power except w/high-comb stock, low safety.

SERIES 3000
CROWN GRADE. . . . . NiB $643 Ex $455 Gd $300
Same as Series 3100, except w/Monte Carlo comb stock.

SERIES 3100
CROWN GRADE. . . . . NiB $643 Ex $455 Gd $300
HVA improved Mauser action. Calibers: .243 Win., .270 Win., .30-

Husqvarna 3000
Crown Grade

Husqvarna 4100
Lightweight

Husqvarna 6000
Imperial Custom

06, .308 Win.; five-round box mag. Bbl.: 23.75 inches. Weight: 7.75 lbs. Open rear, hooded ramp front sights. European walnut checkered stock, cheekpiece, pistol-grip cap; black forend tip, swivels. Made from 1954 to 1972.

SERIES 4000
LIGHTWEIGHT RIFLE.................NiB $699 Ex $433 Gd $297
Same as Series 4100 except w/Monte Carlo comb stock and no rear sight.

SERIES 4100
LIGHTWEIGHT RIFLE................NiB $616 Ex $423 Gd $260
HVA improved Mauser action. Calibers: . 243 Win., .270 Win., 7mm Rem. Mag., .30-06, .308 Win.; five-round box mag. Bbl.: 20.5 inches. Weight: 6.25 lbs. Open rear, hooded ramp front sights. Lightweight walnut stock w/checkered cheekpiece, pistol grip; Schnabel forend tip; swivels. Made from 1954 to 1972.

SERIES 6000
IMPERIAL CUSTOM GRADE .... NiB $877 Ex $633 Gd $409
Same as Series 3100 except w/fancy grade stock; Calibers: .243 Win., .270 Win., .308 Win., .30-06. Made from 1968 to 1970.; three-leaf folding rear sight, adj. trigger.

SERIES 7000 IMPERIAL
MONTE CARLO LIGHTWEIGHT .. NiB $920 Ex $577 Gd $400
Same as Series 4000 Lightweight except w/fancy grade stock; three-leaf folding rear sight, adj. trigger. Calibers: .243 Win., .270 Win., .308 Win., .30-06. Made from 1968 to 1970.

MODEL 8000
IMPERIAL GRADE RIFLE........ NiB $831 Ex $569 Gd $389
Same as Model 9000 except w/jeweled bolt, engraved floorplate, deluxe French walnut checkered stock, no sights. Made from 1971 to 1972.

MODEL 9000
CROWN GRADE RIFLE............... NiB $633 Ex $459 Gd $348
New design HVA bolt-action. Adj. trigger. Calibers: .270 Win., 7mm Rem. Mag., .30-06, .300 Win. Mag.; five-round box mag., hinged floorplate. Bbl.: 23.75 inches. Weight: 7 lbs., 3 oz. Folding leaf rear, hooded ramp front sights. Checkered Monte Carlo walnut stock, rosewood forend tip and pistol grip cap. Made from 1971 to 1972.

SERIES P-3000
PRESENTATION RIFLE .... NiB $1179 Ex $889 Gd $627
Same as Crown Grade Series 3000 except w/select stock, engraved action, adj. trigger. Calibers: .243 Win., .270 Win., 7mm Rem. Mag., .30-06. Made from 1968 to 1970.

Italian Military Rifles

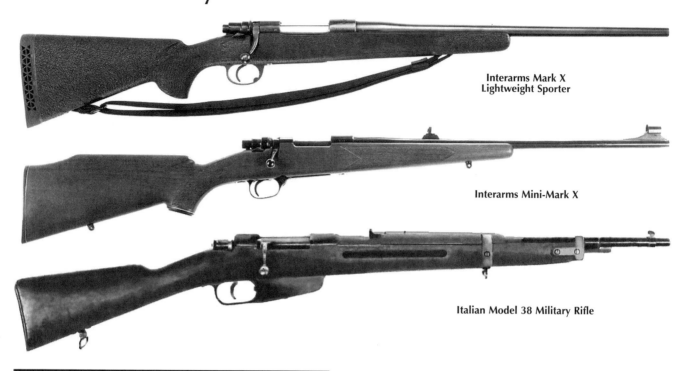

Interarms Mark X
Lightweight Sporter

Interarms Mini-Mark X

Italian Model 38 Military Rifle

INTERARMS RIFLES — Alexandria, Virginia

MARK X ALASKAN . . . . **NiB $708 Ex $447 Gd $321**
Same specs as Mark X Sporter, except chambered for .375 H&H Mag. and .458 Win. Mag. w/3-round magazine. Stock w/recoil-absorbing cross bolt and heavy duty recoil pad. Weighs 8.25 lbs. Made from 1976 to 1984.

MARK X BOLT-ACTION SPORTER SERIES
Mauser-type action. Calibers: .22-250 Rem., .243 Win., .25-06 Rem., .270 Win., 7x57, 7mm Rem. Mag., .308 Win., .30-06, .300 Win. Mag.; five-round mag. (three rounds in magnum calibers). Bbl.: 24 inches. Weight: 7.5 lbs. Adj. leaf rear, hooded ramp front sights. Classic-style European walnut Monte Carlo stock, checkered pistol grip and forearm, black forend tip. QD swivels. Made from 1972 to 1997.
Mark X Standard . . . . NiB $479 Ex $355 Gd $260
Mark X Camo (realtree) . . . . NiB $499 Ex $440 Gd $327
American Field, std. (rubber recoil pad). . . NiB $570 Ex $460 Gd $368
American Field, magnum
(rubber recoil pad) . . . . NiB $689 Ex $566 Gd $408

MARK X CAVALIER. . . . . **NiB $460 Ex $355 Gd $260**
Same specifications as Mark X Sporter except w/contemporary-style stock w/rollover cheekpiece, rosewood forend tip/grip cap, recoil pad. Introduced 1974. Disc.

MARK X CONTINENTAL
MANNLICHER STYLE CARBINE . . . . **NiB $643 Ex $412 Gd $277**
Same specs as Mark X Sporter except w/straight European-style comb stock w/sculptured cheekpiece, French checkering. Double-set triggers, "butterknife" bolt handle.

MARK X LIGHTWEIGHT SPORTER . . . . . . **NiB $445 Ex $355 Gd $260**
Calibers: .22-250 Rem., .270 Win., 7mm Rem. Mag., .30-06 or 7mm Mag. Four- or 5-round magazine. 20-inch bbl. Synthenic Carbolite stock Weight: 7 lbs. Imported from 1988 to 1990. Rintroduced from 1994 to 1997.

MARK X MARQUIS
MANNLICHER-STYLE CARBINE . . . . **NiB $575 Ex $408 Gd $290**
Same specs as Mark X Sporter except w/20-inch bbl., full-length Mannlicher-type stock, metal forend/muzzle cap. Calibers: .270 Win., 7x57, .308 Win., .30-06. Imported from 1976 to 1984.

MINI-MARK X BOLT-ACTION RIFLE . . . . . **NiB $448 Ex $359 Gd $260**
Miniature M-98 Mauser action. Calibers: .243 Win., .223 Rem.; five-round mag. Bbl. 20 inches. Length: 39.75 inches. Weight: 6.25 lbs. Adj. rear, hooded ramp front sights. Checkered hardwood stock. Imported from 1987 to 1994.

MARK X VISCOUNT. . . . . **NiB $440 Ex $368 Gd $258**
Same specifications as Mark X Sporter except w/plain field-grade stock. Imported from 1974 to 1987.

AFRICAN SERIES. . . . . **NiB $1035 Ex $603 Gd $422**
Masuer-type bolt-action. Calibers: .375 H&H Mag., .458 Win. Mag.; three-round mag. Bbl.: 24 inches. Weight: 8 lbs. Three-leaf Express rear, hooded ramp front sights. English-style European walnut stock w/cheekpiece, black forend tip, checkered pistol grip and forearm; recoil pad. QD swivels. Imported from 1974 to 1996 by Whitworth Rifle Co., England.

ITALIAN MILITARY RIFLES — Manufactured by government plants at Brescia, Gardone, Terni, and Turin, Italy

MODEL 38 MILITARY RIFLE. . . . . . . **NiB $165 Ex $120 Gd $85**
Modified Italian Model 1891 Mannlicher-Carcano Military Rifle w/turned-down bolt handle, detachable folding bayonet. Caliber: 7.35mm Italian Service. (Many versions of this model were lated converted to the old 6.5mm caliber.) Six-round box mag. Bbl.: 21.25 inches. Weight: 7.5 lbs. Adj. rear, blade front sights. Military straight-grip stock. Adopted in 1938.

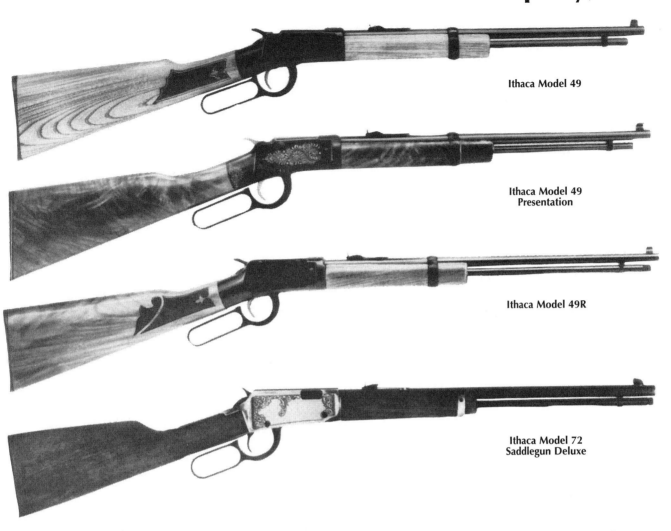

Ithaca Model 49

Ithaca Model 49
Presentation

Ithaca Model 49R

Ithaca Model 72
Saddlegun Deluxe

ITHACA GUN COMPANY, INC. — King Ferry, New York (formerly Ithaca, New York)

MODEL 49 SADDLEGUN LEVER-ACTION
SINGLE-SHOT RIFLE. . . . . **NiB $166 Ex $135 Gd $96**
Martini-type action, rebounding hammer. Caliber: .22 LR, Short. Bbl.: 18 inches. Open sights. Western carbine-style stock. Weight: 5.5 lbs. Made from 1961 to 1978.

MODEL 49 SADDLEGUN — DELUXE . . . . **NiB $220 Ex $167 Gd $121**
Same as standard Model 49 except w/gold-plated hammer and trigger, figured walnut stock, sling swivels. Made from 1962 to 1975.

MODEL 49 SADDLEGUN — MAGNUM . . **NiB $205 Ex $188 Gd $130**
Same as standard Model 49 except chambered for .22 WMR. Made from 1962 to 1978.

MODEL 49 SADDLEGUN —
PRESENTATION . . . . **NiB $333 Ex $239 Gd $166**
Same as standard Model 49 Saddlegun except w/gold-plated hammer and trigger, engraved receiver, full fancy-figured walnut stock w/gold nameplate. Available in .22 LR or .22 WMR. Made from 1962 to 1974.

MODEL 49 SADDLEGUN —
ST. LOUIS BICENTENNIAL. . . . . . . **NiB $366 Ex $330 Gd $169**
Same as Model 49 Deluxe except w/commemorative inscription. 200 made in 1964.

MODEL 49R SADDLEGUN
REPEATING RIFLE. . . . . **NiB $298 Ex $243 Gd $154**
Similar to Model 49 Single-shot. Caliber: .22 LR, Long, Short. Tubular mag. holds 15 LR, 17 Long, 21 Short. Bbl.: 20 inches. Weight: 5.5 lbs. Open rear, bead front sights. Western-style stock w/ checkered grip. Made from 1968 to 1971.

MODEL 49 YOUTH
SADDLEGUN . . . . **NiB $177 Ex $138 Gd $105**
Same as Model 49 except shorter stock for young shooters. Made from 1961 to 1978.

REPEATING CARBINE. . . . . **NiB $379 Ex $300 Gd $208**
Caliber: .22 LR, Long, Short.; tubular mag. holds 15 LR, 17 Long, 21 Short. Bbl.: 18.5 inches. Weight: 5.5 lbs. Open rear, hooded ramp front sights. Grooved for scope mount. Western-style American walnut carbine stock and forearm. Made from 1973 to 1978.

Ithaca Gun Company, Inc.

Ithaca
Model LSA-65 Standard

Ithaca
Model X5-T

Ithaca
Model X-15

Ithaca
BSA CF-2

MODEL 72 SADDLEGUN —
DELUXE . . . . NiB $443 Ex $366 Gd $250
Same as standard Model 72 except w/silver-finished and engraved receiver, octagon bbl., higher grade walnut stock and forearm. Made from 1974 to 1976.

MODEL LSA-55 STANDARD
BOLT-ACTION RIFLE . . . . .NiB $525 Ex $400 Gd $295
Mauser-type action. Calibers: .222 Rem., .22-250 Rem., 6mm Rem., .243 Win., .308 Win.; three-round mag. Bbl.: 22 inches. Leaf sight. Checkered Monte Carlo stock. Mfg. in Finland by Tikka from 1969 to 1977.

MODEL LSA-65 BOLT-ACTION
STANDARD GRADE . . . . NiB $479 Ex $443 Gd $337
Same as Model LSA-55 Standard Grade except in .25-06 Rem., .270 Win. .30-06; four-round mag. Bbl.: 23 inches. Weight: 7 lbs. Made from 1969 to 1977.

MODEL LSA-65 DELUXE . . . . NiB $590 Ex $531 Gd $355
Same as Model LSA-65 Standard Grade except w/special features of Model LSA-55 Deluxe. Made from 1969 to 1977.

MODEL X5-C LIGHTNING
AUTOLOADER . . . . NiB $222 Ex $177 Gd $123
Takedown. Caliber: .22 LR. Seven round clip magazine. 22-inch bbl. Weight: 6 lbs. Sights: Open rear; Ray-bar front. Pistol-grip stock, grooved forearm. Made from 1958 to 1964.

MODEL X5-T LIGHTNING AUTOLOADER TUBULAR
REPEATING RIFLE. . . . . NiB $222 Ex $177 Gd $123
Same as Model X5-C except w/16-round tubular magazine, stock w/plain forearm.

MODEL X-15 LIGHTNING AUTOLOADER. . . .NiB $222 Ex $177 Gd $123
Same specifications as Model X5-C except forend is not grooved. Made from 1964 to 1967.

BSA CF-2 BOLT-ACTION
REPEATING RIFLE. . . . . NiB $510 Ex $366 Gd $277
Mauser-type action. Calibers: 7mm Rem. Mag., .300 Win. Mag., three-round mag. Bbl.: 32.6 inches. Weight: 8 lbs. Adj. rear, hooded ramp front sights. Checkered walnut Monte Carlo stock, rollover cheekpiece; rosewood forend tip. Recoil pad, sling swivels. Imported from 1976 to 1977. Mfd. By BSA Guns Lt., Birmingham, England.

Johnson Model 1941

Johnson Sporting Rifle

Iver Johnson Model M-1

JAPANESE MILITARY RIFLES — Tokyo, Japan. Manufactured by Government Plant

MODEL 38 ARISAKA SERVICE RIFLE . . . . . **NiB $656 Ex $390 Gd $220**
Mauser-type bolt-action. Caliber: 6.5mm Japanese; five-round box mag., Bbl.: 25.38 and 31.25 inches. Weight: 9.25 lbs. w/long bbl. Fixed front, adj. rear sights. Military-type full stock. Adopted in 1905, 38th year of the Meiji reign, hence the designation "Model 38."

MODEL 38 ARISAKA CARBINE . . . **NiB $656 Ex $390 Gd $220**
Same specifications as Model 38 Rifle except w/19-inch bbl., heavy folding bayonet, weight 7.25 lbs.

MODEL 44 CAVALRY CARBINE . . **NiB $1190 Ex $690 Gd $355**
Same specifications as Model 38 Rifle except w/19-inch bbl., heavy folding bayonet, weight 8.5 lbs. Adopted in 1911, the 44th year of the Meiji reign, hence the designation, "Model 44."

MODEL 99 SERVICE RIFLE . . . . . . **NiB $577 Ex $255 Gd $200**
Modified Model 38. Caliber: 7.7mm Japanese; five-round magazine. Bbl.: 25.75 inches. Weight: 8.75 lbs. Fixed front, adj. aperture rear sights. Anti-aircraft sighting bars on some early models. Fixed rear sight on some late-WWII rifles. Military-type full stock, may have bipod. Takedown paratrooper model was also made during WWII. Adopted in 1939 (Japanese year 2599, from which Model 99 designation is derived). Note. The last Model 99 rifles made were of poor quality, some with cast steel receivers. Many are not safe to shoot. Values shown are for earlier models.

JARRETT CUSTOM RIFLES — Jackson, South Carolina

MODEL NO. 2 WALKABOUT
BOLT-ACTION RIFLE . . . . **NiB $4788 Ex $3077 Gd $2043**
Custom lightweight rifle built on Rem. M700 action. Jarrett match-grade bbl., cut and chambered to customer's specs. Short-action calibers only. Pillar-bedded McMillan fiberglass stock. Made from 1995 to 2003.

MODEL NO. 3 CUSTOM
BOLT-ACTION RIFLE . . . . **NiB $4800 Ex $3147 Gd $2090**
Cutstom rifle built on Rem. M700 action. Jarrett match-grade bbl., cut and chambered to customer's specs. Pillar-bedded McMillan classic fiberglass stock finished to customer's preference. Made from 1989 to date.

MODEL NO. 4 PROFESSIONAL
HUNTER BOLT-ACTION RIFLE . . . . . . **NiB $6988 Ex $5876 Gd $4490**
Custom magnum rifle built on Win. M70 "controlled-feed" action. Jarrett m atch-grade bbl. cut and chambered to customer's specs in magnum calibers. Quarter rib w/iron sights, two Leupold scopes w/ QD rings and mounts. McMillan classic fiberglass stock fitted and finished to customer's specs.

JOHNSON AUTOMATICS, INC. — Providence, Rhode Island

MODEL 1941 SEMIAUTO
MILITARY RIFLE . . . . **NiB $7433 Ex $5740 Gd $3328**
Short-recoil operated. Removable, air-cooled, 22-inch bbl. Caliber: .30-06, 7mm Mauser. 10-round rotary magazine. Two-piece wood stock, pistol grip, perforated metal radiator sleeve over rear half of bbl. Sights: Receiver peep; protected post front. Weight: 9.5 lbs. Note: The Johnson M/1941 was adopted by the Netherlands government in 1940-41 and the major portion of the production of this rifle, 1941-43, was on Dutch orders. A quantity was also bought by the U.S. government for use by Marine Corps parachute troops (1943) and for Lend Lease. All these rifles were caliber .30-06; the 7mm Johnson rifles were made for the South American government.

IVER JOHNSON ARMS, INC. — Jacksonville, Arkansas (formerly of Fitchburg, Massachusetts, and Middlesex, New Jersey)

LI'L CHAMP BOLT-ACTION RIFLE . . . . **NiB $225 Ex $146 Gd $90**
Caliber: .22 S. L. LR. Single-shot. 16.25-inch bbl. 32.5 inches overall. Weight: 3.25 lbs. Adj. rear sight, blade front. Synthetic composition stock. Made from 1986 to 1988.

K.D.F. Inc.

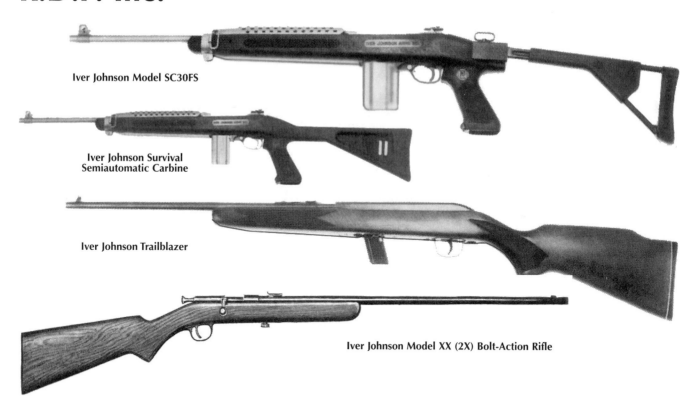

Iver Johnson Model SC30FS

Iver Johnson Survival Semiautomatic Carbine

Iver Johnson Trailblazer

Iver Johnson Model XX (2X) Bolt-Action Rifle

MODEL M-1 SEMIAUTOMATIC CARBINE
Similar to U.S. M-1 Carbine. Calibers: 9mm Parabellum 30 U.S. Carbine. 15- or 30-round magazine. 18-inch bbl. 35.5 inches overall. Weight: 6.5 lbs. Sights: blade front, w/guards; adj. peep rear. Walnut, hardwood or collapsible wire stock. Parkerized finish.

(30 cal. w/hardwood)	NiB $390	Ex $298	Gd $200
(30 cal. w/walnut)	NiB $433	Ex $324	Gd $220
(30 cal. w/wire)	NiB $469	Ex $388	Gd $222
(9mm w/hardwood)	NiB $300	Ex $288	Gd $244
(9mm w/walnut)	NiB $354	Ex $299	Gd $240
(9mm w/wire)	NiB $393	Ex $331	Gd $217

MODEL PM.30
SEMIAUTOMATIC CARBINE. . . . . . NiB $413 Ex $320 Gd $190
Similar to U.S. Carbine, Cal. .30 M-1. Bbl.: 18 inches. Weight: 5.5 lbs. 15- or 30-round detachable mag. Hardwood and walnut stock.

MODEL SC30FS
SEMIAUTOMATIC CARBINE. . . . . . NiB $466 Ex $390 Gd $233
Similar to Survival Carbine except w/folding stock. Made from 1983 to 1989.

SURVIVAL SEMIAUTOMATIC CARBINE. . .NiB $277 Ex &399 Gd $230
Similar to Model PM.30 except in stainless steel. Made from 1983 to 1989.

TRAILBLAZER SEMIAUTO RIFLE . . NiB $277 Ex $160 Gd $125
Caliber: .22 LR. 18-inch bbl. Weight: 5.5 lbs. Sights: Open rear, blade front. Hardwood stock. Made from 1983 to 1985

MODEL X BOLT-ACTION RIFLE . . . NiB $270 Ex $189 Gd $115
Takedown, Single-shot. Caliber: .22 Short, Long and LR. 22-inch bbl. Weight: 4 lbs. Sights: Open rear; blade front. Pistol-grip stock w/knob forend tip. Made from 1928 to 1932.

MODEL XX (2X) BOLT-ACTION RIFLE . . . . NiB $323 Ex $170 Gd $100
Improved version of Model X w/heavy 24-inch bbl.; larger stock (w/forend knob tip). Weight: 4.5 lbs. Made from 1932 to 1955.

K.B.I., INC. — Harrisburg, Pennsylvania

SUPER CLASSIC
Calibers: .22 LR, .22 WMR. .22 Hornet; five- or 10-round capacity. Bolt-action and semi-automatic. Bbl.: 22.6 or 20.75 inches. Lgt.: 41.25 inches. Weight: 6.4 to 6.7 lbs. Blue finish. Oil-finished American walnut Monte Carlo stock w/hardwood grip cap and forend tip. High-polish blued barreled action w/Damascened bolt. Dovetailed receiver and iron sights. Recoil pad, QD swivel posts.

M-1500 SC, .22 LR	NiB $477	Ex $223	Gd $170
M-1500SC, .22 WMR	NiB $289	Ex $233	Gd $177
M-1800-S, .22 Hornet	NiB $455	Ex $377	Gd $256
M-2000 SC, semiauto, .22 LR	NiB $290	Ex $244	Gd $179

K.D.F. INC. — Sequin, Texas

MODEL K15 BOLT-ACTION RIFLE
Calibers (Standard): .22-250 Rem., .243 Win., 6mm Rem., .25-06 Rem., .270 Win., .280 rem., 7mm Rem. Mag., .30-06; (Magnum) .300 Wby. Mag., .300 Win Mag., .338 Win. Mag., .340 Wby. Mag., .375 H&H Mag., .411 KDF Mag., .416 Rem. Mag., .458 Win. Mag.; four-round mag. (standard), three-round in mag. calibers. Bbl.: 22 inches (standard) or 24 inches (magnum). Lgtl.: 44.5 to 46.5 inches. Weight: 8 lbs. Sights optional. Kevlar composite or checkered walnut stock in classic, European or thumbhole style. U.S. manufacture limited to 25 prototypes and pre-production variations.
Standard model. . . . . NiB $1796 Ex $1721 Gd $977
Magnum model. . . . . NiB $1834 Ex $1597 Gd $1106

KDF Model K15
Bolt-Action Rifle

Kel-Tec
Sub-Series Semiautomatic Rifles

KEL-TEC CNC INDUSTRIES, INC. — Cocoa, Florida

SUB-SERIES SEMIAUTOMATIC RIFLES

Semi-automatic blow-back action w/pivoting bbl.; takedown. Caliber: 9mm Parabellum, .40 S&W. Bbl.: 16 inches. Lgt: 31.5 inches. Weight: 4 lbs. Interchangeable grip assembly accepts most double column, high-capacity handgun mag. Hooded post front, flip-up rear sights. Matte black finish. Tubular buttstock w/grooved polymer buttplate and vented handguard. Made from 1997 to 2000.

Sub-9 model (9mm) . . . . NiB $395 Ex $333 Gd $265
Sub-40 model (.40 S&W) . . . . NiB $395 Ex $333 Gd $265

KIMBER RIFLES — Manufactured by Kimber Manufacturing, Inc., Yonkers, New York (formerly Kimber of America, Inc.; Kimber of Oregon, Inc.)

Note: From 1980–91, Kimber of Oregon produced Kimber firearms. A redesigned action designated by serialization with a "B" suffix was introduced 1986. Pre-1986 production is recognized as the "A" series but is not so marked. These early models in rare configurations and limited-run calibers command premium prices from collectors. Kimber of America, in Clackamas, Oregon, acquired the Kimber trademark and resumed manufactured of Kimber rifles. During this transition, Nationwide Sports Distributors, Inc. in Pennsylvania and Nevada became exclusive distributors of Kimber products. In 1997, Kimber Manufacturing acquired the trademark with manufacturing rights and expanded production to include a 1911-A1-style semiautomatic pistol, the Kimber Classic 45.

Rifle production resumed in late 1998 with the announcement of an all-new Kimber .22 rifle and a refined Model 84 in both single-shot and repeater configurations.

MODEL 82 BOLT-ACTION RIFLE

Short-action based on Kimber's "A" Model 82 rimfire receiver w/twin rear locking lugs. Caliber: .22 LR, .22 WRF, .22 Hornet. .218 Bee, .25-20; five- or 10-round mag. (.22 LR); five-round mag. (.22 WRF); three-round mag., (.22 Hornet). .218 Bee and .25-20 are single-shot. Bbl.: 37.63 to 42.5 inches. Weight: 6 lbs. (Light Sporter), 6.5 lbs. (Sporter), 7.5 lbs. (Varmint) or 10.75 lbs. (target). Right- and left-handed actions available, various stock styles.

Cascade (disc. 1987) . . . . NiB $815 Ex $574 Gd $388
Classic (disc. 1988) . . . . NiB $815 Ex $574 Gd $388
Continental . . . . NiB $1477 Ex $1197 Gd $823
Custom Classic (disc. 1988) . . . . . NiB $1031 Ex $833 Gd $579
Mini Classic . . . . NiB $679 Ex $555 Gd $389
Super America . . . . NiB $1307 Ex $1165 Gd $900
Super Continental . . . . NiB $1254 Ex $1390 Gd $925
1990 Classification
All-American Match . . . . NiB $1978 Ex $1165 Gd $789
Deluxe Grade
(disc. 1990) . . . . NiB $1388 Ex $1097 Gd $898
Hunter
(w/laminated stock) . . . . NiB $912 Ex $833 Gd $523
Super America Target
(Government Match) . . . . NiB $954 Ex $876 Gd $690

MODEL 82C CLASSIC BOLT-ACTION RIFLE

Caliber: .22 LR. Four- or 10-round magazine. 21-inch air-gauged bbl. 40.5 inches overall. Weight: 6.5 lbs. Receiver drilled and tapped for Warne scope mounts; no sights. Single-set trigger. Checkered Claro walnut stock w/red buttpad and polished steel grip cap. Reintroduced in 1993.

Classic model . . . . NiB $833 Ex $688 Gd $495
Left-hand model, add $100

Kimber Rifles

Kimber Model 82 Rimfire Classic

Kimber Model 82C Rimfire Classic

Kimber Model 84 Classic

Kimber Model 89 Big Game 375 Caliber

Kimber Model 89 Big Game 375 H&H Caliber

MODEL 84 BOLT-ACTION RIFLE

Same specs as Model 82. Classic Compact medium-action based on a scaled-down Mauser-type receiver. Designed to accept small-base centerfire cartridges. Calibers: .17 Rem., .221 Fireball, .222 Rem., .223 Rem.; five-round mag. Disc. 1988.

Classic (disc. 1988) . . . . NiB $944 Ex $821 Gd $577
Continental . . . . NiB $1337 Ex $1098 Gd $769
Custom Classic (disc. 1988) . . . . NiB $1210 Ex $978 Gd $713
Super America (disc. 1988) . . . . NiB $1925 Ex $1078 Gd $757
Super Continental I (disc. 1988) . . . . . . NiB $1433 Ex $1170 Gd $844
1990 Classifications
Deluxe Grade (disc. 1990) . . . . NiB $1310 Ex $1044 Gd $733
Hunter/Sporter (w/laminated stock) . . . . . NiB $1144 Ex $943 Gd $665
Super America (disc. 1991) . . . . NiB $1988 Ex $1146 Gd $825
Super Varmint (disc. 1991) . . . . NiB $1137 Ex $1187 Gd $825
Ultra Varmint (disc. 1991) . . . . NiB $1189 Ex $1123 Gd $779

MODEL 89 BIG-GAME RIFLE

Long-action based on pre-64 Win. Model 70 and Mauser 98 actions. Three action lengths offered in sthree stock styles. Calibers: .257 Roberts, .25-06, 7x57, .270 Win., .280 Win., .30-06, 7mm Rem. Mag., .300 Win. Mag., .300 H&H Mag., .338 Win. Mag., .35 Whelen, .375 H&H Mag., .404 Jeffrey, .416 Rigby, .460 Wby. Mag., .505 Gibbs and others; five-round mag. (standard calibers) or three-round mag. in mag. calibers. Bbl.: 22 to 24 inches. Lgt.: 42 to 44 inches. Weight: 7.5 to 10.5 lbs. Model 89 African features Express sights on contoured quarter-rib bbl., front sight on band. Bbl.-mounted recoil lug w/integral receiver lug w/two recoil crosspins in stock.

BGR Long Action
Classic (disc. 1988) . . . . NiB $935 Ex $844 Gd $588
Custom Classic (disc. 1988) . . . . NiB $1288 Ex $1044 Gd $745
Super America . . . . NiB $1548 Ex $1270 Gd $908
1990 Classifications
Deluxe Grade Featherweight . . . . NiB $1995 Ex $1490 Gd $1044
Medium . . . . NiB $1866 Ex $1566 Gd $1135
.375 H&H . . . . NiB $1956 Ex $1577 Gd $1145
Hunter Grade (laminated stock)
.270 and .30-06 . . . . NiB $1366 Ex $1105 Gd $800
.375 H&H . . . . NiB $1656 Ex $1356 Gd $944
Super America Featherweight . . . . NiB $2088 Ex $1703 Gd $1213
Medium . . . . NiB $2189 Ex $1760 Gd $1217
.375 H&H . . . . NiB $2788 Ex $2254 Gd $1590
African — all calibers . . . . NiB $5635 Ex $3955 Gd $2766

Knight's Manufacturing Company

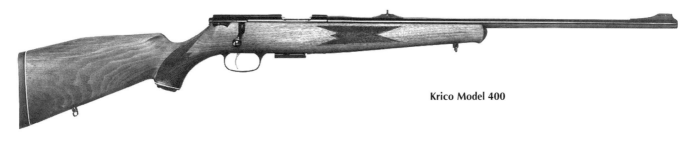

Krico Model 400

KNIGHT'S MANUFACTURING COMPANY — Vero Beach, Florida

SR-15 SEMIAUTOMATIC
MATCH RIFLE . . . . **NiB $1733 Ex $1544 Gd $1103**
AR-15-type. Caliber: .223 Rem. (5.56mm); five- or 10-round mag. Bbl.: 20 inches, free-floating match grade. Two-stage target trigger. Lgt.: 38 inches. Weight: 7.9 lbs. Integral Weaver rail. Matte black oxide finish. Black synthetic stock and forearm. Made from 1997 to 2008.

SR-15 M-4 SEMIAUTOMATIC
CARBINE . . . . **NiB $1520 Ex $1388 Gd $1066**
Similar to SR-15 rifle except w/16-inch bbl. Sights and mounts optional. Fixed synthetic or collapsible buttstock. Made from 1997 to 2008.

SR-15 M-5
SEMIAUTOMATIC RIFLE . . . . . **NiB $1765 Ex $1488 Gd $1165**
Caliber: .223 Rem. (5.56mm). Five- or 10-round magazine. 20-inch bbl. 38 inches overall. Weight: 7.6 lbs. Integral Weaver-style rail. Two-stage target trigger. Matte black oxide finish. Black synthetic stock and forearm. Made from 1997 to 2008.

SR-25 MATCH RIFLE
Similar to SR-25 Sporter except w/free floating 20- or 24-inch match bbl. 39.5-43.5 inches overall. Weight: 9.25 and 10.75 lbs., respectively. Integral Weaver-style rail. Sights and mounts optional. Made from 1993 to 2008.
Model SR-25 LW Match (w/20-inch bbl.) . . . . **NiB $5744 Ex $3289 Gd $2665**
W/RAS (Rail Adapter System), add. $350

SR-25 SEMIAUTOMATIC CARBINE
Similar to SR-25 Sporter except w/free floating 16-inch bbl. 35.75 inches overall. Weight: 7.75 lbs. Integral Weaver-style rail. Sights and mounts optional. Made from 1995 to 2008.
Model SR-25 Carbine (w/o sights) . . . . **NiB $6000 Ex $3927 Gd $1949**
W/RAS (Rail Adapter System), add. $300

SR-25 SEMIAUTOMATIC
SPORTER RIFLE . . . . **NiB $2754 Ex $2409 Gd $1709**
AR-15 style. Caliber: .308 Win. (7.62 NATO); five-10- or 20-round mag. Bbl.: 20 inches. Lgt.: 39.5 inches. Weight: 8.75 lbs. Integral Weavery-style rail. Adj. protected post front, detachable adj. rear sight. Two-stage target trigger. Matte black oxide finish. Black synthetic stock and forearm. Made from 1993 to 1997.

SR-50 SEMIAUTOMATIC LONG
RANGE PRECISION RIFLE . . . . **NiB $6833 Ex $6096 Gd $3597**
Gas-operated semi-automatic. Caliber: .50 BMG; 10-round mag. Bbl.: 35.5 inches, Lgt.: 58.5 inches. Weight: 31.75 lbs. Integral Weaver-style stock. Limited production from 1996 to 2008.

KONGSBERG RIFLES — Kongsberg, Norway. Imported by Kongsberg America L.L.C., Fairfield, CT

MODEL 393 CLASSIC SPORTER
Calibers: .22-250 Rem., .243 Win., .270 Win., 7mm Rem. Mag. .30-06, .308 Win., .300 Win. Mag., .338 Win. Mag.; three- or four-round mag. Bbl.: 23 inches (Standard) or 26 inches (Magnum) Weight: 7.5 lbs. to 8 lbs. Lgt.: 44 to 47 inches. No sights. Dovetailed receiver or optional hooded front, adj. rear sights. Blue finish. Checkered European walnut stock w/rubber buttplate. Imported from 1994 to 1998.
Standard calibers . . . . **NiB $957 Ex $779 Gd $597**
Magnum calibers . . . . **NiB $1289 Ex $1100 Gd $800**
Left-hand model, add $150
W/optional sights, add $75

MODEL 393 DELUXE SPORTER
Similar to Classic model except w/deluxe European walnut stock. Imported from 1994 to 1998.
Standard calibers . . . . **NiB $1017 Ex $900 Gd $599**
Magnum calibers . . . . **NiB $1344 Ex $1117 Gd $809**
Left-hand model, add $150
W/optional sights, add $75

MODEL 393 THUMBHOLE SPORTER
Calibers: 22-250 Rem. or 308 Win. Four-round rotary magazine. 23-inch heavy bbl. Weight: 8.5 lbs. 44 inches overall. No sights, dovetailed receiver. Blue finish. Stippled American walnut thumbhole stock w/adjustable cheekpiece. Imported from 1993 to 1998.
Right-hand model . . . . **NiB $1453 Ex $1344 Gd $644**
Left-hand model . . . . **NiB $1533 Ex $1377 Gd $800**

KRICO RIFLES — Stuttgart-Hedelfingen, Germany. Manufactured by Sportwaffenfabrik, Kriegeskorte GmbH. Imported by Northeast Arms, LLC, Ft. Fairfield, Maine (previously by Beeman Precision Arms, Inc and Mandell Shooting Supplies)

MODEL 260
SEMIAUTOMATIC RIFLE . . . . **NiB $744 Ex $656 Gd $459**
Caliber: .22 LR. 10-round magazine. 20-inch bbl. 38.9 inches overall. Weight: 6.6 lbs. Hooded blade front sight; adj. rear. Grooved receiver. Beech stock. Blued finish. Introduced 1989. Disc.

MODEL 300 BOLT-ACTION RIFLE
Calibers: .22 LR. .22 WMR, .22 Hornet. 19.6-inch bbl. (22 LR), 23.6-inch (22 Hornet). 38.5 inches overall. Weight: 6.3 lbs. Double-set triggers. Sights: Ramped blade front, adj. open

Krico Rifles

Krico Model 420

Krico 640 Varmint

rear. Checkered walnut-finished hardwood stock. Blued finish. Introduced 1989. Disc.

Model 300 Standard . . . . NiB $735 Ex $568 Gd $445
Model 300 Deluxe . . . . NiB $779 Ex $589 Gd $455
Model 300 SA
(Monte Carlo walnut stock) . . . . NiB $897 Ex $744 Gd $553
Model 300 Stutzen
(full-length walnut stock) . . . . NiB $1023 Ex $864 Gd $654

MODEL 311 SMALL-BORE RIFLE
Bolt action. Caliber: .22 LR. Five or 10-round clip magazine. 22-inch bbl. Weight: 6 lbs. Single- or double-set trigger. Sights: Open rear; hooded ramp front; available w/factory-fitted Kaps 2.5x scope. Checkered stock w/cheekpiece, pistol-grip and swivels. Disc. 1962.
W/scope sight . . . . NiB $376 Ex $344 Gd $233
W/iron sights only . . . . NiB $355 Ex $330 Gd $270

MODEL 320 BOLT-ACTION
SPORTER. . . . . NiB $920 Ex $622 Gd $423
Caliber: .22 LR; five-round detachable box mag. Bbl. 19.5 inches. Lgth.: 38.5 inches. Weight: 6 lbs. Single- or double-set triggers. Adj. rear, blade ramb sights. Checkered European walnut Mannlicher-style stock w/low comb and cheekpiece. Imported from 1986 to 1988.

MODEL 340 METALLIC SILHOUETTE
BOLT-ACTION RIFLE . . . . NiB $788 Ex $658 Gd $466
Caliber: .22 LR; five-round mag. 21-inch heavy bull bbl. Match or double-set triggers. Lgth.: 39.5 inches. Weight: 7.5 lbs. No sights. Grooved receiver. European walnut stock in off-hand, match-style configuration. Imported from 1983 to 1988. Disc.

MODEL 360S BIATHLON
RIFLE . . . . NiB $1455 Ex $1188 Gd $687
Straight-pull action. Caliber: .22 LR; Furnished with 5 five-round mags. Bbl.: 21.25 inches w/snow cap. Match trigger w/17 oz. pull. Weight: 9.25 lbs. Biathlon-style walnut stock w/black epoxy finish. Imported from 1991. Disc.

MODEL 360 S2 BIATHLON
RIFLE. . . . . NiB $1423 Ex $1189 Gd $655
Similar to Model 360S except w/pistol grip-activated action. Biathlon-style walnut stock w/black epoxy finish. Imported from 1991. Disc.

MODEL 400 BOLT-ACTION
RIFLE. . . . . NiB $889 Ex $766 Gd $544
Caliber: .22 Hornet; five-round detachable box mag. Bbl.: 32.5 inches. Weight: 6.75 lbs. Adj. open rear, ramp front sights. European walnut stock. Disc. 1990.

MODEL 420 BOLT-ACTION
RIFLE. . . . . NiB $1033 Ex $833 Gd $568
Same as Model 400 except w/full-length Mannlicher-style stock and double-set triggers. Scope optional. Disc. 1989.

MODEL 440 S BOLT-ACTION
RIFLE. . . . . NiB $889 Ex $745 Gd $540
Caliber: .22 Hornet. Detachable box magazine. 20-inch bbl. 36.5 inches overall. Weight: 7.5 lbs. No sights. French walnut stock w/ventilated forend. Disc. 1988.

MODEL 500 MATCH
RIFLE. . . . . NiB $3633 Ex $2988 Gd $1066
Single-shot. Caliber: .22 LR. Bbl.: 23.6 inches. Weight: 9.4 lbs. Kricotronic electronic ignition system. Globe front, match micrometer aperture rear sights. Match-style European walnut stock w/adj. buttplate.

MODEL 600 BOLT-ACTION
RIFLE. . . . . NiB $1177 Ex $1055 Gd $733
Same specs as Model 700 except short-action. Calibers: .17 Rem., .222 Rem., .223 Rem., .22-250 Rem., .243 Win., 5.6x50 Mag., .308 Win. Introduced 1983. Disc.

MODEL 620 BOLT-ACTION
RIFLE. . . . . NiB $1206 Ex $1119 Gd $726
Same as Model 600 except w/short action in .308 only. Full-length Mannlicher-style stock w/Schnabel forend tip. Bbl.: 20.75 inches. Weight: 6.5 lbs. Disc.

MODEL 640 SUPER SNIPER BOLT-ACTION
REPEATING RIFLE . . . . NiB $1863 Ex $1277 Gd $905
Caliber: .223 Rem., .308 Win.; three-round mag. Bbl.: 26 inches. Lgth.: 44.25 inches. Weight: 9.5 lbs. No sights. Drilled and tapped for scope mounts. Single- or double-set triggers. Select walnut stock w/adj. cheekpiece and recoil pad. Disc. 1989.

Lakefield Model 64B

Lakefield Model 92S Target

Lakefield Mark I

MODEL 640 VARMINT
RIFLE . . . . **NiB $997 Ex $844 Gd $638**
Caliber: .222 Rem. Four-round magazine. 23.75-inch bbl. Weight:
9.5 lbs. No sights. European walnut stock. Disc.

MODEL 700 BOLT-ACTION RIFLE
Calibers: .17 Rem., .222 Rem., .222 Rem. Mag., .223 Rem., .22-
250 Rem., 5.6x50 Mag., .243 Win., 5.6x57RWS, 6x62, 6.5x55,
6.5x57, 6.5x68, .270 Win., 7x64, 7.5 Swiss, 7mm Rem. Mag.,
.30-06, .300 Win. Mag., 8x68S, 9.3x64. Bbl.: 24 inches (Standard)
or 26 inches (Magnum). Lgt.: 44 inches. Adj. rear, hooded ramp
front sights. Checkered European-style walnut stock w/Bavarain
cheekpiece, rosewood Schnabel forend tip. Imported from 1983
to date.
Model 700 Hunter . . . . **NiB $1146 Ex $896 Gd $790**
Model 700 Deluxe . . . . **NiB $1244 Ex $1033 Gd $733**
Model 700 Deluxe R . . . . **NiB $1096 Ex $790 Gd $695**
Model 700 Deluxe Stutzen . . . . . . **NiB $1290 Ex $770 Gd $655**

MODEL 720 BOLT-ACTION RIFLE
Same specs as Model 700 except in .27-0 Win. and .30-06.

Full-length Mannlicher-type stock with Schnabel forend tip. Bbl.:
20.75 inches. Weight: 6.75 lbs. Disc.
Sporter model . . . . **NiB $1144 Ex $1043 Gd $728**
Ltd. edition . . . . **NiB $2419 Ex $2179 Gd $1188**

BOLT-ACTION SPORTING
RIFLE . . . . **NiB $733 Ex $634 Gd $438**
Miniature Mauser action. Single- or double-set triggers. Calibers:
.22 Hornet, .222 Rem.; four-round clip mag. Bbl.: 22, 24 or 26
inches. Weight: 6.25 lbs. Open rear, hooded ramp front sights.
Checkered stock w/cheekpiece, pitol grip, black forend tip. Sling
swivels.

CARBINE . . . . **NiB $736 Ex $637 Gd $440**
Same as Krico Sporting Rifle except w/20- or 22-inch bbl., full-
length Mannlicher-type stock. Disc. 1962.

SPECIAL VARMINT
RIFLE . . . . **NiB $736 Ex $637 Gd $440**
Same as Krico Sporting Rifle except .222 Rem. only w/heavy bbl, no
sights. Weight: 7.25 lbs. Disc. 1962.

Magnum Research, Inc.

Magnum Research Mountain Eagle
Bolt-Action Rifle

LAKEFIELD ARMS LTD. — Ontario, Canada

MODEL 64B SEMIAUTOMATIC RIFLE . . . . . NiB $150 Ex $110 Gd $85
Caliber: .22 LR, 10-round mag., Bbl.: 20 inches. Weight: 5.5 lbs. Lgt.: 40 inches. Bead front, adj. rear sights. Grooved receiver. Stamped checkering on walnut-finished Monte Carlo hardwood stock. Imported from 1991 to 1994.

MODEL 90B
BOLT-ACTION TARGET RIFLE. . . . . NiB $476 Ex $359 Gd $232
Caliber: .22 LR; five-round mag. Bbl.: 21 inches w/snow cap. Lgt.: 39.63 inches. Weight: 8.25 lbs. Adj. peep, globe front w/colored inserts. Drilled and tapped for scope mounts. Biathlon-style natural-finished hardwood stock w/shooting rails, hand stop and butthook. Made from 1991 to 1994.

MODEL 91T/91TR BOLT-ACTION TARGET RIFLE
Calibers: .22 Short, Long, LR. Bbl.: 25 inches. Lgt.: 43.63 inches. Weight: 8 lbs. Adj. rear peep, globe front sights w/inserts. Drilled and tapped for scope mounts. Walnut-finished hardwood stock w/ shooting rails and hand stop. Model 91TR is clip-fed repeater. Made from 1991 to 1994.
Model 911 single-shot
Model 91T single-shot. . . . . NiB $378 Ex $299 Gd $148
Model 91TR repeater (.22 LR only). . . . . . . NiB $416 Ex $266 Gd $171

MODEL 92S TARGET RIFLE . . . . . . .NiB $398 Ex $387 Gd $265
Same specs as Model 90B except w/conventional target-style stock. Weight: 8 lbs. No sights. Drilled and tapped for scope mounts. Made from 1993 to 1995.

MODEL 93M BOLT ACTION . . . . . NiB $188 Ex $157 Gd $110
Caliber: .22 WMR. Five-round magazine. 20.75-inch bbl. 39.5 inches overall. Weight: 5.75 lbs. Bead front sight, adj. open rear. Receiver grooved for scope mount. Thumb-operated rotary safety. Checkered walnut-finished hardwood stock. Blued finish. Made in 1995.

MARK I BOLT-ACTION RIFLE. . . . . . . NiB $133 Ex $98 Gd $77
Single-shot. Calibers: .22 Short, Long, LR. Bbl.: 20.5 inches. (19 inches in Youth Model). Smoothbore avail. Weight: 5.5 lbs. Lgt.: 39.5 inches. Bead front, adj. rear sights. Grooved for scope mounts. Checkered walnut-finished pistol-grip Monte Carlo hardwood stock. Blued finish. Made from 1990 to 1994.

MARK II BOLT-ACTION RIFLE
Same specifications as Mark I except has repeating action w/10-round detachable box magazine. .22 LR. only. Made from 1992 to 1994.
Mark II standard model . . . . NiB $137 Ex $120 Gd $80
Mark II Youth model (w/19-inch bbl.). . NiB $132 Ex $111 Gd $83
Mark II left-hand model . . . . NiB $169 Ex $137 Gd $100

LAURONA RIFLES — Manufactured in Eibar, Spain. Imported by Galaxy Imports, Victoria, TX

MODEL 2000X O/U EXPRESS
Calibers: .30-06, 8x57JRS, 8x57JR, .375 H&H Mag,. 9.3x74R; five-round mag., BBl.: 24 inches, separated. Quarter rib drilled and tapped for scope mount. Open sights. Matte black chrome finish. Monte Carlo checkered walnut buttstock, tulip forearm. Weight: 8.5 lbs Custom only. Imported from 1993 to date.
Standard calibers . . . . NiB $3166 Ex $2480 Gd $1723
Magnum calibers . . . . NiB $3790 Ex $3044 Gd 2133

L.A.R. MANUFACTURING, INC. — West Jordan, Utah

BIG BOAR COMPETITION
BOLT-ACTION RIFLE . . . . NiB $2230 Ex $1966 Gd $1429
Single-shot, bull-pup action. Caliber: .50 BMG. 36-inch bbl. 45.5 inches overall. Weight: 28.4 lbs. Made from 1994 to date.

LUNA RIFLE — Mehlis, Germany. Manufactured by Ernst Friedr. Büchel

SINGLE-SHOT TARGET RIFLE. . . . NiB $1033 Ex $788 Gd $558
Falling block action. Calibers: .22 LR. .22 Hornet. 29-inch bbl. Weight: 8.25 lbs. Sights: Micrometer peep rear tang; open rear; ramp front. Checkered cheekpiece stock w/full pistol-grip, semibea-vertail forearm, swivels. Made before WWII.

MAGNUM RESEARCH, INC. — Minneapolis, Minnesota

MOUNTAIN EAGLE BOLT-ACTION RIFLE SERIES
Calibers: .222 Rem., .223 Rem., .270 Win., .280 Rem., 7mm Rem. Mag., 7mm STW, .30-06, .300 Win. Mag., .338 Win. Mag., .340 Wby. Mag., .375 H&H Mag., .426 Rem. Mag; five-round mag (Standard) or four-round mag. (Magnum). Bbl. 24 or 26 inches. . No sights, drilled and tapped for scope mounts. Blued finish. Lgt.: 44 to 46 inches. Weight: 7.75 to 9.75 lbs. Fiberglass composite stock. Made from 1994 to 2000.
Standard model . . . . NiB $1379 Ex $1209 Gd $744
Magnum model. . . . . NiB $1997 Ex $1202 Gd $931
Varmint model (Intro. 1996). . . . . NiB $1498 Ex $1216 Gd $938
Calibers .375 H&H, .416 Rem. Mag., add $325
Left-hand model, add $110

Mannlicher Model L Rifle

Mannlicher Model
M Carbine

Mannlicher Model M Professional

Mannlicher Model
M Rifle

MAGTECH — Las Vegas, Nevada.
Manufactured by CBC, Brazil

MODEL MT 122.2/S BOLT-ACTION RIFLE . . . . NiB $135 Ex $121 Gd $75
Bolt-action. Calibers: .22 Short, Long, LR; six- or 10-round clip.
Bbl.: Free floating, 25 inchesDouble locking bolt. Double extractors.
Red cocking indicator. Safety lever. . Lgt.: 43 inches. Weight: 6.5
lbs. Brazilian hardwood stock, beavertail forearm. Swivels. Imported
from 1994. Disc.

MODEL MT 122.2/R BOLT-ACTION RIFLE. . . . NiB $140 Ex $116 Gd $88
Same as Model MT 122.2/S except w/adj. rear sight and post front
sight. Introduced 1994. Disc.

MODEL MT 122.2T BOLT-ACTION RIFLE . . . . . NiB $151 Ex $122 Gd $93
Same as Model MT 122.2/S except w/adj. micrometer-type rear
sight and ramp front sight. Introduced 1994. Disc.

MANNLICHER SPORTING RIFLES — Steyr, Austria.
Manufactured by Steyr-Daimler-Puch, A.-G.

NOTE: *Certain Mannlicher-Schoenauer models were produced
before WWII. Manufacture of sporting rifles and carbines was
resumed at the Steyr-Daimler-Puch plant in Austria in 1950
during which time the Model 1950 rifles and carbines were
introduced.*

*In 1967, Steyr-Daimler-Puch introduced a series of sporting
rifles with a bolt action that is a departure from the Mannlicher-
Schoenauer system of earlier models. In the latter, the action is
locked by lugs symmetrically arranged behind the bolt head as
well as by placing the bolt handle ahead of the right flank of the
receiver, the rear section of which is open on top for backward
movement of the bolt handle. The current action, made in four
lengths to accommodate different ranges of cartridges, has a
closed-top receiver; the bolt locking lugs are located toward
the rear of the bolt (behind the magazine). The Mannlicher-
Schoenauer rotary magazine has been redesigned as a detachable box type made of Makrolon. Imported by Gun South, Inc.
Trussville, Alabama.*

MODEL L CARBINE . . . . NiB $1466 Ex $1189 Gd $835
Same specs as Model SL Carbine except w/type L action. Weight: 6.2 lbs.
Calibers same as for Model L Rifle. Imported from 1968 to 1996.

Mannlicher Sporting Rifles

**Mannlicher Model SL
Rifle w/Single-Set Trigger**

MODEL L RIFLE . . . . **NiB $2177 Ex $1503 Gd $1009**
Same as Model SL Rifle except w/type L action. Weight: 6.3 lbs. Calibers: .22-250, 5.6x57 (sci. 1991), .243 Win., 6mm Rem., .308 Win. Imported from 1968 to date.

**MODEL L VARMINT
RIFLE.** . . . . **NiB $2107 Ex $1600 Gd $977**
Same specs as Model SL Varmint Rifle except w/type L action. Calibers: . 22-250 Rem., .243 Win., .308 Win. Imported from 1969 to 1996.

MODEL LUXUS BOLT-ACTION RIFLE
Same specifications as Models L and M except w/3-round detachable box magazine and single-set trigger. Full or half-stock w/low-luster oil or high-gloss lacquer finish. Disc. 1996.
Full stock . . . . **NiB $2133 Ex $1790 Gd $1305**
Half stock . . . . **NiB $2733 Ex $1966 Gd $928**

MODEL M CARBINE
Same specs as Model SL Carbine except w/type M action, recoil pad. Weight: 6.8 lbs. Left-hand version w/6.5x55 and 9.3x62 calibers introduced 1977. Imported from 1969 to 1996.
Right-hand carbine . . . . **NiB $1288 Ex $1570 Gd $900**
Left-hand carbine . . . . **NiB $2334 Ex $1964 Gd $1507**

MODEL M PROFESSIONAL RIFLE . . . . . **NiB $2079 Ex $1498 Gd $833**
Same as standard Model M Rifle except w/synthetic (Cycolac) stock, weighs 7.5 lbs. Calibers: 6.5x55, 6.5x57, .270 Win., 7x57, 7x64, 7.5 Swiss, .30-06, 8x57JS, 9.3x62. Imported from 1977 to 1993.

MODEL M RIFLE
Same specs as Model SL Rifle except w/type "M" action, stock w/forendtip an drecoil pad. Weight: 6.9 lbs. Calibers: 6.5x57, .270 Win., 7x57, 7x64, .30-06, 8x57JS, 9.3x62. Made from 1969 to date. Left-hand version in calibers 6.5x55 and 7.5 Swiss. Imported from 1977 to 1996.
Right-hand rifle. . . . . **NiB $1667 Ex $1188 Gd $832**
Left-hand rifle. . . . . **NiB $2317 Ex $1951 Gd $1489**

MODEL S RIFLE . . . . **NiB $1674 Ex $1203 Gd $855**
Same specs as Model SL Rifle except w/type S action; four-round mag., Bbl.: 25.63 inches. Stock w/forend tip and recoil pad. Weight 8.4 lbs. Calibers: 6.5x68, .257 Wby. Mag., .264 Win. Mag., 7mm Rem. Mag., .300 Win. Mag., .300 H&H Mag., .308 Norma Mag., 8x68S, .338 Win. Mag., 9.3x64, .375 H&H Mag., Imported from 1970 to 1996.

MODEL SL CARBINE . . . . **NiB $1664 Ex $1176 Gd $815**
Same specifications as Model SL Rifle except w/20-inch bbl. and full-length stock, weight: 6 lbs. Imported from 1968 to 1996.

MODEL SL RIFLE . . . . **NiB $1744 Ex $1278 Gd $823**
Steyr-Mannlicher SL bolt-action. Calibers: .222 Rem., .223 Rem., .222 Rem. Mag.; five-round detachable rotary mag. Bbl.: 23.63 inches. Weight: 6 lbs. Single or double-set triggers (mechanisms interchangeable). Open rear, hoded ramp front sights. Half European walnut Monte Carlo stock, skip-checkered forearm and pistol grip, rubber buttpad. QD swivels. Imported from 1967 to 1996.

**MODEL SL
VARMINT RIFLE** . . . . **NiB $1233 Ex $1198 Gd $854**
Same specs as Model SL Rifle except in .222 Rem. only. Bbl.: 25.63 inches; no sights. Weight: 7.92 lbs. Imported from 1969 to 1996.

MODEL SSG MATCH TARGET RIFLE
Type "L" action. Caliber: .308 Win. (7.62x51 NATO). Five- or 10-round magazine, single-shot plug. 25.5-inch heavy bbl. Weight: 10.25 lbs. Single trigger. Sights: Micrometer peep rear; globe front. Target stock, European walnut or synthetic, w/full pistol-grip, wide forearm w/swivel rail, adj. rubber buttplate. Imported from 1969 to date.
W/walnut stock. . . . . **NiB $2388 Ex $1956 Gd $1267**
W/synthetic stock. . . . . **NiB $1488 Ex $1131 Gd $709**

MODEL S/T RIFLE. . . . . **NiB $1278 Ex $1564 Gd $931**
Same as Model S Rifle except w/heavy 25.63-inch bbl., weight: 9 lbs. Calibers: 9.3x64, .375 H&H Mag., .458 Win. Mag. Option of 23.63-inch bbl. in latter caliber. Imported from 1975 to 1996.

**MODEL 1903 BOLT-ACTION
SPORTING CARBINE** . . . . **NiB $2590 Ex $1133 Gd $725**
Caliber: 6.5x53mm (aka 6.7x53mm). Five-round rotary mag. Bbl.: 17.7 inches. Weight: 6.5 lbs. Double-set trigger. Two-leaf rear, ramp front sights. Full-length sporting stock w/cheekpiece, pistol grip, trap buttplate, swivels, Pre-WWII.

MODEL 1905 CARBINE . . . . **NiB $1966 Ex $904 Gd $633**
Same as Model 1903 except w/19.7-inch bbl.chambered 9x56mm. Weight: 6.75 lbs. Pre-WWII.

MODEL 1908 CARBINE . . . . **NiB $1910 Ex $909 Gd $640**
Same as Model 1905 except calibers 7x57mm and 8x56mm. Pre-WWII.

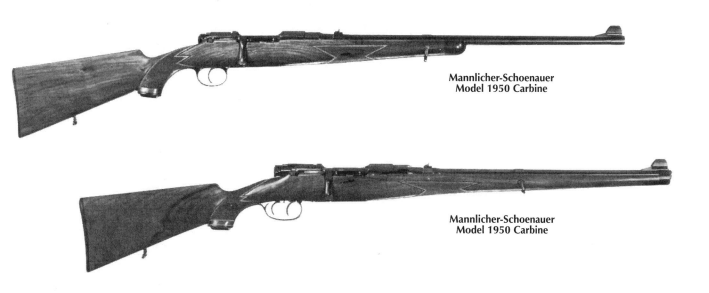

**Mannlicher-Schoenauer
Model 1950 Carbine**

**Mannlicher-Schoenauer
Model 1950 Carbine**

MODEL 1910 . . . . .NiB $1602 Ex $1335 Gd $727
Same as Model 1905 except in .30-06 (7.62x63mm). Pre-WWII.

MODEL 1910 CARBINE . . . . NiB $1623 Ex $1335 Gd $700
Same as Model 1905 except in 9.5x57mm. Pre-WWII.

MODEL 1924 CARBINE . . . . . . NiB $1767 Ex $1543 Gd $1067
Same as Model 1905 except in .30-06 (7.62x63mm). Pre-WWII.

**MODEL 1950 BOLT-ACTION
SPORTING RIFLE** . . . . NiB $1947 Ex $1466 Gd $590
Calibers: .257 Roberts, .270 Win., .30-06. Five-round rotary mag. Bbl.
24 inches. Weight: 7.25 lbs. Single or double-set triggers. Redesigned
low bolt handle, shotgun-type safety. Folding lear open rear, hooded
ramp front sights. Improved half-length checkered stock w/cheek-
piece, pistol grip, ebony forend tip, swivels, Made from 1950 to 1952.

MODEL 1950 CARBINE . . . . NiB $2065 Ex $1567 Gd $997
Same specs as Model 1950 rifle except w/20-inch bbl., full-length
stock. Weight: 7 lbs. Made from 1950 to 1952.

**MODEL 1950
6.5 CARBINE.** . . . . NiB $2060 Ex $1550 Gd $990
Same as other Model 1950 Carbines except in 6.5x53mm, w/18.25-
inch bbl., Weight: 6.75 lbs. Made from 1950 to 1952.

**MODEL 1952
IMPROVED CARBINE.** . . . . NiB $1866 Ex $1444 Gd $905
Same as Model 1950 Carbine except w/swept-back bolt handle,
redesigned stock. Calibers: .257 Roberts, .270 Win., .30-06. Made
from 1952 to 1956.

**MODEL 1952 IMPROVED
6.5 CARBINE.** . . . . NiB $2088 Ex $1091 Gd $623
Same as Model 1952 Carbine except in 6.5x53mm, w/18.25-inch
bbl. Made from 1952 to 1956.

**MODEL 1952 IMPROVED
SPORTING RIFLE** . . . . NiB $1847 Ex $1350 Gd $896

Same as Model 1950 except w/swept-back bolt handle, redesigned
stock. Calibers: .257 Roberts, .270 Win., .30-06, 9.3x62mm. Made
from 1952 to 1956, imported by Stoeger Arms Co.

**MODEL 1956 CUSTOM
CARBINE.** . . . . NiB $2055 Ex $831 Gd $567
Same specs as 1950 and 1952 model carbines except w/redesigned
stock w/high comb. Drilled and tapped for scope mount. Calibers:
.243 Win., 6.5mm, .257 Roberts., .270 Win., 7mm Mag., .30-06
.308 Win. Made from 1956 to 1960.

**CARBINE, MODEL
1961-MCA** . . . NiB $1867 Ex $1278 Gd $990
Same as Model 1956 Carbine except w/universal Monte Carlo
design stock. Calibers: .243 Win., 6.5mm, .270, .308, .30-06. Made
from 1961 to 1971.

**RIFLE, MODEL
1961-MCA** . . . . NiB $2159 Ex $1389 Gd $997
Same as Model 1956 rifle except w/universal Monte Carlo design
stock. Calibers: .243 Win., .270 Win., .30-06. Made from 1961 to
1971.

**HIGH VELOCITY BOLT-ACTION
SPORTING RIFLE.** . . . . NiB $6650 Ex $4156 Gd $2097
Calibers: 7x64 Brenneke, .30-06 (7.62x63mm), 8x60 Mag., 9.3x62,
10.75x68mm. Bbl.: 23.6 inches. Weight: 7.5 lbs. British-style 3-leaf
open rear, ramp front sights. Half-length sporting stock w/cheek-
piece, pistol grip, checkered trap buttplate, swivels. Also produced
in a takedown model. Pre-WWII.

M72 MODEL L/M CARBINE. . . . . NiB $1033 Ex $762 Gd $513
Same specs as M72 Model L/M rifle except w/20-inch bbl. and full-
length stock. Weight: 7.2 lbs. Imported from 1972 to date.

M72 MODEL L/M RIFLE. . . . . NiB $906 Ex $821 Gd $600
M72 Bolt-action, type L/M receiver, front-locking bolt, internal
five-round rotary mag. Calibers: .22-250 Rem., 5.6x57, 6mm Rem.,
.243 Win., 6.5x57, .260 Win., 7x57, 7x64, .308 Win., .30-06. Bbl.:

Marlin Firearms Co.

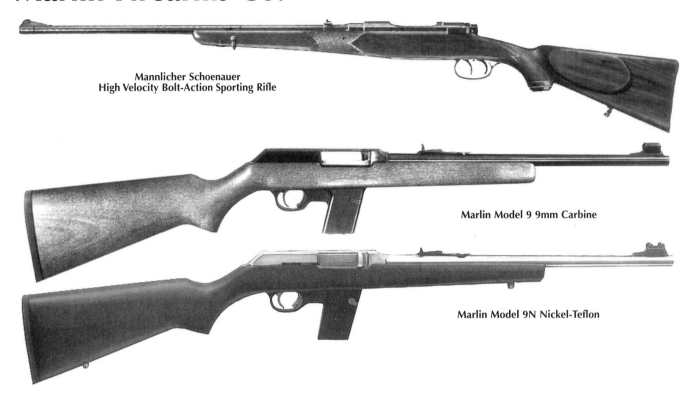

Mannlicher Schoenauer
High Velocity Bolt-Action Sporting Rifle

Marlin Model 9 9mm Carbine

Marlin Model 9N Nickel-Teflon

23.63 inches. Weight: 7.3 lbs. Single or double-set trigger (mechanisms interchangeable). Open rear, hooded ramp front sights. Monte Carlo half stock of European walnut, checkered forearm and pistol grip.Rosewood forend tip, recoil pad, QD swivels. Imported from 1972 to 1981.

M72 MODEL S RIFLE . . . . NiB $866 Ex $756 Gd $544
Same specs as M72 Model L/M rifle except w/magnum action, four-round mag. Bbl.: 25.63 inches. Weight: 8.6 lbs. Calibers: 6.5x68, 7mm Rem. Mag., 8x68S, 9.3x64, .375 H&H Mag. Imported from 1972 to 1981.

M72 MODEL S/T RIFLE . . . . NiB $1455 Ex $1161 Gd $788
Same as M72 Model S Rifle except w/heavy 25.63-inch bbl., weighs 9.3 lbs. Calibers: .300 Win. Mag. 9.3x64, .375 H&H Mag., .458 Win. Mag. Option of 23.63-inch bbl. in latter caliber. Imported from 1975 to 1981.

MODEL SBS FORESTER RIFLE
Calibers: .243 Win., .25-06 rem., .270 Win., 6.5x55mm, 6.5x57mm, 7x64mm, 7mm-08 Rem., .30-06, .308 Win., 9.3x64mm; four-round detachable mag. Bbl.: 23.6 inches. Lgt.: 44.5 inches. Weight: 7.5 lbs. No sights, drilled and tapped for Browning A-Bolt scope configuration. Checkered American walnut stock w/Monte Carlo cheekpiece and Pachmayr swivels. Polished or matte blue finish. Imported from 1997 to date.
Standard calibers . . . . NiB $955 Ex $823 Gd $595
Mountain Rifle (w/20-inch bbl.) . . . . NiB $975 Ex $797 Gd $555
For magnum calibers, add. $50
For metric calibers, add $125

MODEL SBS PRO-HUNTER RIFLE
Similar to the Forester Model, except w/ASB black synthetic stock. Matte blue finish. Imported from 1997 to date.
Standard calibers . . . . .NiB $844 Ex $679 Gd $467

Mountain Rifle (w/20-inch bbl.) . . . . NiB $897 Ex $689 Gd $523
.376 Steyr. . . . . .NiB $887 Ex $679 Gd $513
Youth/Ladies rifle . . . . .NiB $897 Ex $689 Gd $523
For magnum calibers, add $50
For metric calibers, add. $150
W/synthetic stock, add $150

MARLIN FIREARMS CO. — North Haven, Connecticut

MODEL 9 SEMIAUTOMATIC CARBINE
Calibers: 9mm Parabellum. 12-round magazine. 16.5-inch bbl. 35.5 inches overall. Weight: 6.75 lbs. Manual bolt hold-open. Sights: Hooded post front; adj. open rear. Walnut-finished hardwood stock w/rubber buttpad. Blued or nickel-Teflon finish. Made 1985 to 1999.
Model 9 . . . . .NiB $525 Ex $387 Gd $213
Model 9N, nickel-Teflon (disc. 1994) . . . . .NiB $475 Ex $390 Gd $146

MODEL 15Y/15YN
Bolt-action, single-shot "Little Buckaroo" rifle. Caliber: .22 Short, Long or LR. 16.25-inch bbl. Weight: 4.25 lbs. Thumb safety. Ramp front sight; adj. open rear. One-piece walnut Monte Carlo stock w/ full pistol-grip. Made from 1984 to 1988. Reintroduced in 1989 as Model 15YN.
Model 15Y . . . . NiB $200 Ex $130 Gd $98
Model 15YN .NiB $215 Ex $140 Gd $110

MODEL 18 BABY SLIDE-ACTION
REPEATER . . . . NiB $797 Ex $443 Gd $300
Exposed hammer. Solid frame. Caliber: .22 LR, Long Short. Tubular magazine holds 14 Short cartridges. 20-inch bbl., round or octagon. Weight: 3.75 lbs. Sights: Open rear; bead front. Plain straight-grip stock and slide handle. Made from 1906 to 1909.

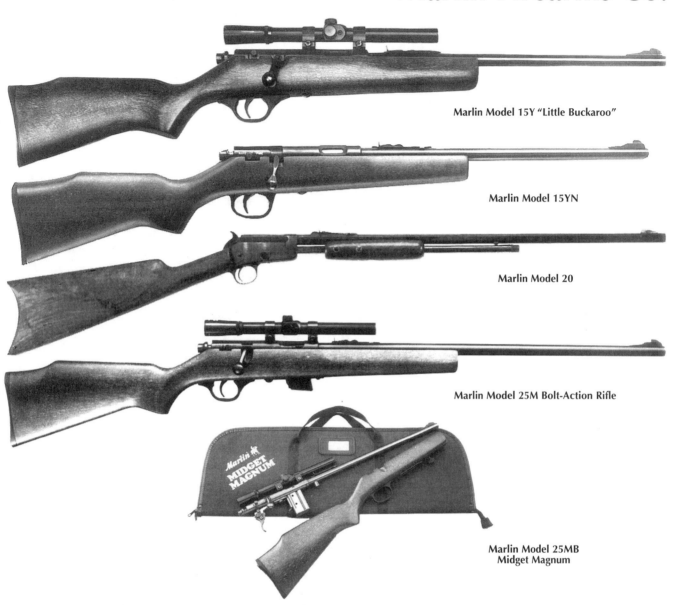

Marlin Model 15Y "Little Buckaroo"

Marlin Model 15YN

Marlin Model 20

Marlin Model 25M Bolt-Action Rifle

Marlin Model 25MB
Midget Magnum

MODEL 20 SLIDE-ACTION
REPEATING RIFLE . . . . **NiB $790 Ex $545 Gd $433**
Exposed hammer. Takedown. Caliber: .22 LR. Long, Short. Tubular magazine: Half-length holds 15 Short, 12 Long, 10 LR; full-length holds 25 Short, 20 Long, 18 LR. 24-inch octagon bbl. Weight: 5 lbs. Sights: Open rear; bead front. Plain straight-grip stock, grooved slide handle. Made from 1907 to 1922. After 1920 was designated "Model 20-S."

MODEL MB 25 BOLT-ACTION RIFLE . . . . . . **NiB $179 Ex $110 Gd $95**
Caliber: .22 Short, Long or LR; 7-round clip. 22-inch bbl. Weight: 5.5 lbs. Ramp front sight, adj. open rear. One-piece walnut Monte Carlo stock w/full pistol-grip Mar-Shield finish. Made 1984 to 1988.

MODEL 25
SLIDE-ACTION REPEATER . . . . **NiB $879 Ex $540 Gd $431**
Exposed hammer, takedown. Caliber: .22 Short (also handles .22 CB caps); 15-round tubular mag. Bbl.: 23 inches. Weight: 4 lbs. Open rear, bead front sights. Plain straight-grip stock and slide handle. Made from 1909 to 1910.

MODEL 25M BOLT ACTION W/SCOPE . . . . **NiB $165 Ex $119 Gd $95**
Caliber: .22 WMR. 7-round clip. 22-inch bbl. Weight: 6 lbs. Ramp front sight w/brass bead, adj. open rear. Walnut-finished stock w/Monte Carlo styling and full pistol-grip. Sling swivels. Made from 1986 to 1988.

MODEL 25MB MIDGET MAGNUM . . . . **NiB $160 Ex $125 Gd $99**
Bolt-action. Caliber: .22; seven-round capacity. Bbl.: 16.25 inches. Weight: 4.75 lbs. Walnut-finished Monte Carlo-style stock w/full pistol grip, abbreviated forend. Brass bead ramp front, open rear sights. Thumb safety. Made from 1986 to 1988.

MODEL 25MG/25MN/25N/25NC BOLT-ACTION RIFLE
Caliber: .22 WMR (Model 25MN) or .22 LR (Model 25N). Seven round clip magazine. 22-inch bbl. 41 inches overall. Weight: 5.5 to 6 lbs. Adj. open rear sight, ramp front; receiver grooved for scope mounts. One piece walnut-finished hardwood Monte Carlo stock w/pistol grip. Made from 1989 to 2003.
Model 25MG (Garden Gun) . . . . **NiB $218 Ex $179 Gd $125**
Model 25MN . . . . **NiB $200 Ex $165 Gd $110**
Model 25N . . . . **NiB $177 Ex $155 Gd $109**
MODEL 25 NC (camo stock), add $50

Marlin Firearms Co.

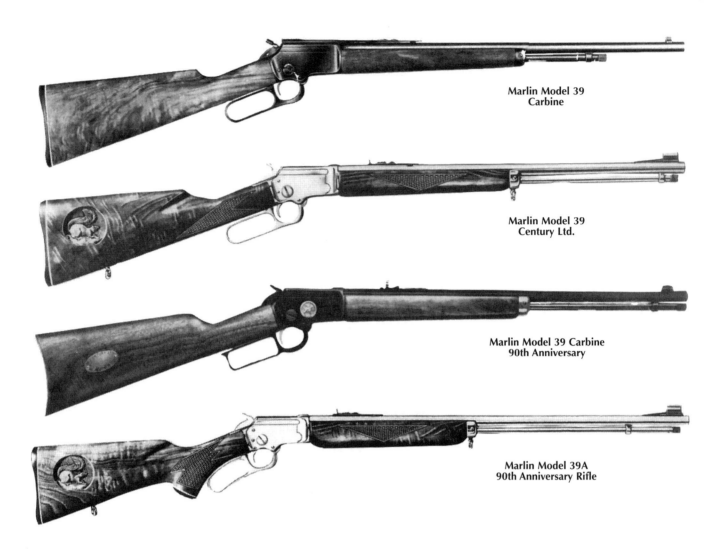

Marlin Model 39
Carbine

Marlin Model 39
Century Ltd.

Marlin Model 39 Carbine
90th Anniversary

Marlin Model 39A
90th Anniversary Rifle

MODEL 27 SLIDE-ACTION
REPEATING RIFLE............. NiB $1159 Ex $900 Gd $644
Exposed hammer. Takedown. Calibers: .25-20, .32-20. Magazine (tubular) holds 7 rounds. 24-inch octagon bbl. Weight: 5.75 lbs. Sights: Open rear; bead front. Plain, straight-grip stock, grooved slide handle. Made from 1910 to 1916.

MODEL 27S .... NiB $900 Ex $579 Gd $388
Same as Model 27 except w/round bbl., also chambered for .25 Stevens rimfire. Made from 1920 to 1932.

MODEL 29 SLIDE-ACTION REPEATER .... NiB $660 Ex $388 Gd $290
Similar to Model 20 w/23-inch round bbl., half magazine only, weight 5.75 lbs. Made from 1913 to 1916.

MODEL 30/30A AND 30AS LEVER-ACTION
Caliber: .30-30; six-round tubular mag. Bbl.: 20 inches; Micro-Groove rifling. Lgt.: 38.25 inches. Weight: 7 lbs. Brass bead front, adj. rear sights. Solid top receiver, offset hammer spur for scope use. Walnut-finished hardwood stock w/pistol grip. Mar-Shield finish. Made from 1964 to 2000.
Model 30/30A .... NiB $290 Ex $198 Gd $160
Model 30AS .... NiB $290 Ex $198 Gd $160
Model 30AS w/4x scope, add........................ $25

MODEL 32 SLIDE-ACTION REPEATER ... NiB $1154 Ex $690 Gd $533
Hammerless. Takedown. Caliber: .22 LR. Long, Short. Tubular magazine holds 15 Short, 12 Long, 10 LR; full magazine, 25 Short, 20 Long, 18 LR. 24-inch octagon bbl. Weight: 5.5 lbs. Sights: Open rear; bead front. Plain pistol-grip stock, grooved slide handle. Made from 1914 to 1915.

MODEL 36 LEVER-ACTION REPEATING CARBINE
Calibers: .30-30, .32 Special; seven-round tubular mag. Bbl.: 20 inches. Weight: 6.5 lbs. Open rear, bead front sights. Pistol-grip stock, semi-beavertail forearm w/carbine bbl. band. Early production w/receiver lever and hammer color case-hardened, remaining metal blued. Late production w/blued receiver. Made from 1936 to 1948. In 1936, designated as "Model 1936" and so marked on the upper tang. In 1937 the model designation was shortened to "36." An "RC" serial number suffix identifies a "Regular/Carbine."
Model 1936 CC receiver
(w/long tang, no SN prefix) .... NiB $900 Ex $744 Gd $500
Model 1936 CC receiver
(w/short tang, no SN prefix)........... NiB $645 Ex $531 Gd $390
Model 1936 CC receiver (w/SN prefix) ... NiB $534 Ex $488 Gd $345
Model 36, CC receiver (w/SN prefix) ..... NiB $508 Ex $433 Gd $300
Model 36, blued receiver (w/SN prefix) ... NiB $477 Ex $390 Gd $289

Marlin Model 39AS

MODEL 36 SPORTING CARBINE
Same as M36 carbine except w/6-round, (2/3 magazine) and weighs 6.25 lbs.
Model 1936, CC receiver
(w/long tang, no SN prefix) . . . . NiB $860 Ex $700 Gd $499
Model 1936, CC receiver
(w/short tang, no SN prefix) . . . . NiB $656 Ex $567 Gd $380
Model 1936, CC receiver (w/SN prefix) . . . NiB $588 Ex $497 Gd $355
Model 36, CC receiver (w/SN prefix) . . . . . NiB $555 Ex $457 Gd $339
Model 36, blued receiver (w/SN prefix) . . . NiB $480 Ex $413 Gd $303

MODEL 36A/36ADL LEVER-ACTION REPEATING RIFLE
Same as Model 36 Carbine except w/a 24-inch bbl., hooded front sight and 2/3 six-round mag. Weight: 6.75 lbs. An "A" suffix denotes Rifle, an "A-DL" suffix denotes a Deluxe model w/checkered stock, semi-beavertail forearm, swivels and sling. Made from 1936 to 1948.
Model 1936, CC receiver
(w/long tang, no SN prefix) . . . . NiB $1180 Ex $1066 Gd $790
Model 1936, CC receiver
(lw/short tang, no SN prefix) . . . . NiB $795 Ex $556 Gd $378
Model 1936, CC receiver (w/SN prefix) . . . NiB $845 Ex $589 Gd $465
Model 36, CC receiver (w/SN prefix) . . . . . NiB $775 Ex $451 Gd $348
Model 36, blued receiver (w/SN prefix) . . . NiB $744 Ex $440 Gd $332
ADL model, add 25%

MODEL 37 SLIDE-ACTION
REPEATING RIFLE. . . . . NiB $644 Ex $442 Gd $237
Similar to Model 29 except w/24-inch bbl. and full magazine. Weight: 5.25 lbs. Made from 1913 to 1916.

MODEL 38 SLIDE-ACTION
REPEATING RIFLE. . . . . NiB $744 Ex $418 Gd $339
Hammerless. Takedown. Caliber: .22 LR, Long, Short; 2/3 tubular mag. holds 15 Short, 12 Long, 10 LR. Bbl.: Octagon, 24 inches. Weight: 5.5 lbs. Adj. rear, ivory bead front sights. Plain shotgun-type pistol-grip buttstock w/hard rubber buttplate; grooved slide handle. About 20,000 made from 1920 to 1930.

MODEL 39 CARBINE . . . . NiB $556 Ex $355 Gd $298
Same as Model 39M except w/lightweight bbl., ¾ mag., capacity 18 Short, 14 Long, 12 LR, slimmer forearm, Weight: 5.25 lbs. Made from 1963 to 1967.

MODEL 39 90TH
ANNIVERSARY CARBINE . . . . . . NiB $1244 Ex $966 Gd $835
Carbine version of 90th Anniversary Model 39A. 500 made in 1960.

MODEL 39 CENTURY
LTD. . . . . NiB $670 Ex $366 Gd $259
Commemorative version of Model 39A. Receiver inlaid w/brass medallion ("Marlin Centennial 1970-1970"). Square lever. Bbl.: 20 inches, octagon. Fancy walnut straight-grip stock and forearm; brass forend cap, buttplate. Nameplate in buttstock. 35,388 made in 1970.

MODEL 39 LEVER-ACTION
REPEATER . . . . NiB $3145 Ex $1189 Gd $1018
Takedown. Case-hardened receiver. Caliber: .22 LR, Long, Short. Tubular mag., holds 25 Short, 20 long, 18 LR. Bbl.: 24 inches, octagon. Weight 5.75 lbs. Open rear, bead front sights. Weight: 5.75 lbs. Open rear, bead front sights. Plain pistol-grip stock and forearm. Made from 1922 to 1938.

MODEL 39A
General specs same as Model 39 except w/blued receiver, round bbl., heavier stock w/semi-beavertail forearm. Weight: 6.5 lbs. Made from 1939 to 1960.
Early model (no prefix) . . . . NiB $1500 Ex $1178 Gd $800
Late model ("B" prefix) . . . . NiB $1166 Ex $895 Gd $644

MODEL 39A 90TH
ANNIVERSARY RIFLE . . . . NiB $1255 Ex $1140 Gd $835
Commemorates Marlin's 90th anniversary. Same specs as Golden 39A except w/chrome-plated bbl. and action, finely checkered stock and forearm of select walnut. Carved figure of a squirrel on right side of buttstock. 500 made in 1960.

MODEL 39A
ARTICLE II RIFLE . . . . NiB $489 Ex $420 Gd $335
Similar to Model 39A. Commemorative National Rifle Association Centennial 1871-1971. "The Right To Bear Arms" medallion inlaid in receiver. Magazine capacity: 26 Short, 21 Long, 19 LR. Bbl.: 24 inches, octagon. Fancy walnut pistol-grip stock and forearm; brass forend cap, buttplate. 6,244 made in 1971.

Marlin Firearms Co.

Marlin Model 56

Marlin Model 57

Marlin Model 60C

Marlin Model 60SS

Marlin Model 62

GOLDEN 39A/39AS RIFLE
Same as Model 39A except w/gold-plated trigger, hooded ramp front sight, sling swivels. Made from 1960 to 1987 (39A); model 39AS made from 1988 to date.
Golden 39A . . . . NiB $479 Ex $300 Gd $190
Golden 39AS (W/hammer block safety) . . . NiB $479 Ex $300 Gd $190

MODEL 39A "MOUNTIE" LEVER-
ACTION REPEATING RIFLE . . . . . . NiB $479 Ex $300 Gd $190
Same as Model 39A except w/lighter, straight-grip stock, slimmer forearm. Weight: 6.25 lbs. Made from 1953 to 1960.

MODEL 39A OCTAGON . . . . NiB $645 Ex $579 Gd $390
Same as Golden 39A except w/oct. bbl., plain bead front sight, slimmer stock and forearm, no pistol-grip cap or swivels. Made in 1973 (2551 produced).

MODEL 39D . . . . NiB $440 Ex $280 Gd $200
Same as Model 39M except w/pistol-grip stock, forearm w/bbl. band. Made from 1970 to 1974.

39M ARTICLE II CARBINE . . . . . . NiB $488 Ex $469 Gd $300
Same as 39A Article II Rifle except w/straight-grip buttstock, square

lever, 20-inch octagon bbl., reduced magazine capacity. 3,824 units made in 1971.

GOLDEN 39M
Calibers: .22 Short, Long, and LR; tubular mag., holds 21 Short, 16 Long or 15 L. bbl.: 20 inches. Lgt.: 36 inches.. Weight: 6 lbs. Gold-plated trigger. Hooded ramp front, adj. folding semi-buckhorn rear. Two-piece straight-grip American black walnut stock. Sling swivels. Mar-Shield finish. Made from 1960 to 1987.
Golden 39M . . . . NiB $445 Ex $335 Gd $266
Octagonal bbl.
made 1973 only . . . . NiB $490 Ex $469 Gd $390

MODEL 39M
"MOUNTIE" CARBINE . . . . NiB $479 Ex $300 Gd $190
Same as Model 39A "Mountie" Rifle except w/20-inch bbl. Weight: 6 lbs. 500 made in 1960.

MODEL 39TDS
CARBINE. . . . . NiB $545 Ex $369 Gd $290
Same general specifications as Model 39M except takedown style w/16.5-inch bbl. and reduced magazine capacity. 32.63 inches overall. Weight: 5.25 lbs. Made from 1988 to 1995.

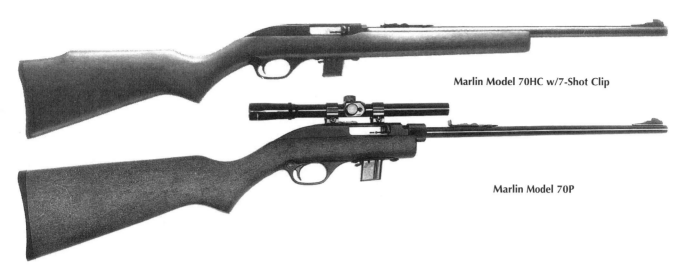

Marlin Model 70HC w/7-Shot Clip

Marlin Model 70P

MODEL 45 . . . . **NiB $390 Ex $290 Gd $198**
Semi-automatic. Caliber: .45 Auto; seven-round clip mag. Bbl.: 16.5 inches. Lgt.: 35.5 inches. Weight: 6.75 lbs. Manual bolt hold-open. Brass bead ramp front, adj. folding rear sights. Drilled and tapped for scope mount. Walnut-finished hardwood stock. Made from 1986 to 1999.

MODEL 49/49DL AUTOLOADING RIFLE
Same as Model 99C except w/two-piece stock, checkered after 1970. Made from 1968 to 1971. Scrollwork on sides of receiver of Model 49DL. Checkered stock and forearm, made from 1971 to 1987.
Model 49 . . . . **NiB $200 Ex $190 Gd $145**
Model 49DL . . . . **NiB $225 Ex $179 Gd $144**

MODEL 50/50E AUTOLOADING RIFLE
Takedown. Caliber: .22 LR; six-round detachable box mag., Bbl.: 22 inches. Weight: 6 lbs. Open rear, bead front sights. Mdl. 50E w/peep rear, hooded front sight. Plain pistol-grip stock, forearm with finger grooves. Made from 1931 to 1934.
Model 50 . . . . **NiB $225 Ex $190 Gd $124**
Model 50E. **NiB $235 Ex $200 Gd $130**

MODEL 56 LEVERMATIC RIFLE . . . . **NiB $345 Ex $250 Gd $149**
Same as Model 57 except clip-loading. Magazine holds eight rounds. Weight: 5.75 lbs. Made from 1955 to 1964.

MODEL 57 LEVERMATIC RIFLE . . . . **NiB $365 Ex $195 Gd $100**
Lever-action. Caliber: 22 LR, Long, Short; tubular mag. holds 19 LR, 21 Long, 27 Short. Bbl.: 22 inches. Weight: 6.25 lbs. Adj. open rear, hooded ramp front sights. Monte Carlo-style stock w/pistol grip. Made from 1959 to 1965.

MODEL 57M LEVERMATIC. . . . . . . **NiB $415 Ex $255 Gd $148**
Same as Model 57 except in .22 WMR; 24-inch bbl., 15-round mag. Made from 1960 to 1969.

MODEL 60 SEMIAUTOMATIC RIFLE . . . . . . **NiB $225 Ex $145 Gd $90**
Caliber: .22 LR; 14-round tubular mag. Bbl.: 22 inches. Lgt.: 40.5 inches. Weight: 5.5 lbs. Grooved receiver. Removeable-hood ramp front, adj open rear sights. Anodized receiver w/blued bbl. Monte Carlo-style walnut-finished hardwood stock w/Mar-Shield finish. Made from 1981 to date. Marketed from 1960 to 1980 under Glenfield logo w/modified stock.

MODEL 60C SELF-LOADING RIFLE . . . . . . **NiB $198 Ex $130 Gd $107**
Caliber: .22 LR; 14-round tubular mag. Bbl.: 22 inches. Lgt.: 40.5 inches. Weight: 5.5 lbs. Screw-adj. open rear and ramb front sights. Aluminum receiver, grooved for scope mount. Hardwood Monte

Carlo stock w/Mossy Oak "Break-Up" camo pattern. Made from 2000 to date.

MODEL 60SS SEMIAUTOMATIC RIFLE
Same specs as Model 60 except w/stainless bbl. and mag. tube. Synthetic, plain birch or laminated black/gray birch stock w/nickel-plated swivel studs. Made from 1993 to date.
W/uncheckered birch stock . . . .**NiB $275 Ex $200 Gd $135**
W/laminated birch stock. . . . .**NiB $270 Ex $197 Gd $125**
W/fiberglass stock. . . . .**NiB $260 Ex $188 Gd $125**

MODEL 62
LEVERMATIC RIFLE. . . . . **NiB $555 Ex $440 Gd $190**
Lever-action. Calibers: .256 Magnum, .30 Carbine. Four-round clip magazine. 23-inch bbl. Weight: 7 lbs. Sights: Open rear; hooded ramp front. Monte Carlo-style stock w/pistol-grip, swivels and sling. Made in .256 Magnum from 1963 to 1966; in .30 Carbine from 1963 to 1969.

MODEL 65 BOLT-ACTION
SINGLE-SHOT RIFLE. . . . . **NiB $139 Ex $93 Gd $70**
Takedown. Caliber: .22 LR. Long, Short. 24-inch bbl. Weight: 5 lbs. Sights: Open rear; bead front. Plain pistol-grip stock w/grooved forearm. Made from 1932 to 1938. Model 65E has rear peep sight and hooded front sight.

MODEL 70HC SEMIAUTOMATIC
Caliber: .22 LR; seven-and 15-round mag. Bbl.: 18 inches. Weight: 5.5 .bs. Lgt.: 37.5 inches. Ramp front, adj. open rear sights. Grooved receiver for scope mounts. Walnut-finished hardwood Monte Carlo stock w/pistol grip. Made from 1988 to 1996.
Marlin model . . . . **NiB $200 Ex $155 Gd $124**
Glenfield model . . . . **NiB $155 Ex $125 Gd $100**

MODEL 70P
SEMIAUTOMATIC. . . . . **NiB $290 Ex $189 Gd $100**
"Papoose" takedown. Caliber: .22 LR. Seven round clip. 16.25-inch bbl. 35.25 inches overall. Weight: 3.75 lbs. Sights: Ramp front, adj. open rear. Side ejection, manual bolt hold-open. Cross-bolt safety. Walnut-finished hard-wood stock w/abbreviated forend, pistol-grip. Made from 1984 to 1994.

MODEL 70PSS
SELF-LOADING CARBINE . . . . **NiB $335 Ex $200 Gd $175**
"Papoose" takedown carbine. Caliber: .22 LR. Seven round clip. 16.25- inch bbl., 35.25 inches overall. Weight: 3.25 lbs. Ramp front and adjustable open rear sights. Automatic last-shot hold open (1996). Black fiberglass synthetic stock. Made from 1995 to date.

Marlin Firearms Co.

Marlin Model 75C

Marlin Model 80C

Marlin Model 80DL

Marlin Model 81DL

MODEL 75C
SEMIAUTOMATIC . . . . **NiB $233 Ex $158 Gd $109**
Caliber: .22 LR. 13-round tubular magazine.18-inch bbl. 36.5 inches overall. Weight: 5 lbs. Side ejection. Cross-bolt safety. Sights: Ramp-mounted blade front; adj. open rear. Monte Carlo-style walnut-finished hardwood stock w/pistol-grip. Made from 1975 to 1992.

MODEL 80 BOLT-ACTION REPEATING RIFLE
Takedown. Caliber: .22 LR, Long, Short; eight-round detachable box mag. Bbl.: 24 inches. Weight: 6 lbs. Open rear, bead front sights. Plain pistol-grip stock. Made from 1934 to 1939. Model 80E w/peep rear, hooded front sights. Made from 1934 to 1940.
Model 80 Standard . . . . **NiB $190 Ex $135 Gd $95**
Model 80E. **NiB $175 Ex $110 Gd $85**

MODEL 80C/80DL BOLT-ACTION REPEATER
Improved version of Model 80. Model 80C w/bead front sight, semi-beavertail forearm made from 1940 to 1970. Model 80DL w/peep rear, hooded blade ramp front sight, swivels; made from 1940 to 1965.
Model 80C . . . . **NiB $200 Ex $155 Gd $100**
Model 80DL . . . . **NiB $165 Ex $110 Gd $90**

MODEL 81/81E BOLT-ACTION REPEATER
Takedown. .22 LR. Long, Short. Tubular magazine holds 24 Short, 20 Long, 18 LR. 24-inch bbl. Weight: 6.25 lbs. Sights: Open rear, bead front. Plain pistol-grip stock. Made from 1937 to 1940. Model 81E w/peep rear sight; hooded front w/ramp.
Model 81 . . . . **NiB $220 Ex $176 Gd $110**
Model 81E. **NiB $245 Ex $195 Gd $139**

MODEL 81C/81DL BOLT-ACTION REPEATER
Improved version of Model 81. Model 81C has bead front sight, semi-beavertail forearm; made from 1940 to 1970. Model 81 DL has peep rear, hooded front sights, swivels. Disc. 1965.
Model 81C . . . . **NiB $239 Ex $188 Gd $100**
Model 81DL . . . . **NiB $220 Ex $199 Gd $110**

MODEL 88C/88DL TAKEDOWN RIFLE
Takedown. Caliber: .22 LR; tubular mag. in buttstock holds 14 rounds. Bbl.: 24 inches. Weight: 6.75 lbs. Open rear, hooded front sights. Plain pistol-grip stock. Made from 1947 to 1956. Model 88DL w/receiver peep sight, checkered stock and sling swiels. Made from 1953 to 1956.
Model 88C . . . . **NiB $200 Ex $145 Gd $100**
Model 88DL . . . . **NiB $200 Ex $145 Gd $100**

Marlin Firearms Co.

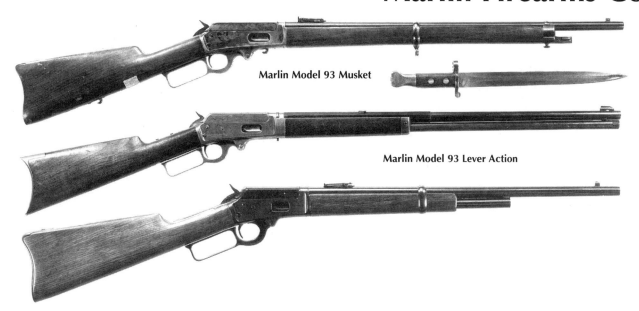

Marlin Model 93 Musket

Marlin Model 93 Lever Action

MODEL 89C/89DL AUTOLOADING RIFLE
Same as Model 88C except w/seven-round clip (12-round in later models); Model 89C. Made from 1950 to 1961. Model 89DL has receiver peep sight, sling swivels.

Model 89C . . . . NiB $200 Ex $145 Gd $100
Model 89DL . . . . NiB $210 Ex $150 Gd $105

MODEL 92 LEVER-ACTION REPEATING RIFLE
Caliber: .22 Short, Long, LR; .32 Short, Long (rimfire or centerfire by changing firing pin); tubular mag. holds 25 Short, 20 Long, 18 LR or 17 Short, 14 Long in .32. Model w/ shorter mag., holds 15 Short, 12 Long, 10 LR. Bbl.: 16 (.22 cal. only), 24, 26, 28 inches. Weight: 5.5 lbs. w/24-inch bbl. Open rear, blade front sights. Plain, straight-grip stock and forearm. Made from 1892 to 1916. Originally designated Model 1892.

Model 92 (.22 caliber) . . . . NiB $1598 Ex $1400 Gd $883
Model 92 (.32 caliber) . . . . NiB $1554 Ex $1255 Gd $956

MODEL 93/93SC CARBINE
Same as Standard Model 93 Rifle except in .30-30 and .32 Special only. Model 93 w/7-round magazine. 20-inch round bbl., carbine sights, weight: 6.75 lbs. Model 93SC magazine capacity 5 rounds, weighs 6.5 lbs.

Model 93 Carbine (w/saddle ring) . . . . NiB $1680 Ex $1423 Gd $1108
Model 93 Carbine "Bull's-Eye"
(w/o saddle ring). . . . . NiB $1439 Ex $1188 Gd $966
Model 93SC Sporting Carbine . . . . NiB $1377 Ex $1076 Gd $915

MODEL 93 LEVER-ACTION
REPEATING RIFLE. . . . . NiB $2833 Ex $2022 Gd $1370
Solid frame or takedown. Calibers: .25-36 Marlin, .30-30, .32 Special, .32-40, .38-55; tubular mag. holds 10 rounds. Bbl.:26 inches, round or octagon standard; also made w/28- and 32-inch bbls. Weight: 7.25 lbs. Open rear, bead front sights. Plain straight-grip stock an dforearm. Made from 1893 to 1936. Designaed Model 1893 prior to 1915.

MODEL 93 MUSKET. . . . . NiB $5610 Ex $ 3766 Gd $2833
Same as Standard Model 93 except w/30-inch bbl., angular bayonet, ramrod under bbl., musket stock, full-length military-style forearm. Weight: 8 lbs. Made from 1893 to 1915.

MODEL 94 LEVER-ACTION
REPEATING RIFLE. . . . . NiB $2655 Ex $1840 Gd $979
Solid frame or takedown. Calibers: .25-20, .32-20, .38-40, .44-40; 10-round tubular mag. Bbl.: round or octagon, 24 inches. Weight: 7 lbs. Open rear, bead front sights. Plain straight-grip stock and forearm (also available w/pistol-grip stock). Made from 1894 to 1934. Before 1906 designated as Model 1894.

MODEL 94 LEVER-ACTION COWBOY SERIES
Calibers: .357 Mag., .44-40, .44 Mag., .45 LC. 10-round magazine. 24-inch tapered octagon bbl. Weight: 7.5 lbs. 41.5 inches overall. Marble carbine front sight, adjustable semi-buckhorn rear. Blue finish. Checkered, straight-grip American black walnut stock w/hard rubber buttplate. Made from 1996 to date.

Cowboy model (.45 LC) . . . . NiB $833 Ex $644 Gd $466
Cowboy II model
(.357 Mag., .44-40, .44 Mag.) . . . . NiB $854 Ex $659 Gd $566

MODEL 97 LEVER-ACTION
REPEATING RIFLE. . . . . NiB $2590 Ex $2066 Gd $1259
Takedown. Caliber: .22 LR,Long, Short; full tubular mag. holds 25 Short, 20 Long, 18 LR. Half-length mag. holds 16 Short, 12 Long, 10 LR. Bbl.: 16, 24, 26, 28 inches. Weight: 6 lbs. Open rear, bead front sights. PLlain, straight-grip stock and forearms (also avail. w/pistol-grip stock). Made from 1897 to 1922. Before 1905 designated as Model 1897.

MODEL 98 AUTOLOADING RIFLE. . . . . . NiB $255 Ex $138 Gd $100
Solid frame. Caliber: .22 LR. Tubular magazine holds 15 cartridges. 22-inch bbl. Weight: 6.75 lbs. Sights: Open rear; hooded ramp front. Monte Carlo stock w/cheekpiece. Made from 1950 to 1961.

MODEL 99 AUTOLOADING RIFLE. . . . . . NiB $255 Ex $138 Gd $100
Caliber: .22 LR. Tubular magazine holds 18 cartridges. 22-inch bbl. Weight: 5.5 lbs. Sights: Open rear; hooded ramp front. Plain pistol-grip stock. Made from 1959 to 1961.

MODEL 99C . . . . NiB $209 Ex $177 Gd $119
Same as Model 99 except w/gold-plated trigger, receiver grooved for tip-off scope mounts, Monte Carlo stock (checkered in later production). Made from 1962 to 1978.

MODEL 99DL . . . . NiB $266 Ex $255 Gd $144
Same as Model 99 except w/gold-plated trigger, jeweled breech bolt, Monte Carlo stock w/pistol-grip, swivels and sling. Made from 1960 to 1965.

Marlin Firearms Co.

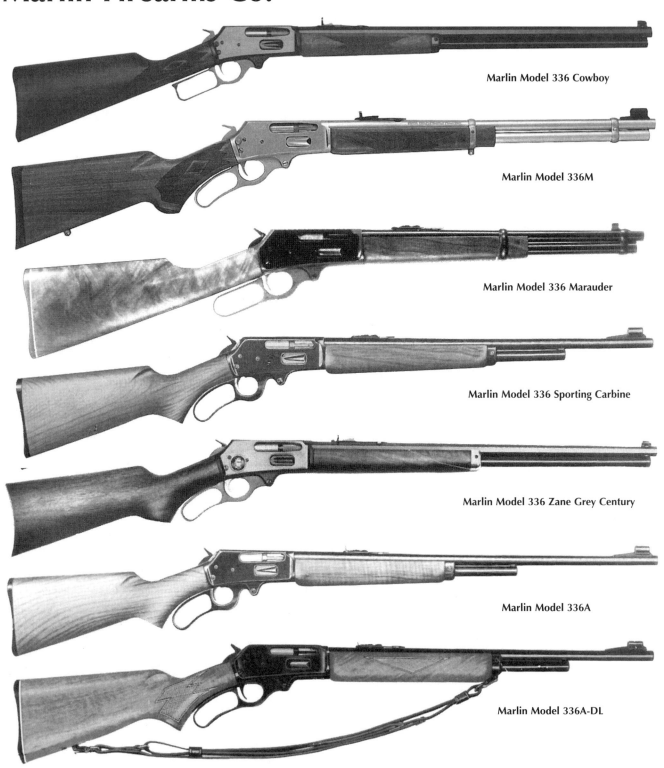

Marlin Model 336 Cowboy

Marlin Model 336M

Marlin Model 336 Marauder

Marlin Model 336 Sporting Carbine

Marlin Model 336 Zane Grey Century

Marlin Model 336A

Marlin Model 336A-DL

MODEL 100 BOLT-ACTION
SINGLE-SHOT RIFLE. . . . . **NiB $200 Ex $123 Gd $90**
Takedown. Caliber: .22 LR, Long, Short. 24-inch bbl. Weight: 4.5 lbs. Sights: Open rear; bead front. Plain pistol-grip stock. Made from 1936 to 1960.

MODEL 100SB . . . . **NiB $120 Ex $90 Gd $65**
Same as Model 100 except smoothbore for use w/22 shot cartridges, shotgun sight. Made from 1936 to 1941.

MODEL 99M1
CARBINE. . . . . **NiB $200 Ex $99 Gd $80**
Same as Model 99C except styled after U.S. .30 M1 Carbine; 9-round tubular magazine, 18-inch bbl. Sights: Open rear; military-style ramp front; carbine stock w/handguard and bbl. band, sling swivels. Weight: 4.5 lbs. Made from 1966 to 1979.

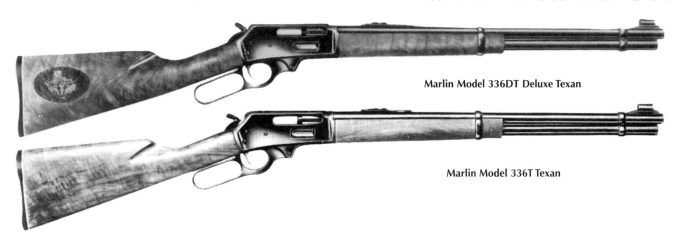

Marlin Model 336DT Deluxe Texan

Marlin Model 336T Texan

MODEL 100 TOM MIX SPECIAL. . . . . NiB $315 Ex $200 Gd $146
Same as Model 100 except w/peep rear sight; hooded front; Sling swivels. Made from 1936 to 1946.

MODEL 101 . . . . NiB $100 Ex $75 Gd $55
Improved version of Model 100 w/beavertail forearm, weighs 5 lbs. Introduced 1951. Disc.

MODEL 101 DL . . . . NiB $119 Ex $85 Gd $70
Same as Model 101 except has peep rear sight; hooded front, swivels. Disc.

MODEL 122 SINGLE-SHOT
JUNIOR TARGET RIFLE. . . . . NiB $135 Ex $95 Gd $75
Bolt action. Caliber: .22 LR, .22 Long, .22 Short. 22-inch bbl. Weight: 5 lbs. Sights: Open rear; hooded ramp front. Monte Carlo stock w/pistol-grip, swivels, sling. Made from 1961 to 1965.

MODEL 322 BOLT-ACTION
VARMINT RIFLE . . . . NiB $597 Ex $390 Gd $275
Sako short Mauser action. Caliber: .22 Rem.; three-round clip mag. Bbl. 24 inches, medium weight. Two-position peep rear, hooded ramp front sights. Checkered stock. Weight: 7.5 lbs. Made from 1954 to 1957.

MODEL 336A
LEVER-ACTION RIFLE. . . . . NiB $570 Ex $400 Gd $335
Same as Model 36A Rifle except w/improved action w/round breech bolt. Calibers: .30-30, .32 Special (disc. 1963), .35 Rem (intro. 1952). Made from 1948 to 1963, reintroduced 1973, disc. 1980.

MODEL 336A-DL . . . . NiB $665 Ex $544 Gd $351
Same as Model 336A Rifle except w/deluxe checkered stock and forearm, swivels and sling. Made from 1948 to 1963.

MODEL 336AS
LEVER-ACTION RIFLE. . . . . NiB $475 Ex $291 Gd $139
Similar to Model 30AS. Caliber: .30-30; six-round tubular mag. Bbl.: 20-inches w/Micro-Groove rifling. Lgt.: 38.25 inches. Weight: 7 lbs. Checkered walnut finish Maine birch pistol-grip stock w/ swivel studs and hard rubber buttplate. Tapped for scope mount and receiver sights. Screw-adj. open rear and ramp front sights. Made from 1999 to date.

MODEL 336C
LEVER-ACTION CARBINE. . . . . . . NiB $559 Ex $398 Gd $290
Same as Model 36 Carbine except w/improved action w/round breech bolt. Original calibers: .30-30 and .32 Special. Made from 1948 to 1983. .35 Rem. intro. in 1953. .32 Special disc. 1963.

MODEL 336 COWBOY
LEVER-ACTION RIFLE. . . . . NiB $600 Ex $445 Gd $377
Calibers: .30-30 Win., .38-55 Win.; six-round tubular mag. Bbl.: 24 inches, tapered octagon. Lgt.: 42.5 inches. Weight: 7.5 lbs. American black walnut checkered stock. Mar ble carbine front sight w/solid top receiver drilled and tapped for scope mount. Mar-Shield finish. Made from 1998 to date.

MODEL 336CS W/SCOPE. . . . . . . NiB $479 Ex $335 Gd $266
Lever-action w/hammer block safety. Caliber: .30-30 Win. or .35 Rem; six-round tubular mag. Bbl.: 20 inches, round, w/Micro Groove rifling. Lgt.: 38.5 inches. Weight 7 lbs. Hooded ramp front , folding rear sights. Solid top receiver drilled and tapped for scope mount or receiver sight. Offset hammer spur for scope use. American black walnut stock w/pistol grip, fluted comb. Mar-Shield finish. Made from 1984 to date.

MODEL 336DT DELUXE TEXAN . . . . NiB $500 Ex $466 Gd $359
Same as Model 336T except w/select walnut stock and forearm, handcarved longhorn steer and map of Texas on buttstock. Made from 1962 to 1964.

MODEL 336M
LEVER-ACTION RIFLE. . . . . NiB $590 Ex $490 Gd $359
Calibers: .30-30 Win; six-round tubular mag. Bbl.: 20 inches, stainless steel, Micro-Groove rifling. Lgt.: 38.5 inches. Weight: 7 lbs. American black walnut stock w/checkered pistol grip. Adj. folding semi-buckhorn rear and brass bead, hooded ramp front sights. Drilled and tapped for receiver sight and scope mounts. Mar-Shield finish. Made from 1999 to date.

MODEL 336 MARAUDER. . . . . . . NiB $600 Ex $485 Gd $300
Same as Model 336 Texan Carbine except w/16.25-inch bbl., weight: 6.25 lbs. Made from 1963 to 1964.

MODEL 336-MICRO GROOVE ZIPPER . . . NiB $845 Ex $633 Gd $390
Same as Model 336 Sporting Carbine but in .219 Zipper. Mde from 1955 to 1961.

MODEL 336 OCTAGON. . . . . NiB $570 Ex $498 Gd $300
Same as Model 336T except chambered for .30-30 only w/22-inch octagon bbl. Made in 1973.

MODEL 336 SPORTING CARBINE. . . . . . NiB $845 Ex $589 Gd $445
Same as Model 336A rifle except w/20-inch bbl., weight: 6.25 lbs. Made from 1948 to 1963.

MODEL 336T TEXAN CARBINE . . . . NiB $365 Ex $277 Gd $228
Same as Model 336 Carbine except w/straight-grip stock. Not availabie in .32 Special. Made from 1953 to 1983. .44 Mag., made from 1963 to 1967.

Marlin Firearms Co.

Marlin Model 336TS Carbine

Marlin Model 444SS

Marlin Model 455 Sporter

MODEL 336TS . . . . **NiB $400 Ex $333 Gd $190**
Lever-action w/hammer-block safety. Caliber: .30-30 Win.; six-round tubular mag. Bbl.: 18.5 inches, Micro-Groove rifling. Lgt.: 37 inches. Weight: 6.5 lbs. ramp front, adj. semi-buckhorn folding rear sights. Straight grip American black walnut stock. Made from 1983 to 1987.

**MODEL 336 ZANE
GREY CENTURY** . . . . **NiB $488 Ex $435 Gd $300**
Similar to Model 336A except w/22-inch octagon bbl. Caliber:. .30-30. Zane Grey Centennial 1872-1972 medallion inlaid in receiver. Select walnut stock w/classic pistol-grip and forearm; brass buttplate and forend cap. Weight 7 lbs. 10,000 produced (numbered ZG1 through ZG 10,000). Made in 1972.

**MODEL 444 LEVER-ACTION
REPEATING RIFLE** . . . . **NiB $477 Ex $390 Gd $235**
Similar to Model 336. Caliber: .444 Marlin; four-round tubular mag. Bbl.: 24 inches. Weight: 7.5 lbs. Open rear, hooded ramp front sights. Monte Carlo stock w/straight grip, recoil pad. Carbine sty;e forearm w/bbl. band; swivels, sling. Made from 1965 to 1971.

MARLIN MODEL 444 SPORTER . . . . **NiB $576 Ex $445 Gd $235**
Same as Model 444 Rifle except w/22-inch bbl., pistol-grip stock and forearm as on Model 336A; recoil pad, QD swivels and sling. Made from 1972 to 1983.

**MODEL 444P (OUTFITTER)
LEVER-ACTION RIFLE** . . . . **NiB $559 Ex $447 Gd $255**
Caliber: .444 Marlin. Five round tubular magazine. 18.5-inch ported bbl., 37 inches overall. Weight: 6.75 lbs. Ramp front and adjustable folding rear sights. Black walnut straight grip stock w/cut checkering and Mar-Shield finish. Made from 1999 to 2002.

MODEL 444SS . . . . **NiB $570 Ex $449 Gd $240**
Same specs as Model 444 except w/hammer safety. Made from 1984 to 2002 (Designated M444 in 2001).

MODEL 455 BOLT-ACTION SPORTER
FN Mauser action w/Sako trigger. Calibers: .30-06 or .308 Win.; five-round box mag. Bbl. 24 inches, medium-weight stainless steel.

Monte Carlo stock w/cheekpiece, checkered pistol grip and forearm. Lyman No. 48 receiver sight, hooded ramp front. Weight: 8.5 lbs. Made from 1957 to 1959.
.30-06 Spfd., 1,079 produced . . . . **NiB $700 Ex $535 Gd $325**
.308 Win., 59 produced . . . . **NiB $800 Ex $610 Gd $475**

MODEL 780 BOLT-ACTION REPEATER SERIES
Caliber: .22 LR. Long, Short. Seven round clip magazine. 22-inch bbl. Weight: 5.5 to 6 lbs. Sights: Open rear; hooded ramp front. Receiver grooved for scope mounting. Monte Carlo stock w/checkered pistol-grip and forearm. Made from 1971 to 1988.
Model 780 standard . . . . **NiB $145 Ex $100 Gd $85**
Model 781 w/17-round tubular mag. . . . . . . **NiB $145 Ex $100 Gd $85**
Model 782 .22 WMR w/swivels, sling. . . . . . **NiB $145 Ex $100 Gd $85**
Model 783 w/12-round tubular mag. . . . . . . **NiB $145 Ex $100 Gd $85**

MODEL 795 SELF-LOADING RIFLE . . . . . . **NiB $165 Ex $130 Gd $115**
Caliber: .22 LR; 10-round clip mag. Bbl.: 18 inches, Micro-Groove rifling. Lgt.: 41 inches. Weight: 5 lbs. Screw-adj. open rear and ramp front sights. Monte Carlo synthetic stock with checkering; swivel studs. Made from 1999 to date.

MODEL 880/881/882/883 BOLT-ACTION REPEATER SERIES
Caliber: .22 rimfire. Seven round magazine. 22-inch bbl. 41 inches overall. Weight: 5.5 to 6 lbs. Hooded ramp front sight; adj. folding rear. Grooved receiver for scope mounts. Checkered Monte Carlo-style walnut stock w/QD studs and rubber recoil pad. Made from 1989 to 1997.
.22 LR . . . . **NiB $220 Ex $177 Gd $115**
Stainless .22 LR . . . . **NiB $269 Ex $200 Gd $150**
Squirrel .22 LR . . . . **NiB $269 Ex $223 Gd $160**
Model 881 w/7-round tubular magazine . . **NiB $244 Ex $175 Gd $110**
Model 882 (.22 WMR) . . . . **NiB $235 Ex $189 Gd $115**
W/laminated hardwood stock . . . . **NiB $277 Ex $189 Gd $120**
Stainless w/Fire sights . . . . **NiB $290 Ex $222 Gd $167**
Stainless .22 LR . . . . **NiB $195 Ex $225 Gd $170**
Model 883
(.22 WMR w/12-round tubular mag.) . . . . . **NiB $235 Ex $179 Gd $120**
W/nickel-Teflon finish. . . . . **NiB $279 Ex $226 Gd $180**
Stainless w/laminated stock . . . . **NiB $297 Ex $200 Gd $177**

Marlin Model 780

Marlin Model 781

Marlin Model 783

Marlin Model 882L

Marlin Model 883N

MODEL 922 MAGNUM
SELF-LOADING RIFLE. . . . . **NiB $390 Ex $244 Gd $160**
Similar to Model 9 except chambered for .22 WMR. Seven round magazine. 20.5-inch bbl. 39.5 inches overall. Weight: 6.5 lbs. American black walnut stock w/Monte Carlo. Blued finish. Made from 1993 to 2001.

MODEL 980 .22 MAGNUM . . . . . . **NiB $290 Ex $167 Gd $135**
Bolt action. Caliber: .22 WMR. Eight round clip magazine. 24-inch bbl. Weight: 6 lbs. Sights: Open rear; hooded ramp front. Monte Carlo stock, swivels, sling. Made from 1962 to 1970.

MODEL 989 AUTOLOADING RIFLE. . . . . . **NiB $210 Ex $144 Gd $110**
Caliber: .22 LR. Seven round clip magazine. 22-inch bbl. Weight: 5.5 lbs. Sights: Open rear; hooded ramp front. Monte Carlo walnut stock w/pistol grip. Made from 1962 to 1966.

MODEL 989M2
CARBINE. . . . . **NiB $250 Ex $145 Gd $100**
Same as Model 99M1 except w/7-round clip. Made from 1966 to 199.

MODEL 990 SEMIAUTOMATIC
Caliber: .22 LR; 17-round tubular mag. Bbl.: 22 inches. Lgt.: 40.75 inches. Weight: 5.5 .bs. Side ejection. Cross-bolt safety. Brass bead ramp front, adj. semi-buckhorn folding rear sights. Grooved for scope mount. American black walnut Monte Carlo stock w/checkered pistol grip and forend. Made from 1979 to 1987.
Model 990 Semiautomatic . . . . **NiB $135 Ex $100 Gd $85**
Model 990L w/14-round mag,
laminated hardwood stock, QD swivels, black recoil pad.
Made 1992 to date . . . . **NiB $208 Ex $155 Gd $110**

Marlin Firearms Co.

Marlin Model 980

Marlin Model 989

Marlin Model 989M2

Marlin Model 990

Marlin Model 990L

Marlin Model 995

MODEL 995
SEMIAUTOMATIC. . . . . NiB $233 Ex $167 Gd $110
Caliber: .22 LR; seven-round clip mag. Bbl.: 18 inches. Lgt.: 36.75 inches. Weight: 5 lbs. Cross-bolt safety. Brass bead ramp from, adj. folding semi-buckhorn rear sights. American black walnut Monte Carlo stock w/checkered pistol grip and forend. Made from 1979 to 1994.

MODEL 1870-1970 CENTENNIAL MATCHED
PAIR, MODELS 336/39. . . . . NiB $2230 Ex $1766 Gd $1180
Presentation-grade rifles in luggage-style case. Matching serial numbers. Fancy walnut straight-grip stock and forearm, brass butt-plate and forend cap. Engraved receiver w/inlaid medallion; square lever. Bbl.: 20 inches, octagon. Model 336 calibers: .30-30; 7-round tubular mag. Weight 7 lbs. Model 39: Caliber: .22 Short, Long, LR; tubular mag. holds 21 Short, 16 Long, 15 LR. 1,000 sets produced. Made in 1970.

MODEL 1894 CARBINE
Replica of original Model 94. Caliber: .44 Rem. 10-round magazine. 20-inch round bbl. Weight: 6 lbs. Sight: Open rear; ramp front. Straight-grip stock. Made from 1969 to 1984.

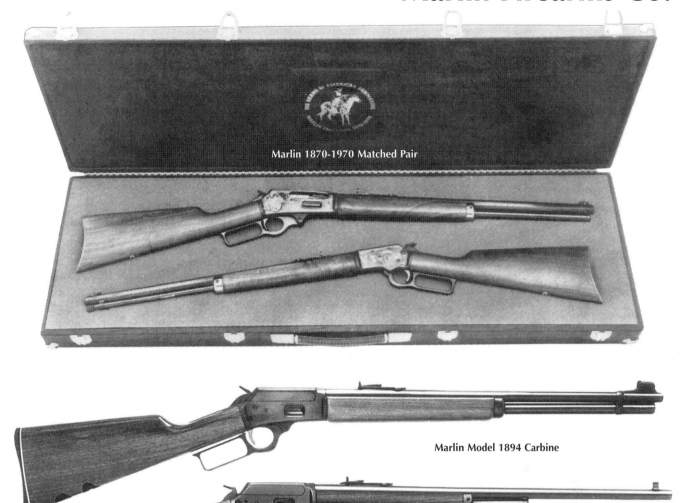

Marlin 1870-1970 Matched Pair

Marlin Model 1894 Carbine

Marlin Model 1894CL

Model 1894 Carbine. . . . . NiB $415 Ex $300 Gd $245
Octagon bbl. (made 1973) . . . . NiB $525 Ex $390 Gd $239
Sporter model
(w/22-inch bbl. made 1973). . . . . NiB $585 Ex $365 Gd $345

MODEL 1894CL
CLASSIC . . . . NiB $743 Ex $545 Gd $355
Calibers: .218 Bee, .25-20 Win., .32-20 Win.; six-round tubular mag. Bbl.: 22 inches. Lgt.: 38.75 inches. Weight: 6.25 lbs. Adj. semi-buckhorn folding rear, brass bead front sights. Drilled and tapped for scope mounts. Straight-grip American black walnut stock w/Mar-Shield finish. Made from 1988 to 1994.

MODEL 1894CS
LEVER-ACTION. . . . . NiB $779 Ex $545 Gd $365
Caliber: .357 Mag., .38 Special; nine-round tubular mag. Bbl.: 18.5 inches. Lgt.: 36 inches. Weight 6 lbs. Side ejection, hammer block safety. Square lever. Bead front, adj. Semi-buckhorn folding rear

sights. Offse hammer spur for scope use. Two-piece straight grip American black walnut stock w/white buttplate spacer. Mar-Shield finish. Made from 1984 to 2002.

MODEL 1894M
LEVER-ACTION. . . . . NiB $490 Ex $443 Gd $233
Caliber: .22 WMR; 11-round tubular mag. Bbl.: 20 inches. Weight: 6.25 lbs. Hooded brass bead ramp front, adj. semi-buckhorn folding rear sighs. Offset hammer spur for scope use. Square lever. Straight-grip American black walnut stock w/white buttplate spacer.

MODEL 1894S
LEVER-ACTION. . . . . NiB $522 Ex $344 Gd $245
Calibers: .41 Mag., .44 Rem. Mag., .44 S&W Special, .45 Colt.10-shot tubular magazine. 20-inch bbl.37.5 inches overall. Weight: 6 lbs. Sights and stock same as Model 1894M. Made from 1984 to 2002.

Marlin Firearms Co.

Marlin Model 1894CS

Marlin Model 1894M

Marlin Model 1894S

Marlin Model 1895
.45-70 (New Model)

MODEL 1895 .45-70 REPEATER . . . NiB $445 Ex $390 Gd $235
Model 336-type action. Caliber: .45-70 Gov't.; four-round mag., Bbl. 22 inches. Weight: 7 lbs. Open rear, bead front sights. Straight-grip stock, firearm w/metal end cap; QD swivels, leather sling. Made from 1972 to 1979.

MODEL 1895
LEVER-ACTION REPEATER . . . . NiB $447 Ex $393 Gd $236
Solid frame or takedown. Calibers: .33 WCF, .38-56, .40-65, .40-70, .40-82, .45-70. Nine round tubular magazine. 24-inch round or octagongon bbl. standard (other lengths available). Weight: 8 lbs. Sights: Open rear; bead front. Plain stock and forearm (also available w/pistol-grip stock). Made from 1895 to 1915.

MODEL 1895G (GUIDE GUN)
LEVER-ACTION RIFLE. . . . . NiB $590 Ex $389 Gd $280
Caliber: .45-70 Gov't.; four-round mag. Bbl. 18.5 inches, ported. Lgt.: 37 inches. Weight: 6.75 lbs. Ramp front, adj. folding rear

sights. Black walnut straight grip stock w/cut checkering and Mar-Shield finish. 2,500 made in 1998.

MODEL 1895M
LEVER-ACTION RIFLE. . . . . NiB $448 Ex $290 Gd $144
Caliber: .450 Marlin; four-round tubular mag. Bbl.: 18.5 inches, ported; Ballard-type rifling. Lgt.: 37 inches. Weight: 6.75 lbs. Adj. folding semi-buckhorn rear, ramp front sights. American black walnut straight-grip stock w/checkering. Vent. recoil pad. Mar-Shield finish. Made from 2000 to date.

MODEL 1895SS LEVER-ACTION . . . . NiB $609 Ex $448 Gd $356
Caliber: .45-70 Gov't.; four-round tubular mag. Bbl.: 22 inches, w/Micro-Groove rifling. Lgt.: 40.5 inches. Weight: 7.5 lbs. Hooded brass bead ramp front, adj. semi-buckhorn folding rear sights. Solid top receiver tapped for scope mount or receiver sight. Off-set hammer spur for scope use. Two-piece American black walnut stock w/fluted comb, pistol grip, sling swivels. Made from 1984 to date (changed to M1895 in 2001).

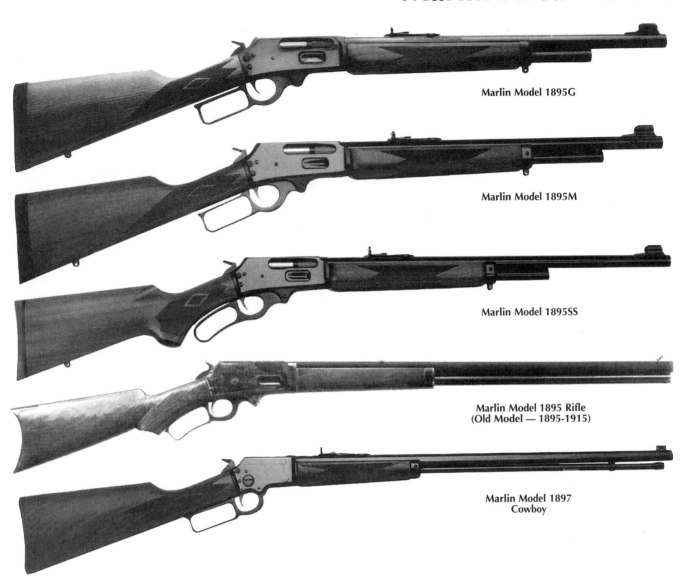

Marlin Model 1895G

Marlin Model 1895M

Marlin Model 1895SS

Marlin Model 1895 Rifle
(Old Model — 1895-1915)

Marlin Model 1897
Cowboy

MODEL 1897 COWBOY
LEVER-ACTION RIFLE. . . . . NiB $643 Ex $489 Gd $365
Caliber: .22 LR; tubular mag. holds 19 LR, 21 Long or 26 Short cartridges. Bbl.: 24 inches, tapered octagon. Lgt.: 40 inches. Weight:
6.5 lbs. Marble front, adj. rear sights; Tapped for scope mount. Black
walnut straight-grip stock w/cut checkering and Mar-Shield finish.
Made from 1999 to 2001.

MODEL 2000 TARGET RIFLE
Bolt-action, single-shot. Five-round adapter kit optional. Caliber:
.22 LR. Bbl.: 22 inches. Lgt.: 41 inches. Weight: 8 lbs. Globe front,
adj. peep or aperture rear sights. Two-stage target trigger. Textured
Kevlar or black/gray composite stock. Made from 1991 to 1995.
Model 2000 (disc. 1995). . . . . NiB $590 Ex $479 Gd $335
Model 2000A w/adj. comb
(made 1994 only) . . . . NiB $643 Ex $522 Gd $355
Model 2000L w/laminated stock
(intro. 1996) . . . . NiB $654 Ex $535 Gd $429

MODEL 7000
Semi-auto, side ejection. Manual bolt hold-open. Cross-bolt safety.
Caliber: .22 LR; 10-round mag. Bbl.: 18 inches. Weight: 5.5 lbs.

No sights; grooved for scope mounts. Matte finish. Synthetic stock.
Made from 1997 to 2001.
Model 7000 . . . . NiB $255 Ex $190 Gd $146
Model 7000T . . . . NiB $390 Ex $290 Gd $220

MODEL A-1
AUTOLOADING RIFLE . . . . NiB $185 Ex $110 Gd $90
Takedown. Caliber: .22 LR. Six round detachable box magazine.
24-inch bbl. Weight: 6 lbs. Open rear sight. Plain pistol-grip stock.
Made from 1935 to 1946.

MODEL A-1C
AUTOLOADING RIFLE. . . . . NiB $185 Ex $110 Gd $90
Same as Model A-1 except w/beavertail forend. Made from 1940
to 1946.

MODEL A-1DL . . . . NiB $185 Ex $110 Gd $90
Same as Model A-1C except w/peep rear sight; hooded front,
swivels.

MODEL A-1E. . . . . NiB $190 Ex $125 Gd $95
Same as Model A-1 except w/peep rear sight; hooded front.

Marlin Firearms Co.

Marlin Model 2000

Marlin Model 2000L

Marlin Model 7000

Marlin Model 7000T

MODEL MR-7 BOLT-ACTION RIFLE
Calibers: .25-06 Rem., .270 Win., .280 Rem., .308 Win., .30-06; four-round mag. Bbl.: 22 inches, w/or w/o sights. Jeweled bolt w/ cocking indicator and three-position safety. Lgt.: 43.31 inches. Weight: 7.5 lbs. Checkered American walnut or birch stock w/recoil pad and swivel studs. Made from 1996 to 1999.
Standard model. . . . . **NiB $555 Ex $380 Gd $277**
W/birch stock, intro. 1998 . . . . **NiB $460 Ex $379 Gd $255**
W/open sights, add. **$50**

MODEL 10 . . . . **NiB $140 Ex $110 Gd $85**
Same as Marlin Model 101 except w/walnut-finished hardwood stock. Made from 1966 to 1979. Later production featuring hot iron-stamped wood pistol grip to stimulate checkering/carving; plain forend.

MODEL 20 . . . . **NiB $779 Ex $435 Gd $310**
Same as Marlin Model 80/780 except w/bead front sight, walnut-finished hardwood stock. Made from 1966 to 1982. Recent production has stamped pistol grip, plain forend.

MODEL 30 . . . . **NiB $280 Ex $133 Gd $100**
Same as Marlin Model 336C except chambered for .30-30 only, w/4-round magazine, plainer stock and forearm of walnut-finished hardwood. Made from 1966 to 1968.

MODEL 30A . . . . **NiB $279 Ex $190 Gd $139**
Same as Marlin Model 336C but chambered for .30-30 only; five-round mag. w/checkered walnut-finished hardwood stock. Made from 1969 to 1983.

MODEL 36G . . . . **NiB $879 Ex $633 Gd $260**
Same as Marlin Model 336C except chambered for .30-30 only, w/5-round magazine, plainer stock. Made from 1960 to 1965.

MODEL 60 . . . . **NiB $200 Ex $124 Gd $79**
Same as Marlin Model 99C except w/walnut-finished hardwood stock. Made from 1960 to 1980.

MODEL 70 . . . . **NiB $188 Ex $95 Gd $65**
Same as Marlin Model 989M2 except w/walnut-finished hardwood stock; no handguard. Made from 1966 to 1969.

MODEL 80G . . . . **NiB $100 Ex $65 Gd $45**
Same as Marlin Model 80C except w/plain stock, bead front sight. Made from 1960 to 1965.

Marlin Firearms Co.

Marlin Model A-1 Autoloader

Marlin-Glenfield Model 10

Marlin-Glenfield Model 30A

Marlin-Glenfield Model 60

Marlin-Glenfield Model 70

Marlin-Glenfield Model 80G

MODEL 81G. . . . . NiB $110 Ex $78 Gd $66
Same as Marlin Model 81C except w/plain stock, bead front sight. Made from 1960 to 1965.

MODEL 99G. . . . . NiB $170 Ex $75 Gd $65
Same as Marlin Model 99C except w/plain stock, bead front sight. Made from 1960 to 1965.

MODEL 101G. . . . . NiB $110 Ex $79 Gd $55
Same as Marlin Model 101 except w/plain stock. Made from 1960 to 1965.

**MODEL 989G
AUTOLOADING RIFLE**. . . . . NiB $179 Ex $110 Gd $79
Same as Marlin Model 989 except w/plain stock, bead front sight. Made from 1962 to 1964.

MAUSER SPORTING RIFLES — Oberndorf am Neckar, Germany. Manufactured by Mauser-Werke GmbH. Imported by Brolin Arms, Pomona, California (previously by Gun South, Inc.; Gibbs Rifle Co.; Precision Imports, Inc. and KDF, Inc.)

Before the end of WWI the name of the Mauser firm was "Waffenfabrik Mauser A.-G." Shortly after WWI it was changed to "Mauser-Werke A.-G." This information may be used to determine the age of genuine original Mauser sporting rifles made before WWII because all bear either of these firm names as well as the Mauser banner trademark.

Mauser Sporting Rifles

Mauser Model ES340

Mauser Model ES350

The first four rifles listed were manufactured before WWI. Those that follow were produced between World Wars I and II. The early Mauser models can generally be identified by the pistol grip, which is rounded instead of capped, and the M/98 military-type magazine floorplate and catch. The later models have hinged magazine floorplates with lever or button release.

PRE-WORLD WAR I MODELS

BOLT-ACTION SPORTING CARBINE
Calibers: 6.5x54, 6.5x58, 7x57, 8x57, 957mm. 19.75-inch bbl. Weight: 7 lbs. Full-stocked to muzzle. Other specifications same as for standard rifle.

W/20-inch bbl. (Type M). . . . . NiB $2489 Ex $2066 Gd $1435
W/20- or 24-inch bbl. (Type S) . . . . . . NiB $2566 Ex $2155 Gd $1486

BOLT-ACTION SPORTING RIFLE
Calibers: 6.5x55, 6.5x58, 7x57, 8x57, 9x57, 9.3x62 10.75x68. Five-round box magazine, 23.5-inch bbl. Weight: 7 to 7.5 lbs. Pear-shaped bolt handle. Double-set or single trigger. Sights: Tangent curve rear; ramp front. Pistol-grip stock, forearm w/Schnabel tip and swivels.

Type A, English export. . . . . NiB $2669 Ex $2256 Gd $1559
Type B. . . . . NiB $1790 Ex $1466 Gd $1080

BOLT-ACTION SPORTING RIFLE,
MILITARY MODEL TYPE C . . . . NiB $3854 Ex $3135 Gd $2189
So called because of stepped M/98-type bbl., military front sight and double-pull trigger. Calibers: 7x57, 8x57, 9x57mm. Other specifications same as for standard rifle.

BOLT-ACTION SPORTING RIFLE
SHORT MODEL TYPE K . . . . NiB $3856 Ex $3139 Gd $2190
Calibers: 6.5x54, 8x51mm. 19.75-inch bbl. Weight: 6.25 lbs. Other specifications same as for standard rifle.

PRE-WORLD WAR II MODELS

MODEL DSM34 BOLT-ACTION
SINGLE-SHOT SPORTING RIFLE . . . . NiB $670 Ex $445 Gd $335
Also called "Sport-model." Caliber: .22 LR. 26-inch bbl. Weight: 7.75 lbs. Sights: Tangent curve open rear; Barleycorn front. M/98 military-type stock, swivels. Introduced c. 1935.

MODEL EL320 BOLT-ACTION
SINGLE-SHOT SPORTING RIFLE . . . . NiB $556 Ex $449 Gd $339
Caliber: .22 LR. 23.5-inch bbl. Weight: 4.25 lbs. Sights: Adj. open rear; bead front. Sporting stock w/checkered pistol grip, swivels.

MODEL EN310 BOLT-ACTION
SINGLE-SHOT SPORTING RIFLE . . . . NiB $499 Ex $420 Gd $298
Caliber: .22 LR. ("22 Lang fur Buchsen.") 19.75-inch bbl. Weight: 4 lbs. Sights: Fixed open rear, blade front. Plain pistol-grip stock.

MODEL ES340 BOLT-ACTION
SINGLE-SHOT TARGET RIFLE . . . . NiB $765 Ex $455 Gd $335
Caliber: .22 LR. 25.5-inch bbl. Weight: 6.5 lbs. Sights: Tangent curve rear; ramp front. Sporting stock w/checkered pistol-grip and grooved forearm, swivels.

MODEL ES340B BOLT-ACTION SINGLE-SHOT
TARGET RIFLE. . . . . NiB $765 Ex $445 Gd $356
Caliber: .22 LR. 26.75-inch bbl. Weight: 8 lbs. Sights: Tangent curve open rear; ramp front. Plain pistol-grip stock, swivels.

MODEL ES350 BOLT-ACTION SINGLE-SHOT
TARGET RIFLE. . . . . NiB $977 Ex $775 Gd $558
"Meistershaftsbuchse" (Championship Rifle). Caliber: .22 LR. 27.5-inch bbl. Weight: 7.75 lbs. Sights: Open micrometer rear; ramp front. Target stock w/checkered pistol-grip and forearm, grip cap, swivels.

MODEL ES350B BOLT-ACTION SINGLE-SHOT
TARGET RIFLE . . . . NiB $970 Ex $668 Gd $490
Same general specifications as Model MS350B except single-shot, weight: 8.25 lbs.

MODEL KKW BOLT-ACTION
SINGLE-SHOT TARGET RIFLE . . . . NiB $944 Ex $667 Gd $544
Caliber: .22 LR. 26-inch bbl. Weight: 8.75 lbs. Sights: Tangent curve open rear; Barleycorn front. M/98 military-type stock, swivels. Note: This rifle has an improved design Mauser 22 action w/separate non-rotating bolt head. In addition to being produced for commercial sale, this model was used as a training rifle by the German armed forces; it was also made by Walther and Gustoff. Introduced just before WWII.

MODEL MM410 BOLT-ACTION
REPEATING SPORTING RIFLE . . . . NiB $2166 Ex $1590 Gd $955
Caliber: .22 LR. Five round detachable box magazine. 23.5-inch bbl. Weight: 5 lbs. Sights: Tangent curve open rear; ramp front. Sporting stock w/checkered pistol-grip, swivels.

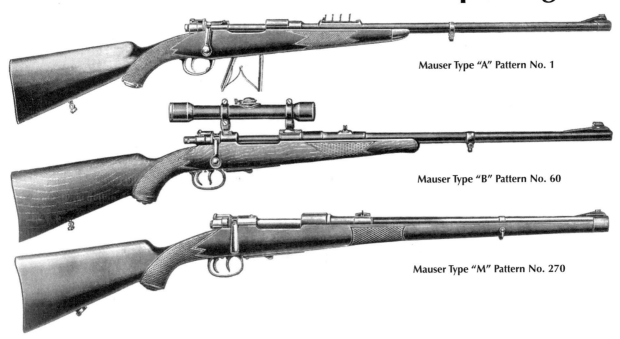

Mauser Type "A" Pattern No. 1

Mauser Type "B" Pattern No. 60

Mauser Type "M" Pattern No. 270

MODEL MM410B BOLT-ACTION
REPEATING SPORTING RIFLE . . . . **NiB $2166 Ex $1590 Gd $955**
Caliber: .22 LR. Five round detachable box magazine. 23.5-inch
bbl. Weight: 6.25 lbs. Sights: Tangent curve open rear; ramp front.
Lightweight sporting stock w/checkered pistol-grip, swivels.

MODEL MS350B BOLT-ACTION
REPEATING TARGET RIFLE . . . . **NiB $1255 Ex $800 Gd $556**
Caliber: .22 LR. Five round detachable box magazine. Receiver and
bbl. grooved for detachable rear sight or scope. 26.75-inch bbl.
Weight: 8.5 lbs. Sights: Micrometer open rear; ramp front. Target
stock w/checkered pistol grip and forearm, grip cap, sling swivels.

MODEL MS420 BOLT-ACTION
REPEATING SPORTING RIFLE . . . . **NiB $1145 Ex $879 Gd $606**
Caliber: .22 LR. Five round detachable box magazine. 25.5-inch
bbl. Weight: 6.5 lbs. Sights: Tangent curve open rear; ramp front.
Sporting stock w/checkered pistol grip, grooved forearm swivels.

MODEL MS420B BOLT-ACTION
REPEATING TARGET RIFLE . . . . **NiB $1156 Ex $922 Gd $633**
Caliber: .22 LR. Five round detachable box magazine. 26.75-inch
bbl. Weight: 8 lbs. Sights: Tangent curve open rear; ramp front.
Target stock w/checkered pistol grip, grooved forearm, swivels.

STANDARD MODEL RIFLE . . . . . . **NiB $339 Ex $210 Gd $159**
Refined version of German Service Kar. 98k. Straight bolt handle.
Calibers: 7mm Mauser (7x57mm), 7.9mm Mauser (8x57mm). Five
round box magazine. 23.5-inch bbl. Weight: 8.5 lbs. Sights: Blade
front; adj. rear. Walnut stock of M/98 military-type. Note: These
rifles were made for commercial sale and are of the high quality
found in the Oberndorf Mauser sporters. They bear the Mauser
trademark on the receiver ring.

TYPE "A" BOLT-ACTION
SPORTING RIFLE . . . . **NiB $5596 Ex $3227 Gd $1975**
Special British Model. 7x57, 30-06 (7.62x63), 8x60, 9x57,
9.3x62mm. Five round box mag. 23.5-inch round bbl. Weight:
7.25 lbs. Mil.-type single trigger. Sights: Express rear; hooded ramp
front. Circassian walnut sporting stock w/checkered pistol-grip and
forearm, w/ or w/o cheekpiece, buffalo horn forend tip and grip

cap, detachable swivels. Variations: Octagon bbl., double-set trigger, shotgun-type safety, folding peep rear sight, tangent curve rear
sight, three-leaf rear sight.

TYPE "A" BOLT-ACTION SPORTING RIFLE,
MAGNUM MODEL . . . . **NiB $5598 Ex $3443 Gd $2745**
Same general specifications as standard Type "A" except w/Magnum
action, weighs 7.5 to 8.5 lbs. Calibers: .280 Ross, .318 Westley
Richards Express, 10.75x68mm, .404 Nitro Express.

TYPE "A" BOLT-ACTION SPORTING
RIFLE, SHORT MODEL . . . . . . **NiB $6149 Ex $4144 Gd $2448**
Same as standard Type "A" except w/short action, 21.5-inch round
bbl., weight 6 lbs. Calibers: .250-3000, 6.5x54, 8x51mm.

TYPE "B" BOLT-ACTION SPORTING
RIFLE. . . . . **NiB $4885 Ex $2544 Gd $2045**
Normal Model. Calibers: 7x57, .30-06 (7.62x63), 8x57, 8x60,
9x57, 9.3x62, 10.7568mm. Five round box magazine. 23.5-inch
round bbl. Weight: 7.25 lbs. Double-set trigger. Sights: Three-
leaf rear, ramp front. Fine walnut stock w/checkered pistol-grip,
Schnabel forend tip, cheekpiece, grip cap, swivels. Variations:
Octagon or half-octagon bbl., military-type single trigger, shotgun-
type safety, folding peep rear sight, tangent curve rear sight, telescopic sight.

TYPE "K" BOLT-ACTION
SPORTING RIFLE . . . . **NiB $6177 Ex $3775 Gd $2856**
Light Short Model. Same specifications as Normal Type "B" model
except w/short action, 21.5-inch round bbl., weight: 6 lbs. Calibers:
.250-3000, 6.5x54, 8x51mm.

TYPE "M" BOLT-ACTION
SPORTING CARBINE . . . . **NiB $5569 Ex $4133 Gd $2455**
Calibers: 6.5x54, 7x57, .30-06 (7.62x63), 8x51, 8x60, 9x57mm. Five
round box magazine. 19.75-inch round bbl. Weight: 6 to 6.75 lbs.
Double-set trigger, flat bolt handle. Sights: Three-leaf rear; ramp front.
Stocked to muzzle, cheekpiece, checkered pistol-grip and forearm,
grip cap, steel forend cap, swivels. Variations: Military-type single
trigger, shotgun-type trigger, shotgun-type safety, tangent curve rear
sight, telescopic sight.

Mauser Sporting Rifles

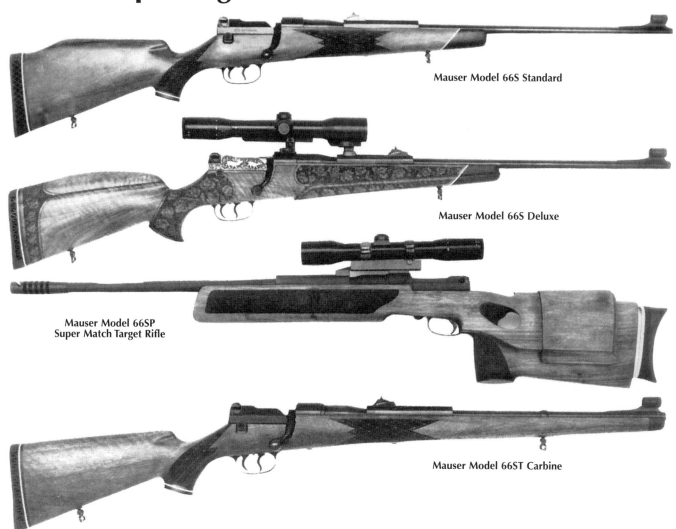

Mauser Model 66S Standard

Mauser Model 66S Deluxe

Mauser Model 66SP
Super Match Target Rifle

Mauser Model 66ST Carbine

TYPE "S" BOLT-ACTION
SPORTING CARBINE . . . . NiB $4300 Ex $2339 Gd $2045
Calibers: 6.5x54 7x57, 8x51, 8x60, 9x57mm. Five-round box magazine. 19.75-inch round bbl. Weight: 6 to 6.75 lbs. Double-set trigger. Sights: Three-leaf rear; ramp front. Stocked to muzzle, Schnabel forend tip, cheekpiece, checkered pistol-grip w/cap, swivels. Variations: Same as listed for Normal Model Type "B."

POST-WORLD WAR II MODELS

NOTE: *Production of original Mauser sporting rifles (66 series) resumed at the Oberndorf plant in 1965 by Mauser-Jagdwaffen GmbH, now Mauser-Werke Oberndorf GmbH. The Series 2000-3000-4000 rifles, however, were made for Mauser by Friedrich Wilhelm Heym Gewehrfabrik, Muennerstadt, West Germany.*

MODEL 66S BOLT-ACTION STANDARD SPORTING RIFLE
Telescopic short action. Bbls. Interchangeable within cal. Group. Single- or double-set trigger (interchangeable). Cal: .243 Win., 6.5x57, .270 Win., 7x64, .308 Win., .30-06. Three round mag. 23.6 inch bbl. (25.6 inch in 7x64). Wt: 7.3 lbs. (7.5 lbs in 7x64). Sights: Adj.open rear, hooded ramp front. Select Eur. Walnut stock, Monte Carlo w.cheekpiece, rosewood forend tip and pistol-grip cap, skip checkering, recoil pad, sling swivels. Made from 1974 to 1995,

export to U.S. disc. 1974. Note: U.S. designation, 1971 to 1973, was "Model 660."
Model 66S. . . . . NiB $4739 Ex $3054 Gd $2044
W/extra bbl. assembly, add. $600

MODEL 66S DELUXE SPORTER
Limited production special order. Model 66S rifles and carbines are available with /elaborate engraving, gold and silver inlays and carved select walnut stocks. Added value is upward of $4500.

MODEL 66S ULTRA
Same general specifications as Model 66S Standard except with 20.9-inch bbl., weight: 6.8 lbs.
Model 66S Ultra . . . . NiB $1754 Ex $1644 Gd $1097
W/extra bbl. assembly, add. $600

MODEL 66SG BIG GAME
Same general specifications as Model 66S Standard except w/25.6-inch bbl., weight 9.3 lbs. Calibers: .375 H&H Mag., .458 Win. Mag. Note: U.S. designation, 1971-73, was "Model 660 Safari."
MODEL 66SG BIG GAME. . . . . NiB $3077 Ex $2100 Gd $1388
W/ extra bbl. assembly, add $600

Mauser Model 99

Mauser Model 201

Mauser Model 3000

Mauser Model 4000

MODEL 66SH HIGH PERFORMANCE . . NiB $1689 Ex $1530 Gd $1109
Same general specifications as Model 66S Standard except w/25.6-inch bbl., weighs 7.5 lbs. (9.3 lbs. in 9.3x64). Calibers: 6.5x68, 7mm Rem. Mag., 7mm S.E.v. Hoffe, .300 Win. Mag., 8x68S, 9.3x64.

MODEL 66SP SUPER MATCH
BOLT-ACTION TARGET RIFLE. . . . . . . NiB $4198 Ex $3700 Gd $2033
Telescopic short action. Adj. single-stage trigger. Caliber: .308 Win. (chambering for other cartridges available on special order). Three round magazine. 27.6-inch heavy bbl. w/muzzle brake, dovetail rib for special scope mount. Weight: 12 lbs. Target stock w/wide and deep forearm, full pistol-grip, thumbhole adj. cheek-piece, adj. rubber buttplate.

MODEL 66ST CARBINE
Same general specifications as Model 66S Standard except w/20.9-inch bbl., full-length stock, weight: 7 lbs.
Model 66ST. . . . . NiB $2635 Ex $1710 Gd $1277
W/extra bbl. assembly, add $600

MODEL 83 BOLT-ACTION RIFLE . . . . . NiB $2215 Ex $2188 Gd $1360
Centerfire single-shot, bolt-action rifle for 300-meter competition. Caliber: .308 Win. 25.5-inch fluted bbl. Weight: 10.5 lbs. Adj. micrometer rear sight globe front. Fully adj. competition stock. Disc. 1988.

MODEL 96 . . . . NiB $677 Ex $633 Gd $455
Calibers: .25-06, .270 Win., 7x64, .308 Win., .30-06, 7mm Rem. Mag., .300 Win. Mag. 22-inch bbl.; magnums 24-inch. Weight: 6.25 lbs. No sights; drilled and tapped for scope. Walnut stock. Five-round top-loading magazine. 3-position safety.

MODEL 99 CLASSIC BOLT-ACTION RIFLE
Calibers: .243 Win., .25-06, .270 Win., .30-06, .308 Win., .257 Wby., .270 Wby., 7mm Rem. Mag., .300 Win., .300 Wby. .375 H&H. Four round magazine (standard), 3-round (Magnum). Bbl.: 24-inch (standard) or 26-inch (Magnum). 44 inches overall (standard). Weight: 8 lbs. No sights. Checkered European walnut stock w/rosewood grip cap available in Classic and Monte Carlo styles w/High-Luster or oil finish. Disc. importing 1994.
Standard Classic or
Monte Carlo (oil finish). . . . . NiB $1156 Ex $1066 Gd $710
Magnum Classic or
Monte Carlo (oil finish). . . . . NiB $1266 Ex $1109 Gd $800
Standard Classic or
Monte Carlo (H-L finish). . . . . NiB $1188 Ex $1098 Gd $775
Magnum Classic or
Monte Carlo (H-L finish). . . . . NiB $1344 Ex $1109 Gd $790

MODEL 107 BOLT-ACTION RIFLE . . . . NiB $365 Ex $277 Gd $210
Caliber: .22 LR. Mag. Five round magazine. 21.5-inch bbl. 40 inches overall. Weight: 5 lbs. Receiver drilled and tapped for rail scope mounts. Hooded front sight, adj. rear. Disc. importing 1994.

MODEL 201/201 LUXUS BOLT-ACTION RIFLE
Calibers: .22 LR. .22 Win. Mag. Five round magazine. 21-inch bbl. 40 inches overall. Weight: 6.5 lbs. Receiver drilled and tapped for scope mounts. Sights optional. Checkered walnut-stained beech stock w/Monte Carlo. Model 201 Luxus w/checkered European walnut stock QD swivels, rosewood forend and rubber recoil pad. Made from 1989 to 1997.
Standard model. . . . . NiB $670 Ex $555 Gd $400
Magnum . . . . NiB $722 Ex $569 Gd $440
Luxus Standard model. . . . . NiB $756 Ex $544 Gd $468
Luxus Magnum model. . . . . NiB $844 Ex $633 Gd $560

Mitchell Arms, Inc.

Midland Model 2700 Bolt-Action Rifle

MODEL 2000 BOLT-ACTION
SPORTING RIFLE . . . . **NiB $539 Ex $355 Gd $290**
Modified Mauser-type action. Calibers: .270 Win., .308 Win., .30-06.
Five-round magazine. 24-inch bbl. Weight: 7.5 lbs. Sights: Folding
leaf rear; hooded ramp front. Checkered walnut stock w/Monte Carlo
comb and cheekpiece, forend tip, sling swivels. Made from 1969 to
1971. Note: Model 2000 is similar in appearance to Model 3000.

MODEL 2000 CLASSIC BOLT-ACTION SPORTING RIFLE
Calibers: .22-250 Rem., .234 Win., .270 Win., 7mm Mag., .308
Win., .30-06, .300 Win. Mag. Three or 5-round magazine. 24-inch
bbl. Weight: 7.5 lbs. Sights: Folding leaf rear; hooded ramp front.
Checkered walnut stock w/Monte Carlo comb and cheekpiece, forend
tip, sling swivels. Imported 1998. The Model 2000 Classic is designed
to interchange bbl. assemblies within a given caliber group.
Classic model .NiB $1696 Ex $ 1377 Gd $1044
Professional model . . . . NiB $3228 Ex $2709 Gd $1995
W/recoil compensator . . . . NiB $3245 Ex $2730 Gd $1100
Sniper model. NiB $2010 Ex $1544 Gd $1120
Varmint model . . . . .NiB $1996 Ex $1528 Gd $965
Extra bbl. assembly, add $950

MODEL 3000 BOLT-ACTION
SPORTING RIFLE . . . . **NiB $570 Ex $440 Gd $400**
Modified Mauser-type action. Calibers: .243 Win., .270 Win., .308
Win., .30-06. Five round magazine. 22-inch bbl. Weight: 7 lbs. No
sights. Select European walnut stock, Monte Carlo style w/cheek-
piece, rosewood forend tip and pistol-grip cap, skip checkering,
recoil pad, sling swivels. Made from 1971 to 1974.

MODEL 3000 MAGNUM . . . . **NiB $635 Ex $486 Gd $379**
Same general specifications as standard Model 3000, except w/3-
round magazine, 26-inch bbl., weight: 8 lbs. Calibers: 7mm Rem.
Mag., .300 Win. Mag., .375 H&H Mag.
MODEL 4000 VARMINT RIFLE . . . . **NiB $466 Ex $377 Gd $269**
Same general specifications as standard Model 3000, except w/
smaller action, folding leaf rear sight; hooded ramp front, rubber
buttplate instead of recoil pad, weight 6.75 lbs. Calibers: .222 Rem.,
.223 Rem. 22-inch bbl. Select European walnut stock w/rosewood
forend tip and pistol-grip cap. French checkering and sling swivels.

GEBRÜDER MERKEL — Suhl, Germany

OVER/UNDER RIFLES ("BOCK-DOPPELBÜCHSEN")
Calibers: 5.6x35 Vierling, 6.5x58r5, 7x57r5, 8x57JR, 8x60R
Magnum, 9.3x53r5, 9.3x72r5, 9.3x74r5, 10.3x60R as well as most
of the British calibers for African and Indian big game. Various bbl.
lengths, weights. In general, specifications correspond to those of
Merkel over/under shotguns. Values of these over/under rifles (in
calibers for which ammunition is obtainable) are about the same as

those of comparable shotgun models currently manufactured.
Model 210 . . . . NiB $5766 Ex $4470 Gd $3210
Model 210E. . . . . NiB $6630 Ex $4900 Gd $3765
Model 240E1. . . . . NiB $7113 Ex $4966 Gd $3412

MEXICAN MILITARY RIFLE — Manufactured by Government Arsenal, Mexico, D.F.

MODEL 1936 MAUSER MILITARY RIFLE . . **NiB $233 Ex $179 Gd $110**
Same as German Kar.98k w/minor variations and U.S. M/1903
Springfield-type knurled cocking piece.

MIDLAND RIFLES — Manufactured by Gibbs Rifle Company, Inc., Martinsburg, West Virginia

MODEL 2100 BOLT-ACTION
RIFLE. . . . . **NiB $413 Ex $335 Gd $228**
Calibers: .22-250, .243 Win., 6mm Rem., .270 Win., 6.5x55, 7x57, 7x64, .308
Win., and .30-06. Springfield 1903 action. Four-round magazine. 22-inch bbl.
43 inches overall. Weight: 7 lbs. Flip-up rear sight; hooded ramp front. Finely
finished and checkered walnut stock w/pistol-grip cap and sling swivels. Steel
recoil bar. Action drilled and tapped for scope mounts. Production disc.1997.

MODEL 2600 BOLT-ACTION RIFLE . . . . . . **NiB $445 Ex $366 Gd $220**
Same general specifications as Model 2100 except no pistol-grip cap,
and stock is walnut-finished hardwood. Made from 1992 to 1997.

MODEL 2700 BOLT-ACTION RIFLE . . . . . . **NiB $443 Ex $284 Gd $220**
Same general specifications as Model 2100 except the weight of
this rifle as been reduced by utilizing a tapered bbl., anodized aluminum trigger housing and lightened stock. Weight: 6.5 lbs. Disc.

MODEL 2800 LIGHTWEIGHT RIFLE . . . . . **NiB $466 Ex $355 Gd $267**
Same general specifications as Model 2100 except w/laminated
birch stock. Made from 1992 to 1994 and from 1996 to 1997.

MITCHELL ARMS, INC. — Fountain Valley, California (formerly Santa Ana, California)

MODEL 15/22 SEMIAUTOMATIC
High Standard-style action. Caliber: .22 LR. 15-round magazine (10-round
after 10/13/94). 20.5-inch bbl. 37.5 inches overall. Weight: 6.25 lbs. Ramp
front sight; adj. open rear. Blued finish. Mahogany stock; Monte Carlo-
style American walnut stock on Deluxe model. Made from 1994 to 1996.

Mitchell Arms, Inc.

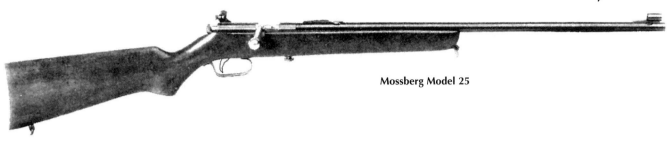

Mossberg Model 25

SP (Special) w/plastic buttplate . . . . NiB $300 Ex $233 Gd $179
Carbine. . . . . NiB $300 Ex $233 Gd $179
Deluxe . . . . NiB $259 Ex $166 Gd $125

MODEL 9300 SERIES BOLT-ACTION RIFLE
Calibers: .22 LR. .22 Mag. Five or 10-round magazine. 22.5-inch bbl. 40.75 inches overall. Weight: 6.5 lbs. Beaded ramp front sight; adj. open rear. Blued finish. American walnut stock. Made from 1994 to 1995.
Model 9302 (.22 LR
w/checkered stock, rosewood caps) . . . . . . NiB $319 Ex $239 Gd $177
Model 9302 (.22 Mag.,
checkered stock, rosewood caps) . . . . NiB $317 Ex $237 Gd $175
Model 9303 (.22 LR, plain stock) . . . . NiB $317 Ex $237 Gd $175
Model 9304
(.22 Mag., checkered stock) . . . . NiB $266 Ex $201 Gd $177
Model 9305 (.22 LR, special stock). . . . . . NiB $221 Ex $179 Gd $235

AK-22 SEMIAUTOMATIC RIFLE . . . . NiB $359 Ex $248 Gd $189
Replica of AK-47 rifle. .22 LR. .22 WMR., 20-round magazine (.22 LR), 10-round (.22 WMR). 18-inch bbl. 36 inches overall. Weight: 6.5 lbs. Sights: Post front; open adj. rear. European walnut stock and forend. Matte black finish. Made from 1985 to 1994.
CAR-15 . . . . NiB $525 Ex $355 Gd $283
Replica of AR-15 CAR rifle. Caliber: .22 LR. 15-round magazine.16.25-inch bbl. 32 inches overall. Sights: Adj. post front; adj. aperture rear. Telescoping buttstock and ventilated forend. Matte black finish. Made from 1990 to 1994.
GALIL 22 SEMIAUTOMATIC RIFLE. . . . . . . NiB $435 Ex $289 Gd $198
Replica of Israeli Galil rifle. Calibers: .22 LR. .22 WMR., 20-round magazine (.22 LR), 10-round (.22 WMR). 18-inch bbl. 36 inches overall. Weight: 6.5 lbs. Sights: Adj. post front; rear adj. for windage. Folding metal stock w/European walnut grip and forend. Matte black finish. Made from 1987 to 1993.

M-16A 22 SEMIAUTOMATIC RIFLE . . . . . NiB $479 Ex $266 Gd $179
Replica of AR-15 rifle. Caliber: .22 LR. 15-round magazine. 20.5-inch bbl. 38.5 inches overall. Weight: 7 lbs. Sights: Adj. post front, adj. aperture rear. Black composite stock and forend. Matte black finish. Made from 1990 to 1994.

MAS SEMIAUTOMATIC RIFLE . . . . NiB $439 Ex $290 Gd $221
Replica of French MAS bullpup rifle. Caliber: .22 LR. 20-round magazine. 18-inch bbl. 28 inches overall. Weight: 7.5 lbs. Sights: Adj. post front, folding aperture rear. European walnut buttstock and forend. Matte black finish. Made from 1987 to 1993.

PPS SEMIAUTOMATIC RIFLE
Caliber: .22 LR. 20-round magazine, 50-round drum. 16.5-inch bbl. 33.5 inches overall. Weight: 5.5 lbs. Sights: Blade front; adj. rear. European walnut stock w/ventilated bbl. shroud. Matte black finish. Made from 1989 to 1994.
Model PPS (20-round magazine). . . NiB $366 Ex $259 Gd $188
Model PPS/50 (50-round drum) . . . NiB $522 Ex $402 Gd $300

O.F. MOSSBERG & SONS, INC. — North Haven, Connecticut (formerly New Haven, Connecticut)

MODEL 10 BOLT-ACTION
SINGLE-SHOT RIFLE. . . . . NiB $335 Ex $190 Gd $120
Takedown. Caliber: .22 LR, Long, Short. 22-inch bbl. Weight: 4 lbs. Sights: Open rear; bead front. Plain pistol-grip stock w/swivels, sling. Made from 1933 to 1935.

MODEL 14 BOLT-ACTION
SINGLE-SHOT RIFLE. . . . . NiB $335 Ex $190 Gd $120
Takedown. Caliber: .22 LR. Long, Short. 24-inch bbl. Weight: 5.25 lbs. Sights: Peep rear; hooded ramp front. Plain pistol-grip stock w/ semi-beavertail forearm, 1.25-inch swivels. Made from 1934 to 1935.

MODEL 20 BOLT-ACTION
SINGLE-SHOT RIFLE. . . . . NiB $335 Ex $190 Gd $120
Takedown. Caliber: .22 LR. Long, Short. 24-inch bbl. Weight: 4.5 lbs. Sights: Open rear; bead front. Plain pistol-grip stock and forearm w/finger grooves, sling and swivels. Made from 1933 to 1935.

MODEL 25/25A BOLT-ACTION SINGLE-SHOT RIFLE
Takedown. Caliber: .22 LR. Long, Short. 24-inch bbl. Weight: 5 lbs. Sights: Peep rear; hooded ramp front. Plain pistol-grip stock w/semi-beavertail forearm. 1.25-inch swivels. Made from 1935 to 1936.
Model 25 . . . . NiB $335 Ex $190 Gd $120
Model 25A (Improved Model 25, 1936–38) . . . NiB $325 Ex $190 Gd $120

MODEL 26B/26C BOLT-ACTION SINGLE-SHOT
Takedown. Caliber: .22 LR. Long, Short. 26-inch bbl. Weight: 5.5 lbs. Sights; Rear, micrometer click peep or open; hooded ramp front. Plain pistol-grip stock swivels. Made from 1938 to 1941.
Model 26B . . . . NiB $335 Ex $190 Gd $120
Model 26C
(No rear sights or sling swivels) . . . . NiB $250 Ex $132 Gd $91

MODEL 30 BOLT-ACTION
SINGLE-SHOT RIFLE. . . . . NiB $335 Ex $190 Gd $120
Takedown. Caliber: .22 LR. Long, Short. 24-inch bbl. Weight: 4.5 lbs. Sights: Peep rear; bead front, on hooded ramp. Plain pistol-grip stock, forearm w/finger grooves. Made from 1933 to 1935.

MODEL 34 BOLT-ACTION
SINGLE-SHOT RIFLE. . . . . NiB $335 Ex $190 Gd $120
Takedown. Caliber: .22 LR. Long, Short. 24-inch bbl. Weight: 5.5 lbs. Sights: Peep rear; hooded ramp front. Plain pistol-grip stock w/ semibeavertail forearm, 1.25-inch swivels. Made from 1934 to 1935.

MODEL 35 TARGET GRADE
BOLT-ACTION SINGLE-SHOT RIFLE . . . . . NiB $440 Ex $300 Gd $166

O.F. Mossberg & Sons, Inc.

Mossberg Model 35A

Mossberg Model 40

Mossberg Model L42A

Mossberg Model 42B

Caliber: .22 LR. 26-inch heavy bbl. Weight: 8.25 lbs. Sights: Micrometer click rear peep; hooded ramp front. Large target stock w/full pistol grip, cheekpiece, full beavertail forearm, 1.25-inch swivels. Made from 1935 to 1937.

MODEL 35A BOLT-ACTION
SINGLE-SHOT RIFLE . . . . **NiB $440 Ex $300 Gd $166**
Caliber: .22 LR. 26-inch heavy bbl. Weight: 8.25 lbs. Sights: Micrometer click peep rear; hooded front. Target stock w/cheekpiece full pistol grip and forearm, 1.25-inch sling swivels. Made from 1937 to 1938.

MODEL 35A-LS. . . . . **NiB $440 Ex $300 Gd $166**
Caliber .22 LR. Same as Model 35A but w/Lyman No. 57 rear sight, 17A front. Target stock w/checkpiece, full pistol-grip and forearm.

MODEL 35B . . . . **NiB $440 Ex $300 Gd $166**
Same specifications as Model 44B except single-shot. Made from 1938 to 1940.

MODEL 40 BOLT-ACTION REPEATER . . . . **NiB $222 Ex $140 Gd $100**
Takedown. Caliber: .22 LR, Long, Short, 16-round tubular magazine. 24-inch bbl. Weight: 5 lbs. Sights: Peep rear; bead front, on hooded ramp. Plain pistol-grip stock, forearm w/finger grooves. Made from 1933 to 1935.

MODEL 42 BOLT-ACTION REPEATER . . . . **NiB $278 Ex $155 Gd $110**
Takedown. Caliber: .22 LR, Long, Short. Seven-round detachable box magazine. 24-inch bbl. Weight: 5 lbs. Sights: Receiver peep, open rear; hooded ramp front. Pistol-grip stock. 1.25-inch swivels. Made from 1935 to 1937.

MODEL 42A/L42A BOLT-ACTION REPEATERS
Takedown. Caliber: .22 LR, Long, Short. Seven-round detachable box magazine. 24-inch bbl. Weight: 5 lbs. Sights: Receiver peep, open rear; ramp front. Plain pistol-grip stock. Made from 1937-38. Model L42A (left-hand action) made from 1937 to 1941.

Model 42A . . . . **NiB $279 Ex $169 Gd $120**
Model L42A . . . . **NiB $288 Ex $179 Gd $130**

MODEL 42B/42C BOLT-ACTION REPEATERS
Takedown. Caliber: .22 LR. Long, Short. Five-round detachable box magazine. 24-inch bbl. Weight: 6 lbs. Sights: Micrometer click receiver peep, open rear hooded ramp front. Plain pistol-grip stock, swivels. Made from 1938 to 1941.

Model 42B . . . . **NiB $289 Ex $190 Gd $100**
Model 42C (no rear peep sight) . . . **NiB $235 Ex $155 Gd $110**

MODEL 42M BOLT-ACTION
REPEATER . . . . **NiB $345 Ex $233 Gd $135**
Caliber: .22 LR. Long, Short. Seven-round detachable box magazine. 23-inch bbl. Weight: 6.75 lbs. Sights: Microclick receiver peep, open rear; hooded ramp front. Two-piece Mannlicher-type stock w/cheekpiece and pistol-grip, swivels. Made from 1940 to 1950.

MODEL 43/L43 BOLT-ACTION
REPEATERS . . . . **NiB $376 Ex $256 Gd $198**
Speedlock, adj. trigger pull. Caliber: .22 LR. Seven-round detachable box magazine. 26-inch heavy bbl. Weight: 8.25 lbs. Sights: Lyman No. 57 rear; selective aperture front. Target stock w/cheekpiece, full pistol-grip, beavertail forearm, adj. front swivel. Made from 1937 to 1938. Model L43 is same as Model 43 except w/left-hand action.

MODEL 43B . . . . **NiB $390 Ex $300 Gd $170**
Same as Model 44B except w/Lyman No. 57 receiver sight and No. 17A front sight. Made from 1938 to 1939.

MODEL 44 BOLT-ACTION REPEATER . . . . **NiB $397 Ex $276 Gd $160**
Takedown. Caliber: .22 LR. Long, Short. Tubular magazine holds 16 LR. 24-inch bbl. Weight: 6 lbs. Sights: Peep rear; hooded ramp front.

O.F. Mossberg & Sons, Inc.

Mossberg Model 42C

Mossberg Model L-43

Mossberg Model 43B

Mossberg Model 44US

Mossberg Model L45A
Left-Hand Model

Mossberg Model 45B

Mossberg Model L46A-LS

Mossberg Model 46B

Plain pistol-grip stock w/semi-beavertail forearm, 1.25-inch swivels. Made from 1934 to 1935.

MODEL 44B BOLT-ACTION
TARGET RIFLE. . . . . **NiB $389 Ex $266 Gd $160**
Caliber: .22 LR. Seven-round detachable box magazine. Made from 1938 to 1941.

MODEL 44US BOLT-ACTION REPEATER
Caliber: .22 LR. Seven round detachable box magazine. 26-inch heavy

bbl. Weight: 8.5 lbs. Sights: Micrometer click receiver peep, hooded front. Target stock, swivels. Made from 1943 to 1948. This model was used as a training rifle by the U.S. Armed Forces during WWII.
Model 44US . . . . **NiB $395 Ex $279 Gd $145**
Model 44US (marked U.S. Property) . . . . . **NiB $395 Ex $279 Gd $145**

MODEL 45 BOLT-ACTION REPEATER . . . . **NiB $254 Ex $178 Gd $117**
Takedown. Caliber: .22 LR. Long, Short. Tubular magazine holds 15 LR. 18 Long, 22 Short. 24-inch bbl. Weight: 6.75 lbs. Sights: Rear peep; hooded ramp front. Plain pistol-grip stock, 1.25-inch swivels. Made from 1935 to 1937.

O.F. Mossberg & Sons, Inc.

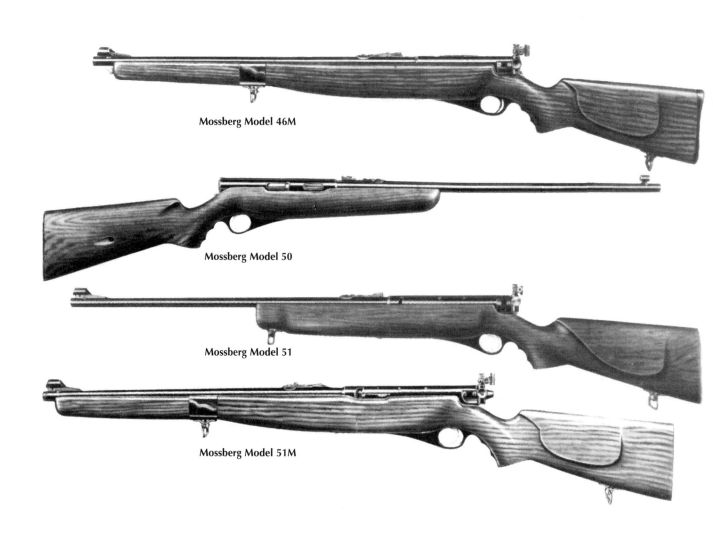

Mossberg Model 46M

Mossberg Model 50

Mossberg Model 51

Mossberg Model 51M

MODEL 45A, L45A, 45AC BOLT-ACTION REPEATERS
Takedown. Caliber: .22 LR. Long, Short. Tubular magazine holds 15 LR, 18 Long, 22 Short. 24-inch bbl. Weight: 6.75 lbs. Sights: Receiver peep, open rear; hooded blade front sight mounted on ramp. Plain pistol-grip stock, 1.25-inch sling swivels. Made 1937 to 1938.
Model 45A . . . . NiB $300 Ex $190 Gd $145
Model L45A (left-hand action) . . . . NiB $655 Ex $355 Gd $279
Model 45AC (no receiver peep sight) . . . . . NiB $249 Ex $177 Gd $123

MODEL 45B/45C BOLT-ACTION REPEATERS
Takedown. Caliber: .22 LR. Long, Short. Tubular magazine holds 15 LR, 18 Long, 22 Short. 24-inch bbl. Weight: 6.25 lbs. Open rear sight; hooded blade front sight mounted on ramp. Plain pistol-grip stock w/sling swivels. Made from 1938 to 1940.
Model 45B . . . . NiB $335 Ex $233 Gd $138
Model 45C (No sights, made 1935 – 1937) NiB $335 Ex $233 Gd $138

MODEL 46 BOLT-ACTION REPEATER . . . . NiB $335 Ex $233 Gd $138
Takedown. Caliber: .22 LR. Long, Short. Tubular magazine holds 15 LR, 18 Long, 22 Short. 26-inch bbl. Weight: 7.5 lbs. Sights: Micrometer click rear peep; hooded ramp front. Pistol-grip stock w/cheekpiece, full beavertail forearm, 1.25-inch swivels. Made from 1935 to 1937.

MODEL 46A, 46A-LS, L46A-LS BOLT-ACTION REPEATERS
Takedown. Caliber: .22 LR. Long, Short. Tubular magazine holds 15 LR, 18 Long, 22 Short. 26-inch bbl. Weight: 7.25 lbs. Sights: Micrometer click receiver peep, open rear; hooded ramp front. Pistol-grip stock w/cheekpiece and beavertail forearm, quick-detachable swivels. Made from 1937 to 1938.
Model 46A . . . . NiB $335 Ex $233 Gd $138
Mdl. 46A-LS (w/Lyman No. 57 receiver sight). . . . NiB $386 Ex $276 Gd $189
Model L46A-LS (Left-hand action) . . . . NiB $644 Ex $355 Gd $269

O.F. Mossberg & Sons, Inc.

Mossberg Model 140B

Mossberg Model 140K

Mossberg Model 144LS

Mossberg Model 146B

MODEL 46B BOLT-ACTION
REPEATER . . . . **NiB $290 Ex $167 Gd $133**
Takedown. Caliber: .22 LR. Long, Short. Tubular magazine holds 15 LR, 18 Long, 22 Short. 26-inch bbl. Weight: 7 lbs. Sights: Micrometer click receiver peep, open rear, hooded front. Plain pistol-grip stock w/ cheekpiece, swivels. Note: Postwar version of this model has full magazine holding 20 LR, 23 Long, 30 Short. Made from 1938 to 1950.

MODEL 46BT . . . . **NiB $344 Ex $229 Gd $176**
Same as Model 46B except w/heavier bbl. and stock. Weight: 7.75 lbs. Made from 1938 to 1939.

MODEL 46C . . . . **NiB $344 Ex $229 Gd $176**
Same as Model 46 except w/a heavier bbl. and stock than that model. Weight: 8.5 lbs. Made from 1936 to 1937.

MODEL 46M
BOLT-ACTION REPEATER . . . . **NiB $344 Ex $229 Gd $176**
Caliber: .22 LR. Long, Short. Tubular magazine holds 22 Short, 18 Long, 15 LR. 23-inch bbl. Weight: 7 lbs. Sights: Microclick receiver peep, open rear; hooded ramp front. Two-piece Mannlicher-type stock w/cheekpiece and pistol-grip, swivels. Made from 1940 to 1952.

MODEL 50
AUTOLOADING RIFLE . . . . **NiB $298 Ex $213 Gd $139**
Same as Model 51 except w/plain stock w/o beavertail cheekpiece, swivels or receiver peep sight. Made from 1939 to 1942.

MODEL 51 AUTOLOADING RIFLE . . . . . . **NiB $298 Ex $213 Gd $139**
Takedown. Caliber: .22 LR. Fifteen-round tubular magazine in buttstock. 24-inch bbl. Weight: 7.25 lbs. Sights: Micrometer click receiver peep, open rear; hooded ramp front. Cheekpiece stock w/ full pistol grip and beavertail forearm, swivels. Made in 1939 only.

MODEL 51M AUTOLOADING RIFLE . . . . . **NiB $275 Ex $154 Gd $123**
Caliber: .22 LR. Fifteen-round tubular magazine. 20-inch bbl. Weight: 7 lbs. Sights: Microclick receiver peep, open rear; hooded ramp front. Two-piece Mannlicher-type stock w/pistol-grip and cheekpiece, hard-rubber buttplate and sling swivels. Made from 1939 to 1946.

MODEL 140B SPORTER-TARGET RIFLE . . . **NiB $254 Ex $186 Gd $134**
Same as Model 140K except w/peep rear sight, hooded ramp front sight. Made from 1957 to 1958.

MODEL 140K BOLT-ACTION REPEATER . . **NiB $248 Ex $197 Gd $123**
Caliber: .22 LR. .22 Long, .22 Short. Seven-round clip magazine. 24.5-inch bbl. Weight: 5.75 lbs. Sights: Open rear; bead front. Monte Carlo stock w/ cheekpiece and pistol-grip, sling swivels. Made from 1955 to 1958.

MODEL 142-A BOLT-ACTION
REPEATING CARBINE . . . . **NiB $277 Ex $233 Gd $166**
Caliber: .22 Short Long, LR. Seven-round detachable box magazine. 18-inch bbl. Weight: 6 lbs. Sights: Peep rear, military-type front. Monte Carlo stock w/pistol-grip, hinged forearm pulls down to form hand grip; sling swivels mounted on left side of stock. Made from 1949 to 1957.

O.F. Mossberg & Sons, Inc.

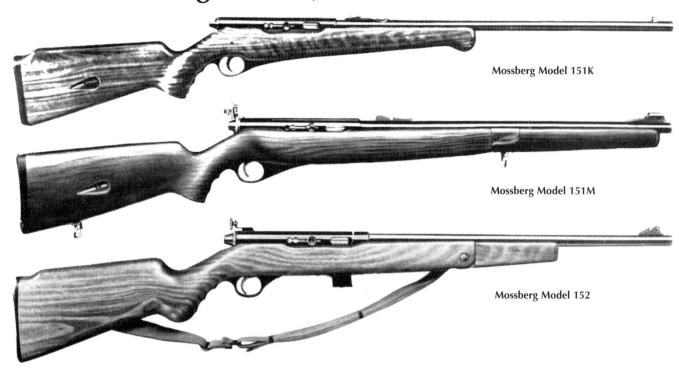

Mossberg Model 151K

Mossberg Model 151M

Mossberg Model 152

MODEL 142K . . . . **NiB $244 Ex $152 Gd $109**
Same as Model 142 except w/open rear sight. Made from 1953 to 1957.

MODEL 144 BOLT-ACTION
TARGET RIFLE . . . . **NiB $390 Ex $288 Gd $215**
Caliber: .22 LR. Seven-round detachable box magazine. 26-inch heavy bbl. Weight: 8 lbs. Sights: Microclick receiver peep; hooded front. Pistol-grip target stock w/beavertail forearm, adj. hand stop, swivels. Made from 1949 to 1954. This model designation was resumed c.1973 to replace Model 144LS, and then disc. again in 1985.

MODEL 144LS . . . . **NiB $385 Ex $277 Gd $205**
Same as Model 144 except w/Lyman No. 57MS or Mossberg S331 receiver sight and Lyman 17A front sight. Made from 1954 to date. Note: Since 1973, this model has been marketed as Model 144.

MODEL 146B BOLT-ACTION REPEATER . . . **NiB $344 Ex $190 Gd $139**
Takedown. Caliber: .22 LR. Long, Short. Tubular magazine holds 30 Short, 23 Long, 20 LR. 26-inch bbl. Weight: 7 lbs. Sights: Micrometer click rear peep, open rear; hooded front. Plain stock w/pistol-grip, Monte Carlo comb and cheekpiece, knob forend tip, swivels. Made from 1949 to 1954.

MODEL 151K . . . . **NiB $290 Ex $193 Gd $130**
Same as Model 151M except w/24-inch bbl., weight: 6 lbs., w/o peep sight, plain stock w/Monte Carlo comb and cheekpiece, pistol-grip knob, forend tip, w/o swivels. Made from 1950 to 1951.

MODEL 151M AUTOLOADING RIFLE . . . . **NiB $366 Ex $199 Gd $138**
Improved version of Model 51M w/same general specifications, complete action is instantly removable w/o use of tools. Made from 1946 to 1958.

MODEL 152 AUTOLOADING CARBINE . . **NiB $276 Ex $197 Gd $135**
Caliber: .22 LR. Seven-round detachable box magazine. 18-inch bbl. Weight: 5 lbs. Sights: Peep rear; military-type front. Monte Carlo stock w/pistol-grip, hinged forearm pulls down to form hand grip, sling mounted on swivels on left side of stock. Made from 1948 to 1957.

MODEL 152K . . . . **NiB $233 Ex $176 Gd $121**
Same as Model 152 except w/open instead of peep rear sight. Made from 1950 to 1957.

MODEL 320B BOY SCOUT TARGET RIFLE . . . . **NiB $233 Ex $176 Gd $121**
Same as Model 340K except single-shot w/auto. safety. Made from 1960 to 1971.

MODEL 320K HAMMERLESS
BOLT-ACTION SINGLE-SHOT . . . . . **NiB $200 Ex $123 Gd $90**
Same as Model 346K except single-shot, w/drop-in loading platform, automatic safety. Weight: 5.75 lbs. Made from 1958 to 1960.

MODEL 321B . . . . **NiB $344 Ex $190 Gd $139**
Same as Model 321K except w/receiver peep sight. Made from 1972 to 1975.

MODEL 321K BOLT-ACTION
SINGLE-SHOT. . . . . **NiB $344 Ex $190 Gd $139**
Same as Model 341 except single-shot. Made from 1972 to 1980.

MODEL 333
AUTOLOADING CARBINE . . . . **NiB $266 Ex $180 Gd $145**
Caliber: .22 LR. 15-round tubular magazine. 20-inch bbl. Weight: 6.25 lbs. Sights: Open rear; ramp front. Monte Carlo stock w/checkered pistol grip and forearm, bbl. band, swivels. Made from 1972 to 1973.

MODEL 340B TARGET SPORTER . . . . **NiB $231 Ex $188 Gd $133**
Same as Model 340K except w/peep rear sight, hooded ramp front sight. Made from 1958 to 1981.

MODEL 340K HAMMERLESS
BOLT-ACTION REPEATER . . . . **NiB $231 Ex $188 Gd $133**
Same as Model 346K except clip type, 7-round magazine. Made from 1958 to 1971.

MODEL 340M. . . . . **NiB $644 Ex $390 Gd $238**
Same as Model 340K except w/18.5-inch bbl., Mannlicher-style stock w/swivels and sling. Weight: 5.25 lbs. Made from 1970 to 1971.

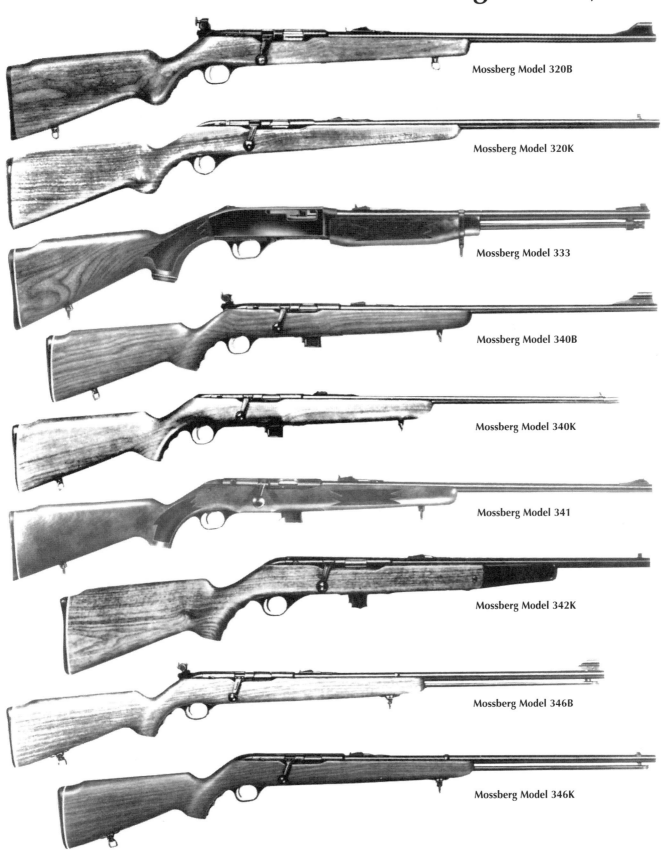

Mossberg Model 320B

Mossberg Model 320K

Mossberg Model 333

Mossberg Model 340B

Mossberg Model 340K

Mossberg Model 341

Mossberg Model 342K

Mossberg Model 346B

Mossberg Model 346K

O.F. Mossberg & Sons, Inc.

Mossberg Model 350K
Autoloading — Clip Type

Mossberg Model 351K
Automatic Sporter

Mossberg Model 352K
Carbine

Mossberg Model 353
Carbine

Mossberg Model 377
Plinkster

MODEL 341 BOLT-ACTION REPEATER . . . NiB $290 Ex $144 Gd $110
Caliber: .22 Short. Long, LR. Seven-round clip magazine. 24-inch bbl. Weight: 6.5 lbs. Sights: Open rear, ramp front. Monte Carlo stock w/checkered pistol-grip and forearm, sling swivels. Made from 1972 to 1985.

**MODEL 342K HAMMERLESS
BOLT-ACTION CARBINE . . . . NiB $240 Ex $150 Gd $113**
Same as Model 340K except w/18-inch bbl., stock w/no cheekpiece, extension forend is hinged, pulls down to form hand grip; sling swivels and web strap on left side of stock. Weight: 5 lbs. Made from 1958 to 1974.

MODEL 346B . . . . NiB $240 Ex $180 Gd $113
Same as Model 346K except w/peep rear sight, hooded ramp front sight. Made from 1958 to 1967.

**MODEL 346K HAMMERLESS
BOLT-ACTION REPEATER . . . . NiB $240 Ex $150 Gd $113**
Caliber: .22 Short. Long, LR. Tubular magazine holds 25 Short, 20 Long, 18 LR. 24-inch bbl. Weight: 6.5 lbs. Sights: Open rear; bead front. Walnut stock w/Monte Carlo comb, cheekpiece, pistol-grip, sling swivels. Made from 1958 to 1971.

**MODEL 350K AUTOLOADING
RIFLE — CLIP TYPE. . . . . NiB $240 Ex $150 Gd $113**
Caliber: .22 Short (High Speed), Long, LR. Seven-round clip magazine.

23.5-inch bbl. Weight: 6 lbs. Sights: Open rear; bead front. Monte Carlo stock w/pistol-grip. Made from 1958 to 1971.

**MODEL 351C
AUTOLOADING CARBINE. . . . . NiB $240 Ex $150 Gd $113**
Same as Model 351K except w/18.5-inch bbl., Western carbine-style stock w/barrel band and sling swivels. Weight: 5.5 lbs. Made from 1965 to 1971.

**MODEL 351K AUTOLOADING
SPORTER. . . . . NiB $240 Ex $150 Gd $113**
Caliber: .22 LR. Fifteen-round tubular magazine in buttstock. 24-inch bbl. Weight: 6 lbs. Sights: Open rear; bead front. Monte Carlo stock w/pistol-grip. Made from 1960 to 1971.

MODEL 352K AUTOLOADING CARBINE . . . . NiB $240 Ex $150 Gd $113
Caliber: .22 Short, Long, LR. Seven-round clip magazine. 18-inch bbl. Weight: 5 lbs. Sights: Open rear; bead front. Monte Carlo stock w/pistol grip; extension forend of Tenite is hinged, pulls down to form hand grip; sling swivels, web strap. Made from 1958 to 1971.

MODEL 353 AUTOLOADING CARBINE . . . NiB $240 Ex $150 Gd $113
Caliber: .22 LR. Seven round clip magazine. 18-inch bbl. Weight: 5 lbs. Sights: Open rear; ramp front. Monte Carlo stock w/checkered pistol-grip and forearm; black Tenite extension forend pulls down to form hand grip. Made from 1972 to 1985.

112

HIGHLIGHTS OF THE RIFLES FROM THE
NRA FIREARMS MUSEUM

ARMALITE, INC.

Armalite AR-7 Explorer Rifle (see page 11)

BALLARD RIFLE LLC

Ballard No. 5 Pacific Rifle (see page 15)

THE NRA NATIONAL FIREARMS MUSEUM

The NRA National Firearms Museum presents America's most significant firearms ranging from a wheellock that came over on the Mayflower to a NYPD Officer's revolver recovered from the ashes of the World Trade Center. The 15 galleries house 3,000 guns that detail and examine the nearly 700-year history of firearms with a special emphasis on firearms, freedom, and the American experience. Highlights include the Robert E. Petersen Gallery, which displays 400 firearms representing the finest collection of high end sporting arms and Gatling guns on public display anywhere in the world, and spectacular examples of firearms engraving. "Hollywood Guns", another featured exhibit, showcases 120 actual guns used in movies and television over the past 80 years, from the first revolver John Wayne used on camera through guns from recent Academy Award Winners. The Museum is also home to a firearms research library available to the public, and the NRA National Firearms Museum Store, known for having the finest selection of firearms books available anywhere.

In 2013, the Museum and Bass Pro Shops opened the NRA National Sporting Arms Museum at Bass Pro's flagship store in Springfield, Missouri. This entirely new museum features more than 1,000 firearms used by sportsmen through the centuries, highlighting themes of Hunting, Conservation and Freedom.

The Museum offers a glimpse into the firearms that built our nation, helped forge our freedom, and captured our imagination.

Website: NRAMuseum.com • Facebook: NRAMuseum • Twitter: NRAMuseum
• Pinterest: NRAMuseum •YouTube: NFMCurator

NATIONAL
FIREARMS
MUSEUM

BROWNING RIFLES

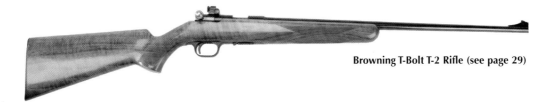

Browning T-Bolt T-2 Rifle (see page 29)

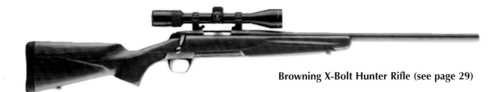

Browning X-Bolt Hunter Rifle (see page 29)

Browning X-Bolt Stainless Hunter Rifle (see page 29)

Browning X-Bolt Medallion Rifle (see page 29)

Browning X-Bolt Composite Stalker Rifle (see page 29)

Highlights of the Rifles from the NRA Firearms Museum

COLT'S MFG. CO., INC.

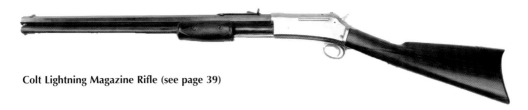

Colt Lightning Magazine Rifle (see page 39)

CHARLES DALY RIFLE

Charles Daly Mauser 98 Rifle (see page 45)

HEYM RIFLES AMERICA, INC.

Heym Model 55B O/U Double Rifle (see page 63)

O.F. MOSSBERG & SONS, INC.

Mossberg Model L Single-Shot Rifle (see page 115)

REMINGTON ARMS COMPANY

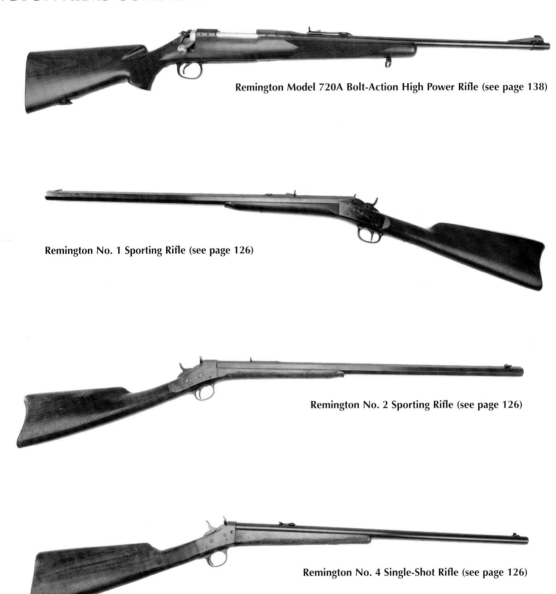

Remington Model 720A Bolt-Action High Power Rifle (see page 138)

Remington No. 1 Sporting Rifle (see page 126)

Remington No. 2 Sporting Rifle (see page 126)

Remington No. 4 Single-Shot Rifle (see page 126)

JOHN RIGBY & CO.

Rigby Model 416 Big Game Rifle (see page 144)

STANDARD ARMS COMPANY

Standard Arms Model G Automatic Rifle (see page 174)

J. STEVENS ARMS CO.

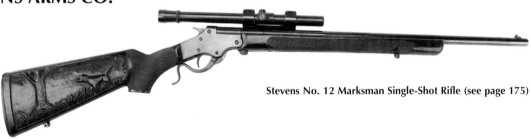

Stevens No. 12 Marksman Single-Shot Rifle (see page 175)

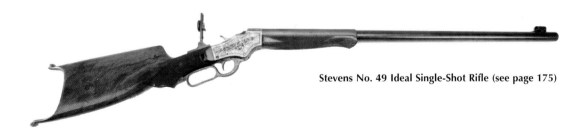

Stevens No. 49 Ideal Single-Shot Rifle (see page 175)

Highlights of the Rifles from the NRA Firearms Museum

U.S. MILITARY RIFLES

U.S. 1898 Krag-Jorgensen Military Rifle (see page 187)

U.S. 1903 Springfield Military Rifle (see page 187)

WEATHERBY, INC.

Weatherby Mark V Accumark Bolt-Action Repeating Rifle (see page 193)

Weatherby Mark XXII Deluxe .22 Automatic Sporter Rifle (see page 195)

WINCHESTER RIFLES

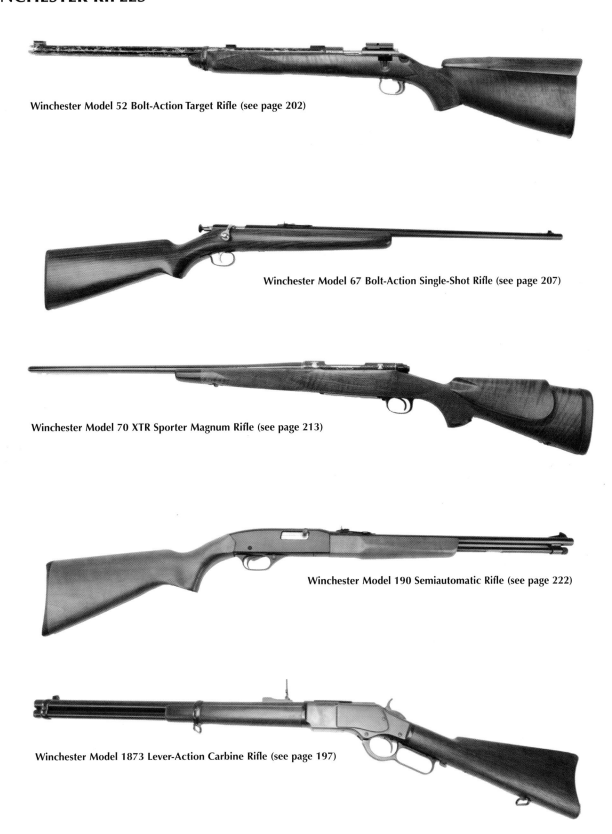

Winchester Model 52 Bolt-Action Target Rifle (see page 202)

Winchester Model 67 Bolt-Action Single-Shot Rifle (see page 207)

Winchester Model 70 XTR Sporter Magnum Rifle (see page 213)

Winchester Model 190 Semiautomatic Rifle (see page 222)

Winchester Model 1873 Lever-Action Carbine Rifle (see page 197)

Highlights of the Rifles from the NRA Firearms Museum

WINCHESTER RIFLES

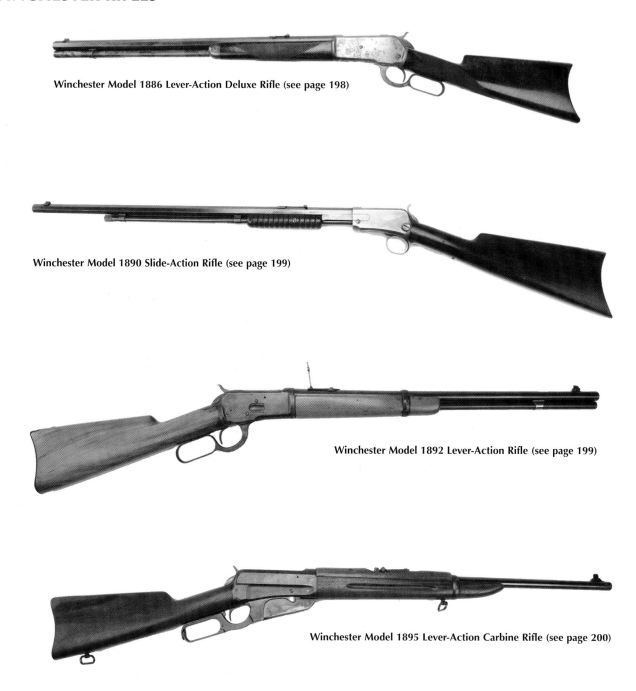

Winchester Model 1886 Lever-Action Deluxe Rifle (see page 198)

Winchester Model 1890 Slide-Action Rifle (see page 199)

Winchester Model 1892 Lever-Action Rifle (see page 199)

Winchester Model 1895 Lever-Action Carbine Rifle (see page 200)

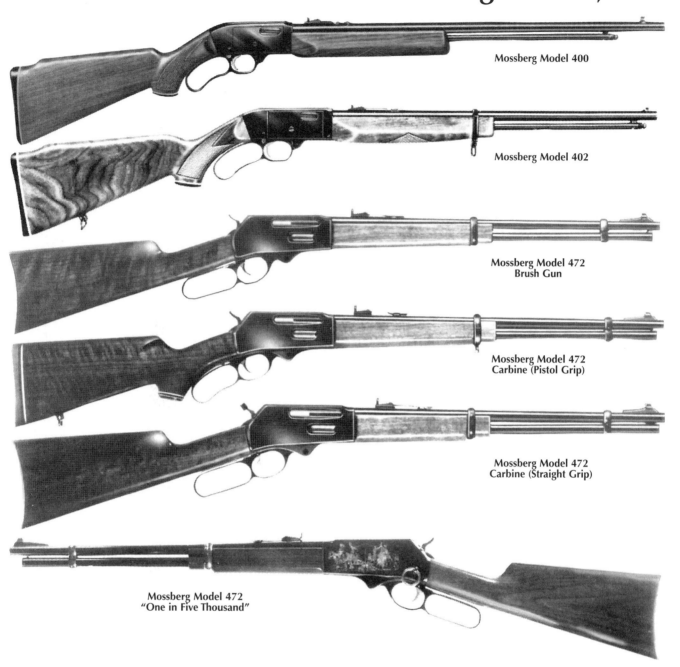

Mossberg Model 400

Mossberg Model 402

Mossberg Model 472
Brush Gun

Mossberg Model 472
Carbine (Pistol Grip)

Mossberg Model 472
Carbine (Straight Grip)

Mossberg Model 472
"One in Five Thousand"

MODEL 377 PLINKSTER AUTOLOADER . . . NiB $275 Ex $200 Gd $155
Caliber: .22 LR. Fifteen-round tubular magazine. 20-inch bbl. Weight: 6.25 lbs. 4x scope sight. Thumbhole stock w/rollover cheekpiece, Monte Carlo comb, checkered forearm; molded of modified polystyrene foam in walnut-finish; sling swivel studs. Made from 1977 to 1979.

MODEL 380 SEMIAUTOMATIC RIFLE . . . . NiB $275 Ex $200 Gd $155
Caliber: .22 LR. Fifteen-round buttstock magazine. 20-inch bbl. Weight: 5.5 lbs. Sights: Open rear; bead front. Made from 1980 to 1985.

MODEL 400 PALOMINO LEVER-ACTION . . . . NiB $390 Ex $242 Gd $161
Hammerless. Caliber: .22 Short, Long, LR. Tubular magazine holds 20 Short, 17 Long, 15 LR. 24-inch bbl. Weight: 5.5 lbs. Sights: Open rear; bead front. Monte Carlo stock w/checkered pistol-grip; beavertail forearm. Made from 1959 to 1964.

MODEL 402 PALOMINO CARBINE . . . . . . NiB $390 Ex $242 Gd $161
Same as Model 400 except w/18.5-inch (1961-64) or 20-inch bbl. (1964-71), forearm w/bbl. band, swivels; magazine holds two fewer rounds. Weight: 4.75 lbs. Made from 1961 to 1971.

MODEL 430 AUTOLOADING RIFLE. . . . . NiB $340 Ex $180 Gd $135
Caliber: .22 LR. Eighteen-round tubular magazine. 24-inch bbl. Weight: 6.25 lbs. Sights: Open rear; bead front. Monte Carlo stock w/checkered pistol grip; checkered forearm. Made from 1970 to 1971.

MODEL 432 WESTERN-STYLE AUTO . . . . . NiB $340 Ex $180 Gd $135
Same as Model 430 except w/plain straight-grip carbine-type stock and forearm, bbl. band, sling swivels. Magazine capacity: 15 cartridges. Weight: 6 lbs. Made from 1970 to 1971.

O.F. Mossberg & Sons, Inc.

Mossberg Model 640K Chuckster

Mossberg Model 640KS

Mossberg Model 640M

Mossberg Model 642K

MODEL 472 BRUSH GUN . . . . NiB $340 Ex $180 Gd $135
Same as Model 472 Carbine w/straight-grip stock except w/18-inch bbl., weight: 6.5 lbs. Caliber: .30-30. Magazine capacity: 5 rounds. Made from 1974 to 1976.

MODEL 472 LEVER-ACTION CARBINE . . . NiB $340 Ex $180 Gd $135
Calibers: .30-30, .35 Rem. Six round tubular magazine. 20-inch bbl. Weight: 6.75 to 7 lbs. Sights: Open rear; ramp front. Pistol-grip or straight-grip stock, forearm w/bbl. band; sling swivels on pistol-grip model saddle ring on straight-grip model. Made from 1972 to 1979.

MODEL 472 ONE IN FIVE THOUSAND . . . NiB $665 Ex $423 Gd $240
Same as Model 472 Brush Gun except w/Indian scenes etched on receiver; brass buttplate, saddle ring and bbl. bands, gold-plated trigger, bright blued finish, select walnut stock and forearm. Limited edition of 5,000; serial numbered 1 to 5,000. Made in 1974.

MODEL 472 RIFLE . . . . NiB $340 Ex $180 Gd $135
Same as Model 472 Carbine w/pistol-grip stock except w/24-inch bbl., 5-round magazine, weight: 7 lbs. Made from 1974 to 1976.

MODEL 479
Caliber: .30-30. Six-round tubular magazine. 20-inch bbl. Weight: 6.75 to 7 lbs. Sights: Open rear; ramp front. Made 1983 to 1985.
Model 479 Rifle . . . . NiB $340 Ex $180 Gd $135
Model 479PCA
(carbine w/20-inch bbl.) . . . . NiB $340 Ex $180 Gd $135
Model 479RR
(Roy Rogers model, 5,000 Ltd. Ed.) . . . . . . NiB $665 Ex $423 Gd $240

MODEL 620K HAMMERLESS SINGLE-SHOT
BOLT-ACTION RIFLE . . . . NiB $290 Ex $179 Gd $133
Single shot. Caliber: .22 WMR. 24-inch bbl. Weight: 6 lbs. Sights: Open rear; bead front. Monte Carlo stock w/cheekpiece, pistol-grip, sling swivels. Made from 1959 to 1960.

MODEL 620K-A . . . . NiB $290 Ex $179 Gd $133
Same as Model 640K except w/sight modification. Made 1960 to 1968.

MODEL 640K CHUCKSTER HAMMERLESS
BOLT-ACTION RIFLE . . . . NiB $335 Ex $228 Gd $136
Caliber: .22 WMR. Five-round detachable clip magazine. 24-inch bbl. Weight: 6 lbs. Sights: Open rear; bead front. Monte Carlo stock w/cheekpiece, pistol grip, sling swivels. Made from 1959 to 1984.

MODEL 640KS . . . . NiB $335 Ex $ 228 Gd $136
Deluxe version of Model 640K w/select walnut stock hand checkering; gold-plated front sight, rear sight elevator, and trigger. Made from 1960 to 1964.

MODEL 640M. . . . . NiB $665 Ex $423 Gd $240
Similar to Model 640K except w/heavy receiver and jeweled bolt. 20-inch bbl., full length Mannlicher-style stock w/Monte Carlo comb and cheekpiece, swivels and leather sling. 40.75 inches overall. Weight: 6 lbs. Made from 1971 to 1973.

MODEL 642K CARBINE . . . . NiB $396 Ex $277 Gd $194
Caliber: .22 WMR. Five-round detachable clip magazine. 18-inch bbl. Weight: 5 lbs. 38.25 inches overall. Sights: Open rear; bead front. Monte Carlo walnut stock w/black Tenite forearm extension that pulls down to form hand grip. Made from 1961 to 1968.

O.F. Mossberg & Sons, Inc.

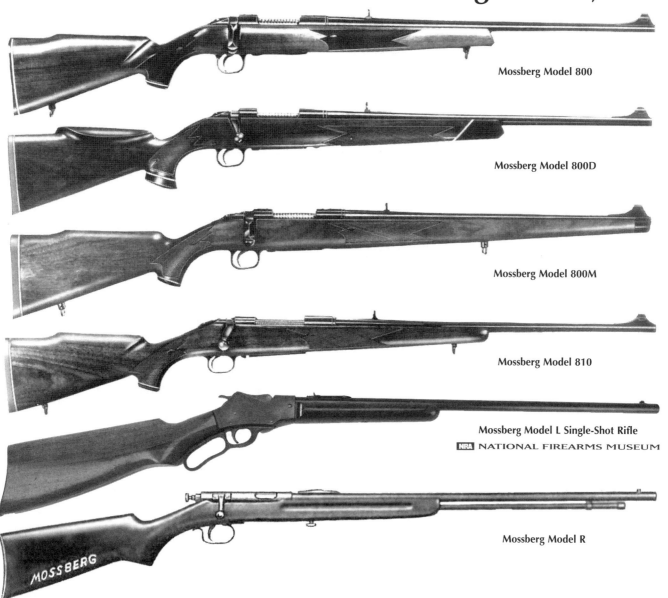

Mossberg Model 800

Mossberg Model 800D

Mossberg Model 800M

Mossberg Model 810

Mossberg Model L Single-Shot Rifle

NRA NATIONAL FIREARMS MUSEUM

Mossberg Model R

MODEL 800 BOLT-ACTION
CENTERFIRE RIFLE . . . . NiB $455 Ex $307 Gd $200
Caliber: .222 Rem., .22-250 Rem., .243 Win., .308 Win.; four-round mag (three rounds in .22). Bbl.: 22 inches. Weight: 7.5 lbs. Folding leaf rear, ramp front sights. Monte Carlo stock w/cheekpiece, checkered pistol grip and forearm, sling swivels. Made from 1967 to 1979.

MODEL 800D SUPER GRADE . . . . NiB $455 Ex $307 Gd $200
Same as Model 800 except not in .222 Rem. Deluxe version w/rollover comb and cheekpiece, rosewood forend tip and grip cap. Weight: 6.75 lbs.

MODEL 800M. . . . . NiB $644 Ex $315 Gd $209
Same as Model 800 except w/flat bolt handle.. Calibers: .22-250 Rem., .243 Win., .308 Win. Bbl.: 20 inches. Weight: 6.5 lbs. Mannlicher-style stock. Made from 1969 to 1972.

MODEL 800VT VARMINT/TARGET . . . . . . NiB $455 Ex $307 Gd $200
Similar to Model 800. Calibers: .222 Rem., .22-250 Rem., .243 Win. 24-inch heavy bbl., no sights. Weight: 9.5 lbs. Made from 1968 to 1979.

MODEL 810 BOLT-ACTION CENTERFIRE RIFLE
Calibers: .270 Win., .30-06, 7mm Rem. Mag., .338 Win. Mag.; detachable box mag (1970 to 1975) or internal mag. w/hinged floorplate (1972 to 1979). Four-round capacity in .270 and .30-06, three rounds in magnum calibers. Bbl.: 22 inches in .270 and .30-06; 24 inches in magnum calibers. Weight: 7.5 to 8 lbs. Leaf rear, ramp front sights. Monte Carlo stock w/checkered pistol grip and forearm, grip cap; sling swivels. Made from 1970 to 1979.
Standard calibers . . . . NiB $390 Ex $333 Gd $232

MODEL 1500 MOUNTAINEER
GRADE I CENTERFIRE RIFLE . . . . . NiB $441 Ex $335 Gd $288
Calibers: .223 Rem., .270 Win., .243 Win., .30-06, 7mm Rem. Mag., Bbl.: 22 or 24 inches. Weight: 7 lbs, 10 oz. Hooded ramp gold bead front, adj. rear sights. Drilled and tapped for scope mounts. Walnut finished checkered hardwood stock. Swivel studs. Imported from 1986 to 1987.

O.F. Mossberg & Sons, Inc.

Musgrave Premier NR5

Musgrave RSA NR1

Musgrave Valiant NR6

MODEL 1500 VARMINT BOLT-ACTION RIFLE
Same as Model 1500 Grade I except w/22-inch heavy bbl. Calibers: .222 Rem., .22-250 Rem., .223 Rem. High-luster blued finish or Parkerized, satin finished stock. Imported from Japan from 1986 to 1987.
High-luster blue . . . . NiB $440 Ex $328 Gd $288
Parkerized satin finish. . . . . NiB $455 Ex $338 Gd $298

MODEL 1700LS CLASSIC
HUNTER BOLT-ACTION RIFLE. . . . . NiB $479 Ex $369 Gd $266
Same as Model 1500 Grade I except w/checkered classic-style stock and Schnabel forent. Calibers: .243 Win., .270 Win. .30-06. Imported from Japan from 1986 to 1987.

MODEL B BOLT-ACTION RIFLE . . . NiB $340 Ex $205 Gd $113
Single-shot.Takedown. Caliber: .22 LR, Long, Short. Bbl.: 22 inches. Open rear, bead front sights. Plain pistol-grip stock. Made from 1930 to 1932.

MODEL K SLIDE-ACTION REPEATER . . . . . NiB $545 Ex $390 Gd $233
Hammerless. Takedown. Caliber: .22 LR. Long, Short. Tubular magazine holds 20 Short, 16 Long, 14 LR. 22-inch bbl. Weight: 5 lbs. Sights: Open rear; bead front. Plain, straight-grip stock. Grooved slide handle. Made from 1922 to 1931.

MODEL L SINGLE-SHOT RIFLE . . . . NiB $850 Ex $535 Gd $429
Martini-type falling-block lever-action. Takedown. Caliber: .22 LR, Long, Short. 24-inch bbl. Weight: 5 lbs. Sights: Open rear; bead front. Plain pistol-grip stock and forearm. Made from 1929 to 1932.

MODEL M SLIDE-ACTION REPEATER . . . .NiB $550 Ex $ 340 Gd $225
Same as Model K except w/24-inch octagon bbl.; pistol-grip stock. Weight: 5.5 lbs. Made from 1928 to 1931.

MODEL R BOLT-ACTION REPEATER . . . . . NiB $379 Ex $265 Gd $190
Takedown. Caliber: .22 LR, Long, Short. Tubular magazine. 24-inch bbl. Sights: Open rear; bead front. Plain pistol-grip stock. Made from 1930 to 1932.

MUSGRAVE RIFLES, MUSGRAVE MFRS. & DIST. (PTY) LTD. — Bloemfontein, South Africa

PREMIER NR5 BOLT-
ACTION HUNTING RIFLE . . . . NiB $460 Ex $375 Gd $288
Musgrave or Mauser action. Calibers: .243 Win., .270 Win., .30-06, .308 Win., 7mm Rem., Mag.; five-round mag., Bbl.: 25.5 inches. Weight: 8.25 lbs. No sights, drilled and tapped for scope mounts. Select walnut Monte Carlo stock w/cheekpiece, checkered pistol grip and forearm, contrasting grip cap and forend tip, recoil pad, swivel studs. Made from 1971 to 1976.

RSA NR1 BOLT-ACTION
SINGLE-SHOT TARGET RIFLE . . . . . NiB $449 Ex $420 Gd $300
Caliber: .308 Win. (7.62 NATO). 26.4-inch heavy bbl. Weight: 10 lbs. Sights: Aperture receiver; tunnel front. Walnut target stock w/beavertail forearm, handguard, bbl. band, rubber buttplate, sling swivels. Made from 1971 to 1976.

VALIANT NR6 HUNTING RIFLE . . NiB $415 Ex $365 Gd $255
Similar to Premier model except w/24-inch bbl., stock w/straight comb, French-style skip checkering; no grip cap or forend tip. Leaf rear, hooded ramp bead front sights. Weight: 7.7 lbs. Made from 1971 to 1976.

MUSKETEER RIFLES — Washington, D.C. Manufactured by Firearms International Corp.

MAUSER SPORTER
FN Mauser bolt-action. Calibers: .243 Win., .25-06, .270, .264 Win. Mag., .308 Win., .30-06, 7mm Rem Mag., .300 Win. Mag; five-round mag (standard calibers), three rounds in magnum calibers. Bbl.: 24 inches. Weight: 7.25 lbs. No sights. Monte Carlo stock w/checkered pistol-grip and forearm, swivels. Made from 1963 to 1972.

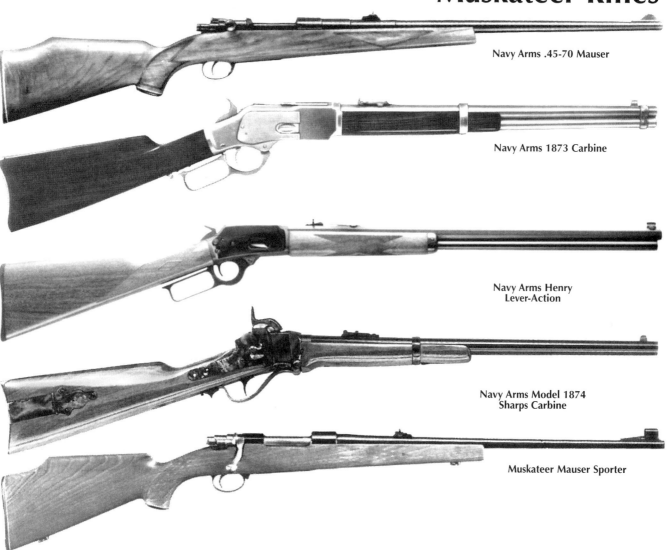

Navy Arms .45-70 Mauser

Navy Arms 1873 Carbine

Navy Arms Henry Lever-Action

Navy Arms Model 1874 Sharps Carbine

Muskateer Mauser Sporter

Standard Sporter . . . . NiB $415 Ex $295 Gd $255
Deluxe Sporter . . . . NiB $459 Ex $380 Gd $276
Standard Carbine . . . . NiB $415 Ex $295 Gd $255

NAVY ARMS — Ridgefield, New Jersey

45-70 MAUSER CARBINE . . . . NiB $333 Ex $227 Gd $160
Same as .45-70 Mauser Rifle except w/18-inch bbl., straight-grip stock w/low comb, weight: 7.5 lbs. Disc.

.45-70 MAUSER RIFLE . . . . NiB $260 Ex $221 Gd $155
Siamese Mauser bolt-action. Caliber: .45-70 Gov't.; three-round mag. Bbl.: 24 or 26 inches. Weight: 8.5 lbs. Open rear, ramp front sights. Checkered Monte Carlo stock. Intro. 1973. Disc.

MODEL 1873 WINCHESTER
BORDER RIFLE . . . . NiB $1077 Ex $869 Gd $378
Replica of Winchester Model 1873 Short Rifle. Calibers: .357 Mag., .44-40, .45 Colt. Bbl.: Blued, octagon. Color case-hardened receiver. Lgt.: 39.25 inches. Weight: 7.6 lbs. Walnut stock. Made from 1999 to 2009.

MODEL 1873 CARBINE . . . . NiB $1033 Ex $756 Gd $399
Similar to Model 1873 Rifle except w/blued receiver, 10-round magazine, 19-inch round bbl. carbine-style forearm w/bbl. band, weighs 6.75 lbs. Disc. Reissued in 1991 in .44-40 or .45 Colt.

MODEL 1873 LEVER-ACTION RIFLE . . . . NiB $1033 Ex $756 Gd $399
Replica of Winchester Model 1873. Case-hardened receiver. Calibers: .22 LR. .357 Magnum, .44-40. 15-round magazine. 24-inch octagon bbl. Weight: 8 lbs. Sights: Open rear; blade front. Straight-grip stock, forearm w/end cap. Disc. Reissued in 1991 in .44-40 or .45 Colt w/12-round magazine. Disc. 1994.

MODEL 1873 TRAPPER . . . . NiB $744 Ex $560 Gd $425
Same as Model 1873 Carbine, except w/16.5-inch bbl., 8-round magazine, weighs 6.25 lbs. Disc.

MODEL 1873 SPORTING CARBINE/RIFLE
Replica of Winchester Model 1873 Sporting Rifle. Calibers: .357 Mag. (24.25-inch bbl. only), .44-40 and .45 Colt. 24.25-inch bbl. (Carbine) or 30-inch bbl. (Rifle). 48.75 to 53 inches overall. Weight: 8.14 to 9.3 lbs. Octagonal barrel, case-hardened receiver and checkered walnut pistol-grip. Made from 1999 to 2003.
Carbine model . . . . NiB $970 Ex $844 Gd $630
Rifle model . . . . NiB $1035 Ex $928 Gd $670

MODEL 1874 SHARPS
CAVALRY CARBINE . . . . NiB $1010 Ex $733 Gd $580
Replica of Sharps 1874 Cavalry Carbine. Similar to Sniper Model, except w/22-inch bbl. and carbine stock. Caliber: .45-70. Imported from 1997 to 2009.

Navy Arms

Navy Arms
Revolving Carbine

Navy Arms
Rolling Block Baby Carbine

Navy Arms
Rolling Block Buffalo Rifle

Navy Arms 1874
Sharps Sniper Rifle

Navy Arms Martini
Target Rifle

MODEL 1874 SHARPS SNIPER RIFLE
Replica of Sharps 1874 Sharpshooter's Rifle. Falling breech, single-shot. Caliber.: .45-70 Gov't. Bbl.: 30 inches. Lgt.: 46.75 inches. Weight: 8.5 lbs. Double-set triggers. Color case-hardened receiver. Blade front, elevation leaf rear sights. Polished blued bbl. Military-style three-band stock w/patch box. Imported from 1994 to 2000.
Infantry model (single trigger) . . . . NiB $933 Ex $790 Gd $630
Sniper model (double set trigger) . . . . . . NiB $2013 Ex $1118 Gd $956

ENGRAVED MODELS
Yellowboy and Model 1873 rifles are available in deluxe models w/select walnut stocks and forearms and engraving in three grades. Grade "A" has delicate scrollwork in limited areas. Grade "B" is more elaborate with 40 percent coverage. Grade "C" has highest grade engraving. Add to value:
Grade "A" . . . . NiB $1023 Ex $779 Gd $615
Grade "B" . . . . NiB $1126 Ex $986 Gd $813
Grade "C" . . . . NiB $1568 Ex $995 Gd $723

HENRY LEVER-ACTION RIFLE
Replica of Winchester Model 1960 Henry Rifle. Caliber: .44-40;

12-round mag., Bbl.: Octagon, 16.5, 22 or 24.25 inches. Weight: 7.5 to 9 lbs. Lgt.: 35.4 to 43.25 inches. Blade front, adj. ladder rear sights. European walnut straight grip buttstock w/bbl. and side stock swivels. Imported from 1985 to date. Brass or steel receiver. Blued or color case-hardened metal.
Carbine model (w/22-inch bbl.,
introduced 1992) . . . . NiB $735 Ex $479 Gd $376
Military rifle model (w/brass frame) . . . . . . NiB $979 Ex $688 Gd $477
Trapper model (w/brass frame) . . . . NiB $735 Ex $479 Gd $376
Trapper model (w/iron frame) . . . . NiB $1055 Ex $800 Gd $479
W/"A" engraving, add $325
W/"B" engraving, add $550
W/"C" engraving, add $950

MARTINI TARGET RIFLE . . . . NiB $556 Ex $379 Gd $330
Martini action, single-shot. Calbers: .444 Marlin, .45-70 Gov't. Bbl.: 26 or 30 inches, half-octagon or octagon. Weight: 9 lbs. Creedmoor tang peep, open middle, blade front sights. Checkered stock w/cheekpiece and pistol grip, Schnabel tip. Introduced 1972. Disc.

Navy Arms

Navy Arms
Yellowboy Carbine

REVOLVING CARBINE . . . . **NiB $635 Ex $540 Gd $400**
Similar to Remington Model 1875 revolver. Case-hardened frame. Calibers: .357 Mag., .44-40, .45 Colt; six-round cylinder. Bbl. 20 inches. Weight: 5 lbs. Open rear, blade front sights. Straight grip stock, brass trigger guard and buttplate. Introduced 1968, disc.

ROLLING BLOCK BABY CARBINE . . . . **NiB $255 Ex $190 Gd $155**
Replica of small Remington Rolling Block single-shot action. Casehardened frame, brass trigger guard. Calibers: .22 LR. .22 Hornet, .357 Magnum, .44-40. 20-inch octagon or 22-inch round bbl. Weight: 5 lbs. Sights: Open rear; blade front. Straight-grip stock, plain forearm, brass buttplate. Imported from 1968 to 1981.

ROLLING BLOCK BUFFALO CARBINE . . . . **NiB $435 Ex $330 Gd $225**
Same as Buffalo Rifle except w/18-inch bbl.; weighs 10 lbs.

ROLLING BLOCK BUFFALO RIFLE . . . . . . **NiB $720 Ex $566 Gd $338**
Replica of Remington Rolling Block rifle, single-shot. Calibers: .444 Marlin, .45-70 Gov't., .50-70. Bbl.: 26 or 30 inches, heavy half-octagon or octagon. Weight: 11 to 12 lbs. Open rear, blade front sights. Case-hardened frame, brass trigger guard. Straight-grip stock w/brass buttplate; forearm w/brass bbl. band. Made from 1971 to 2003.

ROLLING BLOCK CREEDMOOR RIFLE
Same as Buffalo Rifle except calibers .45-70 Gov't. and .50-70 only. Bbl 28 or 30 inches, heavy half-octagon or octagon. Creedmoor tang peep sight.
Target model . . . . NiB $1530 Ex $1109 Gd $775
Deluxe target model (disc. 1998) . . . . . . NiB $1677 Ex $1330 Gd $190

YELLOWBOY CARBINE . . . . **NiB $856 Ex $590 Gd $443**
Similar to Yellowboy Rifle exept w/19-inch bbl., 10-round mag (14 rounds in .22 LR). Carbine-style forearm. Weight: 6.75 lbs. Disc. Reissued in 1991 in .44-40 only.

YELLOWBOY LEVER-ACTION REPEATER . . . . **NiB $1025 Ex $567 Gd $359**
Replica of Winchester Model 1866. Calibers: .38 Special, .44-40. 15-round magazine. 24-inch octagon bbl. Weight: 8 lbs. Sights: Folding leaf rear; blade front. Straight-grip stock, forearm w/end cap. Introduced 1966. Disc. Reissued 1991 in .44-40 only w/12-round magazine and adj. ladder-style rear sight.

YELLOWBOY TRAPPER'S MODEL . . . . . . **NiB $723 Ex $500 Gd $379**
Same as Yellowboy Carbine except w/16.5-inch bbl., 8-round magazine, weighs 6.25 lbs. Disc.

NEW ENGLAND FIREARMS — Gardner, Massachusetts

In 1987, New England Firearms was established as an independent company producing selected H&R models under the NEF logo. In 1991, H&R 1871, Inc. was formed from the residual of the parent company and that took over the New England Firearms facility. H&R 1871 produced firearms under both its logo and the NEF brand name until 1999, when the Marlin Firearms Company acquired the assets of H&R 1871.

HANDI-RIFLE
Single-shot, break-open action w/side lever. Calibers: .22 Hornet, .22-250 Rem., .223 rem., .243 Win., .270 Win., .30-30, .30-06, .45-70; Bbl.: 22 inches. Weight 7 lbs. Ramp front, folding rear sights. Drilled and tapped for scope mounts. Walnut-finished hardwood or synthetic stock. Blued finish. Made from 1989 to 2008.

Handi-Rifle . . . . NiB $335 Ex $254 Gd $145
Synthetic . . . . NiB $290 Ex $22 Gd $128
Synthetic/stainless. . . . . NiB $325 Ex $266 Gd $159
Youth model NiB. . .$300   Ex. . .$233   Gd. . .$144
10th Anniversary model NiB. . .$822   Ex. . .$555   Gd. . .$375
Trapper's Edition NiB. . .$334   Ex. . .$265   Gd. . .$190

SUPER LIGHT HANDI-RIFLE . . . . . **NiB $378 Ex $229 Gd $145**
Cal.: .22 Hornet, .223 Rem., .243 Win. Same as Handi Rifle but with black synthetic stock and forearm, recoil pad. Bbl.: 20-inch special contour w/rebated muzzle. .223 Rem. model includes scope base and hammer extension. Weight: 5.5 lbs. Made 1997 to 2008.

SPORTSTER . . . . **NiB $218 Ex $144 Gd $90**
Cal.: .17 HMR, .17 Mach 2, .22 LR, .22 Mag. Bbl.: 20 or 22 inches, Weaver-style rail, no sights. Adult or youth (.22 LR only) dimensions. Stock and forearm: Black polymer. Made 1999 to 2008.

SURVIVOR . . . . **NiB $297 Ex $195 Gd $115**
Cal.: .223 Rem., .308 Win., .357 Mag., .410/.45 Long Colt. Similar to Survivor series shotgun but with removable forearm and thumbhole stock (both with ammo compartments). Bbl.: 20 or 22 inches, blue or nickel finish. Weight: 6 lbs. Made 1996 to 2008.

NEWTON SPORTING RIFLES — Buffalo, New York. Manufactured by Newton Arms Co., Charles Newton Rifles Corp. and Buffalo Newton Rifle Co.

BUFFALO
SPORTING RIFLE . . . . **NiB $2590 Ex $1800 Gd $970**
Same general specifications as Standard Model, Second Type. Made c. 1922 to 1932 by Buffalo Newton Rifle Co.

MAUSER
SPORTING RIFLE . . . . **NiB $2125 Ex $1633 Gd $1110**
Mauser (Oberndorf) action. Caliber: .256 Newton. Five round box magazine, hinged floorplate. Double-set triggers. 24-inch bbl. Open rear sight, ramp front sight. Sporting stock w/checkered pistol-grip. Weight: 7 lbs. Made c. 1914 by Newton Arms Co.

STANDARD MODEL
SPORTING RIFLE, FIRST TYPE . . . . **NiB $3597 Ex $2044 Gd $1035**
Newton bolt-action, interrupted screw-type breech-locking mechanism. Double-set triggers. Calibers: .22, .256, .280. .30, .33, .35 Newton.; .30-06. Bbl.: 24 inches. Open rear or cocking-piece peep, ramp front sights. Checkered pistol-grip stock. Weight: 7 to 8 lbs. Made circa 1916 to 1918 by Newton Arms Co. Second Type was prototype, never manufactured.

NEWTON SPRINGFIELD . . . . **NiB $1255 Ex $835 Gd $589**
Kit gun including a Marlin-built sporting stock with .256 Newton barrel; Springfield 1903 action. No sights. Original has square-cut bbls. Marked "Newton Arms Col, Buffalo, N.Y." Made from 1914 to 1917.

Norinco

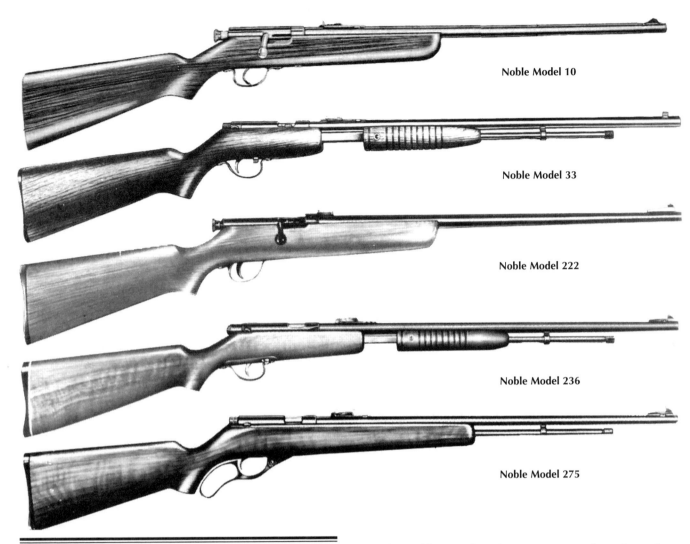

Noble Model 10

Noble Model 33

Noble Model 222

Noble Model 236

Noble Model 275

NOBLE MFG. CO. — Haydenville, Massachusetts

MODEL 10 BOLT-ACTION
SINGLE-SHOT RIFLE. . . . . NiB $121 Ex $89 Gd $73
Caliber: .22 LR. Long, Short. 24-inch bbl. Plain pistol-grip stock. Sights: Open rear, bead front. Weight: 4 lbs. Made from 1955 to 1958.

MODEL 20 BOLT-ACTION
SINGLE-SHOT RIFLE. . . . . NiB $125 Ex $92 Gd $75
Manually cocked. Caliber: .22 LR. Long, Short. 22-inch bbl. Weight: 5 lbs. Sights: Open rear; bead front. Walnut stock w/pistol grip. Made from 1958 to 1963.

MODEL 33 SLIDE-ACTION REPEATER . . . . . NiB $230 Ex $110 Gd $80
Hammerless. Caliber: .22 LR. Long, Short. Tubular magazine holds 21 Short, 17 Long, 15 LR. 24-inch bbl. Weight: 6 lbs. Sights: Open rear; bead front. Tenite stock and slide handle. Made from 1949 to 1953.

MODEL 33A . . . . NiB $115 Ex $89 Gd $69
Same specifications as Model 33 except w/wood stock and slide handle. Made from 1953 to 1955.

MODEL 222 BOLT-ACTION
SINGLE-SHOT RIFLE. . . . . NiB $240 Ex $120 Gd $80
Manually cocked. Caliber: .22 LR. Long, Short. Barrel integral w/receiver. Overall length: 38 inches. Weight: 5 lbs. Sights: Interchangeable V-notch and peep rear; ramp front. Scope base. Pistol-grip stock. Made from 1958 to 1971.

MODEL 236 SLIDE-ACTION
REPEATING RIFLE. . . . . NiB $159 Ex $140 Gd $97
Hammerless. Caliber: .22 Short, Long, LR. Tubular magazine holds 21 Short, 17 Long, 15 LR. 24-inch bbl. Weight: 5.5 lbs. Sights: Open rear; ramp front. Pistol-grip stock, grooved slide handle. Made from 1951 to 1971.

MODEL 275 LEVER-ACTION RIFLE . . . . . . NiB $225 Ex $139 Gd $110
Hammerless. Caliber: .22 Short, Long, LR. Tubular magazine holds 21 Short, 17 Long, 15 LR. 24-inch bbl. Weight: 5.5 lbs. Sights: Open rear; ramp front. Semi-pistol-grip stock. Made from 1958 to 1971.

NORINCO — Manufactured by Northern China Industries Corp., Beijing, China. Imported by Century International Arms; Interarms; KBI and others

MODEL 81S/AK SEMIAUTOMATIC RIFLE
Semi-automatic Kalashnikov-style AK-47 action. Caliber: 7.62x39mm; five-, 30- or 40-round mag. Bbl.: 17 inches. Lgt.: 36.75 inches. Weight: 8.5 lbs. Hooded post front, 500-meter leaf rear sights. Oil-finished hardwood (military style), pistol-grip buttstock, forearm and handguard or folding metal stock. Black oxide finish. Imported from 1988 to 1989.

Parker-Hale
Model 81 Classic

Parker-Hale
Model 87

NIdek 81S (w/wood stock) . . . . NiB $1244 Ex $965 Gd $733
Model 81S (w/folding metal stock). . . . . . . NiB $1266 Ex $1002 Gd $753
Model 81S-5/56S-2
(w/folding metal stock). . . . . NiB $1339 Ex $1027 Gd $755

MODEL 84S/AK SEMIAUTOMATIC RIFLE
Semiautomatic Kalashnikov style AK-47 action. Caliber: .223 (5.56mm). 30-round magazine. 16.25-inch bbl. 35.5 inches overall. Weight: 8.75 lbs. Hooded post front sight, 800 meters leaf rear sight. Oil-finished hardwood (military style) buttstock, pistol grip, forearm and handguard; sporterized composite fiberglass stock or folding metal stock. Black oxide finish. Imported from 1988 to 1989.
Model 84S (w/wood stock). . . . . NiB $1479 Ex $1022 Gd $678
Model 84S-3 (w/folding metal stock) . . . . . . NiB $1688 Ex $954 Gd $669
Model 84S-3 (w/composite stock) . . . . . NiB $1337 Ex $1033 Gd $645
Model 84S-5 (w/folding metal stock) . . . . . . NiB $1613 Ex $981 Gd $687

MODEL AK-47 THUMBHOLE SPORTER
Semi-automatic AK-47 sporterized version. Calibers: .223 Rem. (5.56mm) or 7.62x39mm; five-round mag. Bbl.: 16.25 or 23.25 inches. Lgt.: 35.5 or 42.5 inches. Weight: 8.5 to 10.3 lbs. Adj. post front, open adj. rear sights. Forged receiver w/black oxide finish. Walnut-finished thumbhole stock w/recoil pad. Imported from 1991 to 1993.
5.56mm. . . . . NiB $775 Ex $466 Gd $337
7.62x39mm. . . . . NiB $564 Ex $466 Gd $339

MODEL MAK 90/01 SPORT . . . . . . NiB $733 Ex $455 Gd $337
Similar to Model AK-47 Thumbhole Sporter except w/minor modifications implemented to meet importation requirements. Imported from 1994 to 1995.

OLYMPIC ARMS — Olympia, Washington

PCR SERIES
Gas-operated, semi-automatic. Calibers: .17 rem., .223 Rem., 7.62x39mm, 6x45, 6PPC or 9mm, .40 S&W, .45 ACP (in carbine version). 10-round mag. Bbl.: Fluted, 16, 20 or 24 inches. Weight: 7 to 10.2 lbs. Black composite stock. Post front, adj. rear sights. Flattop receiver drilled and tapped for scope mount. Williams set trigger. Made from 1994 to date.

PCR-1 Ultra Match . . . . NiB $981 Ex $760 Gd $583
PCR-2 Multi-Match ML-1 . . . . NiB $1022 Ex $915 Gd $633
PCR-3 Multi-Match ML-2 . . . . NiB $1070 Ex $959 Gd $654
PCR-4 AR-15 Match . . . . NiB $877 Ex $808 Gd $521
MCR-5 CAR-15 (.223 Rem.) . . . . . . NiB $977 Ex $803 Gd $522

PCR5 CAR-15
(9mm, 40 S&W, .45 ACP) . . . . NiB $903 Ex $794 Gd $538
PCR-5 CAR (.223 Rem.) . . . . NiB $955 Ex $731 Gd $510

BOLT-ACTION SAKO . . . . NiB $755 Ex $575 Gd $456
Cal.: Various from .17 Rem. to .416 Rem. Mag. Bbl.: Fluted; various stock options. Value is for base model without custom options.

ULTRA CSR TACTICAL . . . . . . NiB $1877 Ex $1355 Gd $1033
Cal.: .308 Win. Sako action. Bbl.: Heavy, 26 inches, broach cut. Stock: Bell & Carlson black or synthetic with aluminum bedding. Harris bipod included. Made from 1996 to 2000.

COUNTER SNIPER RIFLE . . . . . NiB $1490 Ex $1266 Gd $1079
Bolt action. Cal.: .308 Win. Bbl.: Heavy, 26-inches. Stock: Camo fiberglass. Weight: 10.5 lbs. Disc. 1987.

SURVIVOR 1. . . . . NiB $455 Ex $276 Gd $264
Converts M1911 into bolt-action carbine. Cal.: .223 Rem., .45 ACP. Bbl.: 16.25 inches. Collapsible stock. Available for S&W and Browning Hi-Power. Weight: 5 lbs.

CAR 97 . . . . NiB $900 Ex $693 Gd $633
Cal.: .223 Rem., 9mm Para., 10mm, .40 S&W, .45 ACP. Similar to PCR-5 but w/ 16-inch button-rifled barrel. A2 sights, fixed CAR stock, post-ban muzzle brake. Weight: 7 lbs. Made from 1997 to 2004.
M-4 version (disc. 2004), add. $75

FAR-15 . . . . NiB $1035 Ex $780 Gd $669
Featherweight model. Cal.: .223 Rem. Bbl.: 16 inches, lightweight, button-rifled, collapsible stock. Weight: 9.2 lbs. Made from 2001 to 2004.

GI-16 . . . . NiB $979 Ex $760 Gd $590
Cal.: .223 Rem. Forged aluminum receiver, matte finish. Bbl.: Match grade, 16 inches, button rifled. Collapsible stock. Weight: 7 lbs. Made 2004 and 2006.

GI-20 . . . . NiB $877 Ex $698 Gd $549
Cal. .223 Rem. Similar to GI-16 except w/20-inch heavy bbl., A-2 lower. Weight: 8.4 lbs. Made 2004.

OA-93 Carbine . . . . NiB $1390 Ex $1133 Gd $966
Based on OA-93 pistol. Cal.: .223 Rem. Bbl.: 16 inches. Flattop receiver. Aluminum side folding stock, round aluminum handguard, Vortex flash supp. Weight: 7.5 lbs. Made 1998 and from 2004 to 2007.

Parker-Hale Limited

Olympic Arms OA-93 Carbine

Olympic Arms LTF Tactical Rifle

Olympic Arms K4B

Olympic Arms K7 Eliminator

OA-93PT . . . . **NiB $1077 Ex $966 Gd $692**
Similar to OA-93 carbine but with aluminum receiver, black matte anodized finish. Bbl.: 16 inches, match grade chromemoly steel with removable muzzle brake, push-button removable stock. Weight: 7 lbs. Made from 2006 to 2007.

LTF TACTICAL RIFLE . . . . **NiB $1338 Ex $1056 Gd $777**
Cal. .223 Rem. Bbl.: 16 inches, fluted or non-fluted w/flash supp. Black matte anodized receiver. Firsh-type forearm, Picatinny rails, Parkerized steel parts. Tube-style stock. Weight: 6.4 lbs.
Fluted bbl., add. **10%**

K3B CARBINE . . . . **NiB $1189 Ex $873 Gd $689**
Cal. .223 Rem. Bbl.: 16 inches, match grade chromemoly steel w/ flash supp. A2 rear sight and buttstock; adj. front post sight.
A3 Flattop receiver, add **$75**
FAR carbine, add **$75**
M4 carbine, add **$75**
A3-TC carbine, add. **$250**

K4B/K4B68 . . . . **NiB $1087 Ex $764 Gd $590**
Cal.: .223 Rem., 6.8 SPC. Bbl.: 20 inches, match grade, chromemoly steel, button rifled; flash supp. Adj. A2 rear sight and front post; A2 buttstock, upper receiver and hand guard. Weight: 8.5 lbs.
Flattop receiver, add **$150**

K4B-A4 . . . . **NiB $1034 Ex $766 Gd $588**
Cal.: .223 Rem. Bbl.: 20 inches w/A2 flash supp.; bayonet lug. Flattop receiver. Adj. post front sight. Firsh handguard, Picatinny rails. Made from 2006 to 2008.

K7 ELIMINATOR . . . . **NiB $1076 Ex $800 Gd $633**
Cal.: .223 Rem. Bbl.: 16 inches, stainless steel w/flash supp.; adj. A2 rear sight and front post; A2 buttstock. Weight: 7.8 lbs.

K8 TARGET MATCH . . . . **NiB $1076 Ex $723 Gd $566**
Cal.: .223 Rem. Bbl.: 20-inch bull bbl., stainless, button rifling; Picatinny flattop upper, A2 buttstock. Weight: 8.5 lbs.

K8-MAG . . . . **NiB $1423 Ex $1150 Gd $976**
Similar to Target Match model. Cal.: .223 WSSM, .243 WSSM, .25 WSSM, .300 WSM. 24-inch bbl. Weight: 9.4 lbs.

K9/K10/K40/K45 . . . . **NiB $1132 Ex $955 Gd $780**
Cal.: 9mm Para., 10mm Norma, .40 S&W, .45 ACP. Blow-back action. Bbl.: 16 inches w/flash suppressor and bayonet lug. Adj. A2 rear sight. Collapsible stock. Weight: 6.7 lbs.

K9GL/K40GL . . . . **NiB $1188 Ex $992 Gd $694**
Similar to K9 series. Cal.: 9mm Para., .40 S&W. Lower designed to accept Glock magazines. Bbl.: 16 inches; flash suppressor. Collapsible stock. No magazine furnished.
A3 upper, add **$125**

K16 . . . . **NiB $962 Ex $710 Gd $577**
Cal.: .223 Rem. Bbl.: 16 inches, free-floating, button rifled. Picatinny flattop upper; A2 buttstock. Weight: 7.5 lbs.
K30R . . . . **NiB $1066 Ex $879 Gd $683**
W/A3 upper, add **$125**

K-30 (.30 carbine) . . . . **NiB $978 Ex $668 Gd $533**
Cal.: 7.62x39mm. Bbl.: 16-inch stainless steel, adj. rear sight. Parkerized steel parts. Six-point collapsible stock.

K68 . . . . **NiB $1198 Ex $978 Gd $645**
Cal.: 6.8 Rem. SPC. Bbl.: 16-inch stainless steel, A2 upper with adj. rear sight and flash suppressor. Matte black anodized receiver, Parkerized steel parts. Six-position collapsible A2 stock w/pistol grip.
W/A3 upper, add **$125**

K74 . . . . **NiB $1027 Ex $903 Gd $645**
Cal.: 5.45x39mm. Bbl.: 16-inches, button rifling; flash suppressor and adj. front sight. Six-position collapsible stock. Weight 6.75 lbs.

PARKER-HALE LIMITED — Birmingham, England

MODEL 81 AFRICAN . . . . **NiB $900 Ex $789 Gd $533**
Same general specifications as Model 81 Classic except in caliber .375 H&H only. Sights: African Express rear; hooded blade front. Barrel-band swivel. All-steel trigger guard. Checkered European walnut stock w/pistol grip and recoil pad. Engraved receiver. Imported from 1986 to 1991.

MODEL 81 CLASSIC
BOLT-ACTION RIFLE . . . . **NiB $745 Ex $627 Gd $435**
Calibers: .22-250 Rem., .243 Win., 6mm rem, 6.5x55, 7x57, 7x64, .308 Win., .30-06, .300 Win. Mag., 7mm Rem. Mag.; four-round mag., 24-inch bbl. Weight: 7.75 lbs. Adj. open rear, hooded ramp front sights. Checkered European walnut pistol-grip stock. Imported from 1984 to 1991.

MODEL 85 SNIPER RIFLE . . . . . **NiB $2730 Ex $2161 Gd $1578**
Caliber: .308 Win.; 10 or 20-round M-15-type mag. Bbl.: 24.25 inches. Lgt.: 45 inches overall. Weight: 12.5 lbs. Blade front, folding aperture rear sights. McMillan fiberglass stock w/detachable bipod. Imported from 1989 to 1991.

Parker-Hale Model 1100
Lightweight

Parker-Hale Model 1200
Super Clip

MODEL 87 BOLT-ACTION
REPEATING TARGET RIFLE..... NiB $1425 Ex $1233 Gd $757
Calibers: .243 Win., 6.5x55, .308 Win., .30-06 Springfield, .300 Win. Mag. Five-round detachable box magazine. 26-inch bbl. 45 inches overall. Weight: 10 lbs. No sights; grooved for target-style scope mounts. Stippled walnut stock w/adj. buttplate. Sling swivel studs. Parkerized finish. Folding bipod. Imported from 1988 to 1991.

MODEL 1000 STANDARD RIFLE .... NiB $460 Ex $359 Gd $248
Bolt-action. Calibers: .22-250, .243 Win., .270 Win., 6mm Rem., .308 Win., .30-06; four-round mag.. Bbl.: 22 or 24 inches. Lgt.: 43 inches. Weight: 7.25 lbs. Checkered Monte Carlo walnut stock w/ satin finish. Imported from 1984 to 1988.

MODEL 1100 LIGHTWEIGHT
BOLT-ACTION RIFLE .... NiB $535 Ex $443 Gd $337
Same specs as Model 1000 except w/22-inch lightweight bbl., hollow bolt handle, alloy trigger guard and floorplate. Weight: 6.5 lbs. Schnabel forend. Imported from 1984 to 1991.

MODEL 1100M AFRICAN
MAGNUM RIFLE.............. NiB $858 Ex $745 Gd $500
Same as Model 1000 except in .404 Jeffrey, .458 Win. Mag.; 24-inch bbl., Weight: 9.5 lbs. Adj. Rear, hooded post front sights. Imported from 1984 to 1991.

MODEL 1200 SUPER CLIP
BOLT-ACTION RIFLE .... NiB $763 Ex $555 Gd $423
Same as Model 1200 Super except in .243 win., 6mm Rem., .270 Win., .30-06, .308 Win. .300 Win. Mag., 7mm Rem. Mag., detachable box mag. Imported from 1984 to 1991.

MODEL 1200 SUPER BOLT-ACTION
SPORTING RIFLE .... NiB $586 Ex $480 Gd $355
Mauser-type bolt-action. Calibers: .22-250 Rem., .243 Win., 6mm Rem. .25-06 Rem., .270 Win., .30-06, .308 Win.; four-round mag. Bbl.: 24 inches. Weight: 7.25 lbs. Folding open rear, hooded ramp front sights. European walnut stock w/rollover Monte Carlo cheekpiece, rosewood forend tip and pistol grip cap. Skip checkering. Recoil pad, sling swivels. Imported from 1986 to 1991.

MODEL 1200 SUPER MAGNUM .... NiB $556 Ex $550 Gd $365
Same specifications as 1200 Super except in 7mm Rem. Mag. and .300 Win. Mag., 3-round magazine. Imported from 1988 to 1991.

MODEL 1200P PRESENTATION .... NiB $580 Ex $459 Gd $344
Same specs as Model 1200 Super except in .243 Win. and .30-06. Scroll-engraved action, trigger guard and floorplate. No sights. QD swivels. Imported from 1969 to 1975.

MODEL 1200V VARMINT....... NiB $557 Ex $498 Gd $425
Same specs as Model 1200 Super except in .22-250 rem., .6mm Rem., .25-06 Rem., .243 Win.; 24-inch heavy bbl., no sights. Weight: 9.5 lbs.

MODEL 1300C SCOUT .... NiB $733 Ex $689 Gd $550
Calibers: .243 Win., .308 Win.; 10-round mag. Bbl.: 20 inches w/muzzle brake. Lgt.: 41 inches. Weight: 8.5 lbs. No sights, drilled and tapped for scope mounts. Checkered laminated birch stock w/QD swivels. Imported in 1991.

MODEL 2100 MIDLAND
BOLT-ACTION RIFLE .... NiB $380 Ex $321 Gd $244
Calibers: .22-250 Rem., .243 Win., 6mm Rem., .270 Win., 6.5x55, 7x57, 7x64, .308 Win., .30-06; four-round mag. Bbl.: 22 or 24 inches (.22-250). Lgt.: 43 inches. Weight: 7 lbs. Adj. folding rear, hooded ramp front sights. Checkered European walnut Monte Carlo stock w/pistol grip. Imported from 1984 to 1991.

MODEL 2700 LIGHTWEIGHT .... NiB $370 Ex $329 Gd $237
Same specifications as Model 2100 Midland except w/tapered lightweight bbl. and aluminum trigger guard. Weight: 6.5 lbs. Imported in 1991.

MODEL 2800 MIDLAND .... NiB $375 Ex $319 Gd $245
Same specifications as Model 2100 except w/laminated birch stock. Imported in 1991.

PEDERSEN CUSTOM GUNS — North Haven, Connecticut; division of O.F. Mossberg & Sons, Inc.

MODEL 3000 GRADE I
BOLT-ACTION RIFLE .... NiB $1034 Ex $809 Gd $544
Mossberg Model 810 action. Calibers: .270 Win., .30-06, 7mm Rem. Mag, .338 Win. Mag.; three-round mag, hinged floorplate. Bbl.: 22 inches (in .270 and .30-06).; 24 inches in magnum calibers. Weight: 7 to 8 lbs. Open rear, hooded ramp front sights. Richly engraved w/silver inlays, full fancy American walnut Monte Carlo stock w/rollover cheekpiece, wraparound hand checkering on pistol grip and forearm, rosewood grip cap and forend tip; recoil pad or steel buttplate w/trap; detachable swivels. Imported from 1973 to 1975.

MODEL 3000 GRADE II........ NiB $733 Ex $480 Gd $377
Same as Model 3000 Grade I except w/less elaborate engraving, no inlays, fancy grade walnut stock w/recoil pad. Imported from 1973 to 1975.

MODEL 3000 GRADE III .... NiB $579 Ex $380 Gd $299
Same as Model 3000 Grade I except no engraving or inlays, select grade walnut stock w/recoil pad. Imported from 1973 to 1974.

Plainfield Machine Company

Pedersen Model 3000 Grade I Bolt-Action Rifle

Pedersen Model 3000 Grade III

Plainfield M-1 Carbine

MODEL 4700 CUSTOM
DELUXE LEVER-ACTION RIFLE. . . . . **NiB $279 Ex $238 Gd $175**
Mossberg Model 472 action. Calibers: .30-30, .35 Rem.; five-round tubular mag. Bbl.: 24 inches. Weight: 7.5 lbs. Open rear, hooded ramp front sights. Hand finished black walnut stock and beavertail forearm, barrel band swivel. Imported in 1975.

J.C. PENNEY CO., INC. — Dallas, Texas

Firearms sold under the J.C. Penney label were mfd. by Marlin, High Standard, Stevens, Savage and Springfield.

MODEL 2025 BOLT-ACTION REPEATER . . . . **NiB $100 Ex $65 Gd $55**
Takedown. Caliber: .22 RF. Eight round detachable box magazine. 24-inch bbl. Weight: 6 lbs. Sights: Open rear; bead front. Plain pistol-grip stock. Manufactured by Marlin.

MODEL 2035 BOLT-ACTION REPEATER . . . . **NiB $100 Ex $65 Gd $55**
Takedown. Caliber: .22 RF. Eight round detachable box magazine. 24-inch bbl. Weight: 6 lbs. Sights: Open rear; bead front. Plain pistol-grip stock. Manufactured by Marlin.

MODEL 2935 LEVER-ACTION RIFLE . . . . . **NiB $210 Ex $170 Gd $121**
Same specifications as Marlin Model 336.

MODEL 6400 BOLT-ACTION
CENTERFIRE RIFLE . . . . **NiB $210 Ex $170 Gd $110**
Same specifications as Savage Model 340.

MODEL 6660
AUTOLOADING RIFLE. . . . . **NiB $115 Ex $90 Gd $75**
Caliber: .22 RF. Tubular magazine. 22-inch bbl. Weight: 5.5 lbs. Sights: Open rear; hooded ramp front. Plain pistol-grip stock. Manufactured by Marlin.

PLAINFIELD MACHINE COMPANY — Dunellen, New Jersey

M-1 CARBINE. . . . . **NiB $227 Ex $166 Gd $135**
Same as U.S. Carbine Cal. .30 M-1 except also in 5.7mm (.30 Carbine necked down to .22 caliber). Ventilated metal handguard and bbl. band w/o bayonet lug. Early models have standard military-type fittings. Made from 1960 to 1977.

M-1 CARBINE,
COMMANDO MODEL. . . . . **NiB $232 Ex $171 Gd $145**
Same as M-1 Carbine except w/paratrooper-type stock w/telescoping wire shoulderpiece. Made from 1960 to 1977.

M-1 CARBINE, MILITARY SPORTER. . . . . . . **NiB $227 Ex $166 Gd $135**
Same as M-1 Carbine except w/unslotted buttstock and wood handguard. Made from 1960 to 1977.

M-1 DELUXE SPORTER. . . . . **NiB $232 Ex $171 Gd $145**
Same as M-1 Carbine except w/Monte Carlo sporting stock. Made from 1960 to 1973.

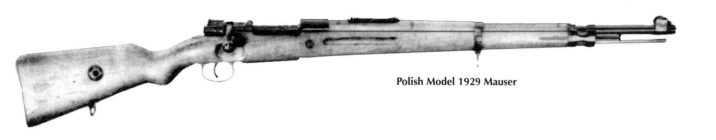

Polish Model 1929 Mauser

POLISH MILITARY RIFLES — Manufactured by Government Arsenals at Radom and Warsaw, Poland

MODEL 1898 (KARABIN 98, K98)
MAUSER MILITARY CARBINE .... NiB $331 Ex $210 Gd $166
Same as German Kar. 98A except for minor details. Made circa 1920.

MODEL 1898 (KARABIN 98, WZ98A)
MAUSER MILITARY RIFLE. .... NiB $289 Ex $180 Gd $145
Same as German Kar. 98 used in WWI except for minor details. Made c. 1921.

MODEL 1929 (KARABIN 29, WZ29)
MAUSER MILITARY RIFLE. .... NiB $331 Ex $210 Gd $166
Same as Czech Model 24, mfd. 1929 thru WWII except for minor details. A similar model produced during German occupation was designated Gew. 29/40.

WILLIAM POWELL & SON LTD. — Birmingham, England

BOLT-ACTION RIFLE .... NiB $2888 Ex $2367 Gd $1699
Mauser-type bolt-action. Calibers: 6x54 through .375 H&H Mag.; three- and four-round mag. Bbl.l: 24 inches. Weight: 7.5 to 8.75 lbs. Folding leaf rear, hooded ramp front sights. Cheekpiece stock, checkered forearm and pistol grip; swivels. Imported by Stoeger from 1938 to 1951.

RAPTOR ARMS COMPANY, INC. — Newport, New Hampshire

BOLT-ACTION RIFLE
Calibers: .243 Win., .270 Win., .30-06, .308 Win.; four-round mag. Bbl.: 22 inches, sporter or heavy. Weight: 7.3 to 8 lbs. Lgt.: 42.5 inches. No sights. Drilled and tapped receiver, optional blade front sight. Blue, stainless or Taloncote rust-resistant finish. Checkered black synthetic Monte Carlo stock w/cheekpiece and vented recoil pad. Imported from 1997 to 1999.
Raptor Sporter model . . . . NiB $255 Ex $190 Gd $155
Raptor Deluxe Peregrine model (disc. 1998) . . . . NiB $258 Ex $195 Gd $159
Raptor heavy bbl. model. . . . . NiB $277 Ex $222 Gd $195
Raptor stainless bbl. model. . . . . NiB $299 Ex $257 Gd $213
W/optional sights, add $40

REMINGTON ARMS COMPANY — Ilion, New York, and Mayfield, Kentucky

To facilitate locating Remington firearms, models are grouped into four categories: Single-shot rifles, bolt-action repeating rifles, slide-action (pump) rifles, and semiautomatic rifles. For a complete listing, please refer to the index.

SINGLE-SHOT RIFLES

NO. 1 SPORTING RIFLE . . . . . NiB $6223 Ex $3856 Gd $2210
Single-shot, rolling block action. Calibers: .40-50, .40-70, .44-77, .50-45, .50-70 Gov't. centerfire; .44 Long, .44 Extra Long, .45-70, .46 Long. .46 Extra Long, .50-70 rimfire calibers. Bbl.: 28 or 30 inches, part octagon. Weight: 5 to 7.5 lbs. Folding leaf rear, sporting front; dovetail bases. Plain walnut straight stock, flanged top, semi-carbine buttplate. Plain walnut forend w/thin, rounded tip. Made from 1868 to 1902.

NO. 1 1/2 SPORTING RIFLE . . NiB $4190 Ex $1200 Gd $1888
Similar to Remington No. 1. Single-shot, rolling block action. Calibers: .22 Short, Long, LR; .25 Stevens, .32 and .38 rimfire; .32-20, .38-40, .44-40 centerfire. Bbl.: 24, 26 and 28 inches; 30-inch part octagon. Made from 1969 to 1902.

NO. 2 SPORTING RIFLE
Single-shot, rolling block action. Calibers: .22, .25, .32, .38, .44 rimfire or centerfire. Bbl.; 24, 26, 28, 30 inches. Weight: 5 to 6 lbs. Open rear, bead front sights. Walnut straight-grip sporting stock w/ knob-tip forearm. Made from 1873 to 1909.
Calibers: .22, .25, .32 . . . . NiB $3575 Ex $2040 Gd $979
Calibers: .38, .44. . . . . NiB $9650 Ex $8129 Gd $5450

NO. 3 HIGH POWER RIFLE
Single-shot, Hepburn falling-block action w/side lever. Calibers: .30-30, .30-40, .32 Special, .32-40, .38-55, .38-72 (high-power cartridges). Bbl. lengths: 26-, 28-, 30-inch. Weight: 8 lbs. Open sporting sights. Checkered pistol-grip stock and forearm. Made from 1893 to 1907.
Calibers: .30-30, .30-40,
.32 Special, .32-40 . . . . NiB $9775 Ex $7956 Gd $5110
Calibers: .38-55, .38-72 . . . . NiB $9688 Ex $8154 Gd $6422

NO. 3 SPORTING RIFLE . . . . . . NiB $9775 Ex $7279 Gd $6788
Single-shot, Hepburn falling-block action w/side lever. Calibers: .22 WCF, .22 Extra Long, .25-20 Stevens, .25-21 Stevens, .25-25 Stevens, .32 WCF, .32-40 Ballard & Marlin, .32-40 Rem., .38 WCF, .38-40 Rem., 38-.38-50 Rem., .38-55 Ballard & Marlin, .40-60 Ballard & Marlin, .40-60 WCF, .40-65 Rem. Straight, .40-82 WCF, .45-70 Gov., .45-90 WCF, also was supplied on special order in bottle-necked .40-50, .40-70, .40-90, .44-77, .44-90, .44-105, .50-

Remington Arms Company

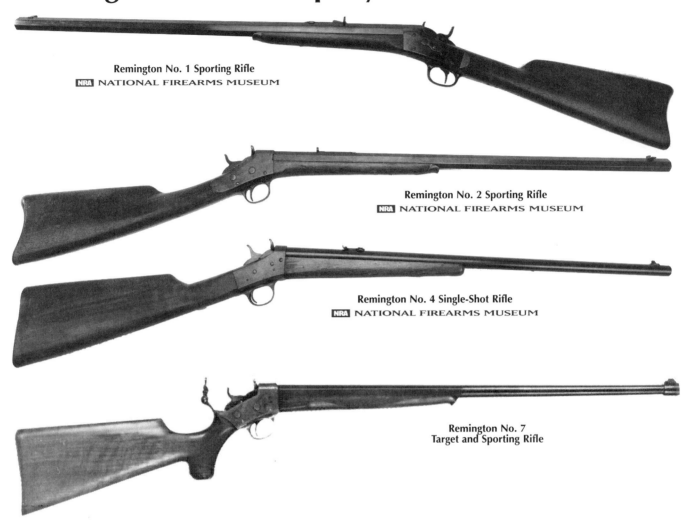

Remington No. 1 Sporting Rifle
NRA NATIONAL FIREARMS MUSEUM

Remington No. 2 Sporting Rifle
NRA NATIONAL FIREARMS MUSEUM

Remington No. 4 Single-Shot Rifle
NRA NATIONAL FIREARMS MUSEUM

**Remington No. 7
Target and Sporting Rifle**

70 Gov., .50-90 Sharps Straight. Bbl. lengths: 26-inch (22, 25, 32 cal. only), 28-inch, 30-inch; half-octagon or full-octagon. Weight: 8 to 10 lbs. Sights: Open rear; blade front. Checkered pistol-grip stock and forearm. Made from 1880 to c. 1911.

NO. 4 SINGLE-SHOT RIFLE . . . . NiB $1630 EX $944 Gd $755
Rolling-block action. Solid frame or takedown. Calibers: .22 Short and Long, .22 LR. .25 Stevens R.F., .32 Short and Long R.F. 22.5-inch octagon bbl., 24-inch available in .32 caliber only. Weight: 4.5 lbs. Sights: Open rear; blade front. Plain walnut stock and forearm. Made from 1890 to 1933.

**NO. 4S MILITARY MODEL 22
SINGLE-SHOT RIFLE . . . . NiB $2650 Ex $2033 Gd $997**
Rolling block action. Calibers: .22 Short, LR. Bbl.: 28 inches. Weight: 5 lbs. Military-type rear, blade front sights. Military-type stock w/ handguard, stacking swivel, sling. Bayonet stud on bbl.; bayonet and scabbard included. This model was the official rifle of the Boy Scouts of America and was called the Boy Scout Rifle. Made from 1913 to 1933.

NO. 5 SPECIAL SINGLE-SHOT RIFLE
Single-shot, rolling block action. Calibers:. 7mm Mauser, .30-30, .30-40 Krag, .303 British, .32-40, .32 Special, .38-55 (high-power

cartridges). Bbl.: 24, 26, 28 inches. Weight: 7 lbs. Open sporting sights. Plain straight-grip stock and forearm. Made from 1902 to 1918. Models 1897 and 1902 military rifles for export market are nearly identical except for 30-inch bbl., full military stock and Weight (about 8.5 lbs.). A carbine was also offered. Military rifles were produced in 8mm Lebel for France, 7.62mm Russian for Russia and 7mm Mauser for the Central and South American government. Also available to the retail market.
Sporting model . . . . NiB $934 Ex $733 Gd $530
Military model . . . . NiB $731 Ex $554 Gd $400

NO. 6 TAKEDOWN RIFLE . . . . NiB $675 Ex $535 Gd $459
Single-shot, rolling-block action. Calibers: .22 Short, .22 Long, .22 LR, .32 Short/Long RF. 20-inch bbl. Weight: 4 lbs. Sights: Open front and rear; tang peep. Plain straight-grip stock, forearm. Made from 1901 to 1933.

NO. 7 TARGET AND SPORTING RIFLE . . . .NiB $9700 Ex $7235 Gd $6755
Single-shot, rolling block Army Pistol frame. Calibers: .22 Short, LR; .25-10 Stevens RF (other calibers on special order). Bbl.: half-octagon, 24, 26 and 28 inches. Weight: 6 lbs. Lyman combination rear, Beach combination front sights. Fancy walnut stock, Swiss buttplate option. Made from 1903 to 1911.

Remington Arms Company

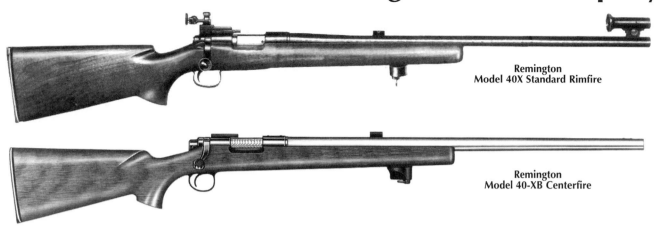

Remington
Model 40X Standard Rimfire

Remington
Model 40-XB Centerfire

MODEL 33 BOLT-ACTION
SINGLE-SHOT RIFLE . . . . **NiB $275 EX $190 Gd $239**
Takedown. Caliber: .22 Short, Long, LR. 24-inch bbl. Weight: 4.5 lbs. Sights: Open rear, bead front. Plain, pistol-grip stock, forearm with grasping grooves. Made from 1931 to 1936.

MODEL 33 NRA
JUNIOR TARGET RIFLE . . . . **NiB $544 Ex $408 Gd $240**
Same as Model 33 Standard except has Lyman peep rear sight, Partridge-type front sight, 0.88-inch sling and swivels, weighs 5 lbs.

MODEL 40X
CENTERFIRE RIFLE . . . . **NiB $2690 Ex $2044 Gd $1107**
Specs same as Model 40X Rimfire (heavyweight). No sights. Calibers: .222 Rem., .222 Rem. Mag., 7.62mm NATO, .30-06 (others on special order). Made from 1961 to 1964.

MODEL 40X HEAVYWEIGHT BOLT-ACTION TARGET RIFLE (RIMFIRE)
Single-shot. Model 722-type action. Caliber: .22 LR. Click-adj. trigger. Bbl.: Heavy, 28 inches. Redfield Olympic sights. Scope bases. High-comb target stock, bedding device, adj. swivel. Rubber buttplate. Weight: 12.75 lbs. Made from 1955 to 1964.
With sights . . . . **NiB $3370 Ex $2133 Gd $1320**
Without sights. . . . . **NiB $2390 Ex $1096 Gd $675**

MODEL 40-X SPORTER . . . . **NiB $3370 Ex $2133 Gd $1320**
Same specs as Model 700 C Custom (listed in this section) except in .22 LR. Made from 1972 to 1977.

MODEL 40X STANDARD BARREL
Same as Model 40X Heavyweight except has lighter barrel. Weight: 10.75 lbs.
With sights . . . . **NiB $579 Ex $416 Gd $322**
Without sights. . . . . **NiB $490 Ex $338 Gd $256**

MODEL 40-XB CENTERFIRE MATCH RIFLE . . . **NiB $590 Ex $466 Gd $380**
Bolt-action, single-shot. Calibers: .222 Rem., .222 Rem. Mag., .223 Rem.,. .22-250 Rem., 6x47mm, 6mm Rem., .243 Win. .25-06 Rem., 7mm Rem., Mag., .30-06, .308 Win., .30-338,

.300 Win. Mag. Bbl. 27.25 inches standard or heavy. No. sights. Weight: 9.25 lbs. (standard bbl.), 11.25 lbs. w/heavy bbl. target stock w/adj. front swivel block on guide rail, rubber buttplate.

MODEL 40-XB RANGEMASTER CENTERFIRE RIFLE
Single-shot target rifle with same specs as Model 40-XB Centerfirle Match. Also in .220 Swift, 6mm BR Rem. and 7mm BR Rem. Stainless bbl. American walnut or Kevlar (weights 1 pound less) target stock with forend stop. Disc. 1994.
Right-hand model . . . . **NiB $835 Ex $600 Gd $444**
Left-hand model . . . . **NiB $835 Ex $600 Gd $444**
Kevlar stock, right-hand model. . . . . . . **NiB $2200 Ex $2011 Gd $1066**
Kevlar stock, left-hand model . . . . **NiB $2200 Ex $2011 Gd $1066**
W/2 oz. trigger, add $125
Repeater model, add. $125

MODEL 40-XB RANGEMASTER
RIMFIRE MATCH RIFLE . . . . **NiB $877 Ex $792 Gd $440**
Bolt-action, single-shot. Caliber: .22 LR. Bbl.: 28 inches, standard or heavy. Target stock w/adj. front swivel block on guide rail; rubber buttplate. Weight: 10 lbs. (standard bbl., no sights); 11.25 lbs. w/ heavy bbl. Made from 1964 to 1974.

MODEL 40-XB
VARMINT SPECIAL RIFLE. . . . . **NiB $1367 Ex $890 Gd $466**
Same specs as Model 40-XB repeater except w/synthetic (Kevlar) stock. Made from 1987 to 1994.

MODEL 40-XBBR BENCH REST RIFLE
Bolt-action, single-shot. Calibers: .222 Rem., .222 Rem. Mag. .223 Rem., 6x47mm, .308 Win. Bbl.: 20 or 26 inches, unblued, stainless steel. No sights. Weight: 9.25 lbs. w/20-inch bbl., 12 lbs. w/26-inch bbl. (Heavy Varmint class); 7.25 lbs. w/Kevlar stock (Light Varmint class). Made from 1974 to 2004, reintro. 2007.
Model 40-XBBR (disc.) . . . . **NiB $3550 Ex $2896 Gd $1600**

Remington Arms Company

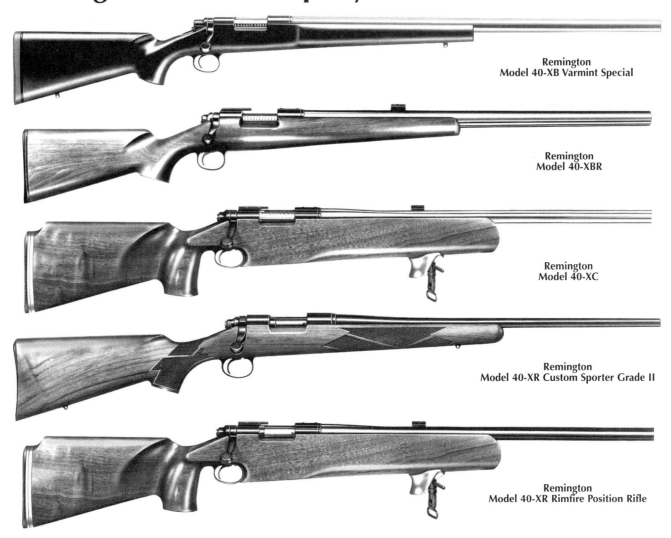

Remington
Model 40-XB Varmint Special

Remington
Model 40-XBR

Remington
Model 40-XC

Remington
Model 40-XR Custom Sporter Grade II

Remington
Model 40-XR Rimfire Position Rifle

MODEL 40-XC NATIONAL MATCH COURSE RIFLE
Bolt-action repeater. Caliber: .308 Win.; five-round mag., clip slot in receiver. Bbl.: 24 inches. No sights. Weight: 11 lbs. thumb-groove stock w/adj. hand stop, sling swivel, adj. buttplate. Disc. 2004, reintro. 2006.
W/wood stock, disc. . . . . NiB $3170 Ex $2834 Gd $1566
W/Kevlar stock, disc. 1994 . . . . NiB $3159 Ex $2833 Gd $1633

MODEL 40-XR CUSTOM SPORTER RIFLE
Caliber: .22 RF. 24-inch contoured bbl. Supplied w/o sights. Made in four grades of checkering, engraving and other custom features. Made from 1987 to date. High grade model disc. in 1991.
Grade I . . . . NiB $1233 Ex $1099 Gd $820
Grade II . . . . NiB $2250 Ex $1833 Gd $1166
Grade III . . . . NiB $3077 Ex $2100 Gd $1310
Grade IV . . . . NiB $5055 Ex $4110 Gd $2966

MODEL 40-XR RIMFIRE POSITION RIFLE
Bolt action, single shot. Caliber: .22 LR. 24-inch heavy bbl. Supplied w/o sights. Weight: 10 lbs. Position-style stock w/thumb groove, adj. hand stop and sling swivel on guide rail, adj. buttplate. Made from 1974. Discontinued 2004.
Model 40-XR Rimfire Position. . . . . .NiB $1266 Ex $1087 Gd $677
KS model (w/Kevlar stock) . . . . NiB $1387 Ex $1100 Gd $700

MODEL 41A TARGETMASTER BOLT-ACTION
SINGLE-SHOT RIFLE. . . . . NiB $296 Ex $190 Gd $137
Takedown. Caliber: .22 Short, Long, LR. 27-inch bbl. Weight: 5.5 lbs. Sights: Open rear; bead front. Plain pistol-grip stock. Made from 1936 to 1940.

MODEL 41AS . . . . NiB $398 Ex $224 Gd $135
Same as Model 41A except in .22 Remington Special (.22 W.R.F.).

MODEL 41P . . . . NiB $323 Ex $200 Gd $135
Same as Model 41A except has peep rear sight, hooded post front sight.

MODEL 41SB . . . . NiB $435 Ex $167 Gd $154
Same as Model 41A except smoothbore for use with shot cartridges.

MODEL 510A TARGETMASTER
BOLT-ACTION SINGLE-SHOT RIFLE . . . . . NiB $255 Ex $170 Gd $130
Takedown. Caliber: 22 Short, Long, LR. 25-inch bbl. Weight: About 5.5 lbs. Sights: Open rear; bead front. Plain pistol-grip stock. Made from 1939 to 1962.

MODEL 510P . . . . NiB $277 Ex $175 Gd $131
Same as Model 510A except has peep rear sight, Partridge front on ramp.

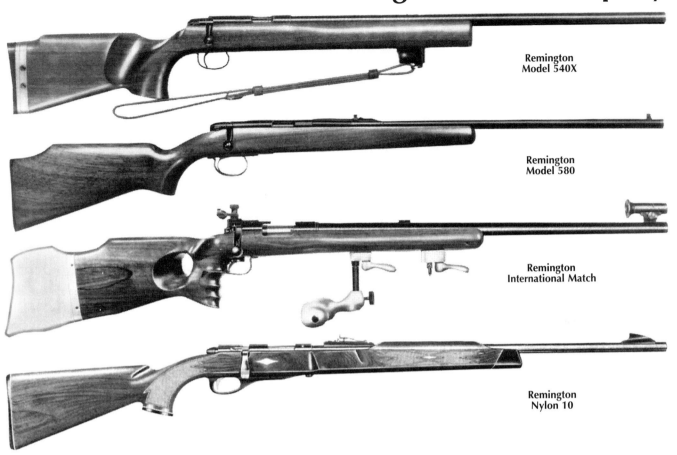

Remington
Model 540X

Remington
Model 580

Remington
International Match

Remington
Nylon 10

MODEL 510-X SB . . . . NiB $390 Ex $248 Gd $190
Same as Model 510A except smoothbore for use with shot cartridges, shotgun bead front sight.

**MODEL 510-X BOLT-ACTION
SINGLE-SHOT RIFLE. . . . . NiB $233 Ex $190 Gd $125**
Same as Model 510A except improved sights. Made from1964 to 1966.

**MODEL 514 BOLT-ACTION
SINGLE-SHOT. . . . . NiB $180 Ex $157 Gd $125**
Takedown. Caliber: .22 Short, Long, LR. 24-inch bbl. Weight: 4.75 lbs. Sights: Open rear; bead front. Plain pistol-grip stock. Made from 1948 to 1971.

MODEL 514BC BOY'S CARBINE . . . . NiB $225 Ex $166 Gd $129
Same as Model 514 except has 21-inch bbl., 1-inch shorter stock. Made from1961 to 1971.

MODEL 514P . . . . NiB $225 Ex $166 Gd $129
Same as Model 514 except has receiver peep sight.

MODEL 540-X RIMFIRE TARGET RIFLE . . . NiB $455 Ex $300 Gd $141
Bolt-action, single-shot. Caliber: .22 R. 26-inch heavy bbl. Supplied w/o sights. Weight: 8 lbs. Target stock w/Monte Carlo cheekpiece and thumb groove, guide rail for hand stop and swivel, adj. buttplate. Made from 1969 to 1974.

MODEL 540-XR POSITION RIFLE . . . . NiB $455 Ex $300 Gd $141
Bolt-action, single-shot. Bbl.: medium weight, 26 inches, no sights. Weight: 8 lbs. Position-style stock w/thumb groove, guide rail for hand stop and swivel, adj. buttplate. Made from 1974 to 1984.

MODEL 540-XRJR. . . . . NiB $415 Ex $335 Gd $200
Same as Model 540-XR except 1.75-inch shorter stock. Made from 1974 to 1984.

**MODEL 580 BOLT-ACTION
SINGLE-SHOT. . . . . NiB $200 Ex $155 Gd $120**
Caliber: .22 Short, Long, LR. 24-inch bbl. Weight: 4.75 lbs. Sights: Bead front; U-notch rear. Monte Carlo stock. Made from 1967 to 1978.

MODEL 580BR BOY'S RIFLE. . . . . . NiB $200 EX $155 Gd $120
Same as Model 580 except w/1-inch shorter stock. Made from 1971 to 1978.

MODEL 580SB SMOOTH BORE. . . NiB $290 Ex $215 Gd $149
Same as Model 580 except smooth bore for .22 Long Rifle shot cartridges. Made from 1967 to 1978.

INTERNATIONAL FREE RIFLE. . . . NiB $1100 Ex $824 Gd $477
Same as Model 40-XB rimfire and centerfire except has free-rifle type stock wth adj. buttplate and hook, adj. palm rest, moveable front sling swivel, 2-oz. trigger. Weight: 15 lbs. Made from 1964 to 1974.

**INTERNATIONAL
MATCH FREE RIFLE . . . . NiB $1133 Ex $1055 Gd $677**
Model 40-X-type bolt-action, single-shot. Calibers: .22 LR, .222 Rem., .222 Rem., Mag., 7.62mm NATO, .30-06 (other calibers on special order). 2-oz. adj. trigger. Bbl.: 28 inches, heavy. Weight: 15.5 lbs. Free-rifle style stock with thumbhole (semi-finished by mfr.), interchangeable adj. rubber buttplate and hook buttplate. Adj. palm rest, sling swivel. Made from 1961 to 1964.

Remington Arms Company

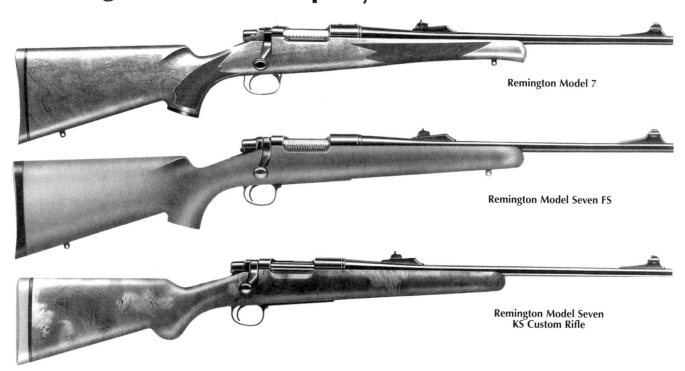

Remington Model 7

Remington Model Seven FS

Remington Model Seven
KS Custom Rifle

**NYLON 10 BOLT-ACTION
SINGLE-SHOT RIFLE** . . . . **NiB $335 Ex $175 Gd $139**
Caliber: .22 Short, Long, LR. Bbl.: 19.13 inches. Weight: 4.25 lbs.
Open rear, ramp blade front sights. Grooved for scope mount.
Brown nylon stock. Made from 1962 to 1966.

BOLT-ACTION REPEATING RIFLES

MODEL SEVEN (7) CF BOLT-ACTION RIFLE
Calibers: .17 Rem. .222 Rem., .243 Win., 6mm Rem., 7mm-08
Rem., .308 Win.; five-round mag. in .17 Rem,. .222 Rem., .223
Rem., four rounds in other calibers. Bbl.: 18.5 inches. Weight: 6.5
lbs. Checkered walnut stock; recoil pad. Made from 1983 to 1999.
.223 Rem. added in 1984.
Standard calibers. . . . . **NiB $525 Ex $459 Gd $325**
.17 Rem & .222 Rem... . . . . **NiB $577 Ex $485 Gd $350**

**MODEL SEVEN (7)
FS RIFLE** . . . . **NiB $559 Ex $490 Gd $356**
Caliber: .243 Win., 7mm-08 Rem., .308 Win. Bbl.: 18.5 inches.
Lgt.: 37.5 inches. Weight: 5.25 lbs. Fiberglass stock reinforced
with DuPont Kevlar at points of bedding and stress. Made from
1987 to 1989.

MODEL SEVEN (7) KS RIFLE. . . . **NiB $2269 Ex $1090 Gd $789**
Calibers: .223 Rem., 7mm-08 Rem., .308 Win., .35 Rem., .350
Rem. Mag. Bbl.: 20 inches. Made in Remington's Custom Shop with
Kevlar stock. Made from 1987 to date.

MODEL SEVEN (7) LS RIFLE. . . . . . **NiB $654 Ex $490 Gd $335**
Calibers: .223 Rem., .243 Win., .260 Rem., 7mm-08 and 308 Win.
20-inch matte bbl. Laminated hardwood stock w/matte brown finish. Weight: 6.5 lbs. Made from 2000 to 2005.

MODEL SEVEN (7) LSS RIFLE. . . . . **NiB $645 Ex $510 Gd $355**
Similar to Model 7 LS except stainless bbl. w/o sights. Calibers: .22-
250 Rem., .243 Win. or 7mm-08 Rem. Made from 2000 to 2003.

**MODEL SEVEN (7) MS
CUSTOM RIFLE.** . . . . **NiB $2655 Ex $2025 Gd $1033**
Similar to standard Model 7 except with laminated full Mannlicher-
style stock. Weight: 6.75 lbs. Calibers: .222 Rem., .22-250 Rem.,
.243 Win., 6mm Rem., 7mm-08 Rem. .308 Win., . 350 Rem. Mag.
Additional calibers on special order. Made from 1993 to 1999.

MODEL SEVEN (7) SS RIFLE . . . . . **NiB $650 Ex $445 Gd $316**
Same as Model 7 except w 20-inch stainless bbl., receiver and bolt;
black synthetic stock. Calibers: .243 Win., 7mm-08 Rem., .308 Win. Made
from 1994 to 2006.

MODEL SEVEN (7) YOUTH RIFLE . . . . . . **NiB $575 Ex $366 Gd $279**
Same as Model 7 w/hardwood stock, 12.19-inch pull. Calibers: .243 Win.,
6mm Rem., 7mm-08 Rem. Made from 1993 to 2007.

**MODEL 30A BOLT-ACTION
EXPRESS RIFLE** . . . . **NiB $644 Ex $522 Gd $361**
Standard grade modified M-1917 Enfield action. Calibers: .25, .30, .32
and .35 Rem., 7mm Mauser, .30-06; five-round box mag. Bbl.: 22 inches.
Weight: 7.25 lbs. Open rear, bead front sights. Walnut stock w/checkered
pistol grip and forearm. Made from 1921 to 1940. Early models had slender
forend with Schnabel tip, military-type double-pull trigger.

MODEL 30R CARBINE . . . . **NiB $655 Ex $540 Gd $433**
Same as Model 30A except w/20-inch bbl., plain stock. Weight: 7 lbs.

MODEL 30S SPORTING RIFLE. . . . **NiB $790 Ex $650 Gd $455**
Special Grade. Same action as Model 30A. Calibers: .257 Roberts,
7mm Mauser, .30-06; five-round box mag. Bbl.: 24 inches. Weight: 8
lbs. Lyman No. 48 Receiver rear, bead front sights. Special high comb
checkered stock with long, full forearm. Made from 1930 to 1940.

MODEL 34 BOLT-ACTION REPEATER . . . . **NiB $210 Ex $166 Gd $137**
Takedown. Caliber: .22 Short, Long, LR. Tubular magazine holds
22 Short, 17 Long or 15 LR. 24-inch bbl. Weight: 5.25 lbs. Sights:
Open rear; bead front. Plain, pistol-grip stock, forearm w/grasping
grooves. Made from 1932 to 1936.

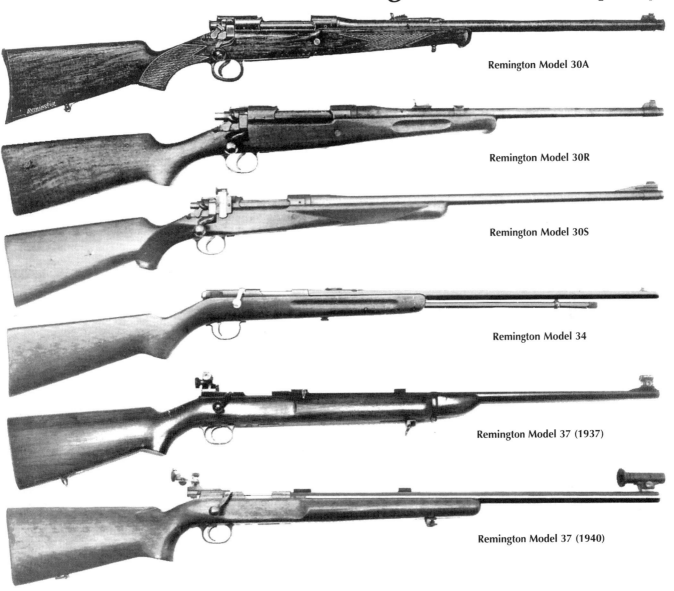

Remington Model 30A

Remington Model 30R

Remington Model 30S

Remington Model 34

Remington Model 37 (1937)

Remington Model 37 (1940)

MODEL 34 NRA TARGET RIFLE . . . . NiB $553 Ex $390 Gd $256
Same as Model 34 Standard except has Lyman peep rear sight, Partridge-type front sight, .88-inch sling and swivels, weight: 5.75 lbs.

MODEL 37 RANGEMASTER BOLT-ACTION TARGET RIFLE (I)
Model of 1937. Caliber: .22 LR. Five round box magazine, single shot adapter also supplied as standard equipment. 28-inch heavy bbl. Weight: 12 lbs. Remington front and rear sights, scope bases. Target stock, swivels, sling. Note: Original 1937 model had a stock with outside bbl. band similar in appearance to that of the old-style Winchester Model 52, forearm design was modified and bbl. band eliminated in 1938. Made from 1937 to 1940.
W/factory sights . . . . NiB $1190 Ex $715 Gd $377
W/o sights. . . . . NiB $1010 Ex $599 Gd $335

MODEL 37 RANGEMASTER BOLT-ACTION TARGET RIFLE (II)
Model of 1940. Same as Model of 1937 except has "Miracle" trigger mechanism and Randle-design stock with high comb, full pistol-grip and wide beavertail forend. Made from 1940 to 1954.
W/factory sights . . . . NiB $1179 Ex $687 Gd $491
W/out sights . . . . NiB $977 Ex $569 Gd $335

MODEL 40-XB
CENTERFIRE REPEATER . . . . NiB $2210 Ex $1088 Gd $779
Same as Model 40-XB Centerfire except 5-round repeater. Calibers: .222 Rem., .222 Rem. Mag., .223 Rem., .22-250, 6x47mm, 6mm Rem., .243 Win., .308 Win. (7.62mm NATO). Heavy bbl. only. Disc.

MODEL 788 SPORTSMAN
BOLT-ACTION RIFLE . . . . NiB $496 Ex $390 Gd $322
Similar to Model 700 ADL except w/straight comb walnut-finished hardwood stock in .223 Rem., .243 Win., .270 Win., .30-06 and .308 Win. Bbl.:.22 inches, adj. sights Weight 7 lbs. Made from 1967 to 1983.

MODEL 341A SPORTSMASTER
BOLT-ACTION REPEATER . . . . NiB $295 Ex $167 Gd $135
Takedown. Caliber: .22 Short, Long, LR. Tubular magazine holds 22 Short, 17 Long, 15 LR. 27-inch bbl. Weight: 6 lbs. Sights: Open rear; bead front. Plain pistol-grip stock. Made from 1936 to 1940.

GRADING: **NiB** = New in Box   **Ex** = Excellent or NRA 95%   **Gd** = Good or NRA 68%

Remington Arms Company

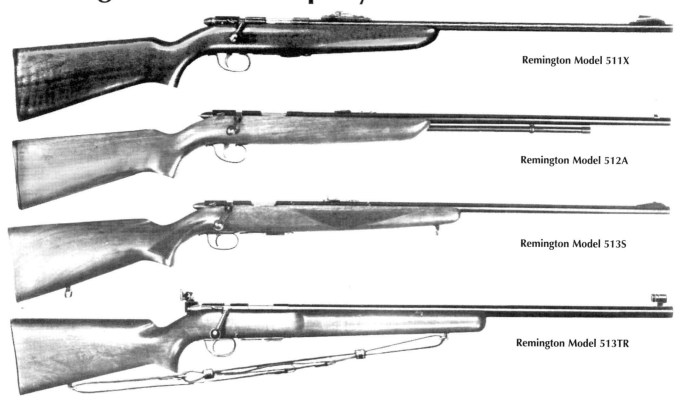

Remington Model 511X

Remington Model 512A

Remington Model 513S

Remington Model 513TR

MODEL 341P . . . . NiB $465 Ex $220 Gd $150
Same as Model 341A except has peep rear sight, hooded front sight.

MODEL 341SB . . . . NiB $533 Ex $280 Gd $198
Same as Model 341A except smoothbore for use with shot cartridges.

MODEL 511A SCOREMASTER BOLT-ACTION
BOX MAGAZINE REPEATER . . . . NiB $266 Ex $188 Gd $145
Takedown. Caliber .22 Short, Long, LR; six-round detachable box mag. Bbl.: 25 inches. Weight: 5.5 lbs. Open rear, bead front sights. Plain pistol-grip stock. Made from 1939 to 1962.

MODEL 511P . . . . NiB $190 Ex $201 Gd $150
Same as Model 511A except has peep rear sight, Partridge-type blade front on ramp.

MODEL 511X BOLT-ACTION REPEATER . . NiB $259 Ex $210 Gd $155
Clip type. Same as Model 511A except improved sights. Made from 1964 to 1966.

MODEL 512A SPORTSMASTER
BOLT-ACTION REPEATER . . . . NiB $269 EX $179 Gd $139
Takedown. Caliber: .22 Short, Long, LR. Tubular magazine holds 22 Short, 17 Long, 15 LR. 25-inch bbl. Weight: 5.75 lbs. Sights: Open rear; bead front. Plain pistol-grip stock w/semi-beavertail forend. Made from 1940 to 1962.

MODEL 512P . . . . NiB $288 Ex $225 Gd $170
Same as Model 512A except has peep rear sight, blade front sights.

MODEL 512X BOLT-
ACTION REPEATER. . . . . NiB $277 Ex $228 Gd $180
Tubular magazine. Same as Model 512A except has improved sights. Made from 1964 to 1966.

MODEL 513S BOLT-ACTION RIFLE . . . . . . NiB $955 Ex $644 Gd $400
Caliber: .22 LR. Six round detachable box magazine. 27-inch bbl. Weight: 6.75 lbs. Marble open rear sight, Partridge-type front. Checkered sporter stock. Made from 1941 to 1956.

MODEL 513TR MATCHMASTER
BOLT-ACTION TARGET RIFLE . . . . . NiB $533 Ex $365 Gd $267
Caliber: .22 LR. Six round detachable box magazine. 27-inch bbl. Weight: 9 lbs. Sights: Redfield No. 75 rear; globe front. Target-style stock. Sling and swivels. Made from 1941 to 1969.

MODEL 521TL JUNIOR TARGET
BOLT-ACTION REPEATER . . . . NiB $459 Ex $345 Gd $234
Takedown. Caliber: .22 LR; six-round detachable box mag. Bbl.: 25 inches. Weight: 7 lbs. Lyman No. 57RS rear, dovetailed blade front sights. Target-style stock; sling and swivels. Made from 1947 to 1969.

MODEL 522 VIPER . . . . NiB $200 Ex $165 Gd $125
Calibers: .22 LR. 10-round magazine. 20-inch bbl. 40 inches overall. Weight: 4.63 lbs. Checkered black PET resin stock with beavertail forend. DuPont high-tech synthetic lightweight receiver. Matte black finish on all exposed metal. Made from 1993 to date.

MODEL 541-S CUSTOM SPORTER. . . . . NiB $825 Ex $675 Gd $500
Bolt-action repeater. Scroll engraving on receiver and trigger guard. Caliber: .22 Short, Long, LR. Five round clip magazine. 24-inch bbl. Weight: 5.5 lbs. No sights. Checkered walnut stock w/rosewood-finished forend tip, pistol-grip cap and buttplate. Made from 1972 to 1984.

MODEL 541-T BOLT-ACTION RIFLE
Caliber: .22 RF; five-round clip. Bbl.: 24 inches. Weight: 5.88 lbs. Checkered walnut stock. Made from 1986 to date. Heavy bbl. model introduced 1993.
Model 541-T Standard . . . . NiB $590 Ex $385 Gd $255
Model 541-T-HB (heavy bbl.) . . . . . . NiB $690 Ex $485 Gd $355

Remington Arms Company

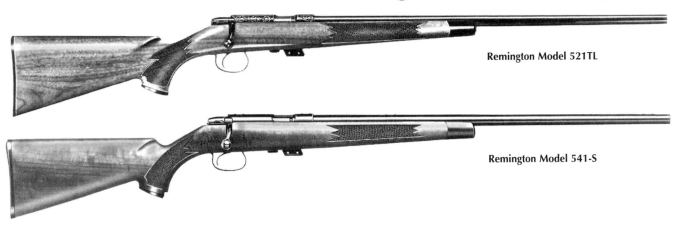

Remington Model 521TL

Remington Model 541-S

MODEL 581 CLIP REPEATER
Same specifications as Model 580 except has 5-round clip magazine. Made from 1967 to 1984.
Model 581 . . . . NiB $ 259 Ex $144 Gd $120
Model 581 (left-hand, made 1969-84) . . . . NiB $257 Ex $142 Gd $118

MODEL 581-S BOLT-ACTION RIFLE. . . . . . NiB $190 Ex $157 Gd $133
Caliber: .22 RF. Clip-fed, 5-round. 24-inch bbl. Weight: 4.75 lbs. Plain walnut-colored stock. Made from 1987 to 1992.

MODEL 582 TUBULAR REPEATER . . . . . . NiB $256 Ex $179 Gd $127
Same specs as Model 580 except has tubular mag.; holds 20 Short, 15 Long, 14 LR. Weight: 5 lbs. Made from 1967 to 1984.

MODEL 591 BOLT-ACTION
CLIP REPEATER. NiB $319 Ex $210 Gd $171
Caliber: 5mm Rimfire Magnum. Four round clip magazine. 24-inch bbl. Weight: 5 lbs. Sights: Bead front; U-notch rear. Monte Carlo stock. Made from 1970 to 1973.

MODEL 592 TUBULAR REPEATER . . . . . . NiB $275 Ex $175 Gd $128
Same as Model 591 except has tubular magazine holding 10 rounds. Weight: 5.5 lbs. Made from 1970 to 1973.

MODEL 600 BOLT-ACTION CARBINE
Calibers: .222 Rem., .223 Rem., .243 Win., 6mm Rem., .308 Win., 35 Rem., 5-round magazine (6-round in .222 Rem.) 18.5-inch bbl. with ventilated rib. Weight: 6 lbs. Sights: Open rear; blade ramp front. Monte Carlo stock w/pistol-grip. Made from 1964 to 1967.
.222 Rem. . . . . NiB $550 Ex $445 Gd $330
.223 Rem . . . . NiB $1109 Ex $923 Gd $715
.35 Rem. . . . . NiB $635 Ex $540 Gd $499
Standard calibers . . . . NiB $510 Ex $390 Gd $335

MODEL 600 MAGNUM . . . . NiB $1044 Ex $800 Gd $645
Same as Model 600 except in .350 Rem. Mag, 6.5mm Mag.; four-round mag. Special magnum-type bbl. wth bracket for scope back-up; laminated walnut and beech stock w/recoil pad. QD swivels and sling. Weight: 6.5 lbs. Made from 1965 to 1967.

MODEL 600 MONTANA
TERRITORIAL CENTENNIAL. . . . . . NiB $990 Ex $755 Gd $559
Same as Model 600 except has commemorative medallion embedded in buttstock. Made in 1964.

MODEL 660 STP
Calibers: .222 Rem., 6mm Rem., .243 Win., .308 Win.; five-round mag. (six rounds in .222). Bbl.: 20 inches. Weight: 6.5 lbs. Open rear, bead ramp front sights. Checkered Monte Carlo stock. Black pistol grip cap and forend tip. Mde from 1968 to 1971.
.222 Rem . . . . NiB $465 Ex $355 Gd $290
Other calibers. . . . . NiB $560 Ex $443 Gd $355

MODEL 660 MAGNUM . . . . NiB $970 Ex $766 Gd $635
Same as Model 660 except in 6.5 Rem. Mag and .350 Rem. Mag.; four-round mag. Laminated walnut and beech stock with recoil pad; QD swivels and sling. Made from 1968 to 1971.

MODEL 700 ADL CENTERFIRE RIFLE. . . . . NiB $535 Ex $365 Gd $266
Calibers: .22-250 Rem., .222 Rem., .25-06 Rem., .243 Win., .270 Win., .30-06, .308 Win., 7mm Rem. Mag; capacity six rounds in .222 Rem., four rounds in 7mm Rem. Mag; five rounds in other calibers. Bbl.: 24 inches in .22-250 Rem. and .222 Rem., .25-06 Rem. 7mm Rem. Mag.; 22 inches in other calibers. Weight: 7 lbs. standard, 7.5 lbs. in 7mm Rem. Mag. Ramp front, sliding ramp open rear sights. Monte Carloo stock w/cheekpiece, skip checkering; recoil pad on magnum calibers. Laminated stock option. Made from 1962 to 2005.

MODEL 700 APR BOLT-ACTION RIFL . . . NiB $2900 Ex $2290 Gd $1998
African Plains Rifle. Calibers: 7mm Rem. Mag., 7mm STW, .300Win. Mag. .300 Wby. Mag., .300 Rem. Ultra Mag., .338 Win. Mag. .375 H&H Mag.; three-round mag. Bbl.: 26 inches on magnum action. Lgt.: 46.5 inches. Weight: 7.75 lbs. Matte blue finish. Checkered classic-style laminated wood stock w/black magnum recoil pad, Made from 1994 to 2004.

MODEL 700 AS BOLT-ACTION RIFLE
Similar to the Model 700 BDL except with non-reflective matte black metal finish, including the bolt body. Weight: 6.5 lbs. Straight comb synthetic stock made of Arylon, a fiberglass-reinforced thermoplastic resin with non-reflective matte finish. Made from 1988 to 1992.
Standard caliber . . . . NiB $555 Ex $440 Gd $339
Magnum caliber . . . . NiB $579 Ex $466 Gd $340

Remington Arms Company

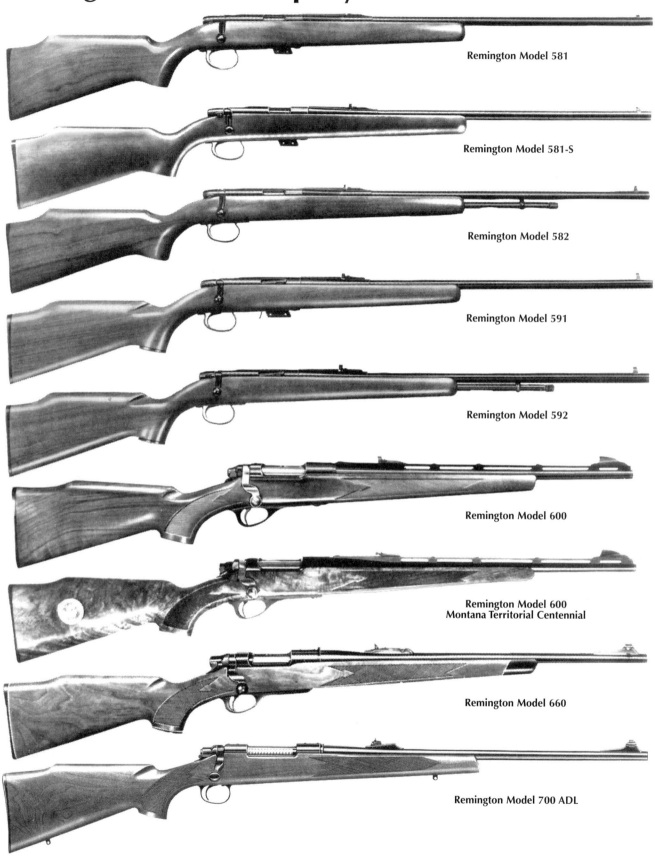

Remington Model 581

Remington Model 581-S

Remington Model 582

Remington Model 591

Remington Model 592

Remington Model 600

Remington Model 600
Montana Territorial Centennial

Remington Model 660

Remington Model 700 ADL

Remington Arms Company

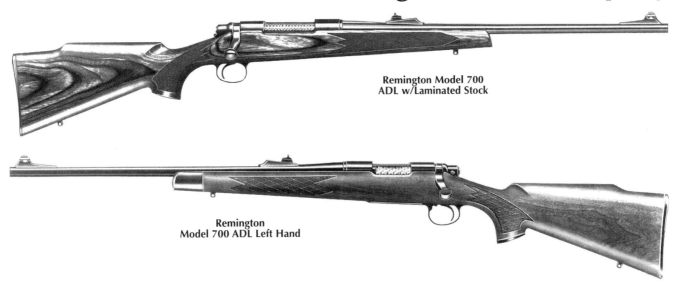

Remington Model 700
ADL w/Laminated Stock

Remington
Model 700 ADL Left Hand

MODEL 700 AWR
BOLT-ACTION RIFLE . . . . **NiB $1566 Ex $1264 Gd $1090**
Alaskan Wilderness Rifle, similar to Model 700 APR except w/24-inch stainless bbl., black chromed action. Matte gray or black Kevlar stock w/straight comb and raised cheekpiece, black magnum recoil pad. Made from 1994 to 2004.

MODEL 700 BDL CENTERFIRE RIFLE
Same as Model 700 ADL except w/hinged floorpate, hooded ramp front sight, black forend tip and grip cap. Cut checkering; QD swivels and sling. Additional calibers: .17 Rem. .223 Rem., .264 Win. Mag., 7mm-08, .280 Rem. .300 Sav., .300 Win. Mag., 8mm Rem. Mag., .338 Win. Mag. .35 Whelen. Bbl.: 24 inches. Magnums have four-round mag, recoil pad. Weight 7.5 lbs. .17 Rem. has six-round mag., Weight: 7 lbs. Made from 1962 to 2004.

Standard calibers.	NiB $810	Ex $466	Gd $333
Magnum calibers and .17 Rem.	NiB $855	Ex $555	Gd $380
Left-hand, .270 Win. and .30-06	NiB $855	Ex $469	Gd $343
Left hand, 7mm Rem. Mag. & .222 Rem. . .	NiB $788	Ex $559	Gd $490

MODEL 700 BDL EUROPEAN RIFLE
Same specs as Model 700 BDL except w/oil-finished walnut stock. Calibers: .243 Win, 270 Win., 7mm-08 Rem., 7mm Rem Mag., .280 Rem., .30-06. Made from 1993 to 1995.

Standard calibers	NiB $490	Ex $422	Gd $366
Magnum calibers	NiB $579	Ex $466	Gd $357

MODEL 700 BDL SS BOLT-ACTION RIFLE
Same as Model 700 BDL except w/24-inch stainless bbl., receiver and bolt. Black synthetic stock. Calibers: .223 Rem., .243 Win., 6mm Rem., 25-06 Rem, .270 Win., .280 Rem., 7mm-08 Rem, 7mm Rem. Mag., 7mm Wby. Mag., .30-06, .300 Win. Mag., .308 Win., .338 Win. Mag., .375 H&H Mag. Made from 1992 to 2004.

Standard calibers	NiB $625	Ex $509	Gd $344
Magnum calibers, add.			$100
DM (detachable magazine), add.			$50
DM-B (w/muzzle brake), add			$125

MODEL 700 BDL
VARMINT SPECIAL. . . . . **NiB $695 Ex $449 Gd $315**
Same as Model 700 BDL except w/24-inch heavy bbl, no sights. Weight: 9 lbs. (8.75 lbs. in .308 Win.) Calibers: .22-250 Rem. .222 Rem. .223 Rem., .25-06 Rem., .243 Win., .308 Win. Made from 1967 to 1994.

REMINGTON MODEL 700 CS BOLT-ACTION RIFLE
Similar to Model 700 BDL except with nonreflective matte black metal finish, including the bolt body. Straight comb synthetic stock camouflaged in Mossy Oak Bottomland pattern. Made from 1992 to 1994.

Standard calibers	NiB $590	Ex $490	Gd $365
Magnum calibers	NiB $635	Ex $500	Gd $370

MODEL 700 CLASSIC
Same specs as Model 700 BDL except w/"classic" stock of high-quality walnut with full-pattern cut checkering, special satin wood finish, Schnabel forend, brown rubber buttpad. Hinged floorplate. No sights. Weight: 7 lbs. Also available in .257 Roberts and .250-3000 Savage. Introduced 1981.

Standard calibers	NiB $916	Ex $588	Gd $369
Magnum calibers	NiB $977	Ex $588	Gd $365

MODEL 700 CUSTOM BOLT-ACTION RIFLE
Same specs as Model 700 BDL except in choice of wood quality, checkering patterns, engraving, metal finishes.

C Grade I	NiB $1965	Ex $1110	Gd $800
C Grade II.	NiB $2490	Ex $1854	Gd $1354
C Grade III	NiB $2988	Ex $2360	Gd $1635
C Grade IV	NiB $4955	Ex $3290	Gd $2990
D Peerless Grade	NiB $2855	Ex $1590	Gd $1122
F Premier Grade	NiB $3634	Ex $2989	Gd $2190

MODEL 700 FS BOLT-ACTION RIFLE
Similar to Model 700 ADL except with straight comb fiberglass stock reinforced with DuPont Kevlar, finished in gray or gray camo with Old English-style recoil pad. Made from 1987 to 1989.

Standard calibers	NiB $600	Ex $479	Gd $259
Magnum calibers	NiB $720	Ex $590	Gd $433

MODEL 700 KS CUSTOM MOUNTAIN RIFLE
Similar to standard Model 700 MTN Rifle, except with custom Kevlar reinforced resin synthetic stock with standard or wood-grain finish. Calibers: .270 Win., .280 Rem., 7mm Rem Mag., .30-06, .300 Win. Mag., .300 Wby. Mag., 8mm Rem. Mag., .338 Win. Mag., .35 Whelen, .375 H&H Mag. Four round magazine. 24-inch bbl. Weight: 6.75 lbs. Made from 1986 to 2008.

Standard KS stock (disc. 1993)	NiB $1899	Ex $1380	Gd $1079
Wood-grain KS stock.	NiB $1139	Ex $899	Gd $655
Stainless synthetic (1995-97)	NiB $2090	Ex $1421	Gd $1008
Left-hand model, add			$100

Remington Arms Company

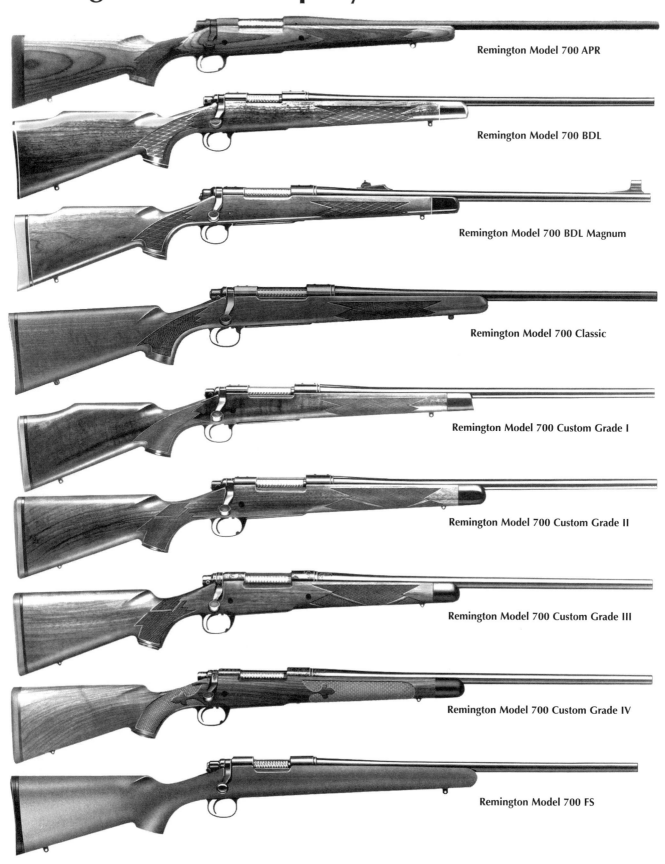

Remington Model 700 APR

Remington Model 700 BDL

Remington Model 700 BDL Magnum

Remington Model 700 Classic

Remington Model 700 Custom Grade I

Remington Model 700 Custom Grade II

Remington Model 700 Custom Grade III

Remington Model 700 Custom Grade IV

Remington Model 700 FS

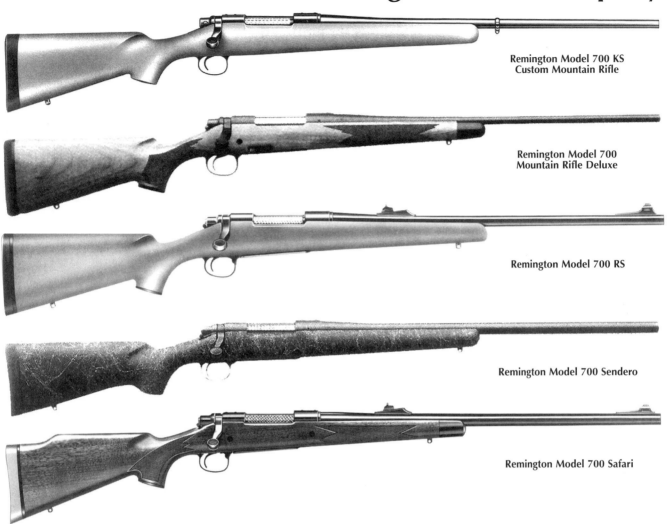

Remington Model 700 KS
Custom Mountain Rifle

Remington Model 700
Mountain Rifle Deluxe

Remington Model 700 RS

Remington Model 700 Sendero

Remington Model 700 Safari

MODEL 700 LS BOLT-ACTION RIFLE

Similar to Model 700 ADL except with checkered Monte Carlo-style laminated wood stock with alternating grain and wood color, impregnated with phenolic resin and finished with a low satin luster. Made from 1988 to 1993.

Standard calibers	NiB $690	Ex $550	Gd $395
Magnum calibers	NiB $779	Ex $598	Gd $443

MODEL 700 MOUNTAIN RIFLE

Similar to Model 700 BDL except with stainless steel bbl. and action. Checkered Monte Carlo-style laminated wood stock with alternating grain and gray-tinted colors impregnated w/phenolic resin and finished with a low-satin luster. Made from 1996 to 2004.

Standard w/blind magazine	NiB $510	Ex $440	Gd $290
Standard w/hinged floorplate (disc. 1994)	NiB $588	Ex $479	Gd $466
DM model (intro. 1995)	NiB $755	Ex $488	Gd $367
SS model (stainless synthetic, disc. 1993)	NiB $500	Ex $443	Gd $309

MODEL 700 RS BOLT-ACTION RIFLE

Similar to the Model 700 BDL except with straight comb DuPont Rynite stock finished in gray or gray camo with Old English style recoil pad. Made from 1987 to 1990.

Standard calibers	NiB $600	Ex $433	Gd $377
Magnum calibers	NiB $677	Ex $535	Gd $390
.280 Rem. (Limited prod.)	NiB $739	Ex $596	Gd $415

MODEL 700 SAFARI GRADE

Big-game, heavy-magnum version of the Model 700 BDL. Caliber: 8mm Rem. Mag., .375 H&H Mag., .416 Rem. Mag. .458 Win. Mag. Bbl.: 24 inches, heavy. Weight: 9 lbs. Blued or stainless finish. Checkered walnut stock or synthetic/Kevlar stock with standard matte or wood-grain finish and Old English-style recoil pad. Made from 1962 to 2000.

Safari Classic/Monte Carlo	NiB $1498	Ex $1044	Gd $610
Safari KS (Kevlar stock, intro. 1989)	NiB $1335	Ex $1155	Gd $927
Safari KS (wood-grain stock, intro. 1992)	NiB $1296	Ex $1133	Gd $900
Safari KS SS (stainless, intro. 1993)	NiB $1577	Ex $1326	Gd $1055
Safari model, left-hand, add			$125

MODEL 700 SENDERO BOLT-ACTION RIFLE

Same as Model 700 VS except chambered in long-action and magnum calibers: .25-06 Rem., .270 Win., 280 Rem., 7mm Rem. Mag., .300 Win. Mag. Made from 1994 to 2002.

Standard calibers	NiB $700	Ex $589	Gd $390
Magnum calibers, add.			$50
SF model (stainless, fluted bbl.), add			$150

MODEL 700 VLS (VARMINT LAMINATED STOCK)

BOLT-ACTION RIFLE .... NiB $890 Ex $555 Gd $390
Same as Model 700 BDL Special. Calibers: .222 Rem., .223 Rem., .22-250 Rem., .243 Win., 7mm-08 Rem., .308 Win. Weight: 9.4 lbs. Bbl.: 26-inch polished blue. Laminated wood stock with alternating grain and wood color impregnated with phenolic resin, satin luster finish. Made from 1995 to date.

GRADING: **NiB** = New in Box   **Ex** = Excellent or NRA 95%   **Gd** = Good or NRA 68%   **137**

Remington Arms Company

Remington Model 720A Bolt-Action High Power
NRA NATIONAL FIREARMS MUSEUM

Remington Model 721A Deluxe

Remington Model 722A

MODEL 700 VS BOLT-ACTION RIFLE
Same as Model 700 BDL Varmint Special except w/matte blue or fluted stainless bbl. Textured black or gray synthetic stock reinforced with Kevlar, fiberglass and graphite with full length aluminum bedding block. Calibers: .250 Rem., .220 Swift, .223 Rem., .308 Win., Made from 1992 to date.
Model 700 VS . . . . NiB $888 Ex $559 Gd $444
Model SF (fluted bbl.) . . . . NiB $790 Ex $677 Gd $535
Model 700 VS SF/SF-P
(fluted & ported bbl.) . . . . NiB $1033 Ex $866 Gd $657

MODEL 720A BOLT-ACTION
HIGH POWER . . . . NiB $1379 Ex $1266 Gd $1108
Modified M-1917 Enfield action. Calibers: .257 Roberts, .270 Win., .30-06; five-round box mag. Bbl.: 22 inches (20 inches in Model 720R, 24 inches in Model 720S). Weight: 8 lbs. Open rear, bead ramp front sights. Pistol grip checkered stock. Made in 1941.

MODEL 721 STANDARD GRADE
BOLT-ACTION HIGH-POWER RIFLE . . . . . NiB $490 Ex $433 Gd $356
Calibers: .270 Win., .30-06. Four round box magazine. 24-inch bbl. Weight: 7.25 lbs. Sights: Open rear; bead front, on ramp. Plain sporting stock. Made from 1948 to 1962.

MODEL 721A MAGNUM
STANDARD GRADE . . . . NiB $655 Ex $499 Gd $439
Caliber: .264 Win. Mag. or .300 H&H Mag. Same as standard model except has 26-inch bbl. Three round magazine and recoil pad. Weight: 8.25 lbs.

MODEL 721ADL/BDL DELUXE
Same as Model 721A Standard or Magnum except has deluxe checkered stock and/or w/select wood stock.
Deluxe Grade . . . . NiB $744 Ex $548 Gd $433
.300 Win. Mag. Deluxe . . . . NiB $790 Ex $775 Gd $600
Deluxe Special Grade . . . . NiB $844 Ex $645 Gd $500
.300 Mag. Deluxe . . . . NiB $833 Ex $680 Gd $567

MODEL 722A STANDARD GRADE SPORTER
Same as Model 721A except in short-action calibers: .222 Rem. Mag., .244 Rem., .243 Win., .257 Roberts, .308 Win., .300 Savage; four- or five-round mag. Weight: 7 to 8 lbs. .222 Rem. intro. 1950, .244 Rem., intro. 1955. Made from 1948 to 1962.
.222 Rem. . . . . NiB $517 Ex $466 Gd $360
.244 Rem. . . . . NiB $500 Ex $380 Gd $275

.222 Rem. Mag. & .243 Win. . . . . . NiB $465 Ex $390 Gd $288
Other calibers. . . . . NiB $466 Ex $398 Gd $270

MODEL 722ADL DELUXE GRADE
Same as Model 722A except has deluxe checkered stock.
Standard calibers . . . . NiB $590 Ex $513 Gd $398
.222 Rem. Deluxe Grade . . . . NiB $690 Ex $579 Gd $455
.244 Rem. Deluxe Grade . . . . NiB $835 Ex $733 Gd $490

MODEL 722BDL DELUXE SPECIAL GRADE
Same as Model 722ADL except w/select wood stock.
Standard calibers . . . . NiB $866 Ex $590 Gd $498
.222 Rem. Deluxe Special Grade . . NiB $866 Ex $590 Gd $498
.224 Rem. Deluxe Special Grade . . NiB $799 Ex $733 Gd $475

MODEL 725 KODIAK
MAGNUM RIFLE. . . . . NiB $4200 Ex $3543 Gd $2300
Similar to Model 725ADL. Calibers: .375 H&H Mag., .458 Win. Mag.; three-round mag. Bbl.: 26 inches with recoil reducer. Weight: 9 lbs. Deluxe, reinforced Monte Carlo stock with black forend tip, recoil pad, swivels, sling. Fewer than 100 made in 1961.

MODEL 725ADL BOLT-ACTION REPEATING RIFLE
Calibers: .222 Rem., .243 Win., .244 Rem., .270 Win., .260 Rem., .30-06; four-round box mag (five rounds in .222). Bbl.: 22 inches (24 inches in .222). Weight 7 lbs. Open rear, hooded ramp front sights. Checkered Monte Carlo stock w/pistol grip, swivels. Made from 1958 to 1961.
.222 Rem., .243 Win., .244 Rem. . . NiB $855 Ex $690 Gd $505
.270 Win. . . . . NiB $767 Ex $659 Gd $467
.280 Win. . . . . NiB $977 Ex $800 Gd $509
.30-06 . . . . NiB $700 Ex $580 Gd $435

MODEL 788 CENTERFIRE BOLT-ACTION
Calibers: .222 Rem., .22-250 Rem., .223 Rem., 6mm Rem., .243 Win., 7mm-08 Rem., .308 Win., .30-30, .44 Rem. Mag.; three-round clip mag (four rounds in .222 and .223). Bbl.: 24 inches in .222 and .223, 22 inches in other calibers. Weight: 7.5 lbs. Blade ramp front, U-notch rear sights. Plain Monte Carlo stock. Made from 1967 to 1984.
.22-250, .223 Rem., 6mm Rem.,
.243 Win., .308 Win.. . . . . NiB $522 Ex $339 Gd $243
.30-30 Win. NiB $555 Ex $434 Gd $319
7mm-08 Rem.. . . . . NiB $733 Ex $423 Gd $333
.44 Mag. . . . . NiB $644 Ex $449 Gd $339

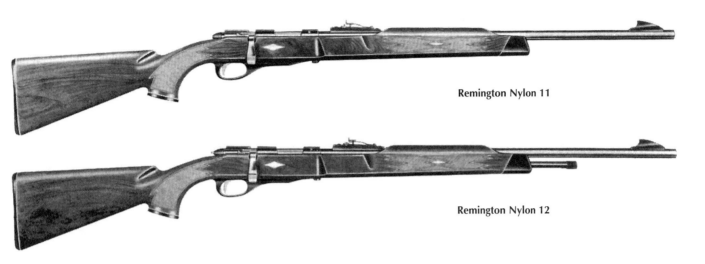

Remington Nylon 11

Remington Nylon 12

NYLON 11 BOLT-ACTION
REPEATER . . . . **NiB $495 Ex $322 Gd $209**
Caliber: .22 Short, Long, LR; six or 10-round clip mag. Bbl.: 19.63 inches. Weight: 4.5 lbs. Open rear, blade front sights. Nylon stock. Made from 1962 to 1966.

NYLON 12 BOLT-ACTION
REPEATER . . . . **NiB $545 Ex $433 Gd $245**
Same as Nylon 11 except has tubular magazine holding 22 Short, 17 Long, 15 LR. Made from 1962 to 1966.

SLIDE- AND LEVER-ACTION RIFLES

MODEL SIX (6) SLIDE-ACTION
REPEATER . . . . **NiB $698 Ex $390 Gd $288**
Hammerless. Calibers: 6mm Rem., .243 Win., .270 Win. 7mm Express Rem., .30-06, .308 Win. 22-inch bbl. Weight: 7.5 lbs. Checkered Monte Carlo stock and forearm. Made from 1981 to 1988.

MODEL SIX (6) SLIDE-ACTION
REPEATER, PEERLESS GRADE . . . . **NIB $2029 EX $1788 GD $1180**
Same as Model Six Standard except has engraved receiver. Three versions made from 1981 to 1988.

MODEL SIX (6) SLIDE-ACTION REPEATER, PREMIUM GRADES
Same as Model Six Standard except has engraved receiver with gold inlay. Made from 1981 to 1988.
Peerless D Grade . . . . **NiB $1977 Ex $1670 Gd $1120**
Premier F Grade . . . . **NiB $4509 Ex $3533 Gd $2410**
Premier Gold F Grade . . . . **NiB $6212 Ex $4944 Gd $3490**

MODEL 12A, 12B, 12C, 12CS SLIDE-ACTION REPEATERS
Standard grade. Hammerless, takedown. Caliber: .22 Short, Long, LR; tubular mag., holds 15 Short, 12 Long, 10 LR. Bbl.: Round or octagon, 22 or 24 inches. Open rear, bead front sights. Plain half pistol grip walnut stock and grooved slide hande. Made from 1909 to 1936.
Model 12A . . . . **NiB $600 Ex $399 Gd $275**
Model 12B
(.22 Short only w/octagon bbl.) . . . . **NiB $733 Ex $549 Gd $366**
Model 12C
(w/24-inch octagon bbl.) . . . . **NiB $623 Ex $544 Gd $355**
Model 12CS
(.22 WRF w/24-inch octagon bbl.) . . . . **NiB $570 Ex $445 Gd $315**

MODEL 14A HIGH POWER
SLIDE-ACTION REPEATING RIFLE . . . . . . **NiB $1077 Ex $798 Gd $643**
Standard grade. Hammerless, takedown. Calibers: .25, .30, .32 and .35 Rem.; five-round tubular mag., Bbl.: 22 inches. Weight: 6.75 lbs. Open rear, bead front sights. PLlain half pistol grip walnut stock and grooved slide handle. Made from 1912 to 1935.

MODEL 14R CARBINE . . . . **NiB $1286 Ex $1044 Gd $590**
Same as Model 14R except has 18.5-inch bbl., straight-grip stock. Weight: 6 lbs.

MODEL 14 1/2 CARBINE . . . . . **NiB $1286 Ex $1044 Gd $590**
Same as Model 14A Rifle except has 9-round magazine, 18.5-inch bbl.

MODEL 14 1/2 RIFLE . . . . **NiB $1688 Ex $1044 Gd $622**
Simlar to Model 14A except in .38-40 and .44-40; 11-round full-length mag.; 22.5-inch bbl. Made from 1912 to 1920s.

MODEL 25A SLIDE-ACTION
REPEATER . . . . **NiB $1094 Ex $744 Gd $500**
Standard Grade. Hammerless, takedown. Calibers: .25-20, .32-20; 10-round tubular mag. Bbl.: 24 inches. Weight 5.5 lbs. Open rear, bead front sights. Plain pistol-grip stock, grooved slide handle. Made from 1923 to 1936.

MODEL 25R CARBINE . . . . **NiB $1190 Ex $745 Gd $533**
Same as Model 25A except has 18-inch bbl. Six round magazine, straight-grip stock. Weight: 4.5 lbs.

MODEL 121A FIELDMASTER
SLIDE-ACTION REPEATER . . . . **NiB $677 Ex $500 Gd $355**
Standard grade. Hammerless, takedown. Caliber: .22 Short, Long, LR; tubular mag. holds 20 Short, 15 Long, 14 LR cartridges. Bbl.: 24 inches, round. Weight: 6 lbs. Plain pistol-grip stock, grooved semi-beavertail slide handle. Made from 1936 to 1954.

MODEL 121S . . . . **NiB $599 Ex $500 Gd $443**
Same as Model 121A except in .22 Rem., Special (.22WRF); 12-round mag. Disc.

MODEL 121SB . . . . **NiB $700 Ex $553 Gd $435**
Same as Model 121A except smoothbore. Disc.

Remington Arms Company

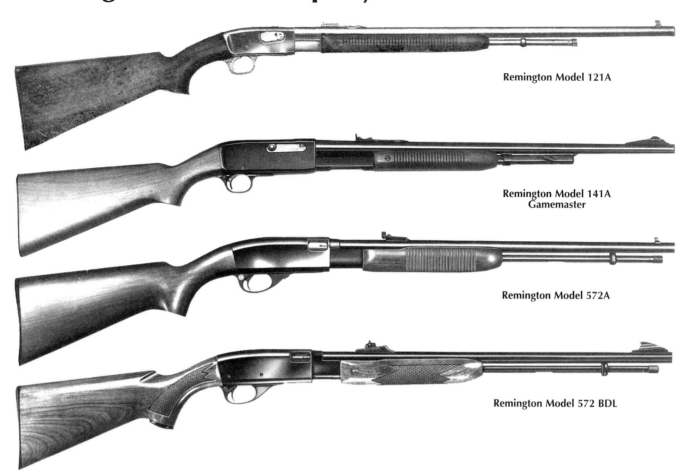

Remington Model 121A

Remington Model 141A
Gamemaster

Remington Model 572A

Remington Model 572 BDL

MODEL 141A GAMEMASTER
SLIDE-ACTION REPEATER . . . . **NiB $543 Ex $359 Gd $267**
Standard Grade. Hammerless. Takedown. Calibers: .30, .32 and
.35 Rem. Five round tubular magazine. 24-inch bbl. Weight: 7.75
lbs. Sights: Open rear; bead front, on ramp. Plain, pistol-grip stock,
semibeavertail forend (slide-handle). Made from 1936 to 1950.

MODEL 572A FIELDMASTER
SLIDE-ACTION REPEATER . . . . **NiB $290 Ex $179 Gd $130**
Hammerless. Caliber: .22 Short, Long, LR; tubular mag., holds 20 Short,
17 Long, 15 LR. Bbl.: 23 inches. Weight: 5.5 lbs. Open rear, ramp front
sights. Pistol-grip stock, grooved slide handle.

MODEL 572BDL DELUXE . . . . **NiB $533 Ex $444 Gd $149**
Same as Model 572A except has blade ramp front sight, sliding
ramp rear; checkered stock and forearm. Made from 1966 to date.

MODEL 572SB SMOOTH BORE . . . **NiB $549 Ex $400 Gd $300**
Same as Model 572A except smoothbore for .22 LR shot cartridges.
Made from 1961 to date.

MODEL 760 BICENTENNIAL
COMMEMORATIVE . . . . **NiB $556 Ex $398 Gd $265**
Same as Model 760 except has commemorative inscription on
receiver. Made in 1976.

MODEL 760 CARBINE . . . . **NiB $480 Ex $390 Gd $245**
Same as Model 760 Rifle except made in .270 Win., .280 Rem., .30-06 and
.308 Win. only, has 18.5-inch bbl., weight: 7.25 lbs. Made from 1961 to 1980.

MODEL 760 GAMEMASTER
STANDARD GRADE SLIDE-ACTION REPEATING RIFLE
Hammerless. Calibers: .223 Rem., 6mm Rem., .243 Win., .257
Roberts, .270 Win., .280 Rem., .30-06, .300 Sav., .308 Win., .35 Rem.
Bbl.: 22 inches. Weight 7.5 lbs. Open rear, bead ramp front sights.
Plain pistol-grip stock, grooved slide handle in early models, later
models wcheckered stock and slide handle. Made from 1952 to 1980.
.222 Rem. NiB $1195 Ex $1021 Gd $744
.223 Rem. NiB $1409 Ex $1135 Gd $739
.257 Roberts . . . . NiB $933 Ex $779 Gd $489
Other calibers . . . . NiB $460 Ex $407 Gd $375

MODEL 760ADL
DELUXE GRADE . . . . NiB $500 Ex $398 Gd $344
Same as Model 760 except has deluxe checkered stock, standard or
high comb, grip cap, sling swivels. Made from 1953 to 1963.

MODEL 760BDL
CUSTOM DELUXE . . . . NiB $655 Ex $449 Gd $325
Same as Model 760 Rifle except in .270 Win., .30-06, .308 Win.
only. Monte Carlo cheekpiece stock, black forearm tip; basket-weave
checkering. Also in left-hand model. Made from 1953 to 1980.

MODEL 760D
PEERLESS GRADE . . . . NiB $2589 Ex $1176 Gd $925
Same as Model 760 except scroll engraved, fancy wood. Made
from 1953 to 1980.

Remington Arms Company

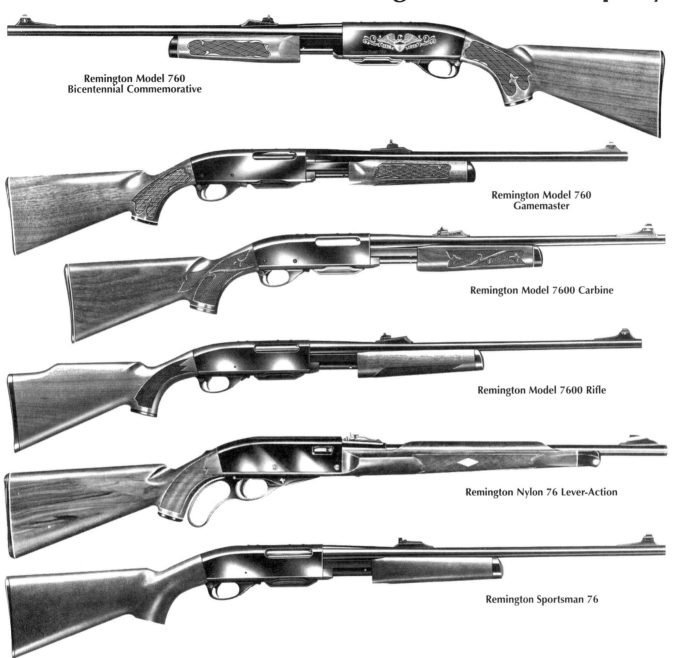

Remington Model 760 Bicentennial Commemorative

Remington Model 760 Gamemaster

Remington Model 7600 Carbine

Remington Model 7600 Rifle

Remington Nylon 76 Lever-Action

Remington Sportsman 76

MODEL 760F PREMIER GRADE
Same as Model 760 except extensively engraved with game scenes and scroll, finest grade wood. Also available with receiver inlaid with gold; adds 50 percent to value. Made from 1953 to 1980.
Premier F Grade . . . . NiB $5200 Ex $3288 Gd $2579
Premier Gold F Grade. . . . . . . NiB $7179 Ex $6088 Gd $4439

MODEL 7600 SLIDE-ACTION
CARBINE. . . . . NiB $698 Ex $449 Gd $366
Same specifications as Model 7600 Rifle except has 18.5-inch bbl. and weighs 7.25 lbs. Made from 1987 to date.

MODEL 7600 SLIDE-ACTION RIFLE. . . . . NiB $700 Ex $451 Gd $370
Similar to Model Six except has lower grade finishes. Made from 1981 to date.

MODEL 7600 SPECIAL PURPOSE. . . . . . . NiB $470 Ex $444 Gd $289
Same specs as Model 7600 except in .270 Win. or .30-06 only. Matte black finish on exposed metal. American walnut stock with non-glare finish.

NYLON 76 LEVER-ACTION REPEATER. . . . NiB $420 Ex $390 Gd $236
Short-throw lever action. Caliber: .22 LR. 14-round buttstock tubular magazine. Weight: 4 lbs. Black (add $700) or brown nylon stock and forend. Made from 1962 to 1964. Remington's only lever-action rifle.

SPORTSMAN 76 SLIDE-ACTION RIFLE . . . NiB $375 Ex $300 Gd $200
Caliber: .30-06, 4-round magazine. 22-inch bbl. Weight: 7.5 lbs. Open rear sight; front blade mounted on ramp. Uncheckered hardwood stock and forend. Made from 1985 to 1987.

Remington Arms Company

SEMIAUTOMATIC RIFLES

MODEL FOUR (4) AUTOLOADING RIFLE
Hammerless. Calibers: 6mm Rem., .243 Win., .270 Win. 7mm Express Rem., .30-06, .308 Win. 22-inch bbl. Weight: 7.5 lbs. Sights: Open rear; bead front, on ramp. Monte Carlo checkered stock and forearm. Made from 1981 to 1988.
Standard model. NiB $722 Ex $465 Gd $365
Peerless Grade (engraved receiver). . . . . NiB $2219 Ex $1266 Gd $909
Premier Grade (engraved receiver). . . . NiB $4155 Ex $3265 Gd $2200
Premier Grade,
(engraved receiver, gold inlay) . . . . NiB $6544 Ex $5233 Gd $3588

MODEL FOUR DIAMOND
ANNIVERSARY LTD. EDITION. . . . . . . NiB $1377 EX $1088 Gd $966
Same as Model Four Standard except has engraved receiver w/ inscription, checkered high-grade walnut stock and forend. Only 1,500 produced in 1981.

MODEL 8A AUTOLOADING RIFLE . . . . . NiB $766 Ex $645 Gd $473
Standard Grade, takedown. Calibers: .25, .30, .32, .35 Rem.; five-round clip mag. Bbl.: 22 inches. Weight: 7.75 lbs. Adj dovetailed open rear, dovetailed bead front sights. Half-moon metal buttplate on plain straight-grip walnut stock and thin, curved forearm. Made from 1906 to 1936.

MODEL 16 AUTOLOADING RIFLE. . . . . . NiB $755 Ex $523 Gd $390
Takedown. Similar to Win. Model '03 semi-automatic rifle. Calibers: .22 Short, LR, .22 Rem. Auto.; 15-round tubular mag. in buttstock. Bbl.: 22 inches. Weight: 5.75 lbs. Open rear, dovetailed bead front sights. Plain straight-grip stock and forearm. Made from 1914 to 1928. In 1918 this model was disc. in all calibers except .22 Rem. Auto.

MODEL 24A AUTOLOADING RIFLE . . . . . NiB $498 Ex $343 Gd $244
Standard grade, takedown. Calibers: .22 Short, LR; tubular mag. in buttstock holds 15 Short or 10 LR. Bbl.: 21 inches. Weight: 5 lbs. Dovetailed adj. open rear, dovetailed bead front sights. Plain straight-grip walnut stock and forearm. Made from 1922 to 1935.

MODEL 81A WOODSMASTER
AUTOLOADER . . . . NiB $590 Ex $498 Gd $300
Standard Grade. Takedown. Calibers: .30, .32 and .35 Rem., .300 Sav. Five round box magazine (not detachable). 22-inch bbl. Weight: 8.25 lbs. Sights: Open rear; bead front. Plain walnut pistol-grip stock and forearm. Made from 1936 to 1950.

MODEL 141A SPEEDMASTER
AUTOLOADER . . . . NiB $500 Ex $326 Gd $249
Standard grade, takedown. Calibers: .22 Short, LR; tubular mag. in buttstock holds 15 Short , 10 LR. Bbl.: 24 inches. Weight: 6 lbs. Open rear, bead front sights. Plain walnut stock and forearm. Made from 1935 to 1951.

MODEL 550A AUTOLOADER. . . . . NiB $366 Ex $222 Gd $129
With "Power Piston" or floating chamber permits interchangeable use of .22 Short, Long, or LR cartridges; tubular mag. holds 22 Short, 17 Long, 15 LR. Bbl.: 24 inches. Weight: 6.25 lbs. Open rear, bead front sights. Plain one-piece pistol-grip stock. Made from 1914 to 1971.

MODEL 550P . . . . NiB $369 Ex $221 Gd $156
Same as Model 550A except has peep rear, blade ramp front sights.

MODEL 550-2G . . . . NiB $388 Ex $279 Gd $200
"Gallery Special." Same as Model 550A except has 22-inch bbl., screw eye for counter chain and shell deflector.

Remington Sportsman 742
Canadian Centennial

MODEL 552A SPEEDMASTER
AUTOLOADER . . . . NiB $339 Ex $229 Gd $133
Caliber: .22 Short, Long, LR. Tubular magazine holds 20 Short, 17 Long, 15 LR. 25-inch bbl. Weight: 5.5 lbs. Sights: Open rear; bead front. Pistol-grip stock, semi-beavertail forearm. Made from 1957 to 1988.

MODEL 552BDL DELUXE. . . . . . . NiB $533 Ex $367 Gd $290
Same as Model 552A except has checkered walnut stock and forearm. Made from 1966 to date.

MODEL 552C CARBINE . . . . NiB $333 Ex $209 Gd $148
Same as Model 552A except has 21-inch bbl. Made from 1961 to 1977.

MODEL 552GS GALLERY SPECIAL. . . . . . NiB $387 Ex $265 Gd $190
Same as Model 552A except in .22 Short only. Made from 1957 to 1977.

MODEL 740A WOODSMASTER AUTOLOADER
Standard Grade, gas-operated. Calibers: .30-06, .308 Win.; four-round detachable box mag., Bbl.: 22 inches. Weight: 7.5 lbs. Plain pistol-grip stock, semi-beavertail forend with finger grooves. Open rear, ramp front sights. Made from 1955 to 1959.
Rifle model . . . . NiB $369 Ex $278 Gd $199
Carbine model . . . . NiB $467 Ex $443 Gd $290

MODEL 740ADL/BDL DELUXE
Same as Model 740A except has deluxe checkered stock, standard or high comb, grip cap, sling swivels. Model 740 BDL has select wood. Made from 1955 to 1960.
Model 740 ADL Deluxe Grade . . . . NiB $480 Ex $566 Gd $410
Model 740 BDL Deluxe Special Grade . . . NiB $480 Ex $566 Gd $410

MODEL 742 BICENTENNIAL
COMMEMORATIVE . . . . NiB $588 Ex $380 Gd $355
Same as Model 742 Woodsmaster rifle except has commemorative inscription on receiver. Made in 1976.

MODEL 742 CARBINE . . . . NiB $522 Ex $355 Gd $260
Same as Model 742 Woodsmaster Rifle except in .30-06 and .308 Win. only, has 18.5-inch bbl., weight 6.75 lbs. Made from 1961 to 1980.

MODEL 742 WOODSMASTER
AUTOMATIC BIG GAME RIFLE . . . . NiB $700 Ex $533 Gd $290
Gas-operated semiautomatic. Calibers: 6mm Rem., .243 Win., .280 Rem., .30-06, .308 Win. Four round clip magazine. 22-inch bbl. Weight: 7.5 lbs. Sights: Open rear; bead front, on ramp. Checkered pistol-grip stock and forearm. Made from 1960 to 1980.

Remington Model 7400

Remington Model 7400 Carbine

Remington Nylon 66
Bicentennial Commemorative

Remington Nylon 66 Mohawk

Remington Sportsman 74

MODEL 742BDL CUSTOM DELUXE..... NiB $523 Ex $433 Gd $300
Same as Model 742 rifle except in .30-06 and .308 Win. only.
Monte Carlo stock, forearm with black tip, basket-weave check-
ering. Available in left-hand version. Made from 1966 to 1980.

MODEL 742D PEERLESS GRADE .... NiB $2590 Ex $2020 Gd $1100
Same as Model 742 except scroll engraved, fancy wood. Made
from 1961 to 1980.

MODEL 742F PREMIER GRADE
Same as Model 742 except w/extensive engraved game scenes and
scroll; finest grade wood. Also available with receiver inlaid with
gold (adds 50% to value). Made from 1961 to 1980.
Premier F Grade .... NiB $5233 Ex $3288 Gd $2270
Premier Gold F Grade........ NiB $7350 Ex $5093 Gd $3466

MODEL 7400 AUTOLOADER
Similar to Model Four w/lower grade finishes. Made from 1981 to date.
Standard .... NiB $559 Ex $433 Gd $310
HG(High gloss finish) .... NiB $559 Ex $433 Gd $310

MODEL 7400 CARBINE .... NiB $559 Ex $433 Gd $310
Similar to Model 7400 Rifle except in .30-06 only, 18.5-inch bbl.
Weight: 7.25 lbs. Made from 1988 to date.

MODEL 7400 SPECIAL PURPOSE....... NiB $476 Ex $434 Gd $289
Same specs as Model 7400 except in .270 Win. and .30-06 only.
Special Purpose black matte metal finish. American walnut stock with
SP non-glare finish.Made from 1993 to 1995.

NYLON 66 APACHE BLACK ...... NiB $279 Ex $169 Gd $130
Same as Nylon 66 Mohawk Brown except w/chrome plated bbl.
and receiver cover, black stock. Made from 1962 to 1984.

NYLON 66 BICENTENNIAL
COMMEMORATIVE .... NiB $597 Ex $433 Gd $259
Same as Nylon 66 Mohawk Brown except has commemorative
inscription on receiver. Made in 1976 only.

NYLON 66MB AUTOLOADING RIFLE.... NiB $500 Ex $325 Gd $244
Similar to early production Nylon 66 Black Apache except with
blued bbl. and receiver cover. Made from 1978 to 1987.

NYLON 66 MOHAWK
BROWN AUTOLOADER........ NiB $450 Ex $275 Gd $230
Caliber: .22 LR. Tubular magazine in buttstock holds 14 rounds.
19.5-inch bbl. Weight: 4 lbs. Sights: Open rear; blade front. Brown
nylon stock and forearm. Made from 1959 to 1987.

NYLON 77 CLIP REPEATER ...... NiB $400 Ex $295 Gd $220
Same as Nylon 66 except has 5-round clip magazine. Made from 1970 to 1971.

Rossi Rifles

Rigby Model 416 Big Game
NRA NATIONAL FIREARMS MUSEUM

Rossi Model 62 Stainless Rifle

Rossi Model 62 Stainless Carbine

Rossi Model 62 WMR Rifle

Rossi Model 62 SAC Carbine

Rossi Model 62 Gallery Rifle

SPORTSMAN 74 AUTOLOADING RIFLE . . . . . NiB $379 Ex $294 Gd $200
Caliber: .30-06; four-round mag. Bbl.: 22 inches. Plain stock and forend. Open rear, ramp blade front sights. Made from 1985 to 1988.

JOHN RIGBY & CO. — Paso Robles, California

MODEL 275 MAGAZINE SPORTING RIFLE. . NiB $6475 Ex $5144 Gd $3576
Mauser action. Caliber: .275 High velocity, 7.57mm; five-round box mag,. Bbl.: 25 inches. Weight: 7.5 lbs. Folding leaf rear, bead front sights. Checkered, sporting-style stock w/half pistol grip. Pre-WWII and current specs similar.

MODEL 275 LIGHTWEIGHT
MAGAZINE RIFLE. . . . . NiB $5110 Ex $4122 Gd $2833
Same as Standard Model 275 except. w/21-inch bbl. Weight: 6.75 lbs.

MODEL 350 MAGNUM
MAGAZINE SPORTING RIFLE . . . . NiB $4332 Ex $3633 Gd $2490
Mauser action. Caliber.: .350 Magnum; five-round box mag. Bbl.: 24 inches. Weight: 7.75 lbs. Folding leaf rear, bead front sights. Checkered sporting stock w/full pistol grip.

MODEL 416 BIG GAME
MAGAZINE SPORTING RIFLE . . . . NiB $7688 Ex $6133 Gd $4286
Mauser action. Caliber: .416 Big Game; four-round box mag. Bbl.: 24 inches. Sgt. 9 to 9.25 lbs. Folding leaf rear, bead front sights. Checkered sporting stock w/full pistol grip.

ROSS RIFLE CO. — Quebec, Canada

MK II MODEL 1910 BOLT-ACTION SPORTING RIFLE
Straight-pull bolt-action with interrupted screw-type lugs. Calibers: .280 Ross, .303 British. Four round or 5-round magazine. Bbl. lengths: 22, 24, 26 inches. Sights: Two-leaf open rear; bead front. Checkered sporting stock. Weight: 7 lbs. Made c. 1910 to end of World War I. Most firearm authorities agree that this and other Ross models with interrupted screw-type lugs are unsafe to fire.
Military model . . . . NiB $2175 Ex $1370 Gd $989
Military Match Target model . . . . . . NiB $10,300 Ex $7225 Gd $3590

ROSSI RIFLES

MODEL 62 GALLERY SAC CARBINE
Same as standard Gallery Model except in .22 LR only with 16.25-inch bbl.; weight 5.5 lbs. Imported from 1975 to 1998.
Blued finish. . . . . NiB $215 Ex $159 Gd $125
Nickel finish . . . . NiB $220 Ex $163 Gd $130
Stainless . . . . NiB $220 Ex $163 Gd $130

MODEL 62 GALLERY MAGNUM . . . . NiB $235 Ex $200 Gd $135
Same as standard Gallery Model except chambered for .22 WMR, 10-shot magazine. Imported from 1975 to 1998.

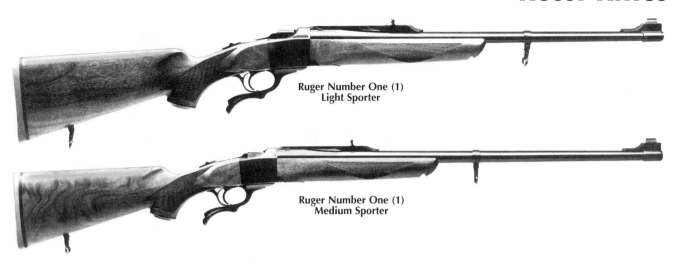

**Ruger Number One (1)
Light Sporter**

**Ruger Number One (1)
Medium Sporter**

62 GALLERY MODEL SLIDE-ACTION REPEATER
Similar to Winchester Model 63. Calibers: .22 LR, Long, Short, .22 WMR; tubular mag. holds 13 LR, 16 Long, 20 Short. Bbl.: 23 inches. Lgt.: 39.25 inches. Weight: 5.75 lbs. Open rear, bead front sights. Straight-grip stock, grooved slide handle. Blued, nickel or stainless finish. Imported 1970 to 1998. Values same as SAC model.

MODEL 65/92 LEVER-ACTION CARBINE
Similar to Winchester Model 92 Carbine. Caliber: .38 Special, .357 Mag. .44 Mag., .44-40, .45 LC; eight or 10-round mag. Bbl.: Round or half-octagonal, 16, 20, 24 inches. Lgt.: 41.5 inches. Satin blue, chrome or stainless finish. Brazilian hardwood buttstock and forearm. Made from 1978 to 1998.

.45 LC	NiB $335	Ex $250	Gd $190
.38/.357, .44 Mag.	NiB $335	Ex $250	Gd $190
W/octagon bbl.	NiB $400	Ex $329	Gd $275
LL Lever model	NiB $510	Ex $396	Gd $280
Engraved, add			$100
Chrome, add			$50
Stainless, add			$50

RUGER RIFLES

NUMBER ONE (1) LIGHT SPORTER. . . . . NiB $1010 Ex $615 Gd $445
Same as No. 1 Standard Rifle except w/22-inch bbl.; folding leaf rear sight on quarter rib, ramp front sight; Henry pattern forearm. Made from 1996 to date.

NUMBER ONE (1) MEDIUM SPORTER . . NiB $1010 Ex $615 Gd $445
Same as No. 1 Light Sporter except has 26-inch bbl. (22 inches in .45-70). Calibers: 7mm Rem. Mag., .300 win. Mag., .45-70 Gov't. Made from 1966 to date. Weight: 8 lbs (7.25 lbs. in 45-70).

NUMBER ONE (1) "NORTH AMERICANS"
PRESENTATION RIFLE . . . . .NiB $53,950 Ex $43,550 Gd $38,770
Same general specifications as the Ruger No. 1 Standard except highly

NUMBER ONE (1) RSI INTERNATIONAL
SINGLE-SHOT RIFLE. . . . . .NiB $1010 Ex $615 Gd $445
Similar to the No. 1 Light Sporter except w/lightweight 20-inch bbl. and full Mannlicher-style forend. Calibers: .243 Win., .270 Win., 7x57mm, .30-06. Weight: 7.25 lbs.

NUMBER ONE (1)
SPECIAL VARMINTER . . . . NiB $1010 Ex $615 Gd $445
Same as No. 1 Standard except w/heavy 24-inch bbl., target scope bases, no quarter rib. Weight: 9 lbs. Calibers: .22-250 Rem., .25-06 Rem., 7mm Rem. Mag., .300 Win Mag. Made from 1966 to date.

NUMBER ONE (1)
STANDARD RIFLE. . . . . NiB $1010 Ex $615 Gd $445
Falling-block, single-shot action. Farquharson-type lever. Calibers: .22-250 rem., .243 Win., 6mm Rem., .26-06, .270 Win., .30-06, 7mm Rem. Mag., .300 Win. Mag. Bbl.: 26 inches. Weight: 8 lbs. No sights, quarter rib for scope mounting. Checkered pistol-grip buttstock and semi-beavertail forearm. QD swives, rubber buttplate. Made from 1966 to date.

NUMBER ONE (1) TROPICAL RIFLE. . . . . NiB $1010 Ex $615 Gd $445
Same as No. 1 Light Sporter except w/24-inch bbl. Calibers: .375 H&H, .404 Jeffrey, .416 Rigby, .458 Win. Mag. Weight: 8.25 to 9 lbs. Made from 1966 to date.

NUMBER THREE (3) SINGLE-SHOT
CARBINE. . . . . NiB $800 Ex $495 Gd $355
Falling-block action with American-style lever. Calibers: .22 Hornet .223 Rem., .30-40 Krag, .357 Win., .44 Mag., .45-70. 22-inch bbl. Weight: 6 lbs. Sights: Folding leaf rear; gold bead front. Carbine-style stock w/curved buttplate, forearm with bbl. band. Made from 1972 to 1987.

Ruger Rifles

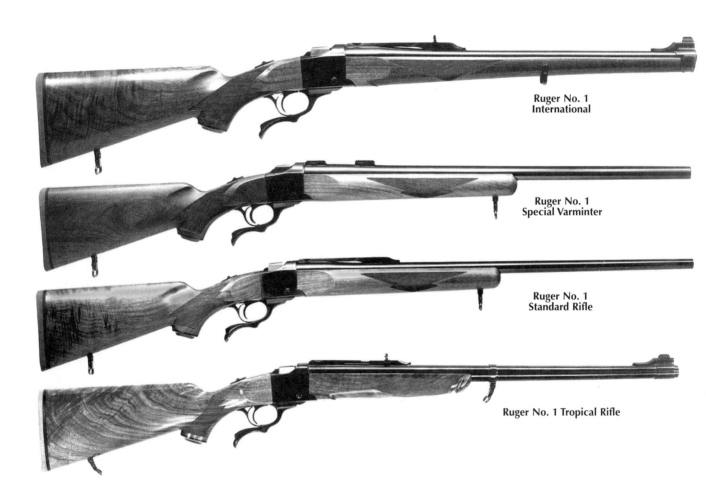

Ruger No. 1
International

Ruger No. 1
Special Varminter

Ruger No. 1
Standard Rifle

Ruger No. 1 Tropical Rifle

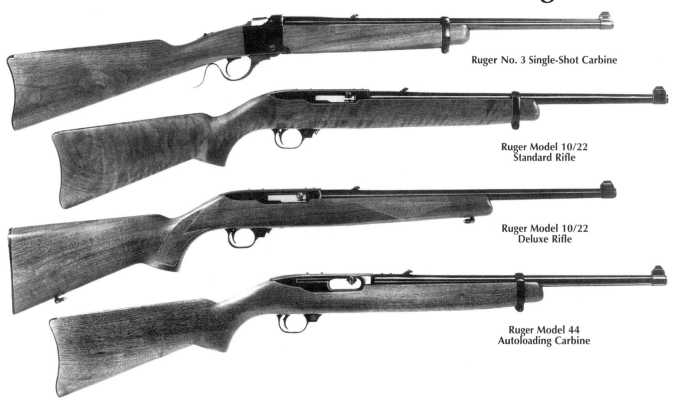

Ruger No. 3 Single-Shot Carbine

Ruger Model 10/22 Standard Rifle

Ruger Model 10/22 Deluxe Rifle

Ruger Model 44 Autoloading Carbine

MODEL 10/22 AUTOLOADING CARBINE

Caliber: .22 LR; detachable 10-round rotary mag. Bbl.: 18.5 inches. Weight: 5 lbs. Folding leaf rear, bead front sights. Carbine-style stock w/ bbl.band, curved buttplate. (Walnut stock disc. 1980.) Made from 1964 to date. International and Sporter versions disc. 1971.

Standard carbine w/walnut stock . . . . NiB $265 Ex $190 Gd $149
International, w/Mannlicher-style
stock (disc. 1971) . . . . NiB $710 Ex $497 Gd $375
RB (w/birch stock, blued finish). . . . . NiB $260 Ex $178 Gd $144
K-10/22 RB (w/birch stock, stainless finish) . . NiB $260 Ex $178 Gd $144
Sporter (w/MC stock,
flat buttplate, disc. 1971). . . . . NiB $260 Ex $178 Gd $144
SP Deluxe Sporter (intro. 1966). . . . . NiB $260 Ex $178 Gd $144
RBI International (blued, intro. 1994) . . . . NiB $690 Ex $488 Gd $377
RBI International (stainless, intro. 1995) . . . . NiB $695 Ex $448 Gd $377

MODEL 44 AUTOLOADING CARBINE

Gas-operated. Caliber: .44 Magnum. Four round tubular magazine (with magazine release button since 1967). 18.5-inch bbl. Weight: 5.75 lbs. Sights: Folding leaf rear; gold bead front. Carbine-style stock w/bbl. band and curved buttplate. Made from 1961 to 1986. International and Sporter versions discontinued in 1971.

Standard model . . . . NiB $588 Ex $434 Gd $335
Model 44 International
(w/Mannlicher-style stock). . . . . NiB $944 Ex $597 Gd $488
44 Sporter (MC stock w/finger groove) . . . . . . NiB $700 Ex $569 Gd $490
44RS Carbine
(w/peep rear sight, disc. 1978) . . . . NiB $695 Ex $487 Gd $388

MODEL 77 BOLT-ACTION RIFLE

Receiver w/integral scope mount base or round top. Short stroke or magnum-length action depending on caliber. Calibers: .22-250 Rem., .220 Swift, 6mm Rem., .243 Win., .250-3000, .25-06 Rem., .257 Roberts, 6.5 Rem. Mag., .270 Win., 7x57 mm, 7mm-08 Rem., Mag., .280 Rem., .284 Win., .308 Win., .30-06, .300 Win. Mag, .338 Win Mag., .350 Rem. Mag.,l458 Win. Mag; five-round

mag. standard, four rounds in .220 Swift; three rounds in magnum calibers. Bbl.: 22, 24 or 26 inches. Weight: 7 lbs (8.75 lbs in .458 Mag.). Round-top model furnished w/folding leaf rear, ramp front sights, integral base models furninshed w/scope rings with or w/o open sights. Stock w/checkered pistol grip and forearm, grip cap, rubber recoil pad, QD swivel studs. Made from 1968 to 1992.

Model 77 w/integral base, no sights . . . . NiB $500 Ex $408 Gd $321
6.5 Rem. Mag., add $100
.284 Win., add $50
.338 Win. Mag., add. $75
.350 Rem. Mag., add $75
Model 77RL Ultra Light, w/no sights . . . . NiB $545 Ex $438 Gd $290
Model 77RL Ultra Light, w/open sights . . . . . . NiB $569 Ex $454 Gd $331
MODEL 77RS w/integral base, open sights . . NiB $569 Ex $454 Gd $331
.338 Win. Mag, .458 Win. Mag.,
standard stock, add $100
Model 77RSC, .458 Win. Mag.,
w/walnut stock, add. $125
W/fancy grade Circassian walnut stock, add. $700
Model 77RSI International w/Mannlicher
stock, short action, 18.5-inch bbl. . . . . NiB $675 Ex $466 Gd $339
Model 77ST w/round top, open sights. . . . . . . NiB $575 Ex $439 Gd $369
.338 Win. Mag., add. $75
Model 77V Varmint
w/integral base, no sights. . . . . NiB $588 Ex $466 Gd $300
Model 77 NV Varmint w/integral base, no sights,
stainless steel bbl., laminated wood stock. . . . NiB $593 Ex $468 Gd $379

MODEL 77 MARK II ALL-WEATHER RIFLE . . . NiB $535 Ex $430 Gd $315
Redesigned Model 77 action. Same specs as Model M-77 Mark II except w/stainless bbl. and action. Zytel injection-molded stock. Caliber: .223 Rem., .243 Win., .270 Win., .308 Win., .30-06, 7mm Rem. Mag., .300 Win. Mag, .338 Win. Mag. Made from 1999 to 2008.

Ruger Rifles

Ruger Model 77 Round Top Receiver

Ruger Model 77
Ultra-Light Carbine

Ruger Model 77
International Carbine

Ruger Model 77
Varmint Rifle

Ruger Model 77 Mark II
All-Weather Rifle

MODEL 77 MARK II BOLT-ACTION RIFLE

Revised Model 77 action. Same specifications as Model M-77 except with new 3-position safety and fixed blade ejector system. Calibers .22 PPC, .223 Rem., 6mm PPC, 6.5x55 Swedish, .375 H&H, .404 Jeffery and .416 Rigby also available. Weight: 6 to 10.25 lbs. Made from 1989 to date.

MKIIR w/integral base, no sights . . . . NiB $545 Ex $423 Gd $314
Left-hand model, add $50
MKII RL Ultralight, no sights . . . . NiB $545 Ex $423 Gd $314
MKII RLS w/open sights . . . . NiB $545 Ex $423 Gd $314
MKII RS w/integral base, open sights . . . . NiB $545 Ex $423 Gd $314
MKII RS Express w/fancy grade French
walnut stock, integral base,
open sights . . . . NiB $1344 Ex $1116 Gd $835
MKII RSI International Mannlicher . . . . NiB $799 Ex $479 Gd $368
MKII RSM Magnum w/fancy grade Circassian
walnut stock, integral base, open sights . . . . NiB $1465 Ex $1143 Gd $870
77VT (VBZ or VTM) MKII
Varmint/Target w/stainless steel action,
laminated wood stock . . . . NiB $480 Ex $403 Gd $288

MODEL 77/.22 HORNET

BOLT-ACTION RIFLE . . . . NiB $556 Ex $445 Gd $339
Redesigned Model 77 action. Same specs as Model M-77 except w/new three-position safety and fixed blade ejector system. Calibers: .22 PPC, .223 Rem., 6mm PPC, 6.5x55 Swedish, .375 H&H Mag., .404 Jeffrey, .416 Rigby. Weight: 6 to 10.25 lbs. Made from 1989 to date.

Model 77/.22RH w/scope rings, no sights . . . NiB $625 Ex $470 Gd $369
Model 77/.22RSH w/rings & sights . . . . NiB $625 Ex $470 Gd $369
W/laminated wood stock . . . . NiB $735 Ex $544 Gd $390

MODEL 77/.22 RIMFIRE BOLT-ACTION RIFLE

Calibers: .22 LR, .22 WMR; 10-round (.22 LR) or 9-round (.22 WMR) rotary mag. Bbl.: 20 inches. Lgt.: 39.75 inches. Weight: 5.75 lbs. Integral scope bases with or w/o sights. Checkered American walnut or Zytel injection-molded stock. Stainless or blued finish. Blued version made from 1983 to date. Stainless introduced 1989.

77/.22R w/scope rings, no sights, walnut stock . . NiB $625 Ex $544 Gd $390
77/.22RS w/scope rings, sights, walnut stock. . NiB $625 Ex $544 Gd $390
77/.22RP w/scope rings, no sights, synthetic stock . NiB $625 Ex $544 Gd $390
77/.22RSP w/scope rings, sights, synthetic stock . NiB $625 Ex $544 Gd $390
K77/.22RP w/stainless scope rings,
no sights, synthetic stock . . . . NiB $625 Ex $544 Gd $390
K77/.22RSP w/stainless scope rings,
sights, synthetic stock . . . . NiB $625 Ex $544 Gd $390
77/.22RM (.22 WMR) w/scope rings,
no sights, walnut stock . . . . NiB $625 Ex $544 Gd $390
K77/.22RSMP (.22 WMR) w/stainless
scope rings, sights, synthetic stock . . . . NiB $735 Ex $579 Gd $437
K77/.22RMP (.22 WMR) w/stainless
scope rings, sights, synthetic stock . . . . NiB $625 Ex $544 Gd $390
K77/.22 VBZ (.22 WMR) w/no sights,
laminated stock (intro. 1993) . . . . NiB $735 Ex $579 Gd $437

Ruger Model 77 Mark II

Ruger Model 77/.22 Rimfire

Ruger Model 77/.44 All Weather

MODEL 77/.44 BOLT-ACTION
Short-action, carbine-style similar to the M77/.22 RH. Caliber: .44 Rem. Mag.; four-round rotary mag. Bbl. : 18.5 inches. Lgt.: 38.25 inches. Weight: 6 lbs. Gold bead front, folding adj. rear sights, integral scope base w/Ruger rings. Blued or stainless finish. Synthetic or checkered American walnut stock w/ rubber buttpad and swivels. Made from 1997 to 2004.
Blued finish . . . . .NiB $625 Ex $544 Gd $390
Stainless finish. . . . . .NiB $555 Ex $350 Gd $245

MODEL 96 Lever-Action CARBINE
Caliber: .22 LR, .22 WMR, .44 Mag.; detachable 4-, 9- or 10-round mag. Bbl.: 18.5 inches. Weight: 5.25 lbs. Front gold bead sight. Drilled and tapped for scop mount. American hardwood stock. Made from 1996 to 2008.
.22 LR . . . . .NiB $379 Ex $255 Gd $180
.22 WMR. . . . . .NiB $390 Ex $275 Gd $195
.44 Mag. . . . . .NiB $390 Ex $275 Gd $195

MINI-14 SEMIAUTOMATIC RIFLE
Gas-operated. Caliber: .223 Rem. (5.56mm); five, 10 or 20-round box mag. Bbl.: 18.5 inches. Weight : 6.5 lbs. Peep rear sight, blade front on removable bbl. band. Pistol-grip stock w/curved buttplate. Handguard. Made from 1974 to 2004.
Blued finish . . . . NiB $725 Ex $579 Gd $375
K-Mini-14/S stainless steel. . . . . NiB $815 Ex $580 Gd $444

Mini-14/5F w/blued finish,
folding stock . . . . NiB $1144 Ex $995 Gd $790
K-Mini-14/SF w/stainless finish,
folding stock . . . . NiB $855 Ex $690 Gd $545
Mini-14 Ranch Rifle w/scope . . . . NiB $800 Ex $590 Gd $400

MINI-30 AUTOLOADER
Caliber: 7.62x39mm (.308 Win.); five-round detachable mag. Bbl.: 18.5 inches. Lgt.: 37.25 inches. Weight: 7 lbs., 3 oz. Peep rear sight, blade front on bbl. band. Designed for use w/telescopic sights. Walnut-stained stock. Blued or stainless finish, Made from 1987 to 2004.
Blued. . . . . .NiB $625 Ex $439 Gd $300
Stainless .NiB $815 Ex $545 Gd $360

PC SERIES SEMIAUTOMATIC CARBINES
Calibers: 9mm Parabellum or .40 S&W. 10-round magazine. 15.25-inch bbl. Weight: 6.25 lbs. Integral Ruger scope mounts with or without sights. Optional blade front sight, adjustable open rear. Matte black oxide finish. Matte black Zytel stock w/checkered pistol-grip and forearm. Made from 1997 to date.
Model PC9 (no sights) . . . . .NiB $510 Ex $440 Gd $300
Model PC4 (no sights) . . . . .NiB $545 Ex $467 Gd $330
W/adjust. sights, add. $50

Ruger Rifles

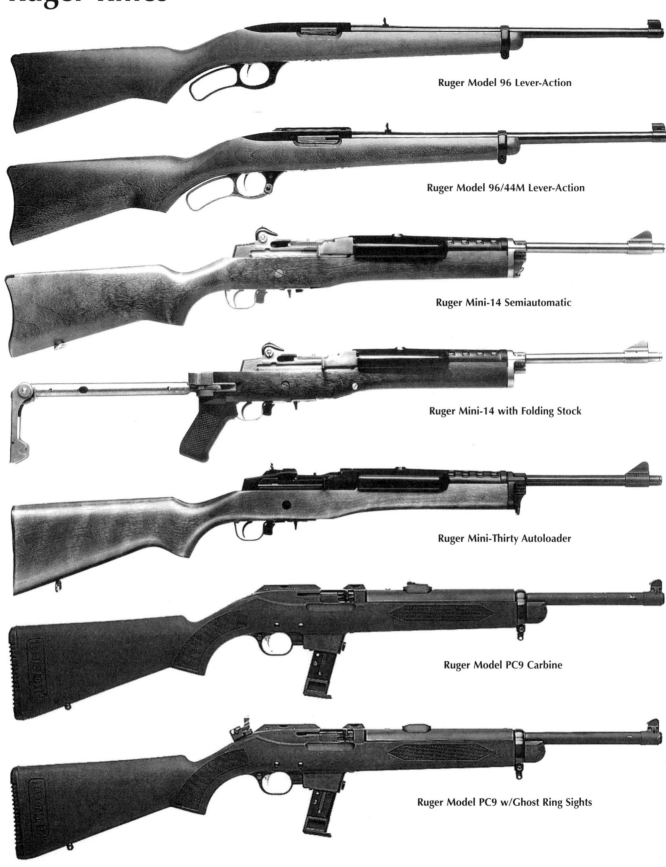

Ruger Model 96 Lever-Action

Ruger Model 96/44M Lever-Action

Ruger Mini-14 Semiautomatic

Ruger Mini-14 with Folding Stock

Ruger Mini-Thirty Autoloader

Ruger Model PC9 Carbine

Ruger Model PC9 w/Ghost Ring Sights

RUSSIAN MILITARY RIFLES — Principal U.S.S.R. Arms Plant, Tula

MODEL 1891
MOSIN MILITARY RIFLE. . . . . **NiB $485 Ex $269 Gd $187**
Nagant system bolt-action. Caliber: 7.62mm Russian; five-round box mag. Bbl.: 31.5 inches. Weight: 9 lbs. Open rear, blade front sights. Full stock w/straight grip. Specs are for WWII version, earlier types differ slightly. In 1916 Remington Arms. Co. and New England Westinghouse Co. produced 250,000 of these rifles on contract with the Imperial Russian Government. Few were delivered to Russian. The balance was bought by the U.S. Government for training in 1918. Many of these rifles were sold to NRA members for about $3 each by the Director of Civilian Marksmanship.

TOKAREV MODEL 40 SEMIAUTOMATIC
MILITARY RIFLE . . . . **NiB $844 Ex $438 Gd $270**
Gas-operated. Caliber.: 7.62mm Russian; 10-round detachable box mag. Bbl.: 24.5 inches w/muzzle brake. Weight: 9 lbs. Leaf rear, hooded post front sights. Full stock w/pistol grip. Differences between models 1938, 1940 and 1941 are minor and do not affect value.

SAKO RIFLES — Riihimaki, Finland. Manufactured by Sako L.T.D.

Formerly imported by Stoeger Industries, Wayne, New Jersey (formerly by Garcia Corp.) until 2000. Imported by Beretta USA from 2001 to date.

MODEL 72 . . . . **NiB $1090 Ex $865 Gd $660**
Single model designation replacing Vixen Sporter, Vixen Carbine, Vixen Heavy Barrel, Forester Sporter, Forester Carbine, Forester Heavy Barrel, Finnbear Sporter, and Finnbear Carbine, with same specifications. All but heavy barrel models fitted with open rear sight. Values same as for corresponding earlier models. Imported from 1972 to 1974.

MODEL 73 LEVER-ACTION RIFLE . . . . . . **NiB $1670 Ex $988 Gd $690**
Same as Finnwolf except has 3-round clip magazine, flush floorplate; stock has no cheekpiece. Imported from 1973 to 1975.

MODEL 74 CARBINE . . . . **NiB $1130 Ex $735 Gd $600**
Long Mauser-type bolt action. Caliber: .30-06. Five round magazine. 20-inch bbl. Weight: 7.5 lbs. No sights. Checkered Mannlicher-type full stock of European walnut, Monte Carlo cheekpiece. Imported from 1974 to 1978.

MODEL 74 HEAVY BARREL RIFLE,
LONG ACTION. . . . . **NiB $1165 Ex $755 Gd $634**
Same specs as short action except w/23-inch heavy bbl., Weight 8.5 lbs. Calibers: .220 Swift, .22-250 Rem., .243 Win., .308 Win. Imported from 1974 to 1978.

MODEL 74 HEAVY BARREL RIFLE,
MEDIUM ACTION. . . . . **NiB $1165 Ex $755 Gd $634**
Same specifications as short action except w/23-inch heavy bbl., weighs 8.5 lbs. Calibers: .220 Swift, .22-250, .243 Win., .308 Win. Imported from 1974 to 1978.

MODEL 74 HEAVY BARREL RIFLE,
SHORT ACTION . . . . **NiB $1195 Ex $900 Gd $650**
Mauser-type bolt action. Calibers: .222 Rem., .223 Rem. Five round magazine. 23.5-inch heavy bbl. Weight: 8.25 lbs. No sights. Target-style checkered European walnut stock w/beavertail forearm. Imported from 1974 to 1978.

MODEL 74 SUPER SPORTER,
LONG ACTION. . . . . **NiB $1165 Ex $755 Gd $634**
Same specs as short action except w/24-inch bbl., Weight: 8 lbs. Magnums have four-round mag., recoil pad. Calibers.: .25-06 Rem., .270 Win. 7mm Rem. Mag., .30-06, .300 Win. Mag. .338 Win. Mag., .375 H&H Mag. Imported from 1974 to 1978.

MODEL 74 SUPER SPORTER,
MEDIUM ACTION . . . . **NiB $1175 Ex $910 Gd $659**
Same specs as short action except Weight: 7.25 lbs. Caliber: .220 Swift, .22-250 Rem. .243 Win. Imported from 1974 to 1978.

MODEL 74 SUPER SPORTER,
SHORT ACTION . . . . **NiB $1175 Ex $910 Gd $659**
Mauser-type bolt action. Calibers: .222 Rem., .223 Rem. Five round magazine. 23.5-inch bbl. Weight: 6.5 lbs. No sights. Checkered European walnut stock w/Monte Carlo cheekpiece, QD swivel studs. Imported 1974. Disc.

MODEL 75 DELUXE . . . . **NiB $1190 Ex $944 Gd $690**
Same specifications as Sako 75 Hunter except w/hinged floor plate, deluxe high gloss checkered walnut stock w/rosewood forend cap and grip cap w/silver inlay. Imported from 1998 to 2006. Disc.

MODEL 75 HUNTER . . . . **NiB $1250 Ex $833 Gd $665**
Bolt-action design available in four action lengths. Fitted with a new bolt featuring three front-locking lugs and an external extractor positioned under the bolt. Calibers: .17 Rem., .222 Rem., .223 Rem., .22-250 Rem., .243 Win., 7mm-08 Rem. .308 Win. .25-06 Rem., .270 Win. .280 Rem. .30-06, 7mm Rem. Mag. .300 Win. Mag.. .300 Wby. Mag, .375 H&H Mag., .416 Rem. Mag.; four-, five- or six-round detachable mag. Bbl.: 22, 24 or 26 inches. Lgt.: 41.75 to 45.6 inches. Weight: 6.3 to 9 lbs. Sako dovetail scope base integral with receiver, no sights. Checkered high-grade walnut stock w/recoil pad and sling swivels. Made from 1997 to 2006.

MODEL 75 STAINLESS SYNTHETIC . . . . . **NiB $1279 Ex $877 Gd $685**
Similar to Model 75 Hunter except chambered for .22-250 Rem., .243 Win., .25-06 Rem., .270 Win., 7mm-08 Rem., 7mm STW, .30-06, .308 Win., 7mm Rem Mag., .300 Win. Mag., .338 Win. Mag. or .375 H&H Mag. 22-, 24-, and 26-inch bbls. Black composite stock w/soft rubber grips inserts. Matte stainless steel finish. Made from 1997 to 2006.

MODEL 75 VARMINT RIFLE. . . . . . **NiB $1456 Ex $835 Gd $656**
Similar to Model 75 Hunter except chambered for .17 Rem., .222 Rem., .223 Rem. and .22-250 Rem. 24-inch bbl. Matte lacquered walnut stock w/beavertail forearm. Made from 1998 to 2006.

MODEL 78 SUPER HORNET SPORTER . . . **NiB $654 Ex $535 Gd $338**
Same specifications as Model 78 Rimfire except chambered for .22 Hornet, 4-round magazine. Imported from 1977 to 1987.

MODEL 78 SUPER RIMFIRE SPORTER . . . . **NiB $587 Ex $466 Gd $335**
Bolt action. Caliber: .22 LR. Five round magazine. 22.5-inch bbl. Weight: 6.75 lbs. No sights. Checkered European walnut stock, Monte Carlo cheekpiece. Imported from 1977 to 1986.

MODEL 85 CLASSIC BOLT-ACTION RIFLE
Caliber: .25-06 Rem. .270 Win., .30-06, .308 Win., .300 Win. Mag., .338 Win. Mag., .370 Sako Mag., .375 H&H Mag., .270 WSM, .300 WSM, 7mm Mag. Detachable mag., single-stage trigger. Checkered walnut pistol-grip stock. Weight: 7 lbs. New in 2009.
Standard calibers . . . . **NiB $1937 Ex $1216 Gd $1019**
Magnum caliber, add $125

Sako Rifles

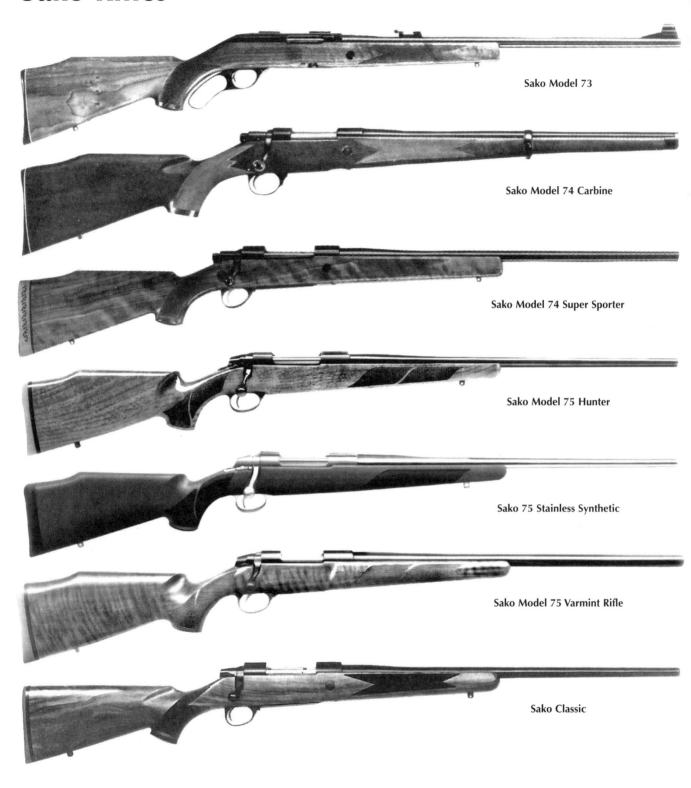

Sako Model 73

Sako Model 74 Carbine

Sako Model 74 Super Sporter

Sako Model 75 Hunter

Sako 75 Stainless Synthetic

Sako Model 75 Varmint Rifle

Sako Classic

Sako Rifles

Sako Deluxe Lightweight

Sako Fiberglass

Sako Finnfire

Sako Finnfire Heavy Barrel

Sako Finnwolf

DELUXE GRADE AI . . . . NiB $1266 Ex $870 Gd $633
Same specs as Standard grade except w/22-line French checkering, rosewood grip cap and forend tip, semi-beavertail forend. Disc.

DELUXE GRADE AII . . . . NiB $1145 Ex $790 Gd $556
Same specs as Standard grade except w/22-line French checkering, rosewood grip and forend tip, semi-beavertail forend. Disc.

DELUXE GRADE AIII . . . . NiB $1477 Ex $1188 Gd $766
Same specifications as w/standard except w/French checkering, rosewood grip cap and forend tip, semi-beavertail forend. Disc.

**DELUXE LIGHTWEIGHT
BOLT-ACTION RIFLE . . . . NiB $1190 Ex $1021 Gd $699**
Same specs as Hunter Lightweight except w/select French walnut stock w/high-gloss finish, hand-cut checkering, rosewood forend tip and grip cap. Imported from 1985 to 1997.

**FIBERCLASS BOLT-ACTION
RIFLE. . . . . NiB $1137 Ex $1077 Gd $644**
All-weather, fiberglass-stock version of Sako-barreled long-action. Calibers: .25-06 Rem., .270 Win., .30-06. 7mm Rem. Mag., .300 Win. Mag. .338 Win. Mag., .375 H&H Mag. Bbl.: 22.5 inches. Lgt.: 44.25 inches. Weight: 7.25 lbs. Imported from 1984 to 1996.

FINNBEAR CARBINE . . . . NiB $1190 Ex $917 Gd $566
Same as Finnbear Sporter except w/20-inch bbl., Mannlicher-type full stock. Imported 1971. Disc.

FINNBEAR SPORTER . . . . NiB $1190 Ex $917 Gd $566
Mauser-type long action. Calibers: .25-06 Rem., .254 Win. Mag., .270, .30-06, .300 Win. Mag., .338 Win Mag., 7mm Rem, Mag., .375 H&H Mag; four- or five-round mag. Bbl.: 24 inches. Weight: 7 lbs. Hooded ramp front sight. Sporter stock w/Monte Carlo cheekpiece, checkered pistol grip and forearm, recoil pad, swivels. Imported from 1961 to 1971.

FINNFIRE BOLT-ACTION RIFLE
Scaled-down Sako-design Mini-Sporter built for .22 LR; five- or 10-round mag. Bbl.: 22 inches. Lgt.: 39.5 inches. Weight: 5.25 lbs. Receiver machined for 11mm dovetail scope rings. Beaded blade front, open adj. rear sights. Blued finish. Checkered European walnut stock. Imported from 1994 to 2005.
Hunter model . . . . NiB $908 Ex $694 Gd $533
Varmint model . . . . NiB $988 Ex $696 Gd $580
Sporter model . . . . NiB $1027 Ex $866 Gd $613

FINNWOLF LEVER-ACTION RIFLE . . . . . . .NiB $975 Ex $733 Gd $621
Hammerless. Calibers: .243 Win., .308 Win. Four round clip magazine. 23-inch bbl. Weight: 6.75 lbs. Hooded ramp front sight. Sporter stock w/Monte Carlo cheekpiece, checkered pistol-grip and forearm, swivels. Available w/right- or left-hand stock. Imported from 1963 to 1972.

Sako Rifles

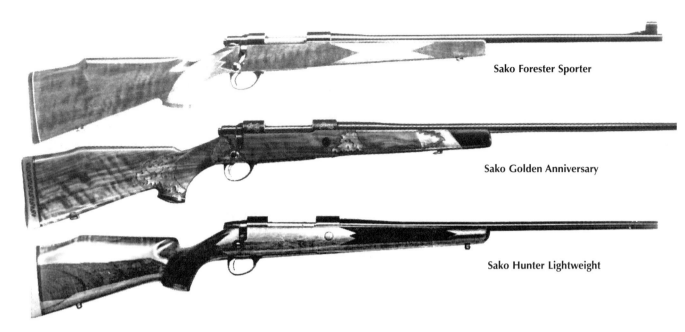

Sako Forester Sporter

Sako Golden Anniversary

Sako Hunter Lightweight

FINNSPORT 2700. . . . . **NiB $808 Ex $597 Gd $466**
Bolt-action centerfire rifle. Calibers: .270 Win., .30-06, 7mm Rem. Mag., .300 Win. Mag. Bbl.: 24 inches. Weight: 8 lbs. Imported from 1984 to 1986.

FORESTER CARBINE. . . . . **NiB $1116 Ex $924 Gd $550**
Same as Forester Sporter except w/20-inch bbl., Mannlicher-type full stock. Imported from 1958 to 1971.

FORESTER HEAVY BARREL. . . . . . **NiB $1423 Ex $988 Gd $713**
Same as Forester Sporter except w/24-inch heavy bbl. Weight: 7.5 lbs. Imported from 1958 to 1971.

FORESTER SPORTER. . . . . **NiB $1130 Ex $1015 Gd $559**
Medium-length Mauser-type bolt-action. Calibers: .22-250 Rem., .243 Win., .308 Win.; five-round mag. Bbl.: 23 inches. Weight: 6.5 lbs. Hooded ramp front sight. Sporter stock w/Monte Carlo cheekpiece, checkered pistol grip and forearm, swivels. Imported from 1957 to 1971.

GOLDEN ANNIVERSARY MODEL . . . . **NiB $2866 Ex $2210 Gd $1570**
Special presentation-grade rifle issued in 1973 to commemorate Sako's 50th anniversary. Numbered 1 to 1,000. Same specs as Deluxe sporter. Long action, 7mm Rem. Mag. Trigger guard and floorplate decorated w/gold oak leaf and acorn motif. Select European walnut stock, checkering bordered w/hand-carved oak leaf pattern.

HIGH-POWER MAUSER SPORTING RIFLE . . . . **NiB $1154 Ex $1033 Gd $831**
FN Mauser action. Calibers: .270 Win., .30-06; five-round mag. Bbl.: 24 inches. Open rear leaf, Partridge hooded ramp front sights. Checkered stock w/Monte Carlo comb and cheekpiece. Weight.: 7.5 lbs. Imported from 1950 to 1957.

HUNTER LIGHTWEIGHT BOLT-ACTION RIFLE
Five-or six-round mag. Bbl.: AI models, 21.5 inches; AII models; 22 inches; AIII models 22.5 inches. Lgt.: 42.5 to 44.5 inches. Weight: 5.75 lbs to 7.25 lbs. Monte Carlo-syle oil-finished European walnut stock; hand-checkered pistol grip and forend. Imported from 1985 to 1997. Left-hand version introduced 1987.
AI (Short Action) .17 Rem. . . . . **NiB $1466 Ex $1224 Gd $1018**
.222 Rem., .223 Rem. . . . . **NiB $1088 Ex $831 Gd $589**

AII (medium action)
.22-250 Rem., .243 Win., .308 Win. . . . . . . **NiB $976 Ex $798 Gd $543**
AII (Long Action) .25-06 Rem.
.270 Win., .30-06 . . . . **NiB $978 Ex $792 Gd $553**
.338 Win. Mag. . . . . **NiB $1154 Ex $976 Gd $735**
.375 H&H Mag. . . . . **NiB $1266 Ex $1044 Gd $766**
Left-hand model (standard cal.) . . . . **NiB $1294 Ex $1088 Gd $773**
Magnum calibers . . . . **NiB $1590 Ex $1277 Gd $945**

LAMINATED STOCK BOLT-ACTION RIFLES
Similar to Hunter Grade except w/stock of resin-bonded hardwood veneers. Available in 18 calibers in AI (short-action), AII (medium-action), AV (long-action), left-hand version in 10 calibers, AV only. Imported from 1987 to 1995.
Short or medium action . . . . **NiB $1043 Ex $890 Gd $577**
Long action/Magnum . . . . **NiB $1108 Ex $902 Gd $645**

MAGNUM MAUSER . . . . **NiB $1588 Ex $1244 Gd $900**
Similar to Standard Model except w/recoil pad and redesigned longer AIII action to handle longer magnum cartridges. Calibers .300 H&H Mag. and .375 H&H Mag. standard at time of introduction. Disc.

MANNLICHER-STYLE CARBINE
Similar to Hunter Model except w/full Mannlicher-style stock, 18.5-inch bbl. Weight: 7.5 lbs. Chambered in .243 Win., .25-06, .270 Win., .308 Win., .30-06, 7mm Rem. Mag., .300 Win., .338 Win., Mag., .375 H&H. Introduced 1977. Disc.
Standard calibers . . . . **NiB $1287 Ex $1021 Gd $734**
Magnum calibers (except .375) . . . . **NiB $1338 Ex $1055 Gd $733**
.375 H&H . . . . **NiB $1366 Ex $1094 Gd $790**

SAFARI GRADE. . . . . **NiB $2576 Ex $1988 Gd $1166**
Classic bolt-action. Calibers: .300 Win. Mag., .338 Win. Mag., .375 H&H. Oil-finished European walnut stock w/hand-checkering. Barrel band swivel, express-type sight rib; satin or matte blue finish. Imported from 1980 to 1996.

SPORTER DELUXE . . . . **NiB $1290 Ex $1045 Gd $687**
Same as Vixen, Forester, Finnbear and Model 74 except w/fancy French walnut stock, w/skip checkering, rosewood forend tip and pistol-grip cap. Inlaid trigger guard and floorplate. Disc.

Sako Mannlicher-Style Carbine

Sako Sporter Deluxe

Sako TRG-21
Target Rifle

STANDARD GRADE AI . . . . **NiB $1077 Ex $823 Gd $440**
Short bolt-action. Calibers: .17 Rem., .222 Rem., .223 Rem. Five round magazine. 23.5-inch bbl. Weight: 6.5 lbs. No sights. Checkered European walnut stock w/Monte Carlo cheekpiece, QD swivel studs. Imported from 1978 to 1985.

STANDARD GRADE AII . . . . **NiB $1090 Ex $840 Gd $456**
Medium bolt-action. Calibers: .22-250 Rem., .243 Win., .308 Win. 23.5-inch bbl. in .22-250; 23-inch bbl. in other calibers. Five round magazine. Weight: 7.25 lbs. Checkered European walnut stock w/Monte Carlo cheekpiece, QD swivel studs. Imported from 1978 to 1985.

STANDARD GRADE AIII . . . . **NiB $1178 Ex $843 Gd $545**
Long bolt-action. Calibers: .25-06 Rem., .270 Win., .30-06, 7mm Rem. Mag., .300 Win. Mag., .338 Win. Mag., .375 H&H. 24-inch bbl. 4-round magazine. Weight: 8 lbs. Imported from 1978 to 1984.

SUPER DELUXE RIFLE . . . . **NiB $2544 Ex $2210 Gd $1344**
Available in AI, AII, AIII calibers. Select European walnut stock w/hand-checkered, deep oak leaf hand-engraved design. Disc.

TRG BOLT-ACTION TARGET RIFLE
Caliber: .308 Win., .330 Win. or .338 Lapua Mag. Detachable 10-round magazine. 25.75- or 27.2-inch bbl. Weight: 10.5 to 11 lbs. Blued action w/stainless barrel. Adjustable two-stage trigger. Modular reinforced polyurethane target stock w/adj. cheekpiece and buttplate. Options: Muzzle break; detachable bipod; QD sling swivels and scope mounts w/1-inch or 30mm rings. Imported from 1993 to 2004.

TRG 21 .308 Win	NiB $2376	Ex $2099	Gd $1545
TRG 22 .308 Win.	NiB $2459	Ex $2288	Gd $1590
TRG 41 .338 Lapua.	NiB $2788	Ex $2690	Gd $1877
TRG-42 (.300 Win Mag. or .338 Lapua) . .	NiB $3154	Ex $2651	Gd $1835

TRG-S BOLT-ACTION RIFLE
Calibers: .243 Win., 7mm-08 Rem., .270 Win., .30-06, 7mm Rem. Mag., .300 Win. Mag., .338 Win. Mag; five-round mag. (standard calibers), four-round in magnum calibers. Bbl.: 22 or 24 inches. Lgt.: 45.5 inches. Weight: 7.75 lbs. No sights. Reinforced polyurethane Monte Carlo stock. Introduced in 1993.
Standard calibers . . . . **NiB $823 Ex $707 Gd $466**
Magnum calibers . . . . **NiB $880 Ex $844 Gd $545**

VIXEN CARBINE . . . . **NiB $1096 Ex $954 Gd $868**
Same as Vixen Sporter except w/20-inch bbl., Mannlicher-type full stock. Imported from 1947 to 1971.

VIXEN HEAVY BARREL . . . . **NiB $1110 Ex $933 Gd $545**
Same as Vixen Sporter except calibers .222 Rem., .222 Rem. Mag., .223 Rem., heavy bbl., target-style stock w/beavertail forearm. Weight: 7.5 lbs. Imported from 1947-71.

VIXEN SPORTER . . . . **NiB $1100 Ex $969 Gd $546**
Short Mauser-type bolt-action. Caliber: .218 Bee., .22 Hornet, .222 Rem. .222 Rem. Mag, .223 Rem.; five-round mag. Bbl.: 23.5 inches. Weight: 6.5 lbs. Hooded ramp front sight. Sporter-style stock w/Monte Carlo cheekpiece, checkered pistol-grip and forearm, swivels. Imported from 1946 to 1971.

GRADING: **NiB** = New in Box   **Ex** = Excellent or NRA 95%   **Gd** = Good or NRA 68%   **155**

Savage Industries

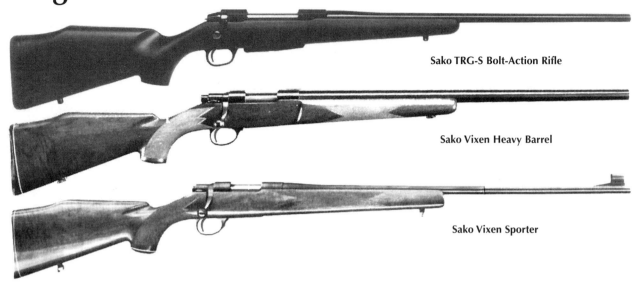

Sako TRG-S Bolt-Action Rifle

Sako Vixen Heavy Barrel

Sako Vixen Sporter

J. P. SAUER & SOHN — Eckernforde, Germany (formerly Suhl, Germany). Imported by Sigarms Exeter, New Hampshire (previously by Paul Company Inc. and G.U. Inc.)

MAUSER BOLT-ACTION
SPORTING RIFLE . . . . **NiB $1457 Ex $1089 Gd $777**
Caliber: 7x57, 8x57 most common; also most popular Continental calibers and .30-06; five-round mag. Bbl.: 22 or 24 inches, Krupp steel; half octagon w/raised matte rib. Double-set triggers. Weight: 7.5 lbs. Three-leaf open rear, ramp front sights. Sporting-style stock w/cheekpiece, checkered pistol grip, raised side panels, Schnabel forend tip; swivels. Also made w/20-inch bbl. and full-length stock. Manufactured before WWII.

MODEL S-90 BOLT-ACTION RIFLES
Calibers: .243 Win., .308 Win. (short action); .25-06 Rem., .270 Win., .30-06 (medium action); 7mm Rem. Mag., .300 Win. Mag., .300 Wby., .338 Win. Mag., .375 H&H Mag (magnum action). Four-round mag. (standard calibers) or three-round mag. (magnum calibers. Bbl.: 20 inches (Stutzen), 24 inches. Weight: 7.6 to 10.75 lbs. Adj. (Supreme) checkered Monte Carlo-style stock, contrasting forend and pistol grip caps, high-gloss finish; or classic-style (Lux) European walnut stock w/satin oil finish. Imported from 1983 to 1989.

S-90 Standard . . . . NiB $1154	Ex $990	Gd $587
S-90 Lux . . . . NiB $1389	Ex $1100	Gd $654
S-90 Safari. . . . . NiB $1397	Ex $1127	Gd $665
S-90 Stutzen . . . . NiB $1144	Ex $994	Gd $477
S-90 Supreme . . . . NiB $1490	Ex $1167	Gd $800
Grade I engraving, add.		$650
Grade II engraving, add		$850
Grade III engraving add		$1200
Grade IV engraving, add.		$1700

MODEL 200 BOLT-ACTION RIFLES
Calibers: .243 Win., .25-06 Rem., .270 Win., 7mm Rem. Mag., .30-06, .308 Win. .300 Win. Mag; detachable box mag. Bbl. (24 inches (American) or 26 inches (European). Interchangeable bbl. Standard (steel) or lightweight (alloy) action. Weight: 6.6 to 7.75 lbs. Lgt.: 44 inches. Stock options: American model w/checkered Monte Carlo-style two-piece stock, contrasting forend and pistol grip caps w/high gloss finish; no sights. European walnut stock w/Schnabel forend, satin oil finish, iron sights. Contemporary model w/synthetic carbon fiber stock. Imported from 1986 to 1993.

Standard model. . . . . NiB $1266	Ex $1093	Gd $700
Lightweight model . . . . NiB $1275	Ex $1033	Gd $580
Contemporary model . . . . NiB $1260	Ex $1017	Gd $565
American model . . . . NiB $1260	Ex $1017	Gd $565
Left-hand model, add		$200
Magnum calibers, add.		$130
Interchangeable barrel assembly, add.		$325

MODEL 202 BOLT-ACTION RIFLES
Caliber: .243 Win., 6.5x55, 6.5x57, .25-06 Rem., .270 Win., .280 Rem., 7x64, .308 Win., .30-06, 7mm Rem. Mag., .300 Win., Mag., .300 Wby. Mag., 8x68S, .338 Win. Mag., .375 H&H Mag.; removable 3-round box mag. Interchangeable 23.6 and 26 inch bbl. Lgt.: 44.3 to 46 inches. Modular receiver drilled and tapped for scope bases. Adj. two-stage trigger w/dual-release safety. Weight: 7.7 to 8.4 lbs. Stock options: checkered Monte Carlo-style select American walnut two-piece stock; Euro-classic French walnut two-piece stock w/semi-Schnabel forend and satin oil finish; Super Grade Claro walnut two-piece stock fitted w/rosewood forend and grip cap w/high-gloss epoxy finish. Imported from 1994 to 2004.

Standard model. . . . . NiB $2660	Ex $1848	Gd $983
Euro-Classic model . . . . NiB $1365	Ex $897	Gd $633
Super Grade model. . . . . NiB $1119	Ex $888	Gd $603

SAVAGE INDUSTRIES — Westfield, Massachusetts (formerly Chicopee Falls, Massachusetts, and Utica, New York)

MODEL 3 BOLT-ACTION
SINGLE-SHOT RIFLE. . . . . **NiB $100 Ex $61 Gd $59**
Takedown. Caliber: .22 Short, Long, LR. Bbl.: 26 inches on pre-WWII models, 24 inches on post-war prod. Weight: 5 lbs. Open rear, bead front sights. Plain pistol-grip stock. Made from 1933 to 1952.

MODEL 3S . . . . **NiB $116 Ex $89 Gd $59**
Same as Model 3 except w/peep rear sight, hooded front. Made from 1933 to 1942.

MODEL 3ST . . . . **NiB $120 Ex $85 Gd $50**
Same as Model 3S except fitted w/swivels and sling. Made from 1933 to 1942.

Savage Industries

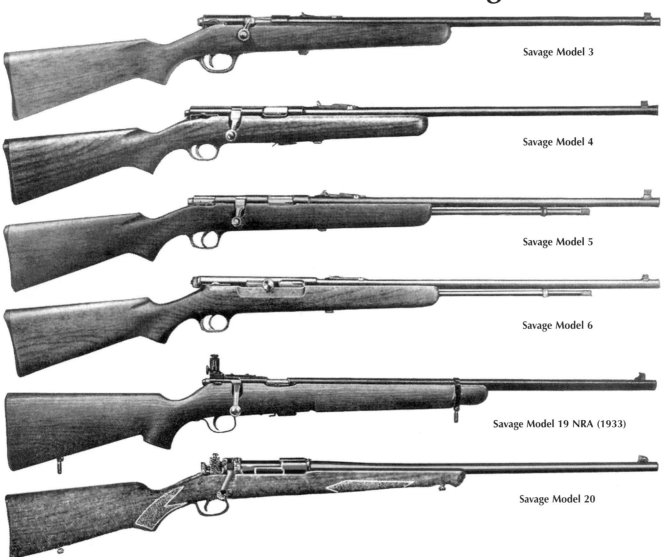

Savage Model 3

Savage Model 4

Savage Model 5

Savage Model 6

Savage Model 19 NRA (1933)

Savage Model 20

MODEL 4 BOLT-ACTION REPEATER . . . . . . NiB $149 Ex $90 Gd $59
Takedown. Caliber: .22 Short, Long, LR; five-round detachable box mag. Bbl.: 24 inches. Weight: 5.5 lbs. Open rear, bead front sights. Checkered pistol-grip stock on prewar models. Early production had grooved forearm. Post-WWII rifles have plain stocks. Made from 1933 to 1965.

MODEL 4M. . . . . NiB $121 Ex $87 Gd $64
Same as Model 4 except chambered for .22 WMR. Made from 1961 to 1965.

MODEL 4S . . . . NiB $130 Ex $78 Gd $47
Same as Model 4 except w/peep rear sight, hooded front. Made from 1933 to 1942.

**MODEL 5 BOLT-ACTION
REPEATER** . . . . NiB $125 Ex $78 Gd $57
Same as Model 4 except w/tubular magazine (holds 21 Short, 17 Long, 15 LR); weight: 6 lbs. Made from 1936 to 1961.

MODEL 5S . . . . NiB $135 Ex $77 Gd $50
Same as Model 5 except w/peep rear hooded front sights. Made from 1936 to 1942.

MODEL 6 AUTOLOADING RIFLE. . . . . NiB $169 Ex $94 Gd $57
Takedown. Caliber: .22 Short, Long, LR; tubular mag. holds 21 Short, 17 Long, 15 LR. Bbl.: 24 inches. Weight: 6 lbs. Open rear, bead front sights. Checkered pistol-grip stock on pre-WWII models. Postwar rifles have plain stocks. Made from 1938 to 1968.

MODEL 6S . . . . NiB $170 Ex $95 Gd $48
Same as Model 6 except w/peep rear, bead front sights. Made from 1938 to 1942.

MODEL 7 AUTOLOADING RIFLE. . . . . NiB $165 Ex $105 Gd $59
Same general specifications as Model 6 except w/5-round detachable box magazine. Made from 1939 to 1951.

MODEL 7S . . . . NiB $165 Ex $105 Gd $62
Same as Model 7 except w/peep rear sight, hooded front. Made from 1938 to 1942.

MODEL 19 BOLT-ACTION TARGET RIFLE . . . . NiB $325 Ex $270 Gd $209
Model of 1933. Speed lock. Caliber: .22-LR. Five round detachable box magazine. 25-inch bbl. Weight: 8 lbs. Adj. rear peep sight, blade front on early models, later production equipped w/extension rear sight, hooded front. Target stock w/full pistol-grip and beavertail forearm. Made from 1933 to 1946.

Savage Industries

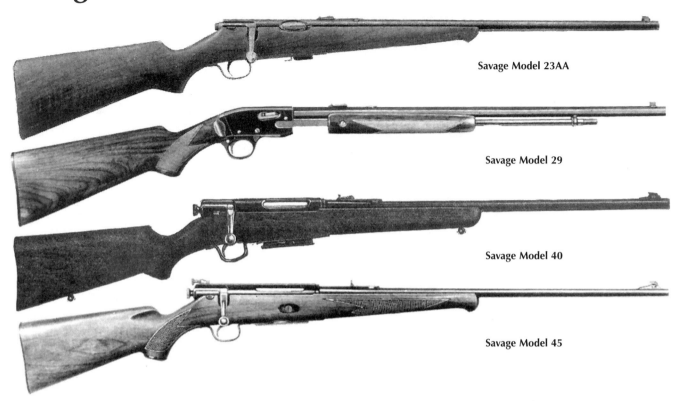

Savage Model 23AA

Savage Model 29

Savage Model 40

Savage Model 45

MODEL 19 NRA BOLT-ACTION
MATCH RIFLE . . . . **NiB $300 Ex $205 Gd $125**
Model of 1919. Caliber: .22 LR. Five round detachable box maga-
zine. 25-inch bbl. Weight: 7 lbs. Sights: Adj. rear peep; blade front.
Full military stock w/pistol-grip. Made from 1919 to 1933.

MODEL 19H . . . . **NiB $575 Ex $340 Gd $265**
Same as standard Model 19 (1933) except chambered for .22
Hornet, w/Model 23D-type bolt mechanism, loading port and
magazine. Made from 1933 to 1942.

MODEL 19L . . . . **NiB $348 Ex $290 Gd $185**
Same as standard Model 19 (1933) except w/Lyman No. 48Y receiver sight, 17A front sight. Made from 1933 to 1942.

MODEL 19M . . . . **NiB $356 Ex $465 Gd $225**
Same as standard Model 19 (1933) except w/heavy 28-inch bbl.
w/scope bases, weight: 9.25 lbs. Made from 1933 to 1942.

MODEL 20-1926
HI-POWER . . . . **NiB $935 Ex $725 Gd $420**
Same as Model 1920 except w/24-inch medium-weight bbl., Lyman
No. 54 peep sight, improved stock. Weight: 7 lbs. Made from 1926
to 1929.

MODEL 23A BOLT-ACTION
SPORTING RIFLE . . . . **NiB $270 Ex $208 Gd $177**
Caliber: 22 LR. Five round detachable box magazine. 23-inch bbl.
Weight: 6 lbs. Sights: Open rear, blade or bead front. Plain pistol-
grip stock w/slender forearm and Schnabel tip. Made from 1923
to 1933.

MODEL 23AA . . . . **NiB $370 Ex $275 Gd $200**
Model of 1933. Improved version of Model 23A w/same general
specifications except w/speed lock, improved stock, weighs 6.5 lbs.
Made from 1933 to 1942.

MODEL 23B . . . . **NiB $330 Ex $235 Gd $179**
Same as Model 23A except in .25-20. Bbl.: 25 inches. Improved stock
w/full forearm. Weight: 6.5 lbs. Made from 1923 to 1942.

MODEL 23C . . . . **NiB $389 Ex $290 Gd $175**
Same as Model 23B except in .32-20. Made from 1923 to 1942.

MODEL 23D . . . . **NiB $415 Ex $300 Gd $220**
Same as Model 23B except in .22 Hornet. Made from 1933 to 1947.

MODEL 25 SLIDE-ACTION REPEATER . . . . **NiB $346 Ex $391 Gd $237**
Takedown hammerless. Caliber: .22 Short, Long, LR; tubular mag.
holds 20 Short, 127 Long, 15 LR. Bbl.: 24-inch octagon. Weight:
5.75 lbs. Open rear, blade front sights. Plain pistol-grip stock.
Grooved slide handle. Made from 1925 to 1929.

MODEL 29 SLIDE-ACTION
REPEATER . . . . **NiB $500 Ex $377 Gd $265**
Takedown, hammerless. Caliber: .22 Short, Long, LR; tubular mag.
holds 20 Short, 17 Long, 15 LR. Bbl.: 24-inch octagon on pre-WWII
models, round on post-war production. Weight: 5.5 lbs. Open rear,
bead front sights. Stock w/checkered pistol grip and slide handle on
prewar models, plain stock and grooved forearm on post-war production. Made from 1929 to 1967.

MODEL 40 BOLT-ACTION
SPORTING RIFLE . . . . **NiB $379 Ex $280 Gd $225**
Standard Grade. Calibers: .250-3000 Sav., .300 Sav., .30-30, .30-06; four-round
detachable box mag. Bb: 22 inches in .250-3000 and .30-30; 24 inches in .300
Sav., and .30-06. Weight: 76.45 lbs. Open rear, bead ramp front sights.

MODEL 45 SUPER SPORTER . . . . . **NiB $423 Ex $265 Gd $220**
Special Grade. Same as Model 40 except w/checkered pistol-grip
and forearm, Lyman No. 40 receiver sight. Made from 1928 to
1940.

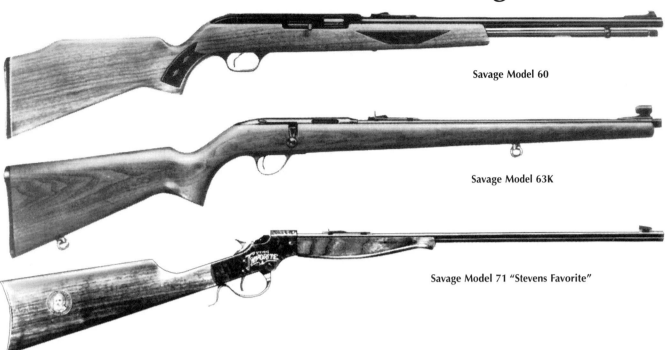

Savage Model 60

Savage Model 63K

Savage Model 71 "Stevens Favorite"

MODEL 60 AUTOLOADING RIFLE. . . . . **NiB $115 Ex $80 Gd $48**
Caliber: .22 LR; 15-round tubular mag. Bbl.: 20 inches. Weight:
6 lbs. Open rear, ramp front sights. Walnut Monte Carlo stock
w/checkered pistol grip and forearm. Made from 1969 to 1972.

MODEL 63K KEY LOCK BOLT-ACTION
SINGLE-SHOT RIFLE. . . . . **NiB $120 Ex $90 Gd $60**
Caliber: .22 Short, Long, LR. Bbl.: 18 inches. Trigger locked w/key.
Weight: 4 lbs. Open rear, hooded ramp front sights. Full-length
stock w/pistol grip, swivels. Made from 1970 to 1972.

MODEL 63KM . . . . **NiB $125 Ex $98 Gd $63**
Same as Model 63K except chambered for .22 WMR. Made from 1970
to 1972.

MODEL 64F AUTOLOADING RIFLE. . . . . . . **NiB $173 Ex $128 Gd $99**
Same general specifications as Model 64G except w/black graphite/
polymer stock. Weight: 5 lbs. Made from 1997 to date.

MODEL 64G AUTOLOADING RIFLE . . . . . **NiB $177 Ex $125 Gd $100**
Caliber: .22 LR; 10-round mag. Bbl.: 20 inches. Weight: 5.5 lbs. Lgt.:
40 inches. Adj. open rear, bead front sights. Receiver grooved for
scope mounts. Stamped checkering on walnut-finished hardwood
stock. Monte Carlo cheekpiece. Made from 1996 to date.

MODEL 71 "STEVENS FAVORITE"
SINGLE-SHOT LEVER-ACTION RIFLE. . . . . . **NiB $229 Ex $114 Gd $98**
Replica of original Stevens Favorite issued as a tribute to Joshua
Stevens, "Father of .22 Hunting." Caliber: .22 LR. 22-inch full-
octagon bbl. Brass-plated hammer and lever. Sights: Open rear;
brass blade front. Weight: 4.5 lbs. Plain straight-grip buttstock and
Schnabel forend; brass commemorative medallion inlaid in butt-
stock, brass crescent-shaped buttplate. 10,000 produced in 1971.

MODEL 90 AUTO-LOADING
CARBINE. . . . . **NiB $194 Ex $161 Gd $126**
Similar to Model 60 except w/16.5-inch bbl. Folding leaf rear, bead
front sights. 10-round tubular mag. Uncheckered carbine-style
walnut stock w/bbl. band, sling swivels. Weight: 5.75 lbs. Made
from 1969 to 1972.

MODEL 93G BOLT-ACTION RIFLE. . . . . . . **NiB $225 Ex $166 Gd $125**
Caliber: .22 WMR; fie-round mag. Bbl.: 20.75 inches. Lgt.: 39.5
inches. Weight: 5.75 lbs. Adj. open rear, bead front sights. Receiver
grooved for scope mounts. Stamped checkering on walnut-finished
hardwood Monte Carlo stock. Made from 1996 to date.

MODEL 93F BOLT-ACTION RIFLE . . . . **NiB $277 Ex $124 Gd $110**
Same specifications as Model 93G except w/black graphite/polymer
stock. Weight: 5.2 lbs. Made from 1997 to date.

MODEL 99A (I). . . . . **NiB $1015 Ex $768 Gd $545**
Hammerless. Solid frame. Calibers: .30-30, .300 Sav., .303 Sav.
Five-round rotary magazine. 24-inch bbl. Weight: 7.25 lbs. Sights:
Open rear; bead front, on ramp. Plain straight-grip stock, tapered
forearm. Made from 1920 to 1936.

MODEL 99A (II) . . . . **NiB $915 Ex $668 Gd $445**
Similar to original Model 99A except w/top tang safety, 22-inch bbl.
Folding leaf rear sight; no crescent buttplate. Calibers: .243 Win.,
.250 Sav., .300 Sav., .308 Win. Made from 1971 to 1982.

MODEL 99B . . . . **NiB $1245 Ex $938 Gd $577**
Takedown. Same as Model 99A. Weight: 7.5 lbs.

Savage Industries

Savage Model 90

Savage Model 99A 1971 Issue

Savage Model 99C

Savage Model 99CD

Savage Model 99DE

MODEL 99C . . . . **NiB $560 Ex $488 Gd $399**
Same as Model 99F except w/clip mag. Calibers: .243 Win., .284 Win., .308 Win.; four-round detachable mag. holds four rounds (three in .284). Weight: 6.75 lbs. Made from 1965 to 1998.

MODEL 99CD . . . . **NiB $698 Ex $599 Gd $389**
Deluxe version of Model 99C. Calibers: .243 Win., .250 Sav., .308 Win. Hooded ramp front sight. Weight: 8.25 lbs. Monte Carlo stock, checkered pistol grip, grooved forearm, swivels, sling. Made from 1975 to 1981.

MODEL 99DE CITATION GRADE . . . . **NiB $955 Ex $679 Gd $490**
Same as Model 99PE except w/less elaborate engraving. Made from 1968 to 1970.

MODEL 99DL DELUXE . . . . **NiB $745 Ex $576 Gd $359**
Post-WWII model. Same as Model 99A. Calibers: .243 Win., .308 Win. Same as Model 99F except w/high comb Monte Carlo stock, sling swivels. Weight: 6.75 lbs. Made from 1960 to 1973.

MODEL 99E CARBINE (I) . . . . **NiB $656 Ex $500 Gd $435**
Pre-WWII type. Solid frame. Calibers: .22 Hi-Power, .250/3000, .30/30, .300 Sav., .303 Sav. w/22-inch bbl.; .300 Sav. 24-inch. Weight: 7 lbs. Made from 1920 to 1936.

MODEL 99E CARBINE (II) . . . . **NiB $709 Ex $505 Gd $457**
Solid frame. Caliber: .250 Sav., .243 Win., .300 Sav., .308 Win. Bbl.: 20 or 22 inches. Checkered pistol-grip stock and forearm. Made from 1960 to 1989.

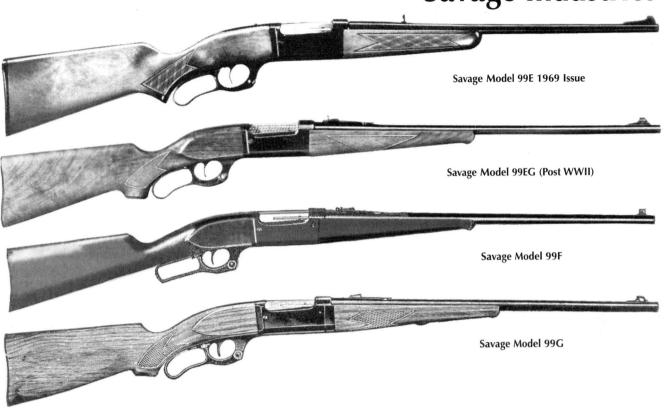

Savage Model 99E 1969 Issue

Savage Model 99EG (Post WWII)

Savage Model 99F

Savage Model 99G

MODEL 99EG (I). . . . . **NiB $877 Ex $687 Gd $476**
Pre-WWII type. Same as Model G except w/solid frame, plain
pistol-grip stock and forearm. Made from 1936 to 1941.

MODEL 99EG (II) . . . . **NiB $1023 Ex $799 Gd $600**
Post-WWII type. Same as prewar model except w/checkered stock
and forearm. Calibers: .250 Sav., .300 Sav., .308 Win. (intro. 1955),
.243 Win., and .358 Win. Made from 1946 to 1960.

MODEL 99F
FEATHERWEIGHT (I) . . . . **NiB $813 Ex $700 Gd $514**
Pre-WWII type. Takedown. Specifications same as Model 99E,
except weight: 6.5 lbs. Made from 1920 to 1942.

MODEL 99F
FEATHERWEIGHT (II) . . . . **NiB $945 Ex $735 Gd $567**
Post-WWII model. Solid frame Calibers: .243 Win., .300 Sav., .308
Win. Bbl.: 6.5 lbs. Made from 1955 to 1973.

MODEL 99G . . . . **NiB $1290 Ex $933 Gd $700**
Takedown. Checkered pistol-grip stock and forearm. Weight: 7.25 lbs.
Other specifications same as Model 99E. Made from 1920 to 1942.

MODEL 99H CARBINE . . . . **NiB $926 Ex $577 Gd $4455**
Solid frame. Calibers: .250/3000, .30/30, .303 Sav. 20-inch special
weight bbl. Walnut carbine stock w/metal buttplate; walnut forearm
w/bbl. band. Weight: 6.5 lbs. Open rear sights; ramped blade front
sight. Other specifications same as Model 99A. Made from 1931 to
1942.

MODEL 99K . . . . **NiB $3854 Ex $2650 Gd $2128**
Deluxe version of Model G w/similar specifications except w/fancy
stock and engraving on receiver and bbl. Lyman peep rear sight and
folding middle. Made from 1931 to 1942.

MODEL 99PE PRESENTATION GRADE . . **NiB $2055 Ex $1700 Gd $854**
Same as Model 99DL except w/engraved receiver (games scenes on
sides), tang and lever. Fancy walnut Monte Carlo stock and forearm w/
hand checkering. QD swivels. Calibers: .243 Win., .284 Rem. .308 Win.
Made from 1968 to 1970.

Savage Industries

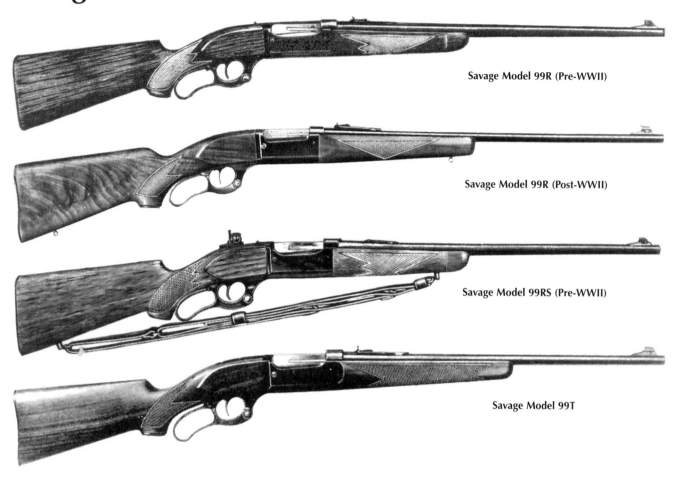

Savage Model 99R (Pre-WWII)

Savage Model 99R (Post-WWII)

Savage Model 99RS (Pre-WWII)

Savage Model 99T

MODEL 99R (I) . . . . **NiB $735 Ex $588 Gd $499**
Pre-WWII type. Solid frame. Calibers: .250-3000 (22-inch bbl.),
.300 Sav. (24-inch bbl.). Weight: 7.5 lbs. Special large checkered
pistol-grip stock and forearm. Specs same as Model 99 rifle. Made
from 1936 to 1942.

MODEL 99R (II) . . . . **NiB $689 Ex $498 Gd $356**
Post-WWII type. Same as prewar models except w/24-inch bbl..
Calibers: .250 Sav., .300 Sav., .308 in., .243 Win., .358 Win. Made
from 1946 to 1960.

MODEL 99RS (I) . . . . **NiB $935 Ex $644 Gd $489**
Pre-WWII type. Same as prewar Model 99R except equipped w/
Lyman rear peep sight and folding middle sight, quick detachable
swivels and sling. Made from 1932 to 1942.

MODEL 99RS (II) . . . . **NiB $756 Ex $600 Gd $467**
Post-WWII type. Same as postwar Model 99RS except equipped w/
Redfield 70LH receiver sight, blank in middle sight slot. Made from 1946
to 1960.

MODEL 99T . . . . **NiB $1690 Ex $1032 Gd $744**
Featherweight. Solid frame. Calibers: .22 Hi-Power, .30/30, .303
Sav. w/20-inch bbl.; .300 Sav. w/22-inch bbl. Checkered pistol-grip
stock and beavertail forearm. Weight: 7 lbs. Specifications same as
other Model 99 rifles. Made from 1936 to 1942.

MODEL 99-358. . . . . **NiB $1156 Ex $903 Gd $657**
Similar to Model 99A except caliber .358 Win. Grooved forearm,
recoil pad, swivel studs. Made from 1977 to 1980.

MODEL 110 SPORTER
BOLT-ACTION RIFLE . . . . **NiB $420 Ex $333 Gd $155**
Caliber: .243 Win., .270 Win., .308 Win., .30-06; four-round mag.
Bbl.: 22 inches. Weight: 6.75 lbs. Open rear, ramp front sights.
Standard sporter stock w/checkered pistol grip. Made from 1958
to 1963.

MODEL 110B BOLT-ACTION RIFLE
Same as Model 110E except with checkered select walnut Monte
Carlo-style stock (early models) or brown laminated stock (late mod-
els). Calibers: .243 Win., .270 Win. .30-06, 7mm Rem. Mag., .338
Win. Mag. Made from 1976 to 1991.
Early model. . . . . **NiB $423 Ex $303 Gd $225**
Laminated stock model. . . . . **NiB $367 Ex $299 Gd $211**

MODEL 110BL . . . . **NiB $439 Ex $369 Gd $267**
Same as Model 110B except has left-hand action.

MODEL 110C
Calibers: .22-250 Rem., .243 Win., .25-06 Rem., .270 Win., .308
Win., .30-06, 7mm Rem. Mag., .300 Win. Mag.; four-round detachable clip mag. (three rounds in magnum calibers). Bbl.: 22 inches.
(24 inches in .22-250). Weight: 6.75 lbs. (magnum calibers 7.75 to
8 lbs.). Open rear, ramp front sights. Checkered Monte Carlo-style
walnut stock (recoil pad on magnum calibers). Made from 1966 to
1988.
Standard calibers . . . . **NiB $468 Ex $413 Gd $239**
Magnum calibers . . . . **NiB $639 Ex $455 Gd $279**

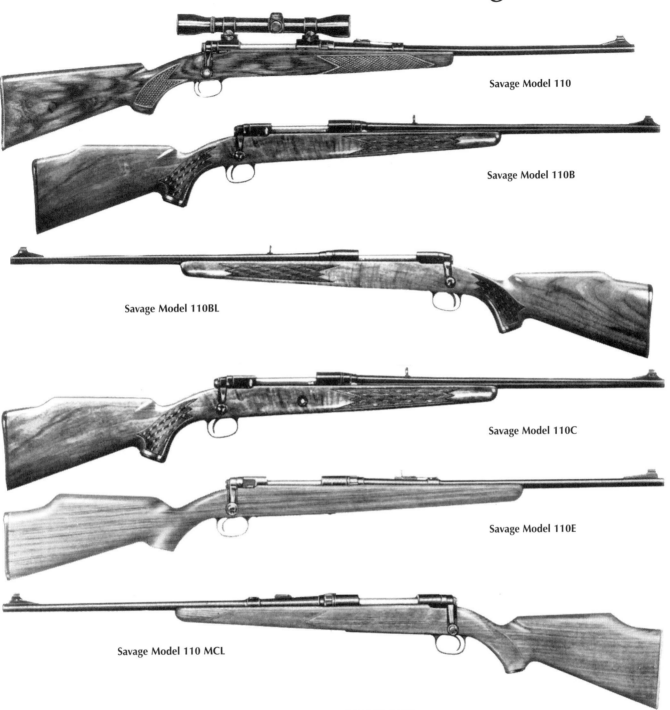

Savage Model 110

Savage Model 110B

Savage Model 110BL

Savage Model 110C

Savage Model 110E

Savage Model 110 MCL

MODEL 110CL
Same as Model 110C except w/left-hand action. Calibers: .243 Win., .30-06, .270 Win., 7mm Rem. Mag. Made from 1963 to 1966.
Standard calibers . . . . NiB $488 Ex $369 Gd $262
Magnum calibers . . . . NiB $459 Ex $350 Gd $255

MODEL 110CY
YOUTH/LADIES RIFLE . . . . NiB $466 Ex $379 Gd $228
Same as Model 110G except with walnut-finished hardwood stock with 12.5-inch pull. Calibers: .243 Win. and .300 Savage. Made from 1991 to 2009.

MODEL 110D
Similar to Model 110C except has internal magazine with hinged floorplate. Calibers: .243 Win., .270 Win., .30-06, 7mm Rem. Mag., .300 Win. Mag. Made from 1972 to 1988.
Standard calibers . . . . NiB $390 Ex $310 Gd $240
Magnum calibers . . . . NiB $453 Ex $390 Gd $259

MODEL 110DL
Same as Model 110D except has left-hand action. Disc.
Standard calibers . . . . NiB $500 Ex $413 Gd $297
Magnum calibers . . . . NiB $535 Ex $430 Gd $319

Savage Industries

Savage Model 110P

Savage Model 110PE

MODEL 110E . . . . NiB $379 Ex $255 Gd $198
Caliber: .22-250, .223 Rem., .243 Win., .270 Win., .308 Win., 7mm rem. Mag., .30-06; four-round box mag. (three rounds in magnums). Bbl.: 20 or 22 inches (24-inch stainless steel in magnums). Weight: 6.75 lbs. 7.75 lbs. in magnum. Open rear, ramp front sights. Plain Monte Carlo stock on early production; later models have checkered walnut-finished hardwood stocks (recoil pad on magnums). Made from 1963 to 1989.

MODEL 110EL . . . . NiB $366 Ex $248 Gd $185
Same as Model 110E except has left-hand action made in .30-06 and 7mm Rem. Mag. Made from 1969 to 1973.

MODEL 110F/110K BOLT-ACTION RIFLE
Same as Model 110E except w/black Rynite synthetic stock, swivel studs. Made from 1988 to 1993. Model 110K has laminated camouflage stock, made from 1986 to 1988.
Adj. sights . . . . NiB $770 Ex $470 Gd $359
W/out sights . . . . NiB $735 Ex $355 Gd $277
Standard calibers . . . . NiB $355 Ex $320 Gd $256
Magnum calibers . . . . NiB $520 Ex $399 Gd $287

MODEL 110FM SIERRA ULTRA LIGHT . . . NiB $376 Ex $336 Gd $244
Calibers: .243 Win., .270 Win., .30-06, .308 Win.; five-round mag. Bbl.: 20 inches. Lgt.: 41.5 inches. Weight: 6.25 lbs. No sights. Drilled and tapped for scope mounts. Black graphite/fiberglass composition stock. Non-glare matte blue finish. Made from 1996 to date.

MODEL 110FP POLICE RIFLE . . . . . NiB $610 Ex $355 Gd $265
Caliber: .243 Win., .270 Win.; four-round mag., Bbl.: 24 inches. Lgt.: 45.5 inches. Weight: 9 lbs. Black Rynite composite stock. Matte blue finish. Made from 1990 to date.

MODEL 110G BOLT-ACTION RIFLE
Calibers: .223 Rem., .22-250 Rem., .243 Win., .270 Win., 7mm Rem. Mag., .308 Win., .30-06, .300 Win. Mag.; five-round (standard) or four-round mag. (magnums). Bbl.: 22 or 24 inches. Lgt.: 42.38 inches. Weight: 6.75 to 7.5 lbs. Ramp front, adj. rear sights. Checkered walnut-finished hardwood stock, rubber recoil pad. Made from 1989 to 1993.
Standard calibers . . . . NiB $408 Ex $309 Gd $220
Magnum calibers . . . . NiB $455 Ex $335 Gd $259
Left-hand, no sights. . . . . NiB $355 Ex $369 Gd $271

MODEL 110GV VARMINT RIFLE . . . . NiB $369 Ex $335 Gd $268
Similar to Model 110G except fitted with medium-weight varmint bbl.; no sights. Drilled and tapped for scope mounts. Calibers: .22-250 Rem. and .223 Rem. only. Made from 1989 to 1993.

MAGNUM 110M MAGNUM . . . . . . NiB $445 Ex $345 Gd $269
Same as Model 110MC except calibers: 7mm Rem. Mag. .264, .300 and .338 Win. 24-inch bbl. Recoil pad. Weight: 7.75 to 8 lbs. Made from 1963 to 1969.

MODEL 110MC . . . . NiB $444 Ex $229 Gd $149
Same as Model 110 except w/Monte Carlo stock. Calibers: .22-250 Rem., .243 Win., .270 Win., .308 Win. .30-06. Bbl.: 24 inches in .22-250. Made from 1959 to 1969.
Model 110MCL. . . . . NiB $400 Ex $215 Gd $135

MODEL 110P PREMIER GRADE
Caliber: .243 Win., 7mm Rem. Mag., .30-06; four-round mag. (three rounds in magnums). Bbl.: 22 inches (24 inch stainless steel in magnums). Weight: 7 Lbs.; 7.75 lbs. in magnums). Open folding leaf rear, ramp front sights. French walnut Monte Carlo stock, rosewood forend tip and grip cap; skip checkering. Sling swivels. Recoil pad on magnums. Made from 1964 to 1970.
Calibers .243 Win. and .30-06 . . . . NiB $798 Ex $645 Gd $459
Caliber 7mm Rem. Mag. . . . . NiB $945 Ex $765 Gd $545

MODEL 110PE PRESENTATION GRADE
Same as Model 110P except has engraved receiver, floorplate and trigger guard. Choice grade French walnut stock. Made from 1968 to 1970.
Calibers .243 Win. and .30-06 . . . . NiB $555 Ex $441 Gd $290
Caliber 7mm Rem. Mag. . . . . NiB $600 Ex $455 Gd $344

MODEL 110PEL PRESENTATION GRADE
Same as Model 110PE except has left-hand action.
Calibers .243 Win. and .30-06 . . . . NiB $825 Ex $745 Gd $500
Caliber 7mm Rem. Mag. . . . . NiB $910 Ex $800 Gd $608

MODEL 110PL PREMIER GRADE
Same as Model 110P except has left-hand action.
Calibers .243 Win. and .30-06 . . . . NiB $675 Ex $485 Gd $365
Caliber 7mm Rem. Mag. . . . . NiB $700 Ex $515 Gd $400

MODEL 110S/110V
Same as Model 110E except Model 110S in .308 Win. only, disc. 1985. Model 110V in . 22-250 Rem. and .223 Rem. w/heavy 22-inch bbl. Lgt.: 47 inches. Weight: 9 lbs. Disc. 1989.
Model 110S. . . . . NiB $397 Ex $315 Gd $240
Model 110V . . . . NiB $416 Ex $322 Gd $248

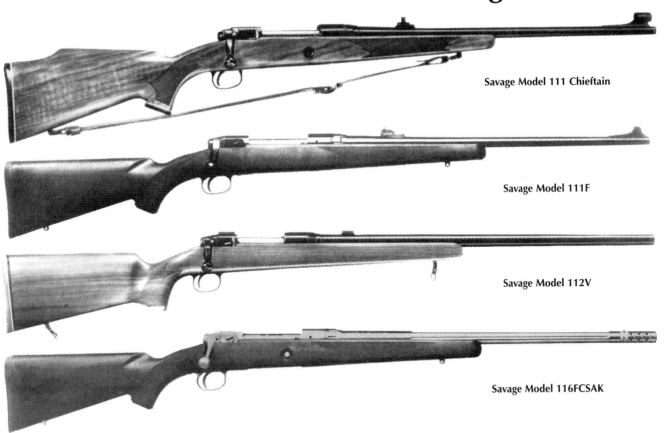

Savage Model 111 Chieftain

Savage Model 111F

Savage Model 112V

Savage Model 116FCSAK

MODEL 111 CHIEFTAIN BOLT-ACTION RIFLE

Caliber: .243 Win., .270 Win., 7x57mm, 7mm Rem. Mag.., .30-06; four-round clip mag. (three rounds in magnums). Bbl.: 22 inches. (24 inches in magnums). Weight: 7.5 lbs (8.25 lbs in magnums). Leaf rear, hooded ramp front sights. Select walnut Monte Carlo stock; checkered pistol grip cap; QD swivels, sling. Made from 1974 to 1979.

Standard calibers . . . . NiB $444 Ex $389 Gd $259
Magnum calibers . . . . NiB $445 Ex $398 Gd $279

MODEL 111F, 11FC, 111FNS CLASSIC HUNTER RIFLE

Similar to the Model 111G except with graphite/fiberglass composite stock. Weight: 6.25 lbs. Made from 1994 to date.

Model 111F (right- or left-hand w/box mag.). . NiB $498 Ex $411 Gd $238
MODEL 111FC (w/detachable mag.) . . . . . NiB $448 Ex $335 Gd $206
Model 111FNS (right- or left-hand
w/detachable mag.) . . . . NiB $469 Ex $355 Gd $228

MODEL 111G, 111GC, 111GNS CLASSIC HUNTER RIFLE

Calibers: .22-250 Rem., .223 Rem., .243 Win., .25-06 Rem. .250 Sav., .270 Win., 7mm-08 Rem., 7mm Rem. Mag., .30-06, .300 Sav., .300 Win. Mag., .308 Win., .338 Win. 22- or 24-inch bbl. Weight: 7 lbs. Ramp front sight, adj. open rear. Walnut-finished hardwood stock. Blued finish. Made from 1994 to date.

Model 111G (right- or left-hand w/box mag.). . NiB $365 Ex $298 Gd $210
Model 111GC (right- or left-hand w/
detachable mag.). . . . . NiB $465 Ex $358 Gd $225
Model 111GNS (w box mag., no sights) . . . NiB $366 Ex $300 Gd $198

MODEL 112BV,112BVSS HEAVY VARMINT RIFLES

Similar to the Model 110G except fitted with 26-inch heavy bbl., laminated high comb wood stock. .22-250 Rem. and .223 Rem. only.

Model 112BV (Made 1993-94) . . . . NiB $520 Ex $378 Gd $266
Model 112BVSS (w/fluted stainless
bbl., intro. 1994) . . . . NiB $556 Ex $422 Gd $315

MODEL 112FVVS, 112FVSS VARMINT RIFLE

Similar to Model 110G except w/26-inch heavy bbl, DuPont Rynite stock. Calibers: .22-250 Rem., .223 Rem., .220 Swift (Model112FVS only). Blued or stainless finish. Made from 1991 to date

Model 112RV (blued finish) . . . . NiB $420 Ex $355 Gd $261
Model 112FV-S (blued finish,
single-shot, disc. 1993) . . . . NiB $533 Ex $445 Gd $398
Model 112FVSS (stainless finish). . . . . NiB $645 Ex $545 Gd $390
Model 112 FVSS-S (stainless finish, single-shot). . NiB $645 Ex $545 Gd $390

MODEL 112V VARMINT RIFLE. . . . NiB $389 Ex $289 Gd $200

Bolt-action, single-shot. Caliber: .220 Swift, .222 Rem., .223 Rem., .22-250 Rem. .243 Win., .25-06 Rem. Bbl.: heavy, 26 inches w/scope bases. No sights. Weight: 9.25 lbs. Select walnut varmint-style stock w/checkered pistol grip, high comb. QD swivels. Made from 1975 to 1979.

MODEL 114C, 114CE, 114CU RIFLES

Calibers: .270 Win., 7mm Rem. Mag., .30-06, .300 Win. Mag.; detachable three- or four-round mag. Bbl.: 22 or 24 inches. Weight: 7 lbs. Ramp front, adjustable open rear sights. (Model 114CU has no sights). Checkered select walnut stock w/oil finish. Red butt pad. Schnabel forend and skip-line checkering (Model 114CE). High-luster blued finish. Made from 1991 to date.

Model 114C (Classic) . . . . NiB $745 Ex $588 Gd $338
Model 114CE (Classic European) . . . . NiB $533 Ex $390 Gd $300
Model 114CU (Classic Ultra) . . . . NiB $540 Ex $400 Gd $310

Savage Industries

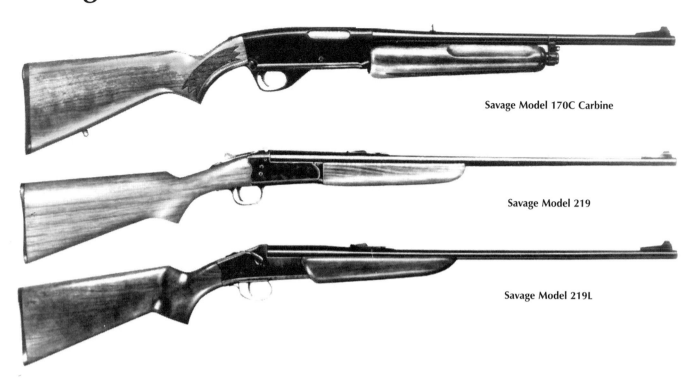

Savage Model 170C Carbine

Savage Model 219

Savage Model 219L

MODELS 116FSAK, 116FCSAK BOLT-ACTION RIFLES
Similar to the Model 116FSK except in .270 Win., .30-06, 7mm Mag., .300 Win. Mag., .338 Win. Mag. Fluted 22-inch stainless bbl. w/adj. muzzle brake. Weight: 6.5 lbs. Made from 1994 to date.
Model 116FSAK . . . . NiB $590 Ex $443 Gd $338
Model 116FCSAK (detachable mag.). . . . . NiB $645 Ex $547 Gd $379

MODELS 116FSC, 116FSS BOLT-ACTION RIFLES
Improved Model 110 with satin stainless action and bbl. Caliber: .223 Rem., .243 Win., .270 Win., .30-06, 7mm Rem .Mag., ,300 Win. Mag., .338 Win Mag.; four- or five-round mag. Bbl.: 22 or 24 inches. No sights. Receiver drilled and tapped for scope mounts. Weight: 7.5 lbs. Black Rynite stock w/recoil pad and swivel studs. Made from 1991 to date.
Model 116FSS . . . . NiB $677 Ex $544 Gd $339
Model 116FSC, detachable magazine . . . . . NiB $688 Ex $554 Gd $349

MODEL 116FSK KODIAK RIFLE . . . . NiB $535 Ex $380 Gd $275
Similar to Model 116FSS except with 22-inch bbl. chambered for 338 Win. Mag. only. "Shock Suppressor" recoil reducer. Made from 1994 to 2000.

MODEL 116-SE, 116-US RIFLES
Caliber: .270 Win., 7mm Rem. Mag., .30-06, .300 Win. Mag (Model 116US); .300 Win. Mag., .338 Win Mag., .435 Express, .458 Win. Mag (Model 116SE); three-round mag. Bbl.: 24 inches (muzzle brake on Model 116SE only). Three-leaf Express sights (Model 116SE only). Lgt.: 45.5 inches. Weight: 7.2 to 8.5 lbs. Stainless finish. Checkered classic-style select walnut stock w/ebony forend tip. Made from 1994 to 2004.
Model 116SE (Safari Express) . . . . . NiB $947 Ex $788 Gd $556
Model 116US (Ultra Stainless) . . . . NiB $660 Ex $498 Gd $400

MODEL 170 PUMP-ACTION
CENTERFIRE RIFLE . . . . NiB $249 Ex $190 Gd $106
Calibers: .30-30, .35 Rem. Three round tubular magazine. 22-inch bbl. Weight: 6.75 lbs. Sights: Folding leaf rear; ramp front. Select walnut stock w/checkered pistol-grip Monte Carlo comb, grooved slide handle. Made from 1970 to 1981.

MODEL 170C CARBINE . . . . NiB $280 Ex $322 Gd $166
Same as Model 170 Rifle except in .30-30 only w/18.5-inch bbl.. Straight comb stock. Weight: 6 lbs. Made from 1974 to 1981.

MODEL 219 SINGLE-SHOT RIFLE . . NiB $225 Ex $119 Gd $67
Hammerless. Takedown. Shotgun-type action with top lever. Calibers: .22 Hornet, .25-20, .32-20, .30-30. 26-inch bbl. Weight: 6 lbs. Sights: Open rear; bead front. Plain pistol-grip stock and forearm. Made from 1938 to 1965.
Model 219L (w/side lever, made 1965–67). . NiB $155 Ex $100 Gd $70

MODEL 221-229 UTILITY GUNS
Same as Model 219 except in various calibers in combination with an interchangeable shotgun bbl. Disc.
Model 221 (.30-30,12-ga. 30-inch bbl.) . . . . . NiB $155 Ex $80 Gd $55
Model 222 (.30-30,16-ga. 28-inch bbl.) . . . . . NiB $155 Ex $80 Gd $55
Model 223 (.30-30, 20-ga. 28-inch bbl.). . . . . NiB $155 Ex $80 Gd $55
Model 227 (.22 Hornet, 12-ga. 30-inch bbl.) . . . . NiB $155 Ex $80 Gd $55
Model 228 (.22 Hornet, 16-ga. 28-inch bbl.) . . . NiB $155 Ex $80 Gd $55
Model 229 (.22 Hornet, 20-ga. 28-inch bbl.) . . . NiB $155 Ex $80 Gd $55

MODEL 340 BOLT-ACTION REPEATER
Caliber: .22 Hornet, .222 Rem., .223 Rem. .225 Win., .30-30; four-round clip mag. (three rounds in .30-30). Bbl.: 20 inches in .30-30, 22 inches in .22 Hornet. Later models have 22-inch bbls. in .30-30, 24 inches in other calibers. Weight: 6.5 to 7.5 lbs. Open rear (folding leaf on later production) ramp front sights. Early models had plain pistol-grip stock; checkered since 1965. Made from 1950 to 1985. Rifles produced between 1947 and 1950 were .22 Hornet Stevens Model 322 and .30-30 Model 325. The Savage rifle was designated Model 340 for all calibers.
Pre-1965 with plain stock . . . . NiB $266 Ex $190 Gd $105
Savage Model 340C Carbine. . . . . . NiB $275 Ex $228 Gd $140

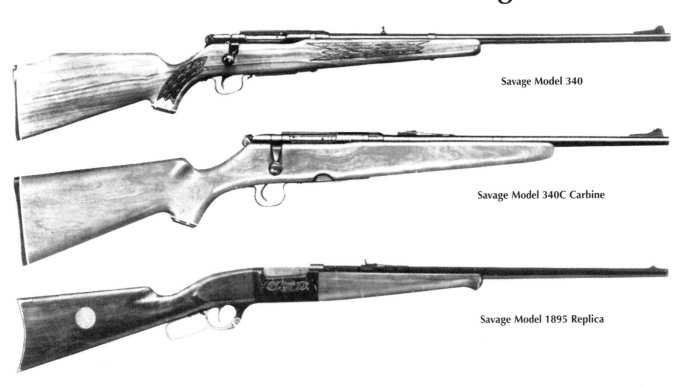

Savage Model 340

Savage Model 340C Carbine

Savage Model 1895 Replica

MODEL 340S DELUXE . . . . **NiB $345 Ex $298 Gd $218**
Same as Model 340 except w/checkered stock, screw in sling swivels; peep rear sight, hooded front sights. Made from 1955 to 1960.

MODEL 342 . . . . **NiB $345 Ex $298 Gd $218**
Designated Model 340 of 1950 to 1955, .22 Hornet only.

MODEL 342S DELUXE . . . . **NiB $355 Ex $325 Gd $225**
Designated Model 340S of 1950 to 1955. .22 Hornet only.

ANNIVERSARY MODEL
1895 LEVER-ACTION . . . . **NiB $6235 Ex $4589 Gd $2240**
Replica of Savage Model 1895 hammerless lever-action rifle. Issued to commemorate the 75th Anniversary (1895 to 1970) of Savage Arms Co. Caliber: .308 in.; five-round rotary mag., Bb.: Full-octagon, 24 inches. Engraved receiver, brass-plated lever. Open rear, brass blade front sights. Plain straight-grip buttstock, Scnhabel-type forend, brass crescent-shaped buttplate. Brass medallion inlaid in buttstock. 9,999 units produced. Made in 1970.

MODEL 1903 SLIDE-ACTION
REPEATER . . . . **NiB $733 Ex $549 Gd $366**
Hammerless. Takedown. Caliber: .22 Short, Long, LR. Detachable box magazine. 24-inch octagon bbl. Weight: 5 lbs. Sights: Open rear; bead front. Pistol-grip stock, grooved slide handle. Made from 1903 to 1921.

MODEL 1904 BOLT-ACTION
SINGLE-SHOT RIFLE. . . . . **NiB $228 Ex $140 Gd $90**
Takedown. .22 Short, Long, LR. 18-inch bbl. Weight: 3 lbs. Sights: Open rear; bead front. Plain, straight-grip, one-piece stock. Made from 1904 to 1917.

MODEL 1905 BOLT-ACTION
SINGLE-SHOT RIFLE. . . . . **NiB $220 Ex $138 Gd $85**
Takedown. .22 Short, Long, LR. 22-inch bbl. Weight: 5 lbs. Sights: Open rear; bead front. Plain, straight-grip one-piece stock. Made from 1905 to 1919.

MODEL 1909 SLIDE-ACTION
REPEATER . . . . **NiB $800 Ex $533 Gd $337**
Hammerless. Takedown. Similar to Model 1903 except has 20-inch round bbl., plain stock and forearm. Weight: 4.75 lbs. Made from 1909 to 1915.

MODEL 1912
AUTOLOADING RIFLE. . . . . **NiB $800 Ex $533 Gd $337**
Takedown. Caliber: 22 LR. only. Seven round detachable box magazine. 20-inch bbl., plain stock and forearm. Made from 1912 to 1916.

MODEL 1914 SLIDE-ACTION
REPEATER . . . . **NiB $520 Ex $344 Gd $239**
Hammerless. Takedown. Caliber: .22 Short, Long, LR, Tubular magazine holds 20 Short, 17 Long, 15 LR. 24-inch octagon bbl. Weight: 5.75 lbs. Sights: Open rear; bead front. Plain pistol-grip stock, grooved slide handle. Made from 1914 to 1924.

MODEL 1920 HI-POWER BOLT-ACTION RIFLE
Short Mauser-type action. Caliber: .250-3000, .300 Savage; five-round box mag., Bbl.: 22 inches in .250-3000, 24 inches in .300 Savage. Weight: 6 lbs. Open rear, bead front sights. Checkered pistol-trip stock w/slender forearm, Schnabel forend tip. Made from 1920 to 1926.
.250-3000 Savage . . . . **NiB $1029 Ex $833 Gd $690**
.300 Savage. . . . . **NiB $969 Ex $755 Gd $588**

Savage Industries

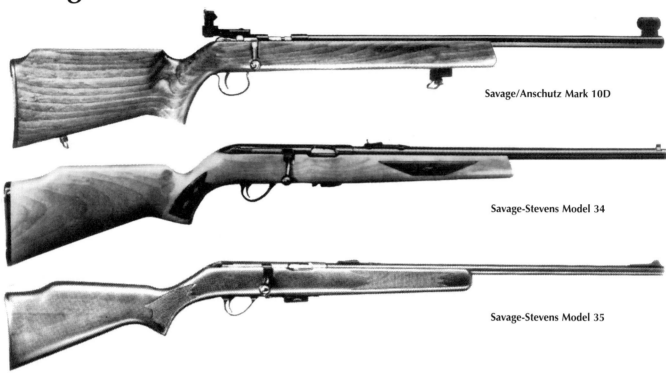

Savage/Anschutz Mark 10D

Savage-Stevens Model 34

Savage-Stevens Model 35

MARK 10 BOLT-ACTION
TARGET RIFLE. . . . . NiB $534 Ex $359 Gd $265
Single shot. Caliber: .22 LR. 26-inch bbl. Weight: 8.5 lbs. Sights:
Anschutz micrometer rear; globe front. Target stock w/full pistol-grip
and cheekpiece, adj. hand stop and swivel. Made from 1967 to 1972.

MARK 10D . . . . NiB $544 Ex $365 Gd $259
Same as Mark 10 except has redesigned stock with Monte Carlo
comb, different rear sight. Weight: 7.75 lbs. Made in 1972.

Note: *In 1965, Savage began the importation of rifles manufactured by J. G. Anschutz of West Germany. Models designated "Savage/Anschutz" Are listed in this section. Rifles marketed in the United States under the Anschutz name are included in that firm's listings. See Anschutz listing for detailed specifications.*

MODEL 54
CUSTOM SPORTER . . . . NiB $766 Ex $639 Gd $400
Same as Anschutz Model 1422D.

MODEL 54M. . . . . NiB $945 Ex $670 Gd $435
Same as Anschutz Model 1522D.

MODEL 64 BOLT-ACTION
TARGET RIFLE. . . . . NiB $655 Ex $512 Gd $335
Same as Anschutz Model 1403.

MODEL 153 BOLT-ACTION
SPORTER. . . . . NiB $697 Ex $488 Gd $349
Caliber: .222 Rem. Three round clip magazine. 24-inch bbl. Sights:
Folding leaf open rear; hooded ramp front. Weight: 6.75 lbs. French
walnut stock w/cheekpiece, skip checkering, rosewood forend tip
and grip cap, swivels. Made from 1964 to 1967.

MODEL 153S . . . . NiB $770 Ex $556 Gd $390
Same as Model 153 except has double-set trigger. Made from 1965 to 1967.

MODEL 164 CUSTOM SPORTER . . . . NiB $775 Ex $561 Gd $195
Same as Anschutz Model 1416.

MODEL 164M. . . . . NiB $660 Ex $454 Gd $300
Same as Anschutz Model 1516.
MODEL 184 SPORTER . . . . NiB $638 Ex $484 Gd $288
Same as Anschutz Model 1441.

NOTE: *J. Stevens Arms Co. (see also separate listings) is a division of Savage Industries. Certain Savage models carry the "Stevens" name.*

MODEL 34 BOLT-ACTION
REPEATER . . . . NiB $190 Ex $125 Gd $88
Caliber: .22 Short, Long, LR. 20-inch bbl. Weight: 4.75 lbs. Sights:
Open rear; bead front. Plain pistol-grip stock. Made from 1965 to
1980.

MODEL 34M. . . . . NiB $190 Ex $146 Gd $98
Same as Model 34 except chambered for 22 WMR. Made from 1969
to 1973.

MODEL 35 . . . . NiB $190 Ex $146 Gd $98
Bolt-action repeater. Caliber: 22 LR. Six round clip magazine. 22-inch
bbl. Weight: 5 lbs. Sights: Open rear; ramp front. Monte Carlo stock
w/checkered pistol grip and forearm. Made from 1982 to 1985.

MODEL 35M. . . . . NiB $219 Ex $140 Gd $100
Same as Model 35 except in .22 WMR. Made from 1982 to 1985.

MODEL 46 BOLT-ACTION
RIFLE. . . . . NiB $190 Ex $136 Gd $100
Caliber: .22 Short, Long, LR. Tubular magazine holds 22 Short, 17
Long, 15 LR. 20-inch bbl. Weight: 5 lbs. Plain pistol-grip stock on
early production; later models have Monte Carlo stock w/checkering. Made from 1969 to 1073.

MODEL 65
BOLT-ACTION RIFLE . . . . NiB $219 Ex $138 Gd $99
Caliber: .22 Short, Long, LR. Five round clip magazine. 20-inch
bbl. Weight: 5 lbs. Sights: Open rear; ramp front. Monte Carlo stock
w/checkered pistol grip and forearm. Made from 1969 to 1973.

Savage-Stevens Model 46

Savage-Stevens Model 65

Savage-Stevens Model 72 — Crackshot

Savage-Stevens Model 73

Savage-Stevens Model 80

MODEL 65M. . . . . **NiB $200 Ex $134 Gd $90**
Same as Model 65 except in .22 WMR, has 22-inch bbl., weighs 5.25 lbs. Made from 1969 to 1981.

MODEL 72 CRACKSHOT SINGLE-SHOT
LEVER-ACTION RIFLE. . . . . **NiB $190 Ex $109 Gd $79**
Falling-block action. Case-hardened frame. Caliber: .22 Short, Long, LR. Bbl.: Octagon, 22 inches. Weight: 4.5 lbs. Open rear, bead front sights. Plain straight-grip walnut stock and forend. Made from 1972 to 1989.

MODEL 73 BOLT-ACTION SINGLE-SHOT . . **NiB $159 Ex $138 Gd $89**
Caliber: .22 Short, Long, LR. 20-inch bbl. Weight: 4.75 lbs. Sights: Open rear; bead front. Plain pistol-grip stock. Made from 1965 to 1980.

MODEL 73Y YOUTH MODEL. . . . . . **NiB $150 Ex $110 Gd $90**
Same as Model 73 except w/18-inch bbl., one-inch shorter butt-stock. Weight: 4.5 lbs. Made from 1965 to 1980.

MODEL 74
LITTLE FAVORITE . . . . **NiB $165 Ex $115 Gd $98**
Same as Model 72 Crackshot except has black-finished frame, 22-inch round bbl., walnut-finished hardwood stock. Weight: 4.75 lbs. Made from 1972 to 1974.

MODEL 80
AUTOLOADING RIFLE . . . . **NiB $215 Ex $170 Gd $125**
Caliber: 22 LR. 15-round tubular magazine. 20-inch bbl. Weight: 6 lbs. Sights: Open rear, bead front. Monte Carlo stock of walnut w/checkered pistol-grip and forearm. Made from 1976 to date. (This rifle is the same as the Model 60 except w/different style checkering, side safety and plain bead front sight.)

MODEL 88
AUTOLOADING RIFLE . . . . **NiB $190 Ex $110 Gd $88**
Similar to Model 60 except has walnut-finished hardwood stock, plain bead front sight. Weight: 5.75 lbs. Made from 1969 to 1972.

Sears, Roebuck & Company

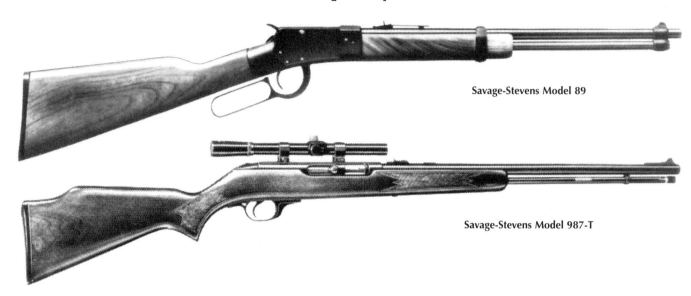

Savage-Stevens Model 89

Savage-Stevens Model 987-T

MODEL 89 SINGLE-SHOT
LEVER-ACTION CARBINE . . . . NiB $121 Ex $90 Gd $66
Martini-type action. Caliber: .22 Short, Long, LR. 18.5-inch bbl.
Weight: 5 lbs. Sights: Open rear; bead front. Western-style carbine
stock w/straight grip, forearm with bbl. band. Made from 1976 to
1989.

MODEL 987-T
AUTOLOADING RIFLE . . . . NiB $217 Ex $166 Gd $129
Caliber: .22 LR. 15-round tubular magazine. 20-inch bbl.
Weight: 6 lbs. Sights: Open rear; ramp front. Monte Carlo stock
w/checkered pistol grip and forearm. Made from 1981 to 1989.

V.C. SCHILLING — Suhl, Germany

MAUSER-MANNLICHER
BOLT ACTION SPORTING RIFLE . . NiB $938 Ex $744 Gd $539
Same general specifications as the Haenel Mauser-Mannlicher
Sporter. (See separate listing.)

'88 MAUSER SPORTER . . . . NiB $900 Ex $722 Gd $515
Same general specifications as Haenel '88 Mauser Sporter.
(See separate listing.)

SCHULTZ & LARSEN GEVAERFABRIK — Otterup, Denmark

MATCH RIFLE NO. 47 . . . . NiB $690 Ex $555 Gd $360
Bolt-action single-shot. Caliber: .22 LR. Set trigger. Bbl.: 28.5
inches, heavy. Weight 14 lbs. Micrometer receiver, globe front
sights. Free-rifle thumbhole stock w/cheekpiece, adj. Shuetzen-type
buttplate; swivels, palm rest.

FREE RIFLE MODEL 54 . . . . NiB $866 Ex $780 Gd $598
Schultz & Larsen M54 bolt-action single-shot; set trigger. Caliber:
6.5x55mm or standard American centerfire calibers. Bbl: 27.5
inches, heavy. Weight: 15.5 lbs. Micrometer receiver, globe front
sights. Free-rifle thumbhole stock w/cheekpiece, adj. Schuetzen-
type buttplate; swivels, palm rest.

MODEL 54J
SPORTING RIFLE . . . . NiB $684 Ex $528 Gd $430
Schultz & Larsen bolt-action. Caliber: .270 Win., .30-06, 7x61
Sharpe & Hart; three-round mag. Bbl.: 24 inches in .270 and
.30-06, 26 inches in 7x61. No sights. Checkered Monte Carlo
stock.

SEARS, ROEBUCK & COMPANY — Chicago, Illinois

MODEL 2C
BOLT-ACTION RIFLE . . . . NiB $159 Ex $119 Gd $95
Caliber: .22RF. Seven round clip mag. 21-inch bbl. Weight: 5 lbs.
Sights: Open rear; ramp front. Plain Monte Carlo stock. Mfd. by Win.

MODEL 42
BOLT-ACTION REPEATER . . . . NiB $159 Ex $119 Gd $95
Takedown. Caliber: .22RF. Eight round detachable box magazine.
24-inch bbl. Weight: 6 lbs. Sights: Open rear; bead front. Plain
pistol-grip stock. Mfd. by Marlin.

MODEL 42DL
BOLT-ACTION REPEATER . . . . NiB $159 Ex $119 Gd $95
Same specs as Model 42 except fancier grade w/peep rear, hooded
front sights, swivels.

MODEL 44DL
LEVER-ACTION RIFLE . . . . NiB $239 Ex $179 Gd $130
Caliber: .22 RF; tubular mag. holds 19 LR. Bbl.: 22 inches. Weight:
6.25 lbs. Open rear, hooded ramp front sights. Monte Carlo pistol-
grip stock. Mfd. By Marlin.

MODEL 53
BOLT-ACTION RIFLE . . . . NiB $289 Ex $198 Gd $155
Calibers: .243 Win., .270 Win., .308 Win., .30-06; four-round mag.
Bbl.: 22 inches. Weight: 6.75 lbs. Open rear, ramp front sights.
Standard sporter pistol-grip checkered stock. Mfd. By Savage.

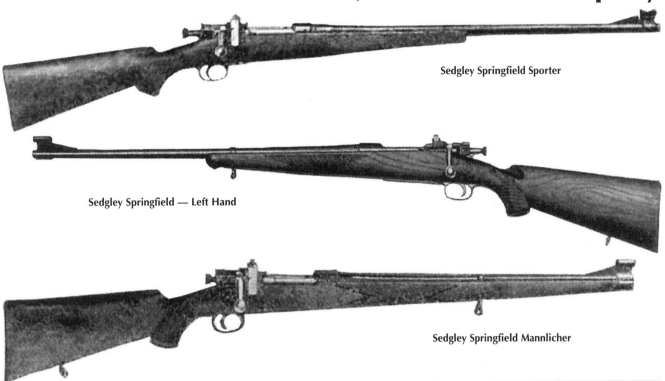

Sedgley Springfield Sporter

Sedgley Springfield — Left Hand

Sedgley Springfield Mannlicher

MODEL 54 LEVER-ACTION
RIFLE. . . . . **NiB $222 Ex $188 Gd $135**
Similar to Winchester Model 94 Carbine. Made in .30-30 only. Mfd. By Win.

MODEL 103 SERIES
BOLT-ACTION REPEATER. . . . . **NiB $229 EX $121 Gd $98**
Same specifications as Model 103.2 w/minor changes. Mfd. by Marlin.

MODEL 103.2 BOLT-ACTION
REPEATER . . . . **NiB $145 Ex $100 Gd $90**
Takedown. Caliber: .22RF. Eight-round detachable box magazine. 24-inch bbl. Weight: 6 lbs. Sights: Open rear; bead front. Plain pistol-grip stock. Mfd. by Marlin.

R. F. SEDGLEY, INC. —
Philadelphia, Pennsylvania

SPRINGFIELD SPORTER. . . . . . . NiB $1290 Ex $1189 Gd $633
Based on Springfield '03 bolt-action. Caliber: .220 Swift, .218 Bee, .22-3000, .22-4000, .22 Hornet, .25-35, .250-3000, .257 Roberts, .270 Win., 7mm, .30-06, Bbl.: 24 inches. Weight: 7.5 lbs. Lyman No. 48 receiver, matted ramp bead front sights. Checkered walnut stock, grip cap, sling swivels. Disc. 1941.

SPRINGFIELD LEFT-HAND SPORTER. . . NiB $1654 Ex $1398 Gd $954
Same as Standard Springfield Sporter except bolt-action reversed for left-hand shooter. Disc. 1941.

SEDGLEY SPRINGFIELD
MANNLICHER-TYPE SPORTER. . . . . . . **NiB $1515 Ex $1479 Gd $1088**
Same as standard Sedgley Springfield Sporter except w/20-inch bbl., Mannlicher-type full stock w/cheekpiece; weight: 7.75 lbs. Disc. 1941.

SHILEN RIFLES, INC. — Enis, Texas

DGA BENCHREST RIFLE. . . . . . NiB $1529 Ex $1244 Gd $977
DGA bolt-action single-shot. Caliber: same as Sporter model. Bbl.: 26 inches, medium-heavy or heavy. Weight: 10.5 lbs. No sights. Fiberglass or walnut stock, classic or thumbhole pattern.

DGA SPORTER . . . . NiB $1567 Ex $1189 Gd $843
DGA bolt action. Calibers: .17 Rem., .222 Rem., .223 Rem. .22-250, .220 Swift, 6mm Rem., .243 Win., .250 Sav., .257 Roberts, .284 Win., .308 Win., .358 Win. Three round blind magazine. 24-inch bbl. Weight: 7.5 lbs. No sights. Select Claro walnut stock w/cheekpiece, pistol grip, sling swivel studs.

DGA VARMINTER. . . . . NiB $1455 Ex $1209 Gd $1155
Same as Sporter except w/25-inch medium-heavy bbl. Weight: 9 lbs.

SHILOH RIFLE MFG. CO. — Big Timber, Montana

SHARPS MODEL 1874 BUSINESS RIFLE. . .NiB $1798 Ex $1703 Gd $1166
Replica of 1874 Sharps No. 3 Sporting Rifle. Caliber: .32-40, .38-55, .40-50 BN, .40-70 BN, .40-90 BN, .45-70 ST., .45-90 ST, .50-70 ST, .50-110 ST. Bbl.: 28 inches, round, heavy. Blade front, buckhorn rear sights. Double-set triggers. Straight-grip walnut stock w/steel crescent buttplate. Made from 1986 to date.

SHARPS MODEL 1874 LONG
RANGE EXPRESS RIFLE. . . . . . . **NiB $1900 Ex $1695 Gd $1210**
Replica of Model 1874 Sharps w/single-shot, falling breech action. Caliber: .32-40, .38-55, .40-50 BN, .40-70 BN, .45-70 ST, .45-90 ST, .45-110 ST, .50-70 ST, .50-90 ST, .50-110 ST. Bbl.: 34 inches, tapered octagon. Double-set triggers. Lgt.: 54 inches. Weight: 10.75 lbs. Globe front, sporting tang peep rear sights. Walnut buttstock w/pistol grip and Schnabel-style forend. Color case-hardened action. Made from 1986 to date.

Sig Swiss Industrial Company

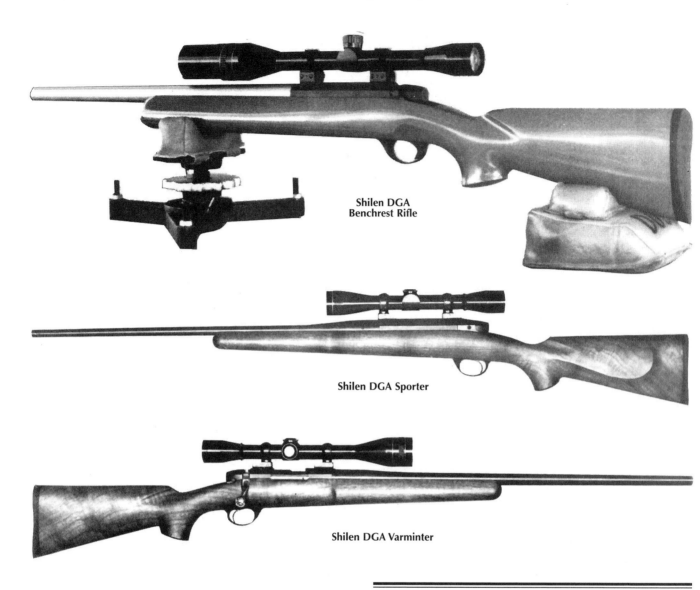

Shilen DGA
Benchrest Rifle

Shilen DGA Sporter

Shilen DGA Varminter

SHARPS MODEL 1874
SADDLE RIFLE . . . . NiB $1257 Ex $1133 Gd $723
Similar to Model 1874 Express Rifle except w/30-inch bbl., blade front sight and buckhorn rear. Made from 1986 to date.

SHARPS MODEL 1874
SPORTING RIFLE NO. 1 . . . . NiB $1355 Ex $1187 Gd $745
Similar to Model 1874 Express Rifle except w/30-inch bbl., blade front sight and buckhorn rear. Made from 1986 to date.

SHARPS MODEL 1874
SPORTING RIFLE NO. 3 . . . . NiB $1150 Ex $1007 Gd $688
Similar to Model 1874 Sporting Rifle No. 1 except w/straight-grip stock w/steel crescent buttplate. Made from 1986 to date.

SHARPS MODEL 1874 MONTANA ROUGHRIDER
Simlar to Model 1874 Sporting Rifle No. 1 except w/24- to 30-inch half-octagon or full-octagon bbl.; Standard or deluxe walnut pistol-grip stock or military-style buttstock. Made from 1989 to date.
Standard model. . . . . NiB $1154 Ex $715 Gd $646
Deluxe model . . . . NiB $1300 Ex $990 Gd $615

SIG SWISS INDUSTRIAL COMPANY —
Neuhausen-Rhine Falls, Switzerland

AMT SEMIAUTOMATIC RIFLE . . . . . . NiB $4798 Ex $3270 Gd $2775
Caliber: .308 Win., (7.62 NATO); five-, 10- or 20-round mag. Bbl.: 18.5 inches w/flash suppressor. Weight: 9.5 lbs. Adj. aperture rear, post front sights. Walnut buttstock and forend w/synthetic pistol grip Imported from 1980 to 1988.

AMT SPORTING RIFLE . . . . NiB $4876 Ex $3129 Gd $2210
Semiautomatic version of SG510-4 automatic assault rifle based on Swiss Army SIGW57. Roller-delayed blowback action. Caliber: 7.62x51mm NATO (.308 Win.). Five, 10- and 20-round magazines. 19-inch bbl. Weight: 10 lbs. Sights: aperture rear, post front. Wood buttstock and forearm, folding bipod. Imported from 1960 to 1988.

PE-57 SEMIAUTOMATIC RIFLE. . . . . . . NiB $6596 Ex $4348 Gd $3100
Caliber: 7.5 Swiss. 24-round magazine. 23.75-inch bbl. Weight: 12.5 lbs. Sights: Adj. aperture rear; post front. High-impact synthetic stock. Imported from Switzerland during the 1980s.

Smith & Wesson
Model 1500DL

Smith & Wesson
Model 1700 LS Classic Hunter

Springfield Armory
BM-59

SMITH & WESSON — Springfield, Massachusetts. Manufactured by Husqvarna, Vapenfabrik A.B., Huskvarna, Sweden, & Howa Machinery LTD., Shinkawa-Chonear, Nagota 452, Japan

MODEL 1500 . . . . **NiB $410 Ex $339 Gd $269**
Bolt-action. Caliber: .243 Win., .270 Win., .30-06, 7mm Rem. Mag. Bbl.: 22 inches (24 inches in 7mm Rem. Mag.). Walnut Monte Carlo stock, cut checkering. Open rear, hooded ramp gold bead front sights. This model was also imported by Mossberg (see separate listing). Imported from 1979 to 1984.

MODEL 1500DL DELUXE . . . . **NiB $410 Ex $339 Gd $269**
Same as Standard model except no sights. Engine-turned bolt, decorative scroll on floorplate, French checkering. Imported from 1983 to 1984.

MODEL 1700 LS "CLASSIC HUNTER" . . . . **NiB $460 Ex $388 Gd $318**
Bolt-action. Caliber: .243 Win., .270 Win., .30-06; five-round mag. Bbl.: 22 inches, no sights. Weight: 7.5 lbs. Checkered walnut stock, Schnabel forend, solid recoil pad. Imported from 1983 to 1984.

MODEL A BOLT-ACTION RIFLE . . . . **NiB $443 Ex $329 Gd $290**
Similar to Husqvarna Model 9000 Crown Grade. Mauser-type bolt-action. Caliber: .22-250, .243 Win., .270 Win., .308 Win., .30-06, 7mm Rem. Mag., .300 Win. Mag; five-round mag. (three rounds in magnum calibers). Bbl.: 23.75 inches. Weight: 7 lbs. Folding leaf rear, hooded ramp front sights. Checkered walnut Monte Carlo stock w/rosewood forend tip and grip cap; swivels. Made from 1969 to 1972.

MODEL B . . . . — **NiB $460 Ex $367 Gd $238**
Same as Model A except w/20.25-inch extra-light bbl., Monte Carlo cheekpiece w/Schnabel-style forearm; weight: 6 lbs., 10 oz. Calibers: .243 Win., .30-06.

MODEL C . . . . **NiB $460 Ex $367 Gd $238**
Same as Model B except w/straight comb.

MODEL D . . . . **NiB $588 Ex $469 Gd $240**
Same as Model C except w/full-length Mannlicher-style forearm.

MODEL E . . . . **NiB $588 Ex $469 Gd $240**
Same as Model B except w/full-length Mannlicher-style forearm.

SPRINGFIELD, INC. — Colona, Illinois (formerly Springfield Armory of Geneseo, Illinois)

This is a private firm not to be confused with the former U.S. Government facility in Springfield, Massachusetts

BM-59 SEMIAUTOMATIC RIFLE
Gas-operated. Caliber: .308 Win. (7.62mm NATO); 20-round detachable box mag. Bbl.: 19.3 inches w/flash suppressor. Adj. military-style aperture rear square post front sights. Direct and indirect grenade launcher sights. Lgt.: 43 inches. Weight: 9.25 lbs. European walnut stock w/handguard or folding buttstock (Alpine Paratrooper model). Made from 1981 to 1990.
Standard model . . . . **NiB $1844 Ex $1329 Gd $911**
Paratrooper model . . . . **NiB $2136 Ex $1779 Gd $1533**

M-1 GARAND SEMIAUTOMATIC RIFLE
Gas-operated. Caliber: .308 Win. (7.62 NATO), .30-06; eight-round stripper clip. Bbl.: 24 inches. Lgt.: 43.5 inches. Weight: 9.5 lbs. Adj.

Standard Arms Company

**Springfield Armory
SAR-8 Sporter Rifle**

**Standard Arms Model
G Automatic Rifle**

NRA NATIONAL FIREARMS MUSEUM

aperture rear, military square blade front sights. "Standard issue" grade walnut stock or folding buttstock. Made from 1979 to 1990.

Standard model...............	NiB $779	Ex $588	Gd $353
National Match model	NiB $900	Ex $799	Gd $489
Ultra Match model	NiB $1000	Ex $808	Gd $589
Sniper model.................	NiB $1254	Ex $876	Gd $665
Tanker model	NiB $954	Ex $677	Gd $498
Paratrooper model (w/folding stock)...........	NiB $1466	Ex $1109	Gd $1066

MATCH M1-A
Same as Standard M1-A except w/National Match-grade bbl w/modified flash suppressor. National Match sights, tuned trigger pull, gas system assembly in one unit. Modified mainspring guide, glass-bedded walnut stock. Super Match M1-A w/premium-grade heavy bbl. Weight: 10 lbs.

Match M1-A	NiB $1277	Ex $1879	Gd $1271
Super Match M1-A	NiB $2695	Ex $1899	Gd $1721

STANDARD M1-A SEMIAUTOMATIC
Gas-operated. Similar to U.S. M14 service rifle except semi-automatic only. Caliber: .308 Win. (7.62 NATO); five-, 10- or w0-round detachable box mag., Bbl.: 25.13 inches w/flash suppressor. Weight: 9 lbs. Adj. aperture rear, blade front sights. Fiberglass, birch or walnut stock. Fiberglass handguard, sling swivels. Made from 1996 to 2000.

W/fiberglass or birch stock......	NiB $1198	Ex $694	Gd $645
W/walnut stock..............	NiB $1398	Ex $1100	Gd $833

M-6 SCOUT RIFLE/SHOTGUN COMBO
Similar to (14-inch) short-barreled Survival Gun provided as backup weapon to U.S. combat pilots. Caliber: .22 LR/.410 and .22 Hornet/.410. Bbl.: 18.5 inches. Lgt.: 32 inches. Weight: 4 lbs. Parkerized or stainless steel finish. Folding detachable stock w/space for fifteen .22 LR and four .410 cartridges. Drilled and tapped for scope mounts. Introduced 1982. Imported from Czech Republic from 1995 to 2004.

First Issue (no trigger guard)...	NiB $1709	Ex $1433	Gd $1067
Second Issue (w/trigger guard)..	NiB $1797	Ex $1439	Gd $1088

SAR-8 SPORTER RIFLE
Similar to H&K Model 911 semi-automatic rifle. Calibers: .308 Win. (7.62x51 NATO); detachable five-, 10- or 20-round mag. Bbl.: 18 or 20 inches. Lgt.: 45.3 inches. Weight: 8.7 to 9.5 lbs. Protected post front, rotary rear sights. Delayed roller-locked blow-back action w/fluted chamber. Kevlar-reinforced fiberglass thumbhole-style wood stock. Imported from 1990 to 1998.

SAR-8 w/wood stock (disc. 1994).......	NiB $1066	Ex $877	Gd $658
SAR-8 w/thumb-hole stock...........	NiB $1127	Ex $976	Gd $679

SAR-48, SAR-4800
Similar to Browning FN FAL/LAR semi-automatic rifle. Caliber: .223 Rem. (5.56mm), .308 Win. (7.62 NATO); detachable five, 10- or 20-round mag. Bbl.: 18 or 21 inches, chrome-lined. Lgt.: 38.25 or 45.3 inches. Weight: 9.5 to 12.25 lbs. Protected post front, adj. rear sights. Forged receiver and bolt w/adj. gas system. Pistol-grip or thumbhole-style synthetic or wood stock. Imported 1985. Reintro. 1995.

W/pistol-grip stock, disc. 1989........	NiB $1788	Ex $1289	Gd $990
W/wood stock, disc. 1989	NiB $2577	Ex $2066	Gd $1500
W/folding stock, disc. 1989	NiB $2854	Ex $2310	Gd $1669
W/thumb-hole stock...............	NiB $1329	Ex $1100	Gd $796

SQUIRES BINGHAM CO., INC. —
Makati, Rizal, Philippines

MODEL 14D DELUXE BOLT-ACTION
REPEATING RIFLE.............. NiB $159 Ex $123 Gd $88
Caliber: .22 LR; five-round box mag. Bbl.: 24 inches. V-notch rear, hooded ramp front sights. Receiver grooved for scope mounts. Pulong Dalaga stock w/contrasting forend tip and grip cap, checkered forearm and pistol grip. Weight: 6 lbs. Disc.

MODEL 15 .... NiB $189 Ex $127 Gd $115
Same as Model 14D except chambered for .22 WMR. Importation disc.

MODEL M16 SEMIAUTOMATIC RIFLE.... NiB $190 Ex $166 Gd $125
Similar to U.S. M-16 military rifle. Caliber: .22 LR; 15-round mag. Bbl.: 19.5 inches w/muzzle brake-flash hider. Rear sight in carrying handle, post front on high ramp. Black-painted mahogany buttstock and forearm. Weight : 6.5 lbs. Importation disc.

MODEL M20D DELUXE .... NiB $277 Ex $227 Gd $131
Caliber: .22 LR. 15-round box magazine. 19.5-inch bbl. w/muzzle brake/flash hider. Sights: V-notch rear; blade front. Receiver grooved for scope mount. Pulong Dalaga stock w/contrasting forend tip and grip cap, checkered forearm/pistol-grip. Weight: 6 lbs. Importation disc.

STANDARD ARMS COMPANY —
Wilmington, Delaware

MODEL G AUTOMATIC RIFLE .... NiB $815 Ex $569 Gd $355
Gas-operated autoloader. Hammerless. Takedown. Caliber: .25-35, .30-30, .25 Rem. .30 Rem; four-round mag. in .35 Rem., five rounds in other calibers. Bbl.: 22.38 inches. Weight: 7.75 lbs. Open sporting rear, ivory bead front sights. Shotgun-type stock. Made circa 1910. This was the first gas-operated

Standard Arms Company

Star
Rolling Block Carbine

Stevens No. 12 Marksman Single-Shot Rifle
NRA NATIONAL FIREARMS MUSEUM

Stevens No. 49 Ideal Single-Shot Rifle
NRA NATIONAL FIREARMS MUSEUM

rifle manufactured in the U.S. The gas port may be closed so that the rifle may be operated as a slide-action repeater.

MODEL M HAND-OPERATED RIFLE . . . . . **NiB $737 Ex $543 Gd $431**
Slide-action repeater w/same specifications as Model G except lacks autoloading feature. Weight: 7 lbs.

STAR — Eibar, Spain. Manufactured by Bonifacio Echeverria, S.A.

ROLLING BLOCK CARBINE . . . . . **NiB $500 Ex $337 Gd $178**
Single-shot similar to Remington Rolling Block Rifle. Caliber: .30-30, .357 Mag., .44 Mag. Bbl.: 20 inches. Weight: 6 lbs. Folding leaf rear, ramp front sights. Walnut straight-grip stock w/crescent buttplate, forearm bbl. band. Imported from 1934 to 1975.

STERLING — Imported by Lanchester U.S.A., Inc., Dallas, Texas

MARK 6 SEMIAUTOMATIC CARBINE . . **NiB $1822 Ex $1177 Gd $987**
Caliber: 9mm Parabellum; 34-round mag. Bbl.: 16.1 inches. Weight: 7.5 lbs. Flip-type rear peep, ramp front sights. Folding metal skeleton stock. Made from 1983 to 1994.

J. STEVENS ARMS CO. — Chicopee Falls, Massachusetts; division of Savage Industries, Westfield, Massachusetts

NO. 12 MARKSMAN
SINGLE-SHOT RIFLE . . . . **NiB $456 Ex $324 Gd $189**
Lever-action, tip-up. Takedown. Calibers: .22 LR, .25 RF, .32 RF. Bbl.: 22 inches. Plain straight-grip stock, small tapered forearm.

NO. 14 LITTLE SCOUT
SINGLE-SHOT RIFLE . . . . **NiB $455 Ex $310 Gd $180**

Caliber: .22 RF. 18-inch bbl. One-piece slab stock. Made from 1906 to 1910.

NO. 14 1/2 LITTLE SCOUT
SINGLE-SHOT RIFLE . . . . **NiB $455 Ex $309 Gd $200**
Rolling block action. Takedown. Caliber: .22 LR. Bbl.: 18 or 20 inches. Weight: 2.75 lbs. Open rear, blade front sights. Plain straight-grip stock, small tapered forearm.

MODEL 15 . . . . **NiB $225 Ex $150 Gd $144**
Same as Stevens-Springfield Model 15 except w/24-inch bbl., Weight: 5 lbs. Redesigned stock. Made from 1948 to 1965.

MODEL 15Y YOUTH'S RIFLE . . . . . **NiB $221 Ex $155 Gd $127**
Same as Model 15 except w/21-inch bbl., short buttstock; weight: 4.75 lbs. Made from 1958 to 1965.

NO. 44 IDEAL
SINGLE-SHOT RIFLE . . . . **NiB $689 Ex $466 Gd $377**
Rolling block lever-action. Takedown. Caliber: .22 LR, .25 RF, .32 RF. .25-20, .32-20, .32-40, .38-40, .38-55. .44-40. Bbl.: 24 and 26 inches, round, half-octagon or full octagon. Weight: 7 lbs. Open rear, Rocky Mountain front sights. Plain straight-grip stock and forearm. Made from 1894 to 1932.

NO. 44 1/2 IDEAL SINGLE-SHOT RIFLE . . **NiB $990 Ex $848 Gd $578**
Falling block, lever-action. Same as Model 44.

NOS. 45-54 IDEAL SINGLE-SHOT RIFLES
Same as Model 44 except w/high-grade finishes, engraving on lever and barrel. Set triggers. The Schuetzen-type rifles (include the Stevens-Pope models) are in this series. Model No. 45 to 54 were intro. in 1896 w/No. 44-type falling block action. These models were disc. c. 1916. The 45-54 series rifles, the Stevens-Pope and higher grade Schuetzen models are highly sought and bring much higher prices than the standard No. 44 and 44.5 rifles.

MODEL 66 BOLT-ACTION
REPEATING RIFLE . . . . **NiB $255 Ex $140 Gd $121**
Takedown. Caliber: .22 Short, Long, LR. Tubular magazine holds 13 LR, 15 Long, 19 Short. 24-inch bbl. Weight: 5 lbs. Sights: Open rear, bead front. Plain pistol-grip stock w/grooved forearm. Made from 1931 to 1935.

J. Stevens Arms Co.

Stevens No. 14 Little Scout

Stevens No. 14.5 Little Scout

Stevens No. 44 Ideal

Stevens Model 87

**NO. 70 VISIBLE LOADING
SLIDE-ACTION** . . . . **NiB $579 Ex $398 Gd $255**
Exposed hammer. Caliber: .22 LR, Long, Short; tubular mag.
holds 11 LR, 13 Long, 15 Short. Bbl.: 22 inches. Weight: 4.5 lbs.
Open rear, bead front sights. Plain straight-grip stock, grooved
slide handle. Made from 1907 to 1934. Nos. 702, 71, 712, 72
and 722 are the same as No. 70 except w/different bbl. lengths
or sights.

MODEL 87 AUTOLOADING RIFLE . . . . **NiB $167 Ex $121 Gd $90**
Takedown. Caliber: .22 LR; 15-round tubular mag. Bbl.: 24
inches (20 inches in later production). Weight: 6 lbs. Open rear,
bead front sights. Pistol-grip stock. Made from 1938 to date.
This model originally bore the "Springfield" brand name, disc.
in 1948.

**MODEL 322 HI-POWER
BOLT-ACTION CARBINE** . . . . **NiB $487 Ex $333 Gd $202**
Caliber: .22 Hornet. 4-round detachable magazine. 21-inch bbl.
Weight: 6.75 lbs. Sights: Open rear; ramp front. Pistol-grip stock.

MODEL 322-S . . . . **NiB $479 Ex $335 Gd $200**
Same as Model 325 except w/peep rear sight. (Same as Savage
models 340S, 342S.)

**MODEL 325 HI-POWER
BOLT-ACTION CARBINE** . . . . **NiB $479 Ex $335 Gd $200**
Caliber: .30-30. Three round detachable box magazine. 21-inch
bbl. Weight: 6.75 lbs. Sights: Open rear; bead front. Plain pistol-grip
stock. Made from 1947 to 1950. (Similar to Savage Model 340.)

MODEL 325-S . . . . **NiB $479 Ex $335 Gd $200**
Same as Model 325 except w/peep rear sight. (Similar to Savage
Model 340S.)

**NO. 414 ARMORY MODEL
SINGLE-SHOT RIFLE** . . . . **NiB $488 Ex $398 Gd $316**
No. 44-type lever-action. Calibers: .22 LR only, .22 Short only.
26-inch bbl. Weight: 8 lbs. Sights: Lyman receiver peep; blade
front. Plain straight-grip stock, military-type forearm, swivels.
Made from 1912 to 1932.

**MODEL 416 BOLT-ACTION
TARGET RIFLE** . . . . **NiB $159 Ex $100 Gd $77**
Caliber: .22 LR. Five round detachable box magazine. 26-inch
heavy bbl. Weight: 9.5 lbs. Sights: Receiver peep; hooded front.
Target stock, swivels, sling. Made from 1937 to 1949.

**NO. 419 JUNIOR TARGET MODEL
BOLT-ACTION SINGLE-SHOT RIFLE** . . . . . **NiB $433 Ex $325 Gd $255**
Takedown. Caliber: .22 LR. 26-inch bbl. Weight: 5.5 lbs. Sights:
Lyman No. 55 rear peep; blade front. Plain junior target stock w/pistol
grip and grooved forearm, swivels, sling. Made from 1932 to 1936.

**BUCKHORN MODEL 053 BOLT-ACTION
SINGLE-SHOT RIFLE** . . . . **NiB $200 Ex $148 Gd $110**
Takedown. Calibers: .22 Short, Long, LR, .22 WRF, .25 Stevens RF. Bbl.: 24
inches, Weight: 5.5 lbs. Receiver peep, open middle, hooded front sights.
Sporting stock w/pistol grip, black forend tip. Made from 1935 to 1948.

BUCKHORN MODEL 53 . . . . **NiB $220 Ex $179 Gd $122**
Same as Buckhorn Model 053 except w/open rear sight and plain bead front sight.

J. Stevens Arms Co.

Stevens No. 414 Armory

Stevens Model 416

Stevens Buckhorn Model 53

Stevens Buckhorn Model 055

Stevens Buckhorn Model 56

BUCKHORN 055 . . . . **NiB $233 Ex $188 Gd $125**
Takedown. Same as Model 056 except single-shot. Caliber: .22 LR, Long, Short. Bbl.: 24 inches. Sporting stock w/pistol grip, black forend tip. Weight: 5.5 lbs. Made from 1935 to 1948.

BUCKHORN MODEL 056
BOLT-ACTION . . . . **NiB $230 Ex $190 Gd $131**
Takedown. Caliber: .22 LR., Long, Short. Five round detachable box magazine. 24-inch bbl. Weight: 6 lbs. Sights: Receiver peep, open middle, hooded front. Sporting stock w/pistol grip and black forend tip. Made from 1935 to 1948.

BUCKHORN
MODEL 56 . . . . **NiB $230 Ex $190 Gd $131**
Same as Buckhorn Model 056 except w/open rear sight and plain bead front sight.

BUCKHORN NO. 057 . . . . **NiB $233 Ex $155 Gd $120**
Same as Buckhorn Model 076 except w/5-round detachable box magazine. Made from 1939 to 1948.

BUCKHORN NO. 57 . . . . **NiB $230 Ex $155 Gd $120**
Same as Buckhorn Model 76 except w/5-round detachable box magazine. Made from 1939 to 1948.

BUCKHORN MODEL 066
BOLT-ACTION REPEATING RIFLE. . . . . . . **NiB $290 Ex $225 Gd $130**
Takedown. Caliber: .22 LR, Long, Short. Tubular magazine holds 21 Short, 17 Long, 15 LR. 24-inch bbl. Weight: 6 lbs. Sights: Receiver peep; open middle; hooded front. Sporting stock w/pistol grip and black forend tip. Made from 1935 to 1948.

BUCKHORN MODEL 66 . . . . **NiB $219 Ex $133 Gd $210**
Same as Buckhorn Model 066 except w/open rear sight, plain bead front sight.

BUCKHORN NO. 076
AUTOLOADING RIFLE. . . . . **NiB $225 Ex $188 Gd $135**
Takedown. Caliber: .22 LR. 15-round tubular magazine. 24-inch bbl. Weight: 6 lbs. Sights: Receiver peep; open middle; hooded front. Sporting stock w/pistol grip, black forend tip. Made 1938 to 1948.

BUCKHORN NO. 76 . . . . **NiB $225 Ex $188 Gd $135**
Same as Buckhorn No. 076 except w/open rear sight, plain bead front sight.

CRACKSHOT NO. 26
SINGLE-SHOT RIFLE. . . . . **NiB $335 Ex $229 Gd $170**
Lever-action. Takedown. Caliber: .22 LR, .32 RF. Bbl.: 18 or 22 inches. Open rear, blade front sights. Weight: 3.25 lbs. Plain straight-grip stock. Small tapered forearm. Made from 1913 to 1939.

J. Stevens Arms Co.

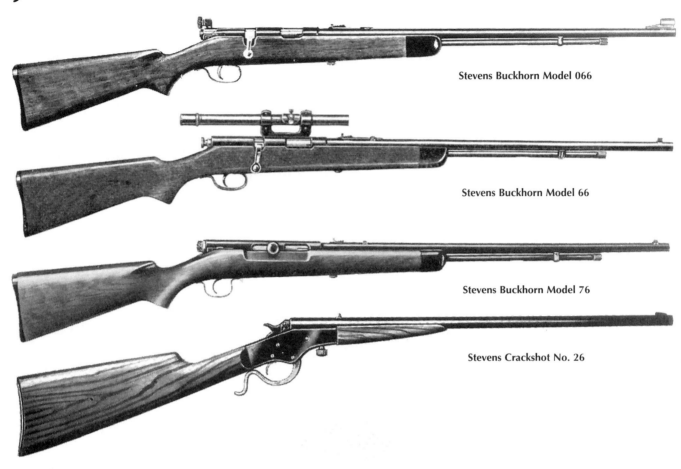

Stevens Buckhorn Model 066

Stevens Buckhorn Model 66

Stevens Buckhorn Model 76

Stevens Crackshot No. 26

CRACKSHOT NO. 26.5 . . . . NiB $325 Ex $220 Gd $195
Same as Crackshot No. 26 except w/smoothbore bbl. for shot cartridges.

FAVORITE NO. 17
SINGLE-SHOT RIFLE . . . . NiB $330 Ex $225 Gd $200
Lever-action. Takedown. Caliber: .22 LR, .25 RF, .32 RF. Bbl.: 24 inches. Round. Weight: 5.4 lbs. Open rear, Rocky Mountain front sights. Plain straight-grip stock. Small tapered forearm. Made from 1894 to 1935.

FAVORITE NO. 18 . . . . NiB $422 Ex $300 Gd $179
Same as Favorite No. 17 except w/Vernier peep rear sight, leaf middle sight, Beach combination front sight.

FAVORITE NO. 19 . . . . NiB $435 Ex $330 Gd $220
Same as Favorite No. 17 except w/Lyman combination rear sight, leaf middle sight, Lyman front sight.

FAVORITE NO. 20 . . . . NiB $420 Ex $325 Gd $215
Same as Favorite No. 17 except w/smoothbore barrel.

FAVORITE NO. 27 . . . . NiB $435 Ex $330 Gd $220
Same as Favorite No. 17 except w/octagon bbl.

FAVORITE NO. 28 . . . . NiB $435 Ex $330 Gd $220
Same as Favorite No. 18 except w/octagon bbl.

FAVORITE NO. 29 . . . . NiB $435 Ex $330 Gd $220
Same as Favorite No. 19 except w/octagon bbl.

WALNUT HILL NO. 417-0
SINGLE-SHOT TARGET RIFLE . . . . NiB $909 Ex $777 Gd $530
Lever-action. Calibers: .22 LR, .22 Short, .22 Hornet. Bbl.: 28-inch, heavy (extra-heavy 29-inch bbl option). Weight: 10.5 lbs. Lyman No. 52L extension rear, 17A front sights; scope bases mounted on bbl. Target stock w/full pistol grip, beavertail forearm. Bbl. band, swivels, sling. Made from 1932 to 1947.

WALNUT HILL NO. 417-1 . . . . . . NiB $900 Ex $750 Gd $521
Same as No. 417-0 except w/Lyman No. 48L receiver sight.

WALNUT HILL NO. 417-2 . . . . NiB $900 Ex $750 Gd $521
Same as No. 417-0 except w/Lyman No. 48L receiver sight.

WALNUT HILL NO. 417-3 . . . . NiB $900 Ex $750 Gd $521
Same as No. 417-0 except w/o sights.

WALNUT HILL NO. 417.5
SINGLE-SHOT RIFLE . . . . NiB $900 Ex $750 Gd $521
Lever-action. Caliber: .22 LR, .22 WMR, .25 RF, .22 Hornet. Bbl.: 28-inches. Weight: 8.5 lbs. Lyman No. 144 tang peep rear, folding middle, bead front sights. Sporting stock w/pistol-grip stock, semi-beavertail forearm, swivels, sling. Made from 1932 to 1940.

WALNUT HILL NO. 418
SINGLE-SHOT RIFLE . . . . NiB $988 Ex $768 Gd $589
Lever-action. Takedown. Calibers: .22 LR only, .22 Short only. 26-inch bbl. Weight: 6.5 lbs. Sights: Lyman No. 144 tang peep; blade front. Pistol-grip stock, semi-beavertail forearm, swivels, sling. Made from 1932 to 1940.

J. Stevens Arms Co.

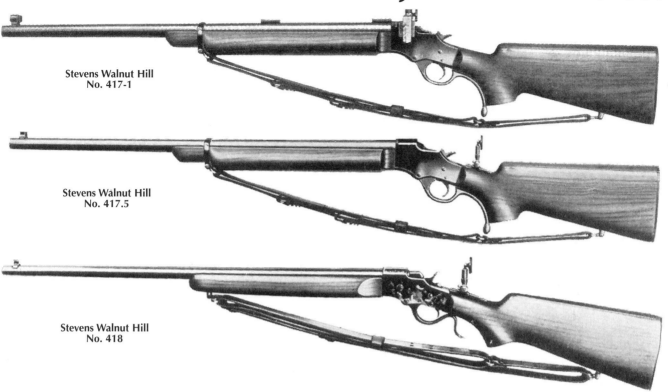

Stevens Walnut Hill
No. 417-1

Stevens Walnut Hill
No. 417.5

Stevens Walnut Hill
No. 418

WALNUT HILL NO. 418.5 . . . . **NiB $988 Ex $768 Gd $589**
Same as No. 418 except in .22 WRF, .25 Stevens RF. Lyman No. 2A tang peep, bead front sights.

MODEL 15 SINGLE-SHOT
BOLT-ACTION RIFLE . . . . **NiB $200 Ex $155 Gd $110**
Takedown. Caliber: .22 LR, Long, Short. 22-inch bbl. Weight: 4 lbs. Sights: Open rear, bead front. Plain pistol-grip stock. Made from 1937 to 1948.

MODEL 82 BOLT-ACTION
SINGLE-SHOT RIFLE. . . . . **NiB $178 Ex $144 Gd $115**
Takedown. Caliber: .22 LR, Long, Short. 22-inch bbl. Weight: 4 lbs. Sights: Open rear; gold bead front. Plain pistol-grip stock w/grooved forearm. Made from 1935 to 1939.

MODEL 83 BOLT-ACTION
SINGLE-SHOT RIFLE. . . . . **NiB $200 Ex $155 Gd $110**
Takedown. Caliber: .22 LR, Long, Short, .22 WRF, .25 Stevens RF. Bbl.: 24 inches. Weight: 4.5 lbs. Peep rear, open middle, hooded front sights. Plain pistol-grip stock w/grooved forearm. Made from 1935 to 1939.

MODEL 84 . . . . **NiB $220 Ex $190 Gd $128**
Same as Model 86 except w/five-round detachable box mag. Pre-1948 versions of this model were designated Springfield Model 84, later known as Stevens Model 84. Made from 1940 to 1965.

MODEL 84-S (084) . . . . **NiB $220 Ex $190 Gd $128**
Same as Model 84 except w/peep rear, hooded front sights. Pre-1948 versions of this model were designated Springfield Model 084, later known as Stevens Model 84-S. Disc.

MODEL 85 . . . . **NiB $244 Ex $199 Gd $139**
Same as Stevens Model 87 except w/five-round detachable box mag. Made from 1939 to date. Pre-1948 versions were designated Springfield Model 85, currently known as Stevens Model 85. Earlier models command higher prices.

MODEL 85-S (085) . . . . **NiB $224 Ex $167 Gd $125**
Same as Model 85 except w/peep rear, hooded front sights. Pre-1948 versions were designated Springfield Model 085, also knows as Stevens Model 85-S.

MODEL 86
BOLT-ACTION . . . . **NiB $224 Ex $167 Gd $125**
Takedown. Caliber: .22 LR, Long, Short. Tubular magazine holds 15 LR, 17 Long, 21 Short. 24-inch bbl. Weight: 6 lbs. Sights: Open rear, gold bead front. Pistol-grip stock, black forend tip on later production. Made from 1935 to 1965. Note: The Springfield brand name was disc. in 1948.

MODEL 86-S (086) . . . . **NiB $230 Ex $172 Gd $128**
Same as Model 86 except w/peep rear, hooded front sights. Pre-1948 versions of this model were designated as Springfield Model 086, later known as Stevens Model 86-S. Disc.

MODEL 87-S (087) . . . . **NiB $233 Ex $215 Gd $156**
Same as Stevens Model 87 except w/peep rear, hooded front sights. Pre-1948 versions of this model were designated Springfield Model 087, later known as Stevens Model 87-S. Disc.

STEYR DAIMLER PUCH A.G. — Steyr, Austria

AUG-SA
SEMIAUTOMATIC. . . . . **NiB $4220 Ex $3366 Gd $2340**
Gas-operated. Caliber: .223 Rem., (5.56mm); 30- or 40-round mag. Bbl: 20 inches standard, optional 16- or 24 inch heavy bbl. w/folding bipod. Lgt.: 31 inches. Weight: 8.5 lbs. Integral 1.5x scope and mount. Green high-impact synthetic stock w/folding vertical grip.

Thompson/Center Arms

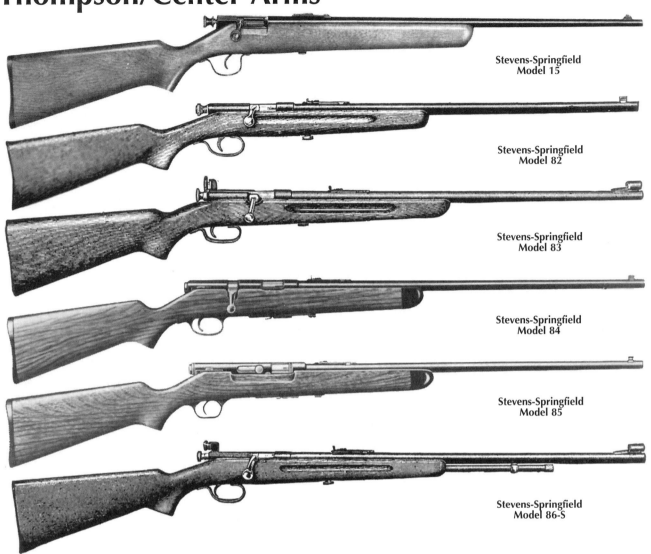

Stevens-Springfield
Model 15

Stevens-Springfield
Model 82

Stevens-Springfield
Model 83

Stevens-Springfield
Model 84

Stevens-Springfield
Model 85

Stevens-Springfield
Model 86-S

SMALL BORE CARBINE . . . . **NiB $440 Ex $300 Gd $166**
Bolt-action repeater. Caliber: .22 LR. Five round detachable box magazine. 19.5-inch bbl. Sights: Leaf rear; hooded bead front. Mannlicher-type stock, checkered, swivels. Made from 1953 to 1967.

STOEGER RIFLE — Manufactured by Franz Jaeger & Co., Suhl, Germany; distributed in the United States by A. F. Stoeger, Inc., New York, New York

HORNET RIFLE. . . . . **NiB $1388 Ex $1008 Gd $659**
Same specifications as Herold Rifle, designed and built on a Miniature Mauser-type action. (See listing under Herold Bolt-Action Repeating Sporting Rifle for additional specifications.) Imported circa 1930s.

SURVIVAL ARMS — Orange, Connecticut

AR-7 EXPLORER . . . . **NiB $180 Ex $155 Gd $98**
Caliber: .22 LR; eight-round mag. Weight: 3 lbs. Polymer stocks. Drift adj. sights. Disassembles into five elements so that bbl.,

action and mag. fit into buttstock. Reassembles w/out tools. Camo, silvertone or black matte finish. Made from 1992 to 1995.

THOMPSON/CENTER ARMS — (Division of Smith & Wesson, Springfield, Massachusetts formerly Rochester, New Hampshire)

CONTENDER CARBINE
Calibers: .22 LR, .22 Hornet, .222 Rem., .223 Rem., 7mm T.C.U., 7x30 Waters, .30-30 Win., .35 Rem., .44 Mag., .357 Rem. Max. and .410 bore. 21-inch interchangeable bbls. 35 inches overall. Adj. iron sights. Checkered American walnut or Rynite stock and forend. Made from 1986 to 2000.

Standard model (rifle calibers)	NiB $466	Ex $287	Gd $198
Standard model (.410 bore)	NiB $459	Ex $280	Gd $210
Rynite stock model			
(rifle calibers)	NiB $390	Ex $290	Gd $245
Rynite stock model (.410 bore). . . .	NiB $390	Ex $300	Gd $244
Youth model (all calibers).	NiB $490	Ex $320	Gd $235
Extra bbl. (rifle calibers), add			$25
Extra bbl. (.410 bore), add			$35

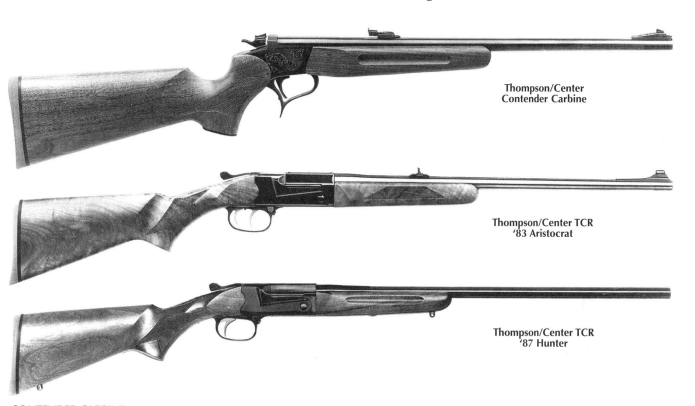

Thompson/Center Contender Carbine

Thompson/Center TCR '83 Aristocrat

Thompson/Center TCR '87 Hunter

CONTENDER CARBINE
SURVIVAL SYSTEM . . . . **NiB $655 Ex $488 Gd $370**
Caliber: .22 LR, .22 Hornet, .222 Rem., .223 Rem., 7mm T.C.U., 7x30 Waters, .30-30 Win., .35 Rem. .44 Mag., .357 Rem. Mag. .410 bore. Interchangeable 21-inch bbls. Lgt.: 35 inches. Adj. iron sights. Checkered American walnut or Rynite stock and forend. Made from 1986 to 2000.

STAINLESS CONTENDER CARBINE
Same as standard Contender Carbine Model, except stainless steel w/blued sights. Calibers: .22 LR, .22 Hornet, .223 Rem., 7-30 Waters, .30-30, .420 bore. Walnut or Rynite stock and forend. Made from 1993 to 2000.
Walnut stock model . . . . **NiB $445 Ex $390 Gd $325**
Rynite stock model . . . . **NiB $490 Ex $425 Gd $300**
Youth stock model . . . . **NiB $467 Ex $388 Gd $287**
Extra bbls. (rifle calibers), add **$25**

TCR '83/ARISTOCRAT MODEL . . . NiB $497 Ex $445 Gd $277
Break frame, over-lever action. Caliber: .223 Rem., .22-250 Rem., .243 Win., 7mm Rem. Mag. .30-06. Interchangeable 23-inch bbls. Lgt.: 23 inches. Weight: 6 lbs, 14 oz. Checkered American walnut stock and forearm, black rubber recoil pad. Made from 1983 to 1987.
Aristocrat model . . . . **NiB $569 Ex $435 Gd $280**
Extra bbl. (rifle calibers), add **$275**

TCR '87 HUNTER RIFLE . . . . NiB $544 Ex $345 Gd $200
Similar to TCR '83 except in .22 Hornet, .222 Rem., .223 Rem., .22-250 Rem,. .243 Win., .270 Win., 7mm-08, .308 Win., .30-06, .32-40 Win. Also 12-ga. slug, 10 and 12 ga. Bbl.: 23 inches standard, 25.88 inches heavy; interchangeable. Lgt.: 39.5 to 43.38 inches. Weight: 6 lbs. 14 oz. to 7.5 lbs. Iron sights optional. Checkered American black walnut buttstock w/fluted forend. Disc. 1992.
Extra bbl. (rifle calibers, 10- & 12-ga. field), add **$250**
Extra bbl. (12-ga. slug), add **$300**

ICON . . . . NiB $1167 Ex $855 Gd $766
Bolt action. Cal.: .22-250 Rem., .270 Win., .30-06, .300 Win. Mag., .308 Win., .30 TC, 6.5 Creedmoor, 7mm Mag. Bbl.: 24 inches. Medium or long action, hinged floor plate (on long action). Stock: Black synthetic or RealTree camo, checkered American walnut, classic walnut or Ultra Wood; pistol grip and forearm. Adj. trigger, cocking indicator, three-shot magazine (on medium action). Jeweled bolt handle. Weaver-style bases. Weight: 7.5 pounds. Guaranteed to shoot 1-inch or less at 100 yards.
Walnut stock models, add **$75**

ICON PRECISION HUNTER . . . . . NiB $1355 Ex $988 Gd $778
Bolt action. Cal.: .204 Ruger, .223 Rem., .22-250 Rem., .243 Win., 6.5 Creedmoor, .308 Win. Bbl.: 22 inches, fluted; 5R button rifling. Tactical-style bolt handle. Stock: Brown synthetic with cheekpiece and beavertail fore end. Detachable 3-round magazine with single-shot adapter. Picatinny rail, adj. trigger, sling studs.

ICON WARLORD . . . . NiB $1366 Ex $1127 Gd $888
Bolt action. Cal.: .308 Win. or .338 Lapua; 5- or 10-round magazine. Bbl.: Fluted, stainless steel, hand lapped. Stock: Carbon fiber tactical style with adj. cheek piece available in OD, flat black or desert sand. Adj. trigger, Picatinny rail. Weight: 12.75 to 13.75 lbs.

VENTURE . . . . NiB $632 Ex $490 Gd $375
Bolt action. Cal.: 270 Win., .30-06, 7 mm Rem. Mag., .300 Win. Mag. Bbl.: 24 inches, tapered match grade with 5R button rifling. Stock: Black synthetic, sporter design, textured grip. Adj. trigger, two-position safety.

VENTURE PREDATOR . . . . NiB $690 Ex $559 Gd $433
Bolt action. Cal.: .204 Ruger, .223 Rem., .22-250 Rem. or .308 Win. Bbl.: 22 inches, fluted, 3-round magazine. Stock: Composite with 100% Realtree Max-1 camo coating; Hogue panels, Weather Shield bolt handle. Weight. 6.75 lbs.

Tikka Rifles

Thompson/Center Icon Warlord

Thompson/Center Model R-55 Classic

Thompson/Center Encore Katahdin

SILVER LYNX. . . . . **NiB $488 Ex $390 Gd $300**
Semi-auto. Cal.: .22 LR. Bbl.: 20 inches, match grade; 5-round magazine, stainless steel action and bbl. Stock: Black composite with Monte Carlo cheek piece. Weight: 5.5 lbs.

MODEL R-55 CLASSIC . . . . **NiB $629 Ex $428 Gd $326**
Semi-auto. Cal.: .17 Mach 2, .22 LR. Bbl.: 22 inches, match grade; adj. rear sight; blue finish. Blow-back action. Smooth Monte Carlo walnut stock. Weight: 5.5 lbs.
R-55 Target . . . . **NiB $677 Ex $466 Gd $389**
R-55 Sporter . . . . **NiB $519 Ex $405 Gd $310**

ENCORE RIFLE . . . . **NiB $788 Ex $521 Gd $379**
Single-shot, break-action. Cal.: Rimfire and centerfire from .17 Mach 2 to .45-70 Gov't. Bbl.: 24 to 16 inches, interchangeable. Hammer block safety, trigger guard opening lever. Stock: Synthetic black, Realtree camo or American walnut; smooth forearm, Monte Carlo stock w/pistol grip.; adj. rear sight.
W/extra blued bbls., add $245
Camo models, add $150
W/thumbhole stock, add $225
.17 Mach 2, add $75
W/stainless bbl., add $400
Hunter pkg. (scope, bases, case), add $300

ENCORE KATAHDIN . . . . **NiB $633 Ex $467 Gd $379**
Same as Encore but with 18-inch blued bbl. Cal.: .444 Marlin, .450 Marlin or .45-70 Gov't. Stock: Black composite. Fiber optic sights, drilled and tapped for scope. Weight: 6.6 lbs. Made from 2002 to 2005.

PRO HUNTER RIFLE. . . . . **NiB $935 Ex $670 Gd $433**
Cal.: Various. Bbl.: 28 inches, stainless steel. Recoil reducing Flex-Tech stock (thumbhole option) in black or camo.
W/camo stock, add $100
W/ extra bbl., add $400

HOTSHOT (CAMO STOCK) . . . . . **NiB $395 Ex $299 Gd $214**
W/pink camo stock, add $25
Youth model. Cal.: 22 LR. Bbl.: 19 inches. Stock: Black synthetic, Realtree AP camo or AP pink camo. Auto safety; drilled and tapped for scope. Weight: 3 lbs.

TIKKA RIFLES — Manufactured by Sako, Ltd. of Riihimaki, Finland, & Armi Marocchi in Italy. Imported by Beretta USA

T3 HUNTER . . . . **NiB $655 Ex $535 Gd $390**
Caliber: .223 Rem., .22-250 Rem., .243 Win., .308 Win., .25-06 Rem,. .270 Win., 6.5x55, .270 WSM, 7mm Rem. Mag., .30-06, .300 WSM, .300 Win. Mag., .338 Win. Mag; Bbl.: 22.5 inches (24.5 in magnum calibers). Weight: 6.75 lbs. Bbl.: 22.5 inches (24.5 in magnum calibers). Weight: 6 .75 lbs. No sights. Walnut stock w/rubber butt pad. Introduced 2003.

T3 LAMINATED
STAINLESS . . . . **NiB $765 Ex $680 Gd $590**
Same as T3 Hunter except w/stainless barrel and action; laminated stock.

T3 LITE . . . . **NiB $555 Ex $489 Gd $410**
Similar to T3 Hunter except w/synthetic stock; weight: 6 pounds, 3 ounces. Introduced 2003.

T3 LITE STAINLESS . . . . **NiB $589 Ex $469 Gd $366**
Same as T3 Lite except w/stainless barrel and action.

T3 TACTICAL. . . . . **NiB $1469 Ex $1210 Gd $1066**
Calibers: .223 Rem., .308 Win.; five-round detachable mag. Similar to T3 Hunter but designed for law enforcement. Bbl.: 20 inches. Black phosphate finish, synthetic stock w/adj. comb. Picatinny rail on receiver, fitted for muzzle brake and bipod use.

T3 VARMINT. . . . . **NiB $844 Ex $700 Gd $567**
Calibers: .223 Rem., .22-250 Rem., .308 Win.; five-round detachable mag. Similar to T3 Hunter except w/heavy bull bbl., synthetic stock, adj. trigger.

T3 VARMINT
STAINLESS . . . . **NiB $844 Ex $700 Gd $567**
Similar to T3 Varmint but with stainless barrel and action.

MODEL 412S DOUBLE RIFLE
Caliber: .308 Win., .30-06, 9.3x74R. Bbl.: 24 inches. Quarter rib machined for scope mounts. Automatic ejectors (9.3x74R only).

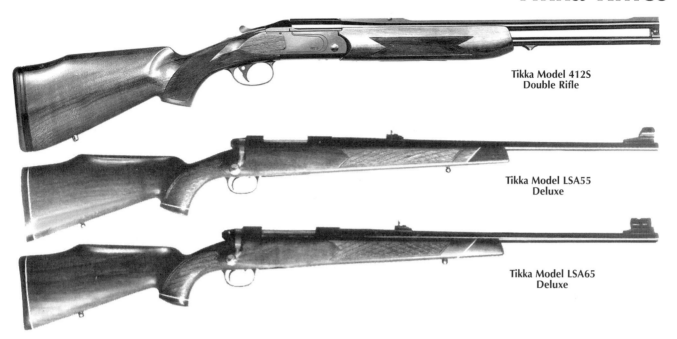

Tikka Model 412S
Double Rifle

Tikka Model LSA55
Deluxe

Tikka Model LSA65
Deluxe

Lgt.: 40 inches. Weight: 8.5 lbs. Ramp front, folding adj. rear sighs. BbL. selector on trigger. European walnut buttstock and forearm. Model 412S was replaced by the 512S version in 1994. imported from 1989 to 1993.

Model 412S
(disc. 1993)...................... NiB $1135 Ex $944 Gd $725
Extra bbl. assembly
(O/U shotgun), add $700
Extra bbl. assembly
(O/U Combo), add $800
Extra bbl. assembly
(OU/rifle), add $1050

MODEL 512S DOUBLE RIFLE
Formerly Valmet 412S. In 1994, the model designation was changed to 512S. Imported from 1994 to 1997.
Model 512S.................. NiB $1559 Ex $1430 Gd $1100
W/extra bbl. assembly (O/U rifle), add $800

LSA55 DELUXE............... NiB $590 Ex $534 Gd $450
Same as LSA55 Standard except w/rollover cheekpiece, rosewood grip cap and forend tip, skip checkering, high-luster bluing. Imported from 1965 to 1988.

LSA55 SPORTER .... NiB $580 Ex $477 Gd $365
Same as LSA55 except has 22.8-inch heavy bbl. w/o sights, special stock w/beavertail forearm, not available in 6mm Rem. Weighs 9 lbs. Imported from 1965 to 1988.

LSA55 STANDARD
BOLT-ACTION REPEATER....... NiB $555 Ex $389 Gd $244
Mauser-type action. Calibers: .222 Rem., .22-250 Rem., 6mm Rem Mag., .243 Win., .308 Win.; three-round clip mag. Bbl.: 22.8 inches. Weight: 6.8 lbs. Folding leaf rear, hooded ramp front sights. Checkered Monte Carlo walnut stock , swivels, Made from 1965 to 1988.

LSA65 DELUXE............... NiB $598 Ex $522 Gd $365
Same as LSA65 Standard except w/special features of LSA55 Deluxe. Imported from 1970 to 1988.

LSA65 STANDARD .... NiB $490 Ex $398 Gd $277

Same as LSA55 Standard except in .25-06 Rem., . 6.5x55, .270 Win., .30-06; five-round mag. Bbl. 22-inches. Weight: 7.5 lbs. Imported from 1970 to 1988.

MODEL M 55
Bolt-action. Calibers: .222 Rem., .22-250 Rem. .223 Rem. .243 Win., .308 Win (6mm Rem. Mag. and .17 Rem. available in Standard and Deluxe models only). Bbl.: 23.2 inches (24.8 inches in Sporter and Heavy bbl. models). Lgt.: 42.8 inches. (44 inches in Sporter and Heavy bbl. models). Weight: 7.25 to 9 lbs. Monte Carlo-style pistol-grip stock. Sling swivels. Imported from 1965 to 1988.

Continental................... NiB $745	Ex $560	Gd $420
Deluxe model................. NiB $808	Ex $579	Gd $443
Sporter...................... NiB $733	Ex $577	Gd $400
Sporter w/sights .... NiB $755	Ex $566	Gd $390
Standard .... NiB $669	Ex $544	Gd $367
Super Sporter .... NiB $833	Ex $466	Gd $398
Super Sporter w/sights .... NiB $900	Ex $478	Gd $514
Trapper .... NiB $755	Ex $556	Gd $443

MODEL M65
Bolt-action. Caliber: .25-06 Rem., .270 Win., .30-06, 7mm Rem. Mag., .300 Win. Mag (Sporter and Heavy bbl. models in .270 Win., .308 Win. and .30-06 only). Bbl.: 22.4 inches. (24.8 inches in Sporter and heavy bbl. models). Lgt.: 43.2 inches (44 inches in Sporter, 44.8 inches in Heavy bbl. models) Weight: 7.5 to 9.9 lbs. Monte Carlo-style pistol-grip stock. Disc. 1989

Continental................... NiB $755	Ex $566	Gd $435
Deluxe Magnum............... NiB $800	Ex $677	Gd $490
Deluxe model .... NiB $770	Ex $587	Gd $467
Magnum .... NiB $709	Ex $540	Gd $440
Sporter .... NiB $579	Ex $555	Gd $398
Sporter w/sights .... NiB $789	Ex $645	Gd $445
Standard .... NiB $670	Ex $690	Gd $479
Super Sporter .... NiB $898	Ex $690	Gd $489
Super Sporter w/sights .... NiB $900	Ex $695	Gd $494
Super Sporter Master .... NiB $1143	Ex $944	Gd $643

MODEL M65 WILD BOAR .... NiB $790 Ex $644 Gd $469
Same specs as Model M65 except w/20-8-inch bbl. Lgt.: 41.6 inches. Weight: 7.5 lbs. Disc. 1989.

Tikka Rifles

Tikka
Model M65 Sporter

Tikka
Model M65 Wild Boar

NEW GENERATION RIFLES
Short-throw bolt made in three action lengths. Calibers: .22-250 Rem., .223 Rem., .243 Win., .270 Win., .308 Win. (medium action), .30-06 (long action), 7mm Rem. Mag., .300 Win. Mag., .338 Win. Mag. (magnum action). Bbl.: 22 to 26 inches. Lgt.: 42.25 to 46 inches. Weight: 7.2 to 8.5 lbs.
Standard calibers . . . . NiB $769 Ex $688 Gd $487
Magnum calibers, add. $50

PREMIUM GRADE RIFLE
Similar to New Generation rifles except w/hand-checkered deluxe wood stock roll-over check-piece and rosewood grip cap and forend tip. High polished blued finish. Imported from 1989 to 1994.
Standard calibers . . . . NiB $923 Ex $755 Gd $488
Magnum calibers, add. $50

BATTUE MODEL
Similar to Hunter Model except designed for snapshooting w/hooded front and open rear sights on quarter rib. Blued finish. Checkered select walnut stock w/matte lacquered finish. Imported from 1991 to 1997.
Battue model (standard w/sights) . . NiB $568 Ex $466 Gd $388
Magnum calibers, add. $50

CONTINENTAL MODEL
Similar to Hunter model except w/prone-style stock w/wider fore-arm. Bbl.: 26 inches, heavy. Caliber: .17 Rem. .22-250 Rem., .223 Rem., .308 Win., (Varmint); .25-06 Rem. .270 Rem., 7mm Rem. Mag, .300 Win. Mag (Long Range). Weight: 8.6 lbs. Imported from 1991 to 2003
Continental Long-Range model. . . . NiB $690 Ex $558 Gd $390
Continental Varmint model. . . . . . . NiB $640 Ex $500 Gd $355
Magnum calibers, add. 40%

SPORTER MODEL . . . . NiB $900 Ex $779 Gd $633
Similar to Hunter model except w/23.5-inch bbl. Caliber: .22-50 Rem., .223 Rem., .308 Win.; five-round detachable mag. Weight: 8.6 lbs. Adj. buttplate and cheekpiece w/stippled pistol grip and forend. Imported from 1998 to 2003.

WHITETAIL HUNTER MODEL
Caliber: .22-250 Rem., .223 Rem. .243 Win., .25-06 Rem., .270 Win., 7mm Rem. Mag., .308 Win., .30-06, .300 Win., Mag, .338 Win. Mag.; three- or five-round detachable box mag. Bbl.: 20.5 to 24.5 inches, no sights. Lgt.: 42 to 44.5 inches. Weight: 7 to 7.5 lbs. Adj. single-stage or single set trigger. Blued or stainless finish. All-Weather synthetic or checkered select walnut stock w/matte lacquered finish. Imported from 1991 to 2002.
Standard model. . . . . NiB $633 Ex $523 Gd $389
Deluxe model . . . . NiB $689 Ex $534 Gd $445
Synthetic model . . . . NiB $689 Ex $534 Gd $445
Stainless model . . . . NiB $689 Ex $534 Gd $445
Magnum calibers, add $50
Left-hand model, add $100

Uberti Rifles

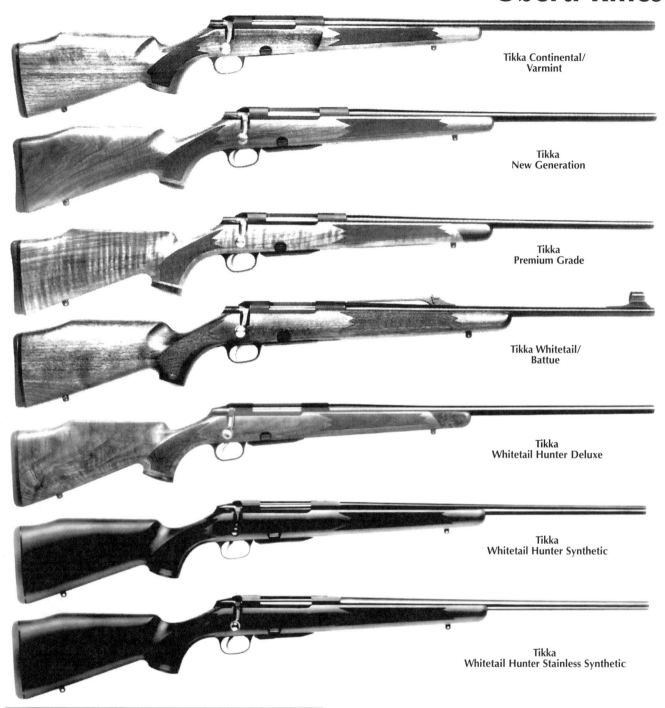

Tikka Continental/
Varmint

Tikka
New Generation

Tikka
Premium Grade

Tikka Whitetail/
Battue

Tikka
Whitetail Hunter Deluxe

Tikka
Whitetail Hunter Synthetic

Tikka
Whitetail Hunter Stainless Synthetic

UBERTI RIFLES — Lakeville, Connecticut. Manufactured by Aldo Uberti, Ponte Zanano, Italy. Imported by Stoeger Industries, Accokeek, Maryland

MODEL 1866 SPORTING RIFLE

Replica of Winchester Model 1866 lever-action repeater. Calibers: .22 LR, .22 WMR., .38 Special, .44-40, .45 LC. Bbl.: 24.5 to 25.25-inches, octagonal. Lgt.: 43.25 inches. Weight: 8.25 lbs. Blade front rear elevator leaf sights. Brass frame and buttplate. Magazine tube, other metal parts blued. Walnut buttstock and forearm.

Model 1866 Rifle . . . . NiB $966 Ex $667 Gd $390
Model 1866 Carbine
(19-inch round bbl.) . . . . NiB $944 Ex $600 Gd $409
Model 1866 Trapper
(16-inch bbl.,
disc. 1989) . . . . NiB $1145 Ex $855 Gd $600
Model 1866 Rimfire
(Indian Rifle). . . . . NiB $744 Ex $523 Gd $379
Model 1866 Rimfire
(Indian Carbine) . . . . NiB $744 Ex $523 Gd $379

Ultra Light Arms Company

Uberti Model
1873 Carbine

MODEL 1873 SPORTING RIFLE
Replica of Winchester Model 1873 lever-action repeater. Calibers: .22 LR, .22 WMR. .38 Special. .357 Mag., .44-40, .45 LC. Bbl.: 24.5 or 30 inches, octagonal. Lgt.: 43.25. Weight: 8 lbs. Blade front, adj. open rear sights. Color case-hardened frame Mag. tube, hammer, lever and buttplate blued. Walnut buttstock and forearm.
Model 1873 Rifle . . . . **NiB $1095 Ex $809 Gd $566**
Model 1873 Carbine
(19-inch round bbl.) . . . . **NiB $790 Ex $666 Gd $445**
Model 1873 Trapper
(16-inch bbl., disc. 1990) . . . . . . **NiB $1095 Ex $809 Gd $566**

HENRY RIFLE
Replica of Henry lever-action repeating rifle. Caliber: .44-40, .45 LC. Bbl.: 24.5 inches, half-octagonal. Lgt.: 43.75 inches. Weight: 9.25 lbs. Blade front, adj. rear sights. Brass frame, buttplate and mag. follower. Bbl., gag. tube and remaining metal parts blued. Walnut buttstock.
Henry Rifle . . . . **NiB $1177 Ex $808 Gd $590**
Henry Carbine
(22.5-inch bbl.) . . . . **NiB $1177 Ex $808 Gd $590**
Henry Trapper
(16- or 18-inch bbl.) . . . . **NiB $1177 Ex $808 Gd $590**
Steel frame, add $100

MODEL 1875
ARMY TARGET . . . . **NiB $455 Ex $360 Gd $300**
Carbine version of Model 1875 single-action revolver. Caliber: .357 Mag., .44-40 Colt; six-round cylinder. Bbl.: 18 inches. Lgt.: 37 inches. Weight: 5.5 lbs. Adj. rear, ramp front sights. Plain walnut stock, polished brass buttplate and trigger guard. Case-hardened frame. Blued or nickel-plated cylinder and bbl. Made in Italy. Introduced in 1987, disc. 1989.
Nickel finish, add $50

ROLLING BLOCK
BABY CARBINE. . . . . **NiB $450 Ex $377 Gd $319**
Replica of Remington New Model No. 4 Carbine. Caliber: .22 LR, .22 WMR, .22 Hornet, .357 Mag. Bbl.: 22 inches. Lgt.: 35.5 inches. Weight: 4.75 lbs. Brass buttplate and trigger guard, blued bbl. Color case-hardened frame. Introduced in 1986.

ULTRA-HI PRODUCTS COMPANY — Hawthorne, New Jersey

MODEL 2200 SINGLE-SHOT
BOLT-ACTION RIFLE . . . . **NiB $235 Ex $166 Gd $120**
Caliber: .22 LR, Long, Short. .23-inch bbl. Weight: 5 lbs. Sights: Open rear; blade front. Monte Carlo stock w/pistol grip. Made in Japan. Introduced 1977. Disc.

ULTRA LIGHT ARMS COMPANY — Granville, West Virginia

MODEL 20 BOLT-ACTION RIFLE
Caliber: .22-250 Rem., .243 Win., 6mm Rem., .250-3000 Savage, .257 Roberts, .257 Ackley, 7mm Mauser, 7mm Ackley, 7mm-08 Rem., .284 Win., .300 Savage, .308 Win., .358 Win; box mag. Bbl.: 22 inches, ultralight. Weight: 4.75 lbs. No sights. Kevlar or graphite-finished synthetic stock, seven colors avail. Non-glare matte or bright metal finish. Medium action avail. in left-hand models. Made from 1985 to 1999.
Standard model. . . . . **NiB $2270 Ex $2056 Gd $1190**
Left-hand model, add $150

MODEL 20S BOLT-ACTION RIFLE
Same specifications as Model 20 except w/short action in 17 Rem., .222 Rem., .223 Rem., .22 Hornet only.
Standard model . . . . **NiB $2467 Ex $2144 Gd $1180**
Left-hand model, add $125

MODEL 24 BOLT-ACTION RIFLE
Same specs as Model 20 except w/long action in .25-06 Rem., .270 Win., .30-06 and 7mm Express only.
Standard model. . . . . **NiB $2350 Ex $2123 Gd $1179**
Left-hand model, add. $125

MODEL 28 BOLT-ACTION RIFLE . . . . . **NiB $2709 Ex $2033 Gd $1190**
Same general specifications as Model 20 except w/long magnum action in calibers .264 Win. Mag., 7mm Rem. Mag., .300 Win. Mag., .338 Win. Mag. only. Weight: 5.75 lbs. Recoil arrester; left-hand model offered.

MODEL 40 BOLT-ACTION RIFLE
Similar to Model 28 except in .300 Wby. and .416 Rigby. Weight: 5.5 lbs. Made from 1994 to 1999.
Standard model. . . . . **NiB $2770 Ex $2055 Gd $1290**
Left-hand, model, add. $125

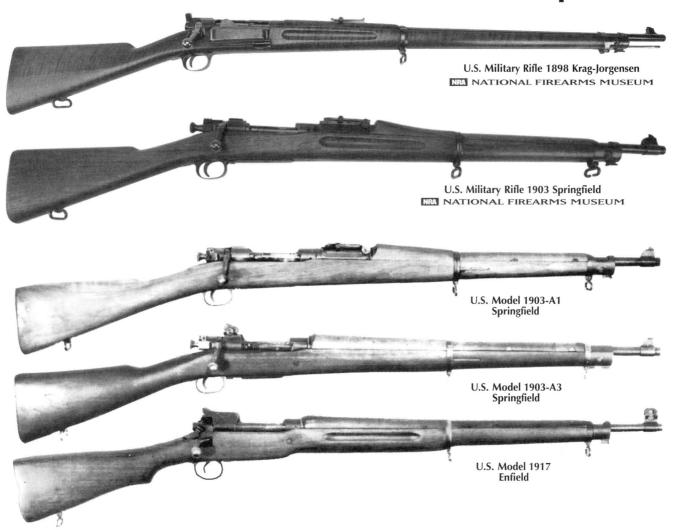

U.S. Military Rifle 1898 Krag-Jorgensen
NRA NATIONAL FIREARMS MUSEUM

U.S. Military Rifle 1903 Springfield
NRA NATIONAL FIREARMS MUSEUM

U.S. Model 1903-A1
Springfield

U.S. Model 1903-A3
Springfield

U.S. Model 1917
Enfield

UNIQUE RIFLE — Hendaye, France. Manufactured by Manufacture d'Armes des Pyrénées Francaises

T66 MATCH RIFLE . . . . **NiB $469 Ex $388 Gd $289**
Bolt-action, single-shot. Caliber: .22 LR. Bbl.: 25.5 inches. Weight: 10.5 lbs. Micrometer aperture rear, globe front sights. French walnut Monte Carlo target stock, bull pistol grip. Wide and deep forearm. stippled grip surfaces. Adj. swivel on accessory track, adj. rubber buttplate. Made in 1966. Disc.

U.S. MILITARY RIFLES — Manufactured at Springfield Armory, Springfield, Massachusetts

MODEL 1898
KRAG-JORGENSEN CARBINE. . NiB $2100 Ex $1879 Gd $1100
Same specs as Model 1898 Rifle except w/22-inch bbl., Weight 8 lbs. Carbine-type stock. Carbine models 1896 and 1899 differ from Model 1898 only in minor details.

MODEL 1898
KRAG-JORGENSEN MILITARY RIFLE . . NiB $2100 Ex $1879 Gd $1100
Bolt-action. Caliber: .30-40 Krag; five-round hinged box mag. Bbl.: 30 inches. Weight: 9 lbs. Adj. rear, blade front sights. Military-type stock, straight grip. These specs apply to models 1892 and 1896, which differ from Model 1898.

MODEL 1903 MARK I SPRINGFIELD . . . NiB $2144 Ex $1844 Gd $945
Bolt-action. Caliber: .30-40 Krag; five-round hinged box mag. Bbl.: 30 inches. Weight: 9 lbs. Adj. rear, blade front sights. Military-type stock, straight grip. These specs apply to models 1892 and 1896, which differ from Model 1898. Same as Standard Model 1903 except altered to permit use of Pedersen Device, which converts the M-1903 to a semi-automatic rifle firing a .30 caliber cartridge similar to a .32 auto pistol round. Mark I rifles have a slot milled in the left side of the receiver that serves as an ejection port when the Pedersen device is in use. Some 65,000 of these units were made but most were destroyed. Only about 20 units are known to exist.

MODEL 1903 NATIONAL
MATCH SPRINGFIELD . . . . **NiB $1755 Ex $1577 Gd $1109**
Same specs as Standard Model 1903 except w/specially star-gauged bbl., Type C pistol grip, stock, polished bolt assembly. Early types have headless firing pin assembly and reversed safety lock. Produced specifically for target shooting.

U.S. Military Rifles

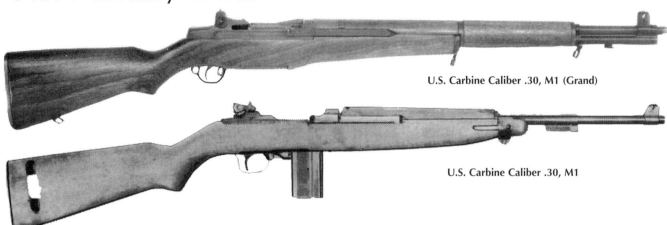

U.S. Carbine Caliber .30, M1 (Grand)

U.S. Carbine Caliber .30, M1

MODEL 1903 SPRINGFIELD MILITARY RIFLE
Modified Mauser-type bolt-action. Caliber: .30-06; five-round box mag. Bbl.: 23.79 inches. Weight: 8.75 lbs. Adj. rear, blade front sights. Military-type straight-grip stock. M-1903 rifles of Springfield manufacture w/serial numbers under 800,000 (1903 to 1918) have case-hardened receivers. Rifles between 800,001 and 1,275,767 (1918 to 1928) were double heat treated. Rifles numbered over 1,275,267 have nickel steel bolts and receivers. Improved heat treatment was adopted in May 1918 with rifle No. 285,207. Three months later, with rifle No. 319,921, the use of nickel steel was adopted. Some production of double-heat-treated carbon-steel receivers and bolts continued. Made from 1903 to 1930 at the Springfield Armory during WWI, M-1903 rifles were also made at the Rock Island Arsenal in Rock Island, Illinois.
W/case-hardened receiver . . . . NiB $5566 Ex $4769 Gd $2250
W/double heat-treated receiver . . . NiB $4410 Ex $3636 Gd $1645
W/nickel steel receiver . . . . NiB $1690 Ex $1530 Gd $977

MODEL 1903 SPRINGFIELD SPORTER. . NiB $1439 Ex $1978 Gd $890
Same general specifications as National Match except w/sporting design stock, Lyman No. 48 receiver sight.

MODEL 1903 STYLE T
SPRINGFIELD MATCH RIFLE . . . . NiB $1633 Ex $1290 Gd $934
Same specs as Springfield Sporter except w/heavy bbl. (26, 28 or 30 inches) scope bases, globe front sight. Weight: 12.5 lbs

MODEL 1903 TYPE A
SPRINGFIELD FREE RIFLE. . . . . NiB $1900 Ex $1544 Gd $1150
Same as Style T except made w/28-inch bbl. only, w/Swiss buttplate; weight: 13.25 lbs.

MODEL 1903 TYPE B
SPRINGFIELD FREE RIFLE. . . . . NiB $3510 Ex $2065 Gd $1400
Same as Type A except w/cheekpiece stock, palm rest. Double-set triggers. Garand fast firing pin. Weight: 14.75 lbs.

MODEL 1903-A1 SPRINGFIELD
Same specs as Model 1903 except may have Type C pistol-grip stock adopted in 1930. The last Springfields produced at the Springfield Armory were of this type. Final serial number was 1,532,878 made in 1939. Late in 1941 Remington Arms Co., Ilion, N.Y., Began producing rifles under government contract with numbers 3,000,001 to 3,348,085. These were manufactured before the adoption of the Model 1903-A3 rifle.
Springfield manufacture . . . . . . NiB $1444 Ex $1266 Gd $845
Remington manufacture . . . . NiB $955 Ex $855 Gd $577

MODEL 1903-A3 SPRINGFIELD. . . . . . NiB $1698 Ex $1492 Gd $978
Same specs as Model 1903-A1 except modified to permit increased production at lower cost. May have straight-grip or pistol-grip stock. Bolt is not interchangeable w/earlier types. Receiver peep sight. Many parts are stamped from sheet steel including the trigger guard and mag. assembly. Quality of these rifles is lower than that of other 1903 Springfields, reflecting the emergency conditions that prevailed when they were produced Mfd. During WWII by Remington Arms Co. and L. C. Smith Corona Typewriters, Inc.

MODEL 1922-M1 22
SPRINGFIELD TARGET RIFLE . . . NiB $1277 Ex $1068 Gd $788
Modified Model 1903. Caliber: .22 LR; five-round detachable box mag. Bbl.: 24.5 inches. Weight: 9 lbs. Lyman No. 48C receiver, blade front sights. Sporting-type stock similar to that of Model 1903 Springfield Sporter issued in 1927. The earlier Model 1922, which is seldom encountered, differs from the Target model chiefly in the bolt mechanism and magazine.

M2 22 SPRINGFIELD TARGET RIFLE . . . NiB $1366 Ex $1123 Gd $580
Same specs as Model 1922-M1 except w/speed-lock, improved bolt assembly. Adj. for headspace. These improvements were later incorporated in many rifle models (M1922, 1922M1). Arms so converted were marked "M1922M2" or "M1922 MII."

CALIBER .30, M1
(GARAND) MIL. RIFLE . . . . . . NiB $1431 Ex $1206 Gd $1166
Clip-fed, gas-operated. Air-cooled semi-automatic. Eight-round clip. Bbl.: 24 inches. Weight: 9.5 lbs. Adj. peep rear, blade front sight. Pistol-grip stock w/handguard. Made from 1937 to 1957. Garand rifles have also been produced by Winchester Repeating Arms Co., Harrington & Richardson Arms Co. and International Harvester Co. Deduct 25% for arsenal-assembled mismatches.

CALIBER .30, M1,
NATIONAL MATCH . . . . NiB $2389 Ex $1775 Gd $730
Accurized target version of the Garand. Glass-bedded stock; match grade bbl., sights, gas cylinder. "NM" stamped on bbl. forward of handguard.

MODEL 1917 ENFIELD MILITARY RIFLE . . NiB $977 Ex $800 Gd $366
Modified Mauser-type bolt-action. Caliber: .30-06; five-round box mag. Bbl. 26 inches. Weight: 9.25 inches. Adj. rear, blade front sights. Military-type stock w/semi pistol grip. This design originated in Great Britain as the Pattern 14 and was mfd. in .303 caliber for the British government in three U.S. plants. In 1917 the U. S. government contracted w/these firms to produce the same rifle in caliber.30-06. The U.S. supplied over 1 million units to Great Britain during WWII. Over 2 million of these Model 1917 Enfields were made, but production ended after WWII.

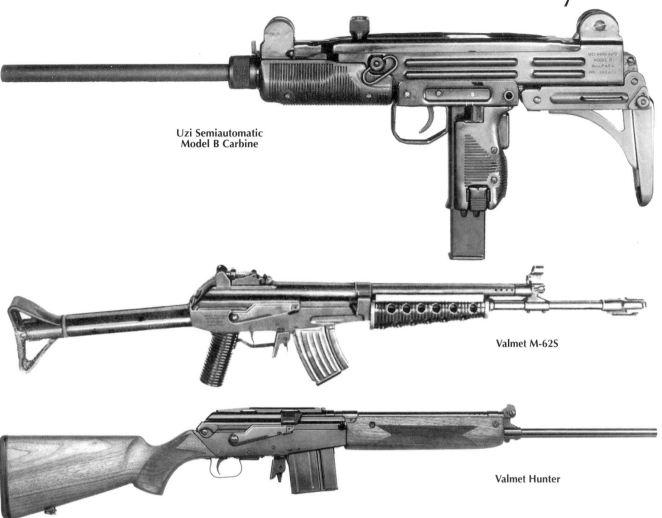

Uzi Semiautomatic
Model B Carbine

Valmet M-62S

Valmet Hunter

CARBINE,
CALIBER 30, M1 . . . . NiB $844 Ex $677 Gd $497
Gas-operated short-stroke piston semi-automatic; 15- or 30-round detachable box mag. Bbl.: 18 inches. Weight: 5.5 lbs. Adj. rear, blade front sight. Pistol-grip stock w/handguard; side-mounted web sling. Made from 1942 to 1945. In 1963, 150,000 surplus carbines were sold at $20 each to members of the National Rifle Association by the Dept. of the Army. For Winchester and Rock-Ola, add 30%. For Irwin Pedersen, add 80%. Quality Hardware Co. did not complete its production run. Guns produced by other manufacturers were marked "Unquality" and command premium prices.

UNIVERSAL FIREARMS, INC. — Miami, Florida

DELUXE CARBINE . . . . NiB $466 Ex $348 Gd $210
Same as standard model except also available in caliber .256, w/deluxe walnut Monte Carlo stock and handguard. Made fro 1965 to 1987.

STANDARD M-1 CARBINE . . . . NiB $375 Ex $246 Gd $175
Same as Standard model except in .256 caliber w/deluxe walnut Monte Carlo stock and handguard. Made from 1965 to 1987.

UZI CARBINE — Manufactured by Israel Military Industries, Israel

SEMIAUTOMATIC MODEL B CARBINE
Calibers: 9mm Parabellum, .41 Action Express, .45 ACP. 20- to 50-round magazine. 16.1-inch bbl. Weight: 8.4 lbs. Metal folding stock. Adj. post-type front, open rear sights. Imported by Action Arms from 1983 to 1989. Selective-fire models imported by UZI America, Inc., from 1983 to 1994.
Model B Carbine (9mm or .45 ACP) . . . NiB $1595 Ex $1276 Gd $1097
Model B Carbine (.41 AE) . . . . NiB $1595 Ex $1276 Gd $1097
Centerfire conversion unit, add $250
Rimfire conversion unit, add. $200

SEMIAUTOMATIC
MINI CARBINE . . . . NiB $2375 Ex $2153 Gd $1535
Similar to Uzi Model 8 except w/19.75-inch bbl., 9mm Parabellum; 20-round mag. Weight: 7.2 lbs. Imported in 1989.

Walther Rifles

Vickers Jubilee
Single-Shot Target Rifle

VALMET — Jyväskylä, Finland

M-62S SEMIAUTOMATIC RIFLE . . . . . . NiB $2590 Ex $2088 Gd $1655
Semi-automatic version of Finnish M-62 assault rifle based on Russian AK-47. Gas-operated floating bolt-action. Caliber: .7.62 mmx39 Russian; f5- w0-round mag. Bbl.: 16.63 inches. Weight: 8 lbs. w/metal stock. Tangent aperture rear, hooded blade front w/ luminous flip-up post front sights. Tubular steel or wood stock. Introduced 1962. Disc.

M-71S . . . . NiB $1988 Ex $1766 Gd $1064
Same specifications as M-62S except in 5.56mmx45 (.223 Rem.), w/open rear sight, reinforced resin or wood stock. Weight: 7.75 lbs. Made from 1971 to 1989.

M-76 SEMIAUTOMATIC RIFLE
Semiautomatic assault rifle. Gas-operated, rotating bolt action. Caliber: .223 Rem. 15- and 30-round magazines. Made from 1984 to 1989.
Wood stock . . . . NiB $1788 Ex $1373 Gd $1055
Folding stock . . . . NiB $1947 Ex $1522 Gd $1140

M-78 SEMIAUTOMATIC RIFLE . . . . . . NiB $1865 Ex $1492 Gd $1170
Caliber: .7.62x51 NATO. Bbl.: 24.13 inches. Lgt.: 43.25 inches. Weight: 10.5 lbs.

M-82 SEMIAUTOMATIC CARBINE . . . . NiB $1748 Ex $1399 Gd $1180
Caliber: .223 Rem. 15- or 30-round magazine. 17-inch bbl. 27 inches overall. Weight: 7.75 lbs.

MODEL 412 S DOUBLE RIFLE . . . . NiB $1095 Ex $1077 Gd $933
Boxlock over-under. Manual or automatic extraction. Calibers: .243 Win., .308 Win., .30-06, .375 Win., 9.3x74R. Bbl.: 24 inches. Weight: 8.63 lbs. American walnut checkered stock and forend.

HUNTER SEMIAUTOMATIC RIFLE . . . . . . NiB $955 Ex $755 Gd $639
Similar to M-78 except in.223 Rem (5.56mm), .243 Win., .308 Win. (7.62 NATO), .30-06; five-, nine- or 15-round mag. Bbl.: 20.5 inches. Lgt.: 42 inches. Wt.: 8 lbs. Adj. combination scope mount/rear, blade front sights. Checkered European walnut buttstock and extended checkered forend and handguard. Imported from 1986 to 1989.

VICKERS LTD. — Crayford, Kent, England

JUBILEE MODEL SINGLE-SHOT-
TARGET RIFLE. . . . . NiB $545 Ex $390 Gd $265
Round-receiver Martini-type action. Caliber: .22 LR. 28-inch heavy bbl. Weight: 9.5 lbs. Sights: Parker-Hale No. 2 front; Perfection rear peep. One-piece target stock w/full forearm and pistol-grip. Made before WWII.

EMPIRE MODEL . . . . NiB $569 Ex $435 Gd $287
Similar to Jubilee Model except w/27- or 30-inch bbl., straight-grip stock. Weight: 9.25 lbs. Made before WWII.

VOERE — Manufactured in Vohrenvach, Germany

VEC-91 LIGHTNING
BOLT-ACTION RIFLE . . . . NiB $2765 Ex $2165 Gd $1540
Electronic ignition system activates caseless ammunition. Caliber: 5.56 UCC (.222 cal.) 6mm UCC caseless; five-round mag. Bbl.: 39 inches. Weight: 6 lbs. Open adj. rear sight. Drilled and tapped for scope mounts. European walnut stock w/cheekpiece. Made from 1992 to date.

VOERE, VOELTER & COMPANY — Vaehrenbach, Germany

MODEL 1007 BIATHLON REPEATER . . . . . NiB $466 Ex $350 Gd $254
Caliber: 22 LR. Five round magazine. 19.5-inch bbl. 39 inches overall. Weight: 5.5 lb. Sights: Adj. rear, blade front. Plain beechwood stock. Imported from 1984 to 1986.

MODEL 1013 BOLT-ACTION REPEATER . . . . NiB $766 Ex $544 Gd $389
Same as Model 1007 except w/military-style stock in .22 WMR. Double-set triggers optional. Imported from 1984 to 1986 by KDF, Inc.

MODEL 2107 BOLT-ACTION REPEATER
Caliber: .22 LR; eight-round mag. Bbl.: 19.5 inches. Lgt.: 41 inches. Weight: 6 lbs. Adj. rear, hooded front. European hardwood Monte Carlo-style stock. Imported in 1986 by KDF, Inc.
Standard model . . . . NiB $439 Ex $278 Gd $255
Deluxe model . . . . NiB $469 Ex $344 Gd $266

WALTHER RIFLES — Manufactured by the German firms of Waffenfabrik Walther and Carl Walther Sportwaffenfabrik

MODEL 1 AUTOLOADING
RIFLE (LIGHT). . . . . NiB $966 Ex $723 Gd $500
Similar to Standard Model 2 but w/20-inch bbl., lighter stock. Weight: 4.5 lbs.

MODEL 2 AUTOLOADING RIFLE. . . . . . . NiB $1045 Ex $690 Gd $533
Bolt-action; manually-operated repeater or single-shot. Caliber: .22 LR; five-or nine-round detachable box mag. Bbl.: 24.5 inches. Weight: 7 lbs. Tangent-curve rear, ramp front sights. Sporting stock w/checkered pistol grip, grooved forearm. swivels. Disc.

Walther Model 1

Walther Model 2

Walther Model GX-1

Walther Model KKM-S

Walther Model U.I.T.
Super Match

OLYMPIC BOLT-ACTION
MATCH RIFLE . . . . NiB $1354 Ex $1095 Gd $800
Single-shot. Caliber: .22 LR. Bbl.: 26 inches, heavy. Weight: 13 lbs. Micrometer extension rear, interchangeable font sights. Target thumbhole stock w/checkered pistol grip, full beavertail forearm covered with corrugated rubber; palm rest. Adj. Swiss-type buttplate; swivels. Disc.

MODEL V BOLT-ACTION
SINGLE-SHOT RIFLE . . . . NiB $645 Ex $544 Gd $368
Caliber: .22 LR. 26-inch bbl. Weight: 7 lbs. Sights: Open rear; ramp front. Plain pistol-grip stock w/grooved forearm. Disc.

MODEL V MEISTERBÜCHSE
(CHAMPION) . . . . NiB $675 Ex $494 Gd $335
Same as standard Model V except w/micrometer open rear sight and checkered pistol-grip. Disc.

MODEL GX-1 FREE RIFLE . . . . . . NiB $1985 Ex $1544 Gd $933
Bolt-action single-shot. Caliber: .22 LR. Bbl: 25.5 inches, heavy. Weight: 15.9 lbs. Micrometer aperture rear, globe front sights. Thumbhole stock w/adj. cheekpiece and buttplate (w/removable hook), accessory rail. Left-hand stock option. Accessories furnished include hand stop and sling swivel, palm rest, counterweight assembly.

MODEL KKJ SPORTER . . . . NiB $1355 Ex $1108 Gd $644
Bolt action. Caliber: .22 LR. Five round box magazine. 22.5-inch bbl. Weight: 5.5 lbs. Sights: Open rear; hooded ramp front. Stock w/cheekpiece, checkered pistol-grip and forearm, sling swivels. Disc.

Weatherby, Inc.

MODEL KKJ-HO . . . . NiB $1543 Ex $1337 Gd $1110
Same as Model KKJ except in .22 Hornet. Disc.

MODEL KKJ-MA . . . . NiB $1321 Ex $1231 Gd $644
Same as Model KKJ except in .22 WMR. Disc.

MODEL KKM INTERNATIONAL
MATCH RIFLE . . . . NiB $944 Ex $669 Gd $609
Bolt-action, single-shot. Caliber: .22 LR. 28-inch heavy bbl. Weight: 15.5 lbs. Sights: Micrometer aperture rear; globe front. Thumbhole stock w/high comb, adj. hook buttplate, accessory rail. Left-hand stock option.

MODEL KKM-S . . . . NiB $1000 Ex $877 Gd $635
Same specifications as Model KKM, except w/adj. cheekpiece. Disc.

MOVING TARGET MATCH RIFLE . . . . NiB $1067 Ex $833 Gd $554
Bolt-action, single-shot. Caliber: .22 LR. 23.6-inch bbl. w/weight. Weight: 8.6 lbs. Supplied w/o sights. Thumbhole stock w/adj. cheekpiece and buttplate. Left-hand stock option.

PRONE 400 TARGET RIFLE . . . . NiB $833 Ex $715 Gd $500
Bolt-action, single-shot. Caliber: .22 LR. 25.5-inch heavy bbl. Weight: 10.25 lbs. Supplied w/o sights. Prone stock w/adj. cheekpiece and buttplate, accessory rail. Left-hand stock option. Disc.

MODEL SSV VARMINT RIFLE . . . . . NiB $770 Ex $697 Gd $488
Bolt-action, single-shot. Calibers: .22 LR, .22 Hornet. 25.5-inch bbl. Weight: 6.75 lbs. Supplied w/o sights. Monte Carlo stock w/high cheekpiece, full pistol grip and forearm. Disc.

MODEL U.I.T. SPECIAL MATCH RIFLE . . . . . NiB $1187 Ex $1070 Gd $833
Bolt-action, single-shot. Caliber: .22 LR. 25.5-inch bbl. Weight: 10.2 lbs. Sights: Micrometer aperture rear; globe front. Target stock w/high comb, adj. buttplate, accessory rail. Left-hand stock avail. Disc. 1993.

MODEL U.I.T. SUPER MATCH RIFLE . . . . . NiB $1169 Ex $1966 Gd $788
Bolt-action, single-shot. Caliber: .22 LR. 25.5-inch heavy bbl. Weight: 10.2 lbs. Micrometer aperture rear; globe front. Target stock w/support for off-hand shooting, high comb, adj. buttplate and swivel. Left-hand stock available. Disc. 1993.

MONTGOMERY WARD — Chicago, Illinois; Western Field and Hercules Models

MODEL 14M-497B WESTERN FIELD
BOLT-ACTION RIFLE . . . . NiB $160 Ex $121 Gd $90
Caliber: .22 RF; seven-round detachable box mag. Bbl.: 24 inches. Weight: 5 lbs. Receiver peep rear, hooded ramp front sights. Pistol-grip stock. Mfg. by Mossberg.

MODEL M771 WESTERN FIELD
LEVER-ACTION RIFLE . . . . NiB $221 Ex $177 Gd $135
Calibers: .30-30, .35 Rem. Six round tubular magazine. 20-inch bbl. Weight: 6.75 lbs. Sights: Open rear; ramp front. Pistol-grip or straight stock, forearm w/barrel band. Mfg. by Mossberg.

MODEL M772 WESTERN FIELD
LEVER-ACTION RIFLE . . . . NiB $235 Ex $190 Gd $131
Calibers: .30-30, .35 Rem. Six round tubular magazine. 20-inch bbl. Weight: 6.75 lbs. Sights: Open rear; ramp front. Pistol-grip or straight stock, forearm w/bbl. band. Mfg. by Mossberg.

MODEL M775
BOLT-ACTION RIFLE . . . . NiB $158 Ex $139 Gd $99
Caliber: .222 Rem., .22-250 Rem., .243 Win., .308 Win.; four-round mag. Weight: 7.5 lbs. Folding leaf rear, ramp front sights. Monte Carlo stock w/cheekpiece, pistol grip. Mfg. by Mossberg.

MODEL M776
BOLT-ACTION RIFLE . . . . NiB $260 Ex $227 Gd $159
Caliber: .222 Rem., .22-250 Rem., .243 Win., .308 Win.; four-round mag. Weight: 7.5 lbs. Folding leaf rear, ramp front sights. Monte Carlo stock w/cheekpiece, pistol grip. Mfg. by Mossberg.

MODEL M778
LEVER-ACTION . . . . NiB $255 Ex $188 Gd $138
Calibers: .30-30, .35 Rem. Six round tubular magazine. 20-inch bbl. Weight: 6.75 lbs. Sights: Open rear; ramp front. Pistol-grip or straight stock, forearm w/bbl. band. Mfg. by Mossberg.

MODEL M780
BOLT-ACTION RIFLE . . . . NiB $265 Ex $237 Gd $168
Caliber: .222 Rem., .22-250 Rem. .243 Win., .308 Win.; four-round mag. Weight: 7.5 lbs. Folding leaf rear, ramp front sights. Monte Carlo stock w/cheekpiece, pistol grip. Mfg. by Mossberg

MODEL M782
BOLT-ACTION RIFLE . . . . NiB $259 Ex $233 Gd $177
Same specifications as Model M780.

MODEL M808 . . . . NiB $155 Ex $133 Gd $90
Takedown. Caliber: .22 RF; 15-round tubular mag. Bbl.: 20 and 24 inches. Weight: 6 lbs. Open rear, bead front sights. Pistol-grip stock. Mfg. by Stevens.

MODEL M832 BOLT-ACTION RIFLE . . . . . . NiB $166 Ex $144 Gd $90
Caliber: .22 RF. Seven round clip magazine. 24-inch bbl. Weight: 6.5 lbs. Sights: Open rear; ramp front. Mfg. by Mossberg.

MODEL M836 . . . . NiB $169 Ex $122 Gd $95
Takedown. Caliber: .22RF. Fifteen round tubular magazine. Bbls.: 20- and 24-inch. Weight: 6 lbs. Sights: Open rear; bead front. Pistol-grip stock. Mfg. by Stevens.

MODEL M865 LEVER-ACTION CARBINE. . . NiB $188 Ex $146 Gd $144
Hammerless. Caliber: .22 RF; tubular mag. Bbl.: 18.5 and 20 inches. Forearm w/bbl. band, swivels, Weight: 5 lbs. Mfg. by Mossberg.

MODEL M894
AUTO-LOADING CARBINE . . . . . . NiB $198 Ex $137 Gd $105
Caliber: .22 RF. Fifteen round tubular magazine. 20-inch bbl. Weight: 6 lbs. Sights: Open rear; ramp front. Monte Carlo stock w/ pistol-grip. Mfg. by Mossberg.

MODEL M-SD57 . . . . NiB $178 Ex $133 Gd $95
Takedown. Caliber: .22 RF; 15-round tubular mag. Bbl.: 20 and 24 inches. Weight: 6 lbs. Open rear, bead front sights. Pistol-grip stock. Mfg. by Stevens.

WEATHERBY, INC. — Atascadero, California (formerly South Gate, California)

CROWN CUSTOM RIFLE . . . . . NiB $8566 Ex $6298 Gd $4470
Caliber: .240 Wby. Mag., .30-06, .257 Wby. Mag., .270 Wby Mag., 7mm Wby. Mag., .300 Wby. Mag., .340 Wby. Mag. Bbl.: made to order. Super fancy walnut stock. Also made w/engraved barreled action including gold animal overlays.

Weatherby, Inc.

Weatherby Mark V Accumark Bolt-Action Repeating Rifle
NRA NATIONAL FIREARMS MUSEUM

Weatherby Mark V Classicmark I

Weatherby Crown Custom

Weatherby Fiberguard

Weatherby Fibermark

DELUXE .378 MAGNUM RIFLE ...... NiB $2233 Ex $2148 Gd $1490
Same specs as Deluxe Magnum plus .378 Wby. Mag. Schultz & Larsen action., 26-inch bbl. Disc. 1958.

DELUXE MAGNUM RIFLE .... NiB $1844 Ex $1623 Gd $1189
Calibers: .220 Rocket, .257 Wby. Mag., .270 Wby. Mag. 7mm Wby. Mag., .300 Wby. Mag., .375 Wby. Mag. Specially processed FN Mauser action. Bbl.: 24 inches (26 inches in .375 Wby. Mag). Monte Carlo-style stock w/cheekpiece, black forend tip, grip cap, checkered pistol grip and forearm; QD sling swivels. Disc. 1958.

DELUXE RIFLE .... NiB $1844 Ex $1623 Gd $1189
Same specs as Deluxe Magnum rifle except chambered for non-Weatherby calibers. Disc. 1958.

FIBERGUARD RIFLE .... NiB $810 Ex $679 Gd $485
Same specifications as Vanguard except w/fiberglass stock and matte metal finish. Disc. 1988.

FIBERMARK RIFLE .... NiB $1377 Ex $1033 Gd $700
Same specs as Mark V except w/molded fiberglass stock in non-glare black wrinkle finish. Non-glare matte black finish on metal parts.

MARK V ACCUMARK BOLT-ACTION REPEATING RIFLE
Weatherby Mark V magnum action. Wby. Mag. calibers: .257, .270, 7mm, .300 , .30-338, .30-378, .340; also 7mm Rem. Mag., 7mm

STW, .300 Win. Mag. Bbl.: 26 or 28 inches, stainless w/black oxide flutes. Lgt.: 46.5 or 48.5 inches. Sgt.: 8. To 8.5 lbs. No sights. Drilled and tapped for scope mounts. Stainless finish w/blued receiver. H-S Precision black synthetic stock w/aluminum bedding plate, recoil pad and sling swivels. Imported from 1996 to date.
.30-338 & .30-378 Wby. Mag.. .... NiB $1654 Ex $1198 Gd $856
All other calibers .... NiB $1589 Ex $1020 Gd $722
Left-hand model, add $100

MARK V ACCUMARK
LIGHT WEIGHT RIFLE .... NiB $1357 Ex $1154 Gd $744
Similar to the Mark V Accumark except w/lightweight Mark V action designed for standard calibers w/six locking lugs. Bbl.: 24 inches, stainless. Weight: 5.75 lbs. Gray or black Monte Carlo-style composite Kevlar/fiberglass stock w/Pachmayr "Decelerator" pad. No sights. Imported from 1997 to 2004.

MARK V CLASSICMARK I RIFLE
Same general specifications as Mark V except w/checkered select American Claro walnut stock w/oil finish and presentation recoil pad. Satin metal finish. Imported from 1992 to 1993.
Calibers .240 to .300 Wby. .... NiB $1135 Ex $884 Gd $566
Caliber .340 Wby. .... NiB $1135 Ex $884 Gd $566
Caliber .378 Wby. .... NiB $1177 Ex $944 Gd $577
Caliber .460 Wby. .... NiB $1313 Ex $1044 Gd $590

GRADING: **NiB** = New in Box   **Ex** = Excellent or NRA 95%   **Gd** = Good or NRA 68%

Weatherby, Inc.

Weatherby Mark V Deluxe

Weatherby Mark V Euromark

Weatherby Mark V Lazermark

Weatherby Mark V Safari Grade

MARK V CLASSICMARK LL RIFLE

Same specifications as Classicmark I except w/checkered select American walnut stock w/oil finish steel grip cap and Old English recoil pad. Satin metal finish. Right-hand only. Imported from 1992 to 1993.

.240 to .340 Wby. (26-inch bbl.). NiB $1589 Ex $1033 Gd $844
.378 Wby. . . . . NiB $1188 Ex $1044 Gd $900
.426 Wby. . . . . NiB $1207 Ex $1044 Gd $1032
.460 Wby. . . . . NiB $1290 Ex $1170 Gd $1056

MARK V DELUXE RIFLE . . . . . . NiB $2633 Ex $1845 Gd $1579

Similar to Mark V Sporter except w/lightweight Mark V action designed for standard calibers w/six locking lugs. Four-or 5-round mag. Bbl.: 24 inches. Lgt.: 44 inches. Weight 6.75 lbs. Checkered Monte Carlo American walnut stock w/rosewood forend and pistol grip caps, diamond inlay. Imported from 1957 to date.

MARK V DELUXE BOLT-ACTION SPORTING RIFLE

Mark V action; right- or left-hand. Calibers: .22-250, .30-06, .224 Wby. Varmintmaster; .240, .257, .270, 7mm, .300, .340, .375 .378, .416, .460 Weatherby magnums. Box mag. holds two to five rounds. Bbl.: 24 or 26 inches. No sights. Weight: 6.5 to 10.5 lbs. Monte Carlo-style stock w/cheekpiece, skip checkering, forend tip, pistol grip cap; recoil pad, QD swivels. Made in Germany from 1958 to 1969; in Japan from 1970 to 1994. Values shown for Japanese production.

.22-250, .224 Wby. . . . . .NiB $1790 Ex $1408 Gd $956
.375 H&H Magnum. . . . . .NiB $1835 Ex $1079 Gd $766
.378 Wby. Mag. .NiB $2239 Ex $1177 Gd $897
.416 Wby. Mag. .NiB $2210 Ex $1433 Gd $833
.460 Wby. Mag. .NiB $2633 Ex $1399 Gd $1069

MARK V EUROMARK BOLT-ACTION RIFLE

Same specs as Mark V rifles except w/Claro walnut stock w/hand-rubbed satin oil finish. Non-glare blued matte barreled action. Left-hand models were made. Imported from 1986 to 1993. Reintro. 1995.

.378 Wby. Mag. . . . . NiB $1855 Ex $1190 Gd $943
.416 Wby. Mag. . . . . NiB $1855 Ex $1190 Gd $943
.460 Wby. Mag. . . . . NiB $1896 Ex $1497 Gd $1108
Other calibers. . . . . NiB $1590 Ex $800 Gd $555

MARK V LAZERMARK RIFLE

Same specifications as Mark V except w/laser-carved stock.

.378 Wby. Mag. . . . . NiB $2022 Ex $1598 Gd $938
.416 Wby. Mag. . . . . NiB $2022 Ex $1598 Gd $938
.460 Wby. Mag. . . . . NiB $1489 Ex $1134 Gd $822
Other calibers. . . . . NiB $1489 Ex $1134 Gd $822

MARK V SAFARI GRADE RIFLE. . . . . . NiB $2300 Ex $1841 Gd $1283

Same specs as Mark V except "Safari style" w/extra capacity mag., bbl. sling swivel. Express rear sight.

MARK V SPORTER RIFLE

Sporter version of Mark V magnum w/low-luster metal finish. Checkered Monte Carlo walnut stock, no grip cap or forend tip. No sights. Imported from 1993 to date.

Calibers .257 to .300 Wby . . . . . . NiB $1488 Ex $920 Gd $723
.340 Wby. Mag. . . . . NiB $1644 Ex $923 Gd $555
.375 H&H . . . . NiB $1588 Ex $923 Gd $555

MARK V LIGHTWEIGHT SPORTER RIFLE. . NiB $1031 Ex $843 Gd $498

Similar to Mark V Sporter except w/lightweight Mark V action designed for standard calibers w/six locking lugs. Imported from 1998 to date

Weatherby, Inc.

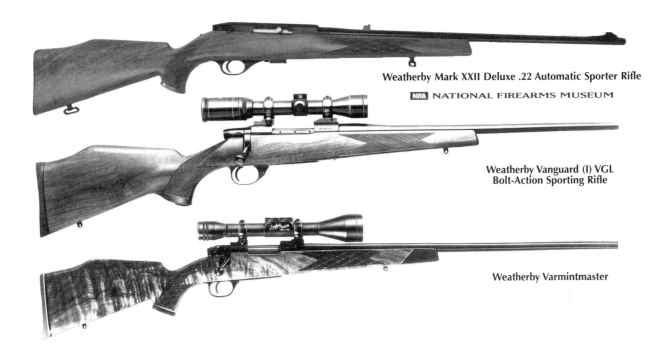

Weatherby Mark XXII Deluxe .22 Automatic Sporter Rifle

NRA NATIONAL FIREARMS MUSEUM

Weatherby Vanguard (I) VGL
Bolt-Action Sporting Rifle

Weatherby Varmintmaster

MARK V STAINLESS RIFLE

Similar to the Mark V Magnum except in 400-Series stainless steel w/bead-blasted matte finish. Weight: 8 lbs. Synthetic Monte Carlo stock w/ aluminum bedding block. Imported from 1997 to 2002.

.30-378 Wby Mag. . . . . NiB $1488 Ex $967 Gd $635
.375 H&H . . . . NiB $1455 Ex $975 Gd $643
All other calibers . . . . NiB $1135 Ex $800 Gd $600
W/fluted bbl., add $150

MARK V (LW) STAINLESS RIFLE . . . . NiB $1146 Ex $833 Gd $500
Similar to the Mark V (standard calibers) except in 400-series stainless steel w/bead-blasted matte finish. Five round magazine. 24-inch bbl. 44 inches overall. Weight: 6.5 lbs. Monte Carlo synthetic stock w/aluminum bedding block. Imported from 1997 to 2002.

MARK V SLS RIFLE

Acronym for Stainless Laminated Sporter. Similar to the Mark V Magnum Sporter except w/stainless 400-Series action and 24- or 26-inch stainless bbl. Laminated wood stock. Weight: 8.5 lbs. Black oxide bead-blasted matte blue finish. Imported from 1997 to date.

.340 Wby. Mag.. . . . . NiB $1257 Ex $1088 Gd $777
All other calibers . . . . NiB $1200 Ex $955 Gd $724

MARK V SYNTHETIC RIFLE

Similar to the Mark V Magnum except w/synthetic Monte Carlo stock w/aluminum bedding block. Bbl.: 24 or 26 inches, standard taper or fluted. Weight: 7.75 to 8 lbs. Matte blue finish. Imported from 1995 to date.

.340 Wby. Mag.. . . . . NiB $1096 Ex $790 Gd $533
.30-378 Wby. Mag.. . . . . NiB $1135 Ex $823 Gd $567
All other calibers . . . . NiB $835 Ex $633 Gd $450
W/fluted bbl., add $125

MARK V ULTRA LIGHT WEIGHT RIFLE

Similar to the Mark V Magnum except w/skeletonized bolt handle;

Bbl.: 24 or 26 inches, fluted stainless. Caliber: .257, 270, 7mm, .300 Weatherby magnums; also 7mm Rem. Mag., .300 Win. Mag. Synthetic Monte Carlo stock w/aluminum bedding block. Weight: 6.75 lbs. Imported from 1998 to date.

Standard calibers . . . . NiB $1648 Ex $1396 Gd $879
Weatherby calibers . . . . NiB $1866 Ex $1545 Gd $1077
Left-hand action, add $200

MARK XXII DELUXE .22 AUTOMATIC

SPORTER, CLIP-FED MODEL . . . . NiB $846 Ex $547 Gd $397
Semiautomatic w/single-shot selector. Caliber: .22 LR. Five and 10-round clip magazines. 24-inch bbl. Weight: 6 lbs. Sights: Folding leaf open rear; ramp front. Monte Carlo-type stock w/ cheekpiece, pistol-grip, forend tip, grip cap, skip checkering, QD swivels. Introduced 1964. Made in Italy from 1964 to 1969; in Japan from 1970 to 1981; in the U.S. from 1982 to 1990.

MARK XXII, TUBULAR

MAGAZINE MODEL . . . . NiB $844 Ex $546 Gd $397
Same as Mark XXII clip-fed model except w/15-round tubular mag. Made in Japan from 1973 to 1981; in the U.S. from 1982 to 1990.

VANGUARD (I) BOLT-ACTION SPORTING RIFLE

Mauser-type action. Caliber: .243 Win., .25-06, .270 Win., 7mm Rem. Mag., .30-06, .300 Win. Mag; five-round mag. (three rounds in Magnum calibers). Bbl.: 24 inches. Weight: 7 lbs., 14 oz. No sights. Checkered Monte Carlo-type stock w/cheekpiece, rosewood forend tip and pistol grip cap. Rubber buttpad, QD swivels. Imported from 1970 to 1984.

Standard model. . . . . NiB $490 Ex $435 Gd $298
VGL model (w/20-inch bbl.,
plain checkered stock, matte finish) . . . . . . NiB $644 Ex $533 Gd $400
VGS model (w/24-inch bbl.). . . . . NiB $440 Ex $388 Gd $335
VGX model (w/higher grade finish) . . . . . . NiB $655 Ex $493 Gd $339

Wickliffe Rifles

VANGUARD CLASSIC I RIFLE . . . . NiB $555 Ex $435 Gd $321
Same specs as Vanguard VGX Deluxe except w/hand-checkered, classic-style stock, black buttpad and satin finish. Calibers: .223 Rem. .243 Win., .270 Win., 7mm-08 Rem., 7mm Rem. Mag., .30-06, .308 Win. Imported from 1989 to 1994.

VANGUARD CLASSIC II RIFLE. . . . NiB $720 Ex $587 Gd $444
Same specs as Vanguard VGX Deluxe except w/custom checkered classic-style American walnut stock, black forend tip and grip cap, solid black recoil pad, satin finish. Imported from 1989 to 1994.

VANGUARD VGX DELUXE. . . . . . NiB $644 Ex $456 Gd $398
Caliber: .22-250 Rem., .243 Win., .270 Wby. Mag., .270 Win., 7mm Rem. Mag., .30-06, .300 Win. Mag. .300 Wby. Mag., .338 Win. Mag; three- or five-round capacity. Bbl.: 24 inches. Lgt.: 44 inches. Weight: 7 to 8.5 lbs. Custom checkered American walnut Monte Carlo stock and recoil pad. Rosewood forend tip and grip cap. High-luster finish. Disc. 1994.

VARMINT SPECIAL BOLT-ACTION RIFLE . . . NiB $654 Ex $447 Gd $368
Caliber: .224 Wby. Mag., .22-250 Wby. Mag.; four-round mag. Bbl. 26 inches, no sights. Lgt.: 45 inches. Weight: 7.75 lbs. Checkered walnut stock. Disc.

WEATHERMARK RIFLE
Mark V bolt-action. Same specs as Classicmark Rifle except w/checkered black Weathermark composite stock. Caliber: .240,. 257, .270, .300, .340 .378, .416, .460 Weatherby Magnum; 270 Win., 7mm Rem. Mag, .30-06, and .375 H&H Mag., Weight: 8 to 10 lbs.   right-hand only. Imported from 1992 to 1994.

Calibers .257 to .300 Wby. Mag.	NiB $798	Ex $616	Gd $452
.340 Wby. Mag.	NiB $835	Ex $647	Gd $445
.375 H&H	NiB $1079	Ex $835	Gd $450
Non-Wby. calibers	NiB $800	Ex $577	Gd $465

WEATHERMARK ALASKAN RIFLE. . . . . . . NiB $700 Ex $544 Gd $433
Same general specifications as Weathermark except w/non-glare electroless nickel finish. Right-hand only. Imported from 1992 to 1994.

WEIHRAUCH — Melrichstadt, Germany. Imported by European American Armory, Sharpes, FL

MODEL HW 60 TARGET RIFLE. . . . NiB $677 Ex $559 Gd $445
Single-shot. Caliber: .22 LR. Bbl.; 26.75 inches. Hooded ramp front sight. Adj. trigger Walnut stock w/adj. buttplate. Push-button safety. Imported from 1995 to 1997.

MODEL HW 66 BOLT-ACTION RIFLE . . . . NiB $645 Ex $477 Gd $335
Caliber: .22 Hornet. Bbl.: 22.75 inches. Hooded blade ramp front sight. Lgt.: 41.75 inches. Weight: 6.5 lbs. Walnut stock w/cheekpiece.

MODEL HW 660 MATCH
BOLT-ACTION RIFLE . . . . NiB $942 Ex $745 Gd $500
Caliber .22 LR. Bbl.: 26 inches. Lgt.: 45. 33 inches. Weight: 10.75. Walnut or laminated stock w/adj. cheekpiece and buttplate. Checkered pistol grip and forend. Adj. trigger. Imported 1991 to 2005.

WICHITA ARMS — Wichita, Kansas

MODEL WCR CLASSIC BOLT-ACTION RIFLE
Single-shot. Calibers: .17 Rem through .308 Win. 21-inch octagon bbl. Hand-checkered walnut stock. Drilled and tapped for scope w/no sights. Right-or left-hand action w/Canjar trigger. Non-glare blued finish. Made from 1978 to date.

Right-hand model	NiB $2578	Ex $2044	Gd $1760
Left-hand model	NiB $3544	Ex $2967	Gd $2178

MODEL WSR SILHOUETTE BOLT-ACTION RIFLE
Single-shot bolt-action. Chambered in most standard calibers. Right- or left-hand action w/fluted bolt. Drilled and tapped for scope mount with no sights. Bbl.: 24 inches. Canjar trigger. Metallic gray Fiberthane stock w/vented rubber recoil pad. Made from 1983 to 1995.

Right-hand model	NiB $2588	Ex $2066	Gd $1439
Left-hand model	NiB $2744	Ex $2190	Gd $1633

MODEL WMR STAINLESS
MAGNUM BOLT-ACTION RIFLE . . . . .NiB $2255 Ex $1938 Gd $1179
Single-shot or w/blind mag. Caliber: .270 Win through .458 Win. Mag. Drilled and tapped for scope mounts, no sights. Adj. trigger. Bbl.: 22 or 24 inches. Hand-checkered select walnut stock. Made from 1980 to 1984.

MODEL WVR VARMINT RIFLE
Calibers: .17 Rem through .308 Win. Three round magazine. Right- or left-hand action w/jeweled bolt. 21-inch bbl. Drilled and tapped for scope mounts. Hand-checkered American walnut pistol-grip stock. Made from 1978 to 1997.

Right-hand model	NiB $2577	Ex $2038	Gd $1289
Left-hand model	NiB $2798	Ex $2260	Gd $1658

WICKLIFFE RIFLES — Wickliffe, Ohio. Manufactured by Triple S Development Co., Inc.

'76 COMMEMORATIVE
MODEL . . . . .NiB $1169 Ex $1044 Gd $939
Limited edition of 100. Same as Deluxe Model except w/filled etching on receiver sidewalls, U.S. silver dollar inlaid in stock, 26-inch bbl. Presentation case. Made in 1976.

'76 DELUXE MODEL. . . . . NiB $522 Ex $415 Gd $331
Same as Standard Model except w/22-inch bbl. in .30-06 only; high-luster blued finish, fancy-grade figured American walnut stock w/nickel silver grip cap.

'76 STANDARD MODEL
SINGLE-SHOT RIFLE. . . . . NiB $443 Ex $300 Gd $217
Falling block action. Caliber: .22 Hornet, .223 Rem., .22-250 Rem., .243 Win., .25-06 Rem., .308 Win., .30-06, .45-70 Gov't. Bbl.: 22 inches, lightweight (in .243 and .308) or 26 inches, heavy sporter. Weight: 6.75 to 8.5 lbs. No sights. Select American walnut pistol grip Monte Carlo stock w/right or left cheekpiece and semi-beavertail forearm. Intro. 1976. Disc.

STINGER MODEL . . . . NiB $433 Ex $300 Gd $217
Falling block single-shot. Caliber: .22 Hornet, .223 Rem. Bbl.: 22 inches, no sights. American walnut Monte Carlo stock w/ Continental-type forend. Made from 1979 to 1980.

TRADITIONALIST MODEL . . . . NiB $441 Ex $339 Gd $200
Falling block single-shot. Caliber: . 30-06, .47-70 Gov't., Bbl.: 24 inches, open sights. Classic style hand-checkered American walnut buttstock and forearm. Made from 1979 to 1980.

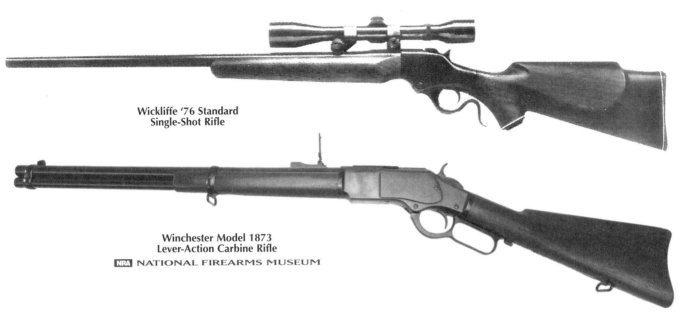

Wickliffe '76 Standard
Single-Shot Rifle

Winchester Model 1873
Lever-Action Carbine Rifle

NRA NATIONAL FIREARMS MUSEUM

WILKINSON ARMS CO. — Covina, California

TERRY CARBINE . . . . **NiB $551 Ex $408 Gd $354**
Semi-automatic, blowback action. Fires from closed bolt. Caliber:
9mm Parabellum; 30-round mag. Bbl.: 15 inches. Lgt.: 30 inches.
Weight: 6 lbs. Dovetailed receiver for scope mounts. Bolt-type
safety. Ejection port w/automatic trap door. Made from 1975. Disc.

WINCHESTER RIFLES — Winchester Repeating Arms Company, New Haven, Connecticut

*Formerly Winchester Repeating Arms Co., and then mfd. by
Winchester-Western Div., Olin Corp., later by U.S. Repeating Arms
Company. In 1999, production rights were acquired by Browning
Arms Company.*

EARLY MODELS 1873–1918

MODEL 1873 LEVER-ACTION
CARBINE. . . . . **NiB $4770 Ex $3933 Gd $2577**
Same as Standard Model 1873 Rifle except w/20-inch bbl.,
12-round magazine; weight: 7.25 lbs.

MODEL 1873 LEVER-ACTION
RIFLE. . . . . **NiB $5088 Ex $3477 Gd $2100**
Caliber: .32-20, .38-40, .44-40; some also chambered for .22 rimfire; 25-round mag. standard, some models made w/six-round half
mag. Bbl.: 24 inches (round, half-octagon, octagon). Weight: 8.5
lbs. Open rear, bead or blade front sights. Plain straight-grip stock
and forearm. 720,610 rifles were made from 1873 to 1924.

Note: *Winchester's Model 1885 Single-Shot rifles were designed
by John M. Browning in a falling block lever-action design manufactured from 1885 to 1920. The rifle was offered in a variety of
models and chambered for the most popular cartridges of the
period, both rimfire and centerfire from .22 to .50 caliber. There*
*are two basic styles of frames: low-wall and high-wall The low-wall
was chambered only for the lower-powered cartridges. The high-
wall was supplied in all calibers and made in three basic types. The
Standard Model for No. 3 and heavier barrels is the type commonly
encountered. The thin-walled version was supplied with No. 1 and
No. 2 light barrels, and the thick-walled action was designed for the
heavier calibers. Made in both solid frame and takedown versions.
Barrels were available in five weights ranging from the lightweight
No. 1 to the extra-heavy No. 6 in round, half-octagon and full-
octagon styles. Many other variations were also made.*

MODEL 1885 HIGH-WALL
SPORTING RIFLE . . . . **NiB $5335 Ex $3100 Gd $2066**
Solid frame or takedown. No. 3, 30-inch bbl., standard. Weight: 9.5
lbs. Standard trigger and lever. Open rear sights; blade front sight.
Plain stock and forend.

MODEL 1885 LOW-WALL
SPORTING RIFLE . . . . **NiB $1550 Ex $1466 Gd $1000**
Solid frame. No. 2, 28-inch round or octagon bbl. Weight: 7 lbs.
Open rear, blade front sights. Plain stock and forend.

MODEL 1885
SCHUETZEN RIFLE . . . . **NiB $10,000 Ex $7860 Gd $5779**
Solid frame or takedown. High-wall action. Schuetzen double-set
trigger. Spur finger lever. No. 3, 30-inch octagon bbl. Weight: 12
lbs. Vernier rear peep sight; wind-gauge front sight. Fancy walnut
Schuetzen stock with checkered pistol-grip and forend. Schuetzen
buttplate; adj. palm rest.

MODEL 1885
SPECIAL SPORTING RIFLE . . . . **NiB $7335 Ex $5550 Gd $5090**
Same specs as Standard high-wall model except w/checkered fancy
walnut stock and forend.

MODEL 1885 SINGLE-SHOT
MUSKET . . . . **NiB $1590 Ex $1171 Gd $878**
Solid frame, low-wall. Caliber: .22 LR, Short. Bbl.: 28 inches, round.
Weight: 8.6 lbs. Lyman rear peep, blade front sights. Military-type
stock and forend. The U.S. Government purchased a large number
of these muskets during WWI for training purposes.

Winchester Rifles

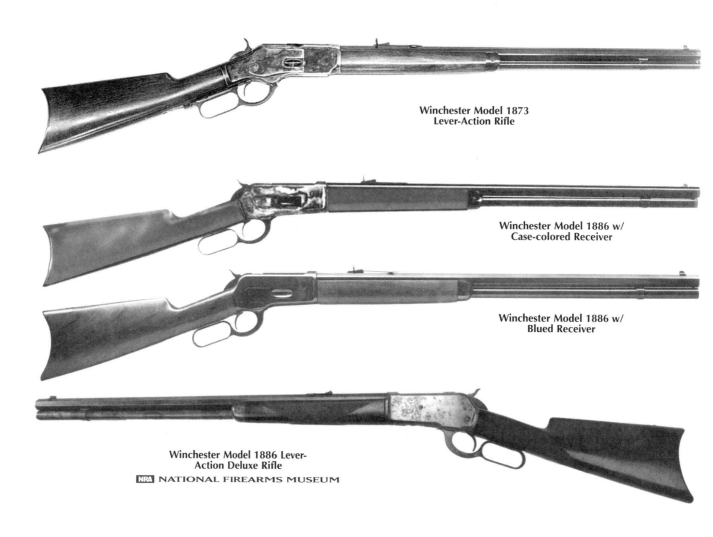

Winchester Model 1873
Lever-Action Rifle

Winchester Model 1886 w/
Case-colored Receiver

Winchester Model 1886 w/
Blued Receiver

Winchester Model 1886 Lever-
Action Deluxe Rifle
NRA NATIONAL FIREARMS MUSEUM

MODEL 1885 SINGLE-SHOT
"WINDER" MUSKET. . . . . **NiB $1488 Ex $1203 Gd $1037**
Solid frame or takedown. High-wall. Plain trigger. 28-inch round
bbl. Weight: 8.5 lbs. Musket rear sight; blade front sight. Military-
type stock and forend w/bbl. band and sling swivels.

MODEL 1886 LEVER-ACTION RIFLE
Solid frame or takedown. Caliber: .38-56, .38-70, .40-65, .40-70, .40-82,
.45-70, .45-90, .50-110. The .233 Win. and .45-70 were the last calibers
in which this model was supplied. Eight-round tubular mag. or four-round
half-mag. Bbl.: 26 inches; round, half-octagon or octagon. Weight: 7.5
lbs. Open rear, bead or blade front sights. Plain straight-grip stock and
forend on standard models, Made from 1886 to 1935.
Standard model. . . . . NiB $7288 Ex $4359 Gd $3100
Takedown model. . . . . .NiB $10,270 Ex $7668 Gd $5790

MODEL 1890 SLIDE-ACTION RIFLE
Visible hammer. Caliber: .22 Short, Long, LR, .22 WRF (not interchangeable). Tubular mag. holds 15 Short, 12 Long, 11 LR; 12 WRF.
Bbl.: 24 inches, octagon. Weight: 5.75 lbs. Open rear, bead front
sights. Plain straight-grip stock, grooved slide handle. Originally
made w/solid frame, after No. 15,499 all rifles of this model were
takedown-type. Rifles with fancy checkered pistol-grip stock, nickel-
steel bbl. can increase value by 100% or more. Made from 1890
to 1932.
WRF, blued model. . . . . NiB $2079 Ex $1754 Gd $1166
.22 LR, blued model . . . . NiB $2148 Ex $2066 Gd $1180
Color casehardened receiver . . . . NiB $6680 Ex $5349 Gd $3730

MODEL 1892 LEVER-ACTION
RIFLE. . . . . **NiB $3477 Ex $2210 Gd $1588**
Solid frame or takedown. Caliber: .25-20, .32-20, .38-40, .44-40;
13-round tubular mag. also seven-round half-mag. Bbl.: 24 inches,
round, octagon, half-octagon. Weight: from 6.75 lbs. Open rear,
bead front sights. Plain straight-grip stock and forend. Models w/
fancy walnut pistol-grip stocks double current value.

Winchester Rifles

Winchester Model 1890 Slide-Action Rifle
NRA NATIONAL FIREARMS MUSEUM

Winchester Model 1892 Lever-Action Rifle
NRA NATIONAL FIREARMS MUSEUM

**MODEL 1892 SADDLE-RING
CARBINE. . . . . NiB $5321 Ex $2549 Gd $1266**
Same specs as Model 1892 except carbine buttstock, forend and sights.
Bbl.: 20 inches. Saddle ring on left side of receiver.

**MODEL 1894 LEVER-ACTION
RIFLE. . . . . NiB $6530 Ex $4739 Gd $3220**
Solid frame or takedown. Caliber: .25-35, .30-30, .32-40, .32 Special,
.38-55; seven-round tubular mag. or four-round half-mag. Bbl.: 26
inches, round, octagon, half-octagon. Weight: 7.35 lbs. Open rear,
bead front sights. Plain straight-grip stock and forearm on standard
models; crescent- or shotgun-style buttplate. Made from 1894 to 1937.
See also Winchester Model 94 for later variations of this model.

**MODEL 1894 SADDLE-RING
CARBINE. . . . . NiB $2866 Ex $1780 Gd $1100**
Same specs as Model 1894 Standard Rifle except w/20-inch bbl.,
carbine buttstock., forend and sights. Saddle ring on left side of
receiver. Weight: 6.5 lbs.

MODEL 1894 STANDARD CARBINE . . NiB $6798 Ex $4890 Gd $3855
Same specs as Saddle Ring Carbine except w/shotgun-type buttstock and
buttplate, no saddle ring. Standard open rear sight. Sometimes called the
"Eastern Carbine." See also Winchester Model 94 carbine.

**MODEL 1895 LEVER-ACTION
CARBINE. . . . . NiB $4297 Ex $3037 Gd $1971**
Same as Model 95 Standard Rifle except w/solid frame only, 22-inch
bbl., carbine style buttstock and forend. Weight: 8 lbs. Caliber: .30-
40 Krag, .30-03, .30-06, .303.

**MODEL 1895 LEVER-
ACTION RIFLE . . . . NiB $3364 Ex $2130 Gd $1266**
Solid frame and takedown. Caliber: .30-40 Krag, .30-03, .30-06, .303
British, 7.62mm Russian, .35 Win., .38-72, .40-72, .405 Win.; four-round
box mag.; five-round mag. in .30-40 and .303. Bbl.: 24, 26, 28 inches;
round, half-octagon, octagon. Weight 8.5 lbs. Open rear, bead or blade
front sights. Plain straight-grip stock and forend (standard). Made from
1897 to 1931.

MODEL (1897) LEE BOLT-ACTION RIFLE
Straight-pull bolt-action. .236 U.S. Navy, 5-round box magazine, clip
loaded. 24- and 28-inch bbl. Weight: 7.5 to 8.5 lbs. Sights: Folding
leaf rear sight on musket; open sporting sight on sporting rifle.
Musket model . . . . NiB $1939 Ex $1777 Gd $1129
Sporting rifle. . . . . NiB $2000 Ex $1808 Gd $1110

MODEL 1900 BOLT-ACTION

SINGLE-SHOT RIFLE. . . . . NiB $628 Ex $499 Gd $356
Takedown. Caliber: .22 Short and Long. 18-inch bbl. Weight:
2.75 lbs. Open rear sight; blade front sight. One-piece, straight-
grip stock. Made from 1899 to 1902.

**MODEL 1902 BOLT-ACTION
SINGLE-SHOT RIFLE. . . . . NiB $490 Ex $369 Gd $269**
Takedown. Same as Model 1900 w/minor improvements.
Caliber: .22 Short and Long, .22 Extra Long, .22 LR. Weight: 3
lbs. Made from 1902 to 1931.

**MODEL 1903
SELF-LOADING RIFLE. . . . . . . NiB $1133 Ex $900 Gd $577**
Takedown. Caliber: .22 WRA; 10-round tubular mag. in buttstock. Bbl.: 20 inches. Weight: 5.75 lbs. Open rear, bead front
sights. Plain straight-grip stock and forearm. Made from 1903
to 1936.

**MODEL (1904) 99 THUMB-TRIGGER BOLT-ACTION
SINGLE-SHOT RIFLE. . . . . NiB $833 Ex $700 Gd $510**
Takedown. Same as Model 1902 except fired by pressing a
button behind the cocking piece. Made from 1904 to 1923.
**MODEL 1904 BOLT-ACTION
SINGLE-SHOT RIFLE. . . . . NiB $469 Ex $388 Gd $267**
Similar to Model 1902. Takedown. Caliber: 22 Short, Long Extra
Long, LR. 21-inch bbl. Made from 1904 to 1931.

**MODEL 1905
SELF-LOADING RIFLE. . . . . NiB $768 Ex $580 Gd $500**
Takedown. Calibers: .32 Win. S. and L., .35 Win. S. and L. Five
or 10-round detachable box magazine. 22-inch bbl. Weight: 7.5
lbs. Sights: Open rear; bead front. Plain pistol-grip stock and
forearm. Made from 1905 to 1920.

**MODEL 1906
SLIDE-ACTION REPEATER . . . NiB $1590 Ex $1077 Gd $733**
Takedown. Visible hammer. Caliber: .22 Short, Long, LR. Tubular
magazine holds 20 Short, 16 Long or 14 LR. 20-inch bbl.
Weight: 5 lbs. Sights: Open rear; bead front. Straight-grip stock
and grooved forearm. Made from 1906 to 1932.

MODEL 1907 SELF-LOADING RIFLE . . . . . NiB $733 Ex $589 Gd $421
Takedown. Caliber: .351 Win. S. and L. Five or 10-round detachable
box magazine. 20-inch bbl. Weight: 7.75 lbs. Sights: Open rear;
bead front. Plain pistol-grip stock and forearm. Made from 1907
to 1957.

MODEL 1910 SELF-LOADING RIFLE . . . . . NiB $910 Ex $700 Gd $533
Takedown. Caliber: .401 Win. S. and L. Four round detachable box

Winchester Rifles

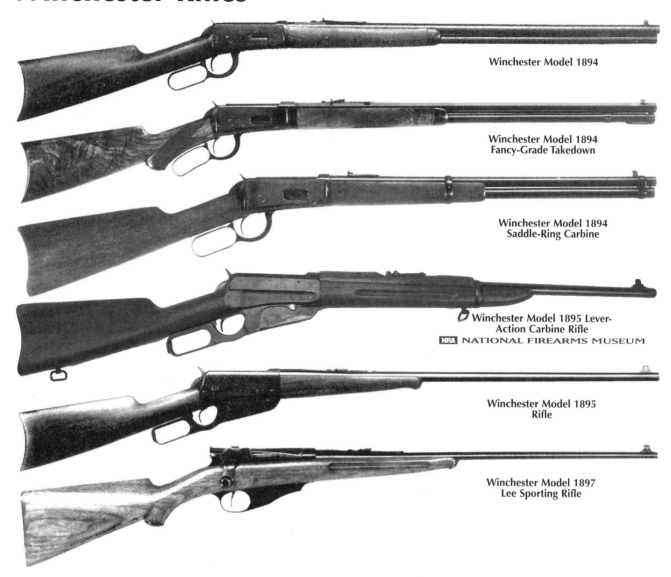

Winchester Model 1894

Winchester Model 1894
Fancy-Grade Takedown

Winchester Model 1894
Saddle-Ring Carbine

Winchester Model 1895 Lever-
Action Carbine Rifle
NRA NATIONAL FIREARMS MUSEUM

Winchester Model 1895
Rifle

Winchester Model 1897
Lee Sporting Rifle

magazine. 20-inch bbl. Weight: 8.5 lbs. Sights: Open rear; bead front. Plain pistol-grip stock and forearm. Made from 1910 to 1936.

MODEL 43 BOLT-ACTION
SPORTING RIFLE . . . . **NiB $855 Ex $679 Gd $480**
Standard Grade. Calibers: .218 Bee, .22 Hornet, .25-20, .32-20 (latter two disc. 1950). Three round detachable box magazine. 24-inch bbl. Weight: 6 lbs. Sights: Open rear, bead front on hooded ramp. Plain pistol-grip stock with swivels. Made from 1949 to 1957.

MODEL 43 SPECIAL GRADE . . . . . **NiB $855 Ex $679 Gd $480**
Same as Standard Model 43 except has checkered pistol-grip and forearm, grip cap.

MODEL 47 BOLT-ACTION
SINGLE-SHOT RIFLE. . . . . **NiB $466 Ex $366 Gd $245**
Caliber: .22 Short, Long, LR. 25-inch bbl. Weight: 5.5 lbs. Sights: Peep or open rear; bead front. Plain pistol-grip stock. Made from 1949 to 1954.

MODEL 52 BOLT-ACTION TARGET RIFLE
Standard 28-inch bbl. first type. Caliber: .22 LR; five-round box mag.

Folding leaf peep rear, blade front sight (other sights were avail.). Scope bases provided. Semi-military-type target stock w/pistol grip. Original model has grasping grooves in forearm. Higher comb and semi-beavertail forearm on later models. Numerous changes were made in this model, most important was the adoption of the speed lock in 1929. Model 52 rifles produced before this change are referred to as "slow lock" models. Last arms of this typer bore serial numbers followed by the Letter "A." Made from 1919 to 1937.
Slow Lock model. . . . . **NiB $900 Ex $622 Gd $370**
Speed Lock model. . . . . **NiB $733 Ex $466 Gd $379**

MODEL 52 HEAVY BARREL . . . . **NiB $1379 Ex $1008 Gd $798**
First type speed lock. Same specifications as Standard Model 52 except has heavier bbl., Lyman No. 17G front sight; weight: 10 lbs.

MODEL 52 INTERNATIONAL MATCH RIFLE
Similar to Model 52D heavy-barrel except w/special lead-lapped bbl., laminated free rifle-style stock with high comb, thumbhole, hook buttplate, accessory rail, hand stop/swivel assembly, palm rest. Weight: 13.5 lbs. Made from 1969 to 1978.
With standard trigger . . . . **NiB $1577 Ex $1103 Gd $922**
With Kenyon or I.S.U. trigger, add **$350**

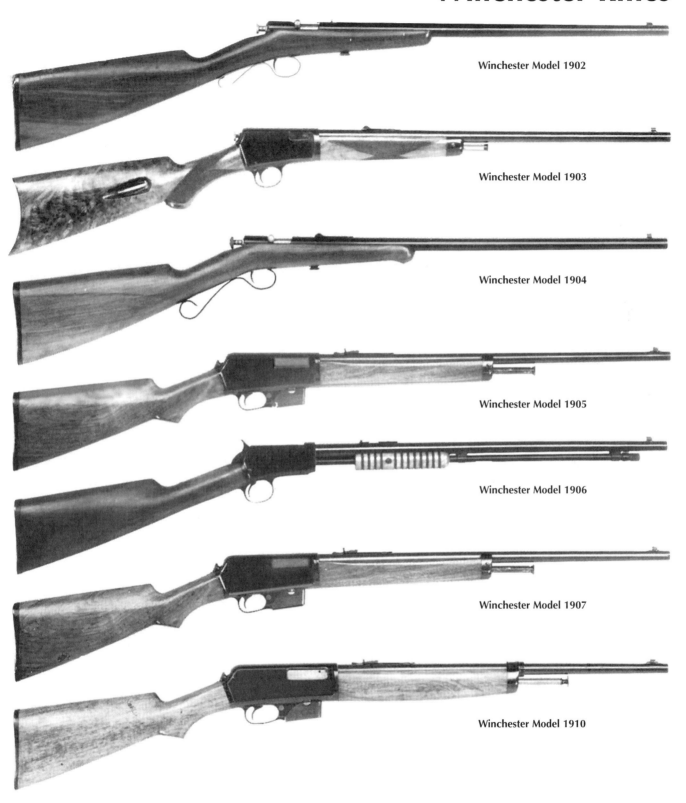

Winchester Model 1902

Winchester Model 1903

Winchester Model 1904

Winchester Model 1905

Winchester Model 1906

Winchester Model 1907

Winchester Model 1910

MODEL 52 INTERNATIONAL PRONE . . NiB $1470 Ex $1133 Gd $900
Similar to Model 520D heavy barrel except w/special lead-lapped bbl, prone stock with full pistol grip, rollover cheekpiece (removable for bore cleaning). Weight: 11.5 lbs. Made from 1975 to 1980.

MODEL 52 SPORTING RIFLE
First type. Same as Standard Model 52 except w/lightweight 24-inch bbl., Lyman No. 48 receiver sight, gold bead front sight on hooded ramp. Deluxe checkered sporting stock with cheekpiece,

Winchester Rifles

Winchester Model 43
Special Grade

Winchester Model 52-B
Bolt-Action Target Rifle

NRA NATIONAL FIREARMS MUSEUM

black forend tip. Weight: 7.75 lbs. Made from 1934 to 1958. Reintro. 1993.

Model 52 Sporter . . . . NiB $4677 Ex $3200 Gd $1590
Model 52A Sporter . . . . NiB $3290 Ex $2733 Gd $1256
Model 52B Sporter . . . . NiB $4633 Ex $2479 Gd $1790
Model 52C Sporter . . . . NiB $5125 Ex $4120 Gd $2798
1993 BAC re-issue. . . . . NiB $644 Ex $500 Gd $433

MODEL 52-B BOLT-ACTION RIFLE

Standard bbl. Extensively redesigned action. Choice of Target or Marksman stocks. Weight: 9 lbs. Wide range of target sights (Lyman, Marble-Goss, Redfield, Vaver, Winchester). Value shown is for rifle w/out sights. Other specs as shown for first type Model 52. Made from 1935 to 1947. Reintro. 1997.

Target model. . . . . NiB $1270 Ex $968 Gd $755
BAC model
(1997 BAC re-issue) . . . . NiB $1270 Ex $968 Gd $755
USRAC Sporting model. . . . . NiB $768 Ex $600 Gd $455

MODEL 52-B BULL GUN

HEAVY BARREL. . . . . NiB $1880 Ex $1144 Gd $600
Same specs s Standard Model 52-B except w/extra heavy bbl., Marksman stock. Weight: 11 lbs. Made from 1940 to 1947.

MODEL 52-C BOLT-ACTION RIFLE

Same as Standard Model 52 except w/improved action, "Micro-Motion" trigger mechanism and new type "Marksman" stock. Made from 1947 to 1961. Bull Gun version from 1952. Value shown is for rifle w/out sights.
Bull Gun (w/extra heavy bbl.,
wt. 12 lbs.) . . . . NiB $1877 Ex $966 Gd $694
W/standard bbl.
(wt. 9.75 lbs.) . . . . NiB $1466 Ex $800 Gd $659
Target model
(w/heavy bbl.). . . . . NiB $1455 Ex $900 Gd $680

MODEL 52-D BOLT-ACTION

TARGET RIFLE. . . . . NiB $1377 Ex $966 Gd $488
Redesigned Model 52 action, single-shot. Caliber: .22 LR. Bbl.: Floating, 28 inches, standard or heavy. No sights, blocks for target scope provided. Weight: 9.75 to 11 lbs. depending on bbl. Restyled Marksman stock w/accessory channel and forend. Stop, rubber buttplate. Made from 1961 to 1978.

MODEL 53 LEVER-ACTION

REPEATER . . . . NiB $2343 Ex $1869 Gd $1333
Modification of Model 92. Solid frame or takedown. Calibers: .25-20, .32-20, .44-40. Six round tubular half-magazine in solid frame model. Seven round in takedown. 22-inch nickel steel bbl. Weight: 5.5 to 6.5 lbs. Sights: Open rear; bead front. Redesigned straight-grip stock and forearm. Made from 1924 to 1932.

MODEL 54 BOLT-ACTION

HIGH POWER SPORTING RIFLE (I). . . . . NiB $1570 Ex $933 Gd $667
First type. Caliber: .270 Win., 7x57mm, .30-30, .30-06, 7.65x53mm, 9x57mm; five-round box mag. Bbl.: 24 inches. Weight: 7.75 lbs. Open rear, bead front sights. Checkered stock w/ pistol grip, tapered forearm w/Schnabel tip. Two-piece firing pin. Made from 1925 to 1930.

MODEL 54 BOLT-ACTION

HIGH POWER SPORTING RIFLE (II) . . . . NiB $1180 Ex $922 Gd $744
Standard Grade, improved type with speed lock and one-piece firing pin. Caliber: .22 Hornet, .220 Swift, .250-3000, .257 Roberts, .270 Win., 7x57mm, .30-06; five-round box mag. Bbl.: 24 or 26 inches (in .220 Swift). Weight: 8 lbs. Open rear, bead ramp front sights. NRA-style stock w/checkered pistol grip and forearm. Made from 1930 to 1936.

MODEL 54 CARBINE (I) . . . . NiB $1566 Ex $922 Gd $744
First type. Same as Model 54 rifle except has 20-inch bbl., plain lightweight stock with grasping grooves in forearm. Weight: 7.25 lbs.

MODEL 54 CARBINE (II) . . . . . . NiB $1865 Ex $1100 Gd $790
Improved type. Same as Model 54 Standard Grade Sporting Rifle except w/20-inch bbl. Weight: 7.5 lbs. This model may have either

Winchester Model 47

Winchester Model 52
Standard Barrel

Winchester Model 52
International Match

Winchester Model 52
International Prone Target

NRA-type stock or lightweight stock found on first-type Model 54 Carbine.

MODEL 54 NATIONAL
MATCH RIFLE . . . . NiB $1722 Ex $967 Gd $679
Same specs and calibers as Standard Model 54 except w/Lyman sights, scope base, Marksman-type target stock. Weight: 9.5 lbs.

MODEL 54 SNIPER'S
MATCH RIFLE . . . . NiB $2489 Ex $1388 Gd $633
Similar to the earlier Model 54 Sniper's Rifle except has Marksman-type target stock, scope bases; weight: 12.5 lbs. Sam calibers as Standard model.

MODEL 54 SNIPER'S RIFLE . . . . NiB $2566 Ex $ 1534 Gd $770
Same as Standard Model 54 except in .30-06 only w/heavy 26-inch bbl., Lyman No. 48 rear peep sight and blade front sight. Semi-milliltary-type stock. Weight: 11.75 lbs.

MODEL 54 SUPER GRADE . . . . NiB $3144 Ex $2057 Gd $1166
Same as Standard Model 54 Sporter except w/deluxe cheekpiece stock, black forend tip and grip cap. QD swivels, 1-inch sling strap.

MODEL 54 TARGET RIFLE . . . . NiB $888 Ex $566 Gd $390
Same as Standard Model 54 except w/24-inch medium-weight bbl. (26 inches in .220 Swift), Lyman sights. Scope bases, Marksman-type target stock. Weight: 10.5 lbs.

MODEL 55 "AUTOMATIC"
SINGLE-SHOT . . . . NiB $379 Ex $290 Gd $210
Caliber: .22 Short, Long, LR. 22-inch bbl. Sights: Open rear, bead front. One-piece walnut stock. Weight: 5.5 lbs. Made from 1958 to 1960.

MODEL 55 LEVER-ACTION REPEATER
Modification of Model 94. Solid frame or takedown. Calibers: .25-35, .30-30, .32 Win. Special. Three round tubular half magazine. 24-inch nickel steel bbl. Weight: About 7 lbs. Sights: Open rear; bead front. Made from 1924 to 1932.
Standard model (straight grip) . . . . NiB $2133 Ex $1670 Gd $1006
Deluxe model (pistol grip) . . . . NiB $2287 Ex $1744 Gd $1140

MODEL 56 BOLT-ACTION
SPORTING RIFLE . . . . NiB $1179 Ex $1143 Gd $700
Solid frame. Caliber: .22 LR, Short; five-or 10-round detachable box mag. Bbl: 22 inches. Weight: 4.5 lbs. Open rear, bead front sights. Plain pistol-grip stock with Schnabel forend. Made from 1926 to 1929.

MODEL 57 BOLT-ACTION RIFLE
Solid frame. Same as Model 56 except in .22 Short (till 1929) and .22 LR; five- or 10-round mag. Semi military-style target stock w/ forend bbl. band; swivels and web sling. Lyman peep rear sight. Weight: 5 lbs. Made from 1926 to 1936.
Sporter model . . . . NiB $888 Ex $654 Gd $500
Target model . . . . NiB $733 Ex $679 Gd $500

MODEL 58 BOLT-ACTION
SINGLE-SHOT . . . . NiB $1056 Ex $800 Gd $598
Similar to Model 52. Takedown. Caliber. .22 Short, Long, LR. 18-inch bbl. Weight: 3 lbs. Sights, Open rear; blade front. Plain, flat, straight-grip hardwood stock. Not serial numbered. Made from 1928 to 1931.

MODEL 59 BOLT-ACTION
SINGLE-SHOT . . . . NiB $1255 Ex $1009 Gd $756

Winchester Rifles

Winchester Model 52-B
Standard Barrel

Winchester Model 52-B
Sporter

Winchester Model 52-C
Heavy Barrel

Winchester Model 53

Winchester Model 54
Super Grade

Improved version of Model 58 w/23-inch bbl., redesigned pistol grip stock. Weight: 4.5 lbs. Made in 1930.

MODEL 60, 60A BOLT-ACTION SINGLE-SHOT
Redesign of Model 59. Caliber: .22 Short, Long, LR. 23-inch bbl. (27-inch after 1933). Weight: 4.25 lbs. Sights: Open rear, blade front. Plain pistol-grip stock. Made from 1930 to 1934 (Model 60); 1932 to 1939 (Model 60A).
Model 60 . . . . NiB $445 Ex $276 Gd $200
Model 60A .. NiB $556 Ex $380 Gd $335MODEL 60A TARGET RIFLE. . . . . NiB $670 Ex $448 Gd $335
Same as Model 60 except w/Lyman peep rear, square top front sights. Semi-military target stock, web sling. Weight: 5.5 lbs. Made from 1932 to 1939.

MODEL 62 HAMMERLESS SLIDE-ACTION REPEATER
Takedown. Caliber: Interchangeable .22 Short, Long, LR; tubular mag. holds 20 Short, 16 Long, 14 LR. Bbl.: 23 inches, round or octagon. Weight: 5.5 lbs. Open rear, bead front sights. Plain pistol-grip stock, grooved semi-beavertail slide handle. Made from 1932 to 1958.
W/round bbl. . . . . NiB $1196 Ex $987 Gd $478
W/grooved receiver . . . . NiB $1255 Ex $1160 Gd $800

W/octagon bbl. . . . . NiB $1766 Ex $1447 Gd $1006
Gallery model, add 50%
Pre-WWII model, add. 30%

MODEL 61 MAGNUM . . . . NiB $2443 Ex $1854 Gd $1000
Same as Standard Model 61 except chambered for .22 WMR; magazine holds 12 rounds. Made from 1960 to 1963.

MODEL 62
VISIBLE HAMMER . . . . NiB $1560 Ex $1288 Gd $1033
Redesigned version of Model 1890. Caliber: .22 Short, Long, LR; bbl.: 23 inches. Weight: 5.5 lbs. Plain straight-grip stock, grooved semi-beavertail slide handle. Also available in Gallery Model chambered for .22 Short only. Made from 1932 to 1959. Pre-WWII model (small forearm) commands 25% higher price.

MODEL 61 SELF-LOADING RIFLE
Takedown. Caliber: .22 LR High Speed only; 10-round tubular mag. in buttstock. Bbl.: 23 inches. Weight: 5.5 lbs. Open rear, bead front sights. Plain pistol-grip stock and forearm. Originally available w/20- and 23-inch bbls. Made from 1933 to 1959. Reintro. in 1997.
W/23-inch bbl.. . . . . .NiB $1144 Ex $996 Gd $573
W/20-inch bbl. . . . . .NiB $2690 Ex $1877 Gd $1133

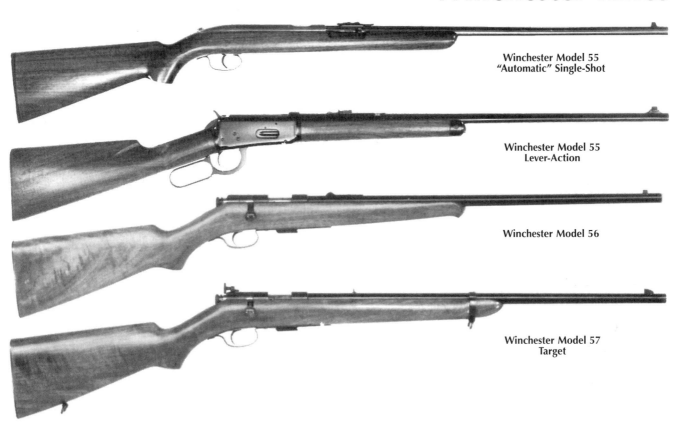

Winchester Model 55
"Automatic" Single-Shot

Winchester Model 55
Lever-Action

Winchester Model 56

Winchester Model 57
Target

W/grooved receiver .NiB $2711 Ex $1912 Gd $995
Grade I (1997 BAC re-issue) . . . . .NiB $700 Ex $576 Gd $488
High Grade (1997 BAC re-issue) . . . . .NiB $705 Ex $579 Gd $490

MODEL 64 DELUXE
DEER RIFLE . . . . NiB $1366 Ex $1109 Gd $777
Same as Standard Model 64. Caliber: .30-30, .32 Win. Special.
Checkered pistol grip and semi-beavertail forearm. swivels and
sling. Weight: 7.75 lbs. Made from 1933 to 1956.

MODEL 64 LEVER-ACTION REPEATER
Standard Grade. Improved version of Models 94 and 55. Solid
frame. Calibers: .25-35, .30-30, .32 Win. Special. Five round
tubular two-thirds magazine. 20- or 24-inch bbl. Weight: About
7 lbs. Sights: Open rear; bead front on ramp w/sight cover. Plain
pistol-grip stock and forearm. Made from 1933 to 1956. Production
resumed in 1972 (24-inch bbl.; caliber .30-30). Disc. 1974.
Original model . . . . NiB $1079 Ex $883 Gd $620
1972–74 model . . . . NiB $490 Ex $339 Gd $216

MODEL 64 .219 ZIPPER . . . . . NiB $4107 Ex $3054 Gd $1978
Same as Standard Grade Model 53 except has 26-inch bbl., peep
rear sight. Made from 1937 to 1947.

MODEL 65 LEVER-ACTION
REPEATER . . . . NiB $5044 Ex $3200 Gd $2555
Improved version of Model 53. Solid frame. Calibers: .25-20 and
.32-20. Six round tubular half-magazine. 22-inch bbl. Weight: 6.5
lbs. Sights: Open rear, bead front on ramp base. Plain pistol-grip
stock and forearm. Made from 1933 to 1947.

MODEL 65 .218 BEE . . . . NiB $5051 Ex $2979 Gd $2000
Same as Standard Model 65 except has 24-inch bbl., peep
rear sight. Made from 1938 to 1947.MODEL 67 BOLT-ACTION
SINGLE-SHOT RIFLE . . . . NiB $345 Ex $259 Gd $200

Takedown. Caliber: .22 Short, Long, LR, smoothbore, .22 WRF.. Bbl.: 27
inches. Weight: 5 lbs. Open rear, bead front sights. Plain pistol-grip stock
(original model had grasping grooves in forearm). Made from 1943 to 1963.

MODEL 67 BOY'S RIFLE . . . . NiB $345 Ex $259 Gd $200
Same as Standard Model 67 except has shorter stock, 20-inch bbl.,
weighs 4.25 lbs.

MODEL 68 BOLT-ACTION
SINGLE-SHOT . . . . NiB $345 Ex $259 Gd $200
Same as Model 67 except has rear peep sight. Made from 1934 to 1946.

MODEL 69 BOLT-ACTION RIFLE'S . . . NiB $450 Ex $366 Gd $200
Takedown. Caliber: .22 Short, Long, LR; five- or 10-round box mag. Bbl.:
25 inches. Weight: 5.5 lbs. Peep or open rear sight. Plain pistol-grip stock.
Rifle cocks on closing motion of the bolt. Made from 1935 to 1937.

MODEL 69A BOLT-ACTION RIFLE
Same as the Model 69 except cocking mechanism was changed to
cock the rifle by the opening motion of the bolt. Made from 1937 to
1963. Models with grooved receivers command 20% higher prices.
Model 69A standard . . . . .NiB $489 Ex $397 Gd $290
Match model w/Lyman No. 57E
receiver sight . . . . .NiB $546 Ex $444 Gd $314
Target model w/Winchester
peep rear sight, swivels, sling . . . . . NiB $690 Ex $567 Gd $389

Winchester's Famous Model 70

*Introduced in 1937, the Model 70 Bolt-Action Repeating Rifle was
offered in several styles and calibers. Only minor design changes
were made over a period of 27 years and more than 500,000 of
these rifles were sold. The original model was dubbed "The rifleman's
Rifle" by the outdoor press. In 1964, a revised version of the Model
70 was introduced with a redesigned action, improved bolt, swaged*

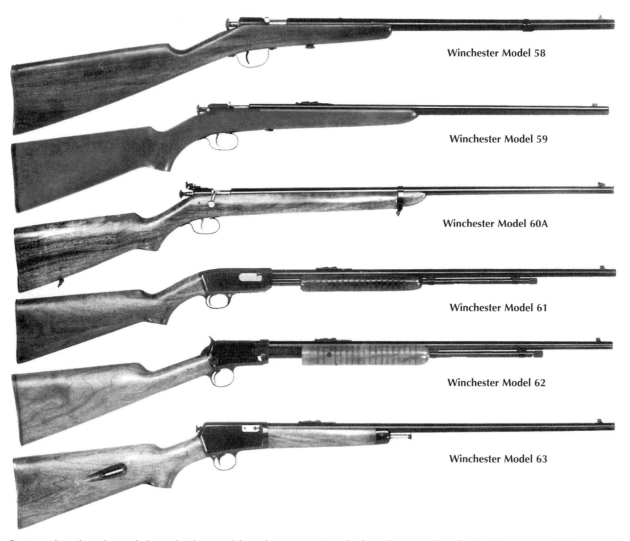

Winchester Model 58

Winchester Model 59

Winchester Model 60A

Winchester Model 61

Winchester Model 62

Winchester Model 63

(free-floating) barrel and restyled stock This model underwent major changes in 1972. Most visible was a new stock with contrasting forend tip and grip cap, cut checkering (instead of impressed as in preceding models), and a knurled bolt handle. The action was machined from a solid block of steel. Barrels were made from chrome molybdenum steel. Other changes in the design and style of the Model 70 followed. The XTR models were added in 1978 along with the Model 70A, the latter w/out the white liners, forend caps and floorplates of earlier models. In 1981, an XTR Featherweight model was added to the lineup, beginning with serial number G1,440,000. This version featured a lighter barrel and fancy checkered stock with Schnabel forend. After U.S. Repeating Arms took over the Winchester Plant the Model 70 went through more changes as described in this section. The Winchester Model 70 in all its variations remains the most popular bolt-action rifle ever manufactured.

PRE-1964 MODEL 70

MODEL 70
AFRICAN RIFLE. . . . . **NiB $8000 Ex $5600 Gd $3779**
Same specs as Super Grade Model 70 except w/25-inch bbl., three-round mag.; Monte Carlo stock w/recoil pad. Weight: 9.5 lbs. Caliber: .358 Win. Mag. Made from 1956 to 1963.

MODEL 70 ALASKAN
Same as standard Model 70 except in .338 Win., Mag., .375 H&H Mag; three-round mag. in .338, four-round in .375. Bbl.: 25 inches.

Standard stock w/recoil pad. Weight: 8 to 8.75 lbs. Made form 1960 to 1963.
.338 Win. Mag. . . . . NiB $4135 Ex $2170 Gd $1166
.375 H&H Mag. . . . . NiB $4355 Ex $2100 Gd $1189

MODEL 70 BULL GUN. . . . . . . **NiB $4467 Ex $3889 Gd $2356**
Same as Standard Model 70 except w/heavy 28-inch bbl., scope bases, Marksman stock, weighs 13.25 lbs. Caliber: .300 H&H Magnum and .30-06 only. Disc. 1963.

MODEL 70 FEATHERWEIGHT SPORTER
Same as Standard Model 70 except w/redesigned stock and 22-inch bbl., aluminum trigger guard, floorplate and buttplate. Calibers: .243 Win., .264 Win. Mag., .270 Win., .308 Win., .30-06, .358 Win. Weight: 6.5 lbs. Made from 1952 to 1963.
.243 Win. . . . . NiB $1790 Ex $1019 Gd $700
.264 Win. Mag . . . . NiB $2164 Ex $1433 Gd $998
.270 Win. . . . . NiB $1869 Ex $1233 Gd $854
.30-06 Springfield . . . . NiB $1043 Ex $888 Gd $596
.308 Win. . . . . NiB $1278 Ex $866 Gd $658
.358 Win. . . . . NiB $4566 Ex $3000 Gd $2043 MODEL 70

NATIONAL
MATCH RIFLE. . . . . **NiB $3376 Ex $1943 Gd $1723**
Same as Standard Model 70 except w/scope bases, Marksman-type target stock. Weight: 9.5 lbs. Caliber .30-06 only. Disc. 1960.

Winchester Model 64
Deer Rifle

Winchester Model 64
Standard

Winchester Model 64
1972-74 Type

Winchester Model 65

Winchester Model 67 Bolt-Action Single-Shot Rifle

NRA NATIONAL FIREARMS MUSEUM

Winchester Model 68

Winchester Model 69

Winchester Model 69 Match

Winchester Model 70
Basic Post-WWII Model

Winchester Model 70
Standard Model

Winchester Model 70
Super Grade

Winchester Model 70
African (1964)

Winchester Model 70
Deluxe (1964)

MODEL 70 STANDARD GRADE

Calibers: .22 Hornet, .220 Swift, .243 Win., .250-3000, .257 Roberts, .270 Win. 7x57mm, .30-06, .308 Win., .300 H&H Mag., .375 H&H Mag.; five-round box mag. (four rounds in magnum calibers). Bbl.: 24 inches standard; 26 inches in .220 Swift and .300 Mag., .25 inches in 375 Mag. Models w/20-inch bbls. were made. Open rear, hooded ramp front sights. Checkered walnut stock. Monte Carlo comb standard on later models. Weight: from 7.75 lbs depending on caliber and length. Made from 1937 to 1963.

.22 Hornet (1937-58) . . . . NiB $3466 Ex $2033 Gd $1266
.220 Swift (1937-63) . . . . NiB $1497 Ex $1266 Gd $879
.243 Win. (1955-63) . . . . NiB $2145 Ex $1077 Gd $910
.250-3000 Sav. (1937-49) . . . . NiB $5433 Ex $3810 Gd $2244
.257 Roberts (1937-59) . . . . NiB $3779 Ex $2088 Gd $1110
.264 Win. Mag.
(1959-63, limited prod.) . . . . NiB $1988 Ex $1154 Gd $877
.270 Win. (1937-63) . . . . NiB $2588 Ex $2000 Gd $1165
7x57mm Mauser (1937-49) . . . . NiB $6970 Ex $4650 Gd $4077
.30-06 Springfield (1937-63) . . . . NiB $3466 Ex $1880 Gd $1299
.300 H&H (1937-63) . . . . NiB $3598 Ex $2079 Gd $1599
.300 Win. Mag. (1962-63) . . . . NiB $2244 Ex $1867 Gd $1265
.338 Win. Mag.
(1959-63, special order only) . . . . NiB $2144 Ex $1675 Gd $1197
.375 H&H (1937-63) . . . . NiB $4676 Ex $4054 Gd $2354
.458 Win. Mag. (1956-63)
Super Grade only . . . . NiB $4000 Ex $2978 Gd $2369

Winchester Model 70 Standard Weight Target Rifle

Winchester Model 70 Bull Gun

Winchester Model 70
(Pre-1964) Standard Model

MODEL 70 SUPER GRADE
Same as Standard Grade Model 70 except w/deluxe stock w/cheek-piece, black forend tip and pistol-grip cap, QD swivels, sling. Disc. 1960. Values for Super Grade models reflect rarity in production and caliber. Values are generally twice that of standard models of similar configuration.

MODEL 70 SUPER GRADE FEATHERWEIGHT
Disc. 1960. Very rare, but wen properly documented will command prices four to five times more than standard production rifles of similar configuration.

MODEL 70 TARGET RIFLE
Same as Standard Model 70 except w/24-inch medium-weight bbl.; scope bases, Marksman stock. Weight: 10.5 lbs. Originally offered in all of the Model 70 calibers, this rifle was available later in .243 Win., and .30-06. Disc. 1963. Values are generally double that of standard rifles of similar configuration.

MODEL 70 TARGET
HEAVY WEIGHT. . . . . **NiB $3160 Ex $2244 Gd $1590**
Same specs as Standard Model 70 except in .243 Win. and .30-06 w/24 or 26-inch heavy-weight bbl. Weight: 10.5 lbs. No checkering.

MODEL 70 TARGET
BULL BARREL. . . . . **NiB $4466 Ex $2587 Gd $1964**
Same specs as Standard Model 70 except w/28-inch heavy-weight bbl. Chambered for .30-06 or .300 H&H Mag., Drilled and tapped for front sight base. Receiver slotted for clip loading. Weight: 13.25 lbs.

MODEL 70
VARMINT RIFLE. . . . . **NiB $2388 Ex $1454 Gd $1145**
Same general specifications as Standard Model 70 except w/26-inch heavy bbl., scope bases, special varminter stock. Calibers: .220 Swift, .243 Win. Made from 1956 to 1963.

MODEL 70
WESTERNER . . . . **NiB $700 Ex $569 Gd $355**
Same as Standard Model 70 except in .264 Win. Mag. (w/26-inch bbl.), .300 Win. Mag; three-round mag. Weight: 8.25 lbs. Made from 1960 to 1963.

1964-TYPE MODEL 70

MODEL 70
AFRICAN . . . . **NiB $595 Ex $397 Gd $335**
Caliber: .458 Win. Mag. Three round magazine. 22-inch bbl. Weight: 8.5 lbs. Special "African" sights. Monte Carlo stock w/ ebony forend tip, hand-checkering, twin stock-reinforcing bolts, recoil pad, QD swivels. Made from 1964 to 1971.

MODEL 70
DELUXE . . . . **NiB $790 Ex $588 Gd $445**
Caliber: .243, .270 Win., .30-06, .300 Win. Mag; five-round mag (three rounds in magnum calibers). Bbl.: 22 inches; 24 inches in magnums. Weight: 7,5 lbs. Open rear, hooded ramp front sights. Monte Carlo stock w/ebony forend tip, hand check-ering. QD swivels. Recoil pad on magnums. Made from 1964 to 1971.

Winchester Rifles

Winchester Model 70
International Army Match (1964)

Winchester Model 70
Mannlicher (1964)

Winchester Model 70
Standard (1964)

Winchester Model 70
Target (1964)

MODEL 70 INTERNATIONAL
ARMY MATCH RIFLE . . . . **NiB $1198 Ex $955 Gd $744**
Caliber: .308 Win (7.62 NATO). Five-round box mag. Bbl.: 24 inches, heavy; no sights. Externally adj. trigger. Weight: 11 lbs. ISU stock w/military-type oil finish, forearm rail for standard accessories. Vertically adj. buttplate. Made in 1971.

MODEL 70 MAGNUM
Caliber: 7mm Rem. Mag., .264 Win., Mag, .300 Win. Mag. .338 Win Mag., .375 H&H Mag.; three-round mag. Bbl.: 24 inches. Weight: 7.75 to 8.5 lbs. Open rear, hooded ramp front sight. Monte Carlo stock w/cheekpiece, checkering. Twin stock-reinforcing bolts, recoil pad, swivels. Made from 1964 to 1971.
375 H&H Mag. . . . . **NiB $1033 Ex $787 Gd $678**
Other calibers. . . . . **NiB $800 Ex $687 Gd $473**

MODEL 70 MANNLICHER . . . . . **NiB $1266 Ex $1090 Gd $789**
Caliber: .243 Win., .270 Win., .308 Win., .30-06; five-round box mag. Bbl.: 19 inches. Open rear, hooded ramp front sights. Weight: 7.5 lbs. Mannlicher-style stock w/Monte Carlo comb and cheekpiece, checkering, steel forend cap, QD swivels. Made from 1969 to 1971.

MODEL 70 STANDARD . . . . **NiB $788 Ex $577 Gd $400**
Calibers: .22-250, .222 Rem., .225, .243 Win., ,270 Win., .308

Win., .30-06; five-round box mag., bbl.: 22 inches. Weight: 7.5 lbs. Open rear, hooded ramp front sights. Monte Carlo stock w/cheekpiece, checkering, swivels, Made from 1964 to 1971.

MODEL 70 TARGET . . . . **NiB $4200 Ex $2765 Gd $1489**
Caliber: .308 Win. (7.62 NATO), .30-06; five-round box mag. Bbl.: 24 inches, heavy. Blocks for target scope mounting. No sights; drilled and tapped for front and rear sights. Weight: 10.25 lbs. High-comb straight-grain one-piece Marksman-type stock, aluminum hand stop, sling swivels, no checkering. Made from 1964 to 1971.

MODEL 70 VARMINT . . . . **NiB $2160 Ex $1576 Gd $1009**
Same as Model 70 Standard except w/24-inch target-weight bbl.; blocks for target scope, No sights. Drilled and tapped for front and rear sights. Available in .22-250, .222 Rem. and .243 Win. Weight: 9.75 lbs. Made from 1964 to 1971.

1972-TYPE MODEL 70

MODEL 70 AFRICAN . . . . **NiB $900 Ex $733 Gd $523**
Similar to Model 70 Magnum except w/22-inch bbl. Caliber: .458 Win. Mag. Special African open rear sight,. Reinforced stock w/ ebony forend tip, detachable swivels and sling, front sling stud attached to bbl. Weight 8.5 lbs. Made from 1972 to 1992.

**Winchester Model 70
African (1972)**

MODEL 70 CLASSIC SM
Similar to Model 70 Classic Sporter except w/checkered black composite stock and matte metal finish. Made from 1994 to 1996.
Model 70 Classic SM . . . . **NiB $765 Ex $595 Gd $355**
.375 H&H . . . . **NiB $935 Ex $765 Gd $535**
W/BOSS, add $150
W/open sights, add $50

MODEL 70 CLASSIC SPORTER
Similar to Model 70 Sporter except w/pre-64-style action w/controlled round feeding, classic-style stock. Optional open sights. Made from 1994 to 2006.
Standard model . . . . **NiB $835 Ex $599 Gd $456**
W/BOSS, add $150
W/open sights, add $50

MODEL 70 CLASSIC SPORTER STAINLESS
Similar to Model 70 Classic Sporter except w/matte stainless steel finish. Weight: 7.5 lbs. No sights. Made from 1994 to 2006.
Standard model . . . . **NiB $875 Ex $679 Gd $365**
Magnum model . . . . **NiB $845 Ex $743 Gd $498**
W/BOSS, add $125

MODEL 70 CUSTOM SHARPSHOOTER
Caliber: .22-250, .223 Rem., .308 Win., .300 Win. Mag. Bbl.: 24 or 26 inches. Lgt.: 44.5 inches. Weight: 11 lbs. Custom fitted, hand-honed action. McMillan A-2 target-style stock.. Matte blue or stainless finish. Made from 1992 to 1996.
Blued model . . . . NiB $2145 Ex $1598 Gd $1195
Stainless model . . . . NiB $2167 Ex $1620 Gd $2125

MODEL 70 CUSTOM SPORTING SHARPSHOOTER
Similar to Custom Sharpshooter model except w/sporter-style gray composite stock. Bbl.: 24 or 26 inches, stainless. Blued receiver. Calibers: .270 Win., 7mmSTW, .300 Win. Mag., Made from 1993 to 2006.
Blued model
(disc. 1995) . . . . NiB $2155 Ex $1635 Gd $1266
Stainless model . . . . NiB $2260 Ex $1723 Gd $1319

MODEL 70 GOLDEN 50TH ANNIVERSARY EDITION
BOLT-ACTION RIFLE . . . . **NiB $1693 Ex $1279 Gd $1039**
Caliber: .300 Win. Mag.,; three-round mag. Bbl. 24 inches. Lgt.: 44.5 inches. Weight: 7.75 lbs. Checkered American walnut stock. Hand-engraved American scroll pattern on bbl., receiver, magazine cover, trigger guard and pistol grip cap. Adj. rear, hooded front ramp sights. Inscription on bbl. reads: "The Rifleman's Rifle 1937 to 1987." Only 500 made from 1986 to 1987.

MODEL 70 FEATHERWEIGHT
CLASSIC . . . . **NiB $735 Ex $520 Gd $449**
Similar to Model 70 XTR Featherweight except w/controlled-round feeding system. Calibers: .270 Win., .280 Rem., and .30-06. Made from 1992 to 2006.

MODEL 70 INTERNATIONAL
ARMY MATCH . . . . **NiB $1095 Ex $944 Gd $654**
Caliber: .308 Win. (7.62mm NATO). Five round magazine, clip slot in receiver bridge. 24-inch heavy barrel. Weight: 11 lbs. No sights, drilled and tapped for front and rear iron sights, and scope mounts. ISU target stock. Introduced 1973. Disc.

MODEL 70 LIGHTWEIGHT . . . . . . **NiB $679 Ex $449 Gd $225**
Caliber: .22-250, .223 Rem., .243 Win., .270 Win., .308 Win., .30-06; five-round mag. (six rounds in .223 Rem.). Bbl.: 22-inch bbl. Lgt.: 42 to 42.5 inches. Weight: 6 to 6.25 lbs. Checkered classic straight-grip stock, swivel studs. Made from 1986 to 1995.

MODEL 70 MAGNUM
Same as Model 70 except .264 Win. Mag., 7mm Rem. Mag., .300 Win. Mag., .338 Win., Mag., .375 H&H Mag.; w/three-round mag. Bbl.: 24 inches, reinforced stock w/recoil pad. Weight: 7.75 to 8.5 lbs. Made from 1972 to 1980.
.375 H&H Magnum . . . . **NiB $655 Ex $533 Gd $400**
Other magnum calibers . . . . **NiB $554 Ex $490 Gd $388**

MODEL 70 STANDARD . . . . **NiB $677 Ex $439 Gd $331**
Same as Model 70A plus .225 Win.; five-round mag. Monte Carlo stock w/cheekpiece, black forend tip and pistol grip cap w/white spacers; checkered pistol grip and forearm. detachable sling swivel.

MODEL 70 STANDARD
CARBINE . . . . **NiB $596 Ex $437 Gd $369**
Same specifications as Standard Model 70 except 19-inch bbl. Weight: 7.25 lbs. Shallow recoil pad. Walnut stock and forend w/ traditional Model 70 checkering. Swivel studs. No sights, but drilled and tapped for scope mount.

MODEL 70 SPORTER DBM
Same specs as Model 70 Sporter SSM except w/detachable box mag. Calibers: .22-250 (disc. 1994), .223 Rem. (disc. 1994), .243 Win., (disc. 1994), .270 Win., 7mm Rem. Mag., .308 Win. (disc. 1994), .30-06, .300 Win. Mag. Made fro 1992 to date.
Model 70 Sporter DMB . . . . **NiB $755 Ex $585 Gd $359**
S-model (w/iron sights) . . . . **NiB $589 Ex $496 Gd $369**

Winchester Rifles

Winchester Model 70
Featherweight

Winchester Model 70
Golden 50th Anniversary

Winchester Model 70
Lightweight

Winchester Model 70
Magnum

Winchester Model 70
Carbine

MODEL 70 STAINLESS
SPORTER SSM. . . . . **NiB $688 Ex $490 Gd $390**
Same specifications as Model 70 XTR Sporter except w/checkered black composite stock and matte finished receiver, bbl. and other metal parts. Caliber: .270 Win., 7mm Rem. Mag., .30-06, .300 Win. Mag. .338 Win. Mag. Weight: 7.75 lbs. Made from 1992 to 1994.

MODEL 70 CLASSIC
SUPER GRADE . . . . **NiB $977 Ex $857 Gd $590**
Calibers: .270 Win. 7mm Rem. Mag., .30-06, .300 Win. Mag., .338 Win., Mag.; five-round mag. (standard), three-rounds in magnums. Bbl.: 24 inches. Lgt.: 44.5 inches. Weight: 7.75 lbs. Checkered walnut stock w/sculptured cheekpiece and tapered forend. Scope bases and rings, no sights. Controlled-round feeding system. Made from 1990 to 1995. Improved in 1999. Disc. 2006.

MODEL 70
TARGET. . . . . **NiB $966 Ex $945 Gd $588**
Caliber: .30-06, .308 Win. (7.62mm NATO); five-round mag. Bbl.: 26 inches, heavy. Weight: 10.5 lbs. No sights. Drilled and tapped for scope mount or open sights. High-comb Marksman-style target stock, aluminum hand stop and swivels. Introduced 1972. Disc.

MODEL 70
ULTRA MATCH. . . . . **NiB $1099 Ex $976 Gd $569**
Similar to Model 70 Target except custom grade w/26-inch heavy bbl. w/deep counterbore, glass bedding, externally adj. trigger. Introduced 1972. Disc.

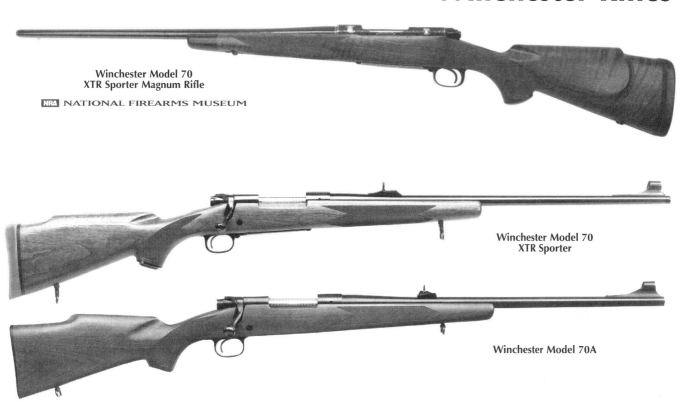

Winchester Model 70 XTR Sporter Magnum Rifle

NRA NATIONAL FIREARMS MUSEUM

Winchester Model 70 XTR Sporter

Winchester Model 70A

MODEL 70 VARMINT (HEAVY BARREL)
Same as Model 70 Standard except w/medium-heavy counter-bored 26-inch bbl. No sights. Stock w/less drop. Weight: 9 lbs. Caliber: .22-250 Rem. .223 Rem., .243 Win., .308 Win. Made from 1972 to 1993. Model 70SHB in .308 Win. only w/black synthetic stock and matte blue receiver/bbl. Made from 1992 to 1993.
Model 70 Varmint................... NiB $699 Ex $633 Gd $390
Model 70 SHB
(synthetic stock, heavy bbl.) .... NiB $745 Ex $635 Gd $440

MODEL 70 WIN-CAM
RIFLE...................... NiB $576 Ex $488 Gd $338
Caliber: .270 Win. and .30-06 Springfield. 24-inch barrel. Camouflage one-piece laminated stock. Recoil pad. Drilled and tapped for scope. Made from 1986 to 1987.

MODEL 70 WINLITE BOLT-ACTION
RIFLE................................ NiB $855 Ex $570 Gd $448
Caliber: .270 Win., .280 Rem., .30-06 Springfield, 7mm Rem. Mag., .300 Win. Mag, .338 Win. Mag; five-round mag. (three rounds in magnum calibers). Bbl.: 22 inches, 24 inches in magnum calibers. Lgt.: 42.5 inches, 44.5 inches in magnum calibers. Weight: 6.25 to 7 lbs. Fiberglass stock w/rubber recoil pad, sling swivel studs. Made from 1986 to 1990.

MODEL 70 WIN-TUFF BOLT-ACTION RIFLE
Caliber: .22-250 Rem., .223 Rem., .243 Win., .270 Win., .308 Win., .30-06. Bbl.: 22 inches. Drilled and tapped for scope mounts. Weight: 6.25 to 7 lbs. Laminated dye-shaded brown wood stock w/ recoil pad. Swivel studs. FWT model made from 1986 to 1994. LW model introduced 1992.
Featherweight model .... NiB $590 Ex $470 Gd $388
Lightweight model (Made 1992–93)...... NiB $590 Ex $470 Gd $388

MODEL 70 XTR
FEATHERWEIGHT.................... NiB $590 Ex $470 Gd $388
Similar to standard Model 70 except w/lightweight checkered American walnut stock, Schnabel forend. Bbl.: 22 inches; hooded blade front, folding leaf rear sights. Stainles steel mag. follower. Weight: 6.75 lbs. Made from 1984 to 1994.

MODEL 70 XTR
SPORTER.......................... NiB $744 Ex $545 Gd $376
Caliber: .264 Win. Mag., 7mm Rem. Mag., .300 Win. Mag., .270 Wby. Mag., .338 Win. Mag.; three-round mag. Bbl.: 24 inches. Weight: 44.5 inches. Weight: 7.75 lbs. Walnut Monte Carlo stock, rubber buttpad. Drilled and tapped for scope mounts. Made from 1986 to 1994.

MODEL 70 XTR
SPORTER MAGNUM.................. NiB $598 Ex $477 Gd $365
Caliber: .264 Win. Mag., 7mm Rem. Mag., .300 Win. Mag., .338 Win. Mag.; three-round mag. Bbl.: 24 inches. Lgt.: 44.5 inches. Weight: 7.75 lbs. No sights; folding leaf rear, hooded ramp front sights optional. Drilled and tapped for scope mounts. Checkered American walnut Monte Carlo-style stock w/satin finish. Made from 1986 to 1994.

MODEL 70 XTR
SPORTER VARMINT .... NiB $825 Ex $477 Gd $365
Same specs as Model 70 XTR Sporter except in .223 Rem. .22-250 Rem., .243 Win. only. Checkered American walnut Monte Carlo-style stock w/cheekpiece. Made from 1986 to 1994.

MODEL 70A .... NiB $545 Ex $380 Gd $315
Caliber: .222 Rem., .22-250 Rem., .243 Win. .25-06 Rem., .270 Win. .30-06, .308 Win.; four-round mag. Bbl. 22 inches (24 or 26 inches in .25-06). Weight: 7.5 lbs. Open rear, hooded ramp front

Winchester Rifles

sights. Monte Carlo stock w/checkered pistol grip and forearm, sling swivels. Made from 1972 to 1978.

MODEL 70A
MAGNUM. . . . . **NiB $476 Ex $313 Gd $236**
Same as Model 70A except w/3-round magazine, 24-inch bbl., recoil pad. Weight: 7.75 lbs. Calibers: .264 Win. Mag., 7mm Rem. Mag., .300 Win. Mag. Made from 1972 to 1978

MODEL 70 ULTIMATE CLASSIC BOLT-ACTION RIFLE
Caliber: .25-06 Rem., .264 Win. Mag., .270 Win., .270 Wby. Mag., .250 Rem., 7mm Rem. Mag., 7mm STW, .30-06, .300 Win. Mag., .300 Wby. Mag., .300 H&H Mag., .338 Win. Mag., .340 Wby. Mag., .35 Whelen, .375 H&H Mag., .416 Rem. Mag., .458 Win. Mag.; three-, four- or five-round mag., Bbl.: 22, 24 or 26 inches, stainless in various configurations including full-fluted tapered round, half-round and half-octagon or tapered full octagonal. Weight: 7.75 to 9.25 lbs. Checkered fancy walnut stock. Made in 1995.
Model 70
Ultimate Classic . . . . **NiB $2350 Ex $2090 Gd $1165**
For Mag. calibers (.375 H&H,
.416 and .458), add **$300**

MODEL 70 LAMINATED STAINLESS
BOLT-ACTION RIFLE . . . . **NiB $2410 Ex $1890 Gd $1265**
Caliber: .270 Win., .30-06, 7mm Rem. Mag., .300 Win. Mag., .338 Win. Mag.; five-round mag. Bbl.: 24 inches. Lgt.: 44.75 inches. Weight: 8 to 8.5 lbs. Gray/black laminated stock. Made from 1998 to 1999.

ADDITIONAL MODEL 70 CHARACTERISTICS

For more information on the Winchester Model 70 series of rifles, consult the Winchester listing in the Gun Trader's Guide, Thirty-Fifth Edition, which contains comprehensive details on the history of this iconic American bolt-action rifle.

MODEL 70 BLACK
SHADOW . . . . **NiB $556 Ex $379 Gd $300**
Caliber: .243 Win., .270 Win., .300 Win. Mag., .308 Win., .338 Win. Mag., .30-06, 7mm STW, 7mm Rem. Mag, 7mm-08 Rem.; three-, four- or five-round mag. Bbl.: 20, 24, 25, 26 inches. Lgt.: 39.5 to 46.75 inches. Weight 6.5 to 8.25 lbs. Composite walnut or gray/black laminated stock. Made from 1998 to 2006.

MODEL 70 CLASSIC
CAMO BOLT-ACTION RIFLE . . . . . . **NiB $990 Ex $887 Gd $554**
Caliber: .270 Win., .30-06 Springfield, 7mm Rem. Mag., .300 Win. Mag; three- or five-round mag. Bbl.: 24 or 26 inches. Lgt.: 44.75 to 46.75 inches. Weight: 7.25 to 7.5 lbs. Mossy Oak composite stock. Made from 1998 to 2006.

MODEL 70 CLASSIC COMPACT
BOLT-ACTION RIFLE . . . . **NiB $3329 Ex $2221 Gd $2069**
Calibers: .243 Win., .308 Win., and 7mm-08 Rem. Three round magazine. 20-inch bbl., 39.5 inches overall. Weight: 6.5 lbs. Walnut stock. Made from 1998 to 2006.

MODEL 70 CLASSIC LAREDO RANGE HUNTER
BOLT-ACTION RIFLE
Caliber: 7mm STW, 7mm Rem. Mag., .300 Win. Mag.; three-round mag. Bbl.: 26 inches. Lgt.: 46.75 inches. Weight: 9.5 lbs. Composite stock. Made from 1996 to 1999.
Classic Laredo . . . . **NiB $788 Ex $675 Gd $500**

W/fluted bbl.
(intro. 1998) . . . . **NiB $833 Ex $733 Gd $513**
Bossa Classic
model . . . . **NiB $800 Ex $689 Gd $466**

MODEL 70
COYOTE . . . . **NiB $976 Ex $695 Gd $500**
Caliber: .22-250 Rem., .223 Rem., .243 Win.; five- or six-round mag. Bbl. 24 inches. Lgt.: 44 inches. Weight: 9 lbs. Medium-heavy stainless steel bbl. w/laminated stock. Reverse-taper forend. Made from 1999. Disc.

MODEL 70 RANGER
COMPACT RIFLE. . . . . **NiB $555 Ex $369 Gd $257**
Push-feed action. Caliber: .22-250 Rem. .223 Rem., .243 Win., 7mm-08 Rem. Mag., .308 Win.; five- or six-round mag. Bbl.: 22 or 22 inches, Adj. Tru-Glo fiber optic sights. Lgt.: 41 inches. Weight: 6.5 lbs. Shorter hardwood stock Matte non-glare finish. Made from 1999 to 2000.

MODEL 70
STEALTH RIFLE . . . . **NiB $920 Ex $700 Gd $449**
Varminter style bolt-action rifle. Calibers: .22-250 Rem., .223 Rem., and .308 Win. Five or 6-round magazine. 26- inch bbl. 46 inches overall. Weight: 10.75 lbs. Black synthetic stock w/Pillar Plus Accu-Block (full-length aluminum bedding block). Matte blue finish. Made from 1999. Disc.

MODEL 71 LEVER-ACTION REPEATER
Solid frame. Caliber: .348 Win. Four round tubular magazine. 20- or 24-inch bbl. Weight: 8 lbs. Sights: Open or peep rear; bead front on ramp w/hood. Walnut stock. Made from 1935 to 1957.
Standard Grade (no checkering, grip cap,
sling or swivels). . . . . **NiB $1366 Ex $1167 Gd $789**
Special Grade
(checkered pistol grip and forearm,
grip cap, QD swivels and sling) . . . . . . **NiB $2144 Ex $1798 Gd $1129**
Special Grade carbine
(w/20-inch bbl., disc. 1940) . . . . **NiB $2675 Ex $2155 Gd $1769**
Standard Grade carbine
(20-inch bbl., disc. 1940) . . . . **NiB $2266 Ex $1880 Gd $1249**

MODEL 72
BOLT-ACTION REPEATER . . . . **NiB $525 Ex $266 Gd $189**
Takedown. Caliber: .22 Short, Long. LR; tubular mag. holds 20 Short, 16 Long, 15 LR. Bbl.: 25 inches. Weight: 5.75 lbs. Peep or open rear, bead front sights. Plain pistol-grip stock. Made from 1938 to 1959.

MODEL 74
SELF-LOADING RIFLE. . . . . **NiB $389 Ex $290 Gd $198**
Takedown. Caliber: .22 Short or .22 LR; tubular mag. holds 20 Short, 14 LR. Bbl.: 24 inches. Weight: 6.25 lbs. Open rear, bead front sights. Plain one-piece pistol-grip stock. Made from 1939 to 1955.

MODEL 75
SPORTING RIFLE . . . . **NiB $600 Ex $299 Gd $210**
Same as Model 75 Target except has 24-inch bbl., checkered sporter stock, open rear sight; bead front on hooded ramp; weight: 5.5 lbs.

MODEL 75
TARGET RIFLE. . . . . **NiB $600 Ex $299 Gd $210**
Caliber: .22 LR. 5- or 10-round box magazine. 28-inch bbl.

Winchester Model 70
Black Shadow

Winchester Model 70
Classic Camo

Weight: 8.75 lbs. Target sights (Lyman, Redfield or Winchester). Target stock w/pistol grip and semi-beavertail forearm, swivels and sling. Made from 1938 to 1959.

MODEL 77 SEMIAUTOMATIC RIFLE,
CLIP TYPE . . . . NiB $322 Ex $190 Gd $133
Solid frame. Caliber: .22 LR. Eight round clip magazine. 22-inch bbl. Weight: 5.5 lbs. Sights: Open rear; bead front. Plain, one-piece pistol-grip stock. Made from 1955 to 1963.

MODEL 77,
TUBULAR MAGAZINE . . . . NiB $379 Ex $267 Gd $200
Same as Model 77 Clip Type except w/tubular mag. holding 15 rounds. Made from 1955 to 1963.

MODEL 88 CARBINE
Same as Model 88 Rifle except has 19-inch bbl., plain carbine-style stock and forearm with bbl. band. Weight: 7 lbs. Made from 1968 to 1973.
Standard calibers . . . . NiB $1335 Ex $1098 Gd $866
.284 Win. . . . . NiB $2095 Ex $1788 Gd $1077

MODEL 88 LEVER-ACTION RIFLE
Hammerless. Caliber: .243 Win., .284 Win,. .308 Win., .358 Win.; four-round box mag. (three rounds in pre-1963 and .284 models). Bbl.: 22 inches. Weight: 7.25 lbs. One-piece walnut stock with pistol grip, swivels. 1965 and later models w/basket-weave ornamentation instead of checkering. Made from 1955 to 1973. .243 and .358 models introduced 1956. .284 introduced 1963. Disc. 1964.
Model 88 (checkered stock) . . . . NiB $1045 Ex $744 Gd $469
W/basketweave checkering. . . . . NiB $1045 Ex $744 Gd $469
.243 Win.. . . . . NiB $1259 Ex $1088 Gd $899
.284 Win. . . . . NiB $2300 Ex $1969 Gd $1655

MODEL 1892 GRADE 1 LEVER-ACTION RIFLE
Similar to the original Model 1892. Caliber: .357 Mag., .44-40, .44 Rem. Mag., .45 LC; 10-round mag. Bbl.: 24 inches, round. Weight: 6.25 lbs. Lgt.: 41.25 inches. Bead front, adj. buckhorn rear sighs. Etched receiver, gold trigger. Blued finish. Smooth straight-grip walnut stock and forearm w/metal grip cap. Made from 1997 to 1999.
Standard Rifle . . . . NiB $677 Ex $558 Gd $425

Short Rifle
(w/20-inch bbl., .44 Mag. only) . . . . NiB $669 Ex $500 Gd $488

MODEL 94
ANTIQUE CARBINE . . . . NiB $588 Ex $448 Gd $290
Same as standard post-64 Model 94 carbine except w/decorative scrollwork and case-hardened receiver; brass-plated loading gate, saddle ring. Caliber .30-030. Made from 1964 to 1984.

MODEL 94 CARBINE
Same as Model 1894 Rifle except 20-inch round bbl., 6-round full-length magazine. Weight: 6.5 lbs. Originally made in calibers .25-35, .30-30, .32 Special and .38-55. Original version disc. 1964.
Pre WWII
(under No. 1,300,000) . . . . NiB $7250 Ex $5988 Gd $3866
Postwar, pre-1964
(under No. 2,700,000) . . . . NiB $865 Ex $700 Gd $530

MODEL 94
CLASSIC CARBINE . . . . NiB $655 Ex $443 Gd $400
Same as Canadian Centennial '67 Commemorative Carbine except without commemorative details; has scroll-engraved receiver, gold-plated loading gate. Made from 1967 to 1970.

MODEL 94
CLASSIC RIFLE . . . . NiB $6744 Ex $5467 Gd $4388
Same as Model 67 Rifle except without commemorative details; has scroll-engraved receiver, gold-plated loading gate. Made from 1968 to 1970.

MODEL 94
DELUXE CARBINE . . . . NiB $845 Ex $600 Gd $400
Caliber: .30-30 Win. Six round magazine. 20-inch bbl. 37.75 inches overall. Weight: 6.5 lbs. Semi-fancy American walnut stock with rubber buttpad, long forearm and specially cut checkering. Engraved with "Deluxe" script. Made from 1987 to 2006.

MODEL 94 LONG BARREL RIFLE. . . . . . . NiB $700 Ex $449 Gd $366
Caliber: .30-30 Win. Seven round magazine. 24-inch bbl. 41.75 inches overall. Weight: 6,5 lbs. American walnut stock. Blade front sight. Made from 1987 to 2006.

Winchester Rifles

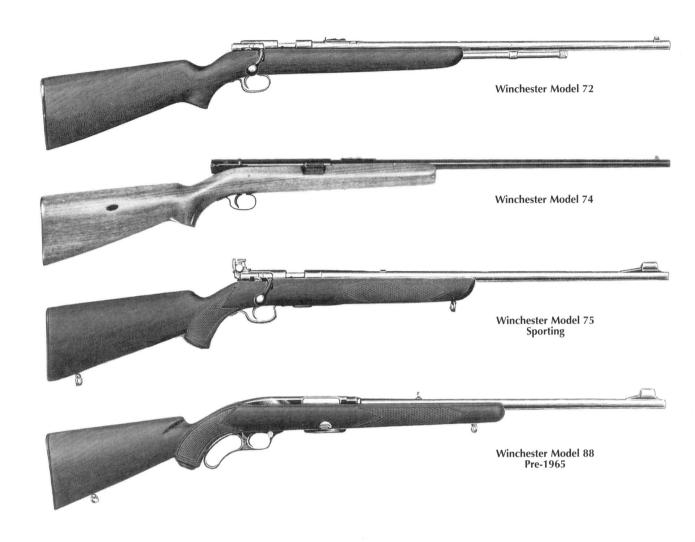

Winchester Model 72

Winchester Model 74

Winchester Model 75
Sporting

Winchester Model 88
Pre-1965

MODEL 94 TRAPPER . . . . **NiB $779 Ex $588 Gd $430**
Same as Model 94 Carbine except 16-inch bbl. and weight: 6 lbs.,
2 oz. Made from 1980 to 2006.

MODEL 94 WIN-TUFF RIFLE . . . . . **NiB $556 Ex $400 Gd $297**
Caliber: .30-30 Win. Six round magazine. 20-inch bbl. 37.75 inches
overall. Weight: 6.5 lbs. Brown laminated wood stock. Made from 1987
to 2006.

MODEL 94 WRANGLER CARBINE
Same as Standard Model 94 Carbine except w/16-inch bbl.
Engraved receiver, chambered for .32 Special and .38-55.
Top-eject model
(disc. 1984) . . . . NiB $623 Ex $414 Gd $331
Wranger II, angle-eject model
(disc. 1985) . . . . NiB $544 Ex $387 Gd $244

MODEL 94 XTR
BIG BORE . . . . **NiB $745 Ex $566 Gd $445**
Model 94 action modified for added strength. Caliber: .375 Win.,
Bbl.: 20 inches. Rubber butttpad. Checkered stock and forearm.

Weight: 6.5 lbs. Made from 1978 to 2006.

MODEL 94 XTR
LEVER-ACTION RIFLE . . . . **NiB $745 Ex $566 Gd $445**
Same specs as standard Angle Eject Model 94 except cham-
bered for .30-30 and 7-30 Waters. Bbl.: 20 or 24 inches.
Weight: 7 lbs. Made from 1985 to 1988 by U.S. Repeating
Arms.

MODEL 94 COMMEMORATIVES

MODEL 94
ANTLERED GAME . . . . **NiB $775 Ex $639 Gd $477**
Standard Model 94 action. Gold-colored medallion inlaid in
stock. Antique gold-plated receiver, lever tang and bbl. bands.
Medallion and receiver engraved with elk, moose, deer and
caribou. 20.5-inch bbl. Curved steel buttplate. In .30-30 caliber.
19,999 made in 1978.

MODEL 94 BICENTENNIAL
'76 CARBINE . . . . **NiB $944 Ex $812 Gd $654**
Same as Standard Model 94 Carbine except in .30-30 Win. Antique

Winchester Model 70
Coyote

Winchester Model 70
Ranger Compact

Winchester Model 70
Stealth

Winchester Model 94
Traditional

silver-finished, engraved receiver. Fancy walnut checkered stock and forearm. Bicentennial medallion embedded in buttstock, curved buttplate. 20,000 made in 1976.

MODEL 94 BUFFALO BILL COMMEMORATIVE
Same as Centennial '66 Rifle except w/black-chromed, scroll engraved receiver w/name "Buffalo Bill." Nickel-plated hammer, trigger, loading gate, saddle ring, forearm cap and buttlplate. Buffalo Bill Memorial Association commemorative medallion embedded in buttstock. "Buffalo Bill Commemorative" inscribed on bbl. Facsimile signature "W.F. Cody, Chief of Scouts" on tang. Bbl.: 20 inches. Six-round mag. Weight: 7 lbs. 112,923 made in 1968.

Carbine . . . . NiB $733 Ex $597 Gd $433
Rifle . . . . NiB $778 Ex $644 Gd $469

CANADIAN CENTENNIAL '67 COMMEMORATIVE
Carbine w/20-inch bbl.; six-round mag. Same as Centennial '66 Rifle except receiver engraved w/maple leaves; black chrome forearm cap, blued buttlplate. Commemorative inscription in gold on bbl. and top tang: "Canadian Centennial 1867-1967". Weight: 7.bs. 90,398 made in 1967.

Carbine . . . . NiB $667 Ex $498 Gd $300
Rifle . . . . NiB $667 Ex $498 Gd $300
Matched carbine/
rifle set . . . . NiB $725 Ex $535 Gd $350

CENTENNIAL '66 COMMEMORATIVE
Commemorates Winchester's 100th anniversary. Standard Model 94 action. Caliber: .30-30. Full-length magazine holds 8 rounds. 26-inch octagon bbl. Weight: 8 lbs. Gold-plated receiver and

Winchester Rifles

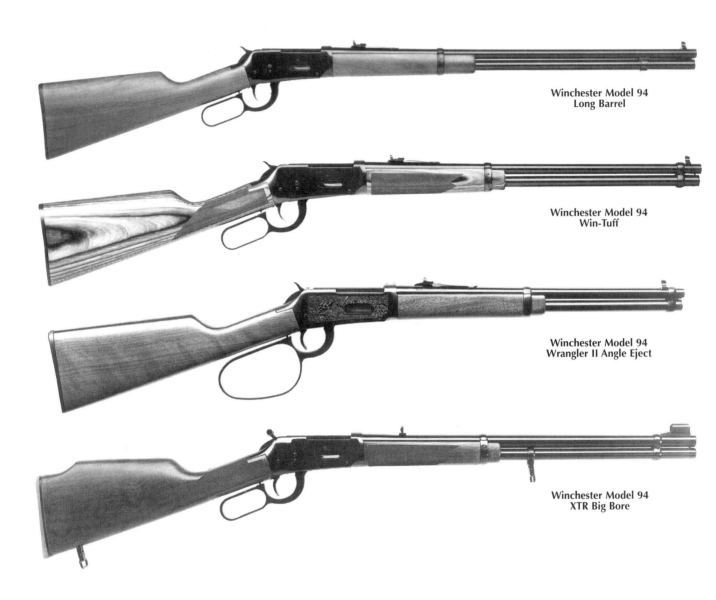

**Winchester Model 94
Long Barrel**

**Winchester Model 94
Win-Tuff**

**Winchester Model 94
Wrangler II Angle Eject**

**Winchester Model 94
XTR Big Bore**

forearm cap. Sights: Open rear; post front. Saddle ring. Walnut buttstock and forearm with high-gloss finish, solid brass buttplate. Commemorative inscription on bbl. and top tang of receiver. 100,478 made in 1966.

Carbine . . . . NiB $727 Ex $537 Gd $353
Rifle . . . . NiB $727 Ex $537 Gd $353
Matched carbine/
rifle set . . . . NiB $1579 Ex $1355 Gd $954

**MODEL 94 CHEYENNE
COMMEMORATIVE** . . . . NiB $966 Ex $755 Gd $642
Available in Canada only. Same as Standard Model 94 Carbine except chambered for .44-40. 11,225 made in 1977.

**MODEL 94 CHIEF CRAZY HORSE
COMMEMORATIVE** . . . . NiB $888 Ex $733 Gd $521
Caliber: .38-55; seven-round tubular mag. Bbl.: 24 inches. Lgt.: 41.75 inches. Walnut stock w/medallion of the United Sioux Tribe; buttstock and forend decorated with brass tacks.

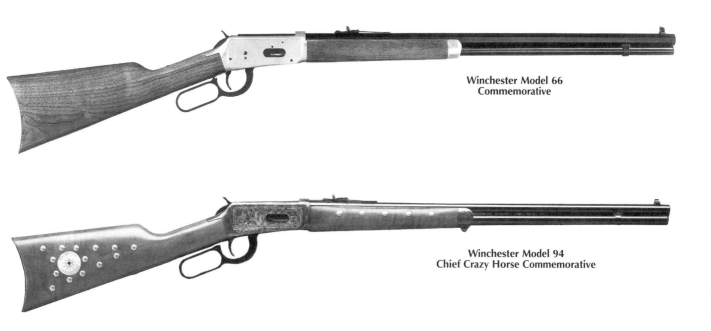

**Winchester Model 66
Commemorative**

**Winchester Model 94
Chief Crazy Horse Commemorative**

Engraved receiver. Open rear, bead front sight. 19,999 made in 1983.

MODEL 94 COLT COMMEMORATIVE
CARBINE SET . . . . **NiB $2689 Ex $2077 Gd $1366**
Standard Model 94 action. Caliber: .44-40 Win. 20-inch bbl. Weight: 6.25 lbs. Features the horse-and-rider trademark and distinctive WC monogram in gold etching on left side of receiver. Sold in set with Colt Single Action Revolver chambered for same caliber.

MODEL 94 COWBOY COMMEMORATIVE CARBINE
Same as Standard Model 94 Carbine except in .30-30 only. Nickel-plated receiver, tang, lever, bbl. bands. Engraved receiver "Cowboy Commemorative" on bbl. Commemorative medallion embedded in buttstock. Curved buttplate. 20,915 made in 1970. One-of -300: Nickel-silver medallion inlaid in stock. Antique silver-plated receiver engraved with scenes of the Old Frontier. Checkered walnut stock and forearm. 19,999 made in 1970.
Cowboy carbine . . . . **NiB $795 Ex $635 Gd $465**
1 of 300 model . . . . **NiB $3275 Ex $2966 Gd $2288**

MODEL 94 GOLDEN SPIKE COMMEMORATIVE
CARBINE. . . . . **NiB $855 Ex $670 Gd $490**
Same as Standard Model 94 Carbine except in .30-30 Win. only. Gold-plated receiver, tang and bbl. band. Engraved receiver, commemorative medallion embedded in stock. 64,758 made in 1969.

MODEL 94 ILLINOIS SESQUICENTENNIAL
COMMEMORATIVE CARBINE . . . . **NiB $622 Ex $398 Gd $287**
Same as Standard Model 94 Carbine except in .30-30 only. Gold-pated buttplate, trigger, loading gate and saddle ring. Receiver engraved with profile of Abraham Lincoln. Commemorative inscription on receiver and bbl.; Souvenir medallion embedded in stock. 31,124 made in 1968.

MODEL 94 LEGENDARY FRONTIERSMEN
COMMEMORATIVE . . . . **NiB $769 Ex $655 Gd $488**
Standard Model 94 action. Caliber: .39-55. Bbl.: 24 inches, round.

Nickel-silver medallion inlaid in stock. Antique silver-plated receiver engraved w/scenes of the Old Frontier. Checkered walnut stock and forearm. 19,999 made in 1979.

MODEL 94 LEGENDARY LAWMEN
COMMEMORATIVE . . . . **NiB $769 Ex $655 Gd $488**
Same as Standard Model 94 Carbine except in .30-30 Win. only. Antique silver-plated receiver engraved with law enforcement action scenes; antique silver-plated bbl. bands. Bbl: 16-inches, Trapper-style. 19,999 made in 1978.Model 94 Lone Star Commemorative Same as Theodore Roosevelt Rifle except yellow-gold plating; "Lone Star" engraving on receiver and bbl., commemorative medallion embedded in buttstock. 30,669 made in 1970.
Rifle or carbine. . . . . **NiB $754 Ex $598 Gd $449**
Matched carbine/rifle set . . . . . . **NiB $1499 Ex $1288 Gd $955**

MODEL 94 NRA
CENTENNIAL MUSKET. . . . . **NiB $700 Ex $597 Gd $479**
Standard Model 94 action. Commemorates 100th anniversary of the National Rifle Association of America. Caliber: .30-30; seven-round mag. Bbl.: 26 inches. Military folding rear, blade front sights. Black chrome-finished receiver engraved "NRA 1871-1971" plus scrollwork. Bbl. inscribed "NRA Centennial Musket." Musket-style buttstock, full-length forearm. Commemorative medallion embedded in buttstock Weight: 7.13 lbs. Made in 1971.

MODEL 94 NRA CENTENNIAL RIFLE . . .NiB $715 Ex $609 Gd $520
Same as Model 94 Rifle except has commemorative details as in NRA Centennial Musket (barrel inscribed "NRA Centennial Rifle"); caliber .30-30, 24-inch bbl., QD sling swivels. Made in 1971.

MODEL 94 NRA
CENTENNIAL MATCHED SET. . **NiB $1400 Ex $1266 Gd $1066**
Rifle and musket in set with consecutive serial numbers. Production figures not available. Rifles offered in 1972 Winchester catalog.

MODEL 94 NEBRASKA CENTENNIAL
COMMEMORATIVE CARBINE . . . . .NiB $1133 Ex $933 Gd $633
Same as Standard Model 94 Carbine except in .30-30 only. Gold-

---

GRADING: **NiB** = New in Box **Ex** = Excellent or NRA 95% **Gd** = Good or NRA 68%

Winchester Rifles

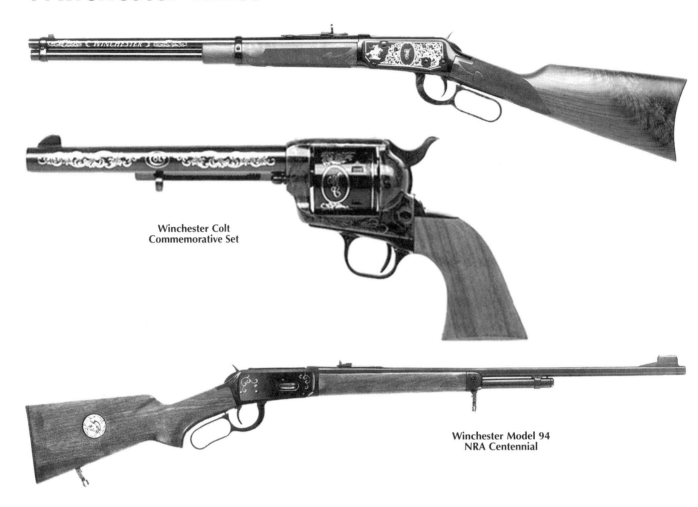

Winchester Colt Commemorative Set

Winchester Model 94 NRA Centennial

plated hammer, loading gate, bbl. band and buttplate. Souvenir medallion embedded in stock; commemorative inscription on bbl. 2,500 made in 1966.

MODEL 94 THEODORE ROOSEVELT COMMEMORATIVE RIFLE/CARBINE
Standard Model 94 action. Caliber: .30-30; six-round half-mag. in rifle, full mag. in carbine. Bbl.: 26 inches, octagon in rifle, Weight: 7.5 lbs; 20 inches in carbine, Weight: 7 lbs. White gold-plated receiver, upper tang and forend cap; receiver engraved with American eagle and inscribed "26th President 1901-1909," and Roosevelt's facsimile signature. Commemorative medallion embedded in buttstock. Saddle ring. Half-pistol grip, contoured lever. 49,505 made in 1969.

Carbine . . . . NiB $733 Ex $560 Gd $398
Rifle . . . . NiB $733 Ex $560 Gd $398

MODEL 94 TEXAS RANGER
ASSOCIATION CARBINE . . . . NiB $769 Ex $654 Gd $498
Same as Texas Ranger Commemorative Model 94 except in special edition of 150 carbines numbered 1 through 150. Hand-checkered full fancy walnut stock and forearm. Sold only through Texas Ranger Association. Made in 1973.MODEL 94 TEXAS RANGER COMMEMORATIVE CARBINE . . . . . . .NiB $655 Ex $496 Gd $400
Same as Standard Model 94 Carbine except in .30-30 only. Stock and forearm of semi-fancy walnut.

MODEL 94 TRAPPER
Same as Model 94 Carbine except w/16-inch bbl. Weight: 6 lbs., 2 oz. Angle Eject model introduced in 1985 also chambered for .357 Mag., .44 Rem. Mag., , .45 LC. Made from 1980 to 2006.
Top eject (disc. 1984) . . . . .NiB $755 Ex $573 Gd $388
Angle eject (.30-30) . . . . .NiB $445 Ex $306 Gd $200
.357 Mag., .44 mag., .45 LC, add $50

MODEL 94 JOHN WAYNE
COMMEMORATIVE CARBINE . . . . .NiB $1597 Ex $1166 Gd $769
Standard Model 94 action. Caliber: .32-40. Bbl.: 18.5 inches. Receiver pewter-plated with over-sized bow on lever. Nickel-silver medallion in buttstock bears a bas-relief portrait of John Wayne. Select American walnut stock w/deep-cut checkering. Intro. by U.S. Repeating Arms in 1981.

MODEL 94 WELLS FARGO & CO.
COMMEMORATIVE CARBINE . . . . . .NiB $770 Ex $544 Gd $339
Same as Standard Model 94 Carbine except in .30-30 Win. only. Antique silver-finished engraved receiver. Fancy checkered walnut stock and forearm, curved buttplate. Nickel-silver stagecoach medallion (inscribed "Wells Fargo & Co. 1852-1977 -125 Years-") embedded in buttstock. 20,000 made in 1977.

MODEL 94 O. F. WINCHESTER
COMMEMORATIVE RIFLE . . . . .NiB $854 Ex $644 Gd $599
Standard Model 94 action. Caliber: .38-55. Bbl.: 24 inches,

Winchester Rifles

Winchester Model 100

octagonal. Receiver satin gold plated with distinctive engravings. Semi-fancy walnut stock and forearm with high-grade checkering.

MODEL 94 WRANGLER CARBINE
Same as Model 94 Carbine except w/16-inch bbl., engraved receiver. Caliber: .32 Special and .38-55. Angle Eject intro. in 1985 as Wrangler II, also chambered for .30-30 Win., .44 Rem. Mag., .45 LC. Made from 1980 to 1986. Reintro. in 1992.
Top eject (disc. 1984) . . . . .NiB $398 Ex $290 Gd $200
Wrangler II, angle eject (.30-30) . . . . .NiB $390 Ex $285 Gd $195
.44 Mag or .45 LC, add $50

MODEL 94 WYOMING DIAMOND JUBILEE
COMMEMORATIVE CARBINE . . . . .NiB $2166 Ex $1812 Gd $1344
Same as Standard Model 94 Carbine except in .30-30 Win. only. Receiver engraved and color case-hardened; brass saddle ring and loading gate, souvenir medallion embedded in buttstock. Commemorative inscription on bbl. 1,500 made in 1964.

MODEL 94 ALASKAN PURCHASE CENTENNIAL
COMMEMORATIVE CARBINE . . . . .NiB $2379 Ex $2006 Gd $1339
Same as Wyoming issue except Alaskan medallion and inscription. 1,501 made in 1967.

MODEL 94 XTR BIG BORE
Model 94 action modified for extra strength. Caliber: .307 Win., 356 Win..375 Win, .444 Marlin. Bbl.: 20 inches.
Top eject (disc. 1984). . . . . .NiB $755 Ex $577 Gd $488
Angle eject (intro. 1985) . . . . .NiB $441 Ex $379 Gd $255
.356 Win. or .375 Win., add $200

MODEL 94 XTR LEVER-ACTION RIFLE
Same specs as Standard and Angle Eject Model 94 except in .30-30 and 7-30 Waters. Bbl.: 20 or 24 inches. Weight: 6.5 to 7 lbs. Made from 1978 to 1988 by U.S. Repeating Arms.
Top eject (disc. 1984). . . . . NiB $744 Ex $ 533 Gd $445
Angle eject (.30-30) . . . . .NiB $744 Ex $533 Gd $445
Deluxe angle eject (.30-30) . . . . .NiB $744 Ex $533 Gd $445
7-30 Waters, add $100

MODEL 100 AUTOLOADING
RIFLE. . . . . .NiB $675 Ex $559 Gd $466
Gas-operated semi-automatic. Caliber: .243 Win., .284 Win. .308 Win.; four-round clip mag. (three rounds in .284). Bbl.: 22 inches. Weight: 7.25 lbs. Open rear, hooded ramp front sights. One-piece stock/pistol grip, basket-weave checkering; grip cap, sling swivels. Made from 1961 to 1973.

MODEL 100 CARBINE. . . . . .NiB $800 Ex $622 Gd $477
Same as Model 100 Rifle except has 19-inch bbl., plain carbine-style stock and forearm with bbl. band. Weight: 7 lbs. Made from 1967 to 1973.

MODEL 121 DELUXE. . . . . .NiB $200 Ex $125 Gd $90
Same as Model 121 Standard except has ramp front sight, stock with fluted comb and sling swivels. Made from 1967 to 1973.

MODEL 121 STANDARD
BOLT-ACTION SINGLE SHOT . . . . .NiB $165 Ex $100 Gd $80
Caliber: .22 Short, Long, LR. 20.75-inch bbl. Weight: 5 lbs. Sights: Open rear; bead front. Monte Carlo-style stock. Made 1967 to 1973.

MODEL 121 YOUTH . . . . .NiB $200 Ex $125 Gd $90
Same as Model 121 Standard except has 1.25-inch shorter stock. Made from 1967 to 1973.

MODEL 131 BOLT-ACTION REPEATER. . . . . .NiB $269 Ex $225 Gd $178
Caliber: .22 Short, Long or LR. Seven round clip magazine. 20.75-inch bbl. Weight: 5 lbs. Sights: Open rear; ramp front. Plain Monte Carlo stock. Made from 1967 to 1973.

MODEL 135 . . . . .NiB $244 Ex $169 Gd $155
Same as Model 131 except chambered for .22 WMR cartridge. Magazine holds 5 rounds. Made in 1967.

MODEL 141 BOLT-ACTION
TUBULAR REPEATER . . . . .NiB $279 Ex $216 Gd $155
Same as Model 131 except has tubular magazine in buttstock; holds 19 Short, 15 Long, 13 LR. Made from 1967 to 1973.

MODEL 145 . . . . NiB $256 Ex $200 Gd $145
Same as Model 141 except chambered for .22 WMR; magazine holds 9 rounds. Made in 1967.

MODEL 150 LEVER-ACTION CARBINE . . . . . .NiB $244 Ex $180 Gd $125
Same as Model 250 except has straight loop lever, plain carbine-style straight-grip stock and forearm with bbl. band. Made from 1967 to 1973.

MODEL 190 CARBINE . . . . NiB $255 Ex $195 Gd $135
Same as Model 190 rifle except has carbine-style forearm with bbl. band. Made from 1967 to 1973.

MODEL 190 SEMIAUTOMATIC RIFLE . . . . . . .NiB $265 Ex $210 Gd $145
Same as current Model 290 except has plain stock and forearm. Made from 1966 to 1978.

MODEL 250 DELUXE RIFLE . . . . . . NiB $300 Ex $233 Gd $150
Same as Model 250 Standard Rifle except has fancy walnut Monte Carlo stock and forearm, sling swivels. Made from 1965 to 1971.

MODEL 250 STANDARD
LEVER-ACTION RIFLE. . . . . NiB $249 Ex $175 Gd $125
Hammerless. Caliber.: .22 Short, Long, LR; tubular mag. holds 21 Short, 17 Long, 15 LR. Bbl.: 20.5 inches. Open rear, ramp front sights. Weight: 5 lbs. Plain stock and forearm on early production; later model has checkered stock. Made from 1963 to 1973.

Winchester Rifles

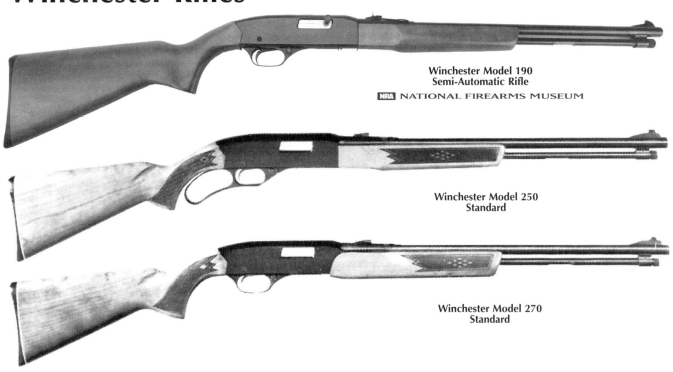

Winchester Model 190
Semi-Automatic Rifle
NRA NATIONAL FIREARMS MUSEUM

Winchester Model 250
Standard

Winchester Model 270
Standard

MODEL 255 DELUXE RIFLE . . . . . . NiB $335 Ex $265 Gd $175
Same as Model 250 Deluxe Rifle except chambered for .22 WMR.
Magazine holds 11 rounds. Made from 1965 to 1973.

MODEL 255 STANDARD RIFLE . . . NiB $265 Ex $198 Gd $144
Same as Model 250 Standard Rifle except chambered for .22 WMR.
Magazine holds 11 rounds. Made from 1964 to 1970.

MODEL 270 DELUXE RIFLE . . . . . . NiB $288 Ex $149 Gd $145
Same as Model 270 Standard Rifle except has fancy walnut Monte
Carlo stock and forearm. Made from 1965 to 1973.

MODEL 270 STANDARD
SLIDE-ACTION RIFLE . . . . NiB $200 Ex $137 Gd $110
Hammerless. Caliber: .22 Short, Long or LR; tubular mag. holds
21 Short, 17 Long, 15 LR. Bbl.: 20.5 inches. Open rear, ramp front
sights. Weight: 5 lbs. Early production had plain walnut stock and
slide handle. Latter also furnished w/plastic (Cycolac) stock. Last
models were checkered. Made from 1963 to 1973.

MODEL 275 DELUXE RIFLE . . . . . . NiB $322 Ex $268 Gd $144
Same as Model 270 Deluxe Rifle except in .22 WMR.; eleven-round
tubular mag. Made from 1965 to 1970.

MODEL 275 STANDARD RIFLE . . . NiB $266 Ex $190 Gd $133
Same as Model 270 Deluxe Rifle except in .22 WMR; eleven-round
tubular mag. Made from 1964 to 1970.

MODEL 290 DELUXE RIFLE . . . . . . NiB $325 Ex $275 Gd $175
Same as Model 290 Standard Rifle except has fancy walnut Monte
Carlo stock and forearm. Made from 1965 to 1973.

MODEL 290 STANDARD SEMIAUTOMATIC RIFLE
Caliber: .22 Long or LR; tubular mag. holds 17 Long, 15 LR. Bbl.:
20.5 inches. Open rear, ramp front sights. Weight: 5 lbs. Plain stock
and forearm on early production, later models w/checkered stocks.
Made from 1963 to 1977.
W/plain stock/forearm . . . . NiB $286 Ex $225 Gd $133

W/checkered
stock/forearm . . . . NiB $300 Ex $255 Gd $156

MODEL 310 BOLT-ACTION
SINGLE SHOT . . . . NiB $330 Ex $288 Gd $185
Caliber: .22 Short, Long, LR. Bbl.: 22 inches. Weight: 5.63 lbs.
Open rear, ramp front sights. Monte Carlo stock w/checkered pistol
grip and forearm, sling swivels. Made from 1972 to 1975.

MODEL 320 BOLT-ACTION
REPEATER. . . . . NiB $370 Ex $300 Gd $210
Same as Model 310 except has 5-round clip magazine. Made
from 1972 to 1974.

MODEL 490 SEMIAUTOMATIC
RIFLE. . . . . NiB $388 Ex $298 Gd $234
Caliber: .22 LR; five-round clip mag. Bbl.: 22 inches. Weight:
6 lbs. Folding leaf rear, hooded ramp front sights. One-piece
walnut stock w/checkered pistol grip and forearm. Made from
1975 to 1977.

MODEL 670 BOLT-ACTION
SPORTING RIFLE . . . . NiB $386 Ex $308 Gd $231
Calibers: .225 Win., .243 Win., .270 Win., .30-06, .308 Win.; four-
round mag. Bbl.: 22 inches. Weight: 7 lbs. Open rear, ramp front
sights. Monte Carlo stock w/checkered pistol grip and forearm.
Made from 1967 to 1973.

MODEL 670 CARBINE . . . . NiB $356 Ex $335 Gd $244
Same as Model 670 Rifle except has 19-inch bbl. Weight: 6.75 lbs.
Calibers: .243 Win., .270 Win., .30-06. Made from 1967 to 1970.

MODEL 670 MAGNUM . . . . NiB $410 Ex $356 Gd $281
Same as Model 670 Rifle except w/24-inch bbl., reinforced stock
w/recoil pad and different checkering pattern. Weight: 7.25 lbs.
Caliber: .264 Win. Mag., 7mm Rem. Mag., .300 Win. Mag. Open
rear, hooded ramp front sights. Made from 1967 to 1970.

Winchester Model 310

Winchester Model 320

Winchester Model 490
Rifle

Winchester Model 670
Bolt-Action Rifle

Winchester Model 670
Magnum

Winchester Model 770

MODEL 770 BOLT-ACTION

SPORTING RIFLE . . . . **NiB $443 Ex $321 Gd $277**
Model 70-type action. Caliber: .22-250 Rem., .222 Rem., .243 Win., .270 Win., .30-06; four-round box mag. Bbl.: 22 inches. Open rear, hooded ramp front sights. Weight: 7.13 lbs. Monte Carlo stock, checkered pistol grip and forend; sling swivels. Made from 1969 to 1971.

MODEL 770 MAGNUM . . . . **NiB $443 Ex $318 Gd $233**
Same as Standard Model 770 except w/24-inch bbl. Weight: 7.25 lbs. Recoil pad. Caliber: 7mm Rem. Mag., 264 Win. Mag., .300 Win. Mag. Made from 1969 to 1971.

MODEL 9422 LEVER-ACTION RIMFIRE RIFLES

Same as Standard Model 94 except chambered for .22 rimfire cartridges. Caliber: .22 Short, Long, LR (Model 9422) or 22 WMR (Model 9422M); tubular mag. holds 21 (or 15) Short, 17 (or 12) Long, 15 (or 11) LR (respectively in M9422 or Trapper model); 11 or 8 WRM (9422 M or Trapper M). Bbl.: 16.5 or 20.5 inches. Lgt.: 33.125 or 37.125 inches. Weight: 5.75 to 6.25 lbs. Open rear, hooded ramp front sights. Carbine-style stock and bbl. band forearm. Stock options: Walnut (standard), laminated brown (WinTuff), laminated green (WinCam). Made from 1972. Disc.

Standard model.	NiB $655	Ex $368	Gd $265
WinCam model.	NiB $690	Ex $376	Gd $254
WinTuff model	NiB $533	Ex $337	Gd $233

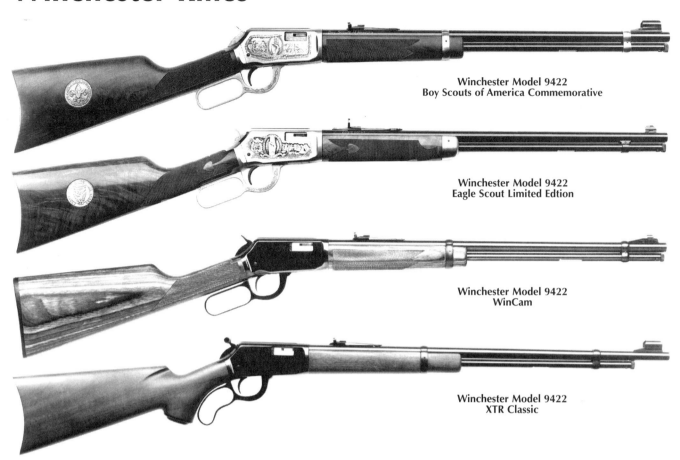

Winchester Model 9422
Boy Scouts of America Commemorative

Winchester Model 9422
Eagle Scout Limited Edtion

Winchester Model 9422
WinCam

Winchester Model 9422
XTR Classic

Legacy model . . . . NiB $844 Ex $577 Gd $300
Trapper model (16.5-inch bbl.) . . . . NiB $765 Ex $456 Gd $268
XTR Classic model . . . . NiB $800 Ex $587 Gd $366
High Grade Series I. . . . . NiB $1389 Ex $1085 Gd $770
High Grade Series II . . . . NiB $1389 Ex $1985 Gd $770
25th Anniversary Edition
Grade (1 of 2,500) . . . . NiB $860 Ex $569 Gd $447
25th Anniversary Edition
High Grade (1 of 250) . . . . NiB $1688 Ex $1233 Gd $1044
25th Anniversary Edition
High Grade (1 of 250) . . . . NiB $843 Ex $667 Gd $490
Eagle Scout
Commemorative (1 of 1,000) . . . . NiB $1448 Ex $1177 Gd $988
.22 WRM, add. 10%

DOUBLE XPRESS RIFLE . . . . . . NiB $3889 Ex $2866 Gd $1744
Over-under double rifle. Caliber: .30-06. Bbl.: 23.5 inches.
Weight: 8.5 lbs. Made for Olin Corp. by Olin-Kodensha in Japan.
Introduced 1982.

**RANGER YOUTH
BOLT-ACTION CARBINE** . . . . NiB $499 Ex $338 Gd $270
Caliber: .223 Rem. (disc. 1989), .243 win, .308 Win.; four-and five-
round mag. Bbl.: 20 inches. Weight: 5.75 lbs. American hardwood stock.
Open rear sight. Made from 1985 to 2006 by U.S. Repeating Arms Co.

RANGER LEVER-ACTION CARBINE . . . . . . NiB $655 Ex $398 Gd $290
Economy version of Model 94.Caliber: .30-30; five-round tubular
mag. Bbl.: 20 inches, round. Weight: 6.5 lbs. American hardwood

stock. Made from 1985 to 2006 by U.S. Repeating Arms Co.

RANGER BOLT-ACTION CARBINE. . . . . NiB $470 Ex $388 Gd $243
Caliber: .223 Rem., .243 Win., .270 Win., .30-06, 7mm Rem. Mag.
(disc. in 1985); three- or four-round mag. Bbl.: 24 inches in 7mm Rem.
Mag., 22 inches in .270 and .30-06. Open sights. American hardwood
stock. Made from 1985 to 1999 by U.S. Repeating Arms Co.

MODEL 1892 GRADE I LEVER-ACTION RIFLE
Similar to the original Model 1892. Caliber: .357 Mag., .44-40,
.44 Rem. Mag., .45 LC; 10-round mag. Bbl.: 24 inches, round.
Weight: 6.25 lbs. Lgt.: 41.25 inches. Bead front, adj. buckhorn
rear sights. Blue finish. Etched receiver, gold trigger. Plain
straight-grip walnut stock and forearm w/metal grip cap. Made
from 1997. Disc.
Standard Rifle . . . . NiB $800 Ex $713 Gd $477
Short Rifle (w/20-inch bbl.,
.44 Mag. only). . . . . NiB $750 Ex $495 Gd $352

**MODEL 1892 GRADE
II LEVER-ACTION RIFLE** . . . . NiB $1388 Ex $1167 Gd $828
Similar to Grade I Model 1892 except w/gold appointments, game scene
on receiver. Chambered in .45 LC only. Limited production of 1,000 made
in 1997.

WINSLOW ARMS COMPANY — Camden,
South Carolina

Winslow Arms Company

Winslow Commander Grade

Winslow Crown Grade

**Winslow Regent Grade
Bushmaster Stock**

BOLT-ACTION SPORTING RIFLE

Action: FN Supreme Mauser, Mark X Mauser, Rem. 700 and 788, Sako, Winchester, Model 70. Standard calibers: .17-222, .17-223, .222 Rem., .22-250. .243 Win., 6mm Rem. .25-06 Rem., .257 Roberts, .270 Win., 7x57, .280 Rem. .284 Win.,.308 Win., .30-06, .358 Win. Magnum calibers: .17-222 Mg., .257 Wby. Mag., .264 Win. Mag., .270 Wby. Mag., 7mm Rem. Mag., 7mm Wby. Mag.,. .300 H&H Mag., .300 Wby. Mag., .300 Win. Mag., .308 Norma Mag., 8mm Rem. Mag., .338 Win. Mag., .358 Norma Mag., .375 H&H Mag., .375 Wby. Mag., .458 Win. Mag. Three-round mag. in standard calibers, two rounds in magnum calibers. Bbl.: 24 inches in standard calibers, 26 inches in magnum calibers. Weight: (w/24-inch bbl.: 7 to 7.5 lbs.; w/26-inch bbl.: 8 to 9 lbs. No sights. Stock options: "Bushmaster " w/slender pistol grip and beavertail forearm; "Plainsmaster" with full curl pistol-grip and flat forearm. Both styles w/Monte Carlo cheekpiece. Values shown are for basic rifle in each grade. Extras such as fancy wood, elaborate carving, inlays engraving will considerably increase these values. Made from 1962 to 1989.

Grade	NiB	Ex	Gd
Commander Grade	NiB $1897	Ex $1565	Gd $1177
Regal Grade	NiB $2066	Ex $1590	Gd $1309
Regent Grade	NiB $2175	Ex $1698	Gd $1433
Regimental Grade	NiB $2966	Ex $2490	Gd $1788
Crown Grade	NiB $3228	Ex $2579	Gd $2188
Royal Grade	NiB $3590	Ex $2666	Gd $2077
Imperial Grade	NiB $4100	Ex $3655	Gd $3000
Emperor Grade	NiB $7000	Ex $5266	Gd $4590

Index

228

229

230

233

NRA NATIONAL FIREARMS MUSEUM

Home to 3,000 of America's most significant firearms

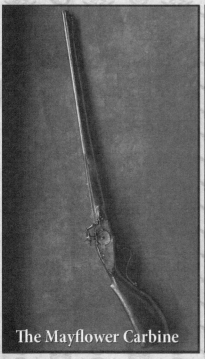

The Mayflower Carbine

JFK's New Frontier Colt

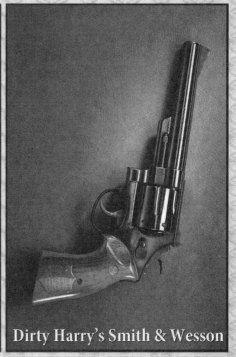

Dirty Harry's Smith & Wesson

NRAMUSEUM.COM

DAILY 9:30AM-5PM | FREE ADMISSION
11250 WAPLES MILL RD | FAIRFAX, VA 22030